Arab–Iranian Relations

Arab–Iranian Relations

edited by
Khair el-Din Haseeb

Centre for Arab Unity Studies

BEIRUT

Published in 1998 by the Centre for Arab Unity Studies
Sadat Tower Building, Lyon Street, Hamra, Beirut, Lebanon

Copyright © the Centre for Arab Unity Studies, 1998

Distributed by British Academic Press
Victoria House, Bloomsbury Square, London WC1B 4DZ

In the United States and Canada distributed by St Martin's Press
175 Fifth Avenue, New York, NY 10010

ISBN 1 86064 156 3

A full CIP record for this book is available from the British Library
A full CIP record for this book is available from the Library of Congress

Manufactured in the UK

Contents

Foreword

By Khair El-Din Haseeb*

I

This book is an English edition of the papers presented at a seminar organized by the Centre for Arab Unity Studies (CAUS) on 'Arab–Iranian Relations: Present Trends and Future Prospects'. The seminar was held in Doha, Quatar, between 11–14 September 1995, and was hosted by the University of Quatar. Over seventy Arab and Iranian scholars and experts participated, in their personal capacity, in preparing the papers, presenting written comments on them and participating in discussions on papers. With the agreement of the Iranian members of the Preparatory Committee of the seminar, formed by the CAUS, Arabic and English languages were both used in all the deliberations of the seminar. In the interest of economy only the papers have been published in this English edition. However, the full text of the seminar's proceedings remains available in the Arabic edition, published by the CAUS in July 1996, and is in the process of being translated and published in Persian.

II

The organization of this seminar on Arab-Iranian relations was part of an over-all academic and research work programme of the CAUS to develop an integrated Arab Strategy in dealing with the geographically neighbouring countries, mainly, Iran, Turkey and Ethiopia. It is in this context that another seminar was organized by the CAUS in 1993 in Beirut on 'The Future of Arab–Turkish Relations' with a wide participation by both Arab and Turkish scholars and experts, and its proceedings was published in both Arabic and Turkish.

The Arab–Iranian relationship is a distinctive one. For, in addition to neighbourhood and many common interests, there was an Arab–Islamic civilization to which Arabs and non-Arabs, Muslims and non-Muslims contributed and shared in. Iran's (Persia's) participation and contribution in this Civilization was dynamic and distinctive. Since the civilizational content of Arab Nationalism is mainly a civilizational Arab-Islamic content, and since this content is not only a historical legacy but a basic source of the present Arab value system, then the theoretical joinder between Arabs and Iranians is of a far broader sort than that exists between Arabs and other neighbouring states, as the seminar on 'The Future of Arab–Turkish Relations' indicated.

Therefore, Arab–Iranian relations are governed by historical and geostrategic ties, ties of mutual interest, and the challenges of contemporary revival. No doubt the new global relations, and the pursuit of a 'new' international order undermining nations, render the aim of narrowing differences between Arabs and Iranians an urgent necessity. The occurrence of the Islamic revolution in Iran added a special importance to Arab–Iranian relations and affirmed the need for greater coordination and cooperation. Unfortunately, events moved sometimes in other directions, especially during the 1980s, with the Iraqi–Iranian war during 1980 to 1988, in which some other Arab Governments were involved. The recent Islamic Summit Conference in Tehran, which was attended by many top Arab leaders, was a major step in the right direction of improving Arab–Iranian relations, but much more follow-up and improvement is needed, if Iran is to be looked at and considered by the Arabs, as it should be, as a part of the Islamic strategic depth to the Arab Nation.

It was therefore felt that there was an urgent need to narrow the differences between Arab and Iranian viewpoints; deepen each side's understanding of the other; strengthen relations and create ties between the various Arab and Iranian elites and between their peoples; explore possibilities for joint effort and closer intellectual and strategic cooperation in the face of the challenges of the current and changing global situation; and, last but not the least, to work hard on conflict resolution and prevention. This seminar was planned and viewed as a serious step in that direction.

III

As to the planning and organization of the seminar, there are certain points which warrant clarification and/or emphasis here.

To begin with, the seminar was organized at the initiative of the CAUS and was independent of any Arab or Iranian official connection and influence, although in planning the seminar the CAUS made every possible effort to alleviate the suspicions of any official circles regarding the motives behind this seminar. The CAUS set up also an independent joint Arab–Iranian Preparatory Committee which met in Beirut and advised the CAUS at the planning stage of the seminar, although final decisions were decided by the CAUS itself. Moreover, in planning the seminar, the interests of Arab and Iranian decision makers to benefit from the outcome of this seminar were among the considerations which the CAUS had in mind.

Therefore, the seminar was a futurist dialogue, at an unofficial level, between Arab and Iranian intellectuals and experts, in their personal capacities, and regardless of their positions in their countries. The CAUS was keen on there being interaction between the Arab and Iranian participants during the seminar as individuals, and not as two delegations or sides facing each other and taking positions to defend official Arab and Iranian views. The CAUS sought a better understanding and to narrow the differences among the Arab and Iranian participants over the topics discussed in the seminar, as independent minds and experts, as far as possible, and that they all resolve, with open minds and hearts, to attempt to arrive at mutual understanding of these issues.

Second, it was the CAUS's hope that the seminar, which was the first direct one of its kind on this subject, serves as a modest beginning for creating, expanding and deepening the interest of Iranian and Arab elites in Arab–Iranian relations and their future, as it was discovered during the planning stage of the seminar that there was very little literature by Arab and Iranian scholars on contemporary affairs and relations of each other. It was also hoped that the seminar and its published proceedings, in both Arabic and Persian editions, would enhance such mutual interest at both the popular and institutional levels. It was hoped that this seminar will ease the way to additional future seminars and conferences on the different dimensions of Arab–Iranian relations.

Third, the CAUS regrets that simultaneous translations could only be provided in Arabic and English; technical and practical constraints having prevented simultaneous translation into Persian. The CAUS hopes, as this seminar proved, that this shortcoming can be avoided in future seminars and conferences.

Fourth, it was regrettable, but perhaps not surprising, that the overflow of some of the historical differences impeded better relations into the seminar. The CAUS was aware of the differences over nomenclature of the Gulf between Arabs and Iranians, and thus made it a point to let each participant, whatever his background, give it the name he or she chooses. But it can hardly be disputed that, whatever name is given, this Gulf is of equal geographic, economic, strategic and historical importance to both nations. Consequently, whether it is called the 'Arabian Gulf', 'Persian Gulf', or even 'Arab–Persian Gulf', facts and realities do not change. What is in need of change are attitudes and intentions among both sides, and we do ourselves and our nations an injustice in looking to exaggerate minor or imaginary differences. The CAUS decided, therefore, to leave in the published Arabic and English editions of the proceedings of the seminar, the specific names of the Gulf used by the different participants, whether in the papers or in the written comments and discussions.

Fifth, on apparently graver issues, such as territorial disputes between the Arabs and Iran, whether the three islands in the Gulf or the Iraq–Iran boundary, the historical experience has consistently shown that the use of force is not the answer. The starting point on such issues, be they major or minor, is that they should be resolved by any means except force, that is, by peaceful means. The logical move is direct negotiations between the disputants, and if this leads to an impasse, then arbitration should be the next choice, whether through a third neutral party or an international arbitration panel. This is not only in deference to sparing both sides the enormous human and economic costs of conflict, and the statistics here are indeed horrifying. It is not only in deference to safeguarding all that we have in common and share, which were eloquently enumerated by the participants in this seminar, it is also to avert intervention by hegemonial powers, as their interest may well differ, and even conflict, with those of the Arab World and Iran.

Sixth, the CAUS was mindful from the start, of the need for all major issues within Arab–Iranian relations to be discussed, based on the belief that objective and civilized mutual dialogue and understanding afford the best way to overcoming the fixations of the past, and to determining the common present and future issues that bear on these relations and their development. There can be no genuine interest in developing these relations if we are to continue living in their past, both the bitter and the sweet. For the study of the past, and the joint and mutual understanding of it, are useful to the extent of their benefiting us with lessons and wisdom for the present and future. We cannot change the past, however much time and effort we expend on studying it, but more important, in CAUS's opinion, is concentration on the present and future, determining joint interests; where we agree and where we disagree; how we can enlarge the areas of our agreement; how we can circumscribe, rationalize and intellectualize our differences; and what we might differ on in the future.

Seventh, the CAUS believes, and is convinced, that the possibilities for contact and accord between Arabs and Iranians are considerable, especially under current regional and international conditions, which constitute challenges to both the Arab and Iranian nations. I do not conceal that I personally always believed, and still believe, in the reality and inevitability of this contact. It was affirmed during my visit in 1994 to Iran, within the framework of preparing for this seminar. I discovered that what the Western media relay to us is quite often a somewhat distorted version of the truth, and perhaps among the most important objectives of this seminar is to affirm the necessity of joint contact and the deepening of mutual understanding, and therefore joint effort.

Finally, as to whether this seminar achieved its initial objectives, the CAUS believes that it proved very beneficial to both sides, not only through achieving a better understanding between Arab and Iranian participants, but also through presenting concrete elements for a plan of action for the future, particularly in pursuit and follow-up of the many proposals and suggestions for enhancing Arab–Iranian relations. Among the most important of these were the need for greater mutual awareness; detailed studies of internal and external constraining influences; an examination of insufficiently addressed topics such as economic development, trading relations, oil policy, arms limitation and even peace itself; image rectification in the media and in schools; the establishment of Arab–Iranian cultural exchange and language centres and programmes; and, of course, additional conferences in future on issues of mutual concern.

The seminar's very occurrence, participation in it by serious and sincere scholars and specialists from both sides, and the above ideas that were exchanged in person, if not in a lengthy similar document, represent, for the CAUS and as no doubt for many in the Arab world and Iran, ample grounds for hope and optimism as to the future of Arab–Iranian relations.

IV

The seminar consisted of two parts, with a number of papers in each. On most issues, two papers were presented; one by an Arab author and a second by an Iranian author. Written comments were presented on each topic, in most cases, by an Arab and an Iranian participant, and was followed by a general discussion. As indicated earlier, and because of economy considerations, the papers only are published in the English edition.

Part I deals with the 'Historical Legacy of Arab–Iranian Relations', on which two papers were presented.

Part II deals with the 'Current Situation and Future Prospects', which covered thirteen topics and an open dialogue. Twenty-five papers were presented on these thirteen topics.

V

It is very difficult to enumerate all the many persons who helped make this seminar a success, but I can assure each and every participant and support staff involved that his or her efforts are most appreciated, even if not directly mentioned here.

To begin with, special thanks to the members of the Preparatory Committee, who helped the Centre in planning this seminar. They included

Jihad El-Zein, Ghassan Ben Jeddou, Fehmi Houweidi, Mohammad Ali Muhtadi, Mahmood, Sariolghalam, Michel Nawfal, Wajih Kawtharani, in addition to the proposals submitted by Ahmad Yusuf Ahmad, Jamil Matar, and Ghassan Salame, which enriched the preparation of the seminar's outline.

A special debt of gratitude is due to Mohammad Sadeq El-Husseini, who was an initiator and encourager of the Centre to propose this seminar, and special gratitude to Ghassan Ben Jeddou who, in addition to his great enthusiasm for holding this seminar, expended much of his time, effort, experience and contacts to organize it and resolve some of its complications; he travelled more than once to Iran, on behalf of the Centre, for this purpose,

I should also take this opportunity to express to Mahmood Sariolghalam, Director General of the Centre for Scientific Research and Middle East Strategic Studies, in Tehran, and to Mohammad Ali Muhtadi, Consultant at the same Centre, the thanks and appreciation of the CAUS for the effort and contacts they undertook to facilitate the holding of this seminar and for following-up the Iranian authors for the preparation of their papers.

I would also like to thank the University of Qatar, its Director and staff, for hosting this seminar and facilitating its holding in Doha. The CAUS cannot but give due credit, appreciation and thanks to Muhammad El-Musfer, of Qatar university, who seized on the idea of holding this seminar in Doha and worked to bring it to fruition, and for all his patience and effort in overcoming and solving the practical problems involved.

Many thanks, as well, to all the support staff, who provided simultaneous translation work and technical support for the participants in this seminar. Many thanks, too, to Mr Hazem Husseini, who undertook the bulk of translation and typing of the manuscript for this English Version.

Finally, it goes without saying that the CAUS is alone responsible for organizing this seminar, just as it is solely responsible for any shortcomings in the exercise.

Beirut, January, 1998

* Director-General of the centre for Arab Unity Studies

One

Historical Ties Between
Arabs and Iranians

1

Arab–Iranian Relations: Historical Background

ABDUL AZIZ AD-DURI*

In order to achieve a better future for Arab–Iranian relations, there must be a better understanding of them. In turning to history, the aim of this chapter is to understand the present through a study of the past. History is the actions of men in a specific terrain at specific times. This means looking carefully at the nature of that terrain, that is the geography of Iran and neighbouring Arab countries. For geography has an impact. The Iranian plateau with its mountainous western edge, and then the Tigro-Euphrates Valley, with its fertile plains and ample waters, are followed by steppes and deserts. The Iranians, then, stand between the highlands, the forbidding mountains and the open plains. Their relations, however, were not confined to the Tigro-Euphrates Valley, but included the Gulf area overlooked by the Iranian highland. This geographic contiguity implies political, civilizational and normal human contact, or possibly collision and conquest. States that emerged in the Iranian highland frequently invaded the rich plains. This happened with the Achamenids, Parthians and Sassanians before Islam, the Buwayhids, Seljuks, Mongols and Safavids after Islam.

States also emerged in the Tigro-Euphrates Valley, such as Assyria, and turned eastwards to prevent attacks on their territories or to expand their power, but they did not advance beyond Iran's west or northwest. As for the powers that invaded Iran, they came from beyond neighbouring countries; for example, the invasion by Alexander of Macedonia. The geographic situation also influences the human. Most inhabitants of the Tigro-Euphrates Valley are from the Arabian Peninsula. Human waves from the peninsula followed natural population increases in a desert environment with few resources, prompting movement to the northeast and northwest. Pre-Islamic migrations from the peninsula entered neighbouring plains but not the mountains; this confirms the migratory patterns that followed the victory of Islam. The mountains remained the eastern limit of Arab movement. The inhabitants of the Iranian highland, on the other hand, came from other peoples to the east or northeast.

The mountains thus became a divider between Arab and Aryan peoples. This geographic and human situation led to the formation of two distinctive cultures/civilizations, each with its own language – Pahlavi in Iran and Arabic in the Tigro-Euphrates Valley and Peninsula. But these cultures were not isolated. Though relatively limited, commercial and cultural ties existed through the ages; but with the arrival of Islam, the impact became wide-scale. Before Islam, there were general direct ties between Iran, the Tigro-Euphrates Valley and the Gulf area. In the Sassanian period, Persia expanded into Iraq and the eastern section (East Khabur) of Mesopotamia. Sassanian suzerainty extended at times to the west of the Gulf and certain shores of Oman. Against this, bedouin pressures on the Tigro-Euphrates Valley, whether in the form of migration or invasion, were continuous; hence the establishment of the kingdom of al-Hirah. While the Lakhmids felt a kinship with the Arabian tribes of the Peninsula, the Persians wanted them as a buffer to these tribes.

The penetration of Arab tribes was limited to Iraq and Mesopotamia. Beyond this, occasional forays would be made at the fringes of the Tigro-Euphrates Valley and, rarely, on the east coast of the Gulf. As for the spread of Iranians into Iraq, it was relatively limited and assumed the form of military garrisons, administrators and landowners; there was no settlement process of any great consequence. In the last third of the 6th century CE, the Persians extended their hegemony to Yemen, following the call by a Yemeni chieftain for their aid in expelling the Abyssinians.

Perhaps the cultural/civilizational ties were wider. Cuneiform characters, and then Aramaic, along with many civilizational terms, entered Pahlavi. A study of influences may also reveal the impact of the ancient civilizations of Iraq. Iran in its turn had a role in the religious formation of the area as Zoroastrianism spread to a limited degree in Iraq (and Mesopotamia), the Gulf and perhaps in other directions. But Manichaeism started from Iraq, and continued to have an impact even after the conquests of Islam. Mazdakism may also have had roots there.

The Islamic conquests changed the political situation in a fundamental way and had a profound impact on the state of civilization. The conquest overthrew the Sassanian state and eliminated the class system and hegemony of Zoroastrianism. Arab tribal groups then came, particularly from Kufa and Basra, to Iran's administrative centres (such as Isfahan, Merv, and Balkh), initially as military garrisons. However, they did not spread to rural areas, and their numbers were generally small compared to Arab extensions elsewhere. Relations were affected, during the first two centuries, by the attitude to Islam. Non-Muslims remained *dhimmis*, free to have their own rights, laws and religious freedom, against the payment of *jizyah* and *kharaj* taxes.

Islam spread by its merit and openness, with hardly any effort from official institutions. The role of sects and opposition groups was important here. The invasion occurred at a time when the Zoroastrian religion was losing the backing of the state, and other Mazdean religions, such as Manichaeism and Mazdakism, found a freedom and clemency they had never known before. We have no record of an increase in taxes in Iran. But there are indications of manipulations by tax collectors, mostly local notables, in the amounts collected, as well as occasional dubious dealings. As for non-Arabs who embraced Islam, presumably what applied to the Muslims in rights and obligations applied to them as well. They became known as the *mawali*. The term *mawla* did not involve a clearly defined social status, but rather, in a society based on tribes and clans, meant 'ally'. Affiliation gave the new Muslim a place in the social structure, but not full social equality.

The *mawali* were not a homogeneous group. Some became the *kuttab* ('secretaries') and then viziers, some jurists and 'ulema (religious scholars) – positions of very high standing; others were merchants who had a major impact on social life. Craftsmen and peasants were also from among the *mawali*, and were looked down upon. Thus, to discuss the *mawali* as though they were a single social group is very risky and a gross oversimplification. It appears that the tribal perspective was the first factor in classifying or demeaning non-Arabs, discouraging their enrolment in the Islamic forces or giving them salaries and provisions, in marked contrast to the Islamic perspective. The differences between the two perspectives, tribal and Islamic, had a role in public life; time and developments tended to favour the Islamic perspective.

There are indications that the *jizyah* was imposed, during the time of the Marwanids, on new converts to Islam. This included some Iranian areas, creating a stir between Muslims, until abrogated by Omar bin Abdel Aziz, only to appear again, and then finally to end in the last years of Hisham bin Abdel Malik. As for the fighting forces, recent research suggests that there were non-Arab garrisons in Syria and Transoxiana, deriving from necessity, whereas from the days of Abdel Malik, Arab fighting forces were being limited. Complete equality in the administration, army, pay and financial obligations needed time to materialize, and their realization moved in line with the gradual preponderance of Islamic precepts in public life.

During the Umayyad period, a large-scale translation took place to Arabize financial registers (*diwans*) in the eastern provinces. The process took half a century to complete, thus enriching Arabic and rendering it the language of administration as well as of culture. Also during this period, the foundations of Islamic and Arabic fields of knowledge were laid down, and the contribution of non-Arabs to them, especially the Persians, began. There were also widespread contacts in new Arab centres, such as Basra and Kufa, including extensive intermarriages between Arabs and *mawali* – an aspect that has not received the attention it deserves. The extent of *wala'* (*mawali*) had a considerable bearing on intellectual and social contact by the Iranians with the Arabs. In Iran, especially Khurasan, Arab mixing with the indigenous peoples was conspicuous. They were affected by the local customs and dress to the point where they at times were indistinguishable. There was also close cooperation between Persian noblemen (*dihqans* and *marzbans*) and the Arabs, but tensions were encountered with the spread of Islam and social development.

Khurasan (and some parts of Iran) became fertile ground for the Abbasid movement that advocated the application of the Book and the *sunnah* and the realization of equality and justice. But the Abbasid movement was not the first to call for these; it was preceded by other movements in the name of Islam's tenets. Non-Arabs did not have parties or associations of their own. The Islamic parties, such as the Kharijite, Shiite and Marj'ite, were initiated by the Arabs, then joined by the *mawali*. These also joined the Abbasid movement and participated in some revolts, including the Abbasid, alongside the Arabs.

One can regard the advent of the Abbasids as the start of a new phase. The first Abbasid period (132–218 AH) was an age of much cooperation between Arabs and Persians. Arab–Iranian relations took on a new form. Persians shared in the government, administration and the army; tribal forces were cancelled; and they were replaced by a standing army of Arabs and Persians. A new capital was established (Baghdad), symbolizing the new image of the state. Its population included Arabs and others; its quarters and suburbs were inhabited by persons of the same origin or profession, and some quarters were for groups from Iranian lands. The cooperation of Persian notables with the Arabs continued, and Khurasan was the Iranian province most closely connected with the Abbasids. It was during this period that the institution of *kuttab* (secretaries) became prominent, with considerable impact on administration and culture. Some Iranian families entered public life (the Barmakids, the Banu Sahl, and Banu Tahir) and played a prominent role therein. Khurasan was the cause of al-Ma'mun's victory over his brother al-Amin and his attaining the caliphate by force. Most of al-Ma'mun's forces were Iranians from Khurasan.

But this widespread cooperation did not last. There was the problem of the relationship between caliph and the vizier, and the palace coalitions that emerged. There was also the adverse impact of the Khurasanite invasion of Baghdad, in addition to the civil strife, which weakened the caliph's army. This led to the introducing of mercenaries/Turks into the army and to far-reaching changes in the centre of power, the most serious being the weakening of the caliphate.

It was in the first Abbasid period that revolts occurred in Iran for the first time. Perhaps the Abbasid movement provoked a certain awareness and stirred certain hopes in Iran. One notes that these revolts broke out among the common people and took on a religious character, goaded on by followers of Mazdeanism (Zoroaster, Mazdak), who were influenced by Islam; no noblemen were among their leaders.

The most serious revolt was that of Babak al-Khurrami in Azerbaijan; most of whose followers were Khurramis (neo-Mazdakites). These revolts were not by Iranian Muslims, but by followers of dualist religions who tried to combine with their own creeds certain Islamic tenets. They opposed the caliphate and its representatives, including large landowners. The revolts showed that the public in Iran did not profit tangibly from the promises of the Abbasid movement. They also suggest that Islam had not yet become very widespread in Iran. This period was one of intense cultural activity, with a meeting of cultures and creeds. It was not expected to be void of wealth, nor was it void of conflict.

Manichaeism was now active in Iraq, its home, and its perspective of interpretation gained ground for it. Its social concepts sometimes contradicted the Islamic. If the word *zindiq* in Zoroastrian writings meant Manichaean, it has since widened to mean any adherent to a dualist creed (non-Zoroastrian) or beliefs that conflict with Islamic tenets. Muslim scholastic theologians (*'ulema' al-kalam*), armed with logic, took the offensive against the *zindiqs*, as did the caliphate.

There was a literary and cultural dialogue between the bearers of Arab Islamic culture (Arabs and Persians) and a group desiring to revive their Sassanian heritage in the humanities and administration. The *kuttab* participated in this, as is evident from the writings of Ibn al-Muqaffa' for example, as well as al-Jahiz's *Risalah fi Dhamm Akhlaq al-Kuttab*, which notes a negative view by some of them (sympathizers of *zandaqa* and Sassanian culture) towards the Islamic cultural base. It was not strange to see some elements reviving their heritage as a means of self-assertion, taking pride in past glories, and taking a stand from prevailing conditions.

Culture may encompass values and ideals about it, literary and social, religious too perhaps, and may go beyond cultural dialogue to transmitting concepts and views that conflict with Islamic values or go further to encroach on Arabic and its defenders. Thus cultural dialogue tends to blend with the political and religious. The participating group was represented by a few non-Arabs, who were naturally unconnected with Islamic parties or sects such as the Kharijites, Shi'ites and others. Baghdad became the principal cultural centre. It was understood that Muslims would borrow from earlier cultures; for after laying the broad lines of their own culture, embodied in Arabic and Islamic studies, they proceeded to enrich it with translations and transmissions from Greece, Persia and India. Transmission from Sassanian culture had begun since the later Umayyad period. Then came an enormous translation effort with the arrival of the Abbasids. The *kuttab* played a role in translating from the Persian and transmitting the Sassanian heritage.

Arabic was the language of culture in *Dar al-Islam* during the first four centuries. Talk of Arab–Iranian relations finds its most resplendent pages in culture. The contribution of peoples of non-Arab origin, especially the Persians, to culture was very substantial; in fact, openness was an important factor in the flourishing and enrichment of Arab Islamic culture, which was embodied in the forms and contents of literature, art and thought generally. We cannot in the space available, deal properly with this broad field; a few simple illustrations will have to suffice. We can return to the beginning to see registers (taxes and expenditures) in the East in Phalli, until they were Arabized in the time of Abdel Malik ibn Marwan and Hisham ibn Abdel Malik. The Sassanian administrative heritage made its impact in the Abbasid period in particular, just as some viziers and *kuttab* played their part too.

Translation began from Persian, in history (*Khudhaya-namah* – 'The Book of Kings') and literature (*adab*), from the Umayyad period. Perhaps the wider translation work in the Abbasid period was in history and literature. It is sufficient to mention *Kalilah wa Dimnah* and *Hazar Afsana* ('Thousand Tales'). Moreover, not only were scientific works translated to Arabic from Syriac, but some were translated from Pahlavi as well. The Jundayshahpur academy's medical sciences were put to widespread use, thanks to translation and writing. One may also point to the arts of Persian architecture, assaying, music and song and their impact on Islamic society. Baghdad attracted scientists from all over the Islamic world, especially from Iran and Transoxiana. We believe that the role of language and culture in the scientific movement did not obscure the impact of environment and locale. For among the great names were Abu Ma'shar al-Falaki from Balkh, Muhammad bin Musa al-Khwarazmi who left valuable works in mathematics and algebra, the famous astronomer Ahmad al-Farghani, the philosopher Abu Nasr al-Farabi, al-Zamakhshari, author of *al-Kashshaf*, and the meritorious historian Miskawayh. But then, what distinguishes man, after all, save his heart and his tongue?

This cultural reality had a profound impact on the cultures that emerged later in Islamic languages such as Persian, Turkish and others. In the 3rd century AH, the first stirrings of autonomous activity began in Iran. This was partly due to the failure of cooperation between the Persian nobility and the Abbasids after al-Ma'mun did away with his vizier, al-Fadl bin Sahl, and to the disappointment of the Persian people with al-Ma'mun's promises when he abandoned Merv and returned to Baghdad. It was the period of the emergence of the first Iranian dynasties in Khurasan, Transoxiana, and Sijistan (the Tahirids, 205–259 AH; the Saffarids, 247–287 AH; the Samanids, 261–389 AH).

While the two dynasties, Tahirid and Samanid, constituted a movement of governors from among the Persian nobility, the Saffarid dynasty was a populist movement in the beginning. And while the Tahirids and Saminids maintained their loyalty to the caliphate and stood against movements in their own areas opposed to the Abbasids, the Saffarids' relations with the caliphate were often negative to the point of collision. Arabic was the language of culture and civilization in these dynasties, but the beginning of poetry in the newly-revived Persian language now manifested itself, though it was a modest beginning and only a few scattered remnants have come down to us. Mention should be made that Yaqub bin al-Laith al-Saffar did not understand Arabic, and this was one reason for the development of Persian poetry in Sijistan. Possibly the Persian poets here were among the first to enter Persian into the metre of Arabic poetry.

Under the Samanid dynasty, it was the new Persian that flourished, and literature and culture too. There emerged poets such as al-Samarqandi, al-Daqiqi and Shahid Balkhi. In the Samanid period as well, some 'ulema sanctioned prayer in Persian, and the *Tafsir* ('Commentaries' on the Qur'an) by Muhammad bin Jarir al-Tabari was translated into Persian. In their time as well, Persian was the language of Samanid bureaucracy, influenced by the *kuttab*, who knew Arabic. Persian was written with Arabic characters.

In the middle of the 4th century AH (10th century CE), a major movement emerged that shook central and west Iran. This was the 'Iranian period' that followed from a movement originating in the Caspian province. The Arabs had not conquered these areas fully, and the coastal province of Gilan in particular had carved a place for itself, opposed the caliphate and ruled through princes who were independent and had memories of pre-Islamic glories. The Zaydi imams had succeeded in converting people, especially the Daylami (Persian) highlanders, to Shi'ism after 250 AH, in a neo-populist movement, and they underscored justice.

The Daylamite chiefs of the Buwayhid line succeeded in forming a political entity extending from west Iran (Rayy) to its south (Shiraz), and expanded to Baghdad and took control of the Abbasid caliphate. The Buwayhids (334–447 AH) achieved the first period of Iranian sovereignty since the Islamic conquests. The Buwayhid emirs themselves were in effective control and shared the official symbols of sovereignty with the caliph. However, they left him only religious affairs and the right to issue diplomas of appointment to their own emirs, since he was the source of legitimacy. Thus emerged the delegation of total authority to the Buwayhid emir by the caliph.

One should draw attention to the financial policy of the Buwayhids and their meting out to soldiers of military fiefs in Iraq rather than salaries. The country returned to an agrarian economy after having been a monetary commercial one. The Buwayhids encouraged Shi'ism, without imposing it. They did not cancel the Abbasid caliphate for practical political reasons, and in deference to people's allegiance to it. They had a role to play in raising the consciousness of the Persians, and they recovered some of the vestiges of the Sassanian kings and claimed descent from them. But the Arabic language continued to be the language of culture, and scientific and cultural movement in all fields was invigorated during the Buwayhid period.

Before the 3rd century AH, Islam prevailed in the towns and urban centres of Iran, whereas the countryside was largely Mazdaean. But through the efforts of the preachers of the Faith, the countryside was brought into the fold of Islam between 850 and 950 CE. In Samanid times, the spread of the Islamic message was strong among Turkish tribes in Central Asia, where the Turkish wave originated. After the Buwayhids, Iran was ruled by Turkish dynasties: the Ghaznavids (366–581 AH), centred in Khurasan and Transoxiana, then the Seljuks (429–540 AH), who ruled over Iran and extended to Iraq and Syria. It was then invaded by the Mongols, from whom emerged the Ilkhanid dynasty (654–751 AH, 1256–1353 CE). Timur then overran the emirates that followed the Ilkhanids (Timurids 771–912 AH, 1370–1506 CE). In the second half of the 15th century CE, the Turcomans established themselves in west and northwest Iran and in Iraq through the states of the Kara–Koyunlu (782–873 AH, 1380–1468 CE) and the Ak-Koyunlu (780–914 AH, 1378–1508 CE).

The Ghaznavids were thoroughly influenced by the Iranians and did not change the fabric of the society and culture they encountered. The *ghuz* movement was a tribal migration; the Seljuks emerged as leaders for them and became the heads of state from Central Asia to Syria and Anatolia. Despite their modest numbers initially, they affected the demographic balance, and the basic elements now became the Persian and Tajik. The contact between Arabs and Persians was replaced by contact between Persians and Tajiks. In the time of the Seljuks, al-Ghazzali established a new relationship between caliphate and sultanate. The Seljuks' authority (*sultan*) was given a legal basis, from which were to follow certain developments in political thought.

The Mongol invasion changed the demographic balance by bringing in new Turkish tribes. It expanded nomadism, destroyed agriculture and urban life and deepened the dualism between 'Turk' and 'Tajik'. The Ilkhanids tried to expand westward, but they could not extend their hegemony beyond the Tigro-Euphrates Valley. The Safavids appeared, and a new age (1501–1722 CE) began. It is justly regarded as 'a major turning point, through which the Iranian nation became conscious of itself and affirmed its origin'. The emergence of the Safavids marks the appearance of the first Persian state to rule all of Iran since the emergence of Islam. It is the state that began unifying Iran and drew the borders that in general match those of the modern state of Iran.

The Safavids trace their descent to Sheikh Safi al-Din (d. 1334 CE), the chief of a Sufi fraternity (*ra's tariqah*) in Ardabil. It is known that the sheikhs of Ardabil were Sunnite, and they had many followers from among Turcoman tribes, from Ardabil through Asia Minor to Syria. But during the period of the great grandfather of Shash Isma'il Khawaja Ali (d. 1427 CE), a conversion to Shi'ism occurred. Then Sheikh Junayd (d. 1460 CE) and his son Haydar (d. 1488 CE) tried to affirm the *jihad* against the infidels in the Caucasus and gave the order a military character. Both died in battle and added martyrdom to their order.

As for the 'Alid link in the Safavid line, that emerged later. The Safavids affirmed it and claimed descent from the seventh imam. There is nothing to suggest a connection with the Turks, because the first verses of Safi al-Din were written in Persian and in a local dialect. But Ardabil, the birthplace of the *tariqah*, affected them and they learned its language, as we can see from the poetry of Shah Isma'il, written in the Turkish of Azerbaijan.

Iran knew of Shi'ism before then, Zaydi principally and, to a limited extent, Imami. But the great part of Iran's population was Sunni. However, Shah Isma'il (who became *ra's tariqah* in 1494 CE), after defeating Shirvan-Shah, then the Turcoman Ak-Koyunlu, entered Tabriz in 1501 CE and declared Shi'ism the official creed. There was nothing under his authority at the time except Azerbaijan; but he later came to dominate all of Iran. The Shah imposed Shi'ism on the country, and it seems to have found acceptance without much resistance.

Shah Isma'il relied for his army originally on Turcoman tribes, *Qizilbash* who accepted the Safavid message, and there were Safavid followers in Anatolia as well. Shah Isma'il distinguished the Safavid state from the Ottoman and gave it a political character. He also continued to spread the Safavid message among Turcomans in east Anatolia. One of these *Qizilbash* (Shah-Quli) incited a rebellion in southwest Anatolia in the spring of 1511 CE and wearied the Ottomans before he was defeated by them later that year. The emergence of a strong Shiite state on the borders of Anatolia, enjoying the loyalty of a large number of tribes living within the Ottoman state, posed a threat to the Ottomans, especially since their state sought the leadership of the Islamic world. Sultan Selim took up the title of caliph in a letter he sent to Shah Isma'il before invading Egypt.

Before this, Shah Isma'il had no sooner subdued the Turcomans of the Ak-Kolunyu in 1507 than he turned on Baghdad and annexed it to his state in 1508. He also visited the holy shrines of Najaf and Karbala. Ottoman policy was to expand westward, but Sultan Selim now turned eastward to confront the Safavids. To protect his flank, he pursued Shi'ites within his territories and suppressed many of them brutally. In 1514, the sultan attacked Iran, the first in a series of Ottoman incursions; and he was victorious over the Shah at Chaldiran (August 1514); he then entered Tabriz, the Safavid capital. The Sultan had then to give up further campaigns for a while; the Shah returned to Tabriz, but he had lost some of his popularity from within and did not resume war. The victory at Chaldiran resulted in the Ottoman annexation of Diyar Bakr (1516) and in ending the 'Dhu'l Qadr' (Dulgadir) dynasty in Mar'ash (southeast Anatolia) and Elbistan to the north of it.

Sultan Selim proceeded towards Damascus (1516) and Egypt (January 1517) and annexed them. He received the allegiance of the Sherif of Mecca and became the Custodian of the Two Holy Mosques. Then Shah Isma'il died (1524) and was succeeded by his son Tahmasp (d. 1576), who faced internal schisms and the domination of Qizilbash emirs. Iran was subjected to four campaigns between 1533 and 1553 by the Ottomans, who reached the height of their power during the reign of Sulayman the Magnificent. The Sultan moved on Baghdad, and by December 1534 had taken the rest of Iraq; then he annexed Basra in 1538. In 1547, Sultan Sulayman occupied Azerbaijan without difficulty. But Tahmasp pursued a scorched earth policy as he retreated, returning to recover his territories when Ottoman forces returned to Istanbul for the winter. The Ottomans did not make any gains save some fortresses in Georgia and the Lake Van fortress, which was turned into a special *vilayet*. In 1552, the Ottoman admiral Piri Reis drove the Portuguese out of Muscat. As Tabriz was subjected to occupation more than once, Tahmasp moved his capital to Qazvin. After the last campaign in 1553, and the Shah's withdrawal as before, the two sides signed the truce of Amasya in 1555, which prevailed for over 20 years.

Iran witnessed internal disputes after the death of Tahmasp. War with the Ottoman was renewed and they expanded into Iranian territory: they established their rule in Shirvan and Daghestan, occupied Azerbaijan and affirmed their presence in the Caucasus. After Shah Abbas (1588–1629) came to power he confronted the excesses of the Uzbeks to the east and Ottoman expansion to the west. He concluded a truce with the Ottomans (1590) and relinquished to them important areas, such as Azerbaijan, Shirvan and Kurdistan. After reorganizing his army, starting with the Uzbeks, he recovered Herat, Mashhad and Merv (1588). Then he turned west and took Bahrain (1602), then recovered Azerbaijan and the Caucasus (1603 and 1604). By about 1607, he had expelled the Ottomans from Safavid lands. Finally, in 1612, the two sides agreed to negotiate on the basis of the Amasya treaty.

A period of inactivity ensued, despite the absence of agreement, until 1623, when Shah Abbas exploited internal differences in the vilayet of Baghdad, and took control of it (January 1624), creating a stir in Istanbul. Ottoman attempts to take Baghdad (1625 and 1629) proved fruitless. Eventually, Murad IV laid siege to it and took it on 25 January 1638. This was followed by the treaty of Zuhab on 17 May 1639, whereby border areas were designated (but borders were not specified) and Iran promised to stop its propaganda and military campaigns in Anatolia. The Afghans occupied Isfahan (the capital since the time of Shah Abbas). Although they did not fully subdue the north or west, for seven years (1722–1729), they ruled while the Safavids remained in Tabriz.

In 1727, the Ottomans broke the peace, and the Afghan commander was obliged to recognize their suzerainty over west Iran and the greater part of the Caucasus. At this time, Nadir Khan, Sheikh of the Afshar (a Turcoman tribe) and supporter of the Safavids represented in Tahmasp II, expelled the Afghans from Isfahan in 1729 and re-established Safavid rule. Nadir recovered Nahavand, Hamadan and Tabriz (1730). Then he moved east towards Khurasan. In his absence, Tahmasp II began conducting forays on the Ottomans in 1731, but with disastrous consequences, having lost Tabriz and Hamadan. In 1733, the Ottomans made a peace with the Iranians, keeping all territories south of the Arax River. Nadir denounced the treaty, deposed Tahmasp and designated the child Abbas III as king (July 1732). He then moved against the Ottomans, occupied Zuhab and laid siege to Baghdad (1733), but lost that battle after reinforcements reached the city. He moved again after renewing his forces and was victorious over the Ottomans, who relinquished Azerbaijan.

Nadir returned to attacking the Ottomans in 1735 and achieved a victory over them near Erivan. In January 1737, he arrived at Mughan and met with the governors and notables of the country. They decided to crown him king. His condition was that they abandon Shah Isma'il's religious practices and declare Shi'ism in Iran the fifth *madhhab* with Sunnism. A document was drawn up and signed by those present, calling on the Ottomans to recognize this Ja'fari *madhhab* alongside the four traditional schools of Sunnism. In 1742, a letter arrived from the sultan, refusing to recognize the Ja'fari *madhhab*. Nadir Shah moved in February of that year and occupied Kirkuk, then Arbil; then he besieged Mosul, but the siege failed. Nadir had good relations with the governor of Baghdad, and he visited the religious sites, both Sunnite and Shiite, in Iraq. On 14 December 1743, a conference was held by the *'ulema* in Najaf (Shiite and Sunnite), and they recognized the Ja'fari *madhhab*. All this was in order to achieve religious reconciliation, though sources interpret these moves as for secular ends. Nadir became preoccupied with domestic troubles, then launched a campaign against the Ottomans and secured a tacit victory. He wrote to the sultan, seeking accord between the sects and referred to him as 'the caliph of the people of Islam'. On 4 September 1746, a treaty was concluded with the sultan, returning the borders to those prevailing before the treaty of Zuhab (1639).

After the assassination of Nadir Shah (1747), a period of chaos and civil strife ensued in Iran. Karim Khan Zand (1750–1779) came to power. His principal military achievement was the capture of Basra from the Otto-

mans in 1776, under his brother's leadership, Sadiq Khan, who continued
to run it even after his brother's death (1779), then abandoned it to enter
into the family struggle for the throne. Such disputes gave the Qajars in
Astarabad an opportunity to move. The Qajars were Turcomans and one of
the Qizilbash tribes; Aqa Muhammad Qajar was able to impose his authority and defeat the Zand by 1795. The start of the 19th century witnessed
the beginnings of Western rivalry in Iran, which affected public life in the
country. Iran lost in the war with Russia some of its territories, including
Caucasian provinces, and, what was worse, Russia imposed capitulations
that encroached on Iran's rights as a sovereign state; this ushered a new era
in Iran's relations with the great powers, as other countries, such as Britain,
quickly followed the Russian lead.

Fath Ali Shah (Baba Khan, 1797–1834) began to pursue a provocative
course in north Iraq (1818), and after negotiations and a pledge by Iran not
to intervene, war resumed (1821–1823). After contacts between the two
states, the first Erzerum treaty was concluded (1823) based on the treaty of
Zuhab. But soon enough, tensions resumed, and the border problems remained. Iran occupied Felahiye and Muhammara (Khorramshahr,
1840–1842). Britain and Russia intervened in the area, for their own interests, and formed a quadripartite commission to demarcate borders. After a
period of deliberations, the second treaty of Erzerum was concluded (1847),
which stipulated leaving to the Ottoman government the western lowlands
in the Zuhab area, and to the Iranian government the mountainous territories east of it. Iran would relinquish its claim to Sulaymaniyyah and its
environs, with a pledge of non-intervention in Kurdish affairs in the region, and the Ottoman state would recognize the sovereignty of Iran on
Muhammara and its port, on Khidr island (Abadan) and on the docking
points and lands of the east bank of the Shatt al-Arab, which belonged to
tribes considered as subjects of Iran. Iranian ships had the right of unre-
stricted navigation in the Shatt al-Arab, from the tip of the Gulf to the
point at which the borders of the two states meet. The two governments
also agreed to appoint commissions and engineers to represent them in
drawing up the borders mentioned in the treaty.

However, implementation of the treaty led to many incidents and disputes over interpretation of the articles relating to borders. This delayed
the demarcation process over half a century. When the Ottoman state entered the First World War, the boundary commission had not yet completed
their task and a relatively small part of the area remained unfinished. Despite an agreement to resolve the issues within two protocols, the first signed
in Tehran in 1911 and the second in Istanbul in 1913, the work of the
authority charged with designating the borders was not completed when
the First World War broke out.

After the War, Turkey ended its historical dispute with Iran, because the new borders between them were no longer in dispute. As for Iraq, it inherited the border problems between Iran and the Ottoman state, including the part that was not finalized; it also inherited the historical differences between Iran and the Ottoman state. Some problems, especially those relating to the border, emerged from the interpretation of a number of paragraphs in the second Erzerum treaty; others emerged from the new conditions that followed the First World War.

Now, after having undertaken this review, shall we speak of a struggle or wars between Arabs and Iranians? It would be difficult to speak of such a struggle with any finality in the periods of the caliphate. One can point to a local revolt against the authorities, such as the revolt of Babak al-Khurrami, or to the emergence of the triumphant Yaqub bin al-Laith al-Saffar, or to an invasion from Iranian territory such as by the Buwayhids and their control of Baghdad. States emerged in Iran between the 11th century and the 15th century; they were generally Turkish, ruling over Iran and expanding westward to frequently include Iraq. Since the emergence of the Safavid state, the situation in the region led to the emergence of two empires. The struggle between Persians and Ottomans had been under way since the days of Shah Isma'il, and it continued between the two sides, through the days of the Safavid state and then the states that succeeded it in Iran, until the First World War.

Throughout four centuries, whenever a strong sultan or ambitious shah emerged, invasions of neighbouring territories would be launched or there would be attempts to recover territories previously lost. The Arabs did not trigger this struggle, but its principal battleground was their land, the Tigro-Euphrates Valley. The people of Iraq were exposed to harm and danger from both sides, sometimes in the name of religion, and they inherited much of the bitterness resulting from this continuous struggle. It might be assumed that ethnic differences played a role in the struggle, but we know that the Safavids relied militarily on the Turcoman tribes in the first stages. Attention may be drawn to language as affirming identity, but Shah Isma'il systematized poetry in the Turcoman dialect and corresponded in it, at a time when the sultan, for his part, used the Persian literary language. Still, these elements did have a lasting effect.

The difference over *madhhab*, which distinguished the identity of each side, had a clear impact. When Iran took up Shi'ism, this was important in affirming its identity and independence from its neighbours to the east (Uzbeks) and west (Ottomans). But Shi'ism did not distinguish Iran from the Arabs. For Shi'ism began with the Arabs and was centred initially in Iraq. Most of its followers, before the Safavids, were Arab. Is religion a link and cause for cooperation and building between two nations in the modern age, or should it take its course towards internecine enmity and harm? Legists dealing with the present, and with personal statutes, have returned to the imamate, and to the four *madhhabs* as well; this in itself is an indication of areas of cooperation and enrichment.

Dispute may be relegated to the geography of the region, but the geographic barriers (mountains) are no longer of historical significance in the modern age. It is to be noted that Iranians, like the Arabs, have a cultural historical identity. This identity continued across the ages, with all their developments and incidents. After centuries of conflict between Iranians and Ottomans, Iran remained by and large within its historical borders, the Ottoman state disappeared, and Iraq retained its Arab Islamic identity. Should we submit to a heritage of bitterness, which we are not an active party to, or should we look at the regional and international conditions, with a view to a better future?

The resplendent pages of the cultural and civilizational side remain by and large with us, in the contributions of the Iranians, alongside the Arabs', to enriching these aspects and expanding their horizons in Arabic during the formative period, thereafter in Arabic and Persian. Shall we look at this cultural history with a positive backdrop for our view of history and the study of it, or shall we look to the negative political points and others? Do we want history to drag us back and obstruct motion, or do we want it as a launching pad towards a better future?

Select Bibliography

*Professor of History and former President of Baghdad University; currently, Professor of History, Faculty of Arts, The Jordanian University, Amman, Jordan.

Arberry, John Arthur. *The Legacy of Persia*. Oxford: Clarendon Press, 1953.

Barthold, W. *Turkestan down to the Mongol Invasion*. London: G.M.S., 1928.

Bosworth, C. E. *The Ghaznavids*. Edinburgh: [n.pub.], 1963.

Boyle, J. A. (ed.). *The Cambridge History of Iran*. Cambridge: Cambridge University Press, 1963, 5 vols.

Browne, Edward Granville. A *Literary History of Persia*. Cambridge: Cambridge University Press, 1953–1956, 4 vols.

— *Encyclopedia of Islam*. 2nd ed., Article 'Iran'.

Frye, N. N. *The Cambridge History of Iran*. Cambridge: Cambridge University Press, 1975, vol. 4.

—*The Heritage of Persia*. London: [n.pb.], 1962.

Khadduri, Majid. *The Gulf War*. Oxford: Oxford University Press, 1988.

Lambton, Ann K. S. *Landlord and Peasant in Persia*. London: Oxford University Press, 1953.

— *Theory and Practice in Medieval Persian Government*. Various reprints. London: Oxford University Press, 1980.

Longrigg, Stephen Hemsley. *Four Centuries of Modern Iraq*. London: Oxford University Press, 1925. New edition. Beirut: [n.pb.], 1968.

Lockhart, L. *The Fall of the Safavid Dynasty and the Afghan Occupation of Persia.* Cambridge: Cambridge University Press, 1958.

Minorsky, Vladimir Fedorovich. *Iranica: Twenty Articles.* Tehran: Tehran University Press, 1964.

—*The Turks, Iran and the Caucasus in the Middle Ages.* Various reprints. London: [n.pb.], 1978.

Nazim, M. *The Life and Times of Sultan Mahmud of Ghazna.* Cambridge: [n.pb.], 1931.

Noldeke, Th. *Das-Iranische Nationalepos.* 2nd ed. Berlin, Leipzig: [n.pb.], 1921.

Perry, John R. *Karim Khan Zand.* Chicago: [n.pb.], 1979.

Rypka, Jan. *History of Iranian Literature.* Dordrecht, Holland: [n.pb.], 1968.

Sadighi, G. H. *Les Mouvements religieux iraniens au Ier et IIIe siècle de l'hégire.* Paris: Les Presses Modernes, 1938.

Savory, R. *Iran under the Safavids.* Cambridge: Cambridge University Press, 1980.

Siddiqi, A. H. *Caliphate and Kingship in Medieval Persia.* Philadelphia: [n.pb.], 1977.

Spuler, B. *Iran in Fruhislamischer Zeit.* Wiesbaden: F. Steiner, 1952.

Von Grunebaum, Gustave Edmund (ed.). *Unity and Variety in Muslim Civilization.* 3rd edition, Chicago, Ill.: University of Chicago Press, 1963. (Comparative Studies of Cultures and Civilizations.)

2

Arab–Iranian Ties: Historical Precedents, Present and Future Confluences

AHMAD LUWASANI*

The historical aspect of Arab-Iranian relations, if dealt with from the standpoint of the course of the two nations, is as difficult as it is interesting; difficult because it spans a long time, truly long, and interesting because their enlightening and noble aspects have contributed much that is beautiful, truly beautiful! I can say with confidence that I know of no nations in human history more different than the Arabs and Iranians, in race, mind, environment and tongue. And yet, their political and social confluence, their intellectual heritage, is greater and richer than any other two nations, even those in which the two are combined.

The Evidence of History

The phrase 'historical aspect in the ties of the two nations', any two nations, suggests, at first glance, military history; the pursuit of conquests, wars, forms of rule and revolutions. In-depth and dynamic history, the history that actually affects peoples, is the civilizational background. What we mean by this is that military conquests, material power and regimentation, important as they are in determining the destiny of a society during various historical eras, fold and shrivel if there is no emotional and spiritual social backdrop of merit. The wars of the Hulaguids, White Hordes, Tartars, Turks, Mongols and their likes were characterized by military force, materialist violence and a destructive tyranny unprecedented in other wars. And yet they passed, their effects soon enough erased, as though they never were.

Furthermore, while conquests and wars in remote times sometimes appear to have played the dominant, or at least the more important, role in history, they in fact arose from a different factor – the economic – which in our view also plays a very important part in conflicts between states and groups, past and present. However, to the military factor with its materialist economic background must be added another, more important one: the social, which serves to bring together or divide peoples, and which has a different background, one that in our view forms the deeper, more far-reaching and active factor in the relations between nations. I mean by this the spiritual or civilizational factor,

I will therefore attempt in this presentation of the history of the two nations to address conquests, wars and warfare states briefly so as to concentrate more, and as deeply as possible, on the ideal civilizational aspect. For this is the route to Arab–Iranian rapprochement, and to the mutual support and reinforcement of the two nations before the new orders, whose mouths are wide open to devour their treasures.

But first we should point out that each of these two nations, thanks to their geographic proximity, formed a barrier that protected the other from outside invasions. Cyrus, with his power and perpetual vigilance in defence, protected his country from attack by the tribes of Hyt, Hawn, Sakka – the so-called Gog and Magog – and other invading nomadic tribes that covered the great steppes of western and central Asia, from the Caucasus and the central lands of the Indian subcontinent. He protected what lay behind his territory to the west, that is the homelands of the Assyrians or Chaldaeans or Canaanite Phoenicians, which at a later stage carried the name of the Arab countries. When the barrier of the east Mediterranean coast fell before Alexander of Macedonia, and Tyre and its island fell after a long and hard siege, the way to the entire east lay open for him. Not only did Fars fall to him, but all of the lands of Iran, enabling him to reach the depths of India effortlessly and easily. And when Iran, which repulsed the Mongol tide before and after Islam, was defeated by the onslaughts of Genghiz Khan, Hulagu and Timur, the tide went beyond it to Mesopotamia to the west, until Timur reached Aleppo and Damascus. It was as though the Lord of these two nations, who joined them in geography and people, had destined and determined, whether they like it or not, that they be one another's support, protector, line of defence and comrade in the common cause.

The Arabic–Islamic Imprint in Iran and the East

Political history shows continuous contact between Arabs and Iranians, from ancient times until the emergence of Islam. Like all similar ties between peoples, these of course had their negative and the positive aspects. But those who look carefully will see that relations on the whole were positive, favouring both sides. We shall mention only two of these, prominent in their history. The first was the campaign of Khosraw Anushirwan (Chosroes I) in Yemen, to expel the Abyssinians, at the appeal of its king,

Sayf bin-dhi-Yazan; he returned to the Arabs their land and to their king
his throne. The poet al-Bukhturi, two and a half centuries later, showed
their appreciation with the verse:

They supported our domain and strengthened its power
Through the protector under the civet's valour.

The second is the alliance between the Persians and their Arab allies,
the Mundhirite princes at al-Hirah. This was such a close alliance that the
Sassanian emperor pledged to Mundhir the education of his crown prince
Bahramjur, who became so engrossed with the Arabs and Arabic that he
spoke the language fluently and eloquently and also used it to write poetry.

While this meeting of the two nations, dating far back, is a meeting of
boundaries, military conquests, economic ties, political alliances and material gain, they were fated to interact and, at a later stage, to enrich social
and civilizational exchange in thought, literature, art and ideas, and in all
forms of aesthetics and spiritualism. This is their great shared legacy. This
civilizational side appeared and multiplied after the emergence of Islam
when the relationship between them developed from one of two states in
defence or attack, cooperation or enmity, to two peoples absorbed and guided
by a noble idealism, relinquishing for its cause national zeal, material gain,
family comfort, even physical existence, all the way to death. Does this
emotional talk reflect a biased attachment, love and appreciation? No! It is
a judgement made on the basis of clear historical fact, evident to whoever
sees the broader realities with the trained student's eye, the eye of the im-
partial critic, the eye of the comparative historian overseeing events and
situations with a totally comprehensive civilized vision. Let us take one
example, or a few examples, from the history of the two nations and their
behaviour after the emergence of Islam to see the subsequent difference in
behaviour and how much higher the civilizational dimension was over national zeal and its limitations.

When the soldiers of Khusraw Anushirwan entered Yemen, expelled
the Abyssinians and restored the Arab King Sayf bin-dhi-Yazan to his
throne, they remained in the conquered areas. They resided there, married,
and gave birth to a generation of men and women who were called in Yemen,
and in history thereafter, the 'sons'. Their birth paralleled the emergence of
the Message of Islam, the hijra of the Prophet. The 'sons' were among those
who believed in the new Message that proceeded from a land other than
their lands, through a Messenger not of their nation. When the Messenger
responded to the summons of his Lord, and the apostasy began among the
Arabs, refusing to pay the zakat to the caliph and his aides, these 'sons' of
Persia fought in it by order of their king. They rose to defend the Arab
Islamic caliphate, opposed to them in lineage, and supported its state, op-

posed to them in nationhood and they backed its system, which contradicted theirs in terms of property, family and class. They did this, while the Sassanian emperor was still on his throne, the haughty empire still standing in its violence and the illusion of its might. It could not even conceive, or its followers conceive, that the Arabs would even think of invading it and march on it with their bare feet.

Why did the 'sons' in Yemen do that? What prompted them and their likes, barely describable as a sovereign invading army, when presumably they were aggressors by virtue of being subjects of the occupying ruling imperial state? More – by the standards of their age, they were expected to not only be subjects, but even equals with those bedouins they ruled over, a collection of weak subjects themselves from among the peoples subordinated to them. What drove them to become defenders, in arms and in person, of a system which in principle and practice struck at their own system? Was it not a passion for ideals that went beyond the attachments of nation, sex, language and family; a spiritual fusion lifting them above the clan, tribe, kinship and a limited plot of land, rendering them a medium enraptured by a Message whose divinity they believed in, a medium ready to die in its defence?

Another example from the history of the two neighbouring nations: the experience of the retreat of the Arab state from the lands of Iran, compared with its retreat from Spain. The Arab Muslims entered Persia in the first quarter of the 1st century AH, with a humanitarian message, neither national nor racial: 'No favouring of Arab over Persian except in piety.' The Islamic conquest extended to cover in a few years the whole of what is today Iran and Afghanistan; shortly thereafter, what is today Armenia, Turkmenistan, Uzbekistan, Tajikistan, Kirghizia, Kazakhistan, the north of the Indian subcontinent, and an important part of western China. The western part of these domains conquered by the Arabs, i.e., that lying on the Mediterranean, had a great political past, a deep sense of nationhood and wide imperial rule rivaling the Romans before them to the west, fully half the entire ancient world. The view of the occupying waves should have been not one of irritation, dispersion or jealousy, but of rage, aggression, hatred and intrigue.

Add to this the fact that those who controlled matters – a few years after the first four caliphs – did not maintain their non-racial and humanitarian ways, but rather ruled as a people with private possessions, blatantly racial, national and dynastic in their manners. For the Umayyad kings who were proferred with the title caliph were like him who said while angrily tearing up the Holy Qur'an:

If you stand before the God on Judgement Day,
Say, O Lord tear me to pieces al-Walid.

Or the one who failed to see in Islam, or its Prophet and his Message, anything but a family struggle for possession and rule, between his Umayyad family and the Hashemite family of the prophets:

I played 'Hashem' with possession but neither
Tiding came nor Inspiration descended.

These rulers and their likes permitted their governors in the east to take the *jizyah* from non-Arab Muslims. Their eternal servant in the Hijaz, al-Hajjaj bin Yusef, ordered that no person lead prayer in the Kaaba except an Arab.[1] Their exchanges at the levels of administration, courts, army, taxation and all public services were on the basis of discrimination between Muslims – Arab and non-Arab – to a point where the non-Arab was dubbed *mawali*, whether as freed slave among them or as always free like the lords of the Arabs. The situation reached a point where one *khariji* fought in defence of Islam – as he understood it and by his standards – and when he got the better of his adversary in battle, he refrained from slaying him when he learned he was Arab. Another *khariji*, after learning that one of the *mawali* married a young lady from the Banu Selim bedouins, got so angry that he rode to Medinah to complain of the grave matter to his Umayyad *wali*, who separated the man from his wife, flogged him two hundred lashes and shaved his head, beard and eyebrows.[2]

This racism was exercised by those calling themselves successors, in a nation whose Prophet said: 'He is not of us who preaches tribal zeal.' The Prophet who freed a slave girl, Maria the Copt, his wife and a mother of the faithful, precisely like Khadijah, Aysheh, Um Salameh, and his cousin Zeinab bint Jahsh. He who said to Salman the Persian, when he was a slave for sale: 'Salman is of us and of the House of God.' It is this racism that led in the Umayyad period to the emergence of the *da'wat al-taswiyyah* in non-Arab Muslim circles, even among sincere believers – many from among the Arabs themselves – followed by Umayyad reaction and angry discrimination against those calling for equality between Arab and non-Arab, whatever his race, for equality in Islam, a reaction that was fomented by determined suspicious persons, creating in that multi-national society a Shu'ubiyyah movement that was fabricated, kindled and inflamed into a canker that ate away at Islamic society and shattered it from within.

How can we envision the feelings of the sons of the conquered countries in the face of this unstable and inhuman situation – in clear violation of Islam – in lands which rulers claimed they were occupying in order to spread the teachings of Islam? Is it strange that they should seek to extirpate this whole religion so long as people of this kind were its lords and masters? Can we not suppose, even by our own standards today, after the advance of humanity centuries and generations, and the emergence of its ideal standards and measures – is it not fair to suppose that they burned with rage over the memories of their past glories, yearned sentimentally for the violence of their own empire, dreamt of the day their state would rise again, a state that would rid them of those occupiers and destroy them, expelling them and even the religion and the teachings they claimed and proclaimed?

Their state emerged – in a very short period of time, less than two centuries from the first conquest of the land. Yes, the Tahirid state emerged, the first Islamic Persian state led by a Persian family. What did it do in the way of revenge? What did it do with the new religion, which toppled its sovereign and his followers who amended the slogans of its nationalism?

It did not abandon its Islam. Rather it imposed itself on the Arabs and others out of love for Islam and a call to correct the deviations of its rulers. It did not call for racial nationalism and nationhood. When other Persian states emerged thereafter – Saminid, Buwayhid, Ziyarid and others – Islam continued with them too, until after the Arab eclipse and the emergence of the smaller Turkish states, after the emergence of the two sectarian states in Isfahan and Istanbul, after the European penetration, and the dominance of Persian language, race and national sentiment. For all that had happened, the land of Pars continued to embrace the Message that came with the Arabian conquest from the Peninsula of the Arabs. Indeed, it rendered it great service, and its sciences too, in all walks of civilized life.

I find it relevant to compare here, very briefly, what followed the eclipse of the Arab conquest in Iran, and what followed its eclipse in Spain. For Iran, despite its royalist, nationalist and racial precedents, and despite the conflict of economic and political interests before the opening of its nation to the Arabs, and despite what it contributed at the civilizational level from itself and from India and Greece, and despite having been the seat of other divine religions – Zoroastrianism, which presumably would make it more hostile to the new religion – and despite the brevity of the period between conquest and eclipse – the Iranians did not abandon the divine spirit that the Arab conquest bore them. In the case of Spain, there was not generally any enmity between it and the Arabs and Muslims before the conquests, except that flowing from military conquest. Nor was there between it and the Arabs – as in the case of the Iranians – any prior political, military, national, religious or civilizational collision that would intensify resentment, hatred and the quest to expel them. Furthermore, Arab rule in Spain lasted for eight centuries, yes, eight centuries; less than a quarter of it would have been sufficient to change the world, revise all understandings, renew all thoughts and feelings, brainwash all succeeding generations and change their systems, aspirations and ideals, as occurred in that same area and others, with the East Syrian Church, with the Greek Orthodox of Syria, the Copts of Egypt, the Greeks of Anatolia, the Berbers of Morocco, the Red Indians of America, the blacks of Africa, and on and on. And yet when the

Arabs left Spain one morning, with them went every vestige of the mission, its civilization, history, thought, literature and aesthetics, as though there was no rule there at all.

Why? Why this big difference in results and connections? Does it not mean that there was unconscious closeness and accord between the spirit of the Arab and Iranian nations, missing between the Arabs and the Iberians in Spain? A joint balance between them – perhaps you could call it an eastern spiritualism of such power and depth as to keep them attached to it even during conflicts of political, economic and emotional interests. It is a balance that should always be noted and benefited from, to help bring the two nations together and exploit opportunities for cooperation to their mutual interest.

A third example from the history of the Arabs and Iranians: the Crusades. The Crusader states of Europe invaded the East to usurp Jerusalem from the Muslims. They were victorious in their campaign, even prolonging their control for tens of years, two centuries in all. But it soon enough waned. The European soldiers even melted into the East, losing their racial, religious and emotional identity. Indeed the names of tens of families – Arab today – in Palestine, Lebanon, Syria and elsewhere, shout with evidence their European origins.

One asks: What is the connection between the Iranian people and this campaign, whose territory was the east Mediterranean coast, having no border with Iran? The answer is that those few meters from the land of Palestine, Lebanon and Syria did not stand alone in the face of Europe, its armies, fleets and aggressive power, until their decline or dissolution. The entire East arose, with its Islamic idealism and adoration of Jerusalem – a Jerusalem that was, and remains, a symbol, meaningful and of significance for it. Such adoration prompted states, families, groups, religious orders and individuals, from Iran especially, and from neighbouring eastern peoples generally, to leave their homes and loved ones, forego their comforts and pleasures, subjecting their lives and existence to death in defence of a Jerusalem they believed was holy, in loyalty to divine spiritual ideals they believed in, not for the sake of Persian, Arab, Turkish, Kurdish, Khawarizmi or other nationalities. Did the great Persian poet Saadi, son of Shiraz, the capital of the province of Fars, who was captured by the Crusaders in Tripoli of Syria, act in defence of the Arabism, of a land or a national colour that contradicted his own? Or again, did Salaheddin Ayubi, when he mustered the armies and crossed the great tracts, he, the Kurdish Aryan, do so in defence of holy Arab Jerusalem?

On the contrary, their love was for the voice that cried from the wilderness of the Arabian Peninsula, and his non-racialist humanity. Because he called for mercy for all the worlds, under the slogan 'he is not of us who preaches tribal zeal', and his echo was the love reflected from the east, from

Iran in particular, and its extremities, in deference to the Arab – politics, state and civilization.

The Impact of Persian Spiritualism in the Lands of the Arabs

Against this, we see a comparable emotional trend, but in the opposite direction. It proceeded from the Near East to the West, from Ur, Palestine and the Hejaz, where the three monotheistic religions emerged and became active, later carrying, gradually, the name Arab countries, to reflect in the East on Iran and its people, in love and appreciation. Whoever surveys the history of the three monotheistic religions, Judaism, Christianity and Islam, all better representatives of civilization than materialism and utilitarianism, clearly sees that the land of Pars and its people had from the beginning a distinct place in them, a good and praiseworthy presence.

Judaism, which suffered the hardship of captivity, dispersion and humiliation, under the rule of Chaldea and at the hands of its King Nebuchadnezzar especially, glorifies Cyrus, King of Persia, who issued after his victory over Nabonides, the last king of the Chaldeans, a proclamation giving freedom to all peoples. And so he freed the Jews from captivity and permitted them to return to Jerusalem to build the temple. The Books of 2 Chronicles, Ezra and Isaiah[3] sing the praises of and glorify Cyrus, even making him a messenger of God to save the Jewish people in particular, whereas his bounty was not for the Jews alone but extended to freedom for all his subject peoples, among whom were his enemies and enemies of the Jews – the Babylonians themselves.

Christianity, which appeared in the land of Palestine, shows us that shepherds of the Persian magis came from the East, following a star that led them to the manger in which the Christ in swaddling cloth was laid after he was born in Bethlehem. At their hands, the miracle of divine guidance to the sincere infant was realized, and the miracle of the inspiration not to return to Herod, lest it lead him to the birthplace of the young child and his person.[4]

Islam, which emerged from the Hijaz, witnessed from the first a prominent Persian presence. For Divine Wisdom destined the Prophet to have around him three individuals from different and separate peoples and nationalities: Suhayb the Roman, Bilal the Abyssinian, and Salman the Persian. What moral weight did history give to each of these three? Suhayb was no different from any other normal individual from among the Companions; there was nothing peculiar about him, though the nation he is identified with was, before the Muslims and Arabs generally, an equal and rival of the Persians. As for the good and sincerely pious Bilal, the most he was noted for was that he was – or became – the Prophet's muezzin. Doubtless this quality returns to his having a good or strong voice, a divine gift, not to any particular personal, intellectual, creative or emotional effort. As for Salman, who left his home in Persia to tour the wide and diverse world of God in search of the truth and answers to questions that only arise in minds of the honourable and the civilized, since the start of his Islam he showed a certain inventiveness before the Companions of the Prophet, and a personality distinctive in faith, morals and loyalty – until he ended up an owned slave and humiliated barber in the racist stratified society of pre-Islamic Hijaz. He became in the end a *wali* over Mada'in (Ctesiphon), a governor of the province of Iraq which was perhaps the richest, most active and influential, and even biggest of the neighbouring provinces conquered. Indeed, the Prophet himself said before his appointment: Who among the Muslims is more important than being a worker or *wali* over a province large or small: 'Salman is of us and of the House [of God]'. The civilized soul of the Persians was reflected in the reign of the Prophet, and in more than one Prophetic *hadith* transmitted by the books of *hadith* and their narrators in various ways, clarifying his saying, which all have transmitted as definite: 'If knowledge were in the Pleiades, a hand from Persia would reach out for it'.

This land included in its past history various peoples – Assyrian, Chaldean, Babylonian, Phoenician, Canaanite, etc., and was surrounded by several different peoples: Medean, Lyddian, Hittite, Greek, Egyptian, Abyssinian, Indian. What, therefore, is the reason for witnessing, from among all these, only the Persian presence in the arrival of the three religions, and in a way that is beautiful, righteous and human? Is there in this an indication of a peculiarity of that nation, a distinction, a preparedness, an open, human civilized nature, I daresay even global nature, rendering them closer and better prepared to exchange aesthetic benefit, especially with the Arabs adjoining them geographically?

And after the Beginnings ...

The student of the region's history of civilization quickly decides that the Iranian Persian arrival was not merely a watching over of the beginnings of the three monotheistic religions, as we mentioned, but played an active role in their emergence. This spanned the entire length of their long history, as well as in the other histories – architectural, cultural and human – of the neighbouring peoples.

In the Old Testament the Books of Ezra, Jeremiah, Daniel, Esther and others speak of the movements of the Persians and their kings, and their doings over their long history: near Lake Urmia (in north west Iran today), which still bears that name, and in Hakmatana (Hamadan today, south of the Khazar Sea, called the Caspian), at Shushan al-Qasr (near Shiraz today, in south central Iran), and elsewhere.

Christianity recognizes that the land of Persia carried to the Indian subcontinent the East Syrian Church writings, present today in ancient Indian inscriptions. The Kisras, Sassanian pleasure-seekers, during the New Year's Day and other celebrations in Mada'in, would have one of them sit as *Mu'adhibban Mu'adhib* (the chief of the *mu'adhibs*, or religious leaders of the Zoroastrian state church) on his right, and the Christian Catholicos (primate of their church) on his left. The Persians, however harsh and long their wars with Christian Rome, permitted freedom of worship, movement and work in those difficult times for the Christians throughout their empire. When the Nestorian and Jacobite Churches split, the Jacobites slaughtered their rivals to a degree worse than any other religious order had done. It reached a point where seven Nestorian philosophers and leaders, fleeing the death and carnage, took refuge with none other than the Sassanian emperor Khusraw Anushirawan who gave them shelter and sent them to the city of learning, Jundishapur, to pursue their work and teach their followers and progeny their knowledge and wisdom. Indeed, many of the Persian pleasure-seekers married Christian women and presented them as queens – as did Anushirawan himself, whose son sought, through his Christian wife, to obtain the throne after his father, or his grandson Khusraw Abriwiz, who first married Mariam, daughter of Caesar, then the Iranian Christian slave girl Shirin. The latter played a role in Persian literature (Sassanian and Islamic), the role of Leila al-'Amerieh the Arab.[5] The remains of the palace that the emperor built for her still stand, despite the passage of more than fifteen centuries, with all their emotion, conflicting sectarian and violent currents and the town in which it stands still carries her sweet name, Shirin's Palace. It proclaims – to whoever cares to know – the loyalty of her lover, the Zoroastrian magi emperor, who was at war with the sons of her Christian faith.

As for the reflection of Persian civilization in Islam, it is broader than can be summarized in lines or pages or even books, however many. It is a history of action and response, cause and effect, give and take, wealth bequeathing wealth, between the two nations of the Arabs and the Persians. It is even the more resplendent chapter of the course of their civilization, if not the whole of their actual and noble history. In language and its many branches – rhetoric, syntax, inflection, eloquence, prosody, lexicography, etc.; in the sciences of medicine, astronomy, mathematics, chemistry, algebra and others; in philosophy, wisdom, logic, ethics, education; in poetry, prose, criticism, fables, folk tales and legends; in denominations, affiliations and separatism; in geography, countries and travel; in history, biographical history and biography; in Islamic jurisprudence, interpretation, discourse, narration and *hadith*; in painting, calligraphy, illumination, ornamentation and wood engraving; in the architecture of copulas, mosques, minbars and minarets; in any field of civilized intellectual and aesthetic endeavour in Islam, the presence of the Persians is there. They delved into them lovingly, studiously, creatively and generously, in Arabic and Persian together! Can we deny the corpus of the contributions? Those of Ibn al-Muqaffa', Abdul Hamid al-Kateb, Sahl bin Harun, Ibn al-'Amid, al-Sahel bin 'Abbad, Ibn Sina, al-Ghazzali, Abu Hunayfah, Ahmad bin Hanbal, Sibawayh, al-Farra', al-Sirafi, Abi 'Ubaydah, al-Zamakhshari, al-Thalibi, Ibn Qutaybah, Abu'l-Faraj al-Isfahani, Nizam al-Mulk, Ahmad bin Faris, al-Azhari, al-Firuzabadi, al-Yaqubi, Abi Zayd al-Balkhi, Farideddin al-'Attar, the Nubakht family, Abu Hayyan al-Tawhidi, Abi Hanifah al-Dinawari, Abi Rayhan Biruni, Abu'l-Fadl al-Midani, al-Nayshaburi, Tabari, al-Tibrisi, al-Kulaymi, Ibn Babawayhi, Nasir al-Din Tusi, Abi Jaafar Muhammad bin Hasan al-Tusi, Abu Bakr al-Razi, al-Bukhari, Muslim al-Nayshaburi, Ibn Najjar al-Qazwini, al-Shahristani, al-Kaabi, Abi Musa al-Nubakhti, Musa Shahwat, Yaser al-Nisa'i, al-Khwarazmi, Omar Khayyam, al-Jihani, al-Istakhri, al-Nasfi, Ibn Miskawayh, Ziyad al-A'jam, al-Taftazani, al-Buzjani, al-Fakhr al-Razi, Mulla Sadra, al-Fayz al-Kashani, al-Bastami, Saadi, Abdel Qaher Jurjani, al-Sakaki, al-Ameli, Badi' al-Zaman al-Hamadani, al-Qazvini, Abi-l-'Abbas al-'Ajami, Mawlana Jalal al-Din Rumi, al-Kasa'i, Abi Ali al-Farisi, Abi-l-Hasan al-'Ameri, Naser Khusraw, al-Sina'i, al-Sijistani, al-Harwi, Shihabeddin al-Suhrawardi, al-Bakharazi, Abdullah al-Ansari, Bayhaqi, and many more among hundreds, even thousands of known minds (with the unknown probably many times more), in all walks of thought and aesthetics. Can anyone deny their prominence in Islamic history? And through it, therefore, the history of civilization and service to mankind?

Thus, the contribution to civilization that joined the two neighbouring rich nations, Arabs and Iranians, is prolific, truly prolific, as well as vast and deep, all across their long and extensive common history.

The Impact of Interaction and Mutual Contribution

Here a question may be raised: Recognizing the civilization contribution conjoining and common to both nations, is it not an obligation that they share economic, social, literary and moral activities generally? What is there to forbid independent civilizational energies, activities, output and creativity by each, showing the strength of each's own contribution and own nationalism?

Perhaps this talk was acceptable in an earlier era or eras, i.e., the phase of independent, complex and haughty nationalism. I am not against nationalism, of course. Who does not love his nation cannot love anyone, and thus cannot win the love of anyone. But there is a big difference between closed nationalism, egocentric, fanatical, vain, haughty, and nationalism that is open, with clear benefits from its particular nationalism, working for cooperation and the exchange of knowledge and material and non-material benefits, strengthening joint interests with others. Wherever man climbs up the ladder of human advancement and global civilization, he exceeds the bounds of his own colour! With the growth of his self, his idealism, and then requirements, grow; they rise and expand in his vision the limits of his own personality and the horizons of his own ambitions and contributions.

As the limits of the world for the Iranians were confined, at one time, between 'Mad' and 'Anzan', the limits of the world at a later stage unified the two provinces. It grew to become all of the Persian Empire, which combined them both. So too the Arab son of Yathrib saw at one time all of the world reduced to the two tribes of Aws and Khazraj; after a time he saw the limits of the world become all of Yathrib, the Medinah of the Prophet, which united Aws, Khazraj and others. This Arab, whose dreams, hopes, conflicts and aspirations were all at the level of 'futile' or 'in vain', began to develop and expand in mind, love and loyalty to the level of the locale of the Message, which packed away 'futile', 'vain' and all the rest. Then on to the state that carried a religious imprint with a national colouration; then to the nation of nations that worked to replace nationalism's genealogical racist colour with the humanist persuasion, with no preference for one above the other except in piety, service and the noble human cause.

Thus, for Iranian and Arab together, as they climbed the emotional, intellectual and civilizational ladder, their homeland grew for them as well! Not only the geographic homeland, but the greater spiritual, emotional and idealistic one, the homeland of the civil state, the state of openness to the whole human world, the homeland for which, and for what it symbolizes, the sons of Thqeef, Kinda and Taghlib left to die at the gates of India, Khwarazm and China, in its defence, and the sons of Firuzabad, Sijistan and Merv left to die at the gates of Kairouan, Granada and Sicily, to spread its message, principles and symbols.

Closed, fanatical nationalism, whose worth remains on the boundary of its geographic domain and individual language, not only means backwardness for its holder, but loss as well, and the limiting of their bounty and benefits. If we quantify the contributions of nations, such as, say for example, that creativity of such and such a nation is 5 units, the contribution of another 10 units, their joint contribution when they meet and interact does not amount to $5 + 10 = 15$ units, but rather to $5 \times 10 = 50$ units. Impregnation generates new energies, rich and wonderful, which often do not cross anyone's mind.

Let us look at Arab output in the domain of civilizational contributions, the intellectual and aesthetic, in whatever field and at whatever level, prior

to the departure from the Arabian Peninsula and interaction with the neighbouring nation or nations: tents, camel, war at the level of Dahis and Ghabra',
erotic poetry and ruined encampments ... 'Black is our reality, red our past'.
And then, after the openness, contact, exchange and impregnations: if this
bedouin who worshipped stone, sacrificed wood, sanctified thunder and
sometimes ate his worshipped when he went hungry – if he and his sons
after him contribute to art, science and thought, and after less than one
century of time, then the history of mankind has never known his likes or
reached his level in ability and sophistication.

Let us look at Iranian output, which predated the Arab in achieving
civil society and its organization. It contributed to the country's history
and humanities, before the Message from the land of the Arabs; and before
the opening and contact and arts, sciences and systems, it conveyed the
wisdom of India and lived and reflected Greek philosophy. This output
developed, improved and was elevated after confrontation and contact, until
it reached the point of abstract philosophical thought, and meditations on
existence, the universe and the Creator, as well as Sufi and mystical forms
of knowledge. No ancient civilization had reached this, neither the legalistic one of Hammurabi in Mesopotamia, nor Akhenaten's [Amenhotep IV]
contemplative, worshipful and transcendental civilization on the banks of
the Nile; nor those that followed them in God's spacious lands and many
peoples.

The types of contact, exchange, cooperation and impregnation in the
historical precedents of the Arabs and Iran are what enabled the medicine
of Ibn Sina (Avicenna) – who never in his life stepped on Arab soil – to
reach Europe, along with his thoughts and philosophy. Through Arabic,
and the civilization of the Arabs, Avicenna's knowledge spread to Europe's
universities, institutes and schools of medicine and there remained for centuries. In the same way Persian literary works in Pahlavi and Dariyyah spread
to the rest of the world through Arabic. The *Hezar Afsaneh* (A Thousand
Legends) and *Hezar Dastan* (A Thousand Tales) – with their Sernedip and
Sindbad, voyages, magic lamps and beautiful stories, appended by the dreams
of the nights of Baghdad and name of Ali Baba, the romance of its caliphs,
the women of its harems, and the interesting intrigues were handed down
to all the world as *A Thousand and One Nights*. The Indian books of wisdom, Oriental literature and its teachings, were given to the world after
they were translated into middle Persian and then into Arabic. Such were
the treasures and literary weapons of the Panchatantra, which became in
Pahlavi *Kalilah and Dimnah*, and of many other works.

The forms of contact, impregnation, cooperation and exchange between
the two nations meant that the poetical stories in Pahlavi, of dance, of the
enjoyment of portraits of imagined love, clever intrigue and entertaining
dialogue were extended to the stories of the Holy Qur'an proceeding from

the land of the Arabs and rendered in the Arab language to portray the Arabian Peninsula, the imagination of its deserts and the virgin purity of its romances. How many an Arab today knows that the romance of Qays bin al-Mulawwah, for example, with his cousin Leila al-'Amerieh, was acted out in Persian decades earlier – on the stages of Dushanbe, Eshqabad, Samarqand and other cities of the Central Asian republics? Or that the poets of Iran transmitted through their odes, music and heroic Persian epics, the literature of the Arab lands, the dreams of their heroes and the sentiments of their people both before and after Islam?

And so, even if a single independent nation could produce creatively, contact, impregnation, cooperation and exchange served to multiply the volume of the output and enhance its quality. As history has taught us this clear, factual scientific account, so it has taught us that, just as contact, impregnation and cooperation across history were the way to mutual gain and benefit for both nations, interruption, enmity and remoteness were the way to damage, harm and loss: the way to gain and the way to damage are parallel, not only at the level of thought, arts and expression but also at the level of practical and good living, at the level of their economies and entire political existence, in place, independence, cohesion, beliefs and power.

The strong and spacious state that incorporated the two nations at one time within one giant nation, impelling its lord to say to the passing cloud that did not thunder forth its copious waters, 'go wherever you will, for the levy you bear will return to me', was transformed by backwardness, repulsion, jockeying for position, sectarian and nationalist fanaticism into nations, then states, and then provinces. The tragedy represented for those who were sincerely jealous of their state, not only its sundering and proliferation but, even worse, its spiritual sundering, variance of purpose, declining ambitions, distortion of beliefs and displacement of aspirations.

The two nations' joint history has here been discussed briefly, in the context of events that took place before the fall of Baghdad, before the Mongol invasions, the subsequent conflicts of petty states (Arab, Persian, Zanji, Kurdish, Mamluk, Ghaznavid, Turkish, Seljuk, etc.), the dominance of the two empires – the Iranian and the Ottoman – the age of European scheming with the Sykes–Picot agreement and all that followed. The extent of the sterility of both in their contribution to civilization in these long centuries is painful to witness.

Yathrib Today

We have mentioned before the possibility of accepting the idea of independent action by the Arabs and their neighbours in an earlier era, enabling acceptance of an overbearing independent nationalism. Today, times have changed and the realities of the world have changed. The development that caused the Awsis and Khazrajis to exceed the bounds of their tribes to the level of Yathrib, the single city that brought them together, and after that caused the cities – Yathrib, Mecca and all the others – to come together within a wider, more comprehensive national unit that combined them, and from there – in the next era – rendered Arabs, Persians and others parts of a single creed combining them all – this development we ourselves have reached today. Our turn has arrived. The state that was established after the emergence of Islam and extended to the east, west and north, then south, until it stood within a few decades at the front ranks of the states of the world, was by the standards of its age, and even subsequent centuries, so vast as to have boundaries that were effectively global. This state has also shrunk, not only in geography, area, people and the energy to form the armies of old, but also by the standards of our age. For example, even China, which was the symbol of remoteness, and was almost unreachable in the eyes of the peoples of the Near East and Middle East in those days, to the point where the Prophet said, 'Seek out knowledge even if it is in China', that same China I can reach in a matter of hours today, far less than the duration of a horse's ride from Damascus to Homs, or Rayy to Hamadan, or Old Cairo to Alexandria, or Tunis to Qayrawan. And with the telephone, broadcasting station, television, satellites, I can know today, within an hour, or maybe even minutes, the news of China's people and of the visitors to its rulers.

Yes, our old world has grown small, that same world that we used to see as so big, spacious and great that nothing could be bigger or greater. Our pride in it has similarly diminished; so too has our appreciation of the size of our tribe or city or country. Our Yathrib, which we look towards today to include our Aws and Khazraj, Persian and Arab, has become the whole world. This emerging and urgent situation, with all its possibilities and dangers, has been recognized by reforming intellectuals, political scientists, sociologists and other scholars for many years. Through this channel calls for international regional unions emerged, and unifying political, social or economic coalitions; indeed, the European continent, despite its multiplicity of states, many languages, disparities in level and different religious sects, has begun the gradual march towards unity, from the economic common market to a broader and deeper political and social unity.

Europe, which is the stronger scientifically, its people psychologically more sophisticated, and the more capable after years of colonialism and economic accumulation – is this Europe the more qualified for union or cooperation or interdependence? Or is it rather the Arabs and Iranians are located at the cross-roads of the three continents, possess oil, sustain large consumer markets, and a population united in its religion and history? Is Europe with its multiplicity of peoples and various races, many languages, and different social persuasions more qualified for union, or at least for cooperation and interdependence, or is it rather the Arabs and Iranians, who form only two nations, speak only two languages, share one civilization bestowing on them far more than Europe's civilization, the more competent and prone to cooperation, exchange and interdependence?

If we pose this query that includes a comparison between the situation of the Arabs and Iran on the one hand, and that of the states of Europe on the other, which have established a common market between them as a prelude to social and then political union, so as to face the power of the greater world, how can strong and forceful Arab and Iranian cooperation not be necessary in the face of a single superpower, the United States of America, whose strength has multiplied and become uncontrollable? It can use – and will invariably use – its massive economic and military might to direct the world according to its interests and whims as the Arab poet[6] predicted it in his verse when he said: 'The atmosphere was cleared for you, so lay and twitter!'[7]

The US has not disappointed either the poet or the analysts. It laid and twittered when it proceeded, after the first signs of the Soviet Union's collapse, to announce its adoption of a new world order, a single system organizing the whole world, a system it has deigned to lead and direct according to rules and considerations whose correctness and merit it decides.

The New World Order and its Backdrop

A world order led by the US can never be relied upon or be reassuring, because the power of government in the US does not proceed from its conduct in the interest of American society, people and national interests as such, but from the electoral and economic interests of that same authority first and foremost. And this is affected by, indeed tied to, its Jewish community, as any student or observer who keeps up with world affairs knows. For the American Jew, as for those in other countries of the world generally, Israel comes before the country he resides in, carries its nationality and benefits from its wealth.

The new world order is a greater threat to the Arabs and Iranians than any other nation of the world because of the state of Israel. Israel for other nations is a state that has its economy, army and technology. These nations and states compete or cooperate with it, just as they compete or cooperate with every other state and strengthen or sever their politial and economic ties with it. Israel says openly that it will not settle for this with its neighbours, even if it does with others. What is required is what it calls normalization – but what this means is economic penetration and hegemony, a personal, moral and spiritual invasion.

I know that here a question appears and may have lingered from several paragraphs back: Israel was erected on part of Arab land, with no geographic link with Iran, so why bring Iran into the question? The motive is that Israel is a state with two special traits. First, it is an independent nationalist sectarian state with its own race and own language, and therefore colliding with the Arabs. Second, it is a theocracy, with a religious persuasion it says is divine, and so is at odds with all opposing or neighbouring divine persuasions, Muslim and Christian. In this regard, the two nations of the Arabs and Iran, and others in the region, even world, meet.

Iran opposes Israeli encroachment on Arab land, and calls openly to fight this state, which sees as one community among others of *dhimmis* (which it says it respects, as Islam obliges it to). As a state, however, this community poses a serious threat not only at the civilian political level but also historical level, reactivated today at the level of creed, civilization, national identity and spirit. For centuries, Christians and Muslims together, and sometimes righteous Jews have pointed to Talmudic beliefs laid down by some rabbis after the Captivity, that is since the 5th century BC, for the preservation of their community, its unity and its eventual return to rebuild its temple. These beliefs, incorporated in the first five books of the Torah, include dangerous and erroneous teachings. The greater danger in them is that they do not stop – as the other revealed religions and philosophic and theological works do – at guiding the spiritual and ethical life of their communities, but instruct their people to invade other societies and religions and destroy their energies,[8] and then, at another, deeper and more penetrating level, to revise non-racialist spiritual and moral beliefs and distort them.[9]

Revision, alteration and distortion of beliefs, ideals, intellectual, emotional and civilizational assumptions are the greater destroyers of a nation's character and the first factor towards splitting its ranks and sundering its unity. Iran, which Israeli expansionism has not touched, may accept or reject the judgement that Israeli encroachment into ideas, beliefs, faith and civilization is no less dangerous than geographic encroachment. In any event, Iran constitutes a support and ally for the Arabs in the geographic and civilizational conflict of both with Israel. The Arabs should profit from this ally, and should look upon every voice, position or call reminding of differences and leading to separation between the Arabs and Iran as suspect, serving the common enemy, and a loss to the Arabs and Iran together. The Arabs should be drawn into alliance and cooperation with all the peoples, states and powers whose interests coincide with those of the Arabs: neighbouring states, the common faith, oil and economy, regional geographic ties, sharing in confrontation of the injustices against the peoples of what has been dubbed the 'Third World' and 'developing countries'. The shocks have been quite sufficient to wake up from the slumber of vanity and empty self-confidence represented by that Palestinian official[10] who said in the 1950s: 'We the Palestinians do not want anyone's help, neither from the Islamic states nor from the states of the region, not even from the Arab states; we alone will throw Israel into the sea!' God rest his soul in death as in life, for He has taken him before he could see Israel end in fact in the sea, but not the sea of the west 'Mediterranean' that he had in mind ... unfortunately.

The Incentive and the Preparation

The success of any major cause requires certain elements, principally two: vision and organization. By vision we mean the target sought and the incentive that inflames and motivates the heart of its bearer. As for organization, it is planning, preparation and good performance so as to reach that target. The target for the modern Jew was set and ready since tens of centuries or more. Nothing was lacking but the incentive and flame of yearning for that target dreamt of and sought after by his ancestors since the Captivity and throughout the Diaspora. The flame drove him to follow the route to the target, the route of planning, preparation and performance, the long and arduous route of organization; long because of the extent of distance and time that were expected to be traversed, with no guarantee of success; arduous because of the smallness of his numbers before those of his adversaries, whose land he sought to expropriate, the smallness of his presence before the greatness of the [Ottoman] Empire that he sought to dismember a part of, and the smallness of his capacities before a nation that he will confront in location, society and wealth. Despite these, he persevered; he persevered because the decision of a strong will is not stopped by the ease or difficulty of a task. The task may well increase his determination when severe, arduous and difficult.

And yet, are aim, incentive and preparedness always sufficient for success? This is the assumption, especially if the aim is good and noble. If the man with a cause has an adversary lacking in spiritual incentive over it, or lacking in planning and preparation, then his chance for success will surely multiply. Yes, Israel emerged because the Arabs, in confronting it, lacked planning, preparation and good performance; even if the incentive – nationalist, religious, patriotic or even for profit – were present, the difference with the Arab in confronting the Jew, the difference in opinion, aim, understanding and approach, prevented his achieving a singular plan and good performance. This is his downfall, which the Jew worked on and will continue to work on, directly, sustaining and influencing it.

My essay deals only with the historical aspect, the past lessons of the relationship between the Arab and Iranian nations, and leaves the matter of 'organization', that is planning, programmes of preparation and future joint effort to other contributors. And so we touch on part of these aspects. However, we have taken note that now Israel is what constitutes the danger for both of them, politically, militarily, economically and – more important – socially, spiritually and civilizationally. We consider it a duty to conclude by maintaining, again, the importance of the aspect of 'vision', that is, the embodiment of the aim and the necessity of always keeping alive the emotional and moral incentive of their peoples.

I say keep alive the emotional and moral incentive, because incentive is what releases man's energies, to the point where he can move mountains, kindled by the flame of adoration, such that he burns himself for the victory of the principle. This incentive that corrects the marches of nations and destinies of peoples often fades after a period of time because of excessive affluence, or the absence of a provocative enemy, or an excess of materialistic interests and greed, or a loss of the flame of love towards the nation. Arabs and Iranians and all lovers of justice need to keep this incentive lofty, strong and vocal in its rejection of the rape of the land, occupation of people's homes, slavery and humiliation. It is an incentive borne, implemented and defended by intellectuals, writers and authors.

From this standpoint, and based on historical precedents and their political logic, it is very clear that the battle with the Zionists will be won. Even if it takes many decades or even eras, Israel will disappear. We do not say this out wishful thinking, nor out of religious or sectarian zeal, but because the Talmudic teachings rest on inhuman and illogical grounds that cannot succeed. They rest on – as we have said – the tenet that the Jews alone are God's chosen people. The teachings of both Christianity and Islam, call for right, justice, love and good will to all mankind! By contrast to the calls of the Gospels, such as 'love your enemies and pray for those who persecute you',[11] and of the Holy Qur'an, such as 'We sent thee not, but as a Mercy for all creatures',[12] no single people to the exclusion of others, we read in the Old Testament hundreds of examples in teachings that say to the Jews, 'you are a people holy to the Lord your God ... and you shall destroy all the peoples that the Lord your God will give over to you, your eye shall not pity them.'[13]

When will a state that is based on such doctrines be brought down? I know that the battle is difficult and will probably be long. Yet Israel is not as powerful as it seems. The weakening factors in its society are many, its difficulties more than ours. Its human resources are as nothing compared to ours; nature and geology has not provided it with the same resources; its population has been raised in different educational systems which reflect the different environment and societies of the countries it came from. The conceptual, interpretational and methodological differences between the groups that make it up are many. The reserve of emotional zeal the Zionists looked forward to before the establishment of their state has petered out. Perhaps more important is that current within Israel that rejects all the beliefs of the scribes – in faith, conduct and religion – which rejects the states' ideology as racism and fights it. Accordingly, this nation contains, as does ours, a Cain and Abel, and, like us, zealotry and openness can be found among its people, and racism and humanism. 'Of the people of Moses there is a section who do justice in the light of truth.'[14]

So begin, and follow up, you people of the mind and the pen your intellectual and human *jihad* against the racism and hegemony of these usurpers. 'Against them make ready your strength to the utmost of your power,'[15] in speech, dialogue, drama or philosophy. 'And slacken not in following up the enemy: if ye are suffering hardships, they are suffering similar hardships; but ye have hope from God, while they have none.'[16]

Notes

*Chairman, School of Oriental Studies, Lebanese University, Beirut, Lebanon.

1.   From Said Abdel Fattah Ashour, *Arab–Iranian Relations*, p. 25.
2.   Ibid., p. 25. Quoted from al-Afghani in Ahmad Amir, *The Dawn of Islam*, Part 1, p. 23.
3.   The Bible, 2 Chronicles 36:22 and 23; Ezra, all of chapter 1, 5:13 and 14, 6:3; and Isaiah, 44:28 and 45:1–7.
4.   The Gospel according to St Matthew, 2:1–12.
5.   Shirin, the 'Leila' of Persia, had two knights or 'Qays'; the first, emperor Kisra Abriwiz himself, who formally took her as wife and placed her, a commoner, above the seven high families, making her – in a reversal of the ways of the emperors – a queen unrivalled by the wives; the second was the first engineer of his army, Farhad (Farhat in Arabic), who cut a tunnel through a mountain to carry gazelle milk to his beloved Shireen, so she could bathe in it every morning to preserve her beauty; he committed suicide when he was told, falsely, that Shireen had died.
6.   The *Jahiliyyah* poet Tarfa bin al-Abed.
7.   'The Room's Expanse', as in the *Diwan* (p. 43): 'What a great tomb you have … to occupy'.

8.   In the Old Testament, there is not one but two texts, one can even say ten texts, along the following lines: 'When thou comest nigh unto a city to fight against it, then proclaim peace on it … and if it make thee answer of peace … all the people that is found therein shall be tributaries unto thee, and they shall serve unto thee … And if it will make no peace with thee … thou shalt smite every male thereof with the edge of the sword … But of the cities of these people … thou shalt save alive nothing that breatheth'. Deuteronomy, 20:10–17.
9.   In Christianity, the Apostle Paul complained, from the start of that era, of

revisions in teachings, whether at Ephesus in Anatolia or among the Galatians, by some whom he saw as perverting the gospel of Christ and turning it into 'another gospel' in order to trouble their people. (Epistle of Paul the Apostle to the Galatians, 1:6–7). In Islam, we see the Holy Qur'an describing the hurt of the Arabs by the Jews in the Peninsula during the emergence of Islam, to the point where they accepted the claims and allegations of the Jews that the prophets and messengers cannot but be from the Israelites; hence the Arabs' surprise by 'a Warner came from among them' (the Holy Qur'an, Part 26, *Surat Qaf, ayah* 2). As for the post-Qur'anic Islamic heritage, the 'Israelite' talk is more widespread than generally realized.

10. The late Ahmad Shuqayry.

11. The Gospel according to St Matthew, 5:43, and the Gospel according to St Luke, 6:28.

12. Part 17, *Surat al-Anbiya', ayah* 107.

13. Deuteronomy, 7:6 and 16.

14. The Holy Qur'an, Part 9, *Surat al-A'raf, ayah* 159.

15. Ibid., Part 10, *Surat al-Anfal, ayah* 60.

16. Ibid., Part 5, *Surat al-Nisaa, ayah* 104.

Two

Arab–Iranian Economic Ties: Current Situation and Future Prospects For Development

3

Geo-Economics of OPEC Members
in theMiddle East

ALI SHAMS ARDEKANI[*]

United to Succeed

Among the major developments in the post-World War history of international relations was the formation of the Organization of Petroleum Exporting Countries (OPEC). Though this was not the first union of developing countries, in time it became one of the most influential – and controversial – global economic and political bodies.

OPEC was a union of states formed primarily for the pursuit of economic objectives. Many bilateral and multilateral unions and alliances of Third World countries had fallen victim to political wrangling among members. Indeed, in the interests of a global system based on the centrality of two power blocs, the survival of any independent union of developing nations, in spite of the ever-present sources of division among members, was a miracle in itself. That OPEC was formed, endured, and actually came to serve the interests of a group of developing countries, was a tribute to the political maturity and foresight of most of its members.

These bore their fruit when, in a concerted effort to defend their economic interests, OPEC countries took the step forward by securing more realistic prices of oil. The events of the early 1970s proved to the Third World that, once they distinguish their common interest and join hands to realize it, even a highly inequitable world economic structure would be unable to prevent their progress.

Stages of Reaction

Equally interesting was the reaction of the outside world, in particular that of advanced industrial countries, to the behaviour of OPEC. At the time of its formation in 1960 it was viewed as a curiosity rather than a power to be

41

reckoned with. Although the oil industries of some of its members were still, wholly or in part, controlled by Western companies, and although those companies engaged in tacit or even open collusion between themselves, the exertion of great influence over the international market by indigenous governments of oil-exporting countries seemed improbable. To this was added the expectation of political rivalries and conflicts among these countries. There can be no doubt that, if Western powers did take time to look at the prospective role of OPEC in the world economy, they saw in it no more than a temporary club set up with much wishful thinking.

This attitude changed when the members came together to concentrate on what they saw as their joint objective. It is interesting that, at the time when OPEC decided to flex its substantial muscle in the oil market in the 1970s, the old political and even military disputes were quite rife among members. What probably took the world by surprise, more than the systematic moves by OPEC in the direction of raising prices, was the fact that member countries came to treat the Organization's mandate as something independent of their internal and international political objectives and ambitions.

Of course, it was not just the talent and dexterity of a few men of vision in the governments of the member countries that made OPEC an unusual success. There were a number of structural reasons as well; for example, the decision to raise prices came at a time when the Western world had become accustomed to sustained economic growth helped by low prices of raw materials, above all energy, which were decided by consumers themselves. Contrary to the basic rules of economics, increased demand for oil had not led to a proportional rise in its price. As far as consumer countries were concerned, crude oil was a commodity subject to marginal cost pricing. However, that oil was not a renewable substance, and that the earth had limited reserves of it hardly struck anyone at the time. Nor did the fact that by uncontrolled consumption, great environmental costs were inflicted on the globe.

These were some of the reasons that OPEC spokesmen cited for their decision. And in time, some of these shortcomings were remedied. However, the 'shock' that the industrial world experienced at the hands of a group of well-organized Third World countries prompted them to speedy reaction. Part of this reaction was in line with the overall interests of both the producer and the consumer nations. Higher energy costs resulted in rapid technological moves to make better use of oil. But to prevent the history of OPEC from setting a precedent for other Third World countries to follow, less constructive, and at times more insidious, moves were also initiated. These were meant to achieve two aims: first, to restore the old balance of economic power between the producers and consumers and, second, to prevent OPEC from gaining the initiative in the oil market.

To reverse the order of economic relations between the two economic regions in the industrial North and the oil-exporting South, the former created the International Energy Agency in 1975 with the aim of dealing a counter-blow to OPEC, albeit in slow motion. It took eight years to consolidate, mainly by creating a so-called 4,000-million barrel of crude oil 'strategic reserve' of crude oil or the equivalent of 120 days' oil consumption by the Western Alliance. The Alliance originally had two wings: a military one, NATO, and a general economic one, the OECD. Now it created a third, the IEA. The IEA was used to break OPEC's strength. What led to the IEA's success was mainly the policies of OPEC members and their feuds, intentional or inadvertent, over the newly-found collective power of a group of developing countries with its centre of gravity in our region. In other words, the regional geo-economic factor, which could have continued to be the cornerstone of our collective strength, became the fuel of our feuds.

Counter Crisis

The process of reversing the changes in the 1970s bore fruit within a decade. On the one hand, the rise in industrial commodity prices soon overtook what had been gained in the oil market. On the other hand, various measures were adopted to weaken OPEC from without and within. Indeed, within a decade it was not the consumers who were biting their nails with anxiety over an oil crisis. The tables had been turned at a most inappropriate time. There is little doubt that some of the factors that led to the weakening of OPEC were 'externally' induced, though without fertile grounds within the Organization, they would not have taken root. Most others were the result of actions, or the lack of them, that had crippled many other similar unions of developing nations. Indeed, the germs of discontent and tendencies towards disintegration could hardly have afflicted a robust and healthy body of nations. These are the problems that OPEC must not fall prey to.

Reversal

With the severe 'producer-felt' oil shock of 1986, a new and unpleasant phase began within OPEC. The sharp decline in oil prices was the result of the inability of OPEC in several areas. It had failed to adapt its market policies to the new consumption trend in industrial countries and had, in several instances, succumbed to the old temptation to bow down to those political motives that could only undermine intra-OPEC unity of purpose. More significantly, the main point of strength of OPEC – that the collective Organizational goals should transcend those of individual members – had been lost.

This set into motion a vicious cry of disintegration, goaded on by 'non-Organizational' objectives. The period of the 1980s had been a time of heavy politicization for OPEC. But thanks to the victory of the Islamic Republic in my country, the 1980s began with another hour of glory for OPEC, with a new peak price reached in the world markets. The Organization's internal health had been under severe attack despite the fact that member countries' representatives did their best to uphold the established tradition of avoiding volatile political issues within the Organization; the decade witnessed two heinous wars that pulled members apart and placed them in opposing factions. The result was the fact that the outside world could no longer be certain of OPEC presenting a solid front in price and quota setting sessions. Political likes and dislikes had crept into the process of decision-making, and members began to accuse each other of seeking to subvert each other's states by the use of the 'oil weapon'. This was one important factor that started, or at least nurtured, the vicious cycle. The other was born out of the cycle itself.

Geo-economic Face

This latter factor came with doubts concerning the efficacy of OPEC's remedial measures among some of the members. Unfortunately, some of these members were of the opinion that, with more haggling among themselves and between them and consumers, OPEC had already reached the end of its useful life. Indeed, they believed that it could prove more of a handicap than an asset. With this in mind, and no doubt to the satisfaction of OPEC's old enemies, some members began to talk about quitting the Organization for good. Comparing their own short-term conditions with those of non-OPEC oil producers, they came to the conclusion that they might be better off without the obligation to follow strict quotas set collectively and, increasingly, with hard feelings of being left behind.

Without a few courageous attempts at leading members to set aside their non-oil disputes in deference to their oil consensus, OPEC might have gone out of existence before the end of the decade. However, it has increasingly become clear that the future of OPEC lies within a new geo-economic context that is at the same time more circumspect in geographical, and more cohesive in organizational, attributes. In 1992, Ecuador gave in to the temptation of a 'life of freedom' and left OPEC. Since then, several centrifugal tendencies have also been experienced, whether by design or by accident.

OPEC's present membership can be divided into two categories. The bulk of the output comes from the Persian Gulf region, which produces over 70 per cent of OPEC oil. Those countries are also highly dependent on their export of oil for their livelihood and the success of their development programmes. The other category includes members who, either out of lack of confidence in OPEC's future or because of changes in their economic structures, are less dependent on OPEC or on their oil. Countries like Gabon have at times threatened to leave the Organization and in this some other members have sympathized with them. Countries like Indonesia have experienced a change in their economic features involving far less emphasis on oil exports as a main source of foreign exchange.

Some other members have moved closer to organizations outside OPEC. Venezuela is an active member of the OLADE, while Nigeria and Gabon, and of course Libya, are active within OPEC. To these must be added a few more facts. Apart from Iraq, which at present is restricted to produce-for-export, most other members are producing more or less at near full capacity. Exceptions are Saudi Arabia and Iran, which, on the basis of 1994 figures, had spare capacities. All these factors may mean that the future of OPEC is closely linked with events in the Persian Gulf or, at most, the Middle East regions. In other words, the countries of the region are inevitably linked together because of their common interest in maintaining their powerful presence in world oil markets. If the policies of OPEC are again reorganized to maximize the collective economic interests of members, these countries must come closer together and try to harmonize many aspects of their economic and even political attitudes and actions. Of course, the existence of the OAPEC cannot be ignored, an organization that includes the Arabic-speaking members of OPEC. However, since the Iraq–Kuwait war, the OAPEC has lost much of its significance. And besides, the mandate of OAPEC does include oil production and pricing issues.

Shared Attributes

This does not mean that OPEC will be necessarily better off with fewer members. In fact, the larger its membership, the greater its presence in the world, provided that the same spirit of cooperation among members and their individual and collective devotion to their common objectives are present. The question is: is the resurrection of OPEC as it was in its prime probable?

The processes mentioned above, including both talk of arbitrary decisions by some members to leave OPEC and structural changes in the economies of some that render them less interested in the Organization, seem to indicate the likely emergence of OPEC as more of a regional geo-economic centre of gravity than, as in its former role, an international source of major events.

If this is the case, then the grounds are already laid for an important geo-economic bloc. However, its formation depends on a number of pre-requisites, which are almost entirely at the discretion of its members. These have to materialize in order to fortify the natural elements of unity that already exist among them.

The reality of cultural, religious and historical similarities have been mentioned. But there may also exist other elements of unity. Among these, economic facts may play an important role. The economic structures of regional oil producers can be shaped to become complementary. Some of these countries have sufficient internal human and natural resources to develop diversified economic structures. Iran, Iraq and Saudi Arabia are such countries. Others can provide excellent markets for the outputs of these countries while themselves specializing in such fields as commerce and related services. This bloc can then establish a close link with the adjacent regions of Central Asia and the Caucasus, where, again by both cultural and economic imperatives, there are fertile grounds for their cooperation with countries of the Persian Gulf area. Put together, the overall formation would be able to do more than simply stabilize the price of their oil.

Out of about 20 million barrels per day of OPEC's current production, almost 17 million barrels are produced in our region, of which around 15 million barrels are exported. If we could be wise enough to put our heads together such that our collective wisdom adds only one dollar to the international price of oil, the region's oil revenues will increase by over $5 billion annually. Unfortunately, our efforts went in the opposite direction, leading to a price cut per barrel of at least ten dollars for the last ten years, and thus accruing a collective loss of almost $5 billion to the region. If we divide this loss over the 100 million people of our region, even new-borns have already lost $5000 per head. There has never been a more voluntary transfer of wealth from a region, i.e., the Persian Gulf oil producers, to a region that is for the most part richer, i.e., the wealthy industrialized countries.

Positive and Negative Measures

No matter how strong the 'natural pull', we are here dealing with independent sovereign states that control the destiny of their nations. In the past, negative political tendencies to engage in conflict and collision have often defeated the positive forces of unity. In time, with the power of mass media, the weeds of animosity could grow strong enough to suffocate the ancient flower of friendship and brotherhood. Thus, a lot rests with the political authorities of the regional countries, for realizing the great benefits of unity. These positive and negative forces can be briefly enumerated. As a very sensitive region, the Middle East in general, and the Persian Gulf area in particular, has for a long time occupied, and will continue to occupy, an important place in the global equation drawn by major powers. Their aim is to assume an inevitable presence in regional political and economic transactions.

The question is whether such a presence is really essential, and whether without it, regional countries will be worse off. The record of the way the major powers have used the region for their own purposes shows that this has had little to do with the interests of the region's people themselves. On the contrary, the interests of the foreign powers have been best served when those of the region's people and governments have been neglected. In a word, It has usually been a negative and, at best, zero sum game in which the supposed gain of one side is made by accruing losses on the others, thus always leading to collective weakening.

It is not difficult to demonstrate how these unhealthy interests have been served, where they were able to sow the seeds of discord. In that direction, the region experienced two heinous and horrible wars that marred almost a whole decade. In none of them did the war-mongers come any nearer to the realization of their objectives, illegitimate though they were. The result of millions of lives lost and billions of dollars squandered, was lost opportunities to develop the economies of the regional countries within a decade, while countries less deserving than these advanced in leaps and bounds. The result was leaving everyone poorer behind, creating an air of suspicion and distrust, and regression to far lower ranks, in the world division of economic and even political power and prestige, for nations that at one time looked set for rapid economic and social progress.

Even now, the process of depleting the human and material resources of the region for futile aims has not come to an end. Today, when everyone has learned how naive is the idea of achieving fame and fortune by brute force in this day and age, the threat of direct confrontation among regional peoples may have diminished. But not the equally debilitating evil of preparing for a war in a ridiculous situation of armed peace. It may seem an exaggeration, but this situation can be no less damaging than direct warfare, since it is far more inconclusive and, for this reason, unnerving.

Instead of seeing the need to pool our resources together, we are devoting our efforts to erecting dubious and ominous barriers between ourselves. Millions of dollars go into the purchase of arms and ammunition which, at least one hopes, are never going to be used; and they probably will not, unless someone is foolhardy enough to be swayed by the temptation of those who wish to relentlessly continue their lethal trade. This is the negative factor facing us today. But past experience has shown us the way to overcome that as well. There were times when, faced with the need to keep a solid front against external pressure, members who were almost at the brink of direct military confrontation had their representatives turn a blind eye to the hawks at home and join in a broad smile before the cameras. Those threats of war passed, but the benefits of the smiles remain.

Today, there are several points of dispute among regional members of OPEC. We do not want to pass judgement on them and describe most of them as 'non-issues', which they are. But assuming that these differences are as real as can be, people who have the same state of mind and share so many positive attributes must be truly void of statesmanship to fail to resolve them by the prime gift of man: speech with reason. What should be avoided is relenting to the sworn enemies of ourselves and our Faith, who fear nothing more than our solidarity behind a single banner.

There are so many different states in this region, with so many different governments, politics and general outlooks. They and their people are entitled to their differences. But behind all these, there is a strong current of similarities of world-view and temperament, which must be utilized in serving at least two purposes: *first*, to forestall any attempt by our enemies at driving a wedge between us, which they are skilful enough to do by presenting themselves as friends; and *second*, to believe that our economic futures can be best realized by our close cooperation, where we find so extensive a common ground.

*Secretary General, Iran Chamber of Commerce, Industries and Mines, Tehran, Iran.

4

Contemporary Arab–Iranian Economic Relations

JASSEM KHALED AL-SAADOUN*

Introduction

A wise world is governed by interests. The radical changes that recently followed the collapse of bi-polarity rendered economic factors preponderant in conflicts of interest. We are now anticipating a new world configuration that will most probably be governed by tri-polarity, but of a different sort: with time the importance of military force will decline and there will be a simultaneous increase in the importance of economic potentials. In the process of formation of poles for world leadership in the future, all available tools of strength will be utilized to take control of relevant resources. At present, and until the end of the first decade of the next century, the advanced states contribute 73 per cent of global GDP. Their relative share is expected to decrease to 67 per cent, although in absolute terms it will increase. The former Second and Third Worlds, which contain 89 per cent of the world's population, will struggle for the remaining third of global GDP. The Third World is likely to divide into three groups. The *first* would be directly tied to the new leading poles, by geography or by conflict of polarization; this group might give more than it takes, but it will be in better shape. The *second group*, by virtue of consciousness or size, will attempt to form smaller blocs or co-operatives, to defend its interests and form a better negotiating position. It may succeed both ways, widening the benefits of mutual potentials and widening benefits from their relations with others. The *third group* is a scattering of states lacking the merits of the first group, and unwilling or unable to comprehend their situation or the changes taking place around them, and the consequences for their peoples and future. The relative, and perhaps absolute, contribution of such states or groups to global output will decline, with all that this entails in the way of serious economic, political and social implications.

49

The Arabs and Iran share similar traits that render them candidates for any of these divisions. On the one hand, they constitute, by virtue of location and resources, material for conflict between the future blocs that seek to dominate them and place them within key spheres of influence. On the other hand, they are also two ancient, progressive and historical civilizations that are classic examples of conflict as well as understanding, thus possessing the importance in location and population to enable them to enter the associational experiences of south east and central Asia or even India and China. In a third respect they also qualify for decline and greater fragmentation, either for internal reasons, through a squandering of resources and the pursuit of unsuccessful development approaches, or for external reasons, as they may be crushed by the conflict of a world well aware of their weak will or their deteriorating condition.

The author faces a predicament in that his argument may be disputed from the start as too theoretical, or that it is an illusion to consider the Arab region as a unit or bloc in relation to Iran. It is reasonable, and there are historical precedents, both ancient and modern, to speak of a unified Iran. But it is very difficult, at least at present, to write about a unified Arab will on this particular track or that. For the Arabs, through their destructive inter-country and intra-country conflicts that undermine economic construction – something which Iran shares – have made it difficult, perhaps even impossible, to envision a single will between them, or between them and others. Accordingly, it will be a difficult task to defend my argument and to generate wholehearted enthusiasm for support of my thesis of the urgent need to prod Iran and the Arabs into the second anticipated category of the states of the Third World.

The paper will be divided into two main parts and a conclusion. In the *first* part I will discuss the 'status quo' in the Arab region and Iran and at their periphery in an attempt to create grounds for proceeding into the second part. In the *second* part, on 'prospects for the development of economic relations', I will attempt to discuss the three alternatives previously mentioned, concentrating on the mutual benefits to be reaped from the second alternative. The *conclusion* is an attempt to summarize the most important points or ideas in the paper, and will anticipate the discussion, possibly even enrich it, by trying to highlight the weak points in it.

The Status Quo

Twenty-six years after the family of Reza Pahlavi assumed power in Iran, and with the consequences of the Second World War and weakness of the old protectorate state – Britain – patriotic nationalist sentiment exploded. Dr Mosaddeq assumed the premiership in 1951 and nationalized the

British–Iranian Oil Company, at a time when Iran was the most important oil producer in the region. With prospects of oil being discovered in the Arab region – Bahrain in small quantities in 1927, Kuwait in commercial quantities before and after the Second World War – and with signs of nationalist and patriotic movements in the Arab region as well, such as the July 1952 revolution, conflicts of interest took a violent form. Plans were made to topple Mosaddeq and return the Shah, with US–British assistance, with General Zahedi ousting Prime Minister Mosaddeq. Afterwards, Iran assumed the role of stabilizer and defender of a region that grew in importance in the energy-exporting market. The Shah liked to be called 'policeman of the Gulf', and he played that role; perhaps this misuse of resources and their distribution was one reason for the subsequent fall of the empire. A revolution then occurred that was similar to Iran's Constitutionalist Revoltution at the beginning of this century. However, its results were different, for it turned into a fundamental change on the domestic scene and in external relations, entering, from the start, into confrontation with former allies; further unveiling its position was the collapse of the Soviet Union.

Iran's relations with neighbouring Arab states were at their worst during the 1980s when Iran entered, at the start of that decade, a violent and destructive military conflict with its largest neighbour, Iraq. The war was financed from the oil revenues of the two warring states. Arab neighbouring states also contributed their share in the interest of Iraq and, with few exceptions, the states of the region incurred financial deficits after registering surpluses up to the beginning of the 1980s. The financing of the war was the main cause of this situation. Along with the depletion of resources, mutual suspicion weakened the negotiating strength of each state neighbouring Iran. This greatly limited the possibilities for domestic or inter-country reform and, consequently, created a weak negotiating position before others. Matters were made even worse with the Iraqi occupation of Kuwait, the impact of which did not stop at the border of neighbouring Arab states but extended to the entire Arab arena. In addition to turning those states which still had financial surpluses into deficit states, and increasing the deficits of those already in the red, it further eroded the negotiating position of the Arab side. Among the consequences was a weakening of the Arab position in the Middle East peace negotiations, the ease of alternatives to inter-Arab co-operation, and actual and potential weakening of the oil market.

The situation within Iran and the Arab region, and at their peripheries, tended towards instability. The Islamic countries neighbouring Iran endured difficult political and economic strains. Border problems, different forms of government, and religious, political, tribal and sectarian divisions in some Arab states, fuelled the breakdown of their hopeless economic situations and drove them to extremism. In such a situation, looking towards the public interest was weakened and subordinated to interests that grow more glaring in the world about us; the language of slogans that cannot be applied came to dominate, as have particularist interests within each country, embodied in parties, sects, movements or interest groups.

I believe that research work should proceed from this *fait accompli* confronting us, with an admission to all its sins and implications. The researcher must estimate, as much as possible, the opportunity cost of such a *fait accompli*. Accordingly, I will present, in the remainder of this part, a statistical survey of the current state of affairs which may enable us to identify the costs of its continuation.

The Arab Region

The Arab world occupies 10.2 per cent of the surface of the globe and constitutes 4.3 per cent of its population. Its GDP amounted to $508 billion in 1993, at current prices. Per capita GDP amounted to $2117. The region contains 62 per cent of the world's oil reserves and almost 21 per cent of its gas reserves. However, caution is necessary when dealing with these figures, as they may not reflect the reality: there are some illogical motivations that can lead to exaggeration in certain countries' estimates of these reserves, due to disputes over production quotas.

Total commodity exports amounted to $142 billion, most of which are crude oil exports (68.5 per cent). Commodity imports amounted to $127 billion, resulting in a limited trade surplus of $15 billion. Inter-country trade represents no more than 9 per cent of foreign trade. The trade surplus becomes a deficit of about $1 billion, in the current accounts of the same year, if exports, services and imports are added, as total exports amounted to $160 billion and total imports $161 billion. The debt of borrower states is about $153 billion, representing 82 per cent of their total GDP; debt servicing takes away some 31.5 per cent of net exports. The volume of debt represents almost 30 per cent of total Arab GDP for 1993, and its servicing takes away about 11.4 per cent of Arab exports.[1]

The *Economics and Business* magazine[2] (*Al-Iqtisad wa'l-Amal*) refers to two international reports on some additional indicators on the Arab condition. These state, for example, that real growth in the GNP over the last decade was the lowest for five groups of developing countries. It stood at 1.4 per cent, representing a decrease in the standard of living, with the proportion of the poor increasing from 30.6 per cent to 33.1 per cent of the population in 1995, whereas the proportion decreased on average for developing countries from 30.5 per cent to 29.7 per cent. Military expenditures in the Arab world in 1990 stood at 275 per cent of expenditures on health and education and 169 per cent of expenditures on health and education for the whole of the developing world, including the Arab world.

These figures, as we have already commented, are weak indicators, because there is not much difference if some states are added and others dropped, or at least these are the possible readings of the figures under present Arab conditions. Placing this fact aside for the moment, we find that the size of the aggregate Arab economy is, when we unify the base year 1993, small by comparative standards, despite its large area and population. Measured by GDP at market prices, it is about 4.9 times larger than the Norwegian economy, although Norway's population does not exceed 4.33 million, half the size of the Italian economy, and only 6 per cent larger than the ailing Spanish economy, where unemployment is 24.5 per cent.[3] More important, the various components of Arab GDP, which is dominated by primary materials and agricultural output, are fundamentally different. For example, oil production represents 20 per cent of GDP, whereas the compared economies show an extremely complex production of goods and services that provide comparative advantage in the market. To secure the advantages of specialization of function, division of labour and economies of scale, these economies are inclined towards union, despite their awareness of its implications, such as relinquishing absolute sovereignty, and despite enmity between them and a history of two contemporary world wars.

Once we turn to the features and performance of country economies in the Arab world, the picture appears more complicated. Perhaps we can explain part of the socio-political chaos by highlighting certain country economic indicators. For example, in Algeria GDP growth in real terms was negative for three out of five years during the present decade (1990–94), and inflation ranged between 16.7 per cent in 1990 and 35 per cent in 1994. The debt servicing ratio reached 78 per cent of revenues from net exports of goods and services during 1994. The current account saw a surplus in four out of five years; however, this could be attributed to a decrease in currency exchange rates against the US dollar for the same period, which dropped to 20.6 per cent of its value at the beginning of the decade.

In Morocco, growth in real terms was negative in two out of five years of this decade. The current account registered a deficit over the five years, and the Moroccan dirham depreciated by about 8 per cent against the US dollar. This did not greatly reflect on inflation rates, which were 4.9–8 per cent.

Real growth in Bahrain was moderate for three out of five years, from 1.3 per cent in 1991 to 1 per cent in 1994, reaching 2.5 per cent in 1992 and 4 per cent in 1993. Inflation does not appear to be a problem at this time, as the Bahraini dinar remains pegged to the dollar; but such subsidy policies have their cost, especially as the current account has been in deficit for five years.

In Egypt, growth was moderate in three out of the five years – 1–1.5 per cent – but generally positive. Inflation rates have been curbed to some extent, reaching their minimum level of 7.5 per cent in 1994, having stood at 19.7 per cent in 1990. Despite a large trade deficit, the current account witnessed a surplus due to exports of services, while debt servicing decreased from 30.8 per cent in 1990 to 14.3 per cent in 1994. The Egyptian pound remained fairly stable against the US dollar between 1991 and 1994, having lost about 40 per cent of its value between 1990 and 1991.

Saudi Arabia realized a moderate growth rate of 1 per cent in 1993, and negative real growth of 3 per cent in 1994, having realized high growth in the three previous years. The current account registered a continuous deficit over the five years, with control on the rate of inflation and a stable exchange rate for the Saudi riyal against the US dollar.

The situation was much worse for other Arab countries, such as Yemen, Libya and Sudan. For Somalia and Djibouti, it was outright tragic. As for the remainder, they do not diverge much from what was stated above.

Projecting these indicators onto the political and social planes undoubtedly helps explain the weakness of central authority in most Arab countries and the emergence of the phenomena of official and unofficial violence – costs that invariably reflect adversely on major economic indicators. In attempting to defuse internal pressures, inter-Arab relations are harmed, whether intentionally or not, by virtue of geographic proximity. Violence or tension is exported across borders, compounding the adversity and the waste of scarce resources devoted to possible confrontations between brethren. Alternatively, internal pressure and pressure from neighbours led in most cases to a lack of rational judgement on the issues by the decision-making authority, thus weakening the possibility of institutionalized political decision-making and creating a gap between the assumed and the actual.

Iran

Iran is, of course, a country with a single central authority. There is nevertheless a similarity in reading where the economic indicators and their effects are concerned, both inside and around it, and this in turn can raise pressures within or from neighbouring territories.

Iran's area is 1.636 million km², or 11.7 per cent of the area of the Arab world and 1.2 per cent of the surface of the globe. Its population is 61 million, or 25.4 per cent of the population of the Arab world, 1.1 per cent of the global population. GDP at market prices stood at $61.5 billion, making per capita GDP $1008. Per capita GDP expressed in dollars fell sharply in 1994 to $25.1 billion, because of the sharp drop in the rate of exchange of the Iranian rial – from 1170 to 2900 to the dollar – a decline that continued in 1995.

Real growth was estimated at minus 4 per cent in 1994, after positive growth rates were realized in the first three years of the decade, ranging from a maximum of 9.9 per cent in 1990 to a minimum of 2 per cent in 1993. Inflation varied between 7.6 per cent and 23 per cent in 1992, stabilizing around 20 per cent in 1993 and 1994.

By applying strict import policies, Iran was able to realize a marginal surplus in its current account in 1993 and 1994, after enduring relatively high deficits in the previous two years. Due to partial liberalization of the exchange rate, as part of monetary policy instruments, the rate of exchange of the Iranian rial decreased to 2.3 per cent of its value between 1990 and 1994.

Iran's foreign debt amounted to $23.5 billion or 92.5 per cent of the total GDP for 1994, in dollar terms, after its debts at the beginning of the decade amounted to only $9 billion. Short-term projections do not seem promising. Iran is subject to additional pressures from the West, especially the United States, as it is accused of accelerating its nuclear programme, sponsoring terrorism, opposing a Middle East peace agreement and the Salman Rushdie case. In addition, there are the pressures that oil states are generally subjected to, especially the borrower states, and Iran is one of these. Such pressures follow from the deterioration of oil prices, real and nominal, and Iran supposedly lost $3.7 on every barrel between 1992 and 1993.

Political and social breakdowns doubtless occurred in the wake of these economic indicators, leading to the weakening of central authority, as was the case with the Arab states. One indicator was the fall in the ratio of voters during presidential elections in 1993 to 58 per cent, and the decrease of the President's share of the vote in these elections to 63 per cent. The problem is that there is a time lapse between the emergence of the economic indicators and their consequences on the political and social plane. The lag may be long or short, depending on objective considerations such as the specific characteristics of a particular society and culture, or the degree of freedom of expression permitted, and on non-objective considerations such as exaggerated security measures. Nevertheless, a sustained negative trend in economic indicators cannot, whatever the considerations, cancel the trend towards extremism, violence and more fragmentation in every direction. The Iranian revolution was originally the product of such a situation, and the Soviet Union is another, neighbouring example.

Until the end of the last decade, the strategic importance of Iran for the West was great, because of its long border with the former Soviet Union. More important was containment of the latter, and preventing its access to the Gulf through Iran. Then suddenly, the containment of Iran, in the hope of safeguarding the world's oil and pipelines, became a top priority from the West's point of view; hence the US trade sanctions on Iran. It is true that there is a fundamental difference here between the US and Europe, with signs of dissent by Japan, but the difference is not in general principle as much as in approach. The US sanctions against Iran seek to expedite the deterioration of the country's economic indicators to the point where they compel the central authority to effect a basic change in its positions on the nuclear programme and on Arab–Israeli peace negotiations, or even change the regime itself, which is accused by the US of sponsoring terrorism. Although it is an individual act so far, its initial results can be seen in the imposition by the Iranian government of a high and fixed rate on the dollar (3000 rials to the US dollar) and obliging exporters to deposit foreign currency earnings in the Central Bank. This has resulted in a rise in the black market exchange rate to 7000 rials to the dollar, as an initial consequence; but this rate then fell to 5000 rials to the dollar, which suggests inflationary pressures that could lead to a further drop in real income, with all its social and political consequences.

Moreover, the United States interfered and applied pressure to prevent Iran from expanding northward into joint enterprises with Azerbaijan on the Caspian Sea. It was also denied participation with a consortium of foreign companies in an agreement valued at $7.4 billion, despite the extreme importance of Iran for facilitating the marketing of Azerbaijan's oil exports.

For Iran, neighbouring territories do not appear stable, and perhaps for the most part, constitute additional pressure on it. To the West, Iraq constitutes a unique situation of potential instability, as a result of the damaging effect of two Gulf wars. In Iran there are between 500 thousand and a million Iraqi refugees, adding to the burden of Iranian refugees from the south of the country, destroyed by the war. To the north, on the common border with Iraq and Turkey, there is a state of permanent instability that may be aggravated by the absence of a central authority in the Kurdish parts of Iraq and the continuous confrontations between them and Turkish authorities. Also, in both Turkey and Iraq, there are armed Kurdish political groups hostile to the authorities in Iran, and there is always the possibility of using them to pressure Iran. To the east there is Afghanistan, torn apart by civil wars, and it is believed that there are about a million Afghan refugees in Iran. These factors not only constitute pressure in every direction, but also create another burden for a government already over-burdened.

Pakistan's situation is certainly better than its neighbour's, Afghanistan; but it has its own internal and regional problems, as well as difficult economic conditions; it is not in a position to export stability, but it is enough that it does not export instability.

Although one is permitted to regard Turkey as a relatively stable state, and though Turkey and Iran are in the same sphere of economic co-operation, which includes Pakistan, Afghanistan and the six Islamic states from the remains of the Soviet Union, there is traditional historical rivalry between them that will continue. This rivalry occasionally surfaces through mutual recriminations over interference in the internal affairs of this country or that. It is sufficient that large tracts of the former Soviet Union were territories with close connections to Turkey and Iran; here there are potential seeds of future dispute, which could be further complicated by the great powers taking the side of one party against the other. Turkey is also clearly inclined towards Europe; it is not unlikely that, under changing conditions, this inclination will be put into practice in the context of the policy of containment. This trend could be accelerated by the Turkish government's current moves against rivals in local Islamic movements.

To the extent that East and West constitute a problem, the North may find itself in a similar situation. The signs of states forming from the remains of the Soviet Union carry indications of possible widespread and costly instability. Given Iran's ambition to strengthen ties with contiguous and non-contiguous Islamic republics, and the possibility of confrontation with the West over this ambition, the breakdown of domestic conditions could export instability to Iran. Although Turkmenistan is in a better situation than its neighbours, with per capita GDP in 1993 at $2515, it endured very high inflation, reaching 3102 per cent in 1993, because of too few goods and services and the sharp drop in the exchange rate of its currency tied to the Russian rouble, which multiplied 1600-fold since the start of the decade until 1994. In Azerbaijan, the other country neighbouring Iran, per capita income amounted to $1029, and inflation stood at 1571 per cent and 2000 per cent in 1993 and 1994 respectively. In Kirghizistan, per capita income was $483 and inflation 1209 per cent; in Tajikistan, $214 and 2195 per cent, and in Uzbekistan, $228 and 821 per cent.

All these states have experienced negative real growth since the beginning of the 1990s, explained, at least in part, by the changeover to market economies. Georgia, Armenia and Russia experienced similar economic conditions, which also makes them candidates for export of some of the political and social instability we see at the present time.[4]

That leaves the Arab Gulf states, separated by only a short distance from Iran. By virtue of their share in oil wealth, comparative political stability and lower population density, they constitute the least costly border extensions and the most important, from Iran's point of view, for exchanges of interests. Although we will deal with this subject in the next section, conditions do not appear to be ripe for benefiting from even a minimum of joint interests, unless genuine efforts and sacrifices are exerted. The strategic importance of the region, the experience of the Iraqi invasion, fear of rumoured exports of revolution and sectarian disputes, fuelled by the border dispute over Abu Musa, Greater Tumb and Lesser Tumb Islands – all these render difficult the possibilities for a breakthrough in this regard.

Briefly, Iran and the Arab world share a basic trait, summed up in the warped economic indicators within them and at their peripheries – weak growth rates, rising inflation, flawed foreign trade structures and a growing foreign debt. All of these must surely have contributed to a rise in unemployment and drop in real wages. Unemployment figures are not published, or in most cases are incorrect. The lack of political and social stability is itself a sign of these indicators. The recurring scenario begins with the strengthening of internal security and the military, which become devious: the *first* serving to confront domestic unrest, the *second* to confront unrest at the periphery or even draw on it to distract attention from the domestic scene. This leads to more severe warping, with the military sector financed at the expense of the civilian – a waste of resources that are already scarce. In an attempt to support this trend and confront its consequences, attention is focused on addressing short-term problems and expanding subsidies for goods and services, even jobs and exchange rates; these, apart from further undermining the competitiveness of the economy and adding to the burden of public finances, are difficult, even impossible, to endure over the short term, thus fuelling entry into a more dangerous phase that borders on chaos. Here timing is of the essence, to avoid the higher costs of confrontation, through a system of domestic policies and economic programmes, some of them external, and relinquishing the exaggerated rhetoric over sovereignty and looking towards the region or the peripheries.

Prospects for the Development of Economic Relations

With the collapse of bi-polarism, the world will tend, it seems, towards multi-polarism, but on economic grounds. Part of the resources that went into the military sector may be made available for financing civilian sectors; the security apparatus may turn to specializing in other fields, particularly the economic, and acquire capability in economic intelligence. There may be a reshuffling of the situation and different alliances may emerge to create new military camps. Such new alliances will be reflected in the principal economic indicators, i.e., growth, unemployment, internal and external budget deficits.

It seems that a major advance has occurred in the world about us in this regard. In addition to a unified Europe and North America (NAFTA), extending to Central and South America, and Japan's efforts in Asia, there are regional organizations as well, with perhaps the most active in Asia.

These states are linked into other systems or associations, such as the Group of Seven (G-7), and some are key participants in the meetings of other economic organizations and take unilateral actions to the point of direct military intervention, for defending present and future economic interests. Some aspects of policy making, which used to be regarded as sovereign and may not be interfered in or discussed, have become subject to direct and major intervention, such as interest rate policy, bolstering foreign exchange rates, and even financial policies and associated shortages or surpluses affecting the competitiveness in trade of this country or that. Doubts over the US Administration's desire for a stable exchange rate for the dollar, which its trade rivals accuse it of, was a problem; the US hostility towards subsidies on agricultural output or European aircraft manufacturing was another; its reaction to Japan's trade policy (rice, automobiles and even airline services) was a third; and US failure to sign an agreement liberalizing financial services was, and remains, a problem. The composition of official delegations has come to include, at heart, businessmen who work to market their output of goods and services and secure the interests of their states indirectly. This is evident from the words of a former US President, who said that every billion in exports means creating 20 thousand local jobs. Embassy facilities to further this new policy have been created and embassies are now staffed more by specialists in economics than politics and intelligence, and a major part of government now lies in the performance of embassies in realizing their country's interests by marketing its output of goods and services.

After the conflict of nationalisms in Europe, which led the world into two destructive wars within a quarter century, the idea of a European common market emerged in 1957. The motive was security; it was hoped that by linking up economic interests a barrier would be built against destructive inclinations. With time, the market developed to include the arch enemies – Britain, Germany, France and perhaps, later, Russia – within a detailed and well-studied economic union. Perhaps it will develop into a political union, through which the Germans will achieve what they could not achieve by war.

In the Americas, trade agreements have brought together Mexico, the United States and Canada, and the United States and Mexico. The US intervened to rescue Mexico during its latest crisis, fearing a major breakdown and a collapse of its dependence on the US, i.e., the import of instability. In Asia, there does not seem to be an enmity stronger than that between Japan on the one hand, and Korea and China on the other; yet trade, technical exchange and capital flows are gradually increasing between them. Perhaps Japan in Asia will repeat the experience of Germany in Europe. The geographic division is too simplistic; conflict between the new poles does not recognize geographic boundaries. The conflict over the remains of the Soviet Union between US companies and others is intense, and the resumption of full relations between the US and Vietnam was motivated largely by pressure on US businessmen and companies to improve their competitiveness there.

Between the Arabs and Iran stands a recent and bloody conflict in which most neighbouring Arab states took the side of Iraq. The conflict led to various degrees of regression on both sides and planted many seeds of distrust and enmity. This is a natural outcome of bloody confrontations, and it is not possible to shorten the timespan that will be needed to overcome such feelings. Even if they were to be overcome, it is very difficult to speak of a union of neighbouring Arab states, much less assume an acceptable stand by this group towards Iran. It is also difficult to assume a unified Iranian position, despite the difference, for Iran continues to live under the shadow of the revolution and the adverse economic pressures that facilitate the substitution of a rational institutional position with propaganda and lecturing on central authority. But let us skip over these facts and delve into the assumed benefits of theoretically inspired stages of economic cooperation.

Can the Arab region and Iran benefit from better relations to allay the impact of attempts to undermine the status quo? Can they both cope with such attempts when they do not take steps towards major reform, including regional cooperation on the pattern of most great powers of the world and those aware of the requirements for achievement in the future? The answer does not appear complicated. The route to bolstering the negotiating strength of both parties and making available resources and their re-distribution is without doubt in the direction of serious and close cooperation; the alternative course is intolerable. The point of entry to this cooperation, by the dictates of geography, resource division and even the division of potential pain, can only begin with Iran and its Arab neighbours. The financial situation that is reflected in burgeoning internal and external deficits, the growing debt on both sides and its ramifications for growth, unemployment, exchange and inflation rates, renders expenditure on sound oil policies a principal way out for neighbouring states and Iran over the short and medium-term. The waste of resources, or their misappropriation because of mutual suspicion and distrust, has made them the biggest spenders on armament and defence in the world; whereas the re-distribution of these resources and more constructive efforts would considerably allay potential pressures. Moreover, expanding absorption capacity, through exchange of capital and investment opportunities, would form a natural basis for improving the political and economic climate, if success can be achieved in coordinating policies and reducing tensions.

The Arab world and Iran possess 72 per cent of the world's fixed reserves of oil. Iran and its Arab neighbours share certain joint oil and gas fields. The demand for oil may increase in absolute terms from 69 mbd to about 90 mbd by the year 2010, and its relative share in energy demand may range between 36 per cent and 39 per cent, compared with the present 40 per cent. The International Energy Agency anticipates demand for oil to become an indicator of two major variables, global economic growth and population increase. The Agency expects world GNP to grow by 60 per cent between the beginning of the 1990s and the end of the first decade of the next century, with a possible partial drop of the growth per unit in need for energy units. The Agency also expects that growth against rising energy demand will increase by 40 per cent over its current volume.

Economic growth rates will vary between groups. The lowest will be at 2.7 per cent per annum for both Western Europe and the United States, and the highest will be for China and Southeast Asia, at 5.5 per cent; this will modify the distribution of regional shares in world GNP. But what is important is its application to trade partnerships, for there will be an accelerating growth in the Asian states' demand for oil and this will increase their trade partnerships with the states of the region, all rapidly growing economies. The share of nine major Asian states – Japan, China, India, South Korea, Indonesia, the Philippines, Thailand, Malaysia and Singapore – was 10.4 mbd in 1988. This figure rose to 13.7 mbd in 1993 and is expected to reach 18.3 mbd in 1998, according to the published projections of British Petroleum Company. These states may constitute one of the new poles, and they are indeed speaking of joint interests.

Reinforcing trends towards greater demand for oil is a possible increase in world population by 1.9 billion between the last decade of this century and the end of the first decade of the next, raising the total population from 5.3 to 7.2 billion. Some 11 per cent of the world's population – that of the areas of the Organization for Economic Cooperation and Development (OECD) – consume about 56 per cent of the world's annual output of oil, though their relative share in consumption will decrease to 48 per cent by the year 2010. These forecasts could be affected in a decisive way by the results of an increasingly shrinking world and the impact of emulation of major advances in transport and communications. The proportion of trade partnerships with states or associations in the Third World could therefore increase substantially.

More important in terms of its effect on the states of the Middle East are developments in supply. The International Energy Agency, in its general report for 1994, expects the advanced states, especially the United States, to fail to compensate for loss in their production, with Britain, Norway and Canada increasing production. The US will thus gradually raise its dependence on imports, above 1991 levels, by 58 per cent of its production. It is also expected that oil supplies will decrease in most producer areas, either because of wells entering the lower output phase or because of increased domestic consumption due to economic and population growth. Growth in supply from producer areas to advanced states (OECD) during this period (1991–2010) is expected to be about -0.7 per cent, and in the remains of the Soviet Union -0.2 per cent. Supply will increase by 0.13 per cent for non-OPEC producer states, 0.9 per cent for the rest of the world, and 4.4 per cent for the Middle East and Venezuela. If we translate these into absolute figures, the share of the Middle East and Venezuela needs to increase from the present 20 mbd to between 40 and 45 mbd by the year 2010, or about half the world's production, which constitutes most of what is available for export. If we exclude Venezuela, which holds only 10 per cent of fixed reserves of global oil, the discussion and the importance of production, export and reserves will focus on Iran and neighbouring Arab states.

It is logical and natural that consumer countries will try, now and in the future, to weaken the negotiating position of the states of the region so as to obtain one of the principal entry points to development – energy – at cheap prices. It is also natural that a permanent state of instability will prevail and that a mechanism will be created to fuel this trend within the strategies of consumer states, perhaps consisting of attempts to undermine the status quo at clearly demarcated red lines. The Iraq–Iran war was viewed within this context, and the Iraqi occupation of Kuwait was a major step in reinforcing it. Either way, one cannot but view the situation from the standpoint of our own short-sightedness and capacity to weaken our negotiating position. The fear that this will be the case proceeds from the escalating strategic importance of the region, and the possibility of sharper conflict over it leading to a very large margin of loss in oil prices, both nominal and real. A number of studies point to real oil prices as being at early twentieth-century levels, before the major price increases of 1973, and lower than their level in the last century. Real prices will remain, at best, unchanged until the end of the next decade. Developments since 1991 suggest that oil prices are declining on average, in real or nominal terms, despite the near total absence of one principal producer from the market, for Iraq at present produces no mre than 500–600 thousand barrels per day.

One of the first points of entry to cooperation based on mutual interests, a logical entry point to wider cooperation between the Arabs and Iran, is to agree on a joint effort to improve the conditions of trade of their common commodity, oil, which constitutes almost the whole of their foreign currency earnings. If they do not do this, any breakdown arising in a country of the region will be because of the continuation of the status quo, and it will not spare the other countries. Perhaps the example of Cuba and the United States, or the US intervention in Haiti to prevent new migrations and the export of violence and surplus labour, provide a warning that we should learn from. Chevron Corporation, for example, suggests that the movement of oil prices presupposes $17–27 to the barrel, and these prices are now below the minimum. Each additional dollar to the price of oil means an annual increase in oil income for the Middle East of around $6–6.5 billion, of which around $5.5 billion are for Iran and neighbouring Arab states. Without doubt, the coordination of their negotiating position would add a larger margin to their returns and would mean, at the very least, an additional capacity to confront short- and medium-term bottlenecks.

The other point relates to the indirect impact of changing the current approach into one of cooperation. This involves the re-distribution of already scarce resources and the possibility of channelling part of them into civilian instead of military sectors. A report by the US Agency for Monitoring Armament and Arms Control, published in *Le Monde Diplomatique* (May 1995), indicates that the states of the Middle East have spent, since the end of the second Gulf war, 20.1 per cent of their GNP and 54.8 per cent of their public expenditures, on arms. If this is true it is terrifying. *Time* magazine indicated that the US, which controls 70 per cent of arms sales in the world today, and 13 per cent in 1986, has sold the two principal arms importers during the period 1990–93 some $64 billion in arms; 60.3 per cent of these went to Saudi Arabia ($30.4 billion), Egypt ($4.4 billion) and Kuwait ($3.8 billion), which ranked first, third and fourth, respectively, in the list.[5] A draft study by Gary Sick of Columbia University indicates that the Gulf Cooperation Council states purchased $82.5 billion in arms between 1986 and 1993, equivalent to 31 per cent of total world arms sales. It is known that Iraq exhausted its resources, and the resources of its neighbours, in the service of its military sectors during its two wars, and that part of the resources were used to develop outlawed weapons whose stocks, or their mechanisms and modes of manufacture and transport, have been destroyed. It is also known that the economic situation of Iraq is extremely bad at present. Even so, it is possible that expenditures on security and defence will swallow up what remains, thus exacerbating a miserable situation. According to the same source, Iran spent $2 billion annually on arms during the period 1990–94, most of it from its scarce foreign currency resources, and at the expense of other sectors. Perhaps to avoid these pressures, Iran will turn to developing sources of outlawed weaponry, which are cheaper, more destructive and have greater deterrent value. But such a strategy, apart from provoking great power response, and the possibility of burdening it with a higher cost margin because of the economic countermeasures being applied, also conflicts with the great powers' strategies in marketing their stocks of conventional weapons.

It is known that the prime motivation for arms policies and, to a great extent, expenditure on internal security is distrust and suspicion of the intentions and tendencies of bordering states. This applies to neighbouring Arab states with respect to one another. It seems that efforts are being exerted to resolve outstanding border problems between neighbouring Arab states, including recognition by Iraq of Kuwait's border, resolving the Saudi–Yemeni and Saudi–Omani border disputes, and signs of a resolution of Qatari–Bahraini and Saudi–Kuwaiti differences. No doubt a positive Iranian move to resolve the dispute over the three islands would be regarded as a major step in improving relations with neighbouring states, provide a message of good will, and reduce the chances of using it as raw material for opposing strategies.

In general, the capacity to use the weaponry purchased by these states is restricted to the red limits adopted by the great powers, and does not exceed minor changes on the borders of Iran and neighbouring Arab states. The experience of the two Gulf wars and change in the stance of the great powers, as indicated in the course of the war and by how much these red limits were exceeded, is an example for the present and a message for the future. The second Gulf war, according to an estimate by the International Monetary Fund, caused a 4 per cent loss in the GDP of the entire Middle East, an increase of 2.5 per cent in the rate of inflation, and a change in the current account of the region from a $10 billion surplus to a $43 billion deficit, apart from direct losses in excess of $600 billion. Without doubt the region cannot cope with any additional confrontations, marginal or major. Ultimately, nothing at all will be accomplished by either party in any conflict.

If this is the extent of squandered resources, and of the destruction resulting from confrontation, and if the margin for present and future achievement is limited and costly for any party pressing for confrontation, is it illogical to work according to the European and Asian logic, towards making cooperation a priority over tendencies towards destruction? Both Germany and Japan reached the top by saving resources for civilian works, and are models of the miracle of economic comeback; they are also candidates for dominance over the two associations of states that they could not dominate by war. The confrontation between Malaysia and Singapore ended in 1963 with a presentation of two successful models of economic achievement; both are included now in a successful economic cooperation plan. The Arabs and Iranians have two civilizations that are classic examples of the ancient and progressive, whatever may be said of their current backwardness. The efforts within them to halt the prevailing breakdown, among the conditions of which is a halt to the squandering of resources in confrontation, must not be stopped, nor should any effort to move feelings and sentiments forwards towards the positive.

Finally, there are private and public savings that will accrue to the two parties. The Arab and Iranian markets remain large markets, with their population of 300 million, half-way in size to the European and American market – in numbers, not purchasing power. Iran and the neighbouring

Arabs both need tens of billions of dollars for investment in the oil production sector alone, so as to double their absorption capacity and address the possible increase in demand for oil. Current and future financial conditions do not permit governments to make available such funds from their own resources. This situation, in its turn, may open the way to dangerous possibilities leading to selling oil or keeping it underground to safeguard wells and increase future production capacity. It seems that since the end of the 1980s, there have been states that took steps in this direction. Moreover, some borrower states have borrowed more than they can repay, while the creditor institutions or states are sufficiently powerful to impose their custody over the oil. If this occurs, it will render control from the supply side, i.e., oil production, impossible, over and above the inability of the states of the region to meet their financial obligations impelling them to accept the principle of sharing their oil reserves.

One of the ways out of this situation is to realize economic cooperation and reduce tensions in order to create a better political and investment climate. This conceivably could lead to a gradual redressing of the balance between the public and private sectors in each country, by presenting opportunities for investment and sharing in the development of the oil sector and by recalling some of the flight capital abroad. Such a climate could also permit the exchange of surpluses in production factors at regional level and coordinate specialization of function and division of labour; these would increase inter-country trade between the Arabs and Iran, presently at an all-time low if we exclude re-exports from the United Arab Emirates to Iran. Iran may provide neighbouring Arab states that have high per capita income and high import ratios with much of their agricultural needs, and the capital of these states may contribute to developing Iran's agricultural and food processing capabilities. Iran may also benefit from its location as a connecting link to the Republics that emerged from the remains of the Soviet Union; this could expand the scope of cooperation and reduce current pressures and potential for instability. More important, cooperation and exchange of interests, given a real need by both parties, would create a mechanism for conflict prevention in future, or at least keep it to a minimum, and this is a major achievement.

What Iran and the Arabs both need is a reduction in the potential for breakdowns from within and on the peripheries. For Iran, the region and neighbouring Arab states seem to be the best entry points to both. Their common interests as holders of the largest reserves of oil, the presence of mutual distrust and suspicion bleeding the two sides of scarce resources, the presence of a market with high purchasing power and public and private financial surpluses – all these constitute major grounds for cooperation. For the Arab region, i.e., the neighbouring Arabs, there are two additional justifications for cooperation. They are prepared to begin taking steps that some of their states have already taken, but they need encouragement from Iran, so as to reduce the pressures on them from states with different, sometimes opposing, perceptions and objectives, whose policy decisions they in turn have the capacity to influence. The option of cooperation may yield short-term benefits on two fronts – a reduction in the level of political tension, and an improvement in the political and economic climate. It is possible that the first would be reflected in oil revenues and resource allocation, while the anticipated gradual improvement in the political and economic climate would curb potential breakdowns; it may also be reflected in the investment climate within and between local economies, which in turn would attract part of the public and private flight capital abroad – an important element for rebuilding these economies. The initial outcome of such cooperation could also put the Arabs and Iran onto a new course, approximating the increasingly cogent and time-proven one of Asia, and the resulting economic association may, on the one hand, develop to include others, and, on the other, increase the negotiating strength of this association before others.

Conclusion

It is not easy to write about the state of development and prospects for economic relations between the two associations, when it is difficult to assume that they are associations to begin with. Furthermore, just as writing about the status quo requires an information base that enables one to elucidate current trends and provides markers to declared or undeclared public policy, the first requirement for writing about potentials is the ability to make assumptions that have a basis in reality. Such an information base is unfortunately unavailable. I have, therefore, in this paper attempted to present indicators of the status quo in both Iran and the Arab world, and on the potential for breakdowns, using these as motivation to find ways out of our difficulties, one of which is economic and regional cooperation. We have been outdistanced in this approach by associations of states that no one ever imagined possible and whose individual members have in some cases far worse histories of enmity than the Arabs and Iran – even over the last few years. These associations did not need to adopt theoretical models to begin forms of cooperation – customs unions, common market, economic union, comprehensive coordination of economic policies; all that was needed was to strike up arrangements that have a basis in reality, lead to tangible results in the short term, and serve as an entry point to later advancement.

Oil is regarded as a source of daily income in foreign currency. Any movement in its prices through an initial and respectable agreement, in lieu of any policy, will immediately reflect on revenues in the public finance and lead to a series of positive effects. Cooperation in oil is considered a sound *first* point of entry into cooperation between Iran and neighbouring Arab states. They currently possess 72 per cent of the world's fixed oil resources. More important, by virtue of their current production quotas, the indicators of new discoveries and negative supply trends, with an escalation in absolute increases in demand, they will increase in relative importance as holders of reserves, and therefore oil exports. Their state of fragmentation and conflict will make them easy prey to hostile strategies, and it will be possible for others to obtain from them any quantity of oil at prices that, with time, will be lower in purchasing power than oil prices before the first increase in 1973. States whose burden of internal and external debt is growing, whose real growth rates are declining or becoming negative, with unemployment and inflation rates and pressures on rates of exchange rising, will without doubt be vulnerable to all forms of political and social extremism. A confrontation between extremisms might lead such states to mortgage oil or sell it in the ground if that is possible. With that, they would have lost the present and the future. But it is something that can be avoided, in part or in full, by accepting what these states do not accept under normal conditions – namely regional cooperation at the expense of certain feelings or certain feeble tenets of sovereignty.

The *second* point of entry, which is a consequence of the first, is to work towards alleviating tension between Arab and Arab, and between neighbouring Arabs and Iran, in the hope that such a course would curb the imbalance in distribution of scarce resources between the two sectors, military and civilian. Iraq has financed two wars, and the amount of destruction from both exceeds a thousand billion dollars. The Middle East has imported weaponry since the end of the second Gulf war to the order of 54.8 per cent of its public expenditures, and the Gulf Cooperation Council spent around $82.5 billion on weaponry between 1986 and 1993, or the equivalent of 31 per cent of total global arms sales. It is believed that what is spent on security and defence in neighbouring Arab states exceeds what is spent in the whole of the civilian sector, despite the difference in number between the two sectors, the civilian being considerably larger. Such a course cannot but lead to greater economic misery and fetter the other principles that underlie security, as happened in the Soviet Union and in other examples of the Second and Third Worlds. What is important is that the experience of confrontation in the recent past yielded nothing but material and moral destruction, and the strategic importance of the region for the new/old great powers will not permit more than minor changes in the results of confrontation. The world's experience has proven the success of models that rest on civilian achievement and the realization of what war failed to realize. There can be no doubt that the gradual reduction of tension and the growth of a new political and security climate would lead to the creation of a mechanism for increasing areas of cooperation, where initiative could very well become spontaneous.

Finally, an improvement in the political and security climate would certainly have positive economic consequences, including a tangible improvement in investment climate, and it is in the interests of Iran to expand and extend its trade into markets with high purchasing power. There will be a great need to recover flight capital or a part of it, and it will be a reason for creating new job opportunities. There will also be a great need for capital to expand the productive capacity of oil wells and to face increases in demand; the reopening of the oil sector to the private sector will return a certain balance to the public sector.

But this course, which appears logical, is not new, and it embodies many dangers. The purpose of its presentation is merely to initiate a joint dialogue with a party that presumably is aware of the dangers of pursuing an opposite course. Perhaps dialogue will create a vision supporting the trend towards cooperation. But it will definitely face several multifaceted dangers: the *first* is that there are fanatical parties and groups on both sides which are not aware of the dangers of deteriorating conditions and the experiences of the world around them, or do not care for reasons that are not objective, or are politically short-sighted. These forces are influential and active. The *second* is that the Arab world's experience in pursuing such approaches has been one of failure; it is very difficult for it to accept a unified association through mere talk; all hope is pinned on the possibility of awareness of the pains of the brethren, the dissension, the pressures of the present situation and the trend in the world around us. *Third*, such a course conflicts with the strategies of great powers pursuing their own interests over the rubble of a party that is in a weak negotiating position. They will work to keep it that way so long as that remains possible.

Notes

* Director General, Al-Shal, Economic Consultants, Kuwait.

1. Arab League, et al., *The Unified Arab Economic Report*, September 1994.
2. See *Economics and Business* magazine, A second reading of Arab socio-economic conditions – the Arab world between wealth and poverty indicators, vol. 17, no. 188 (August 1995), pp. 24–9. See also: UNDP, *Human Resources Development Report 1993*, Beirut: Centre for Arab Unity Studies, 1993. The two reports the figures refer to are: The World Bank, *World Development Report, 1992* , Washington, DC: World Bank; Cairo: Al-Ahram, 1992; and *World Development Report, 1993*, Washington, DC: World Bank; Cairo: Al-Ahram, 1993.
3. The German economy represents 3.37, the French economy 2.47, and the

British economy 1.95 or double the Arab economy. The Economist Intelligence Unit (E.I.U.), *Country Annual Reports, World Outlook*, 1995.

4.   All data on Iran and neighbouring Arab and non-Arab states from two basic sources: *ibid.* various pages, and Economist Intelligence Unit (E.I.U.), *Country Profile, Iran, 1994/1995*.

5.   *Time*, no. 12 (December 1994).

Three

Mutual Awareness between Arabs and Iranians

5

Mutual Awareness between Arabs and Iranians

WAJIH KAWTHARANI*

'Mutual Awareness': Towards a Definition

The awareness by one group of another is a form of image of self vis-à-vis
the other; that is, it is an image of the other, formed in a collective imagination deriving from long historical experience and the exercise of types of
relations through complex modes of conflict, identification, trade, contact
and kinship. With that, it turns into an image of selfhood, formed through
interaction with the other's image. In other words, one can say that mutual
awareness in the Iranian–Arab case reflects a process of interaction between two historical consciousnesses by these two peoples or nations. By
historical consciousness is meant not only the past that is portrayed or repeated in collective historical memory but also elements of the present and
its challenges, and future dreams and objectives. In this shared time zone
(past, present, future), the places giving root to the conscious image of self
and the others overlap, making it difficult to distinguish between the levels,
components or connecting links of this image or that. Perhaps the choice
of the word 'image' to express the embodiment of awareness and consciousness in the words, acts and stances of people and rhetoric of their elites,
follows essentially from a bid to understand the implications of this overlap
with the looking glass image through which one observes. The looking
glass reflects an image of the reality. It is plain that between the image and
the actual object lies a barrier of comparative difference, and at the same
time it connects links and media.

In the case of the Iranians and Arabs, these connecting media may be
applied to the image in the looking glass, as follows:

1 The image of mutual awareness by the two nations through the looking
   glass of Islam.

2 The image of mutual awareness by the two nations through the looking glass of nationalism.
3 The image of mutual awareness by the two nations through the looking glass of sectarianism.
4 The image of mutual awareness by the two nations through the looking glass of political, economic and population geography.

A clarification is in order on the use of the looking glass concept, for there is no perfect looking glass as such. Every one of these glasses reflects on the others its own images, presenting polychromatic and multi-dimensional pictures, even if these carry a dominant colour or a chief dimension. Thus, the dominant colour or chief dimension may be Islamic, including and incorporating the national context, or it may be nationalist centred in Islam, or a chauvinist nationalism that negates Islam, or something purely utilitarian – making the state's interests and its economic and political geography the extent of its 'national security', with a functional employment of Islam and nationalism together. The picture can at times be a complex blend of all these elements.

To simplify matters and become more familiar with the images of mutual awareness between Iranians and Arabs towards the problematics of nationalism and Islam and the resultant political choices at the level of the state, revolution, unity, and relations between religion and politics, a treatment on the following lines is proposed.

The nationalist problematic between Iranians and Arabs and the political choices.

1 The crisis of the Islamic body politic and Arab nationalism: independence from the 'sultanate' and a formula for 'unity'.
2 The current ideological problematic and the issues of 'unity', 'revolution' and *marja'iyat* (authoritative reference).

The Nationalist Problematic and the Political Choices

Morteza Mutahhari draws a connection between a nation's persuasions and its political and strategic choices, regionally, globally and culturally, by saying:

If it is decided that this basis in determining the limits of the Iranian nation is the Aryan factor, the ultimate end of that is proclivity towards the Western world. But this proclivity in our national and political mission involves submissions and consequences, the most serious being a severance with neighbouring Islamic nations that are not Aryan and an attachment to Europe and the West. At the exact opposite, if we make the foundation of our nation our intellectual, behavioural and social heritage over the past fourteen centuries, then we would have a different mission and other costs, opposed to the aforementioned. Therein, Arab, Turk, Indian, Indonesian and Chinaman would become our friends, even kinsmen.[1]

But what needs to be added to Mutahhari's statement is that the division of choices is not determined by a decision of government, party, elite or intellectual, even if this 'decision' and its consequences and claims played a role in setting long-range trends and currents of thought. The evolution of choice in the process of the national or Islamic persuasion is more complex than the process of 'decision-making'. Iran's 'Islam', for example, is in a way permeated by its 'nationalism' too, and one would not be far from the truth to say that the very Islamic current in Iran carries an Iranian nationalist ring. We sense this in Mutahhari's *Islam and Iran*. In this book, considerable historical and documentary effort is exerted to prove the following hypothesis: 'That the Iranian nation contributed more to Islam than any other nation, and the ancient and rich civilization of Iran provided a great service to Islamic civilization'.[2]

On the other hand, it would also not be far from the truth to say that an Iranian nationalist current represented by such symbols as Mohammed Musaddiq, Ali Shari'ati and Mehdi Bazargan, overlaps with Islamic expressions and perceptions as forces of awakening and mobilization in the Iranian revivalist experience.

Observe that the overlap between Islamism as a human liberation drive and nationalism as a national drive, within the context of 'nation-state', does not imply a contradiction or exceeding of bounds in either of the two currents. The first current (the Islamic) enters Iranian nationalism in its Islamic frame; the second (nationalist or patriotic) enters Islam as a civilizational, cultural and mobilizing process. Such is the case of the 'Iran Liberation Movement'.[3]

Even here one does not see, as mentioned previously, a sharp contradiction between the two Iranian perceptions of nationalism and Islam, except in the area of form of government and its practices. The latter, important as it is, will be treated separately in this paper.

What does make one pause over the image of Iranian awareness towards both nationalism and Islamism is extremism, in either direction:

The first direction: the tendency towards an image of Iran as chauvinist nationalist or Aryan, not content with ignoring the influence of Islam across 14 centuries of history, but making Iranian nationalism, ideological expansionist, hegemonial and fanatical towards geographical, cultural or ethnic neighbours. This trend and its cultural precepts and political programmes was nurtured ideologically by the regime of the Shah at one stage in Iran.

The second direction: the tendency to rush towards an Islamist image, cancelling the ethnic and national particularities and the elements of diversity and difference in the life of communities and peoples. Whatever the

justification for this independent rational judgment in interpretation of the
Law (*ijtihad*) in the understanding of Islam as a universal religion or politics of an order, translating this vision into policy and practice suggests a
centralized regional policy towards neighbours and policies of substitution
or cancellation before the will of the other, and penetration of other, different societies on the pretext of what has come to be termed in the literature
of that trend as 'exporting revolution'. This tendency, a reminder of the
theory of 'perpetual world revolution' in the literature of Trotskyist Marxism, paved and still paves the way in practice – however well-meaning – to
regional policies that do not differ much in actual outcome from the politics of racist nationalism or chauvinism, where the 'region state' or 'centre
state' or 'base state' (all of which mean much the same thing in political
geography) is turned into a centre for decision-making on behalf of others
or a mandate over them, even if the decision-making process adopts Islamic jurisprudence through the 'deputy imam' (*na'ib imam*) or 'authority
of the jurist of the Law' (*wilayat al-faqih*) – which are Shiite interpretations within other interpretations, as we shall see – to a centre presenting a
politico-religious rhetoric influencing and influenced by – whether intentionally or not – the precepts of the region state and the interests of economic
and strategic geography. The '*Shari'ah* policy' is turned into a cover and
pretext for internal and external political conflicts.

Accordingly, one notes that within the economic, security and strategic
concepts of the centre state, the images of Persian and Aryan consciousness
do not readily agree with the images of centralized Islamic consciousness
arising from human and existential *ijtihad*, even if this *ijtihad* is given a
sacred or divine character.

Was there not a meeting in the Iraq–Iran war of border disputes and
regional nomenclature ('Persian Gulf', 'Khuzistan', etc.) with Islamic and
Persian ideologies?[4] In geo-strategy and security, each alone cannot readily
unite the collective image of the state/nation towards the other.

Mohammed Hasanein Heikal, in his book *The Ayatollah's Guns*, picks
up on this discrepancy by saying: 'In fact, one of the contradictions of the
Iraq–Iran war is that the driving spirit of the Iranian forces' steadfastness
was more nationalism than religion ...', adding that 'this war has become
for the Iranians a national war, exactly as the Russians fought for Mother
Russia and not for Communism.' He concludes by saying: 'Thus did
Khomeini see within his own lifetime the Islamic content of his revolution
lose its glitter to nationalism, which he said he placed little store by.'[5]

One notes, on the other hand, that the Iranian Islamic view of other
nationalisms involves confusion, misinterpretation and, for some, aggression. A number of Islamic ideologists (international) and affiliates of the
Iranian Islamic model have taken to deprecating nationalist thinking in the
Islamic world in an unjustly and unfairly critical way. Kulami Siddiqi, who

is a friend of Iran and director of the Islamic Institute in London, considers that 'the political entities most submissive and subservient to the West are the rubble of the nation state in the Islamic world', and any nationalist movements in it 'were part of a plan by Western civilization to break up traditional Islamic societies into small communities subservient to colonialism' and 'all this transpired through a Westernized elite estranged from their heritage and origins'.[6]

In general, much ideological effort has been waged against nationalisms principally, and in particular Arab nationalism,[7] with no attempt made to understand the context of its historical origin as an alternative to the decline of the sultanate in Islamic history, or to understand its trends and contents in the course of its development since the turn of this century. Some spared no effort to organize a conference for the purpose of attacking nationalisms, in particular Arab nationalism,[8] and a senior Iranian official did not hesitate to compare Arab nationalism with Zionism,[9] though these were not the general rule in all Iranian thinking or in every phase.

All these took place during events that mobilized historical recollections and reflected through their looking glass one-dimensional images of mutual conflict awareness between the nationalist groups. The contribution of the Arab nationalists, or specific individuals among them, to this nationalist debate was just as sharp and selective.

In addition to the illusions and dreaming of the Iraqi regime in its private imagining of the 'battle of Qadisieh', spilling considerable ink to embellish the books and attract conferences and seminars on the subject, it also drew on historical orations and texts of Arab historians and thinkers with a nationalist bent, to revive the one-dimensional understanding and discrimination of the old *Shu'ubiyyah* [anti-exclusivism] movements and applications of 'Iran' and 'Iranism', which are regarded as 'attempts to tear down Arab Islam'. It also utilized the 'Arab politics of the Caliph Omar' as a reference for Arab nationalist thinking, extolling the politics of the Umayyad state, which, some nationalist historians allege, emerged from 'the ties of the Arabs, their unity and sense of mutual interest in expanding this state', and this through 'the linkage of the Arabic language and manners with Islam, giving it (the language) a sacred character'. This analysis, in its ultimate and final political ideological understanding, posits an interpretation of the *mawali*, *Shu'ubiyyah* and other various social uprisings; their great men in the imaginings of the contemporary Arab nationalist historian are 'hateful' or adventurous 'frauds', their notables 'weak', hence 'the failure of the books to record their chronicles'.[10]

These same views in some contemporary nationalist intellectual circles are translated into the summoning of statements viewed as challenges and dangers to Arab nationalism. Among these is the Marxism and the religious challenge represented by the *Salafiyyah* Islamic reform movements.

This challenge is viewed as a continuation of 'the *Shu'ubiyyah* in history' and resistance to 'minorities' and 'Persians' in the Arab nation. Finally, there is the challenge of fragmentation and the reality of individual countries.[11]

The Iraqi–Iranian horror was not limited to the effect of summoning such historical images for employment in recent political rivalry. Rather this horror began to show its impact in the strategic and futurist studies of Arab researchers regarding the expected role of neighbouring states.

However degenerate the images in the vision of some Iranians and Arabs, or incorrect the assumptions in the minds of some researchers, what is ignored in every case is a neutral and scientific approach to socio-political conflict in Islamic history, which is recorded as a nationalist chronicle. Also overlooked is the history of the emergence of modern nationalist consciousness and the pathway of its political ideological trends in the provinces of the Islamic world, prompting the twin nationalist extremism – Iranian and Arab – towards selective conflict and rivalry that negates what is common to both and what is positive in their common historical experience; it also negates the problematics, which may well be positive and understandable at a certain stage, negative and hindering at another.

Consequently, to avoid such selectivity made hostage by the allegations of the images of memory and ideological looking glasses shaped by the pressures of events, and to be systematic in historical approach and future vision, in search of a realistic awareness of what happened at a particular time and place and its implications for the future, which renders urgent a cooperative arrangement between the corners of the Islamic world in discussing a 'new Middle East order', we present below our understanding of the Arab nationalist problematic, its origin, the context of its interactions with cultural particularities, and the geography of the Arab corner in the domain of Islam.

The Crisis of the Islamic Body Politic: the Problematic of Nationalism

The problematic of nationalism in the provinces of the Islamic world attached to the Ottoman sultanate emerged in the context of the crisis of the sultanate before the pressures of its disintegrating internal structure, the failure of administrative and political reforms and the pressures of foreign interventions directed towards inflicting greater disturbances and fragmentation in Islam's social structure and the unity of its state.[12] Turkification and Ottomanization, which were one ideological–political trend that sought to respond with solutions to this crisis, managed through the revolts of 1908 and 1909 to dominate Ottoman politics and lead it in the direction of a centralized Ottoman state based on a Turkish majority in the institutions of state and in political, economic and cultural decision centres.

One result of the victory of this trend and its preponderance over the organs and institutions of the state is that it alerted nationalities previously alienated from decision centres and devoted to their own language, culture and intellectual and civilizational role. Arab reformers who had sided with the Turkish insurrectionists against despotic rule and for the application of the Constitution, were among the first to be alienated. The Arabic language, which is the language of the Holy Qur'an, *Shari'ah* (Islamic Law) and Islamic civilization together, was targeted for vilification, scorn and distortion. It was then that Arab nationalist awareness appeared, and largely in response to this challenge, an awareness of the internal problematic, which was expressed at the time by a crisis in Arab–Turkish relations. In this specific sense, Arab awareness had an Islamic cultural content; it was manifest in the defence by some Arab intellectuals of the Arabic language as the language of the *Shari'ah*, the need for unity among Arabs and Turks, and their remaining in a single state out of attachment to Islam and for the sake of salvaging what remained of its state.[13]

Even so, there are other aspects that warrant mentioning with regard to the nationalist problematic, distinct from the Ottoman state and opposed to or remote from Islam. Among these aspects are:

1 The convergence of certain calls for independence with international partition plans in the policies of certain great powers at that time.
2 The inclusion of certain callers for independence from the Ottoman state, in the name of Arabism, in the policies of foreign embassies, consulates and ministries. Among these were figures prominent in Arab political associations at the First Arab Conference (1913).
3 The attractiveness of Western national liberal thought for local elites, at a time when the Islamic world was subject to the yoke of despotic governments, using Islam as their cloak and feigning the role of protector of the Faith and its spokesman (the politics of Abdel Hamid II and other sultans).

These aspects constituted, at the moment of victory for the Allies in World War I, complements to the process of self-determination in the provinces of the Islamic world. As a result, this nationalist current was misconstrued by some reformists and became a contributing factor to fragmentation and breakdown at the time (the position of Shakib Arslan, for example).

Actually, if this was by and large the correct picture at the time, the call of Arabism did not achieve after the First World War – especially in the Arab Near East – a monolithic opposition to the politics of regional, confessional and sectarian fragmentation pursued by Western politics from that time until the Nasserist phase, nor was Arabism, at the popular and mass level, dissociable then from its Islamic dimension.

The question is: how did Islamic revivalist and restorational thought confront this nationalist problematic in its Ottoman and Western eras?

Within the context of the growing crisis in the Ottoman sultanate during the late 19th and early 20th centuries, an Islamic intellectual current formed in which we note, from its public positions and the writings of its authors, an attempt to give Islamic answers to this problematic. From the issuing of *Al-'Urwah al-Wuthqah* by Jamaleddin al-Afghani and Mohammed Abduh to *Al-Manar* magazine under the editorship of Rashid Ridha; from the writing of Abdul Rahman al-Kawakibi on *Aspects of Despotism* and *Um al-Qura*, to the writings of Arslan and his activism and positions; from the response of the religious scholars (*'ulema*) of the Najaf and *ijtihad* advocates for Jamaleddin to issue a *fatwah* (religious edict) forbidding tobacco in order to bring down the English treaty in Iran, to their support for Ottoman conditionalism and the Ottoman army against the English occupation of Iraq – throughout these texts and positions runs an Islamic undercurrent whose message presents the outlines of a programme of resistance to a number of problematics raised by the danger of the collapse of Islam's body politic under the external pressure of Western hegemony and the internal pressure of sultanic despotism.

The nationalism problematic stands out here as two-faced: On the one hand, nationalist sentiment emerges as patriotism in opposition to Western occupation and in accord with gradual unification of the concept of nation in Islam, along with a defence of land, home and homeland. In this context, for example, the National Party in Egypt drafts the slogan, 'Egypt for the Egyptians', and the slogan thereby becomes a way of confronting British colonialism, a confirmation of attachment to the Ottoman sultanate and part of a more general Islamic position. Some Arab reformers also advocated administrative decentralization, in deference to the multiplicity of nationalities in the Ottoman state.

On the other hand, nationalist sentiment also emerges as advocating independence from the Ottoman state, and accords with plans for international spheres of influence and a confrontation with the secular side of Islam in other provinces, such as Syria. In this context, the elitist secular current in Syria advocated independence from the Turks, in the wake of which remained a vague political position later made worse by partition agreements, secret diplomatic reports and many tongue-in-cheek intellectual theories that called for shunning Islam and relegating to it the onus of 'backwardness, darkness and periods of decline' (*The Selective Current* and writings by Abdul Rahman al-Shabandar, for example).

Before these twin problematics on nationalism at the turn of the 20th century, the Islamic current expressed through the intellectuals and *'ulema* mentioned earlier suggests an attempt to answer the following question:

how can we avoid using national consciousness as a tool for fragmentation or a mount from which calls for foreign occupation are made? And how can nationalism fall in line with a broader Islamic consciousness?

Jamaleddin al-Afghani had broached, before then, this issue in a number of articles and reflections. He held the Islamic bond as the more comprehensive; mindful of the importance of race in the formative history of peoples and nations, nevertheless he did not consider it part of the 'national psyche' but rather 'the incidental faculties of self on which necessities leave their mark.'[14] These necessities are the singularity of economic interests for a group, or self-defence or maintaining rights. 'If the necessities for this type of tribal entity fade, it too must fade just as it had to emerge.'[15] The remover of this necessity is 'the oneness of God' in Islam. He says: 'The necessity is nullified by relying on a judge before which powers become small and cower before the greatness of his strength, and before whom persons naturally submit; to him they are equal before one another, and he is the All, Conqueror of the heavens and the earth.'[16]

Progression up the ladder of unification and on the basis of the functional principle of lesser ties growing in fields of unification into a broader unity, here incorporates the tie of Arabism, as bearer of the message and voice of *Shari'ah* and language of Qur'an, not as a tie of blood or tribal genealogy.

He says: 'The march of the Arabs and their deputations into countries was to spread the religious message first.' The Arab deputations carried with them the highest virtues, whose nobility was manifest splendidly, such as in scorning falsehood, honouring pledges, showing absolute fairness, freedom and equality ... and relief for the troubled, generosity and courage ... The hearts of nations thus opened to receive the Arab deputations into their countries, whether in war or in peace, and the first introduction was usually acceptance and then permission to work, which enabled them to reach high positions. 'Yes, the biggest reason and strongest factor behind the Arabization of these nations was the noble virtues and high integrity that the Arabs brought, with their fortitude and the courage of their heroes.'[17]

Arabism in the sense that Jamaleddin presents it draws the Arabs to other Islamic peoples and the non-Arab Islamic peoples to the Arabs. It is a cycle of attraction, not repulsion.[18] When al-Afghani wrote these words and reflections, the colonialist danger was threatening the peoples of the Islamic world. The target of the confrontation, on the cultural front and at the level of the body politic in the East, was Islam as a potential attracter, unifier and detonator of dissenting energies.[19] If Islam is compared in this context with the patriotic and nationalist sentiments of the peoples confronting the occupying powers, then it is the pinnacle of common ties and priorities for societies' self-defence, in a dialectical process advancing by its bond to what is higher and more comprehensive.

In political practice, al-Afghani stands out as a dynamic model in the affirmation of the veracity of this thought. Who follows his political career and his calls across the Islamic world is struck by this capacity to penetrate, influence and follow up in detail on the events of every country, draft the appropriate position for every situation, and travel quickly from one country to another. What is startling in all this is his vision of a comprehensive Islamic strategy where a sense of history complements political awareness, as manifest in his emphasis on three corners from which the experience of centralized states in Islamic history would emerge, and through which can be monitored the prospects for revival in the Islamic world: Egypt, Iran, and the Ottoman sultanate (Turkey).

This Islamic intellectual current reaches completion with its integration of the nationalist problematic within the Islamic logic in Kawakibi's theory in the Islamic league. If al-Afghani had proposed that the Ottoman sultanate remain the heart of this league and its framework, al-Kawakibi proposed that the caliphate be transferred to an Arab imam of Quraysh ancestry[20] and that an Islamic league be formed whose preparatory conference embody the *umm al-qura* ('mother of all towns') and distribute its tasks on the basis of the competencies and dispositions of the Muslim nations. Al-Kawakibi proposes entrusting specific tasks to each of the peoples of the Islamic league.[21]

If this vision seems utopian politically, at least in approach it calls for adopting a functional perspective when dealing with what is distinctive among Islamic nations, a vision that aims at achieving a certain balance in the unity of the Islamic league, where no nationalism dominates another, even if cloaked in Islam as 'a religious colouration', to use Ibn Khaldun's words.

The suffering of this Islamic current was to increase the more it confronted the nationalist problematic in combination with the crisis of the Ottoman state and its gradual transformation into a Turkish nationalist state. The effect of this suffering was to become clear in the positions and writings of Rashid Ridha, Shakib Arslan and others.

The first proceeded to place much store by the possibility of constitutional reform, to accord with the *shura* (counsel) in Islam, only to find himself struck by the Turkification movement and the bloody politics of Jamal Pasha. So he turned to the possibility of reviving Islam from the Hijaz (the Arab revolt), only to be demoralized by the Sykes–Picot agreement, Balfour declaration and Hussein–MacMahon correspondence. He returned to looking towards Turkey, and Mustapha Ataturk's movement specifically, conferring on the latter the salvaging of what can be salvaged. Hope prompted him to propose to his friend Shakeeb Arslan that he contact the Turks to mend Arab–Turkish relations, propose that the caliphate remain with them, and even have Mustapha Kemal return to Islam to be acknowledged as sultan over the Muslims.[22]

But Mustapha Kemal had a contrary course in mind. Soon enough the Lausanne treaty closed off all these possibilities, leaving only one road open for Turkey: secular nationalism. With that, the Islamic current in the Arab countries, as in other Islamic countries, suffered a severe blow, and Islamic thought became stricken with apprehensions, doubts and hesitation, despite the 'caliphate conferences' that were held and that ended with the postponement of discussion of the caliphate. Some countries also witnessed movements by sultans and kings and by Western diplomatic circles, to pick the fruit of the political vacuum.

Here one must beware that the decisive factor in weakening the Islamic body politic is not solely the cancellation of the caliphate by Mustapha Kemal. The institution of the sultanate had for all practical purposes become utterly powerless. It lost its 'Islamic legality' when it failed to resist the foreigners, much less submit to them and accept their plans. Hence the rallying, even by Islamists, to the side of the resistance represented by Mustapha Kemal before the Lausanne treaty.

But what researchers have failed to appreciate is that a series of popular uprisings from within the Islamic body politic were viciously suppressed by the advanced European war machine: from the revolt of Abdul Karim al-Khitabi to that of Omar Mukhtar; from urban popular uprisings in Egypt to the revolt in Iraq by the *'ulema* of Najaf, to the Greater Syrian revolt – the features of the Arab Islamic resistance were diffused and dispersed, but all were prompted by the logic of Islamic dissent, which continued to gush forth from the indigenous Islamic body politic at the time.

The victory of the Western powers over these revolts, by force, as discussed in the historical documents and related in popular memory, paved the way for another approach within elitist Arab politics. The role model generally became, and to varying degrees, the image of Ataturk's regime in Turkey and the regime of the Shah in Iran.

With that, and with the suppression of expressions of resistance in Arab and Islamic societies and the emergence of Ataturk's model in Turkey and the Shah's regime in Iran, secular nationalist political currents began to form that became remote from Islam. Indeed, some of their proponents and thinkers relegated to Islam the causes of defeat and backwardness, or else Islam was made part of party or political platforms.

This served to complicate the nationalist and Islamic problematic, for it deepened the rift between the Islamic position and the imported nationalist formula of Europe's experiences and theoreticians, especially for the Arab Near East, and in particular Syria, where the experience of Ottoman Turkification was harsh and the indigenous society had many religious denominations, requiring a political statement that speaks of unity and patriotism without religion.

But the problematic did not extend beyond this particular geographical–historical confine.

In North Africa, nationalist consciousness merged with Islam and was even rooted in it. The Ottoman state, especially during the Turkification phase, did not leave, as it did in Damascus and Beirut, memories of siege, hunger, forced conscription and the gallows. Rather it was an 'Islamic state' that sought to protect the ports of the Muslim south Mediterranean, and so it remained in the memory of 'popular recollection' and books ever since the 16th century.

Accordingly, the Islamic position in North Africa did not find itself in conflict with nationalism. Indeed, the Islamic expression was sometimes part of the nationalist expression; often both were merged in a single political and cultural platform – separateness from the colonialist and defence of national and cultural identity together. This Frantz Fanon clearly noted, especially in his study of the Algerian revolution.

Whoever reviews the Islamic intellectual currents through their texts and advocates in Egypt and the Arab Maghreb (Ben Badis, Ilal al-Fasi, Hasan al-Banna), in addition to a great many authors, can find no place for a nationalist problematic provoking opposition or rejection of Islamic tenets. The terms nation, patriotism, Arab unity and Islamic unity are incorporated within a functional integrative framework directed towards unification.[23]

So how and when and where did these problematics emerge as a conflict between Islamic consciousness and nationalist consciousness?

We have said that the opposition occurred when nationalist sentiment expressed itself through certain local elites, corresponding, intellectually and practically, to European nationalist doctrines that indulged in hegemony, exclusivism, expansionism and domination. They also presented a philosophy of conduct that was anti-religion; this was clearly the case in French secular nationalism.

This insofar as approach is concerned. But there remain other factors, linked to the geographic, demographic and historical features of certain parts of the Islamic world. Syria, for example, has a specific demographic situation and specific historical experience with the phase of centralization and Turkification. Similarly, Iran, Turkey and India had a particular historical experience in terms of the relationship between nationalism and Islam.[24]

The experience was characterized by sharp enmity in certain quarters between nationalist thought and Islamic thought. Abu'l A'la al-Mawdudi regards nationalist thought as 'diabolical', a scourge on Europe and the local elites that would mimic it.[25] Mawdudi, in this strong stance, not only reflects a certain standard in approach and conviction when distinguishing between European nationalist thought and Islamic thought; he is also reflecting, politically and in the actual practical drift of things, the historical possibility of fragmentation and schism in the operation of local nationalisms in India and Pakistan[26] and Iran and Turkey.

Perhaps this divisive tendency in the function of nationalism there is what made a certain Muslim author, Kulami Siddiqi, stop and think. It prompted him to spread opposition to nationalism at all levels of discussion, without due regard to regional distinctions in the historical experiences. He makes nationalism throughout a fabrication of colonialism and a means for cleaving the Islamic nation.[27]

The Islamic current in Iran and Turkey confronted Aryan nationalist thinking, from the angle of disputes over the designation of a reference point in ideas, and the designation of its rules and sources of inspiration. Aryan nationalist thought is linked with two points here, both in conflict with Islamic effort. On the one hand, it identifies with Aryan civilization, which restored to the historical picture a Turkish or Iranian continuity that dates from pre-Islamic times; on the other hand, it is inclined to mimic a modern Western civilizational model that prevailed during the era of Western domination over Islamic peoples. The two most important embodiments of these were the Shah's regime in Iran and Ataturk's regime in Turkey.

Consequently, it is natural for Islamic thought in Iran and Turkey, given these two regimes, to take a negative drift towards nationalist thought as something European, or Aryan thought as hostile to Islam.

Here Morteza Mutahhari's observation is in place – that Iran must choose between Islam or Aryan nationalism – as we noted in the first part of this study.[28] We may summarize by saying that some aspects of nationalist awareness that formed in non-Arab Islamic nations, from Turkey to Iran, acquired intellectual and political overtones remote from political Islam. This was the situation in the Persian Aryan case and the Turanian Turkish case.

It is noteworthy here that the distinction between these two particular cases led to discrimination within Arab nationalism as well. The Turanian Turkish and Aryan Persian cases are similar at the Arab level to the Egyptian–Pharaonic case, Lebanese–Ph*oenician and Syrian–Assyrian, despite variations in extent of representation and importance of each of these civilizations in history.

As to Arabism (if we exclude the neo-nationalist expressions that sought to keep clear of Islam in certain areas and among certain elites), it was more often than not integrated with cultural Islam; it even presented a restored Islam in tongue, Qur'an and heritage. The battle between Arabism and Islam, or rather between nationalist currents and Islamic currents in the land of the Arabs, is due to confusion in theoretical understanding and to errors in the strategies and plans of political activity, that is, in party work and approaches.

The result was a deepening of the rift between unity through reason,

which is supported by Islam and Arabism together, and political party activity, whether Islamic or nationalist. Political parties (Islamic or nationalist),
and the politics of countries, both employ reason and religion in their particular political and power plans. When these plans differ, reason and religion
are subject to dispute, schism and fragmentation; when they accord, effort
is exerted to make them accord, as we can see from the recent coming
together of Arab nationalists and Islamists. Political accord is, of course,
important, but on condition that this accord is systematized within a platform that accommodates difference, believes in plurality, even defends it;
not because it is a timely thing for a political project to have, but because it
is a pre-condition for intellectual and human interaction and a way to the
knowledge and reality that no one may claim a monopoly on. Perhaps the
political mentality that rules the thought of nationalists and Islamists is
one and the same, giving political precedence to the rational and scientific.[29] When the 'political' is an element of unification and accord, it soon
becomes transformed into an element of fragmentation and conflict. Perhaps the ordeal of Nasserism and the Muslim 'brotherhood' was that they
were of this culture type, that is, a mentality that discourages diversity and
embodies a singular unity, especially regarding the exercise of power.

I suspect that the Iranian political experience is not far from this mental
frame, where the relationship of its parts is concerned, for it is a relationship of negation and exclusion. What is disturbing, truly disturbing, is that
this negative culture type of mentality in mutual awareness is also what
dominates in the relationship – and the images of the relationship – between Iranians and Arabs.

There is a singular intellectual phenomenon that continues to attract
attention by its intellectual–political energy and extent of awareness, accommodation and impact: the phenomenon of 'Jamaleddin al-Afghani'.
Here is a phenomenon that is over a century old, presenting a great lesson
on the extraordinary capacity to exceed and incorporate difference and
diversity in the national and sectarian affiliations of the Islamic world. The
thought of Jamaleddin al-Afghani was not limited to a specific nationality
or sect; he influenced Sunnis as much as Shi'ites. It has been said that
'Jamaleddin did not like to be considered as loyal to one nation of the
Muslims, fearing that this would provide an excuse for the colonialists to
incite other Muslim nationalities against him'.[30] It has also been said that,
when asked about his religion, he was content to reply 'Islam'. Perhaps
because of this inclination towards unity in intellectual–political action,
contemporary researchers of various nationalities and sects in the Islamic
world are unclear over where to place Jamaleddin's nationality and sectarian affiliation. Thus emerged the pushes and pulls of those who would
make him Asadabadi and those who would make him Afghani, or those
who say he is 'Shiite' and those who say he is 'Sunnite'.

Are there intellectual elites today who can so act or so embrace, and display such flexibility all across the Islamic world? This question we pose today in the vast sea of research on mutual awareness over issues of unity, authoritative reference and revolution, and in light of the ideological problematic that cloaks the reality with a thick outer cover of various imaginings.

The Current Ideological Problematic: the Issues of 'Unity', 'Revolution' and Marja'iyat

At the Arab level, there have been many examples of unification thought during this century, in experience and programmes. The idea of 'Arab unity' took many paths, and these vacillated between the unified nation state experience – bringing the Arabs together under a single nation state – and the association experience, whether federal or confederate, between two states or more. The forms of the unification experience found practical expression, with some materializing, as with the Egyptian–Syrian union in which Arab nationalists had high hopes that it would become the nucleus of a larger and more comprehensive unity, and the emergence of cooperative councils, such as the Gulf Cooperation Council, or unions, such as the Association of Maghreb Countries.[31] But the practical experience that evolved from the Arab order, in the context of its formation within the world order, and institutionalized as 'state-countries' in the Arab countries, is the experience of cooperation and joint effort within the institutions of the League of Arab States.

It is true that this League, which formed, and continues to form, a least common denominator of cooperation between the Arabs, and where the second Gulf war served to intensify its contradictions, predicaments and continuous failures to this day, was not to meet the ambition of Arab collective awareness as translated by the unification image of Arab nationalist ideology and its parties and elites. Despite this, it remains a comparative institutionalization of the actual Arab reality and its increasing deterioration – a fact of history that needs to be redressed, revived and developed as a basis for unity, deriving from the bases of the joint Arab effort embodied in a shared infrastructure, integrated market, and fair employment of Arab investments for the purpose of balanced human resources development in the Arab region, all of which serve to ease the disparities in social structure, health, education and nutrition between countries and between strata. They would also assist in shaping other forms of authority and civil society, where currents of public opinion can pressure for and share in decision-making and peaceful change.

But this future image remains one possibility out of several, given the great international and regional transformations at work. The experience of a peaceful settlement to the Arab–Israeli conflict and the idea of 'Middle Easternism' confront this possibility with one of two paths:

1 Either greater Arab withdrawal before the Middle Eastern project that Israel is preparing to play a pivotal and hegemonial role in, and that allocates tasks for markets and resources in accordance with the Israeli view.[32]

2 Or a meeting of the challenge by exceeding the Middle Eastern idea in its Israeli–US image, to reshape and redraft it from the milieu of the geo-civilizational reality and historical geography of the Arabs[33] and the Islamic world, i.e., a recovery of the concepts of 'Arab unity' and 'Islamic unity' and their adaptation to the reality.

I had earlier taken up the concept of Islamic unity, as one form of ideas and projects, beginning with the idea of the Islamic league, which Jamaleddin called for at the turn of the 20th century, to the idea of an Islamic commonwealth, which Malek bin Nabi called for in the 1950s and 1960s, a work of the reality and particularities controlling the conditions of the states of the Islamic world and their paramount concern for Jerusalem.

Within the framework of this reality one can now nominate the 'Islamic Conference Organization' as a complement to the summit of the League of Arab States, to provide the more comprehensive formula, going beyond the Middle Eastern, and with greater consistency with the history of the peoples of the region, its geography, culture, civilization, and memory and interests too. But this aspiration has conditions and points of entry, Arab conditions on the one hand and Islamic regional conditions on the other.

By Arab conditions is meant achieving a threshold of stability and Arab solidarity, and domestic Arab peace; its entry point is reconciliation at all levels.[34] Perhaps the level that is more critical and sensitive for this reconciliation is between the politics of the Arab regimes and politics of the opposition, especially the Islamic opposition, which seeks a form of government that believes in power sharing and a society able to criticize, oppose and induce peaceful change.

By Islamic conditions (conditions of Islamic geographic contiguity, especially in the Turkish and Iranian corners) is meant achieving a minimum of appreciation and awareness of peoples' joint interests, especially in the equitable and vital distribution of the sources and uses of strategic wealth (oil, water, passageways and ports) and at the level of development policy, democracy in issues of demographic and ethnic overlap and diversity at border areas. Such issues are not solved by 'border' policies as much as by democratic, developmental and humanitarian policies.

In the case of the Iranian neighbour (the subject of this book),[35] from among the theses of 'Islamic unity', and in its minimal content that is the

Islamic Conference Organization, there arise obstacles, discrepancies in mutual policy, and ideological images in elitist consciousness that do not, in my view, contribute to a climate of solidarity or assist in the growth of joint awareness over the destinies of the Islamic world's peoples in this changing world of rapid and overpowering transformations.

If we leave the subject of border problems and geography to the other discussions of the seminar, we stand before certain issues that relate to conceptual awareness, which has a definite impact on the pathways of joint Islamic effort between Iranians and Arabs. Among these are: a disturbing historical memory, the concept of Islamic revolution and Islamic unity, the issues of democracy, diversity and *marja'iyat* (authoritative reference).

1. Historical Memory

Historical memory often, even always, confuses between the political, strategic and economic needs of states on the one hand, and the ethnic, cultural and sectarian particularities of communities on the other. In the case of the Arab-Iranian historical memory, wars of expansion, border disputes and plans of domination over land and water passages and energy sources became mixed up with national and sectarian differences. The history of conflict and difference, the most prominent Iranian and Arab historians have written, entered into memory as though it were a history of national (Arab–Persian) or sectarian (Sunnite–Shiite) conflict. This memory contains its own feeding ground, in terms of sources of modern history, from the Safavid–Ottoman conflict up to the latest Iraq–Iran war. But the Ottoman–Safavid wars, their settlements, the Erzerum treaty (1847) and its various ramifications and developments until the Algiers agreement in 1975 – all show clearly the actual causes of the conflict. These causes, even if presented in national, Islamist or sectarian rhetoric, operate and continue to operate in terms of the interests of the state's leaders and ruling elites and the strategic geo-political vision dominating them. For what is rhetoric but a form of ideological expression, a distortion and concealment of reality and a functional utilization that meets a need for mobilization and militarization of this strategic vision, according to what has been termed 'the national security of the state'.[36]

2. The Concept of Islamic Revolution and Islamic Unity

Contemporary Islamic movements, in any country of the Islamic world, do not provide a realistic or likely understanding of 'Islamic unity' that can be investigated in the present age. Indeed, its internal differences at the political and power levels have reached the point of combat and warfare within individual countries (Afghanistan, for example). The ideas of 'Islamic unity' formulated at the beginning of the 20th century in the form of the 'Islamic league' (Jamaleddin), and sometimes the 'caliphate' in the 'twenties (the caliphate conference held after Mustapha Kemal abolished the Ottoman caliphate), then Malek bin Nabi's return in the 1950s and 1960s to re-express it as an 'Islamic commonwealth' that can accommodate the emergence of national liberation movements in the Asian–African framework of Islam – all these remained ink on paper. In fact, soon enough the author of the African–Asian idea, in his introduction to the 1971 edition of his book carrying the same title, despaired any transformation of Bandung into a civilizational reality or 'Islamic unity' into a historical reality.[37]

The programmes of contemporary Arab Islamic awakening politics are devoid of concern for this issue, devoting themselves to the concerns of political opposition to the authority of their countries, governments and regimes, and to the central slogan of applying the *Shari'ah*.

As for unity, the many Arab Islamic writings here rely on talk about the institution of the 'caliphate'; they recall it as a unifying institution for Muslims, and recall bids to recover its legality as the general authority over the Muslims[38] and as a symbol of existential longing for periods of history whose last chapters were the 'Ottoman sultanate' that carried, belatedly and for political and logistical reasons, the title of 'caliphate'.[39]

Strangely, this reminder on the conditions, which *'ulema* of the 'twenties and 'thirties admitted were unrealistic and difficult to realize, during their participation in the caliphate conferences held at the time,[40] was not followed up by most Islamic authors with criticism of the historical experience of the system of the caliphate,[41] as exercised in history, and how the caliphate changed, by dominance or by takeover, until it settled on 'arbitrary tenets' in the form of sultanates and *walayahs* of the sultanate.

We suspect that authors of Islamic movements downplay such criticism[42] and avoid it for many reasons, in part due to the ideological function served by a recovery of the history of the Islamic caliphate as a symbol of 'Islamic unity' and an Islamic phase far from tyranny.[43] In part also by its association with the violence of a political ideology in which religion and politics become one, and which played the role of 'legal precedent' for the 'guide' or chief of a group, or their 'imam' in daily life, where the adjectives 'religious' and 'sacred' are not subject to criticism. Perhaps the term that Abu'l A'la al-Maududi used, taken from Seyyed Qotob, *al-hakimieh al-ilahieh* (the divine rule), is the prevalent form of expression in Arab Islamic political literature.

Democracy, Pluralism and Marja'iyat

From the Iranian side, certain facts come to our attention that are suggestive for the treatment of the problematic of joint Iranian–Arab awareness
on this question. One of these is that Khamen'i translated many works by
Seyyed Qotob into Persian during the 'seventies. It goes without saying
that translation at that level and under such circumstances is not merely
academic. In addition to expressing a radical Islamic 'revolutionary mobilization' afforded by the rhetoric of Seyyed Qutb in Iran against the policy of
Westernization in the era of the Shah, it is also an expression of concur-
rence over the need to establish an 'Islamic state' institutionalizing
al-hakimieh al-ilahieh (the expression that summed up the incorporation of
the caliphate with the application of the *Shari'ah* in the Sunnite Arab message), and in the Iranian–Shiite case, institutionalizing the theory of the
'authority of the jurist' (*walayat al-faqih*), which Imam Khomeini had refined during his studies at that time. The concept of *walayat al-faqih* is an
ijtihad notion expanded from the field of the authorities (*walayat*) of the
'deputy imam' and powers of the 'conventional reference' (*marja' al-taqlid*)
in Shiite thought, to provide in this situation a rank of 'general authority' or
'general rule' for the infallible Imam (*al-imam al-ma'sum*) in an age that is
yet to be.[44] Doubtless this *ijtihad*, which the 'charisma' of the leader permitted at its moment of interaction with the psychology of Iran's pious and
resentful masses, surpasses two Islamic conditions:

It exceeds the Sunnite condition in the issue of the caliphate. It exceeds
the prevailing Shiite condition that had, until now, come to rest on a 'diversity of conventional authorities' and a role for the jurist varying from political
aloofness to an advisory or guiding capacity for rulers, as well as resisting
foreign occupation without aspiring for the exercise of direct rule.

With the eruption of the revolution, the psychology of the masses blazed,
as did their reactions and drive and support for the revolution. This impact
was not confined to the Iranian masses but also encompassed the Arab
masses and major nationalist and leftist trends; it even caught the attention
of foreign intellectuals and correspondents.

But soon enough the political and intellectual trends began to diverge at
the level of images of the revolution's pathways, publicists, politics, impacts
and claims. With the regional and international complications that accompanied the Iraq–Iran war and escalation and increase in abduction of foreign
hostages on Lebanese territory, which many liked to call an 'arena' (in view
of its laxity), and with the rise of war propaganda here and there, the quiet
and critical voice of rational awareness of the gravity of the situation, could
not get through; it barely made itself felt in the researchers, seminars, conferences and cultural activities of the 'Fao' and 'Saddam's Qadisieh' rallies.

What is important here is not only the review of the methods of nationalist and sectarian advertising in the two sides, but also the presentation of
the critical intellectual images by the spokesmen for the *walayat al-faqih* in
Arab awareness.[45] First of all, one should call to mind the suppression of
the historical evidence, or nearly so, originating with an Arab Lebanese
imamate *faqih*, Sheikh Muhammad Jawad Mughanieh. When the book
Islamic Government was published, he wrote a bold yet quiet pamphlet to
Imam Khomeini, entitled 'Khomeini and the Islamic State'. The book was
not destined to enter circulation!

Sheikh Mughanieh saw the *walayat al-faqih* to be a partial and limited
authority. He says: 'It was confirmed, by unanimous consent and with clear
wording, that to the just exerciser of *ijtihad* goes authority of *fatwah* and
judging over courts of law, public *waqf*, absentee wealth, legal incompetence in the absence of a personal guardian and over inheritance of the
heirless, in addition to elaboration on the books of jurisprudence, while
there is dispute over whether the *faqih* has authority over other matters'.[46]
Moreover, the Islam of a government or state does not, in his view, lie in
government by the *faqih*, but in any government that does right. He says:
'Whatever state that does right is Muslim, even if its men are not *faqihs*;
and if it does wrong, it is in no way Islamic, even if its members are graduates of the Najaf or Azhar'.[47]

Actually, the view of Sheikh Mughanieh is not new in the imamate
jurisprudence current. It is part of a juridical conventionalism that goes a
long way in focusing on the independent *marja'-i taqlid* towards politics,
politicians and heads of government and state, so as to safeguard the *faqih's*
active influencing of society and nation and serve as a public conscience
(the Kho'ie school). This tradition is shared by many Shiite *faqihs*, Iranian
and Arab. Thus, its importance lies first in opening the door to dialogue, in
a situation of slogan-spreading and dominance of the political, especially
in Iran and on every plain. It is also suggestive of a diversification in *ijtihad*
in imamate jurisprudence, the long and short of it being a maintenance of
diversity in the *marja' al-taqlid* and disputing the absolutism of *walayat al-
faqih*.

Sheikh Mohammed Mahdi Shamseddine takes a significant step forward in understanding this matter, by extracting it from the domain of
discussion over the extent and size of the authority of the *faqih* to re-exam-
ine the heart of the matter and propose an alternative to the *walayat al-faqih*:
'The *faqih* has no authority over people', and 'there is no legitimacy now for
an imamate or caliphate, and the sole legitimacy is establishing a modern
state to preserve the fixed tenets of the *Shari'ah*'.[48] In his view, the trend is
towards a civil state and civil society, because jurisprudence has two domains: private jurisprudence with arbitrary tenets (religious observances),
and public jurisprudence (relating to society, economy, foreign and state

policies). The bulk of these is a kind of 'vacuum zone' amenable to reason and inference by *ijtihad* from both Islamic and non-Islamic texts and other culture zones.[49]

If we draw attention here to the Arab character of these opinions and *ijtihad* judgments, it is not because they express an Arab awareness different from Iranian awareness, but because they emanate from an Arab locale, especially Lebanese, which permits freedom of thought, *ijtihad* and expression. One is duty-bound to bring back to mind that there are Iranian sources of authority who do not agree with the theory of 'absolute' authority, preferring to keep silent or aloof in view of the uni-polar nature of the Imam's leadership at the time.

We suspect that this polarity is what drove Islamists in the world, especially Arab Islamists, to regard the theory of *walayat al-faqih* in the Khomeini sense as the sole Shiite theory of government, rather than one of several Shiite theories. Consequently, we see that this theory provoked a sharp objection from Arab Islamists as denying the *shura*. For it is understood as the continuity and extension of prophethood to the infallible imamate, and what applies to the Imam applies to the Deputy Imam. 'His acts and words are binding on the Muslims and must be carried out' (it is so understood) is a maxim that critics protest. Sheikh Rashed al-Ghannoushi writes on the assumption that this position is held by all imamate Shi'ites, a position that rejects diversity; he writes: 'I state clearly that the forgiveness, even enthusiasm shown by many Sunnite intellectuals to the support of the Islamic masses for their imamate Shiite brethren and defence of the revolution of Islam in Iran, even if they suffer by this oppression and confrontation with their own regimes, was not generally met with a positive response from their Shiite brethren, except with much sweet talk about Islamic unity. At a deeper level, most of our brethren were not apparently rendered by the revolution any the less decidedly certain of the correctness of their reading of Islam, its history, and the alleged corruption of any other reading, and it only made them more scornful of the efforts of the nation and the culture and movements that emerged from it. Those held hope of change in people's belief in and attachment to an imamate infallibility, severing its commands and dogmatic notions and allegations, both new and old. It was a deceptive hope and fruitless aspiration, as the nation stripped away most of its history of diversity, and all that it has to its credit is to maintain on what is left that self-same approach.'[50]

In the context of reproaches, he criticizes Imam Khomeini for saying, 'Among the essentials of our Faith is that our imams hold positions neither kings nor prophets have held.' To this he responds: 'I considered this the religious scholar's humiliation, to recur in subsequent editions of the book, and how this troubled me.'[51]

This is a sample of the forms of Arab Islamic understanding towards the concept of *walayat al-faqih*. We selected it from an Islamic publicist who is known for his moderation, sense of dialogue and support for the Islamic revolution in Iran. One last matter that warrants consideration in this study is the issue of *marja'iyat*, which provoked and continues to provoke controversy; disputes over it imply a difference in awareness and perception as to its position, role and centre of influence.

This can be seen by following up the debate over *marja'iyat* after the demise of three leading authorities, one after the other, following Imam Khomeini's death: Imam Kho'i, Seyyed Kalbekani and Sheikh Araki. Perceptions on this issue are many and disparate, not only at the level of *ijtihad* regarding the authority's size and extent, but also, and fundamentally, in its vacillation and swinging between political overlordship and juridical foresight. We should take note that in this swinging motion enters, in a fundamental way, the element of place and location, i.e., the geo-political framework of the locale of the 'higher authoritative reference' (*marja' a'la*) and the range of his effort.

It goes without saying that the movement was, during the later stage, drawn into political factors and regional considerations evident in two elements:

1 The exceptional situation of elites and the *'ulema* of the Najaf under the Iraqi regime.
2 The new phenomenon of emergence of an Islamic state in Iran that speaks of *walayat al-faqih*.

Let us recall here that the Najaf Institute suffered much from the tyranny of the Iraqi regime, its interference and policy of assassination, oppression, and pursuit and exile of the *'ulema* and their families, sons and followers. This led to a huge gap in the juridical sciences of the Institute, and a paralysis rendering impossible the traditional mechanism of sending forth authorities in the 'territories' and rendering very difficult the regulation of the scholastic hierarchy in it, which is based on a tacit admission of the greater foresight of the *marja' a'la*. Nevertheless, Shiite authoritative references outside Iraq (in Lebanon, the Arab Near East and perhaps in Iran) who continued to adhere to this approach (the Najafi approach and Kho'i line) took an independent course from states and parties and saw in the act of designation or appointment, a deviation from Shiite convention and the system and traditions of *marja'iyat*.[52]

On the other hand, we note that those concerned with *marja'iyat* found themselves, for the first time in history, before a new phenomenon 'consisting of an attempt by an Islamic state based on the theory of *walayat al-faqih* to appoint the *marja' a'la* of religion at a time when the system of *marja'iyat* was such that a *marja' a'la* may come forth from outside its borders and policies, or may be non-Iranian in nationality or reside outside Iran'.[53]

The irony prompting reflection here is that the thesis of combining political authority with religious reference, embodied in Imam Khomeini, is difficult to apply on Iran's heads of state now. Some researchers see the Council of Experts selecting Khomeini principally for political reasons, while the matter of *taqleed* continues to operate within an independent relationship based on trust in the foresight of the assembly of *muqledin* (emulators) and their *muqallad* (authority emulated).[54]

Also noticeable is the emergence of views in Iran disinclined to discussing the designation of a *marja' a'la* from Iran and in Iran; they see an absence of authoritative references outside Iran and call for the merger of the position with that of *walayat al-faqih*.[55] It is well-known that the call to locate the *marja'iyat* in Iran, even merge the position with that of *walayat al-faqih*, derives from political and circumstantial considerations and conceptions peculiar to the Islamic state in Iran, how it understands the issues of 'unity', 'revolution' and 'relation of religion to politics', foreign policies, and the question of freedom and diversity in Islamic societies.

We believe that some Iranian heads of state feel the need for activating the ideological institutionalizing rhetoric of *walayat al-faqih*, at a time when state and society in Iran suffer a duality in rhetoric. There is the political rhetoric that seeks openness, diversification, realism and reverse brain drain among Iranian experts and thinkers, as conveyed by the President of the Republic. And there is the ideological political rhetoric that maintains a singular radicalism and a religio-political hard line that rejects freedom of thought beyond the standards it sets; this is embodied in *walayat al-faqih*.[56] If we may permit remarks by an Arab researcher on the awareness of this issue (Shiite *marja'iyat* and its place), we should propound the following:

If the object is to achieve a threshold of 'Islamic unity' in the Islamic world, and in the domain of our topic, between Iranians and Arabs, it is more than certain that neither the 'caliphate' nor the *'walayat al-faqih'* is the realistic and appropriate formula to achieve this end or work towards it; unless there exist regional or national accountancy for the 'Iranian Islamic experience' on the one hand and the 'Arab Islamic experience' on the other. In which case the accounts are concealed by geo-political and economic undercurrents that promptly surface during crises, whether bearing a nationalist cloak or sectarian or both together.

If the object is to achieve 'Islamic unity' in the form of solidarity and cooperation, its connecting forms should proceed through coordination between regional, economic, cultural, scientific and religious policies such that they can translate into various levels:

1 The level of states, whose most appropriate framework is perhaps the 'Islamic Conference Organization', in order to develop the latter into a

'League of Islamic States'.
2 The level of [non-governmental] civil societies, where institutions, associations, parties, universities and research centres can meet to create
intellectual currents, a general opinion and centres of pressure and lobbying; all of this is conditional on the initiative of civil and domestic
society in Iran and the Arab countries.

If such is the situation, then the most appropriate Shiite formula for
pursuit of this line is maintaining diversity in *marja'iyat,* which is something likely to remain anyway because of deep-rooted Shiite tradition. The
question remaining now is, can the process of debate in Shiite *'ulema* circles
produce, through tacit admission, a hierarchy of *'ulema* who in turn yield a
marja' a'la who has the greater ability?

Let the place and locale follow from productive debate on this *a'lamiyyah,*
for this would not only be a mastery of jurisprudence and its foundations in
the conventional sense, but a mastery of the knowledge of the age as well
and an ability to keep up with new developments. Greater ability here is
thus global, and it cannot possibly dissociate itself today from universalism.
But to become so, its location frame must be a setting of democracy and a
civil society availing freedom of expression, the spread of opinion to the
broadest groups, and follow up of international issues and problems. The
marja' taqlid, in the mondial age, is no longer a conventional *marja'iyat* for
Shi'ites only but is clearly a centre of decision-making and counsel, or should
have been.

Where is an appropriate place for this role? As I write these words, a
dialogue on the function and role of Lebanon comes back to mind. Some
saw this role, and operated it, as an 'arena' for conflict between regional
powers and international politics. Others saw it, and operated it, as a 'po-
dium' or window of civilization on the world. I find myself in this dialogue
as a referee for the latter view. This leads me to ask now, is it not more
fitting for Shiite *a'lamiyyah* to exercise its role as a *marja' al-taqlid* for Shi'ites
and centre of diffusion onto the Islamic world and the world at large, affecting and being affected, from the civilizational window of the Lebanon,
instead of turning this locale into a regional political arena, as occurred
during the past 15 years of war?

I have spoken at some length on this point because it sums up, in my
view, a basic dimension in the dimensions of awareness and observed images in the various looking glasses alluded to in the introduction. This
dimension is important and must complement the others for Iranian–Arab
relations, the foremost being: the geo-political, or border, interests and
locational issues. There should not lurk at bottom of these relations a thick
crust of nationalist, sectarian or Islamist ideologies, nor must this crust be
allowed to surface, through the media or the raising of banners, for then

deeper and deeper pits will be dug into historical memory and a distorted or misleading looking glass image in mutual awareness might be conjured.

Notes

* Faculty of Arts and Humanities, Lebanese University.

1.   Morteza Mutahhari, *Islam and Iran*, 3 vols., (Beirut: Dar al-Ta'aruf, n.d.), p. 22.

2.   Ibid., p. 257.

3.   Mehdi Bazargan founded the 'Iran Liberation Movement' in 1961. He consulted on this with the leader Muhammad Mosaddeq. It is noteworthy that the Islamic struggle waged by Bazargan with Ayatollah Taleqani operates in a frame where religion does not mix with politics, yet both act in unison at what Bazargan calls 'the borderline between religion and politics', which is the border between 'too much and too little', whether in terms of joining or in terms of dissociating. Students of Bazargan see him as 'a bridge between the old national movement and the latest Islamic revolution, i.e., between Mosaddeq and Khomeini'. (See Mehdi Bazargan, *The Borderline between Religion and Politics*, preface and translation by Fadel Rasul, (Beirut: Dar al-Kalimah, 1979), pp. 10, 27).

4.   A circular was issued by the UN Secretariat, dated 14 August 1994, on the use of the term 'Persian Gulf'. It contained another reminder to adhere to 'the approved expression "Persian Gulf" in all documents, correspondence and publications issued by the Secretariat', and affirmed 'commitment to use this expression in full, that is, Persian Gulf, and the inadequacy and incorrectness of adopting the term 'Gulf' alone, even in cases of repetition'. The Embassy of the Islamic Republic of Iran in Beirut, which translated and circulated the text, remarks: 'Accordingly, the term "Gulf" or any other term at variance with "Persian Gulf" is a violation of objective and historical fact.'. Memorandum issued by the General Secretariat of the UN, 18 August 1994.

5.   Mohamed Hasanein Heikal, *The Ayatollah's Guns: The Story of Iran and the Revolution*, (Cairo: Dar al-Shuruq, 1983), p. 269.

6.   Kulami Siddiqi, *Unity and Shiism in the Politics of Islam and Transgression*, (London: The Islamic Institute, 1984), pp. 19–20.

7.   A recurring theme in some Iranian Islamic literature is that there is no place for nationalism in Islamic government or society, that it was 'a tool of imperialism and the Crusades for the purpose of confronting Islam', or that nationalism originates in imperialism. One Iranian researcher, Ali Muhammad Naqavi, gives 'the example of the nationalism that beleaguered the Islamic world, Istanbul, Cairo, Beirut, concurrently with late 19th-century colonialist expansionism; it set the Arabs and Turks against one another.' The researcher devotes a chapter in his book to show how the Arab nationalist movement joined up with colonialism ever since the movements of the Sherif Hussein and the secret Arab societies. See Ali Muhammad Naqavi, *Islam and Nationalism*, (Tehran: Islamic Propagation Organization, 1984), pp. 12 and 27–39.

8.   An example of this is the conference on 'The Impact of Nationalism on the Nation', organized by the Islamic Institute in London, 31 July–3 August 1985.

9. Personal communication from Abu'l Hasan Bani Sadr to columnist Michel Nawfal, *An-Nahar* daily (Beirut), 25/12/1979.

10. For a typical article on this approach in examining the historical roots of Arab nationalism, see: Saleh Ahmad al-Ali, 'Arab Nationalist Sentiment Across History: The Components of Arab Nationalism and its Manifestations Across History', paper presented to the Colloquium on the Development of Arab Nationalist Thought: Researches and Discussions, organized by the Centre for Arab Unity Studies (CAUS), with the participation of the Iraq Scientific Academy, the Union of Arab Historians and the Arab Research and Studies Institute, (Beirut: CAUS, 1986), pp. 15–19.

11. Saadoun Hamadi, 'Arab Nationalism and the Contemporary Challenges', paper presented to the Colloquium on the Development of Arab Nationalist Thought: Researches and Discussions, organized by the Centre for Arab Unity Studies, pp. 337–62.

12. We shall restrict ourselves here to presenting the problematic of nationalism in contemporary Islamic history, especially areas that were part of the vilayets of the Ottoman state. This does not mean that the problem did not already exist in earlier stages of Islamic history. However, what distinguishes the problematic of contemporary nationalism is its embodiment of a political awareness intent on establishing a specific nationalist state on the basis of ethnic affiliation and a fixed geographic–political border; whereas the national problematic in the early stages of Islamic history was restricted to the emergence of tribal entities competing for places within the state or for establishing new states. Then, the limits of the state was not determined, for its people, by ethnic or national boundaries but rather by the capacity of a tribal entity to rival others in extending the scope of Islam on the one hand and the scope of the market and ways of dominating it for the state's coffers on the other. This was in fact the situation of non-Arab dynasties that established such sultanates as the Buwayhid, Seljuk, Ilkhanid and, finally, the Safavid and Ottoman.

13. See the writings of Rashid Ridha on this position in: Rashid Ridha, *Selected Political Writings from 'Al-Manar' Magazine*, preface and explanatory text by Wajih Kawtharani, (Beirut: Dar al-Talee'ah, 1980), pp. 146–69.

14. Jamaleddin al-Afghani, *The Complete Works of Jamaleddin al-Afghani*, edited by Mohammed 'Amarah, (Cairo: Dar al-Kitab al-Arabi, 1968), pp. 34–5.

15. Ibid., p. 34.

16. Ibid., p. 34.

17. Ibid., p. 316.

18. Morteza Mutahhari says that the Persians 'not only regarded Arabic as the language of the Arabs but also as the language of Islam and Muslims generally', for it is 'an international language of Islamic orders'. See Mutahhari, *Islam and Iran*, p. 66.

19. The French orientalist Louis Masignon described it as a kind of 'Islamic Bolshevism', in his article on 'Islamic Demands'.

20. Some researchers see in this proposal an Arab nationalist calling by al-Kawakibi, along the lines of Neguib 'Azouri's call in 1905. However, such a comparison is without historical justification and is a distortion of al-Kawakibi's views.

21. Abdul Rahman al-Kawakibi, *The Mother of All Towns*, pp. 355–66.

22. See Mohammed Rashid Ridha, *The Caliphate or Greater Imamate*, pp. 73–6, and Shakib Arslan, *Mr Rashid Ridha or a Brotherhood of 40 Years*,

(Damascus: Ibn Zeydun Press; Cairo: Dar al-Kitab al-Masriyyah, 1937), p. 314.

23.   See document by Hasan al-Banna on his position on Arab unity and Islamic unity, in *Al-Hiwar* magazine (Summer 1986), pp. 168–9.

24.   See Tariq al-Bishri, 'Between Islam and Arabism', *Al-Hiwar* (Summer 1986), pp. 15–32.

25.   Abu'l A'la al-Maududi, *We and Western Civilization*, p. 77.

26.   Al-Bushri, *op. cit.*, pp. 21–2.

27.   Siddiqi, *Unification and Schism in the Politics of Islam and Transgression*, pp. 27, 31.

28.   Mutahhari, *Islam and Iran*, p. 22. See part 1 of this study.

29.   For a commentary on the nationalist–Islamic conference held in Beirut, 10–12 October 1994, compare Wajih Kawtharani, 'Nationalists and Islamists and a Single Political Culture', *Al-Hayat* daily, 2–3/11/1994.

30.   Quoted in Mutahhari, *op. cit.*, p. 51.

31.   For more details, see: *Arab Unity: Experience and Prospects*, researches and studies of the colloquium organized by the Centre for Arab Unity Studies (Beirut: CAUS, 1989), in particular Ahmad Tarbin, 'Unification Projects in the Contemporary Arab Order', pp. 409–46.

32.   This Israeli view was presented in Shimon Peres, *The New Middle East*, London: Element, 1993.

33.   In the course of writing this research report, the Alexandria summit was held between President Mubarak, President Asad and King Fahd (28–29 December 1994), to give, through its talks and communique, hope in reviving the Arab League, and a possible ambition to 'gather the capacities of the Arab nation in an Arab economic frame that can serve Arab interests'. The statement also noted that 'the cooperation between the three states forms a fundamental basis for joint Arab effort', consisting of a historical possibility for a potential and expected role for the Arab triangle (Cairo–Damascus–Riyadh) as the hub of the Arab wheel. This triangle is also equipped to play an important role in the wider Islamic wheel, as it forms a corner of the Islamic triangle (Arab–Turkish–Iranian).

34.   It is necessary and useful to reflect at length on the indefatigable Sheikh Mohammed Mahdi Shamseddine, the Chairman of the Supreme Islamic Shiite Council, and his call in recent years for a comprehensive reconciliation throughout the Arab nation. See his open letter to Presidents Assad and Mubarak on the occasion of their meeting 1 May 1990, entitled: 'International Change and the Tasks of Arab Islamic Effort', *Minbar al-Hiwar*, no. 18 (Summer 1990). In this letter the Sheikh proposed several practical ideas, including 'a united Arab–Islamic entity'.

35.   See 'Colloquium on Turkish–Arab Dialogue' organized by the Centre for Arab Unity Studies, 15–18 November 1993, in which I presented a research report that I consider supplementary to this one, entitled 'The Place of Arab–Turkish Relations in the Islamic World'. The works of this colloquium were published in a book under the title, *Arabs and Turks: Future Dialogue, Researches and Discussions of the Seminar Organized by the Centre for Arab Unity Studies*, Beirut: CAUS, 1995.

36.   For a historical look at this mixing and an effort to dismantle it in the Safavid–Ottoman case, see Wajih Kawtharani, *A Study in Two Historical Experiences: Ottoman and Safavid–Qajar*, Beirut: Dar al-Rashed, 1979. See also Saad al-Ansari, *Five Centuries of Iraqi–Iranian Relations*, Beirut: Dar al-Huda, 1987.

37.   Compare Malek bin Nabi, *The Afro–Asian Idea in Light of the Bandung Con-*

ference, Damascus: Dar al-Fikr, 1979.

38. Compare the writings of Abbas Madani and Ali Bilhaj and the literature of the Islamic Liberation Party. One can also turn to references in Rashid al-Ghannushi, *Civil Liberties in the Islamic State*, (Beirut: CAUS, 1993), pp. 150–70.

39. On the problematic of the caliphate and sultanate and the functional relationship between them, see: Kawtharani, *The Muslim Jurist and the Sultan, a Study in Two Historical Experiences: Ottoman and Safavid–Qajar*.

40. The position of most *'ulema* participating in the caliphate conference (1926) was to postpone this issue and call for additional conferences; Rashid Ridha's position was summarized in the establishment of an *'ijtihad* school of thought'. See *Memoirs of the Islamic Caliphate Conference*, (Cairo: n.p., 1926), vol. 27, part 5, pp. 370–76.

41. The writings of Sheikh Mohammed Mahdi Shamseddine, to the best of my knowledge, are an exception. His criticism of the historical experience of the sovereign in Islamic history, in relation to the succession by necessity that was allocated usurping sultanates and emirates, and its disagreement with 'the theory of the general authority of the *walayat al-faqih*', becoming the backdrop of a thesis arguing 'the authority of the nation over itself', which in turn led to the statement of establishing the modern institutional state, does not conflict with the arbitrary tenets of the *Shari'ah*, as an alternative to the [Sunnite] caliphate or surrogate for the Shiite imamate [authority of the *faqih*]. See Mohammed Mahdi Shamseddine, *The System of Government and Administration in Islam and the Islamic Body Politics: Towards a Legalistic and Historical Foundation*, Beirut: Jami'iyyah Research Institute, 1992.

42. Some researchers believe the authors of 'Islamic fundamentalism', such as Hasan al-Banna, Mawdudi and Seyyed Qotob, 'do not glorify Islamic history or see in it a guide or director'; if they exclude the first four orthodox caliphs, they regard them, or some of them, as a model of Islamic rule. Compare Ahmad Moussalli, *Islamic Fundamentalism: A Study in the Political Ideological Statement of Seyyed Qotob*, (Beirut: Al-Nasher Printing and Publishing, 1993), p. 217. In my view, if this is true, it is also true that they avoid criticising this history, for criticism does not mean entering into its legality or illegality from the religious standpoint but rather dismantling the functional relationship between the *faqih* and the sultan, between jurisprudence and politics. Put differently, Islamic authors avoid rushing into the field Ibn Khaldun rushed into six centuries ago – the relationship between the religious function and the sultanic plan or *'asabiyyah*; or, in Ibn Khaldun's words, the connection between the *'asabiyyah* and the message. Thus, they avoid – even if they regard the orthodox caliphs as the model – a study of the tribal, interests and political backgrounds in the non-*shura* activity, even at specific stages, of these four caliphates. The problem is always in the projection of the 'sacred' over the 'political'; this 'sacred' that dominates human action is what prevents the emergence of a historical awareness that can profit from the corpus of history and its experiences.

43. Rashed al-Ghannoushi asks in his book mentioned earlier: 'How do we explain the tyranny that emerged in Islamic history?' He avoids dismissing the reasons for the transformation in applying the principle of the *'shura'* towards rule of the one; he also skips over the periods of tyranny in the history of the sultanic state that replaced the caliphate, to throw the weight of the tyranny and its violence on the West and the modern age, by saying: 'The ugliest tyranny known in

our history is in those eras that rendered the legality of rule in the Islamic world derivable not from Islam and its nation but from allegiance and subordination to the West'. Al-Ghannushi, *Civil Liberties in the Islamic State*, p. 37. Here we cannot but pay tribute to Ibn Khaldun, who was certainly braver than the historians and *'ulema* of today in severing the 'sacred' from positivist politics, even if coloured by religion, through his discovery of how the *'asabiyyah* works and the function of the religious message in 'strengthening *'asabiyyah*', as he put it. For details, see Wajih Kawtharani, 'Of Flaws in Our Perception of Our History', *As-Safir* daily, 29 November 1994.

44.   Ayatollah Khomeini, *Islamic Government*, (Beirut: Dar al-Tali'ah, 1979), pp. 70–80. Among the statements of the Imam was: 'The jurists today are the competent authority over the people, just as the Prophet (was God's competent authority over them)' (p. 80).

45.   This does not mean that Arab awareness has no counterpart in Iran. There were Iranian juridical trends opposed to the power of *walayat al-faqih* generally. Among these were Ayatollah Talqani, Shari'atmadari, and, earlier, Mirza al-Na'imi, who restricted this authority to the courts as well as certain probate matters.

46.   Muhammad Jawad Mughanieh, *Khomeini and the Islamic State*, (Beirut: Dar al-'Ilm Li'l Malayeen, 1979), pp. 60–1.

47.   Ibid., p. 66.

48.   See conversation with Sheikh Mohammed Mahdi Shamseddin in *Al-Nur* magazine, 4:22 (October/November 1994).

49.   Mohammed Mahdi Shamseddin, in a dialogue with *Minbar al-Hiwar* on democracy and *shura* in civil society: *Minbar al-Hiwar*, 34 (1994).

50.   Al-Ghannushi, *Civil Liberties in the Islamic State*, p. 144.

51.   Ibid., pp. 143–4.

52.   For more details, and a defence of this trend, see Abdel Majid al-Kho'ie, '*Marja'iyat* as Extension of Succession to the Prophet and Imams: Its Independence between Political and External Influences', *Al-Nour*, 3:33 (February 1994).

53.   Laith Kubbeh, '*Marja'iyat* between Political Overlordship and Juridical Foresight', *Al-Nour*, 3:33 (February 1994), p. 26.

54.   Ibid.

55.   On the *marja'iyat*, Seyyed Ali Khamene'i defined his position as nominating for it 'the experts' and five other persons to the centre of the authority. He saw no necessity or need for 'bearing this burden in Iran' because, as he put it, 'thank God there are many men of *ijtihad* in Qom and elsewhere … competent to do this. So what need is there to place this burden on top of the heavy burden laid on me by God?' Seyyed Khamene'i corrects the situation by announcing his acceptance of this centre outside Iran. He says: 'Of course, for outside Iran is a different ruling; I accept what they would have me bear, because if I do not bear this burden it will be lost'. Full text in *Al-'Ahd* (16 December 1994), p. 3. The discrepancy between the internal and the external in Iranian awareness of the *marja'iyat* issue raises more than one question: Since there are many proper *marja's* within Iran, why are they not themselves proper for outside Iran? Why do national borders not open to the *marja'iyat* of Khamene'i and close to the other authorities? Does it make sense for the Arab region to be devoid of *'ulema* capable of being *marja's*?

56.   Some media sources reported that '134 Iranian intellectuals signed a statement calling for freedom of expression, permitting them to express their thoughts and have their banned books issued. *Islami Jamhurieh* daily, which supports the

leader of the revolution, responded to the statement with an article entitled, "Do Not Open Our Cases", accusing the petitioners of being "Mossad and CIA agents … and communist and royalist enemies of the revolution receiving orders from their Western and Israeli masters …" It described them as "bacteria and vermin of society, the remains of the street thugs who worked for the CIA and Mossad". For Ayatollah Janati, a member of the Council of Experts, his position was declared as "also against the petitioners", stressing that the criterion of freedom of expression is 'say what corrupts' and 'say what is appropriate'. It is a reminder of the criteria of totalitarianism; the Soviet Union, for example, placed a single standard for good and evil, right and wrong. From *An-Nahar* daily (weekly supplement), 17/12/1994.

6

Mutual Awareness between Arabs and Iranians

HADI KHESROSHAHI*

Introduction

Arabs and Iranians share many cultural, political and social characteristics because of their long-standing contacts in most aspects of civilization. This identity and contact became deeply rooted and all-encompassing under Islam as the common faith, the common way of life and the intellectual and political movement on which Islamic systems of government in all their different forms were based. Indeed, these systems were thoroughly intermeshed for long periods of time, until the advent of the Western invasion of Islamic countries, which put an end in the late 19th and early 20th centuries to the political institution of the caliphate and the Islamic empire in all Islamic countries, after which European powers proceeded, often deceitfully, to carve up the Muslim world creating bitter divisions which have fuelled territorial, ethnic and national conflicts. A generation emerged that was unable to view things in terms of the common history, but was ruled by the preoccupations of imperialist culture, discriminating between Muslims on the basis of country, territory or nationality. In response to this there have been, throughout the Arab and Islamic world, calls for a return to Islam with Islamic Iran at the forefront. These movements have begun to fight Western imperialism, and seek to bring down the barriers and bridge the imagined gaps between the nationalities and the territories of the Muslims. In order to grasp, if only in a general and brief way, the depth and dimensions of mutual awareness between Arabs and Iranians, we shall examine the question under four headings: Arab nationalism and Islam; Arab unity and Islamic unity; Iranian nationalism and Islam; The Islamic Revolution in Iran.

Arab Nationalism and Islam

How can one appraise nationalist thought or nationalist feeling from an Islamic point of view? Is the Muslim individual entitled to close connections with his own nationality and history, especially as many forms of these ties may introduce positive and fruitful aspects in his life, contributing to a conscious and responsible understanding of Islam? Many Muslims have asked this question, and many a pen has been put to work on it, particularly as the Arab Muslim's loyalty to his nationalism or Arabism is special and unlike any other nationalist loyalty. If there is a feeling of contradiction between the two loyalties, Islamic and Arab, how can we address this feeling? How can the nationalist tie to Arabism be made to deepen attachment to Islam? And is it possible to subordinate nationalism, for the sake of creating a wider and more universal tie, one that embraces it and other nationalisms as well?

The subject used to be broached from the standpoint of the call of nationalism versus the call of Islam, the assumption being that they contradict each other. This is not true. Experience has shown that carelessness in the choice of words opens doors to imaginary conflicts and to struggles between parties who are not in disagreement. It is possible to define several terms relating to this study, such as 'nationalism' or 'Arab nationalism' or the 'Arab nationalist movement'. Each of these terms has its own meaning and particular significance, although they may have points in common. But when examined and discussed with the aim of deriving basic concepts and tenets that bear on the life of the Muslim, then such terms take on different connotations and have different implications.

All too often these terms became objects of squabbles over definition and disputes between philosophers and authors, whether Arab or Western. Consequently they have surfaced as various assumptions and forms of argument, within sharp intellectual disputes that led to a deepening of the negative side of nationalist attachment. Nationalism is the expression of belonging to a nation, defined as a group of people who share a sense of loyalty, a feeling created by common formative elements, chiefly language; on this all scholars agree, notwithstanding their disagreement over the relative import of each element within the stock of common formative elements. This loyalty is not a creed, nor is it a philosophy; rather it is 'a social and psychological fact of history'. Consequently, the sense of belonging of the Muslim, be he or she Egyptian, Iraqi, Syrian, Algerian or otherwise, to this Arab nation is part of the reality of their organic tie to Arab society, no different than the Quraishite's sense of belonging to Quraish or the Khazrajite's belonging to Khazraj. Thus, the question of what is Islam's position on this tie is meaningless, because this tie is a natural, social and neutral condition like any other neutral social condition.

Such a condition may acquire a frame whose content involves lofty aims of right, justice and perfection, or an abject content and aim directed to falsehood, oppression and corruption. Moreover, one can argue that the individual's attachment to family, tribe, clan or nation is an innate psychological feeling. When the Prophet began his Mission, the 'mother of all towns' [Mecca] turned against him at first, and he and his Message encountered such dissension and harm from its residents that he had to leave it as a muhajir. And yet he missed it, its mountains, valleys and all that was in it, when he was in exile. And there was nothing in that longing to even scratch the perfection of his Islam, or encroach on his place as the leader of the nascent Islamic nation, about which the Almighty has said: 'And verily this Brotherhood of yours is a single Brotherhood, and I am your Lord and Cherisher: therefore fear Me [and no other].'[1]

Arab nationalism, as a natural social condition, thus found its spiritual identity and humanist creed in Islam. We can say that the true dawn of history for the Arab nation came only with Muhammad who united the Arabs under the banner of Islam. Before Muhammad the Arabs had lived in perpetual conflicts and wars that tore them apart, whether for partisanship and honour as in the wars of Dahess, Ghabra and Bassus, or for traditional tribal motives. Through his mission, their history came to be as part of the history of Islam.

Nationalism – in particular Arab nationalism is a political movement, not simply a matter of group loyalty. Its purpose is to turn the historical and civilizational reality of the Arab nation into a 'unified political entity', irrespective of the other special traits that shape the vital and historical features of the nation, the *ummah*. This alone is the meaning of the nationalist movement, and anything else circulated by the followers of the various nationalisms, to give them a positive or progressive image, is nothing more than playing with words or drawing on other notions to further obscure the matter, like the epithets of Arab nationalism as having a socialist character, or basically Islamic, or whatever else.

Thus, nationalism is a historical fact as well as a natural, neutral social condition. Yet Islam is a universal religion which regulates human life on the basis of guidelines in belief, thought and organization; it is a universal Message that the prophets and apostles transmitted from their Lord, Who completed and explained in detail its laws and rites by the Inspiration sent down to the Prophet Muhammad, a Qur'an manifest and a *sunnah* detailed and honoured, a movement that is living, and a leadership to raise its banner that came from his household (on whom be peace) and the devoted of his Companions.

Islam was able to render the Arabs – as it rendered other nationalities who believed in Islam and raised its banner – a strong entity and a great civilization, moving forth to conquer, 'open', other lands, some of which had previous histories and unique civilizations of their own. The Islamic conquests sometimes Arabized them, as in the case of the ancient civilizations of Egypt, Assyria and Babel, or the conquering armies of Islam entered as liberators of lands still under the heel of the two great empires, the Roman and the Persian. It is with this liberation that many of these once subjugated nations began to acquire a special sense of history. This liberation and faith in Islam rendered the history of the region the history of Islam and of its heroes – Muhammad, his virtuous household, his devoted Companions and whoever walked in their footsteps. It was led by Muslim leaders who were from every race in the realm of Islam.

And so the first thing that comes to mind, quite unconsciously, when a person says that he is an Arab, is that he is Muslim, and what other reason is there for that than the inseparability of Arab and Arabism from Islam? Nationalism as an organized political force appeared only in modern times, with the appearance of secular governments, especially that of the Turkish Committee of Union and Progress in the first decade of this century, after the liquidation of the Ottoman Islamic Caliphate and oppression of non-Turkish elements, especially the Arab. After the Ottoman Islamic Caliphate collapsed and the empire disintegrated, several trends developed. Two of these were particularly important and constituted the new alternative to overcoming the phase of past adversity left over from the policy of Ottoman rulers, particularly in the Arab countries.

The first trend was purely secular, and can be labelled the Westernization current which effectively became an ally of the Western imperalist plan in the region. Its intellectual basis lay in the call to adopt the Western model in full. The ideas of this trend derived from hostility to both Arabism and Islam, alleging that Islamic thought and Arab culture are sterile, incapable of recovering by their own means or of their own volition, and the only way to escape the wretched Ottoman legacy is to learn from the West, mimic it and follow it in every respect, even in dress and eating habits, as well as in thought, norms, culture and ethics. This trend was adopted by some elites and social classes in the Arab and Islamic countries, who fantasized with theories and excelled in habits imported from the West, and how many are the examples and manifestations of this trend in our Muslim Arab society today?

This trend was irrevocably hostile to Islam and Arabism, though Arabism as a nationalist movement is a term that comes from the West itself. The second trend is an Arab nationalism that accords with Islamic thinking in opposing Western imperialism and resisting its forms of subjection or walking in its footsteps. Advocates of this trend worked for the establishment of an independent unifying entity. But they disagreed over whether Islam should provide the legislative as well as the intellectual and spiritual content that should be adhered to by the Arabs. All advocates of nationalism hold Islam as a legacy, but they disagreed over attachment to this legacy, both qualitatively and quantitatively, to the point where nationalist currents emerged that altogether rejected Islam, describing it as rooted in the establishment. They limited attachment to legacy and history, and they endorsed secular ideas; this resulted in their falling into the hands of the West because they adopted, consciously or unconsciously, a purely Western secularist current. Nationalism was transformed from pride in attachment to Islam, in bearing its universal Divine Message and disseminating it to all the corners of the earth, and in adoption of a universal unifying system, to mere nationalist movements that wanted to create of their own accord a philosophy of life and social and moral system in place of Islam. And so they fell into the trap of fumbling with and running behind the new secularist notions that were intended for no more than rivalling or fighting the original Islamic idea.

These nationalisms became like a frame that was cracking and splitting at the seams under the weight of ideas that were alien to their original identity and a source of oppression. For despite its commitment to calling for and working as a movement of liberation from hegemony and imperialism the features of nationalism qua Islam began to gradually disappear. This was the case of some Arab nationalist factions that converted into a Marxist movement that was totally internationalist. Islam for them no longer amounted to anything but history, without any real presence, except to the extent or character defined by their own Marxist materialist analysis of Islamic history and legacy.

The same occurred with those who toted catchy slogans, like socialism. They tried to reconcile these both with the intellectual pretensions of Europe and dissociation from Western civilization. They promoted Arab socialism by incorporating it within the Arab framework they advocated and by avoiding the sensitivity of the ummah to any slogan or philosophy tied to the world of the imperialists, West or East. By giving socialism an Arab cloak, they tried to hide the fact that it was foreign, historically and intellectually, but the cloak failed and was unable to win the Muslim Arab ummah over to the essentially foreign nature of socialism.

Arab society possesses a language, history, character and spirituality that is inseparable from Islam, including belief in the Almighty God. How can the advocates of Arab socialism possibly reconcile Islam with the socialism of imperialists and atheists in contradiction with it?

Arab nationalism is unlike any other nationalism, for it is not only race but culture and language. Perhaps culture and language are the basic pillars that distinguish the Arabs from others. Once we recognize this fact we will begin to understand the difficulty in separating Arabism from Islam. Defining these notions poses no problem. The Qur'an was revealed in Arabic and those who seek an understanding of Islam through it must approach the tenets we have referred to above. On the other hand, if we extract Arabic culture from Islamic culture, there would be no Arabic culture left to speak of. One may say that Arabism and Islam are in fact two sides of the same coin. In which case the dispute originates from the overt extremism of advocates of nationalism and their rejection of Islam on the one hand, and the reaction of some Islamists who wished to abandon Arabism altogether on the other hand.

There is another issue. Islam is founded on equality between various peoples and nationalities. The Prophet said 'No favouring of Arab over Persian except in piety' – a command diametrically opposed to the Jewish concept of 'God's chosen people'. Islam was able to establish equality between the Arabs – from whom came the Prophet Muhammad with their language as the language of the people of Paradise and the Holy Qur'an – and with all other peoples and nationalities who embraced Islam in a position of equality that was total in rights and obligations. Armed with this philosophy Islam extended beyond Arabia to new civilizations and was no longer a purely Arab religion. Arabic spread with the spread of Islam and the Qur'an, and the Arabs were the first to carry the *amanah*, the 'sacred trust', of Islam, in faith, diffusion and jihad. As we have already said on the tie between Arabism and Islam, the Holy Qur'an was revealed in an Arabic tongue, manifest to an Arab Apostle in the 'mother of all towns' and the 'place of hijrah' and its surroundings. The choice of time, place, apostle and man in Islam are by Divine Decree, not human will, and Islam is as much a responsibility to provide as it is an honour and honouring. Membership of the Islamic *ummah* is governed by three pillars, brought together in the ayah: 'You are the best of peoples evolved for mankind, enjoining what is right, forbidding what is wrong, and believing in God'.[2] Honour in Islam is piety, and piety is faith and effort.

Arab Unity and Islamic Unity

The Arab nation did not emerge as a single ummah with a mission except through Islam. Before Islam, the southern Arabian Peninsula was under the occupation and suzerainty of the Abyssinians, and then the Persians. In Yathrib and many other towns on the route between Hejaz and Syria, there were well-entrenched gatherings of Israelites. As for the Arabs, they spread out from their original homeland, the Arabian Peninsula, to other settled areas such as Syria, Iraq, the Nile Valley and remainder of North Africa, which were under the suzerainty and occupation of the Romans (Byzantines) and Persians. There was no one who spoke authentic Arabic in those lands except a few small groups. Then Islam came and rid the Peninsula of foreign occupation and dominance, united it under its banner, and conquered those areas where Arabs had settled outside the Arabian Peninsula. Arabic emerged as its language and Islam its eternal Message. The first Islamic state was born there, and the Arabs sowed its first Islamic seed. A great Islamic civilization flourished in every way under its aegis. Its missionary character was consolidated, and it carried the torch of guidance to the countries of the world, its banner spreading eastward and westward. If it was not for Islam, the Qur'an and the Islamic civilization that emerged in their wake, it is quite likely that the Arabs would have been dispersed between several nations of different languages and dialects, remaining at the mercy of those dominating their lands in the Peninsula and other places they inhabited. It is also likely that the Arabs would not have reached a unity of language, society, history and mission, nor would they have been able to spread and exert a spiritual, linguistic cultural and civilizational influence on all parts of the world. The return to the spirit of Islam and its original fountainhead is sufficient to obstruct the conspiracy of division and fragmentation confronting the Islamic and the Arab world, and sufficient, therefore, to recover the ancient glory of Islam and the unity of its sons of every race, nationality and colour, leading to an international Islamic union. Its unity, revival, integration, flourishing and freedom from the greed of the ambitious and aggression of the aggressors would bestow on it glory and pride. All these are part and parcel of the Islamic objectives and of the call for fortifying Islam and rendering the Islamic nation one nation. Moreover, the call for Arab unity is not separable from its being a call for Islamic unity, for the overwhelming majority of the Arab race embrace Islam and therefore on them rests the onus of its call.

The first to sow the seeds of dispersion and difference between the Arabs and initiate discord between them were the Umayyads, when they deviated from the purpose of the Islamic empire and assumed the authority of succession (the caliphate) unjustly and by oppression. The destiny of the Muslims became a game for them, playing which they played according to their tendencies, cravings or preoccupations. And so conflict began between the Arabs of Iraq and those of Syria, and the animosity continued for many years. Then the Umayyads sowed fanaticism and dissension between the Muslim Arab tribes that Islam had united and liberated and lifted above the habits of the Jahiliyyah and its erroneous practices; they did this for political aims and objectives, to enable them to rule their domain and establish their authority at the expense of the Muslims. Dissension among the Arabs spread to the rest of the Muslims who had recently embraced Islam and had left their former religions for the new Faith. These were obliged to become attached to Arab tribes, and they were labelled mawali ('allies' or 'affiliates') to differentiate them from Arab Muslims. Some historical studies go so far as to say that Umayyad rulers had at first discouraged the embrace of Islam by non-Arabs, discriminating against them in the payment of offerings, gathering taxes and so on. Although the Umayyads held the banner of Islam as a universal religion (for all men), they divided the Arabs and Muslims in order to seize power, and this resulted in a return of some Jahiliyyah habits and consequently in the fragmentation of Islamic unity and Arab unity. Meanwhile, they ruled the Islamic empire as a centralized system under Arab control, and this impeded unity between Arab and non-Arab Muslims and even between the Arab Muslims themselves.

The Abbasids were no better than the Umayyads when they assumed the caliphate of Islam. They adopted a racist nationalist form of discrimination that created a state of perpetual rivalry and conflict between nationalities for positions of power. This served to weaken and divide the Abbasid dynasty and, eventually, led to its downfall. The same was the case for the Ottoman Empire, which devised new techniques in order to exploit national divisions amongst the ummah. Perhaps the principal reason for the emergence of modern nationalist movements, specifically the Arab nationalist movement at the beginning of this century, was the secularist parties and the national and political discrimination of the Turkification policy applied by them when they became influential in the Ottoman Empire.

In looking at the Arab reality today and the problems and apprehensions shaking the Arab Muslim nation, we are driven to think about the great danger threatening the Arabs and Muslims. The imperialists have worked to weaken the Arabs as a deterrent force to those waiting for a chance to attack, by preventing the emergence of unity, provoking conflicts and disputes between Arab Islamic states, weakening Islam as a unifying moral force in all its spiritual, political, social and economic dimensions, and using techniques and ways of provoking racial and sectarian conflict, even resorting to distortion of the Islamic faith itself through certain suspicious religious currents. Moreover, the establishment of Zionist Israel within the Arab nation constitutes a destructive factor for Arab unity and Islamic unity. Israel has worked for the gradual division and fragmentation of the Arab region; its occupation of Palestine has extended to Lebanon in a blatant and bold way. These facts must be confronted in order to diagnose a correct and sound treatment for building Arab unity anew and deepening the spirit of Islamic union between all Muslims.

Such a treatment can be summarized as follows:

1. Returning to the spirit of Islam as a gathering and unifying force.
2. Securing the minimum of Arab Islamic solidarity.
3. Subduing the Zionist entity and highlighting its weak points.
4. Correcting the relationship between Arab and Islamic states, especially those neighbouring the Arab world. As Islamic Iran is among the neighbouring Islamic states, it should play a role and bear its major responsibilities in this regard.
5. Extending bridges of understanding and brotherhood between the many nationalities belonging to Islam, especially minorities, such that the natural rights they always enjoyed under Islam are safeguarded, in religion, society and culture.
6. Fighting the deviant and destructive parties and groups formed by im-

perialism to strike at the essence of the Arab nation and sunder the unity of the Muslims.

Iranian Nationalism and Islam

Fourteen hundred years have passed since the Iranians abandoned their ancient doctrines to embrace Islam. During these centuries, hundreds of millions of Iranians were born and nurtured in Islam and lived their lives according to it. The relationship between the Iranians and Islam indeed pre-dates the conquest. In 31 AH, Islam found its way to a large number of Persians residing in Yemen, who submitted of their own will and desire to the commandments of the Qur'an.[3] They sought to spread Islamic law by inner devotion and will, and they sacrificed much in the fight against apostates and the enemies of Islam. It is sufficient to mention Salman al-Farsi as among the first to embrace Islam. The narrations attributed to the Prophet on Salman and his nation are many; these include the narration from Ibn 'Abd al-Barr's Al-Isti'ab fi Ma'rifat al-Ashab ('On Acquiring Knowledge of the Companions'): 'If faith were in the Pleiades, Salman would have reached out for it', or according to another narration, 'men of Persia would have reached out for it'. According to Hadrat Aisha: 'Salman would sit in counsel with the Messenger of God so far into the night that he almost outmatched us to the Messenger of God.'[4] And there are other narrations from the Prophet and his virtuous household, God bless them all in this regard.

The history of Islamic conquests to the east and west of the world speaks of the jihad of Iranians who sacrificed their lives for Islam, in devotion to the faith and in defence of it against seditious elements from within and the foreign infidels. The spread of Islam in the countries of the East, such as India, Pakistan, Kashmir, Bangladesh, Bengal, Turkey, Bulgaria, the Caucasus, Tajekistan, Tashkand, Afghanistan, Tibet, Malaysia, Indonesia and the islands of the Indian Ocean – these were the Islamic impact of the Iranians, who carried Islam with them on trade routes and by sea to the furthest reaches of Asia. The Iranian Muslims also played a major role in spreading Islam into west and north Africa, as well as to the European continent and Asia Minor.[5] As for the Islamic conquest of the land of Pars, the victory of the Muslims prevailed in spite of the fact that the Persian Empire, which along with the Roman Empire ruled the world, was noted for its power. It should be mentioned that the Persians at the time were ahead of the Muslims, in terms of military strength and organization, weaponry, war materials and sheer numbers. Consequently, no one could have predicted the defeat of the Sassanians at the hands of the Arab Muslims.

Among the important factors behind the victory of the Muslims, apart

from the power of their faith, the manifest goals of religion in their historical mission, and their confidence of triumph and victory, was the lack of
serious resistance by the Iranians masses who had lived under the oppression of Sassanian rule. One historian estimates that the number of people
within the bounds of the Persian Empire totalled nearly 140 million, a
large number of whom were soldiers, whereas the Muslim mujahidin conquering Iran and Rome hardly numbered 60, 000.[6] However, the Iranians
were tired of the Sassanian dynasty with its oppressive and harsh rule, the
corruptions of government, society and religion and the prevailing caste-
like system of stratification. For example, religious law permitted carpenters
to learn how to read and write, as the right of teaching and learning was
restricted to the sons of notables and priests of the pagan fire temples.
Zoroastrianism had reached such a level of corruption that the Iranians
could find nothing in it to fill their hearts with belief. Thus, if Islam had
not entered Iran then, Christianity would have seized the opportunity to
dominate the religious thought of the Iranian nation, instead of Islam, as
an alternative to Zoroastrianism. The Iranian soldiers' dislike for their religion and government not only prompted them not to resist the Muslim
Arabs, but also to help them in many ways.

E. G. Browne writes: 'It is indisputable that most of those who abandoned Mazdakism and embraced Islam were convinced and willing to do
so. For instance, we notice that four thousand Persian soldiers embraced
Islam after the war of Qadisieh and followed the Muslim conquerors and
helped them to open Jalulaa, then settled in Kufa, in addition to other groups
who embraced Islam in droves according to their will and desire ...' Saheb
Zamani says: 'Persians were not only attracted to the universal aspects of
Islam, but also found in the Islamic goals and hopes what they had been
desperately missing for many centuries, and what they had been eager and
sacrificing their lives to reach ... '[8] The Islamic conquest had a profound
and permanent effect on the Iranians. For Islam spread quickly and widely
in Iran and imbued people with the morals of the new religion. They dis-
pensed with many of their old habits and traditions, and they cancelled all
rituals imposed by their former religions; more, people began to learn the
Arabic language, and there emerged from them eminent scholars and outstanding authors who enriched the Islamic legacy and left an impact that
remains with us to this day.[9]

Thus, the Iranians advanced with Islam and formed, with time, a great
power that played a major role in changing the direction of the Islamic
empire. We cannot show in this brief treatment all that the Iranians had
bequeathed to Islam, but we can point briefly to one historical fact among
many that attest to this. A hundred years after the Islamic conquest, the
Iranians formed a formidable military force. After most Muslims came to
abhor the Umayyad Caliphate for its distortion and deviation from Islamic

teachings, and for its injustice and oppression – or, at best, those Muslim collaborators who deviated with them towards the tribalism of the jahiliyyah – they were able to transfer the caliphate from the house of Umayyah to the house of Abbas, whose slogan was recovering the caliphate to the 'ulwiyyin ('divine'). When the Abbasids deviated in the caliphate and weakened, the Islamic Caliphate broke up into petty dynasties, Muslim in name only. At that point, the Iranians became politically independent in the entrench- ment of the principles of Islam and the call to its mission. Among the consequences of this was that some Iranians, who had since the beginning of the 3rd century AH still held previous religions, such as Mazdakism and Christianity, were converted to Islam by faith and choice.

One historian has said: 'Until that time, there were many churches and fire temples in Iran, but then they disappeared, little by little turning into mosques.' The author of Ahsan al-Taqasim says about the religions then in Khorasan: 'There are many Jews, few Christians and a variety of Mazdakeans.'[10] Iranians were responsible for the development of Islamic sciences across fourteen centuries of Islamic history, Iranian Muslims em- braced a considerable expanse of this, rarely rivalled by any other Islamic country, and influencing every corner of the civilization of Islam and up to this very day. Among their achievements were in the sciences of *fiqh* (Is- lamic jurisprudence), hadith (Prophetic traditions), *tafsir* (exegesis or commentary) and *kalam* (a branch of philosophy), in addition to literature and philosophy, and all their associated sciences. Thus, the schools of Nishapur, Herat, Balkh, Merv, Bukhara, Samarkand, Rayy, Qom, Isfahan and all the cities of Iran became centres of assiduous scientific activity, where hundreds of Muslim 'ulema (religious scholars) emerged. Many of these scholars also excelled in the natural sciences, such as medicine, physics, chemistry and other fields. We note that the authors of the six Sahihs of the Sunnites, and the four of the Shi'ites, were all Iranian, of whom six were from Khorasan. Among the many scholars were: Muhammad al-Tusi, Muhammad bin Ismail al-Bukhari, Muslim bin al-Hajjaj al-Qushayri al- Nishapuri, Ahmad bin Shu'ayb al-Nasa'i, Abu Dawud al-Sijistani, Muhammad bin Issa al-Tirmidhi, Ahmad bin Hussein al-Bayhaqi, Sheikh Muhammad bin Ali bin Hussein bin Babawayh al-Qummi al-Sadduq, Sheikh Muhammad bin Yaqub al-Kulini, Muhammad bin Majah, and hun- dreds of other eminent scholars. In addition, two of the four imams of the Sunnites being Iranians from Khorasan: Abu Hanifah al-Nu'man bin Thabet and Ahmad bin Hanbal, though one lived in Kufa and the other in Baghdad.

In general, the Iranians contributed much to the consolidation of the rules and principles of Islamic literature, culture and thought. One very noticeable phenomenon is that Iranians excelled in the grammar and syn- tax of the Arabic language and in Arabic literature. Zamakhshari of Khwarazm, author of *Al-Kashshaf* and *Al-Mufassal fi'l-Sarf wa'l-Nahu*, was one of the most eminent of Iranian scholars. Al-Tha'alibi al-Nishaburi, author of *Yatimat al-Dahr fi Mahasen Udaba' Ahl el-'Asr* and *Sirr-al-Adab fi Majari Kalam al-'Arab* on Arabic literature, is the greatest pride of the Iranian *'ulema*. We may mention here some scientific works written by Iranian scholars in the Islamic sciences, such as the *Tafsirs* of Ali bin Ibrahim al-Qommi, al-'Ayashi Muhammad bin Mas'ud and Al-Nu'mani; the *Tafsir al-Tibian* by Sheikh al-Tusi, the *Majma' al-Bayan* by Sheikh Ahmad al-Tabari, *Jami'a ul-Bayan* known as the *Tafsir* of al-Tabari, *Al-Kashshaf* by Zamakhshari, which is the most famous and definitive *tafsir* of the Sunns, *Mafatih al-Ghaib* by Fakhr al-Din Razi, and many other *tafsirs*.

On narration and Prophetic hadith, we may mention *Al-Kafi* by al-Kalini al-Razi, *Man la Yahdaruh al-Faqih* by Ibn Babawayh al-Qummi, *Bihar-ul-Anwar* by Muhammad al-Majlisi, *Tahdhib al-Ahkam* and the *Sahih* by al-Bukhari, the Sahih of Muslim, the Sahih of al-Tirmidhi, and many others, including books written by Iranian 'ulema across the centuries and up to the present day. Iranian Muslims opposed every attempt at rejection or distortion of their Islamic faith and cause. For example, when some began calling for the recovery of the old Persian religion, like Sanabad, Babak and Mazyar,[11] they were confronted with a violent reaction; the people rose as one against them and they were killed as apostates against the True Religion of Islam.

The Islamic Revolution in Iran

The Islamic Revolution in Iran is regarded as, by far, the most striking feature of the last third of the 20th century. It is also the most important event in the history of Islam, in view of the circumstances surrounding the outbreak of the revolution and its ways of moving and uniting the masses, the very reverse of the forms of revolution invented by the Third World – achieving change through military coups.

One of the most important features of the revolution in Iran is its salient Islamic aspect, which coloured the revolution from the start, determining its identity and imperatives in the proposal of solutions to issues, in accordance with the Islamic unity view. The Islamic revolution was a popular revolution that was not limited to one social class to the exclusion of others, and does not favour one community over another. Despite diversity in national composition and the many minorities in Iran, the population united in creating the Islamic revolution and making it a success, especially when we note that the Shah's regime used to fuel enmity and dissension between the various nationalities and minorities. Iranian society includes, in addition to a Persian majority, other nationalities; the most important are the Arab, Turkish, Kurdish and Baluchi. All endured the oppression and injustice of the Shah and his regime. Thus, the Islamic revolution was an important gain for everyone and embodied a great vision of solidarity. Perhaps this was the most important reason for the success and continuity of the revolution. The forces of international hegemony, especially the American, knew this, and began to take steps to halt the Islamic revolutionary tide. They sought to play on sensitive issues, from which they would proceed to implement their strategies for derailing the revolution while still in its infancy. Among these were the provocation of nationalist sentiments amongst Iran's minorities against the revolution.

In this regard, a Western diplomat who was in Tehran at the start of the success of the Islamic revolution alleged: '... The government has many explosive problems ... it is enough that it has a problem of minorities ... it is a timebomb ready to explode at any moment ... this issue could threaten all of Iran in the present and in future ... '[12] *News of the World* magazine, a US periodical known to be directly tied to the US Defense Department and having close connections with the CIA, wrote in one of its issues: 'Iran is likely to become the Lebanon of the Gulf.'[13] It was hinting at racial disturbances that might threaten the security and sovereignty of Iran, as had happened in Lebanon before. And so the US, to carry out its plots for aborting the Islamic revolution, resorted to inciting nationalities and minorities on the pretext of defending their rights and self-determination, as happened in Kurdistan, for example, where some rebelled during the revolution, raising nationalist placards at one point and sectarian placards at another. These attempts failed, however.

One of the priorities of the Islamic revolution was to consolidate the principle of Islamic unity instead of territorial or national unity. Islamic unity was not a mere slogan, but a reality and goal through which the revolution managed over the years to assimilate all nationalities under the banner of the original Islam of Muhammad, which does not recognize race or nationality as a basis of distinction, restricting it instead to taqwa, the true single standard. The Islamic revolution had proposed a very important starting point for the establishment of Islamic government in Iran, that is loyalty to Islam and Islam alone. This is the basis of dealings in the Islamic order, and there is no place for nationalist loyalty except from a human frame that expresses, in its own special social way, harmony with Islam and the Islamic Republic's system. Imam Khomeini drew attention to this in many of his speeches and instructions to the Muslims. He would not permit accommodation with the advocates of nationalist tendencies or calls for autonomy for nationalities or minorities, because this would lead to the fragmentation of the Islamic state – although the Islamic order is not like that of the Shah who oppressed nationalities.

One of the important points that the forces of hegemony relied on and built their hopes on was exploitation of advocates of Arab nationalism in

Iran to stand up against the Islamic revolution, because of what the Arabs endured in suffering and oppression under the Shah. Indeed, the author of *Iran fi Rub' Qarn* wrote of the Arabs during the rule of the Shah: 'The policy of terror and collective killing and hanging continues in the region of Khuzestan, where the number of Arab victims exceeded the number of Autumn's leaves, and where thousands of people have emigrated because of oppression and because of the miserable economic situation that is a part of the extermination policy.'[14]

From the first weeks of the declaration of the Islamic Republic, the forces of hegemony worked to incite the Arab inhabitants, on the pretext of calling for their national and historical rights in the area, suggesting to them that there is an opportunity for this now, especially as the strategic, economic and geographic place enjoyed by this region poses a threat to the Islamic revolution, as oil revenues are the principal resource of the country.[15] With this proposal, the US hegemony lit the flame of dissension through a regime ruling by oppression over Iraq. The required war was launched in the face of the Islamic revolution, on the pretexts of nationalism or defence of the eastern gate of the Arab nation from the Persian tide and on defending the rights of the Arabs in Khuzestan. But what was startling, even for the Arabs of Khuzestan who collaborated with the Iraqi regime, was that the matter was not one of defence of Arabism or a call for national rights, but a conspiracy by the forces of hegemony to undermine the popularity of the Islamic revolution which involved Arabs, Persians and all the other nationalities in Iran. The harm inflicted by the war and its destructive consequences was the same for the Arabs of Khuzestan as for the other nationalities, if not more so, as the areas destroyed by the war bear witness. But the US and its ally, the Iraqi regime, miscalculated, for the wars led to the unification of the Iranian Muslim peoples in all their nationalities. The people of Khuzestan, Arabs and non-Arabs, took an honourable stand against the invaders, bore arms and resisted the occupiers in all areas of the war.

The Islamic revolution in Iran was able to deal with Arab and Islamic issues of destiny in a principled and fundamental way, based on Islamic interests, not narrow territorial or national interests. This stance allowed it to unmask many of the regimes that profess Arabism and Islam, and it exposed the falsity of the loud claims and slogans they raise. The position of the revolution is clear and firm on the Palestinian question, 'the number one cause of the Arabs and Muslims'. We will not go into details here, given the many ramifications of this subject. We will only mention what the leader of the Islamic revolution, Imam Khomeini, has said: 'Israel is an entity that took possession of the wealth of Iran and the Muslims' sacred places in Palestine. It has been created to crush the Muslim peoples and colonize them. It is a germ of corruption that was planted in our heart and we must unite to extirpate it. It is one of the origins of our problems. Israel is the second ally of the Shah – after the United States – opposing the hopes of Muslims, and for this reason it must be eliminated ... '

Palestine is an Islamic issue that concerns the destiny of all the Muslim peoples, whether Arab, Persian or others. So, too, are Bosnia-Herzegovina, Kashmir and other contemporary Islamic issues. In Iran, Islam is the only criterion for the revolution's concern and connection with Muslim issues anywhere, not the criterion of profit or interests or political gains that rule the relations of other regimes professing revolution or progressivism or defence of human rights. In its actual dealing with local and international issues and events, the Islamic revolution has proven its credibility and positive influence on much of the decision-making in favour of the Islamic cause. For instance, the entry of Iran into the Islamic Conference Organization was a turning point in the history of the organization, giving it new strength embodied in the high spirit of the Islamic revolution and its serious bid to resolve the problems of Muslims and Islamic states. This led its transformation from a largely cosmetic organization, with decisions that were not reflected in the political relations governing its member states and entrenchment of the flawed policies of the regimes tied to the forces of international hegemony, to one that is characterized by, at the minimum, the existence of one voice crying for justice from one of the participants of this organization.

As to the institutional structure of the Islamic state, many cultural, media and political centres have been established, for the purpose of strengthening Muslims, whatever their nationality or denomination, at the popular as well as the official level. With that, Iran's Islamic revolution was able to proceed to address other difficulties and problems connected with the cultural, educational and political lives of the Muslims. Through a policy of building on common factors and proceeding from fixed tenets to realize complementarity between them and between all Islamic peoples and states, first and foremost being the Arab peoples and states, with focus on states inclined towards liberation and independence, uninfluenced by the tactics and pressures of international hegemony.

Notes

* Director, Centre for Islamic Studies, Qom, Iran.

1. The Holy Qur'an, *Surat al-Mu'minin, ayah* 52.
2. Ibid., *Surat Al-i-'Umran, ayah* 110.
3. Abu Ja'far bin Jarir al-Tabari, *Tarikh al-Tabari*, vol. 2, p. 654.
4. Al-Sayed Muhsin al-Amin, *A'yan al-Shi'a*, vol. 7, p. 286.

5.   Murteza Mutahhari, *Islam and Iran*, translated by Muhammad Hadi al-Yusifi, vol. 1, p. 73.

6.   Said Nafisi, *The Social History of Iran* (in Persian).

7.   *Tarikh-e Adabiyat-e Iran*, vol. 1, p. 299. Translation into Persian of E. G. Browne's *Literary History of Persia*, Cambridge University Press, 4 vols., 1902–24.

8.   *Dibajah Ray Bar Rahbari*, p. 255.

9.   *Islamic Horizons* magazine, no. 3, p. 104.

10.   Abu Abdullah Muhammad bin Ahmad al-Maqdisi, *Ahsanu Taqasim fi Ma'rifat al-Aqalim*, p. 323.

11.   Abu'l Hasan Ali ibn al-Athir, Al-Kamel fi'l-Tarikh, 13 vols., (Beirut: Dar Sader, 1965–67), vol. 6, p. 473.

12.   Mahmoud an-Najjar, *Ath-Thawra al-Iraniah was Ihtimatal al-Khatar fil Khalij*, p. 98

13.   Ibid., p. 99.

14.   *Iran fi Rub' Qarn* ('Iran across a Quarter Century'), p. 25.

15.   From Najjar, op. cit., p. 104.

FOUR

The Political and Media Message of Governments and Elites and its Impact on Arab–Iranian Ties

7

The Media and Arab–Iranian Relations

FEHMI HOUWAIDI*

With the increasing influence of the media in this era, it no longer really matters whether you right or wrong; what matters is what the media says about you and what category it puts you in. And because the media has come to take advantage of its dangerous role in shaping public opinion, the art of media disinformation has become a science taught at schools of journalism. These arts have become a weapon of political and of armed conflict. And what is disinformation but character assassination? Through it you can liquidate your rival and ruin him politically through the media alone.

One can still recall the news story that was fabricated and injected into the US media within 30 minutes of the Oklahoma blast. The 'tip' that was circulated was that two persons with 'Middle Eastern faces' were seen running from a car at the site of the incident. This 'tip' played an instrumental role in pointing the finger of accusation at Arabs and Muslims from the very first moment, with all the infamous and adverse consequences that followed from this, not least of which were 200 incidents of assault against Arabs and Muslims in the first 50 hours after the blast, according to the findings of Arab–American Council sources announced subsequently.

When the truth was revealed, and it became known that the culprit or culprits were American, the source of the news item was not found. But we need not exert ourselves to know that it was a hostile party experienced in disinformation, fabricating and injecting it in the shock of the moment that pervaded the country after the explosion, and succeeding in venting tension and feelings of hatred against Arabs and Muslims. His approach was very simple; just two lines comprised of 20 words at most.

Consider also a story published by *Al-Sharq Al-Awsat* daily (London) last July. The gist of the item was that the 'Islamic Jihad' movement is investigating the embezzlement of $2 million deposited by one of its leaders in his own bank account, money that was originally counterfeit dollars paid by Iran to the movement which 'laundered' it in Europe. After the laundering, one of the 'Jihad' leaders seized the money and deposited it in his own account.[1]

When the story is analysed, we find that it contains the following explosive suggestions: Iran is behind the 'Islamic Jihad' movement and provides
it with millions of dollars; Iran thus resorts to counterfeiting and deception
since it provides this presumed support in counterfeit dollars; the 'Jihad', a
name that has an important place in Islamic consciousness, is involved in
laundering counterfeit dollars in Europe; innocent Europe fell victim to
evil Muslims, the Islamic Republic and the 'Islamic Jihad' movement, who
traffic in counterfeit dollars; the men of 'Islamic Jihad' are not honourable
mujahidin but are in fact corrupt, in view of one of their leaders not only
circulating counterfeit dollars, but also going on to embezzle the money
after it was replaced with real dollars! The average reader of an article like
this naturally feels contempt and outrage with Iran, the 'Jihad' movement,
jihad itself, and all who are associated with Islam.

Although the leadership of the movement, represented by its Secretary
General, Fathi Al-Shoqaqi, issued a statement denying the entire story (17
July), the damage had already been done. Specialists in fabrication and character assassination can endorse what a newspaper publishes in the first story
and ignore the denial of the same in the follow-up story!

We have no further examples to show the danger of the media when
used to mislead rather than enlighten. It is a danger that increases as the
media falls under the control of the state or serves to reflect its directives, as
in all non-democratic states; for here the media is placed in the service of
policy and becomes a spokesman for authority instead of society.

Shadows adversely affecting Relations

If we look closely at media positions, both Arab and Iranian, with respect
to relations between the two sides, we find that their most prominent feature is that they reflect government positions, especially during the period
immediately following the outbreak of war between Iran and Iraq the year
after the Islamic revolution.

A close examination of the themes of the Arab media shows that most
Arab states sided with the Iraqi regime and by and large affirmed its statements. The media worked to promote these statements as a form of support
or backing for Iraq, which declared from the outset that it was waging a
defensive war by the Arab nation against the 'Persian peril', and was not
motivated by particularist calculations or interests. The media of the few
states that did not support Iraq were characterized by balance and moderation. This was especially the case with Syria and, to some extent, Lebanon.

It is very clear that the eight years of war seriously marred Arab–Iranian
relations, causing a complete polarization and a deepening of the rift between the two sides from an early point. This rift was filled with fears and

adverse impressions which have remained in one form or another until to-day – 16 years after the revolution.

A proper examination of the position of Arab media must distinguish between two phases in Arab–Iranian relations. The *first* is the phase of the Iraq–Iran war (1980–88); the *second* is the post-war phase. By a twist of fate, the interval of the war paralleled the first victory of the Islamic revolution and the assumption of leadership of the state by Imam Khomeini, in what we may go so far as to call the First Islamic Republic. As for the *second* phase, it coincided with the death of Imam Khomeini in 1989 and the subsequent emergence of the Second Republic.

The shadows of war were not the only factor to adversely affect Arab–Iranian relations. There were other issues that brought the two sides together on some occasions, pitted them against each other on others. Prominent among these were the following:

1. The collapse of the nationalist plan, after the death of President Gamal Abdel Nasser, and the entry of the Arab world into a state of limbo, with all the dissolution and fragmentation that this entailed.
2. The increase in Western influence generally, and US influence in particular, whether after the expulsion of Russian advisers from Egypt, leading to its gradual entry into the US orbit (rendered definite after the collapse of the Soviet Union), or after the Iraqi invasion of Kuwait, the ultimate result of which was a noticeable increase in Western and US influence in the Arab world generally and the Gulf area in particular.
3. The signing of the peace agreement between Egypt and Israel in 1978, which led to the removal of Egypt from the greater part of the Arab–Israeli conflict and subsequent weakening of the entire Arab front.
4. The decline in the importance of the Palestine question, especially after the Madrid conference, which opened Israel's appetite to dealing with the Arab and Islamic worlds, while jumping over the Palestine question without resolving any of its fundamental issues.
5. The collision between certain Arab regimes, foremost being the Egyptian, and the Islamic situation, one of the most important outgrowths of which was the Islamic revolution in Iran.

These issues led to greater alienation between the Arab world and Iran, and not only in the political sphere; the reverberations automatically entered the media sphere, in view of the association between media and politics in most countries of the Arab world.

This study will focus on the position of Egyptian media towards Arab–Iranian relations. There are a number of reasons for doing so, perhaps the most prominent being that Egypt is the largest Arab country and its media has the largest impact on the Arab world. In monitoring this media position, we shall distinguish between the two stages of during and after the Iraq–Iran war.

The Media during the Iraq–Iran War

We have said that most Arab states sided with Iraq, and this prompted most Arab media to adopt Baghdad's position and statements, as expressed through Iraqi media, for the winning of the battle. It is true that the Egyptian regime at the time, under President Anwar Sadat, had other reasons to oppose the Islamic revolution, including his close ties with the US, which prompted him to receive the Shah of Iran, who was not welcomed in any other country after the revolution except Egypt. However, while this may have served to reinforce the motives, it did not affect the results.

We would not be exaggerating to say that the position of Egyptian media at that time was the same as that of almost every other Arab media forum. This prompts us to argue that the majority took a single position on the Iranian issue during the war. Rivalry and distrust formed the underlying theme during this period, and this translated into treatments that deliberately sought to provoke suspicion and heap accusations.

We will not labour the media position during the course of the war, which is over and done with now and a part of history. Of much greater concern is the phase that followed, which remains with us to the present day. Consequently, we shall here lump together the key points of the Egyptian media theme, which, as we have said, reflected the trend in Arab media at the time to join the side of Iraq.

From our monitoring of the situation, we find that the most important key points are five:

1. *Iran seeks to export the revolution to all parts of the Arab world.* Exploiting this to the fullest, for purposes of promotion, were the statements of certain supporters of the revolution. They expressed, at the moment of victory, their aspiration to export the revolution to the whole of the Arab world. Irrespective of whether these statements were exaggerated or not, what is certain is that the phrase 'export of the revolution' was a source of apprehension that was implanted and generalized in Arab political and media messages at the time, an apprehension that continues to have reverberations even now.

2. *Iran has ambitions in the Gulf area.* The evidence was ready at hand and did not need to be contrived; it was embodied in the issue of the three islands: Abu Musa, Greater Tunb, and Lesser Tunb. This issue was regarded, and continues to be regarded, as tantamount to a first step in achieving Iran's aspirations and ambitions in the Gulf area..

3. The war between Iraq and Iran is tantamount to a new round of historical conflict between Arabs and Persians. Some Iraqi researchers made
an effort to establish grounds for this remark, seeking to select historical
facts that serve to prove that conflict between the two sides is, at one
and the same time, historical and eternal.
4. The war is an expression of confrontation between Arabism and Islam,
with Iraq and the Arab nation on one side, and Iran on the other. Arab
elites engaged in much dialogue on the connection between the two,
with some supporting the idea of split and confrontation, others calling
for a bridge between the two pillars.
5. The war opened up the issue of Sunni–Shiite relations; many newspaper articles were written, Arab markets were drowned in new books or
reprints of old, and some tapes were issued that sought to disparage the
Shiite faith and demonstrate its shortcomings, then deepen the rift between followers of both sects, even though Shi'ites are not only to be
found in Iran but represent a large portion of the populations of Iraq
and Bahrain and reside throughout the Gulf, Saudi Arabia and Syria,
where their population totals nearly 10 million.

All in all, the media and political theme, which sought to win the battle
of confrontation with Iran during the interval between 1980 and 1988, did
not hesitate to cross a number of red limits and squander the strategic interests of the *ummah*, through bids to escalate the conflict between Arabs
and Persians, between Arabism and Islam, or between Sunnism and Shi'ism,
paying no attention to the impact on the future and heedless of the importance of Iran's strategic importance to the Arab nation as a potential ally in
the confrontion with Israeli.

The Position after the End of the War – Six Observations

When the war ended, there was no longer any convincing excuse to continue rallying to the side of the Iraqi regime or continue the media campaigns
against Iran. Then the Iraqi invasion of Kuwait occurred in 1990, and the
door was opened to a total reconsideration of the issue of Arab–Iranian
relations, most clearly in the Gulf area and Saudi Arabia. But relations
with Egypt remained tense, and this was reflected in the Egyptian national
dailies in particular, which for the most part expressed the inclinations of
the regime.

If we look closely at the record of Egyptian media from 1990 until today
(1995), we note that Egyptian dailies alternated between three positions:

First, the provocative hostile Most official dailies adopted this position,
and some secularist opposition dailies too, such as *Al-Wafd w'al-Ahali*. The

former had reservations over the Islamic situation, the latter was hostile to it. These dailies expressed the official Egyptian policy line in its cautious, sceptical, and sometimes hostile position towards Iran. We can even go so far as to say that dailies such as *Al-Akhbar* and *Al-Gumhourieh* went overboard on the issue, exceeding the limit designated for them on provocation and hostility.

Second, the quiet, sympathetic Most opposition dailies adopted this position, in particular the Islamic opposition represented by the Labour Party and its daily, *Ash-Shaab*, which tried to take a different position and to explain the other side of the story that the advocates of political Islam call for. These saw a need for a rapprochement with Iran and appreciated the importance of this in confronting the strategic enemy represented by Israel and the West.

Third, the neutral, objective This position appeared in a few official dailies on rare occasions, due to extenuating circumstances (such as the Population Conference) or as a result of personal initiatives to analyse the issue rationally and quietly (as in the speech of Mohammed Hasanein Heikal). But this did not last long, and its impact was soon lost before the campaigns of counter-mobilization.

If we thumb through the pages of this issue and delve into detail, we can register the following observations regarding the theme of the Egyptian media.

The First Observation

The three main official dailies (*Al-Ahram, Al-Akhbar, Al-Gumhourieh*), in addition to some opposition dailies such as *Al-Wafd*, are brim-full of claims and descriptions about Iran. They talk at length about hatred for the Arabs and Egypt, the Persian peril to the region, the export of revolution, Iran's engagment in and encouragement of terrorism etc.

The Chairman of the Board of Directors of *Al-Gumhourieh*, Samir Ragab, says: 'Iran thrived over the past years on deception, forgery, trafficking in principles, engaging in terrorism and bloodshed, and abetting theft, deception, crookedness and deceit.'[2] Also in *Al-Gumhourieh*, Ragab presents a long list of accusations against Iran, concluding by equating Persians with Hindus in their evil intentions towards Islam and Muslims.[3]

In *Al-Ahram* daily, its editor-in-chief Ibrahim Nafe' wrote that Iran is plotting for hegemony over the region. It is therefore a threat to the national security and strategic and vital interests of the Arab nations, a threat that stems from Persian hostility towards the Arabs. Iran seeks to undermine Egypt and to continually exhaust and bleed its forces by exporting terrorism to it. At the end of his article, he warns that Iran is seeking to become an heir to the old imperialism, through the imposition of its hegemony on neighbouring states and subordinating the governments of these states to vassalage and compelling them to become its satellites.[4]

In *Akhbar al-Youm* daily, its editor-in-chief Ibrahim Abu Saadeh writes that Iran's leaders have used every legal and illegal trick in the book to try to implement their plots for an explosion that would shake the internal front and topple the system of government in Egypt, and the Iranian regime has plotted to topple and swallow up every Gulf state. He goes so far as to conclude that Iran is behind and orchestrates all internal problems aimed at creating a disturbance that might shake security and stability in an Arab country.[5]

In *Al-Akhbar* daily, Abu Saadeh accused Iran of being behind the terrorism that Algeria has suffered for years, is behind the civil war in Lebanon, supports extremist groups in Egypt with money and weapons, desires hegemony over Yemen and the transformation of its land into one large camp to shelter and train extremists, and has ambitions on the wealth of the Gulf.[6]

In *Al-Wafd* daily, which speaks for the secularist opposition Wafd Party, the editor-in-chief Gamal Badawi wrote: 'Iran has sinister intentions and seeks to spread dissension between Muslims so that the road may be opened for it to establish a greater Persian Shiite empire.' He described the Iranians with the phrase, 'they who do great mischief on earth'![7]

The Second Observation

Some national dailies held a position that called for cutting all ties with Iran and opposing any improvement in these ties; at the same time, they roused the Gulf states and goaded them to remain as adversaries of Iran.

In *Al-Akhbar*, Ibrahim Abu Saadeh launched a sharp attack on Ambassador Ahmad Nameq, head of the office charged with handling Egyptian interests in Iran, for seeking to improve relations with Iran. He accused him of personally desiring to become 'an ambassador tried and true' (his own words) after tiring of being merely the head of an office handling interests, the wrong man for the right place.[8]

This criticism was published because Ambassador Nameq complained in an interview with the Egyptian daily *Ash-Shaab* that some Egyptian authors were harming Egyptian–Iranian relations. He said that he wished to convey invitations to a number of Iranian personalities to visit Egypt and to hold seminars that would bring the two peoples closer together.

In the same daily, the Egyptian Foreign Ministry responded to Abu Saadeh, defending the ambassador and renewing confidence in him, saying that he is doing his job within the general foreign policy framework of the state, that it is his duty to narrow differences between the two countries, and the Foreign Ministry is convinced that the ambassador did not do anything to warrant such an attack against him or such a travesty of his right.[9]

Also in *Al-Akhbar*, under the title 'Reconciliation: When and With Whom?', Abu Saadeh attacked those who would seek rapprochement or reconciliation with Iran, describing them as 'weaklings and servants of money, insisting on exonerating the butchers of Tehran from any involvement in their crimes, servants of the Iranian dollar who sell their conscience along with their party newspapers at its doors, offices and counters ...' In *Al-Gumourieh* daily, its editor-in-chief Samir Ragab deplored the position of the Gulf states and their silence and submission to Iran, calling on them to change their positions towards it.[10]

Ragab also deplored in *Al-Gumhourieh* a statement attributed to Prince Sultan bin Abdel Aziz, Saudi Arabia's defence minister, who said that his country believes that Iran does not represent a threat to Saudi Arabia or the Arab region.[11]

Before that, Ragab had deplored in the daily of the ruling National Party, *Mayo* ('May'), statements from Damascus that Iran is a Gulf state and has interests and concerns over security arrangements for that area. Ragab called for the rallying of Arab states against Iran.[12]

In *Al-Akhbar* daily, the managing editor, Galal Dweidar, mentioned that President Mubarak opposed every attempt by Iran to resume relations, the excuse being that Tehran wants to use diplomatic relations in order to make Cairo its springboard for spreading its ideas and setting the stage for domination and hegemony.[13]

The Third Observation

Nationalist dailies repeatedly adopted the position of accusing Iran as having a hand in supporting the violence waged by some Islamist groups in Egypt. Noticeable in this regard is an article written by Samir Ragab in *Al-Gumhourieh*, where he says: 'The investigations in the states where extremist cells have been caught recently, will reveal that Iran and Sudan are the two supporting these cells and plotting to carry out terrorist operations.'[14] What is curious in this remark is that the author discussed the results of the investigations before they took place!

As for Ibrahim Abu Saadeh in *Al-Akhbar*, he wrote under the title 'Reconciliation: When and With Whom?': 'It is definite that Egypt has confirmation of Iran's collusion in all terrorist activities that many Arab states have endured ...' He adds: 'It is inconceivable that the Egyptian government would issue one statement after another condemning the Iranian regime as being behind all terrorist incidents and crimes without its have sufficient proof; it is unacceptable for the government of a large state such as Egypt to direct specific accusations at the Iranian regime without having at hand what would prompt it to direct this serious accusation that is the severest that any state can direct against another.'

The editor-in-chief of *Al-Ahram*, Ibrahim Nafe', warned of Iran's moves, writing: 'Iran reveals its stronger relations with Pakistan and Afghan resistance groups, and the attempts to strengthen its ties with the Central Asian Islamic republics in the Soviet Union, so as to encircle the Gulf area and attempt to create a network of close ties with this area, centered in west Asia, within the framework of a new Middle Eastern order as an alternative to the Arab order.'[15] Also in *Al-Ahram*, Nafe' warned of the militarization of Iran and its purchase of weaponry from China, Korea, Russia and Eastern Europe.[16]

The Fourth Observation

The nationalist dailies formed a truce with Iran and modulated their position and counter-mobilization campaign on certain exceptional occasions, such as the International Conference on Population and Development (September 1994), especially after the Iranian delegation participated in this conference. There had been rumours that Iran might follow suit with Saudi Arabia and boycott the conference. Despite this period of truce, which extended for no more than two months, the change that occurred in the media was eye-opening, indicative of the fact that nationalist papers adhered to the official line welcoming Iran's participation and considering it a positive and praiseworthy step.

The Egyptian nationalist press gave prominence to what President Husni Mubarak said on 8 September 1994, that Iran by its attendance of the Population Conference and its Islamic cooperation deserved commendation.

After this signal, Samir Ragab, editor-in-chief of *Al-Gumhourieh* daily, wrote that the Population Conference helped prepare for an opportunity for Egyptian–Iranian rapprochement, and the peoples of the two countries have one religion, irrespective of the difference between the two sects, Sunnite and Shiite, with coordination of positions and ongoing contacts a starting point towards the recovery of these relations and their development.[17]

Al-Ahram daily published a statement by the foreign minister, Amr Mousa, who said: 'Egypt's tie with Iran is historical, and rapprochement will return once again; what has occurred in the way of tense relations in the past is something that will pass, and it is inevitable that the two countries will become closer.'[18]

On the other hand, *Al-Ahram* permitted publication of an article by

Abbas Maliki, the director of the Centre for Political and International Studies in Iran's Foreign Ministry and deputy foreign minister. In it he spoke of the possibility of building a common ground for political, economic and cultural understanding, and said that dialogue is the only way to overcome differences. His article carried an introduction by *Al-Ahram* columnist Lutfi al-Khouli.[19]

The official press also permitted front-page coverage of statements by the chairman of the Iranian delegation to the Conference, Hujjat-ul-Islam Muhammad Ali Taskhiri, who expressed hope that this rapprochement would be the start of cooperation between the two countries in other fields, especially the political, and the Conference is an opportunity for a new start in relations between Egypt and Iran, while there is full cooperation and coordination aimed at reaching a document that agrees with Islamic values ... [20]

Al-Gumhourieh daily conducted a lengthy dialogue with Abbas Maliki, focusing on the correction of certain mistaken notions prevailing about the Islamic Republic.[21]

Although the International Conference on Population helped to achieve a certain temporary rapprochement between the countries, as apparent from the news and commentaries published by the press, the first steps towards that rapprochement could be seen nearly three months beforehand, when the Non-aligned Conference was held in Cairo and the Iranian foreign minister Ali Akbar Velayati participated in it. It was the first visit by the foreign minister to Egypt since the Islamic revolution.

Al-Ahram daily gave prominence to a statement by Velayati in which he said that the Non-aligned Movement gained a vitality embodied in the Cairo conference.[22] Two days later, *Al-Ahram* also gave prominence to a statement by President Hashemi Rafsanjani, in which he denied any intention by his country to export the Islamic revolution abroad. He said that Tehran desires good relations with all the Arab states.[23] He also expressed his readiness to resume diplomatic relations with Egypt, resolve outstanding problems with Saudi Arabia and begin talks with the United Arab Emirates to resolve the issue of the disputed islands.

It appears that an atmosphere of optimism pervaded Cairo media circles at that time. This can be seen from newspaper reports published then, which include the following:

1 *Al-Aalam Al-Youm* daily mentioned that there is a trend towards normalization of relations between Egypt and Iran; the two countries are seeking to turn a new page in relations, overcome differences and support issues on which there is agreement, such as Islamic and Non-aligned Movement issues.[24]

2 *Al-Hayat* (London) daily published a statement by President Rafsanjani, in which he said that Iran does not intend to sever ties with states that normalize relations with Israel, and relations with the Arab states are being re-appraised and improved.[25] *Al-Hayat* also published a statement for Amr Mousa, Egypt's foreign minister, in which he said that relations with Iran will witness greater improvement and Iran is a state linked to Egypt and the Arab world by ancient ties of friendship and common interests; the current dispute should not become the rule.[26]

Noteworthy here is that these statements were not published in the nationalist dailies, which usually take the point of view of the authorities; this in turn suggests that the position of the authorities did not change, but remained anxious and cautious.

The Fifth Observation

Islamic opposition dailies held a different point of view. There was a noticeable bid for calm and a call for rapprochement and reconciliation. *Ash-Shaab* daily, which speaks for the Labour Party, published several articles along these lines, including an article entitled 'We Will Not Bend to the Enemies of God and Fight Iran'. The article warned that the real enemy of the *ummah* is Israel, not Iran. It also warned against vacillation before Israel, the danger of falling into its orbit and following its deadly advice to frighten Arab rulers over Iran. It was mentioned that Israel talks about Iranian terrorism because Iran supports the Lebanese and Palestinian revolutionaries against Israel.

Elsewhere, *Ash-Shaab* devoted considerable space to an interview with Hujjat-ul-Islam Muhammad Ali Taskhiri, who stressed that Iran is not a Persian but an Islamic state, and does not differentiate between Arab or Turk or Kurd or Persian. He said that Iran rejects this racist tone and adheres carefully to Islam, which views all men as equal; he called for a unified position by the Islamic *ummah* to resist the plots of its enemies and not be swayed by the fabrications and occurrences injected between Islamic countries.[27]

The daily *Al-Haqiqah* printed an article along these lines by its chief editor, Muhammad Amer, who said of relations with Iran: 'The Arabs supported Iraq in its war against Iran, then discovered that they made a serious mistake, after Saddam pounced on Kuwait, which had long supported him in his war against Iran.' He asks: 'What makes the Arabs, especially officials in Egypt, continue their boycott of Iran, a Muslim state that has its weight in the world? Why do we insist on losing a major power by our hostility, for which there is no justification, towards Iran?' Amer indicated that we are hardly able to differentiate between friend and enemy, and do not reflect on the events that we have encountered, and the only one to benefit from all this is our mutual enemy. He concluded by calling on Egypt to re-establish relations with Iran. He gave as an example the Palestinians, who concluded a peace agreement with Israel, and the Arab states are gradually opening up to it, while Egypt continues to insist on enmity with Iran.

The Sixth Observation

The televized dialogue conducted by Mohammed Hasanein Heikal with President Hashemi Rafsanjani drew noticeable interest from the Egyptian press, which published excerpts from it, while *Al-Araby* daily, which speaks for the Nasserite Party, published the text in full.[28] The dialogue brought up a number of points: appraisal of the experience of the Islamic revolution, Islamic economics, denial of the accusation of terrorism, the need for dialogue with Egypt, the belief that the principle of *ijtihad* in Islamic jurisprudence can accord with the needs of the age, the belief that Iran has succeeded in presenting a modern Islamic model that agrees with the conditions and needs of the age and has organized state affairs on the basis of Islamic education (*ma'aref*) and law (*Shari'ah*).

Although this talk is similar to what was said by Adel Hussein in *Ash-Shaab* daily, perhaps because of Heikal's prominence in Arab and Egyptian circles it did not endure the attacks and abuse that Hussein had to face.

Heikal maintained an objective and positive position on Egyptian–Iranian relations, which was manifest on another occasion with the holding of the 'Seminar on Arab–Iranian Relations', organized by the Centre for Research and Political Studies in Cairo University. Here he presented a lecture that all nationalist and opposition dailies published excerpts of, while *October* magazine, also nationalist, published the full text of the lecture in its 16 June 1994 issue.

Among the things that Heikal said in the lecture was that it is possible to envision the outbreak of contradictions between neighbouring or rival states, but this need not necessarily lead to the kind of enmity we see between Egypt and Iran. He added that the matter needs a political management who define of their own will goals and design of their own will means by which to achieve these goals; this is the crux of international relations.

Heikal decided that the over-sensitivity towards the Iranian revolution pre-dated the talk of terrorism, on which no one presented any evidence verifying collusion by Iran. He affirmed President Rafsanjani's denial of any connection with the events that occurred in Egypt, and he discussed with enthusiasm his keenness to improve relations and re-normalize them.

Heikal also said that Cairo itself was behind the crisis in relations with Iran, and hence responsible for the state of enmity prevailing, which has no justification in principle or in terms of national or regional interests. It was Cairo that began the enmity, at a time when the Arab masses were sympathetic to the Islamic revolution, gave asylum to the Shah on the pretext of the 'village morals' claimed by President Sadat, and invented the oil story (i.e., the fabrication that the Shah gave Egypt oil during the 1973 war). He mentioned – on the basis, he said, of reliable and published information – that Cairo subsequently became a headquarters for various covert operations and a meeting place of forces seeking to change the situation in Iran by a military coup. Iran reacted with anger and dismay over Egypt's position, which developed into mutually hostile political and media campaigns. Heikal also expressed his surprise that the principal dispute with Iran now is the peace process in the Middle East. He said: 'For a number of years, we severed our relations with the Shah of Iran because he had ties with Israel. Today we sever our relations with the revolution because it opposes our ties with Israel.'

Heikal concluded as follows: 'I say without hesitation that I place the greater part of the blame on Egypt for the poor relations with Iran, because hostility to the revolution is no justification, neither in terms of interest nor principle. Notwithstanding this, it is not too late for reappraisal, reconsideration and reconciliation.'[29]

Summary

The question remains: does this picture genuinely express the vision of the Egyptian elite on relations with Iran?

My answer to this is that, first and foremost, it serves to monitor the trends in Egyptian media. If emphasis is placed on the writings of leading editors, the editor-in-chief in the nationalist press has the stronger and wider impact, he is the conductor of the newspaper's chorus, his words expressing its basic line, which in fact is the official line of the state. We have seen how media mobilization became sharper, then calmed and adopted a conciliatory tone, according to the rise and fall of the barometer of political relations.

So long as this situation remains, I would say that the general trailing of the Arab media behind politics prevented, and continues to prevent, it from exercising its role in enlightening, guiding and sharpening public awareness and mobilizing it in defence of the higher interests of the *ummah*. This trailing has not only rendered the press a tool in political battles, but has also committed it to political priorities, with all their fluctuations. We thus find the nationalist Egyptian press, for example, sharp in its attacks on Iran and conciliatory in its talk over Israel. A correspondent who travels to Iran becomes a target of accusation and suspicion and the point is held against him, but his repeated visits to Israel are normal and not to be reproached.

Nevertheless, the enlistment of the press in politics is not the only element influencing the themes of the Egyptian media towards Iran. Some segments of the secularist elite among Egyptian intellectuals have taken a position on Iran based on the fact of conflict between the two camps, secular and Islamic, which the country is witnessing. Accordingly, they do not deal with Iran from a strategic standpoint that calls for winning it over to the Arab side and investing its influence on the side of confronting the Israeli challenge and Western hegemony. Rather, they choose to overrule such strategic interests with considerations of internal conflict. The internal 'Islamic–secularist' clash has influenced, to a great extent, the positions of not a few secularist intellectuals on Iran. Some elements of the Egyptian Left stand at the forefront of these intellectuals; their organ, *Al-Ahali* daily, is regarded as a forum for continuing opposition to any rapprochement or reconciliation with Iran.

Nevertheless, we cannot discount patriotic intellectuals of the Mohammed Hasanein Heikal variety who chose a more objective position, placing the higher interests of the *ummah* first and aware of the importance of positive ties between Egypt and Iran, though there is no real dispute between the two countries.

I suspect that enlarging the scope of this particular segment, which is small and not very vocal, through continuous dialogue and enrichment of awareness and understanding, is very important.

There remains the position of Islamic intellectuals, or the press that expresses the Islamic line and sympathizes with it. In our view, these adopt the same positive line that patriotic intellectuals are inclined towards, even if their Islamic sympathies are combined with the national and strategic considerations that we have mentioned. But the elements of this line occupy a limited place in the media, given the limits of their own forums.

Before the callers for dialogue, understanding and reconciliation, and the callers of support for the higher interests of the *ummah* and mustering of forces to confront its true enemies, lies a long road that they will have to tread and bear with its hardships in order to achieve their aim. There is no choice in the matter.

Notes

* *Al-Ahram* daily, Cairo, Egypt.

1.   *Ash-Sharq Al-Awsat* ('The Middle East'), 15 July 1995.
2.   *Al-Gumhourieh*, 21 May 1993.

3. *Al-Gumhourieh*, 9 February 1993.
4. *Al-Ahram*, 27 November 1992.
5. *Akhbar al-Youm*, 21 November 1992.
6. *Al-Akhbar*, 10 August 1992.
7. *Al-Wafd*, 31 May 1993.
8. *Al-Akhbar*, 5 August 1992.
9. *Al-Akhbar*, 10 August 1992.
10. *Al-Gumhourieh*, 11 August 1993.
11. *Al-Gumhourieh*, 3 May 1993.
12. *Mayo*, 23 November 1992.
13. *Al-Akhbar*, 17 November 1992.
14. *Al-Gumhourieh*, 1 October 1994.
15. *Al-Ahram*, 21 December 1991.
16. *Al-Ahram*, 27 November 1992.
17. *Al-Gumhourieh*, 13 September 1994.
18. *Al-Ahram*, 9 September 1994.
19. *Al-Ahram*, 26 October 1994.
20. See *Al-Akhbar*, 13 September 1994, and *Al-Ahram*, 11 September 1994.
21. *Al-Gumhourieh*, 11 October 1994.
22. *Al-Ahram*, 6 June 1994.
23. *Al-Ahram*, 8 June 1994.
24. *Al-Aalam Al-Youm*, 10 June 1994.
25. *Al-Hayat*, 7 June 1994.
26. *Al-Hayat*, 21 July 1994.
27. *Al-Hayat*, 21 July 1994.
28. *Al-Araby*, 6 December 1993.
29. See *October* magazine, June 1994.

8

The Iranian and Arab Elites and the Evolving Rationality

MASHAALLAH SHAMS AL-WAEZIN*

I

The political and media message of some Iranian elites, and its impact on Arab–Iranian relations, are addressed in this paper, along with other aspects of Arab–Iranian relations. Hopes are high that Iranian and Arab elites will help each other in enabling their societies to realize their noble goals. This can be achieved by reliance on their common heritage and common suffering, misgivings and hopes.

In reality, this subject should be discussed from a new and more serious angle, by addressing the issue of the conflict between modernization and our roots; the issue has in fact been on the tables since the beginning of this century.

Indeed, the issue has been part of the parlance of Iranian political rhetoric since the Constitutional revolution (1324, Islamic calendar) at the start of this century. The revolution was a product of the structural contradictions in Iranian society and was based on the progressive thinking of prominent figures such as Jamaleddine. In fact, the revolution drew traditional and non-traditional forces together in the social arena. After the Constitutional revolution, three strands of opinion regarding modernization were formed. This process had been a source of major change in Europe and the West in general. I will refer to that change briefly.

The first strand of opinion considered the Constitutional revolution as a springboard from which Iranian society could undergo a radical structural transformation affecting all institutions of Iranian society. The advocates of this strand regarded Iran's dependence on the West, and the Western lifestyle prevailing in Iran, as a necessity. They also used to think that the adoption by Iranian society of the 'modern approach' is the highest expres-

136

sion of patriotism, in the eyes of the elite. Hassan Takey Zada was one of the most prominent symbols of this trend. He was quoted as saying that Iran should be totally dependent on the West: 'One of the main duties of Iranians is to absorb and spread European patterns of civilization unconditionally. We should follow Europe and embrace its customs, traditions, science, industry, lifestyle, and all forms and aspects of European life, except language. In other words, Iran should, implicitly and explicitly, become a Western state, in body and soul'.[1]

The second strand of opinion stands at the other end of the spectrum. It was very active during the Constitutional revolution, operating under the slogan 'the legitimate government', and constituted a strong reaction to the modernization revolution. The advocates of this strand rejected elections by universal suffrage and favoured total dependency on the legal and religious dimensions. Sheikh Fadlallah Al-Nouri and Mr Kazem Al-Yazedi are some of the prominent figures who have espoused this way of thinking, and they are two of the main leaders of the movement Mashrouat (in Persian).

The third strand of thinking is a moderate one. The advocates of this strand welcome Western achievement and modernization, especially the modern concepts of universal suffrage and popularly elected regimes. However, the main goal of the advocates of this strand is to bestow some local flavour on contemporary concepts and to harmonize between these concepts and religious teachings. This is an attempt to look at religion from outside the confines of religion. Some of the prominent figures of this movement were Allamah Al-Mirza Al-Na'ini, Akhawand Al-Khorasani, Mullah Abdullah Al-Mazendrani and, subsequently, Mr Hasan Al-Mudarres, the liberal religious scholar whose name became famous during the authoritarianism of Reza Khan (the father of the former Shah).

In the Arab world, the situation was similar, with minor differences, particularly during the first and second decades of this century. The minor differences could be ascribed to the state of the Arab world following the collapse of the Ottoman Empire, and the attempts by Arab intellectual elites to fill the void in legitimacy and continue the struggle against colonialism. At any rate, any study of the course of change in the Arab world at the beginning of this century would suggest three trends: traditional, modern and moderate. The conflicts that pitted the advocates of these various lines against each other continued in the Arab world until the fifties; in other words, until the revolution that took place in Egypt in 1952. One may point, by way of example, to the sharp conflicts between Muhammad Abu'l Fadl Al-Gizawi, the President of Al-Azhar, and Abdel Rahman Qurrah, the Mufti of Egypt, the main representatives, respectively, of the traditionalists and the nationalists, during the year 1928. This conflict continued until the occurrence of a deep change in the perspective of Al-Azhar towards new phenomena in the political scene, that is, until the term of Sheikh Mustapha Al-Mouraghi as President of Al-Azhar, in 1938.

II

Since the thirties, many events have left their mark on the rhetoric of cultural and political elites. In the Arab world, social movements dominated, operating on the nation–state principle and revolving around socialism. But this principle failed to achieve its goal, despite the great impact it had on people. Nasserism, too, was unable to provide answers to questions of capitalism, shared goals, religious teachings and cultural issues. This failure was due to the fact that both socialism and Nasserism accorded with the goals of Marxism, which is rootless, its pragmatic philosophy limited.

In Iran, a nationalist movement emerged that embraced as its nationalist model the Kemalist experience in Turkey, which revolved around the West. Only in 1979, during the Iranian revolution, did the situation change. Great importance is attached to the study of this period in history, be it in Iran or in the Arab world, that we may better understand the divisive factors that plagued relations between Arab and Iranian cultural–political elites.

Towards the beginning of this century, when the winds of modernization began to sweep across the Arab world and Iran, a new configuration surfaced in the social arena of the region. The elites in Iran and the Arab world became interested in the current message of the West, a West whose line was governed by changes specific to Western societies, while what was needed from these elites was bridges of understanding between one another and arriving at a common solution to social dilemmas. The intellectuals in Iran and the Arab world took a one-dimensional position towards culture and the value system underlying it; they became consumers of notions from the West, rather than benefiting from what is positive in it, such as the capacity to accept criticism. This state of mind continued for decades, until it became the rule among the 'enlightened'.

The only dialogue evident between the Arab world and Iran was over the models imported from abroad. It is true that social movements in Iran and the Arab world had a great impact, in particular the independence movements, the nationalization drive (1952), the revolution of free officers in Egypt, and the Algerian revolution. These events played a major role in connecting the Iranian and Arab elites. But the ties were short-lived and fleeting. The political situation, and regional and international developments, played a key role in separating or breaking these few ties.

For instance, the pro-West regime in Iran greatly circumscribed links between Iranian and Arab elites, because of its distress with how the situation was developing in the Arab world, which concentrated on nationalism, socialism and alignment with the East (the former Soviet Union). It reached a point in Iran where translation and publication of books by Arab authors was an invitation to many problems. Moreover, one could no longer walk the route of Arab–Iranian relations, because of the prevalence of the socialist nation-state concept. The problem burgeoned to such an extent that the two sides were compelled to resort to third parties, in the East or West, to understand each other's positions.

One of the impediments to good relations was the lack of any direct contact between the Iranian and Arab elites, due to political reasons. However, this was not the only hurdle. Indeed, in the sixties and seventies Iran was one of the main pillars of US presence and policy in the region; it also held many responsibilities regarding the implementation of Western policy. Anti-Arab rhetoric became a political strategy sponsored by the planners. The cultural rhetoric was aimed at isolating Iran from its neighbours and replacing the common cultural heritage with Western concepts. This trend acquired so much momentum that mobility in the region was suppressed, ostensibly in deference to the Iranian national interest. The media, especially newspapers, endorsed the policy of isolation from neighbouring Arab states and confrontation with progressive currents in the Arab world.

III

Following the triumph of the Islamic revolution in 1979, hopes were high that Iranian policy would undergo a full turn. A new generation of enlightened clergy came to power and adopted a new message deriving from ideological tenets that would serve to bridge gaps. The new message revolved around enmity to the West and struggling against world imperialism and its regional agents, such as the Zionists. The ruling religious elite presented the slogan of the unity of the Islamic world before imperialist hegemony and called for learning from what the previous models had led to. They also regarded Islam as the only way to rescue the region from its political problems and the backwardness that has been accumulating for decades. There was an unprecedented increase in visits between Arab and Iranian clerical elites, so much so that the names of Arab scholars, especially those who contributed to recent religious revivalism, were written alongside the names of prominent enlightened Iranian scholars. The issue of Palestine, the cause par excellence of the Arab world, became the issue of the hour for Iran. However, these high hopes did not continue, most unfortunately, as they should have done, because there were suspicious elements that operated here and there to change the new situation.

The first signs of these moves came with the outbreak of the Iraq–Iran war, which so expanded in scope as to create a new alignment of forces at the regional level. Iranians believe that this war was a conspiracy hatched to topple a revolution that extended the hand of friendship and opened possibilities for cooperation with the Arab world.

Even more regrettable is that a number of Arab regimes opposed the nascent Iranian revolution as something useless apparently, though one may perhaps exclude here Syria, Libya and, to some extent, Algeria. In any case, this situation had a background of extremism from both sides. In Iran, some of the political literature took on stronger ideological and nationalist overtones, in both form and content. On the ideological side there was the slogan of exporting the nascent gains of the revolution, made by zealous and extremist supporters of the revolution. Nationalists, for their part, began to promote the idea of turning inward and keeping Iran away from the issues of the Arab world, on grounds of historical sensitivities and the conflicts inherited from the colonialist era.

Here one can also point to the policies of the United States, which went to great lengths to prevent the occurrence of any rapprochement between Iran and the Arab world, because of the loss of a strategic foothold in a region that brims with instability. All these factors combined to prevent the enlightened among Iranians and Arabs from advancing towards the objective of mending ties between the two sides. These factors and obstacles were so intensified as to curtail even intellectual and cultural exchange.

Among the first results of this new state of affairs was that the elites of Iran and the Arab world returned to the old approach of relying on third parties, especially Western sources, to understand one another's positions. Thus, the current towards rapprochement between Iran and the Arab world was seriously weakened.

On the other hand, the collapse of the former Soviet Union, and the fall of socialist ideology, created a deep intellectual crisis at the regional level. The impact of this crisis in Iran was manifest in a near total collapse of Marxist currents and a sharp decline in leftist tendencies, with a comparable rise in conventional right-wing currents and emergence of a New Right. In this context, enlightened clerical officials introduced rationality in their approaches so as to rise above the intellectual crisis. They worked for a new understanding on the various issues, after having arrived at fundamental questions regarding the rule of religion, its concepts and theoretical roots.

From my own follow-up of the trend in intellectual change in the Arab world, I can say that something is taking shape in the region, perhaps similar to the intellectual developments in Iran. But with one difference: in Iran, rule of religion is going through a difficult phase, and rationality and critical thinking are gradually replacing emotionalism, while in the Arab world the phase is still one of emotionalism for some strata, the beginnings of applying rationality for intellectual–clerical elites.

I agree with Hisham Sharabi, when he said that secular enlightenment trends in the Arab world find themselves torn between two contradictory patterns of thinking and history: The first contradiction is internal and finds expression in the confrontation between the secular and the Islamist; the second contradiction is external and finds expression in different ways of dealing with the West, its global capitalist system and hegemonial culture. The current intellectual debates between thinkers and authors such as Samir Amin,[2] Ali Harb,[3] Muhammad Abed Al-Jabiri[4] and Mustapha Hijazi,[5] are a reflection of these contradictions.

However, I do not think that these enlightened clergy are themselves particularly far from the contradictions, because I believe that the clergy suffer from another contradiction, which returns to their rationalist understanding of religion. Such an understanding of religion is not consistent with the presentation of a coarse image of religion. I do not altogether agree with Arab intellectuals who say that the West and some extremist fundamentalist currents colluded in presenting a negative picture of Islam.

IV

Accordingly, it appears that there are favourable factors within both sides, the Iranian and the Arab, to establish contacts and dialogue between intellectual elites. In Iran at the present moment currents are forming that consider contact with Arab neighbours an urgent necessity for achieving joint effort. Perhaps the experience of the enlightened Iranian clergy across 16 years of religious rule would be very useful and necessary for enlightened Arab intellectuals. In Iran those who are both enlightened and religious did not accept to be categorized as objective allies of the West in its conflict with any religious government or Islamic movement, despite the fundamental conflict between their point of view and that of the ruling political regime. They believe that dialogue and rationality are the best approach to improving the situation. This is an important development, shifting roles and moving the government from a position of adversary to one of neutral in the arena of intellectual conflict. Ultimately, it will lead to pluralism in religion and politics, which is extremely important. Although the Iranian experience has not reached the end of the difficult phase, its prospects show a clear vision of a successful future. It is possible that this experience would be very beneficial for enlightened Arabs, especially those who preferred, in some societies, to become the intellectual arm of the ruling regimes because of their hostility to the externalities and extremist behaviour of Islamist currents. It should be kept in mind that in Iran is a strong religious government supported by a wide popular base, and it can announce, unilaterally, a way of interpreting religious ideas, manifest it, and impose it. Thus, religious currents in the Arab world may be more willing to engage in dialogue with the various intellectual currents in the present phase, because of their having no political authority.

In the Arab world, much ink has flowed on the need for ties with neighbouring states such as Iran and Turkey, to confront the future challenges. Such a shared conclusion between the two sides suggests the possibility of establishing a close contact that must not be ignored. If the points that have been mentioned are concerned with defining the locale of enlightened and enlightening groups, other reasons multiply the necessity of establishing such contact.

We are all aware of the international alliance against Iraq, after the war, as among the final links in the chain of transformations of the last decade, regionally and internationally. A new situation has emerged at the regional level and in the balance of power and alignments of regional powers from the structural standpoint. The Middle East and its peoples are obliged now to pay a big price for a situation that they did not share in making. And so we need to establish a new balance to confront the global dangers and threats towards the whole region. The first step on this road is to open the societies of the region to the new rationality. It appears that religious and political pluralism, and removal of all forms of provocation by political authority, can rescue the region from the current problems and dilemmas.

The enlightened and intellectual elites have a very vital role to play in this field. The approach of rationality by all parties is a definite necessity. When this becomes available, it will be possible to attach hope to the next round of dialogue on joint regional issues, understanding, ties and solidarity between the peoples of the Middle East. We want this seminar to be a step in that direction, God willing.

Notes

* Editor-in-chief, *Kiyan* cultural magazine, Tehran, Iran.

1. *Kawah* magazine, reprint, no. 36 (January 1920), pp. 1-2.
2. Samir Amin, 'Culture and Ideology in the Contemporary Arab World', *Al-Tareeq* (Beirut), vol. 52, no. 1 (May 1993), p. 78.
3. Ali Harb, *Criticism of the Truth: The Written and the Actual*, Part 2, (Beirut: The Arab Cultural Centre, 1993), p. 83.
4. Muhammad Abed Al-Jabiri, *Problems of Contemporary Arab Thought*, (Beirut: Centre for Arab Unity Studies, 1989), p. 172.
5. Mustapha Hijazi in: *Positions* (Beirut), Winter–Spring 1993, p. 55.

Five

The Image of Arabs and Iranians in Schoolbooks

9

The Image of the Arabs in Iranian Schoolbooks

GHOULAM ALI HADDAD ADEL*

It is impossible to depict, assess and analyse 'the image of the Arabs in Iranian schoolbooks' unless we fully take into account 'the Islamic revolution in Iran'. Generally, this is a paper on 'the image of the Arabs as seen by the Iranian government' in this century; it is divided into two main parts: before and after the Islamic revolution. The image of the Arabs is totally and intrinsically different in each part. Prior to the Islamic revolution, politicians and theoreticians in charge of education in Iran were pursuing a policy based on nationalism and racism, thus imitating Western nationalists and imperialist foreign powers that used to control Iran. Here are some of the main characteristics of this period:

1. When trying to identify the Iranian national identity in past and present history, precedence was given to Iranian nationalism over Islam.
2. Utmost importance was accorded to what is known as 'ancient' Iran; the ideas and goals prevailing over that period were commended, whereas any shortcomings and any political or social deficiencies were overlooked.
3. An attempt was made to describe the Islamic conquest of Iran as an act of barbarism and savagery; a conquest carried out by uneducated nomads, having no civilization whatsoever. The conquerors took on a great and prosperous city, causing its decline and backwardness until today.
4. Paying little or no attention to the Muslim communities and the Arab world.
5. Following blindly Western policies and way of life, especially the policy of the United States concerning the Arabs, the Arab world and the Palestinian cause.
6. An attempt was made to make people believe that conversion to Shi'ism is an Iranian response to the Arab onslaught on Iran.

On the other hand, since the year 1357 AH/1979 CE, the Islamic government of Iran has been taking a number of decisions, based on the following:

1. Express reservations when there is an attempt to establish a contradiction between Iranian nationalism and Islam. On the other hand, Islam and Muslims should be considered as pillars of Iranian nationalism, similar to the most important characteristics of Iranian culture, such as language, customs, literature and basic laws.
2. Refrain from heaping praise on 'ancient' Iran when trying to assess objectively the social and political situation in pre-Islamic Iran.
3. Consider the fall of the Sassanian dynasty in terms of its weakness before the strong faith of the Arab Muslims. Furthermore, the Iranian people advocated redressing any injury and establishing what is right while expressing their outrage against Sassanian government.
4. Depict Iranian society as a member of the larger Islamic family. The Arabs are members of the *ummah* (nation) as well. Hence, communicating with the Arabs is of great importance, the more so as Iran is located in the Middle East.
5. Follow an independent policy as regards the Arab–Israeli conflict and defend the Palestinian cause against the West, especially the United States.
6. Consider Shi'ism as part and parcel of Islam, while disregarding any nationalist element in our analysis; more importantly, deny its being an emotional response by the Iranians to the Arabs' campaign.

In light of these points, let us try to depict the image of the Arabs in the textbooks of Iranian schools, briefly of course, with a special emphasis on the position of the Iranian government in the years prior to the Islamic revolution.

Iran and Islam

While there is enough emphasis on Iran as a nation-state, on the Iranian identity and even on the various communities that make up the Iranian citizenry, it seems that any reference to Islam is meant to indicate that it is the backbone of Iranian national identity and the pillar of Iranian culture over the last 14 centuries.

In fact, the writers and curricula-designers did not intend to show any contradiction between Iran and Islam. On the contrary, they attempted to identify Iran as an Islamic country. As a result, Islamic beliefs feature in a different way in textbooks in the past and in the present. Great care was taken to delete any references that might offend Muslims, especially the Arabs, or weaken or undermine their unity.

One should not forget that a few intellectuals who are secular have been criticizing any reference to Islam in textbooks. It should be said that those intellectuals are still clinging to pre-revolution views and ideas. They describe the textbooks in Iran's schools as 'religious', irrespective of the subject being taught, be it a Persian language course, a history course, or social studies.

The ideas held by these detractors stem from their belief that patriotism devoid of religion is stronger than patriotism marked by religion. Undoubtedly, there were a number of exaggerations that gave credence to their allegations.

Schoolbooks in Iran

Schoolbooks in Iran no longer attempt to whip up nationalist, chauvinist feelings, referring to ancient Iran as the ideal lost city. We read in the schoolbooks, as well, about the positive aspects of Iranian society before Islam, but without overlooking the shortcomings and the social deficiencies that plagued the former Iranian government. Finally, a course on history is still given – the pre-Islamic revolution history that is.

Current Texts

The causes behind the defeat of the Sassanian army before the Arab army, as well as the weakness and internal collapse of the Sassanian dynasty, are testimony to the inefficiency, injustice and dictatorship wielded by Parviz.

In the current schoolbooks, unlike the former ones, the monarchy is no longer godlike or perfect. On the contrary, because of the dictatorial nature of any monarchy, it is the cause of the disasters and the problems afflicting the Iranian people in the past and in the present. To illustrate this, there is a book entitled *Shahnamah*, written by Ferdawsi, in which there is the story of 'The Shoemaker'. The shoemaker was ready to cut the budget deficit resulting from the war, from his own pocket, provided his son could attend school. The King turned down the offer because of the ideas prevailing at that time. Indeed, blue collar workers were not allowed to enjoy the perks and privileges of the upper class, including education. Although this story existed, it was not included in the textbooks printed before the revolution, because it was deemed to be trouble-stirring. Today, Iranian textbooks contain references to the faith of the Arab Muslims; they contain, as well, a list of the positive results of the conversion to Islam in Iran, the role of Islam in improving the society, and finally the big role played by Iranians in education and modernization. This same idea was expressed by Murtaza Mutahhari in the book he wrote, before the triumph of the revolution, under the title: *The Mutual Services between Islam and Iran*.

In order to draw the attention of the readers to this aspect, here is an extract taken from a schoolbook before the revolution (from a Persian language course printed in 1352 AH/1974 CE):

The downfall of the Sassanian monarchy was brought about by a group of Arabs living in the desert. Prosperity, order and well-being were replaced by chaos, destruction and worry. The throne of the king was replaced by the rostrum; the land of Fereidun, Kaykhusraw, Zardusht, Esfandiar, Ardashir, Shahpur, Parviz was replaced by the lair of the fox and the nest of the eagle. The wicked camel-breeders and herb-eaters are controlling our sons, Kaoh, Rustam, Koderz and Joupirah. The blood of the Persians, Turks and Arabs was flowing together and was testimony to betrayal, bribery, fear and lack of chivalry; the bottom line being the suppression of liberties. Good taste, beauty and greatness were eliminated, only to be replaced by Semitic roots; these Semitic roots supplanted the Aryan roots.

The Islamic Ummah

In Iranian schoolbooks, the Islamic *ummah* (nation) is depicted as a single entity comprised of small units called: people. So the Iranian people are members of the *ummah*. In which case, no one pretended that one is superior to the other. In fact, the various ideas and thoughts were drawn from the Qur'an, specifically the following verse: 'Verily the most honoured of you in the sight of God is [he who is] the most righteous of you.'[1] The idea of 'Muslim brotherhood' was mentioned in another verse: 'The Believers are but a single Brotherhood'.[2] So, to respect this unity is essential and paramount. Therefore, and for the first time after the revolution, a textbook was made specifically for pre-university studies under the title: *The Geography of Islamic Countries*.

Probably, it is the first book of its kind, and it is going to be included in the curriculum of the Literature and Humanities Department in the preparatory stage.

Schoolbooks no longer contain the story of Shahpur, the one with the broad shoulders who managed to poke a hole through the shoulders of the Arabs, or managed to string them together using a rope, to take as hostages. Instead, now, all schoolbooks contain Islamic stories as well as details of the events that took place while the Prophet was alive and which are related to events in Arab society. Many stories about the Arabs in Arab society were mentioned.

It is important to say that, despite the outbreak of war – a war imposed by the Iraqis on the Iranian people – following the triumph of the Islamic revolution, a war which continued for eight years and caused many disasters, much loss in life and property, and despite the support of some Arab countries for Iraq, despite all this, never was there any mention of Arab fanaticism. Never was there any attempt to fan the flames of racism as a main element in this war. Even when 'Bloody Friday' was referred to in one or two chapters, when Iranian visitors and pilgrims were slaughtered in God's holy sites, never was it said that the reason was Arab fanaticism. Some of the main steps that were taken following the triumph of the Islamic revolution were the publication of schoolbooks aimed at strengthening the ties between Iranians and Arabs, and to teach the Arabic language at school after the elementary level and before university.

The aim is not only to teach the Arabic language, but to pave the way for communication with the Arab world, as far as future generations are concerned. A number of Arabic texts were translated, containing various concepts from old and contemporary sources. One of these texts is entitled *The Big Country*; another is under the title *Ibn al-Haytham, the Arab–Egyptian World*; there is also a poem written by Ibn al-Wardi, the widely known Arab author and poet. The work done by some of the greatest writers and poets also figured in the schoolbooks: Sharif Rezaa, Imam Shafi'i, Daabal, Farazdaq, Safi-el-Din al-Hali, and finally Jeha, the character of fiction.

In the elementary and intermediate levels, a number of independent chapters in history books are devoted to the reign of the three caliphs. In the Department of Literature and Humanities, the history book contains chapters about the history of Islam and Islamic caliphs, and about the period between the *Jahiliyyah* and the end of the 14th century, concentrating on the geography of the Arabian Peninsula. In the history book of the first year elementary, some chapters are devoted to the civilization of Mesopotamia. In the history book of the third grade, there is a paper on the emergence of Islam and Arab countries, from the beginning until the end of the Abbasid era.

Following the triumph of the Islamic revolution, a major shift took place as regards the content of schoolbooks in the Islamic Republic of Iran. The change of content affected the Palestinian cause and the Arab–Israeli conflict in all school levels, in most textbooks, especially on language, religion, history and Arabic language. Other issues were also incorporated into the textbooks, such as Zionism, the plot hatched to occupy Palestine, the sorry fate of the Palestinians, the state of the Lebanese people, the struggle of the Arab people and Muslims in general against occupation.

A big attempt was also made in Iran to raise the awareness of the young generation about the Palestinian cause, so that they do not forget the need to struggle to rescue occupied Palestine. In addition to that, pictures of Arab men and women, Arab poems and songs, were included in the textbooks.

Unlike the old texts, conversion to Shi'ism is not portrayed as an Iranian response to the Sunni Arabs, in the new texts. Shi'ism is widespread in Iran for reasons and causes different from those put forward by Iranian nationalists, i.e., that most Iranians were until the year 1000 AH Sunni and that the authors of the *Sahihs* were Sunni from Bukhara, Tarmaz, Nishapur and the Caspian. This assumption has no scientific basis.

In a nutshell, according correct importance to the Arabs and Arab issues in Iranian schoolbooks is an idea that stems from the importance of Islam. Indeed, the link between Islam and the Qur'an, which is written in Arabic, cannot be broken. Moreover, Islam began in the Arabian Peninsula, from where it spread later on.

One of the main issues regarding the Arabs and their image in Iranian schoolbooks is the Palestinian cause. Special attention was devoted to this issue in the past. Today, however, most cultural issues and contemporary civil movements have not been getting enough attention. This sad state is due to many reasons, prominent among which was the eight-year-old war. Indeed, the war created an atmosphere unconducive to any discussions about cultural issues in the Arab world. Moreover, there is no cultural exchange taking place currently, the more so, as we all know, that the repercussions of the war are still being felt. Indeed, there are still some dark clouds plaguing the ties between the Arab world and Iran.

It can be said that Iran is less mentioned in Arab schoolbooks than the Arabs in Iranian schoolbooks. The reason for this is fairly simple: when talking about Islam, one has to take the Arabs into account, whereas this link does not exist as far as the Arabs are concerned.

Finally, it seems that all Iranian cultural and educational trends are not represented in the Arab world, including schoolbooks. Moreover, most facts and data about Iran are not contained in Arabic schoolbooks despite the fact that Iran and the Arab world have been sharing 14 centuries of common history, geographic proximity and religious and cultural similarities. This sad situation is very painful to endure, and it created a feeling best described by an Iranian poet who said: 'Look at the separation between me and my love, like two eyes that can never visit one another.'

Summary

It can be said that the definition of 'pre-revolutionary Iran' in schoolbooks in the Islamic Republic of Iran is not yet final. This may have been the result of the coming to power of the Pahlavi family in the wake of Iran's shahdoms before Islam and the Iranian people brought down the Pahlavi regime, as it did its predecessors, with the victory of the revolution. This does not mean that we should provide a lengthy discussion on the shahdoms of Iran; rather we draw attention to the absence of a fixed definition of Iran's ancient history, due to the people's hatred for the Pahlavi regime.

The Palestinian cause and the cause of Jerusalem are conveyed in school-books as follows:

1. In the Persian language book, 2nd elementary, under the lesson: 'A Letter from a Palestinian Child'.
2. In the Persian language book, 3rd elementary, under the lesson: 'A Youth from Palestine'.
3. In the Arabic language book, 1st intermediate, under the lesson: 'A Portrait of Jerusalem'.
4. In the Arabic language book, 2nd intermediate, within the new system, under the lesson: 'On the Intifadah'.
5. In the Arabic language book, 3rd secondary Humanities, under the two lessons: (i) 'O Jerusalem – A Poem', (ii) 'Newsreel – The Intifadah'.

Historians mention that the Shoemaker went to Anushirwan to finance the army, in exchange for allowing his son to go to school. Anushirwan refused and replied that the lower classes are not entitled to education.[3]

In the book *Social Instructions*, for 4th grade elementary, there is a lesson entitled 'The Islamic *Ummah*'. Here is an extract from it:

The Islamic *ummah* is made up of all the Muslims in the world. All Muslims believe in the One God, in the Prophet Muhammad and in the Holy Book, the Qur'an. They all turn their faces to the prayer niche when praying. Corrupt governments are trying in all parts of the Muslim world to find a pretext to highlight any differences in colour or race of the Muslims, in an attempt to drive a wedge between them. We, the Muslims in Iran, are an integral part of the Islamic *ummah*; we seek to become united with the rest of the Muslims around the world.

Shahpur I spearheaded a campaign through the Persian Gulf into the Arabian Peninsula. He killed many Arabs, who had attacked Iran when he was a child. Shahpur burned their cities. Historians say: Shahpur gave instructions that a hole should be poked into the shoulders of the Arabs, that they should be strung by a rope. Therefore, the Arabs have named him the 'broad-shouldered'. (This is an extract from a 4th elementary history book, 1346 AH.)

Notes

* Faculty of Arts and Humanities, Tehran University, Tehran, Iran.

1.   The Holy Qur'an, *Surat al-Hujurat*, *ayah* 13.
2.   Ibid., *ayah* 10.
3.   From *Social Instructions*, for 4th Grade Elementary, (Tehran: n.p., 1373 AH), p. 123.

10

The Image of the Iranians in Arab Schoolbooks

TALAL ATRISSI*

Introduction

Analysing the content of schoolbooks has become a norm in various research fields; it enables us, through the study of what the text says and what
it does not say, to identify the cultural, political, ethical and social values
and concepts.

States and political parties and organizations have often made use of the
world of schoolbooks, as well as other sources of knowledge, to convey or
emphasize what they view to be correct, whether about themselves or about
others. While the self-image invariably takes the best possible form, the
image of the other is often subjected, whether good or bad, to the needs
and demands of political and ideological 'interests'.

Content analysis has studied the history, geography, national education,
reading and literature of schoolbooks, because this kind of books, in contrast to scientific books, enables the authors to rewrite history or convey
the ideas and concepts according to their wishes or to the state's policies
and ideology. In this respect, many books, papers and theses that have
adopted content analysis of schoolbooks to search for the hidden images of
the various peoples, religious concepts and traditions, have been published.

The importance of this kind of study lies in probing the texts that usually appear to have a seemingly objective or positive outlook, in order to
discover an indirect channel for forming views, opinions and loyalties, especially when those addressed are of school age, i.e., the stage when their
concepts and values are formed.

Israel, for example, asked Egypt and Jordan, after signing the peace treaties with them in 1978 and 1994 respectively, to amend the academic
curricula in these two countries so as to delete any word, idea or text re-
motely related to the previous hostility against it, to ensure that new
generations' thinking and awareness conform to the new political facts, and

to ensure that textbooks will not run contrary to the 'mutual interests'.

In our study of 'the image of Iranians in Arab schoolbooks', we too resorted to the study of history and geography books to analyse what these books convey to the students of the intermediate level, who are between 12 and 16 years of age. This stage is very important in the formation of awareness and opinion, being the stage when one starts to search for his or her identity and loyalties, thus allowing for a maximum margin of influence that surpasses what could be achieved in a previous stage and establishes a base for what might be achieved at a later stage.

Since the victory of the Islamic revolution, Iranian relations with the Arabs have been quite diverse. They ranged between alliance and support, to tension and severing of diplomatic relations, to outright war and extreme hostility. To demonstrate this diversity, we chose samples from different countries that best reflect these contradictory stands.

We analysed each series of books that we received from each Arab country on its own, trying, for example, to define the image of Iran and the Iranians that is presented by Egyptian history and geography schoolbooks. And we also tried to determine if there was one image or a number of images. We repeated the same analysis with all the other books, bearing in mind that the only national education series we received was from Iraq.

To define the image of the other (Iran in this case), we had to define how these books present the image of their own countries, the role of these countries, as well as their policies and their leaders, as contrasted with that of the other countries, whether friendly or not.

Yet, as it was inconvenient to follow up all the details of the self-image, lest it blur the initial image we are trying to portray, we decided that we would only refer to the self-image when it is contrasted with the image of the other, whether it is presented positively or negatively and even when it is totally absent.

Moreover, we did not attempt in this paper to study all the contents of the schoolbooks, which include the images of the Arabs, the Europeans, and the Africans, as well as the images of the liberation movements, Islam, the West and the Zionists. Nor did we study the number of times a certain word or concept or the name of a leader or president appeared. Despite the fact that they are considered important elements in any content analysis, we had to refrain from using them so as not to exceed the main topic of our study.

We have chosen five sets of history, geography and national education books (75 books) that represent five countries: Syria, Iraq, Morocco, Egypt, and Saudi Arabia.

In our choice of these countries, we tried to represent all the various patterns of relations with Iran, so as to establish how their policies are reflected in their schoolbooks: does the image of alliance, or hostility, each country has pursued conform with the image drawn in its schoolbooks? Or does Iran have two different images?

It would have been better if the samples were more comprehensive, to include, for example, all the Arab Gulf countries and all the Arab Maghreb countries. But, in addition to the fact that we could not acquire the books in time, we believe that the samples we have chosen reflect to a great extent the essential features of Iran in the Arab schoolbooks, especially as countries like Egypt, Syria, Saudi Arabia and Iraq had had, since the victory of the Islamic revolution, i.e. in the last 15 years, clearly different relations with Iran ranging from alliance to hostility, to accusations and severing of relations, and of course to the direct war whose repercussions have not unfolded completely yet.

We preferred to analyse each set of books separately, so as to draw the elements of the picture it presents. We could have compared the same element in all the Arab schoolbooks, but we chose not to, because it might be very complicated, and because the first method enables the reader to review the image presented in the books of each country. Moreover, we have outlined in the conclusion all the common points among the various sets as well as their differences.

It is important to emphasize that we do not discuss the political or historical events, but instead quote them as they are written in the texts, whether we believe that they are true or not. It is evident that much of what the history books, for example, present as facts was disputed by the researchers themselves. But the aim of this kind of research is not to highlight or prove any facts, which could initiate a prolonged discussion, but rather to take the text as it presents itself and interpret it in a way that enables us to define the features of the image we are looking for in the clearest possible way.

The copies of the Arab schoolbooks we ordered are new editions that were published between 1992 and 1994. The first editions of these books were published at a previous date, and some of them go back to 1980, i.e. to the period that witnessed the beginning of the great transformation in Iran after the victory of the Islamic revolution, and the beginning of its relations with the Arab countries, which witnessed many ups and downs in the political, military and security spheres.

Furthermore, the period between 1980 and 1994 has witnessed, especially in the last five years, some fundamental changes in the relations of Iran with the Arab world in general, and with each Arab country in particular. The war with Iraq came to an end, and diplomatic relations with some countries were restored after a long breakdown, while relations with others improved. We therefore looked for the impact of these changes in the schoolbooks to evaluate the extent to which the image of the self, and of the other (Iran), had changed – especially as most of these books talk about the changes and renovations in 'the current edition in our hands'.

The Image of the Iranians in Iraqi Schoolbooks

The image of the Iranians (Persians) in the Iraqi schoolbooks is clear-cut, and so strongly stated that it leaves nothing to clarify or interpret. It is a stereotype image that has undergone no change since the dawn of Islamic history. The transformations that took place over the centuries did not change the picture that is presented in Iraqi history, geography and national schoolbooks. The Iranian is always that mean racist Persian who conspired against the Arab nation, its unity and its language, as well as the Islamic Arab civilization, since the era of the Orthodox Caliphs and until 'Saddam's glorious Qadisieh'. Moreover, the Persian collaborated with foreigners to achieve these goals, and realize his own ambitions as well.

Each time the Persians are mentioned, they are the invaders, an absolute evil that has to be deterred, being a constant danger that threatens the nation and its fate. All the problems of Muslims and Arabs, all the sectarian conflicts and unrest, as well as the attempts to undermine their civilization, may as well be, if we are to rely on these books, the product of Persian conspiracies.

How do the books express this image?

We should mention from the start that the image that will be described in the following pages cannot be separated from the self-image; that is, the image that includes, at one and the same time, the Arab nation, Iraq, the Ba'th Party, and the Iraqi president, with considerable variation between one element and the other, as we shall see. The dialectical relationship between the two images seems absolutely necessary. For the extent of the Persian peril does not become clear unless it is compared with the glory of the Arab nation and its civilization; furthermore, the extent of the leader's power, or that of the party or the state, is not demonstrated except when it faces a critical, comprehensive and long-term conspiracy. In this context, to defend the state is to defend the nation, and to fight the state is to fight the nation.

Through a process of trying to link the components of the image with the concepts that were introduced by the three sets of history, geography and national education books, we were able to determine the elements of the image, and we are going to outline them under separate headings for the sake of classification, despite the fact that they overlap in many instances and could not, therefore, be readily separated.

The Persians have been the Nation's Enemy since the Dawn
of the Message of Islam

Since the beginning of the Message of Islam, the Persians have maintained
their intense hatred of the Arabs and Islam. The Arabs confronted them in
the 'first Qadisieh battle' and thwarted their schemes, but they continued
to conspire throughout the Umayyad and Abbasid eras, to undermine the
unity and sovereignty of the Arab Empire. 'The unity of history is manifest
through the Iraqis' solidarity against the dominance of foreigners, whether
they were Persians, Mongols, Ottomans or British, who have tried to exploit them, fragment their unity and take hold of their land and riches.'[1]

These [common] goals were the slogan of Iraqis and the Arabs, as they confronted
the Persians on [the day of] Dhu Qar. The Arabs realized these goals when they
rallied under the leadership of the most honourable Prophet Muhammad.[2]

'The brave Iraqis held fast against the attempts of the Persians, Ottomans and the
British to occupy their lands and plunder their riches'.[3]

As for Chosroes, the Persian king whom the Messenger sent a letter to call him to
Islam, he was furious when he read the letter, and showed all his deep-rooted
hatred for the Arabs when he tore the letter. The other [kings] responded in a
good and respectful manner, and some sent gifts in acknowledgement of his Message and Prophethood.[4]

(a) The First Qadisieh Battle
The faith of the leader Saad [bin Abi Waqqas] made him take the initiative for
negotiation, but the Persians refused this offer for peace [the call to Islam and
return of the Arab lands and rights to their Arab owners] and they were determined to continue their aggression, and threatened to exterminate the Arabs.[5]

Then the history book starts to describe the details of the battle itself,
with special emphasis on Arab courage, the death of Rustum, the Persian
commander, and the Persian defeat.

By the end of the battle, the blood of the martyrs watered the soil of Iraq, the land
of pan-Arabism and sacrifice. Had it not been for such a courageous stand, the
land would not have been liberated from the usurping Persian occupiers.[6]

(b) Persian Plotting against Arabism and Islam

The Persian conspiracies against Arabism and Islam mounted in the aftermath of
the decisive victory at Qadisieh, the liberation of Iraq and the fall of their Persian
Empire. Exploiting the humanitarianism of the Arabs, they chose Caliph Omar
bin al-Khattab as their target and plotted to assassinate him ... But although the
Caliph was assassinated, the Arab nation continued its march and carried its Mes-

sage to the whole world. The Persians started to conspire by arousing persecutions and disturbances that led to the martyrdom of Caliphs Uthman (and Ali bin Abi Taleb). Thus, the Persians were responsible for the assassination of the three Caliphs.

The same accusation is repeated in the fourth volume of the series.[7]

In its treatment of the emergence of Islam and the rise of the Arab Empire during the era of the Prophet and the Orthodox Caliphs, the fourth volume says:

While Caliph Omar was preoccupied with establishing the basis of the Empire ... he was about to liberate all the Arab lands, were he not assassinated by a Persian criminal (Abu Lu'lu'ah), the slave of Mughira bin Shi'ba, for the Persians have harbored intense hatred for the Arab nation after the Arab victory in the battle of Qadisieh in the year 15 AH.[8]

(c) The Plots of the Umayyad Era

The Persians maintained their hostility against the Arab nation and its united empire in the Umayyad era. That was manifested in two main fields: the first is the religious and ideological hostility. This kind of hostility is marked by *Shu'ubiyyah* (racial discrimination) and atheism, since the Persians wanted to undermine the Islamic religion and tried to distort the Qur'an and the *Sunnah*. They stabbed the Arabic language, the symbol of the Arabs' national unity and their source of pride, contested the lineage of the Arabs and denounced the noble Arab values such as generosity, bravery and honesty. The Arab nation confronted these subversive schemes and thwarted their plans.

The second is the political hostility through which the Persians tried to undermine the building of a strong empire by means of promoting sedition and disturbances and taking part in them. They took part in Al-Mukhtar Al-Thakafi riot, and when the Arab Empire was able to defeat it in the year 76 AH, they supported the mutiny of Ibn Al-Ash'ath, and when it was defeated in the year 84 AH, they supported the rebellion of Abdullah bin Mu'awiyah, whose defeat in 129 AH signaled the collapse of all Persian schemes due to the firm stand of the Arab Empire.[9]

(d) The Plots in the Abbasid Era

'The Persian hostility to the Arab Empire escalated in the Abbasid era.' This same paragraph was repeated, along with the two main fields of hostility in the Umayyad era: ideological and religious and political conspiracies. One of their most prominent hostile movements was the conspiracy of Abu Muslim Al-Khorasani against the Abbasid caliphate, followed by the mutiny of Sinbaz Al-Majusi. Both revolts were crushed by Abu Jaafar Al-Mansur. Then, during the reign of Harun Al-Rashid, the Persian Barmakids plotted against the Abbasid caliphate, but the Caliph thwarted their plot and crushed their revolt. Caliph Al-Ma'mun was also quick to crush the revolt of the Persian Bani Sahl. The caliphate's national and historic efforts were magnificent, for they confronted all Persian conspiracies, whether political or ideological, with a firm and bold stand, and crushed them and thwarted their plots. Jurists and intellectuals like Abi Hanifah, Jaafar As-Sadiq, Al-Jahiz, Al-Asma'i and Ibn Qutaybah ... have in their turn confronted the Persian nationalistic *Shu'ubiyyah* movement ... [10]

In the fourth volume of the same series, the same Persian threats and conspiracies against the Arab Empire are repeated:

The Abbasids gave the Persians a share in running the affairs of the Empire, but they were kept under the close surveillance of the Arab Caliphs, who grew aware of the threat the Persians posed to the Empire, as they dominated its institutions; so they got rid of them ... The Abbasids' crushing of the Persians was a natural reaction, having misbehaved and exploited their positions to the extent of threatening the Abbasid entity and the Arabism of their Empire.[11]

(e) The Persians: A Foreign Challenge and a Hostile External Invasion of Arab and Islamic Civilization

In the course of its history, the united Arab Empire encountered various kinds of foreign challenges that threatened its unity and sovereignty. Some of the most important of these challenges were:

1. The Buwayhid invasion: the Buwayhids were one of the Persian peoples who took advantage of the hardships encountered by the unified Arab Emire. They assumed a hostile policy against the Arab nation and tried to subvert the aspects of the Arab civilization in Iraq ... and promoted sectarian disturbances.
2. The Seljuk invasion: these were Turkish peoples who inhabited Iran, and they took advantage of the unrest in the unified Arab Empire to practice the same aggressions as the Buwayhids.
3. The European invasion.
4. The Mongol invasion: these were a barbarian people who came from Central Asia. The Persians, who hate Islam and the Arabs, allied with them.[12]

The Arab army fought many important battles after they were victorious in the Qadisieh battle. They moved forward to the remaining Arab countries, to liberate the Arab lands from the foreign dominance in general and the Persian dominance in particular. They also confronted all the conspiracies and the subversive movements that were plotted by the Persians, who were motivated by hatred of the Arab Empire.[13]

Persian Hostility continues in the Modern Age

The Persians' hostility against the Arabs, and Iraq in particular, continued in the various historical periods. The Safavids allied with the colonialists to serve their expansionist goals. Shah Reza Pahlavi occupied Ahwaz and an-

nexed it to the Iranian territories. He also gained control of the three islands in the Arabian Gulf.

(a) The Persian Safavid Invasion

Shah Ismail used religion as a pretence for his expansion in Iran and the
neighbouring regions. Iraq was among the first countries Shah Ismail sought to
occupy. He adopted a racist policy in the city [Baghdad] that was concealed by
sectarianism. But he faced mounting resistance from the Iraqis … During their
rule, the Safavids did not accomplish anything worth mentioning in Iraq. On the
contrary, they encouraged the Persian merchants to plunder the riches of Iraq.
And they neglected agriculture and irrigation canals.[14]

The Persians began to collaborate with the colonialist Portuguese to achieve their
expansionist goals in the Arabian Gulf.[15]

When the Portuguese gained control of the Hormuz Strait, Shah Ismail of the
Safavid dynasty sent an envoy in the year 1515 … asking them to give him ships to
invade [Bahrain and Qatif], and he allied with them to achieve his aggressive
goals. The Persians also collaborated with the other European invading powers to
control the Arab lands, and the Arabs had to fight the Persian–European alliance
that wanted to take their lands.[16]

Although Iraq fell under Ottoman control, the Persian ambitions in Iraq did not
cease. The Persian forces occupied Baghdad in 1622 … As for Basra, it managed
to resist the Persian invasion; and Afraisab, the Ottoman officer of Arab origin,
succeeded in establishing an independent authority in the city that was able to
hold out against many Persian military campaigns.[17]

Although the Ottomans signed many agreements and treaties with the Persians, in
which they agreed that they would not interfere in the affairs of Iraq and its borders where under Ottoman rule, the Persians violated all these treaties at the expense of the Iraqi lands and the Iraqi waters in Shatt al-Arab.[18]

When Muhammad Reza Pahlavi succeeded his father, he maintained the same
aggressive policy against Iraq, in spite of all Iraqi good will gestures to establish
mutual understanding and friendly relations.[19]

The Ottomans and the Persians introduced, during their successive dominance of
Iraq, many heresies and wrong practices to the Islamic religion.[20]

When Shah Reza PAHLAVI ruled Iran, the Persian ambitions in the Arabian Gulf
increased. In 1925 he was able, through his armed forces and the cooperation with
the British, to occupy the Ahwaz region, annexing it to Iran, and bringing down
the Arab rule in that region.[21]

(b) The Iranians' ambitions in the Shatt al-Arab

In our contemporary era, no state can change its [geographical] location without violating the rights or sovereignty of another state, as was the case in the attempts of Iran to expand into Shatt al-Arab and the mainland at the expense of Iraq, and the occupation of the three islands (Greater Tunb, Lesser Tunb, and Abu Musa) in the Arabian Gulf on 31 December 1971.[22]

Muhammad Reza PAHLAVI resumed the same aggressive policy against Iraq. He used the policy of immigration to the Arabian Gulf to efface its Arab identity. When the revolution of 17–30 July broke out, the Shah's regime was among the first parties that were hostile to it, because he knew that his Persian ambitions could not be realized if the Baath revolution was successful.[23]

The challenges the Arab nation faces in the modern and contemporary age could be summed up as follows: (i) Colonialism, (ii) Zionism, (iii) racist Iranian ambitions, (iv) the *Shu'ubiyyah* (as 'Iranian nationalism'), (v) fragmentation, and (vi) cultural, economic and social backwardness.[24]

The Iranians' ambitions in Shatt al-Arab go back a long time, about 400 years, when Iraq was under the control of the Ottoman Empire and Iran used to be called the Persian land ... .[25]

Following a historical account of the agreements and treaties that were concluded between the Persians and the Ottomans, over the borders between Iraq and Iran, we read the following:

All the treaties were violated by the rulers of Iran, since the policy of the Persian state has always relied on stalling in implementing the treaties, to take advantage of any future chance for a new expansion.[26]

The arrogant Iranian expansionism and a twist of fate prompted Iran to denounce in 1935 the second Erzerum Treaty of 1847 ... Then Iran began to pursue its claims and mounted a large military incursion in Shatt al-Arab'. Later, after the 17–30 July revolution broke out in 1968, and in coordination with the Zionist entity, Iran declared unilaterally in April 1969 cancellation of the 1937 Iraq–Iran treaty and began to plan new expansionist moves.[27]
In 1975 the circumstances were favourable to sign the treaty of Algeria ... Iraq honoured all its commitments, and tried to establish a relationship with Iran based on good neighbourliness and common interests ... But Iran, both before the so-called Islamic revolution[28] and after it, refused to implement the article concerning territorial borders and tried to stall, although it got half of Shatt al-Arab.[29]

(c) Saddam's Glorious Qadisieh

The 'second Qadisieh' that Iraq fought against 'the Persians' is a continuation of the first one, on both sides of the front: the chivalrous Arabs defending their land and dignity, and the aggressive Persians motivated by greed and conspiracies; Iraq is the Arab party, which is defending the whole of the Arab nation against the Persian peril that endangers the eastern flank of the Arab nation. The indirect preparation for the 'glorious Qadisieh' begins by highlighting two elements: the two main parties to the battle, Iraq and Iran. The first is the object of historical ambitions, due to its place and role; the second is the bearer of these ambitions, because it wants revenge for the first Qadisieh.

It was not limited to a propaganda campaign against Iraq. Rather it developed into interference in Iraq's internal affairs, and shelling and destroying of many Iraqi border towns and cities. Then on 4th September 1980, Iran launched a series of military attacks that used artillery, infantry, armoured vehicles and the air force ... as a prelude to a decisive air strike against Iraq, but they did not know that Iraq was making a new history, and that made it accept the military challenge ... [30]

The successive military invasions increased the awareness of the Iraqi people of their country's position, and made them always ready to resist the challenges, and made their army always vigilant to sacrifice for its country.[31]

This shows the importance of [Iraq's] geographical location as the faithful guard of the eastern frontiers of the Arab homeland [the Iranian border] ... Moreover, Iraq's position at the head of the Arabian Gulf imposed on it a historical responsibility to protect the Arab identity of this body of water.[32]

In accordance with the national responsibility Iraq assumed, due to this geographical position, it utilised all its capabilities and potentials to identify and confront the foreign ambitions ...[33]

Moreover, due to its geographical position on the Arabian Gulf ... Iraq acquired a special importance in the region as one of its countries and the strongest country that can repel aggression in the region. Iraq will not remain idle and will confront this foreign aggression that aims at challenging the independence and Arabism of the Gulf region.[34]

(d) Reasons for the Battle's Name

It is the everlasting heroic epic that the Iraqi people fought to defend Iraq and the Arab nation; it is the battle in which the Iraqi people achieved victory against the racist Khomeinist Persian enemy. It was named Saddam's Qadisieh, after the victorious, by God's Will, leader Saddam Hussein, who led the marvelous heroic battles ... just as leader Saad bin Abi Waqqas did in the first Qadisieh about 14 centuries ago.[35]

Our ancestors' Qadisieh has been revived by the hero of Arabism and Islam, leader Saddam Hussein, and against the same Persian enemy ...[36]

(e) The Reasons for the War

The war broke out because the Iranians refused to respond to the Iraqi demand for adopting a good neighbour policy. The revolutionary government of Iraq welcomed the new government in Iran that assumed power after the fall of the Shah in 1979. But Khomeini and his aides adopted a hostile policy against Iraq from the very first day they assumed power, and instead of responding positively to the Iraqi call of establishing good and neighbourly relations, they increased their assaults against the party and the revolution, and their aggression on the border villages and areas. They launched a campaign of Khomeini conspiracy and subversion inside Iraq ...[37]

The Iraqis had to respond, especially as the Iranian officials declared that they wanted to occupy Iraq:

On the 4 September 1980, the racist Khomeini regime launched its armed aggression ... The Iranian officials began to declare that they wanted to occupy Iraq. The Iraqi leadership decided to retaliate against the aggression and the penetration of the Iranian armed forces into the Iraqi lands.[38]

The detailed account of the reasons for war is accompanied by a change from the general (Iran) to the specific (Khomeini regime); thus, the enemy and the target became more clearly defined. And once again, the reader is reminded of the collaboration between the Iranians and the colonialists, in this case the 'Khomeini regime', and Zionism, without failing to touch on the usual self-praise and glorification of the Ba'th doctrine.

The reasons that led the Khomeini regime to launch its aggression against Iraq and continue the war are:

1. The Ba'th ideology, drawn from the spirit of the Message of Islam and the glorious heritage of the Arab nation, is considered a threat to the backward Khomeini ideas.
2. The Persian racist hatred towards Iraq and the Arab nation since ancient times, which Khomeini has used religion to mask.
3. The military in Iran imagined that the conflict with Iraq will enable them to regain the position and influence they lost when Khomeini came to power.
4. The Khomeini regime wanted to use the war as a means to draw the attention of the Iranian peoples away from economic, social and political problems in Iran.
5. The Zionist encouragement of Iran in its aggression against Iraq ... for Iraq poses a big threat to the Zionist entity.[39]

In addition to analysing the reasons of this war, the lessons explain, throughout the series, how 'Saddam's Qadisieh' created a new life for the Iraqi people, developed the military industry, safeguarded national unity, manifested the heroism of the various units of the Iraqi army, proved to be the road to liberation of Palestine and rescue of the Arab nation and the Islamic world from Khomeini dominance and aggression, which collaborated with Zionism against Arabism.[40]

Moreover, a whole chapter in the 3rd Year Intermediate *National Education* book is dedicated to 'the implications of the glorious Qadisieh of Saddam and its role in the march of Iraqi society'.[41] This chapter ends with a series of questions that reaffirm the chapter's concepts about the aggression of the Khomeini regime, its collaboration with Zionism and the Iraqis' love of fighting for their country.[42]

To match the threat that is represented by the enemy with its historical and present ambitions, the schoolbooks draw a picture of Saddam Hussein the leader as possessing all the qualities and dimensions enabling him to face the threats and challenges imposed on Iraq and the Arab nation. Thus, all chapters of all Iraqi schoolbooks have highlighted, whenever possible, the role of the leader Saddam Hussein, who has replayed the role of the historic leader Saad bin Abi Waqqas and whom they pray God to preserve. This led to the overlapping of the three poles: Saddam Hussein, Iraq and the Arab nation. The role of the first is to protect the other two, while the threat faced by the second pole is a threat to the whole nation; the defence led by the first in Iraq is a defence of the whole nation as well as Arabism. All this is accompanied by the constant reminder that Iraq is the stronger party, always ready to repel aggression, and the Persian enemy is the one who violates all agreements and has not accepted any calls for peace and dialogue:

The Qadisieh of our ancestors has been revived by the hero of Arabism and Islam, leader Saddam Hussein.[43]

Saddam's Qadisieh is a new Arab renaissance, in which the Iraqis have recaptured the heroism of their great grandfathers, who held the banner of Islam ... such as Saad bin Abi Waqqas, Khalid bin Al-Walid and Salaheddine Al-Ayyoubi.[44]

The leader Saddam Hussein is the embodiment of all the values of honour and nobility in our nation and its humane values ... [45]

It was called Saddam's Qadisieh after the leader, whom God has triumphed, Saddam Hussein, who led all the magnificent victorious battles and established victory and peace.[46]

President Saddam Hussein has led this heroic epic ... and became a symbol of the Iraqis and their unity in war, victory and peace.[47]

As for the field of comprehensive development, leader Saddam Hussein is the first architect ... [48]

In one critical battle, Saddam Hussein did the planning ... to ensure the victory of Iraq and the Arab nation in the glorious battle of Qadisieh.[49]

The leader-president (may God protect him) played the major role in the second Qadisieh.[50]

The leader-president led the counter-attack against the enemies.[51]

Iraq was successful, thanks to its great leader, in thwarting all the plots of imperialism and Zionism.[52]

The role of Iraq and the 17–30 July glorious revolution is to defend the Arabism of the Gulf and the Arab nation and oppose the Iranian occupation of the Arab islands.[53]

Then, in an attempt to make the concept of nationalism and Arab unity take root, we notice that the fourth part of the *National Education* series resorts to reminding the reader of Persian racism:

The racist nationalism is fanatical, arrogant and usually resorts to violence as a means of imposing hegemony over other peoples and nations; the racist Persians and Zionists are two cases in point. On the other hand, a humane nationalism is characterized by sublimation and the spirit of cooperation ... as is the case of our Arab nation throughout the various historic stages.[54]

(f) Other Negative Aspects of the Iranian Image

As the books we are studying repeat in almost all chapters the same notion about the Iranian aggression, they sometimes link this 'Iranian aggression' with the 'American Atlantic aggression' in the 'mother of battles', and the Zionist plans in the region. We also have to bear in mind that this battle itself – the battle the Americans called 'Desert Storm' to liberate Kuwait from the Iraqi occupation – is not dealt with in these books, except in a few words to indicate that it was an aggression that was defeated. This means that these books do not even try to explain the nature of this war, and they simply reduce it to an aggression. In contrast, nearly all the chapters are full of inflammatory propaganda against Persian aggression. And each lesson contains photographs and ends with a set of questions that repeat the same notions about the Iranian racial aggression, bearing in mind that there are no questions concerning the 'mother of battles' or Zionism. And while each book dedicates long paragraphs or even chapters to talk about Saddam's Qadisieh, 'the mother of battles' is only mentioned as a quick reference to the American Atlantic aggression against Iraq. The same is true with regard to Israel. Apart from the reference to occupied Palestine as part of the Arab land, there is no incitement like the one against the Persians or Iran in general.

The Iraqis fought the aggressive invaders ... as they did when they fought the aggression of the Iranian regime or when they stood against the American–Atlantic–Zionist aggression.[55]

Today, they continue their struggle to make the present and build the future in

Saddam's glorious Qadisieh and in the immortal battle of the mother of battles ...[56]

Observations on the Image Presented

In addition to the sharp and protruding elements that constitute the dark and harsh image of Iran, there is but one reference in the second and third intermediate geography books in which Iran is mentioned without any description whatsoever; that is, without calling it either Islamic or aggressive and racist. It is merely a neighbouring country. Even when the book talks about the island of Abu Musa, it does not accuse Iran of occupying it.[57] Moreover, when the geography book talks about the distribution of the population and the religious factor in Iraq, Iran is mentioned in a neutral manner. 'The presence of the shrines and the holy places increases the people's visits to the cities of Karbala and Najaf ... as well as the people from some other countries, such as Iran, Pakistan and India ... '[58] This very element, 'the presence of shrines and holy places' which attracts the Iranians to the Iraqi cities, is considered in the history book[59] as a 'fifth column that acts inside the Iraqi society to serve the interests of the foreign powers' ... It should be mentioned that both books (the history book and the geography book) are meant to be studied by students of the same year (third intermediate), and they were reprinted in 1994. Furthermore, not only does the geography book[60] mention Iran in a neutral manner, it also contains a single sentence that calls for positive relations with 'the Iranian peoples and the Turkish people'.[61] But this is a single statement that is never repeated in any of the other books we studied. When they talk about the 'mother of battles' and after they link it with the Iranian aggression, the reference to the Iranian exploitation of this battle is made only once: 'Through the execution of the colonialist plot in the internal affairs, and the arousing of its misled bands to practice certain acts of subversion, plunder and murder of the innocents'.[62]

In addition to the image of the Iranian who exploited the tri-partite aggression (American–Atlantic–Zionist), the 'mother of battles', the third part of the history series mentions once only (not repeated in any of the other parts) the rulers of Saudi Arabia and Kuwait, 'the agents of the colonialist forces who were charged with the task of draining the Iraqi economy',[63] 'certain Arab parties', especially 'those hostile to the party and the revolution, who encouraged the Khomeini regime to launch its aggression against Iraq',[64] and 'that alliance of traitors of the nation with the felonious Iranian enemy in its aggression against the eastern flank of the Arab homeland, and their alliance with the American–Atlantic–Zionist aggression in their aggression against Iraq ... '[65]

Based on these characteristics, which have been constantly repeated in the history, geography and national education books, the various components of a certain image of the Iranian neighbour are accumulated in the mind of the student in the three or four years of his intermediate stage. The elements of this image could be outlined, irrespective of the order they appear in the books, as follows:

1. Iran constantly repeats its Persian history; it did not undergo any change, even after the Islamic revolution, which the books do not even mention.
2. Khomeini and his aggressive policy is a continuation of the former Shah's policies, while Saddam Hussein is a continuation of the policies of the early Arab leaders.
3. The Persians want to avenge the first Qadisieh.
4. The Persians are responsible for the killing of the three Caliphs: Omar, Uthman and Ali.
5. The Persian is always inclined to be aggressive and does not accept any peace initiative proposed by the Arab leader.
6. The Persians are a fifth column who always resort to sedition and turmoil.
7. The Persians are invaders who like to dominate.
8. The Persians are against the Arabism of the Gulf and Arab nations.
9. The Persians are against Arab civilization.
10. The Persians are against the unity of the Iraqi people and the unity of the Arab nation, its language, and its national identity.
11. The Persians always collaborate with the colonialist forces against the Arabs.
12. Persian nationalism is a racialist nationalism, while Arab nationalism is humanist.

In contrast to all these detailed elements of the Persian image, the Arab image (the Iraqi in particular) is of one who defends his country, makes all sacrifices, does not commit an aggression and is always the first to call for peace. On the other hand, the image of the Americans and even that of the Zionists disappears behind the total blackout imposed on 'Desert Storm', whether in respect of its reasons or its events. It is summarized as 'the mother of battles', which was an aggression the Iraqis were able to hold out against and eventually defeat, just as they were victorious in the second Qadisieh. Yet, this battle needs no elaboration, nor even illustration with photographs, in contrast to the case of the war with Iran, despite the fact that new editions of these books were published 1992–93, four years after the end of the Iraq–Iran war.

The single quick reference to good neighbourliness with Iran would not leave any impact in the midst of the hostile attributes that are repeated hundreds of times. Therefore, it could be concluded that the image Iraqi schoolbooks draw of Iran still reflects the policies and emotions of war and enmity. And it seems that there is no inclination to change this picture, even in the new editions.

The Image before the War

But there is another image, contradicting the image portrayed by the 'war books'. It returns to pre-revolution Iran. We can infer from the elements of this image what can be called a shifting, unfixed image of Iran in Iraqi schoolbooks. It is an image that is directly and sharply affected by the policies of the state and its peaceful or belligerent relations with Iran. Perhaps the researcher would discover, at another level, the scope of the change that affected notions, information and historical and geographic facts between one phase and the other. In contrast to the last phase, here we find Iran absent from the school curricula for the four years of the intermediate stage.[66] There is no mention of its defects or virtues in history, geography or education books, or even in reviews, Islamic civilization and literary texts ... while there is no disappearance, on the other hand, of praise of self, creed and system.

When some books of recent years, for that stage of schooling, point to Iran, one can see a 'positive' stance in them, in contrast to the same books adopted during the war years, and in contrast to the same historical events that these books turned to as justification for the sharp and belligerent stance towards Iran we have noted. For example, the *Modern History*[67] book, in the chapter on nationalist movements in the Near East, mentions 'the nationalist awakening that began in Iran since the call of Jamaleddin Al-Afghani to fight European colonialism ... and the patriotic movement against the tyranny of the Shah and foreign influence in 1896 ... '[68] Subsequent texts of the same book carried other 'positive' signs, appreciating Shah Reza Pahlavi's policy of 'reforming the economic and administrative situation of the country, drawing on German and Italian engineers, and American financiers to organize the financial affairs of the Iranian government ... and showing concern for reviving the country's economy by introducing factories and encouraging national industries'.[69] They affirm the positive historical cooperation between the two countries. This same text refers, in discussion of Iran's foreign policy, to the charter concluded on 8 July 1937 in Saadabad, between Turkey, Iraq, Iran and Afghanistan, 'whereby these four states have decided to consult with one another in foreign policy'.[70]

We also do not find a trace of 'the deadly hatred for the Arabs and Muslims that the Kisra, king of the Persians, showed when the Prophet sent him a letter inviting him to embrace Islam'.[71] Rather, the book *History of Arab and Islamic Civilization* limits itself to mentioning 'the letters and dispatches sent by the Prophet to the kings and princes of his time, and to Kisra and Caesar, calling on them to embrace Islam before he engages them in war'.[72] We do not find here the accusation that the Persians were behind the murder of the three Caliphs Omar, Uthman and Ali. The same history book limits itself to talking about the death of Abu Bakr, the assassination of Omar 'at the evil hands of Abu Lu'lu'ah, slave of Mughira bin Shi'ba',[73] 'the death of Uthman after being caliph for twelve years', and 'the martyrdom of Ali as he prayed in Kufa, after a dastardly assassination carried out by Abder Rahman bin Muljam'.[74]

As for the problems of 'the contiguous lands of the Arabs' brought up in the *General Geography* for Fourth General classes,[75] it is only represented in 'the existence of lands inhabited by Arab communities under the control of foreign states'. The book limits itself to referring to two basic problems – 'the Somalian Arab lands under Ethiopian and Kenyan control ... and Ethiopian domination over Eritrea'.[76] It altogether ignores the border and non-border problems with Iran, which became, as we have seen in the 'war books', a principal source of every design on Arab lands. Zionism, on the other hand, figures prominently in the book, with detailed accusations of its conspiracies and the conspiracies to occupy Palestine and other Arab lands through the wars of 1956, 1967 and 1978, with an affirmation that Zionist expansionism and accompanying aggression is a new Nazism 'that is regarded as more dangerous and a greater threat to the peace and security of peoples, in particular the Arab people, who have only one way to confront it and no other – through popular war and armed struggle ... '[77]

The Image of Iranians in Syrian Schoolbooks

The image of Iran that is drawn in the Syrian history and geography schoolbooks is rather placid. Revising the Iranian role throughout the different historical stages does not make Iran a repulsive and aggressive country, like the image presented in the Iraqi schoolbooks. The Persians are not the only ones who, in certain historical circumstances, from the Umayyad era to the contemporary age, threatened the Arab nation or annexed certain parts of it. There were also the Turks, the Mongols and the Crusaders. In addition, we have the Zionists, who represent the greatest colonialist threat in modern history. As for Iran today, it is an Islamic republic.

The Persians in the Historical Framework

(a) The Negative Aspect

This aspect was manifest through the activities of non-Arab Muslims (*mawali*), who stood against the Umayyads. It then continued with the infidels (*zanadiqa*) – a group composed mainly of Persians with atheist inclinations, who competed with Caliph Harun Ar-Rashid with their administrative expertise – and the Racists (*Shu'ubiyyah*) who tried to dominate and degrade the Arabs. The pattern continued until Iran, supported by the British, occupied some Arab islands and territories before it became an Islamic republic.

The Persian *mawalis* tried to overthrow the Umayyads, and they supported the Hashemites as a result of the Umayyads' violence in suppressing the opposition's revolutions ... And because the Umayyads did not treat them like the Arabs after they adopted Islam ... they were prepared to join any revolution that aimed to overthrow Umayyad rule.[78]

The *mawalis* are non-Arab Muslims, who grew in number in the aftermath of the fall of the Persian Empire ... Although they adopted Islam, some of them were still eager to rebuild their Empire. Thus, they conspired against security since the era of Caliph Omar, who was killed by Abu Lu'lu'ah, a Persian *mawali*. The Umayyads, who felt that the *mawali* were dangerous, denied them the right of being equal to the Arabs or appointment to top government posts.[79]

In the Abbasid era, 'Abu Jaafar Al-Mansur was successful in rooting out the *zanadiqa*, a group with atheist inclinations of a Persian majority, who were still influenced by their old culture, and who joined Islam to veil their own designs and undermine Islam and Arabism ...[80]

The Barmakids, who became prominent during the reign of Harun Ar-Rashid, were a 'Persian dynasty whose ancestor, Barmak, was a Magian who worked as a custodian of the fire temple in Balakh. Many of them became prominent at the beginning of Ar-Rashid's reign, who used to rely on them. But they soon took over the affairs of the empire, without going back to him. Thus, they competed with the Caliph with their ascending power and dominance, and he had to get rid of them and put an end to their influence.[81]

The *mawali*, led by the Persians and Turks, supported the Abbasid Empire, not only so as to be equal with the Arabs, but also to take over the government and regain their past glory. Thus, they entered into a struggle for power with the Arabs.[82]

This power struggle finds its origin in 'the Persians' old expertise in administration, especially as they occupied important posts in the Abbasid governments'. This competition between the Arabs and the Persians continued and was manifest in the conflict between Al-Amin and Al-Ma'mun. After Al-Amin became Caliph, the Arabs rallied around him because his mother was Arab, while the Persians rallied around Al-Ma'mun because his mother was Persian.[83]

The Arabs' dissatisfaction with the increasing influence of the Persians was demonstrated in many revolts, the most important of which was 'the revolt of Abdullah
bin Ali, an uncle of both Al-Mansur and As-Saffah, who considered the pledge of
allegiance to Al-Mansur as invalid and called on the people to pledge their allegiance to himself. He was supported by his military commanders, along with most
of the inhabitants of the Sham region, in a gesture that reflected their anger with
the increasing influence of the Persians ... And the revolt of Nasr bin Shabith Al-
Akili that was fomented by the increase of Persian influence during the reign of
Al-Ma'mun ... as well as many other revolts in the Sham and Iraq, which the
government was able to crush'. Rivalry was not confined to Arabs and Persians,
but included Turks as well.[84]

On the other hand, the *Shu'ubiyyah* is:

a Persian movement that acted under the pretense of equality with the Arabs, but
which went as far as trying to dominate and degrade them, as well as undermining
Islam and its teachings. This was accompanied by reviving its own religion and
cultural and linguistic heritage. This movement was motivated by *first*, the Persian
regret over the loss of their great empire, overthrown by the Arabs, whom they
considered inferior to them, and *second*, the social and economic hardships suffered
by the *mawalis*, which they blamed the Abbasid Caliphate for. Moreover, the
Shu'ubiyyah movement manifested the following: (i) Atheism, aimed at destroying
Islam, which was carried and called for by the Arabs. (ii) Revival of the Persian
heritage, and maintaining that Persians are better than Arabs. (iii) Trying to undermine the Arabs by showing their defects ... Distinguishing between the Arabs
and the Religion of Islam that came to all humankind.
The Arabs defended their language and demonstrated its greatness ... taking pride
in their ethics ... and illustrating their role in the spread of Islam ... Many defenders of Arabism emerged. Some of these were Arabs, like Al-Asma'i, while others
were of non-Arab origin, such as Al-Jahiz and Ibn Qutaibah ... [85]

The phase of Buwayhid influence, during the period when the Abbasid
caliphate was weak, is considered one of three stages: the Turkish influence
stage, the Seljuk influence stage, and the Buwayhid influence stage. 'The
Buwayhid princes shared the Caliph his authorities. One of the most important of those was Adud Al-Dawlah ... His reign was one of relative
stability ... He built mosques and hospitals in Baghdad and promoted sciences and arts.'[86]

The battle of Qadisieh, which was a basis of educational guidance in the
history and even geography schoolbooks of Iraq, is seen here as one of
many battles the Arabs fought in the course of their struggle with neighbouring nations. 'Towards the end of their rule, the Persians tried to defeat
the Mundhirites and rule over Al-Hira, but they were confronted by the
Arabian tribes in the battle of Dhu Qar (610 CE) and the Arabs were victorious. This battle acquired a nationalist character that had its impact on the
wars of liberation to drive the Persians out of the Arab territories in the
battles of Qadisieh and Buwayb'.[87]

The Arab territories Iran 'plundered', such as Ahwaz or the Arab islands in the Gulf, could not be considered an exceptional aggression or a deep-rooted hatred.[88] It is rather a 'part of the history of the colonialist struggle in the region that led to the usurpation of other parts [of the Arab territories]: the Alexandretta province, the cities of Ceuta and Melilla and the Cap des Trois Fourches islands in Arab Morocco with Spain ... '[89]

And when the Syrian schoolbooks present a historical treatment of the Persian takeover of the Arab land (Ahwaz), it concentrates – in a chapter of six pages – on the previous Iranian kings, in the period when they were fighting with the Ottomans over the province. The Britain 'started to strengthen its relations with Iran and supported Reza Pahlavi, who is known for his hostility towards the Arabs ... until the Islamic revolution was able to overthrow his son Muhammad Reza PAHLAVI.[90]

(b) The Positive Aspect

In addition to the remarks that indicate, in their general way, a negative aspect to the Persian historical role from an Arab perspective, represented by the Persian penetration of influential posts in the Arab empire, the same Syrian schoolbooks present another, parallel picture. This picture depicts the Persians as part of the world of old civilizations, which they took part in building and which they were also able to influence as well as be influenced by. They also built great Islamic cities that became scientific and intellectual centres. 'The oldest civilizations were established in Mesopotamia, Syria, the Nile Valley and the southern part of the Arabian Peninsula ... These were followed by the emergence of other civilizations in India and Persia.'[91]

In the same book, we find, in a chapter that deals with civilizations, a survey of the Persian civilization. It states: 'The Persian civilization, in contrast with the other civilizations, is characterized by the administrative organization that divided the empire into vilayets (provinces) ... the Judiciary and the establishment of justice, religious doctrines, writing and architecture.'[92]

In Persia, the most important industries were cotton weaving, linen, and carpets ... Egypt, Spain, the Arab Maghreb, Persia and Khurasan were trade centres ... [93]

The impact of the Persians and their habits extended to neighbouring Arab regions, which used to celebrate certain Persian feasts during the Abbasid era: The Nawruz (beginning of Spring), the Mahrajan (beginning of Winter) ... The eastern regions were also influenced by the Persian feasts.[94]

The school at Jundishapur that was established during the reign of the Persian King Sabur I, was 'a source of Greek culture ... and its influence on the Arabs was evident in the field of medicine ... '[95]

On the academic level, and especially in the domains of writing or translation:

A number of writers of Persian origin translated their people's heritage into Arabic ... In addition, the Arabs were familiar with Persian literature and proverbs ... On the social level, the Arab people were influenced by Persian habits in dining, dress and feasts ... The judges and high government officials donned tall head-pieces ...[96]

The Arabs [before Islam] were familiar with the medicine of neighbouring peoples, such as that of the Persians and the Indians.[97]

And when the second intermediate history book talks about the foreign invasion of the Arab homeland during the Abbasid era, a chapter of 15 pages (pp. 141–56) talks about the Crusader and Mongol invasions only: 'As for the colonialist ambitions in the outskirts of the Arabian Peninsula, it does not involve the Persians (as in the case of the Iraqi books), for we find Portuguese, Dutch and British ambitions only'.[98]

As for the current status of Iran, it is quite different than its previous history. The definition presented by Lesson 24, which introduces Iran as one of the countries of Asia, states that it is 'a republic, where an Islamic popular anti-Zionist revolution has emerged ... It supports liberation movements.'[99]

Although this is what the lesson considers sufficient as a political definition of Iran (the rest of the lesson deals with the climate, population, location, resources, etc.), it is the only country that receives such a positive definition. The lessons that deal with all other countries, including Turkey, India and even African countries, start directly with the location and borders, without any introduction on the political system.[100]

Moreover, the *History of Modern Times*, Vol. II, dedicates a special lesson to the Islamic revolution in Iran, in which it briefly (no more than two pages) outlines the reasons and circumstances that led to the revolution. It ends by emphasizing the corruption of the Shah's regime, which 'the Islamic revolution, led by Ayatollah Al-Khomeini, was able to defeat on February 11, 1978'. It also states that 'the Islamic Republic of Iran withdrew from CENTO and joined the Non-Aligned Movement in 1979. It also recognized the Palestine Liberation Organization and closed the Embassy of the Zionist State'.[101]

On the other hand, the other revolutions that are discussed in the book are dealt with rather extensively. The Chinese revolution, for example, was treated in two chapters of 18 pages (135–52), and the Vietnamese revolution was also dealt with in two chapters of 14 pages. In contrast, the Iranian revolution was covered in two pages only (178–9).

Observations and Conclusions

The Syrian schoolbooks do not present a dark image of the Iranians. And even when they do, they do not consider it a result of an aggressive tendency or a deep-rooted hatred; they merely present it as events. And when these books talk about the anti-Arab movements, they do not single out the Persians, but talk in an objective manner about these movements 'that included many Persians'. They also explain the social and political reasons that made the Persians or the *mawalis* revolt. But all this does not lead to a special and promising image of Iran; rather it is referred to as an Islamic republic whose policies differ from those of the Shah, without any praise or exaggeration.

The elements of this image are presented in a context of a series of historical and current events. Concentration in more than one book on the Arabian lands occupied by the Persians or Iran does not prevent them, when they talk about the contemporary history, to focus on the Islamic transformation in Iran and in its policies. That is, there is a general commitment in these books to see Iran from a nationalist Arab perspective that stresses Arab rights on the one hand, and, on the other, viewing Iran from an objective perspective that does not neglect the changes it has witnessed. Furthermore, the developments in Iranian–Arab relations, especially the eight-year war with Iraq, are not mentioned in these books. This means that they avoid discussion of the contemporary Arab–Iranian struggle or its causes and consequences.

But the other element that is strongly emphasized, and considered by the Syrian books as the greatest threat to the Arab nation, is the Zionist element, before which pales the negative side of the Iranian image. For the Zionist threat is a racist threat, its colonialism typical of the colonial settler-states transforming into a thrust of imperialism into the Arab homeland, its tasks to fluster national liberation movements, increase backwardness and fragmentation, thwart Arab development plans by creating tensions and threaten peace and security in the region.[102] On the other hand, Iran was never described in this manner, or called such even in its old Persian history.

The Image of the Iranians in Egyptian Schoolbooks

More than any other image, the Egyptian schoolbooks are dominated by the self-image. The common factor between the two secondary series of the history and geography books is Egypt, which is always present, whether studying ancient civilizations, contemporary history, geography of the Arab homeland or the Nile Basin, and, of course, in the books entitled *Egypt My*

Homeland and *Egypt and the World*. Thus, Egypt nearly fills all the academic texts that the students are supposed to study in History and Geography. Moreover, this image does not rely on any basis of comparison that could indicate its existence, strength and importance. Rather it is enough to speak about 'the heritage of the past and the deep-rooted civilization'. But this does not mean that the other images are totally absent. We have the image of the Arab homeland, the Persian, the Israeli, the African and others.

Nevertheless, these books do not present a clear and sharp image of the Iranians. Talking about the Iranians is restricted to their role in some remote historical events. The more these books approach the present, the less pronounced the image, until it becomes invisible, as if Iran is not in the same geo-political region Egypt is part of. Furthermore, what could be considered as an Iranian image in the past is not one of foe or enemy. The events these books narrate are presented in a calm and chronological manner.

The Image of the Persians in Ancient History

When the geography book talks about the ancient history of the Persians, it merely indicates that they were 'unable to drive away the Arab tribes who came from the Yemen to the fertile region west of the Euphrates, in a place called al-Hira. Then the Persians made them their allies against the attacks of the other Arab tribes. In addition, they could help the Persians, in their war against the Byzantines'.[103]

But this does not mean that the Persians did not have a civilization. This fact is stated in one of the questions at the end of the lesson, which reads: 'Why was the civilization of the Mundhirites and the Ghassanids affected by that of the Yemeni, Persian and Byzantine?[104]

The Persians are mentioned several times in the same historical framework:

Some of the Arab tribes knew the Monotheistic Religions, while the Persians spread Judaism in Yemen.[105]

During the reign of Omar bin al-Khattab, the Arabs were able to achieve decisive victories against Chosroes in Persia.[106]

But some of the *mawalis* were saddened by the fact that their empire was destroyed and that they became subject to the Arabs. Thus, one of them, Abu Lu'lu'ah Fairuz, the Persian Magian, plotted to kill Omar and stabbed him with a poisoned dagger.[107]

Iraq became a part of the Persian Empire, until it was invaded by Alexander the Great in the year 220 BC ... The Persians then entered Iraq for the second time, and it became a battleground on which the Romans and Persians fought, until it was conquered by the Arabs in 622 CE. Iraq then entered into a new prosperous era, the Islamic Era.[108]

And in the context of emphasizing the importance of the Arab homeland and its strategic location, the Persians are treated as one of the major political powers that tried to dominate the Arab homeland since ancient times:

The Persians took control of the seas that surround the Arab homeland, so as to take hold of its land. The Romans tried to do the same thing in the second century before Christ. In addition, the Mongol Asian invasion and the European Crusader campaigns were waged for the same purpose.[109]

As for the battle of Qadisieh, in which the Persians were defeated by the Muslim Arabs, it is not treated as an occasion that calls for taking pride in Arabism or being sceptical of the Persians' intentions and defaming them.[110]

It was merely a historical event, and one of the stages of the Islamic conquest. 'When Abu Bakr was finished with the apostasy war, he sent an army led by Khalid bin al-Walid to conquer Iraq and seize it from the Persians. Khalid was successful in entering Hira ... and when Omar became Caliph, he sent an army of 20 thousand strong, led by Saad bin Abi Waqqas, to Iraq. This army confronted the Persians and defeated them at the locale of Qadisieh on 15 AH/637 CE. Yazdigird, the king of Persia, fled ... And he was dealt a decisive blow by the Arab army ... Persia became a part of the Islamic Empire, and the Persians embraced Islam and the Arabs called them *mawali*'.[111]

But when we research the Abbasid era, the Persians are once again considered as non-Arabs who took part in the fragmentation of the nation:

The first indications of fragmentation began in the second Abbasid era, when the caliphs sought the assistance of non-Arab elements such as the Persians, who played an important role in establishing the Abbasid Empire in the beginning, and the Turks ... These elements took advantage of the weakness of the Abbasid caliphate ...[112]

But these roles the Persians played, and their defeat by the Muslim army, did not conceal in the Egyptian textbooks their sophisticated civilization, which the Arabs interacted with and learned from.

The Islamic conquests led to Arab contact with the old civilizations, the Greek, Roman, Persian, Indian and Chinese.[113]

Influenced by the Persians, the Arabs adopted the *diwan* system in the Islamic administration.[114]

A translation movement emerged, and books were translated from Greek, Indian and Persian into Arabic.[115]

Iranians in the Modern Age

As we approach the modern age, the old Iranian image disappears, and it is replaced by an image that is neutral in all the conflicts over borders and territories, even those with the Arabs. For the Egyptian books do not lay stress on the Iranian occupation of the three islands, Lesser Tunb, Greater Tunb and Abu Musa, or the Ahwaz region, as is the case in the Iraqi and Syrian schoolbooks.

Hormuz, for example, is 'an important strait that joins the Arabian Gulf and the Gulf of Oman. It is bordered by Iran from the north and northeast, and by Oman from the west and southwest. There are some rocky islands near it, such as the islands of Quthum and Abu Musa. Its importance is demonstrated by the fact that it is the only sea outlet for a number of countries'.[116]

This book does not remind us of the role of this strait in the Iraq–Iran war, which is also mentioned in the Egyptian history and geography books, but it does not fail to talk about the British occupation of Bab al-Mandab because of its importance 'since 1839, and British had occupied the island of Bureim 40 years earlier'.[117]

The land borders of the Arab homeland continue southward until they reach the northern end of the Arabian Gulf, where they extend in the middle of a number of contiguous plains in both Iran and Iraq (the plain of Shatt al-Arab). This region is disputed between these countries, and this has not yet been resolved.[118]

And while the Syrian and Iraqi schoolbooks talk about occupied regions in the Arab world, such as Ahwaz and the Alexandretta province, the Egyptian books do not see any continuing occupation except in Palestine. 'The Arab nation acquired a strategic [military] importance, since it controls the major air, sea and land routes. This made the colonialist great powers fight over it since the end of the 18th century, and divide it into small states. The Arab nation struggled for liberation, until all its states, with the exception of occupied Palestine, gained independence'.[119]

Moreover, what has been said about Iranian ambitions or threats against the Arab nation, as well as its history and culture, is not seen as such in Egyptian schoolbooks: 'The natural boundaries of the Arab nation prevented the infiltration of non-Arab elements, including the Turkish and

Persian elements, except on a small scale that did not have an impact on the character of the Arab nation'.[120]

The Egyptian books do not detail the events of the eight-year war between Iraq and Iran, nor do they outline its political and military causes. They do not even indicate the time the war began, in the aftermath of the victory of the Islamic revolution – a major transformation that is also not mentioned. The only indication of this war is in the context of commending Egypt's role, activity and participation in regional, international, Islamic and Arab organizations. In this context, there is mention of a resolution that was issued by the Islamic Conference, which was 'an appeal calling both Islamic warring states (Iran and Iraq) to halt all military operations and resort to negotiations to solve their problems'. It also formed 'a committee to seek the consent of both states to achieve these goals'.[121]

Iran, therefore, is an Islamic state, just like Iraq. Moreover, neither Iran nor Iraq is an aggressor, since the international resolutions do not so state, but merely call on both parties to resolve their current problems through negotiations. This neutral attitude is evident also when the schoolbooks deal with each Arab country, avoiding any reference to differences, whether with other Arab countries or with non-Arab neighbouring countries such as Iran; but this applies to the new editions of books published during the academic year 1994–95. Even when the subject of the lesson is Iraq and there is mention of its population figure by the 1988 census, no link is made with the war with Iran and the obvious loss of lives that was one of the results of the war. It seems that refraining from dealing with political problems or military wars is intentional, in contrast to the official Egyptian policy that has taken a clear position on the Iran–Iraq war or the Iraqi occupation of Kuwait. When the books treat the subject of the contemporary history of Kuwait, there is no mention whatsoever of its occupation by Iraq, or of the second Gulf war, which Egyptian armed forces took part in as part of the international alliance of forces.

The Enemy is not Iran

But what is noticeable in this educational policy, as inferred from the Egyptian schoolbooks, is the concentration on the various historical stages of Israeli aggression and usurpation of Palestine, which is repeated in a clear and distinct manner. But this does not mean that the peace process and the Camp David accord, which Egypt signed with Israel, are not mentioned in some of these books.

The Arab used oil as an economic weapon in the October 1973 war, when they banned its export to the foreign countries that helped Israel in its aggression against the Arabs ... [122]

When reference is made to the role of Egypt and the Arab League in confronting Arab problems, the example of the Palestine Question is again the illustration:

... The Arab armies intervened in the aftermath of the establishment of the state of Israel on the Palestinian territories in 1948. They almost succeeded in their attempt to drive the Zionists out of Palestine, were it not for the intervention of the European states and the United States ... [123]

In the book entitled *The Geography of the Arab Homeland and its History in the Islamic Era*, meant for the second intermediate class, more than one chapter is dedicated to explaining, in detail, the Palestine cause, including the Balfour Declaration, the Palestine War in 1948, the tri-partite aggression on Egypt in 1956, the Zionist aggression in 1967, the October war in 1973, the peace agreement between Egypt and Israel, and the Palestinian *intifadah*.[124] Moreover, the questions at the end of the lessons, which aim at grounding the ideas in the mind of the student, stress the usurpation of Palestine, the *intifadah* and the tripartite aggression against Egypt.[125] On the other hand, the books do not mention any such details, negative or positive, when discussing modern Iran.

The call for Arab integration, which concludes the book *Geography of the Arab Homeland* for second intermediate, is not directed against any of the Arabs' neighbours. Rather it has an economic basis, 'for the realities of the contemporary problems and the regional and international circumstances have made the adoption of the principle of economic integration between countries extremely important, since there is no longer any place for small and fragmented entities in a world of giant economic and political associations.'[126]

Observations and Conclusions

Egyptian schoolbooks are interested only in concentrating on the role of Egypt and its civilization, which extends to its regional environment and its relations with the rest of the world. Thus, the titles and the chapters of Egyptian history and geography books discuss the African, Arab and international spheres that Egypt wishes to stress it belongs to. These spheres can be arranged according to the titles of the books, as follows:

Egypt, My Homeland
The Geography of the Arab Homeland
The Geography of the Arab Homeland and its History in the Islamic Era
The Modern History of Egypt and the Arabs
Egypt and the World

Egypt and the Civilizations of the Ancient World

Thus, there is no special interest in, or concentration on, Iran. And the books do not have a positive or negative image, if we set aside the old historical events that are related to the Persians' role. On the contrary, these books try to present, as we mentioned earlier, a neutral Iran, without trying to deprive it of its Islamic character. It can be further said that this is true for all Egyptian relations these books deal with. There is no political, security or border problem with any other state or political movement, with the exception, as mentioned earlier, of the focus on Zionist aggression, the usurpation of Palestine, the peace with Israel, and the Palestinian uprising. The tense Egyptian–Iranian relations, severed diplomatic relations and attacks of the media of each country towards other countries, have formed a negative image in the public opinion of both countries. But this image was not entered into Egyptian schoolbooks.

The Image of the Iranians in Moroccan Schoolbooks

The main section in all Moroccan history schoolbooks, for both elementary and secondary stages, is concern with Morocco and its history. This section may make up in certain cases two-thirds of the whole book (12 out of 19 chapters of the history book for 7th elementary). And since Morocco is a member of the Association of Maghreb Countries, including Tunisia, Algeria and Libya, Moroccan schoolbooks dedicate a number of chapters to talk about these countries, in addition, of course, to material on Morocco.

Iran does not have any particular image in Moroccan schoolbooks. But its absence does not seem intentional, for the concentration on Morocco and the Maghreb does not warrant any positive or negative reference to Iran. The themes the chapters of these books draw for themselves are the Arab and African spheres. And even when they convey to the student the experiences of other nations, they choose these experiences randomly, without any logical sequence or justification. They start, for example (the 7th primary grade), with Europe between 13th and 17th centuries; then they move to the Islamic East (al-Mashriq), and finally to the Islamic West (al-Maghreb) and the founding of the Maghreb states and civilization.

Another book (8th primary) surveys what happened in Europe and America between 17th and 19th centuries, and then it moves to the Muslim world and Africa, focusing on the Maghreb and its states. As for the modern age, it discusses the most important international developments until the end of the Second World War, and then it moves to the liberation movements of the world, starting with al-Mashriq al-Arabi and then the

Maghrib al-Arabi, where it dedicates a separate chapter to each country (Algeria, Tunisia, Morocco).

The 9th grade book deals with the liberation movements in the Far East and Africa. Then it moves from the ancient civilization to the supremacy of Islamic civilization in the Middle Ages, and then the emergence of the Maghreb states and civilization (1st secondary).

The liberation movements discussed in the history book of the 2nd secondary year are the nationalist movements in Europe. And when this book deals with the resistance against European expansionism in the Muslim world, al-Maghrib al-Arabi absorbs the largest part of these lessons.

And when one of the history lessons deals with the general developments in Turkey and the Arab countries (the history book of the 3rd secondary), it does not find a place for Iran, whether it talks about the liberation movements, or any of the other features attributed to many of the European, African and Muslim world countries, especially those of the Maghreb. Thus, Iran is not present. This means that the transformations it witnessed, such as the victory of the Islamic revolution, the war with Iraq, or even its border and island problems, are also absent. The Moroccan student learns to belong to Morocco first and last, and the Maghreb in which Morocco lies. Furthermore, all these lessons do not describe any country as being a friend or an enemy; they only present certain historical events, such as those of the Palestinian cause and the Arab–Israeli conflict, which end with the international recognition of the PLO in 1974. As for belonging to the Arab nation, as the Syrian, Iraqi and even Egyptian books emphasize, it simply is not there, and there is no reference to such a sense of belonging.

Because Iran does not have any borders with Morocco, or any historical relations with the Maghreb region, its absence from the history and geography books becomes natural. The only image the history books present is that of the Persian who played a role in Islamic history. Furthermore, this image does not leave any negative impression, or convey any feeling of hatred. On the contrary, it presents a balanced picture that relates the historical events all researchers agree on, without going into discussion of ideologies or racial and political provocation. 'The Abbasid caliphate, which unified the Islamic East, ended with the fall of Baghdad; then attempts by other dynasties, like the Mamluk and Safavid, to unify the region emerged'.[127]

The same neutral attitude, and absence of a political environment that could reveal hatred or enmity, is maintained when the history books define the Safavid dynasty:

The Safavid dynasty emerged in Iran in the aftermath of the deterioration of the Mongol empire and emergence of petty dynasties. The Safavid dynasty was founded by Shah Ismail ... one of the followers of Sheikh Ishaq Safi El-Dine, whose chroniclers consider him to be a descendant of the Shiite Imam Musa al-Kazim.

Sheikh Safi El-Dine is the founding father of the Safavid dynasty ... And since its establishment, the Safavid dynasty was engaged in successive conflicts with the Sunni Ottoman Empire, which sought to join all the Islamic world under its rule ... The Safavid dynasty reached the peak of its power during the reign of Shah Abbas al-Kabir. After his death, it began to deteriorate quickly, until it fell in 1148 AH/1735 CE.[128]

The Persians are also mentioned when the lessons deal with Islamic history and the Abbasid era. The Abbasids had relied heavily on the Persians to manage the affairs of government, which 'made the caliphate system influenced by the Sassanian system of government, which in turn was based on the principle of divine right of kings ... '[129] But this is not meant as a value judgement. It is simply stating facts in a way consistent with how Persian civilization is dealt with, for the method of military organization adopted by the Orthodox Caliphs was also obtained from the Persians: 'To enroll in the army and its various ranks and leadership ... '[130] The Safavids were also concerned with civilization ... They also organized the army and established certain military industries, like guns, which they manufactured with the help of the British. They constructed roads and canals, as well as rest houses and caravansaries all over Iran. They also promoted cultural life, especially in the fields of jurisprudence, philosophy and natural sciences. Furthermore, architecture was a field they particularly excelled in. The Safavids were not concerned with establishing a caliphate, as the Mamluks did; rather, they founded a Shiite state whose sect is different from the Sunnite in the remainder of the Islamic East.[131]

The two history books (1st secondary and 7th elementary) do mention Persian civilization, when they draw a chart showing the chronology of ancient civilizations. They cite one of the old books to talk about the grandeur of the art of tapestries in the Safavids' country.

Even the *mawalis*, whom the other Arab history books claim to be racists of a Persian majority, the history book of the 1st secondary offers a 'fair' image of, in which it lists the political and social reasons that led to the deprival of their rights. It also lists the fields they excelled in. But it does not indicate the race they belonged to.

The *mawalis* were the largest social group in number. They were the native population of the conquered lands, who adopted Islam, and whose majority used to work in farming and handicrafts. During the time of the Umayyads, the status of the *mawali* was affected by Arab policy, which aimed at monopolizing political power, leadership and wealth, a policy of superiority towards some of the Persian middle and lower classes, which was evident in the inequality of treatment they received in many areas.

This policy was reflected in the support of the Persian *mawalis* for the Abbasid movement. Then when the Abbasid movement succeeded, it permitted the Persians to participate in the high ranks of government and administration.

The distinction of the *mawalis* in the Abbasid era was evident in their intellectual contributions, especially in the fields of religion and the legal sciences. They became judges and directors, and gained a wide reputation as well as influence and power in many Islamic lands.[132]

Thus, there are no elements in the Moroccan history and geography books that could form a contemporary image of Iran. It is a trans-boundary country with no direct relations or problems with Morocco. Consequently, the transformations of contemporary Iran are also absent. On the other hand, the civilization and colonialist history of European countries is discussed in these books, probably because Morocco has more direct contacts with these than any other country. This may also be due to the concentration on Morocco and the Maghreb, and the absence of the concept of the Arab nation, which is not referred to in any of the history and geography books for all stages. Iran and its problems with the Arab countries are also absent. For the books divide the Arabs into Mashriq and Maghreb, and the focus is on the Maghreb countries alone.

The Image of Iranians in Saudi Schoolbooks

History and geography in Saudi Arabia are taught in the intermediate and secondary stages. There are 34 textbooks that cover both courses, almost evenly divided. The lessons focus mainly on two fundamental themes: the Islamic world, and Saudi Arabia. These themes are under the following headings: the prophets and their messages; the Islamic Empire during the reign of the Orthodox Caliphs; the Islamic Empire during the Umayyads, Abbasids and Ottomans; the internal and external waves of aggression against the Islamic world; historical Muslim personalities; the fundamental message and biography of Muhammad bin Abdel Wahhab; the Saudi state in its three stages, and the biography of its kings in the modern age; the Zionist threat and the history of the Palestine Question; and the features of modern civilization. These same headings are repeated in the geography books (the geography of the Islamic world and its countries, the geography of Saudi Arabia and its relations with these countries), and they occupy the major part of the programme, leaving only a few lessons for natural and population geography.

In all these lessons, there does not seem to be a special image of Iran. The scope of interest in all Islamic countries leaves no special place for Iran. On the other hand, the good relations Saudi Arabia enjoys with the

Arab and Islamic nations do not extend to Iran, despite the fact that there is a big difference in the emphasis on relations between one country and another. And although the battles the Persians fought against the Muslim armies in the early conquests are narrated in detail, the image of contemporary Iran is not affected by what the Persians had done in the past. Moreover, the image itself remains in its historical framework, without any direct or indirect provocation against the Persians as a people or as being hostile to the Arabs. Talking about their remote history is no more controversial to the reader than the image of the Mongols' savagery. Therefore, it can be said that the image of Iran is, in the first place, the image of ancient Persia, with no attempt to link it or link its people with contemporary Iran.

Persian Battles against the Islamic Armies

These battles started during the reign of the first Orthodox Caliph, who sent Khalid bin al-Walid at the head of an army to Iraq, to fight the Persians who 'refused the invitation to Islam'. The most important battles between the Persians and the Muslims were:

1. Al-Jisr, at the Euphrates River; this was the only battle won by the Persians.
2. Al-Buwayb, also on the Euphrates; the Persians were defeated and their commander killed.
3. Al-Qadisieh, west of Hira; the Persians were defeated after they had lost 30 thousand soldiers.
4. Al-Mada'in (Ctesiphon); the Persian capital fell to the hands of the Muslims.
5. Nahawand; in this battle, the Persians tried to regain what they lost, but were defeated. The Muslims took over Nahawand, and Persia's cities began to fall into Muslim hands.[133]

On the battle of Qadisieh, we notice that, while the other Arab schoolbooks refer to this as an important battle fought against the Persians, the history book of the first intermediate[134] stands alone in presenting a detailed account of four pages on all the Persian battles against the Islamic armies, including number of casualties, military tactics of siege, counterattacks, withdrawal and endgame ... But this detailed description is but a recording of chronological events, without accusing the Persians of harbouring a special hatred towards the Arabs. Thus, the general picture is one of heroism of the Muslim army during its confrontation with a stronger and better equipped army.

The Arab conquests in the Umayyad era are treated in a similar manner:

Persia and Khurasan were conquered during the reign of the Orthodox Caliphs. The Umayyads continued the conquest in the East: Qutaibah bin Muslim conquered the most important kingdoms, such as that of Takharistan, Khwarazm and Saghad, whose most important cities are Bukhara and Samarkand ... Not only did Qutaibah conquer these kingdoms, but he also called on their people to embrace Islam ...[135]

The Abbasids grew aware, since the beginning of their rule, of the danger represented by Abu Muslim al-Khurasani, not by the *mawalis* or Persians, as other books have it. They realized his ambitions ... and his great influence over the people of Khurasan ... When he was killed, some Persian extremists revolted against the Empire. Al-Mansur fought them and crushed them.[136]

The Persians, too, and as mentioned by the other Arab schoolbooks, had a role to play in the weakening and fall of the Abbasid Empire:

The Abbasid Empire gave equal treatment to all its Muslim subjects, and paved the way for some of the Persians who were looking, since the Umayyad era, for a chance to overthrow the Arabs. This policy brought in some new peoples, such as the Turks, the original Egyptians and North Africans, who were not concerned with the interests of the Empire as much as their own interests.[137]

As for the *Shu'ubiyyah*, one of the main causes of the weakening and decline of the Umayyad Empire, there is no mention of its Persian origin:

The *Shu'ubiyyah* appeared among the non-Arab Muslims, known as the *mawalis*, who saw that the Umayyads were relying on the Arab tribes to occupy all the important posts, despite the fact that the Persians constituted a large part of the population. They resorted to persecution and supported any movement that rose against the Umayyad Empire.[138]

As ministers during the rule of Harun ar-Rashid, the Persians 'were able to convince him to appoint Al-Ma'mun as heir apparent of Al-Amin and as a ruler of Khurasan. They also convinced him of appointing Al-Qasim as a ruler of Arabia. And that was considered the first division the Islamic Empire underwent.'[139] The Persians who helped the Abbasids were rewarded by 'the highest civil and military posts. But they tried to overthrow the caliphs and restore the old order of Persia ... Nevertheless, the Abbasid caliphs crushed them.'[140]

The Safavid State and the Shiite Sect

The Safavid state is discussed in the context of the states that were competing over the central Islamic lands. The Safavid state ruled over Iran, parts of Iraq and the eastern part of Anatolia, with Tabriz as its capital. It was headed by Shah Ismail al-Safavi, who was famous for his expansionist ambitions and his partiality towards the Shiite sect.[141]

Shah Ismail tried to spread the Shiite doctrine in Anatolia and incited rebellion against the Ottomans ... until he was defeated by the Ottoman Sultan Selim I.[142]

The Saudi schoolbooks fail to point to any kind of cultural or civilizational interaction resulting from the contacts between the Persians and the Muslim Arabs.

Nationalism as a Reactionary Call

Saudi schoolbooks stress the importance of the Islamic identity, as evident in the lessons and introductions of the history and geography books, 'which draw the attention of the student to the fact that the Islamic world is but one nation, regardless of across how many continents its countries are spread'.[143] However, the Arab world enjoys a special position in this [Islamic] world (elaborated on in one chapter only), which is due neither to Arabism nor to the common nationalism, but because of its religious importance as the origin of the Celestial Books.[144]

Nationalism did not play any role in shaping this world. Moreover, it was never called for, nor was there an interest in it. Thus, the Saudi schoolbooks ignore any mention of nationalism or the Arab nationalist call in modern Arab history. When these books discuss the importance of the Arab world and its desire for liberation, both political and economic, from Ottoman rule, they only mention that the countries of the Arab world have struggled to achieve these goals and have changed from backward states into developing states. Furthermore, the fundamental condition for these countries to become a strong nation is by 'implementation of the Islamic *Shari'ah* (Law) and strengthening of faith in the Muslims' hearts'.[145]

The words 'homeland' and 'nationalism' do not have a place in Saudi schoolbooks, whether for incorporation or even in talking about those who believe in them. There is only an Arab world and some Arab states: 'Some of the lands of the Arab world have been graced with a huge source of prosperity, as much as the Arab world's countries can produce' ... 'The countries of the Arab world consume only a small portion of their oil' ... 'The states of the Arab world that oil pipes pass through its territories' ... 'The Arab world occupies an excellent geographic position'. 'The Zionist entity was founded as a base for colonialist and Zionist interests in the heart of the Arab world'.[146]

In addition to avoiding any reference to the Arab homeland or nation or

nationalism, as the Syrian, Egyptian and Iraqi books do, and in addition to
emphasis on belonging to the Islamic world and its one nation, the Saudi
schoolbooks maintain that, after communism and heretical religious calls,
nationalism 'is one of the elements of internal aggression against the Islamic world in the modern age. It is a secular calling and a new kind of
'asabiyah known to many nations in the past ... Arab nationalism is a fanatical ideological and political movement that calls for the glorification of
the Arabs and founding of a unified Arab state, on the basis of bonds of
blood, kinship and history instead of the ties of religion. It is a reverbera-
tion of nationalist thought that had previously emerged in Europe'.[147]

As to how it was established: 'Many countries, and especially Britain,
which aimed at occupying the Islamic East, encouraged and promoted the
call of Arab nationalism ... ' Moreover, 'the purely nationalist call is a reactionary call ... ' Sheikh Ibn Baz describes it as 'a pre-Islamic call that aims
at fighting Islam ... and doing away with its rulings and teachings ... It
was initiated by Western Christians for the purpose of fighting Islam and
destroying it in its own home with ornate rhetoric ... It is a false call, a
grave error, a patent deceit, an abominable ignorance and a malicious plot
against Islam and the Muslims.'[148]

In contrast, we have the concept of the Islamic world, 'which refers to all
the countries Islam entered and left its impact on ... It includes all Muslims all over the world ... who share the same history that starts with the
establishment of Islamic rule in Medinah al-Munawwarah and the Muslim conquests ... ' The Muslims possess all elements of power that enable
their nation to occupy the place it deserves, as ordained in the Holy Qur'an:
'You are the best of nations evolved for Mankind'.[149]

Iran: An Old Islamic Image

As a result of this Islamic, not nationalist, loyalty, these books view Iran as
part of the Islamic nation and not as a racist or nationalist enemy. It is 'an
Islamic country that had a great civilization ... The Iranians, an Indo–
European race, have settled in this country in ancient times and built villages
and cities and founded civilizations; many of its monuments still stand today ... The ancient Iranians adopted the Magian religion, which was
introduced by Zoroaster and is based on polytheism and fire worship. Islam spread quickly in Persia ... and it rescued its inhabitants and brought
them ... to the embrace of Islam ... and great good poured onto the land.'[150]

The history of Iran ends with Iran embracing Islam. There is no mention of all contemporary developments, whether before the Shah or after
the victory of the Islamic revolution. When the geography book talks about
the Iranian population and their language, it only says 'that the Persian

language is the official language. It is written with the Arabic alphabet, and every nationality has its own language, in addition to the Persian language, bearing in mind that all religious schools for all these communities teach the Arabic language'.[151] We are not told if teaching Arabic is an old or new practice; learning Arabic has become obligatory in all schools after the victory of the Islamic revolution. Furthermore, the absence of the modern and contemporary aspects of Iranian history does not extend to all the countries or issues discussed in the Saudi history books. For example, talking about Afghanistan is associated with support of Saudi Arabia to Afghanistan against the [former] Soviet Union. 'The Islamic republics used to be a part of the former Soviet Union'.[152]

The books give other examples of contemporary disputes, such as the West Sahara problem between Morocco and Algeria, the problems of Kashmir and Pakistan, presented as internal conflicts between the sons of the Islamic nation that colonialism was the cause of.[153]

The Self-Image: The Kingdom of Saudi Arabia is the Basis of Islamic Solidarity

The image of Saudi Arabia is drawn within the framework of the Islamic world. In this context, it is a picture of a country that always takes the initiative to safeguard the Muslims' unity and solidarity and elevate their nation's prestigious position. Thus, Saudi Arabia has sought to follow this course throughout the reign of all its leaders, including the custodian of the two Holy Mosques (King Fahd). In accordance with the teachings of Islam, it contributed both money and effort to an unimaginable extent. It was also the first to participate in anything that would unify the Arabs and their stand.

After the late King Abdel Aziz, King Faisal continued to raise the banner of Islamic solidarity. He proceeded to explain this call for Islamic solidarity on every occasion ... The late King Faisal translated words into deeds, whether as his policy or in a degree of generosity that was unimaginable.

Faisal's call for Islamic solidarity is not something new to Islam and the Muslims, for it is rooted and originates in the teachings of Islam ... According to these tenets ... can King Faisal's call for Islamic solidarity really be regarded as a *Salafi* [fundamentalist] call, or is it not instead a response to the age of global coalitions and the age of the atom? Thus, he fulfills the wish of his great predecessor, the late King Abdel Aziz, who sought to maintain the Arabian Peninsula as the land of descent of Islam and fountainhead of Light.[154]

King Khalid bin Abdel Aziz followed his predecessor's plan in calling for Islamic solidarity ... For his part, the custodian of the two Holy Mosques, King Fahd bin Abdel Aziz, continues to make every effort for the sake of the call of Islamic solidarity. He has reaffirmed that he intends to follow the path of his pious predecessors in considering Islam as the basis of the internal and external policies of Saudi Arabia. The role of Saudi Arabia in promoting the idea of Islamic solidarity is fundamental ... ever since its originator, the late King Faisal bin Abdel Aziz, began to call for it ... It has also played a major role in founding the League of the Islamic World, and in ensuring the success of the Islamic Summit Conference in Rabat and the Islamic Conference of Foreign Ministers of Islamic States in Jeddah.[155]

Saudi Arabia also supported the causes of the Arab countries: 'It was always the first to take part in anything that could unite the word of the Arabs and strengthen their ranks, and it always supported any general Arab effort.'[156]

King Abdel Aziz was at the head of those who supported the Palestinians, both morally and materially, to defend themselves and their country. The leaders of Saudi Arabia have always considered the Palestinian cause as the 'main Arab and Islamic cause'.[157] The late King Faisal 'proceeded to unify the Muslims' word and ranks'.[158] Thus, the image of Saudi Arabia is composed of the following elements:

1. Saudi Arabia is the heart of the Islamic world, and the place where its Qiblah is located.
2. The Islamic civilization that promoted human progress originated from here.
3. The Kingdom is accomplishing major achievements in all scientific, economic, cultural and engineering fields.
4. The Kingdom is assuming a major role in solving the world's oil problems.
5. It is playing a major role in solving the urgent problems of Islamic countries.[159]

Saudi Arabia and Iran

When Saudi schoolbooks talk about Saudi Arabia's relations with Arab and Islamic countries, the part dealing with Iran is rather cold compared to others. These books do not talk about the nature of the problems between the two countries since the victory of the Islamic revolution (the complications related to the Hajj and the tensions in their relations generally), but rather focus on the historical side of the relationship and then proceed quickly to current relations, which are confined to oil issues and Iranian participation in the Hajj:

Iran's relations with the Kingdom of Saudi Arabia are old and historic, and go back to the time the Arabs conquered that country to spread Islam. As for the present time, Iran and Saudi Arabia enjoy close relations based on religious ties and the common interests in the field of economic cooperation, especially in oil issues ... A large number of Iranian pilgrims attend the Hajj each year.[160]

But when it comes to other Islamic countries, like Turkey and Pakistan, relations become extremely warm, united by the word of unity and support of Islam, especially the Palestinian cause. 'Turkey has old and historic relations with the Kingdom. They currently enjoy very close relations that are based on Islamic ties that join their peoples in support of Islam. These ties are further consolidated by economic cooperation and regular visits to arrive at unified views on issues of common interest, and to draw plans to support the causes of the Islamic states and solve their problems, especially the cause of Palestine'.[161]

Saudi Arabia and Pakistan are linked 'by unbreakable ties of Islamic brotherhood and spiritual affection ... Pakistan is also one of the important Islamic states that responds favourably with the Muslims on the Palestinian cause'.[162]

The bonds with the countries of the Arab world are also based on religion, support for Muslim causes and cooperation in the various fields. Of these ties, the only ones that apply in the Iraqi case are religion and cooperation in the field of oil. 'Even Iraq is tied with the Kingdom by the bonds of religion, blood, language and common borders. The two countries are linked together by cultural and economic ties, especially with regard to the oil issue ... And they are both members of the League of Arab States'.[163]

The image of relations with Iraq is similar to Iran, for there is no mention in both of the contemporary problems, and the ties are merely historical. If we compare this with Saudi Arabia's relations with other Arab countries, we discover how big the difference in tone is. The Kingdom 'works with Libya to uphold the rights of the Arabs. The relations of the two countries will develop and consolidate, for both countries are great pillars in the defence of Islam and Muslim rights, both materially and morally'.[164] With Morocco there is 'a special relationship to support oppressed Muslim peoples in Palestine, the Philippines and elsewhere ...'[165]

As for Jordan, the two countries have, in addition to close relations in the area of international politics, and economic and cultural cooperation, a common enemy. These relations are further enhanced by the financial and military aid Saudi Arabia donates to strengthen the Jordanian front, 'which is steadfast in the face of the Zionists and their ambitions, and victory, God willing, will be soon achieved'.[166]

For Egypt, Saudi Arabia's relations with this country are multilateral. They are also growing and strengthening, owing to the unity of faith, lan-

guage, blood and common goals that aim to serve Muslims. 'These relations are further enhanced through economic and cultural ties, as well as
the diplomatic representation that seeks to unify the views, principles and
means to serve Islamic and political causes, in particular the Palestinian
cause, whether materially or morally, in all international forums'.[167]

Thus, the nature of these ties is similar to all the Arab and Islamic countries, with the exception of Iraq and Iran. It is as if there is a 'dual exclusion'
at work, putting both countries outside the realm of warm relations enjoyed by other Islamic and Arab countries with Saudi Arabia, but without
revealing their problems with the Kingdom or considering them, simultaneously, like the other countries.

Even in the case of a very dangerous event such as the Iraqi occupation
of Kuwait, this incident is mentioned only once and without detail. Moreover, it is referred to in the context of commending the role and policies of
Saudi Arabia. 'The impact of the merits of the Cooperation Council for
the States of the Arabian Gulf became evident through the various unifying steps in various fields, as well as the unified stand that its states, and the
Kingdom in particular, took to defend Kuwait and free it from the aggression of the Iraqi ruler ... '[168]

On the other hand, the Saudi role in the war for the liberation of Kuwait, in 'Desert Storm' or even before that (in the Iraq–Iran war), is
completely ignored, with no reference whatsoever to it.

How was the Image Formed?

Arab schoolbooks do not present a single image of Iran. The elements of
this image vary from one state to another, according to the local and regional policies of each state. We can nevertheless conclude that the image
of Iran is divided into two parts or levels: the new and the old.

The old image goes back to the stage of the Persian Empire and its
defeat by the Muslim conquering army. At this level, the Arab schoolbooks
present a more or less similar image, when they detail the historical aspect
of this image, such as the stages of development of the Message of Islam or
the reigns of the caliphs. They differ only in details, provocation or non-
interference on the course of events. While the Saudi books explain in detail
the nature of the battles the Muslim army fought against the Persians,
without any ideological additions or comments, the Iraqi books concentrate on ideological propaganda and neglect the part relating to events on
the battlefield: 'Because the Persians are the enemies of Islam and Arabism,
who tried to undermine the Qur'an and the Arabic language'. These books
consider the 'first Qadisieh battle' as a sign of the 'second Qadisieh, Saddam's
Qadisieh' that is going to take place in the modern age. On the other hand,

the Syrian, Moroccan and Egyptian books do not make any political or ideological projections when they deal with this battle, and the Egyptian books tend to go over it rather quickly, without even going into detail.

The elements that form the indirect historical image are the *mawali*, the *Shu'ubiyyah*, and the Persian ambitions. In this respect, the Iraqi books stand alone in considering the *mawali* and *Shu'ubiyyah* as purely Persian movements that serve Persian ambitions, which tried to either undermine, penetrate or conspire against the Arab Empire. In contrast, the Syrian, Egyptian and Moroccan books do not have the same evaluation of the historical role of both the *mawali* and the *Shu'ubiyyah*, for they list the reasons that led to the Empire's persecution of these *mawali*, 'some of whom were Persians', in the course of its discrimination against non-Arab Muslims. Moreover, while all the Arab schoolbooks point to Persian civilization, providing examples and shedding light on its interaction with Islamic civilization, the Iraqi books do not refer to any of these issues and maintain an approach of direct accusation against the Persian role.

In addition, these books distinguish between the image of the old Iran and the contemporary one. They do not consider the current Iran, along with its rulers and policies, as an extension of its old Persian hostile history. The Iraqi books stand alone in their emphasis on such an extension, giving Iran a Persian background and the same ambitions, which have undergone no change from the dawn of the Message of Islam until the Islamic revolution. But the distinction between the two Irans stops short of highlighting the positive aspects and maintains what we can call a kind of neutrality. If these books refrain from accusing Iran of being Persian, as a reminder of its old historical ambitions, they do not also point to the victory of the Islamic revolution in Iran, leaving it as an ordinary country without any positive or negative aspects, or they even ignore it completely. All the Arab schoolbooks, with the exception of the Syrian books, ignore the new status of Iran as an Islamic republic whose policies are different from those of the Shah. Such a neglect could be due to their apprehension over the Islamist movements' calls for change and revolution, which Iran, some allege, 'supports and encourages'.

Content analysis of Arab schoolbooks also shows that they do not always reflect the nature of the relations between most of the Arab countries and Iran. This is particularly true with respect to Egypt, Saudi Arabia and Morocco. Egyptian–Iranian relations are severed at the diplomatic level, and they have been quite tense, with each party accusing the other of various charges for years. Yet the Egyptian schoolbooks do not reflect these realities; they only discuss the historical role of the Persians, totally ignoring contemporary Iran. They do not indicate the positive aspects of this state, or even the damage it has done by 'supporting terrorism', as repeatedly alleged by Egyptian officials and mass media. The Saudi books adopt a similar approach, although the intermittent tension that Saudi–Iranian relations witnessed has not completely ended yet. Iran in these books is merely one of the Islamic states of the Islamic world, which has certain ties with Saudi Arabia.

Moroccan schoolbooks completely ignore Iran, though it should be kept in mind that diplomatic relations between the two countries were only restored two years ago. The only countries that reflect the true nature of their relations with Iran are Syria and Iraq. Iraq has reflected its war with Iran in its history, geography and national education books, through provocative language that goes back to the eight-year war period, notwithstanding the fact that the war stopped five years ago. And the Syrian books reflect, for their part, the good relations and alliance Syria has made with Iran since the victory of the Islamic revolution. The Syrian books do not allow Arab nationalist history, which accuses Iran of occupying Arab territories, to prevail over the contemporary transformations Iranian policies have witnessed. Thus, they dedicate a special lesson to Iran, but they do not touch on the internal or regional problems and wars that Iran faced.

On the other hand, the self-images of both Saudi Arabia and Iraq contribute, in their turn, to this attack on Iran, as does ignoring it in their schoolbooks. Iraq presents itself, especially after its war with Iran, as the defender of the Arab nation, while Saudi Arabia presents itself as the basis of Islamic solidarity and champion of Muslim causes in the world. And since Iran has assumed a similar role, it is natural to ignore the competing party.

Can the Negative Aspects of the Iranian Image be Corrected?

We can say that the strongest negative elements are found in the Iraqi schoolbooks. These books need to free themselves of the psychological, political and ideological climates that accompanied the devastating war between the two countries. This might not be difficult or impossible, since the two countries have begun to put behind them the era of war. Moreover, such a change would undoubtedly affect certain fundamental aspects of the Iraqi academic curriculum.

As for the books of the other countries, the negative impact is implicit and disguised. Furthermore, it is so subtle and indirect that it cannot be seen except by a trained eye, or by a teacher who wants to link his nation's history and geography with the current policies of his state. If the teacher does not volunteer for such an elaboration, all these books need some minor changes, provided that they do not deprive Iran of its due, whether as an Islamic nation or as a revolution that was a turning point in the present and future relations of the regional states. Furthermore, establishing good relations between Iran and the Arab countries will, in time, make the presence of the negative aspects in the academic Iranian image totally unjustified.

But which comes first – changing the curriculum or improving the relations? It is undoubtedly the latter.

Notes

* Director General, Centre for Strategic Studies, Research and Documentation, Beirut, Lebanon.

1. *National Education* for 1st Year Intermediate, (Baghdad: Ministry of Education, 1994), p. 15.
2. Ibid., p. 17.
3. Ibid., p. 60.
4. *Arab Islamic History* for 2nd Year Intermediate, (Baghdad: Ministry of Education, 1994), pp. 24–5.
5. Ibid., p. 44.
6. Ibid., p. 46.
7. Ibid., p. 57.
8. *History of Arab Islamic Civilization* for 4th Year General, (Baghdad: Ministry of Education, 1994), p. 38.
9. *Arab Islamic History* for 2nd Year Intermediate, *op. cit.*, p. 74.
10. Ibid., pp. 87–8.
11. *History of Arab Islamic Civilization* for 4th Year General, *op. cit.*, p. 42.
12. *Arab Islamic History* for 2nd Year Intermediate, *op. cit.*, p. 88.
13. *History of Arab Islamic Civilization* for 4th Year General, part 3, *op. cit.*, pp. 75–6.
14. *The Modern and Contemporary History of the Arab Homeland* for 3rd Year Intermediate, *op. cit.*, p. 13.
15. *History of Arab Islamic Civilization* for 4th Year General, part 3, *op. cit.*, p. 14.
16. *The Modern and Contemporary History of the Arab Homeland* for 3rd Year Intermediate, *op. cit.*, pp. 17 and 22.
17. Ibid., p. 21.
18. Ibid., p. 103.
19. Ibid., p. 104.
20. Ibid., p. 22.
21. Ibid., p. 103.
22. *General Geography* for 4th Year General, *op. cit.*, p. 217.
23. *The Modern and Contemporary History of the Arab Homeland* for 3rd Year Intermediate, *op. cit.*, p. 104.
24. Ibid., p. 112.
25. *General Geography* for 4th Year General, *op. cit.*, p. 218.
26. Ibid., p. 218.
27. Ibid., p. 219.
28. The only time that the Islamic revolution is mentioned in any talk about Iran, despite interjection or cynicism in the phrase.
29. Ibid., p. 219.
30. Ibid., p. 220.

31.   *The Geography of Iraq and some Neighbouring States* for 3rd Year Intermediate, (Baghdad: Ministry of Education, 1994), p. 5.
32.   Ibid., p. 6.
33.   Ibid., p. 6.
34.   *General Geography* for 4th Year General, *op. cit.*, p. 231.
35.   *The Modern and Contemporary History of the Arab Homeland* for 3rd Year Intermediate, *op. cit.*, p. 105.
36.   *Arab Islamic History* for 2nd Year Intermediate, *op. cit.*, p. 47.
37.   *The Modern and Contemporary History of the Arab Homeland* for 3rd Year Intermediate, *op. cit.*, p. 105.
38.   Ibid., p. 106.
39.   Ibid., p. 106.
40.   Ibid., pp. 106-8. Also, *National Education* for 1st Year Intermediate, *op. cit.*, pp. 47, 91, 93–6; and *Arab Islamic History* for 2nd Year Intermediate, *op. cit.*, pp. 50 and 60.
41.   *National Education* for 3rd Year Intermediate, part 3, (Baghdad: Ministry of Education, 1994), 12 pp.
42.   Ibid., p. 49.
43.   *Arab Islamic History* for 2nd Year Intermediate, *op. cit.*, p. 47.
44.   *The Modern and Contemporary History of the Arab Homeland* for 3rd Year Intermediate, *op. cit.*, p. 38.
45.   *Arab Islamic History* for 2nd Year Intermediate, *op. cit.*, p. 47.
46.   *The Modern and Contemporary History of the Arab Homeland* for 3rd Year Intermediate, *op. cit.*, 47.
47.   Ibid., p. 106.
48.   Ibid., p. 107.
49.   Ibid., p. 111.
50.   Ibid., p. 114.
51.   Ibid., p. 114, and part 4, pp. 75–6.
52.   Ibid., p. 114.
53.   *National Education* for 1st Year Intermediate, *op. cit.*, pp. 17, 25, 27, 47; part 3, p. 21; part 4, p. 15.
54.   *National Education and Socialism* for 4th Year General, (Baghdad: Ministry of Education, 1994), p. 21.
55.   *National Education* for 1st Year Intermediate, *op. cit.*, p. 11.
56.   Ibid., pp. 17, 95–6.
57.   *Geography of the Arab Nation* for 2nd Year Intermediate, (Baghdad: Ministry of Education, 1994), p. 18.
58.   *The Geography of Iraq and some Neighbouring States* for 3rd Year Intermediate, *op. cit.*, p. 10.
59.   Ibid., p. 99.
60.   Ibid.
61.   Ibid., p. 114.
62.   *The Modern and Contemporary History of the Arab Homeland* for 3rd Year Intermediate, *op. cit.*, p. 114.
63.   Ibid.
64.   Ibid., p. 106.
65.   *National Education and Socialism* for 4th Year General, *op. cit.*, p. 31.

66.   See those books that we were able to review, returning to the period before the war with Iran: *Modern History, History of Arab and Islamic Civilization, General Geography*; also, books on economics, sociology, review and texts, literature, guidance review, Islamic education, national education.

67.   *Modern History* for 5th Year Arts, 22nd ed., (Baghdad: Ministry of Education, 1980).

68.   *The Modern and Contemporary History of the Arab Homeland* for 3rd Year Intermediate, *op. cit.*, p. 265.

69.   Ibid., p. 303.

70.   Compare 'image of war' presented in Ibid., p. 304.

71.   *Arab Islamic History* for 2nd Year Intermediate, *op. cit.*, pp. 24–5.

72.   *The History of Arab Islamic Civilization* for 4th Year General, 4th printing, Baghdad: Ministry of Education, 1980 [released before the war].

73.   Ibid., p. 48.

74.   Ibid.

75.   *General Geography* for 4th Year General, 3rd printing, Baghdad: Ministry of Education, 1981 [released before the war].

76.   Ibid., pp. 153–7.

77.   Ibid., p. 153.

78.   *History of the Arabs in the Abbasid Age* for 2nd Intermediate, (Damascus: Ministry of Education, 1994–95), p. 12.

79.   *History of the Arabs in the Umayyad Age* for 1st Intermediate, (Damascus: Ministry of Education, 1994–95), p. 51

80.   *History of the Arabs in the Abbasid Age* for 2nd Intermediate, *op. cit.*, p. 25.

81.   Ibid., p. 27.

82.   Ibid., p. 55.

83.   Ibid., p. 60.

84.   Ibid., pp. 61–2.

85.   Ibid., pp. 64–5.

86.   Ibid., p. 71.

87.   *History of Arab Civilization* for 1st Year Secondary, (Damascus: Ministry of Education, 1994–95), p. 13.

88.   *Modern and Contemporary History of the Arabs* for 3rd Year Secondary/Arts, (Damascus: Ministry of Education, 1994–95), p. 357.

89.   Ibid., p. 367.

90.   *A Modern History of the Arabs* for 3rd Year Intermediate, (Damascus: Ministry of Education, 1994–95), pp. 120 and 125.

91.   *History of Arab Civilization* for 1st Year Secondary, *op. cit.*, p. 7.

92.   Ibid., pp. 40 and 42.

93.   Ibid., pp. 121 and 126.

94.   Ibid., p. 139.

95.   Ibid., p. 163.

96.   Ibid., pp. 184–5.

97.   Ibid., p. 224.

98.   *Modern and Contemporary History of the Arabs* for 3rd Year Secondary/Arts, *op. cit.*, p. 118.

99.   *Principles of General Geography and the World* for 1st Year Intermediate, (Damascus: Ministry of Education, 1993–94), p. 131.

100. Ibid., pp. 131–51.

101. Ibid., pp. 178–9.

102. *History of Modern Times* for 2nd Year Secondary/Arts, part 2, (Damascus: Ministry of Education, 1993–94), pp. 106–7; *A Modern History of the Arabs* for 3rd Year Intermediate, *op. cit.*, p. 97; *The World Human Geography and Economy and its Major Problems* for 2nd Year Intermediate, (Damascus: Ministry of Education, 1993–94), pp. 102–4.

103. *The Geography of the Arab Homeland and its History in the Islamic Era* for 2nd Year Intermediate, (Cairo: Ministry of Education, 1994–95), p. 127.

104. Ibid.

105. Ibid., p. 132.

106. Ibid., p. 151.

107. Ibid.

108. *Egypt and the Old World Civilizations* for 1st Year Secondary, (Cairo: Ministry of Education, 1994–95), p. 137.

109. *The Geography of the Arab Homeland* for 2nd Year Secondary, (Cairo: Ministry of Education, 1994–95), p. 11.

110. Compare Iraqi schoolbooks here.

111. *The Geography of the Arab Homeland and its History in the Islamic Era* for 2nd Year Intermediate, *op. cit.*, p. 157.

112. Ibid., p. 172.

113. Ibid., p. 174.

114. Ibid., p. 177.

115. Ibid., p. 188.

116. *The Geography of the Arab Homeland* for 2nd Year Secondary, *op. cit.*, p. 9.

117. Ibid., p. 17.

118. Ibid., p. 18.

119. *The Geography of the Arab Homeland and its History in the Islamic Era* for 2nd Year Intermediate, *op. cit.*, p. 10.

120. Ibid., p. 18.

121. Ibid., p. 109.

122. Ibid., p. 78.

123. Ibid., p. 105.

124. Ibid., pp. 106–8.

125. Ibid., p. 111.

126. Ibid., p. 219.

127. *History* for 7th Year Basic Education, (Rabat: Ministry of National Education, 1991), p. 39.

128. Ibid., p. 44.

129. *History* for 1st Year Secondary, (Rabat: Ministry of National Education, 1994–95), p. 70.

130. Ibid., p. 74.

131. *History* for 7th Year Basic Education, *op. cit.*, p. 46.

132. *History* for 1st Year Secondary, *op. cit.*, pp. 83–4.

133. *The Biography of the Prophet and History of the Islamic Empire* for 1st Year Intermediate, (Riyadh: Ministry of Education, 1994), p. 71. Also, *The Biography of the Prophet and History of the Islamic Empire* for 1st Year Secondary, (Riyadh: Ministry of Education, 1993), pp. 49–50.

134. *The Biography of the Prophet and History of the Orthodox Caliphs* for 1st Year Intermediate.

135. Ibid., p. 105.

136. Ibid., p. 121.

137. Ibid., pp. 52–3.

138. *History of the Islamic World* for 2nd Year Intermediate for Girls, (Riyadh: General Presidency for the Education of Girls, Support Agency for Educational Advancement, 1993), p. 86.

139. Ibid., p. 105.

140. Ibid., p. 121.

141. Abdullah Saleh Al-'Atheemein, *Aspects of Muslim History from the End of the Abbasid Empire to the Present Day* for 3rd Year Intermediate, (Riyadh: Ministry of Education, 1994), p. 35.

142. Ibid., p. 36.

143. *Geography of the Islamic World* for 2nd Year Intermediate for Girls, (Riyadh: General Presidency for the Education of Girls, Support Agency for Educational Advancement, 1993), p. 4.

144. Ibid., p. 38.

145. Ibid., p. 40.

146. Ibid., p. 43.

147. *The Biography of the Prophet and History of the Islamic Empire* for 1st Year Secondary, *op.* cit., pp. 87–8.

148. Ibid., pp. 88–9.

149. *The History (Islamic Empire)* for 2nd Year Secondary, (Riyadh: General Presidency for the Education of Girls, Support Agency for Educational Advancement, 1993), pp. 72, 74–5 and 79. These notions are repeated in the girls' history book for the same level; the verse of the Holy Qur'an is from *Surat Al-i-Umran, ayah* 110.

150. *The History (Islamic Empire)* for 1st Year Secondary, (Riyadh: General Presidency for the Education of Girls, Support Agency for Educational Advancement, 1993), pp. 50–1.

151. *The Regional Geography of the Islamic World* for 3rd Year Secondary for Girls, (Riyadh: General Presidency for the Education of Girls, Support Agency for Educational Advancement, 1993), p. 103.

152. *Geography of the Islamic World* for 2nd Year Intermediate for Girls, *op. cit.*, p. 79.

153. *The History (Islamic Empire)* for 2nd Year Intermediate, *op. cit.*, p. 84.

154. Ibid., pp. 202–6.

155. Ibid., p. 208.

156. *History of the Kingdom of Saudi Arabia* for 3rd Year Secondary, (Riyadh: Ministry of Education, 1993), p. 132.

157. Ibid., p. 134.

158. *Geography of the Islamic World* for 2nd Year Intermediate, *op. cit.*, p. 14.

159. Ibid., p. 38.

160. *Geography of the Islamic World* for 2nd Year Intermediate for Girls, *op. cit.*, p. 55.

161. Ibid., p. 49.

162. Ibid., p. 63.

163. *Geography of the Islamic World* for 2nd Year Intermediate, *op. cit.*, p. 56.
164. Ibid., p. 105.
165. *Geography of the Islamic World* for 2nd Year Intermediate for Girls, *op. cit.*,
p. 26.
166. Ibid., p. 72.
167. Ibid., p. 92.
168. Ibid., p. 133.

Six

The Status of Arab and Iranian Women

The Status of Women in Contemporary Iran: Trends and Prospects

MASSOUMEH EBTEKAR*

Much elucidation is still needed both on the attitude of Islam and the Islamic state towards women as well as the actual status of women in religiously based governments such as the Islamic Republic of Iran. The aggressive 15-year-old media campaign against Islamic Iran has left many scars yet unhealed.

Over the past decade, a considerable wealth of writing has emerged from a variety of perspectives on the conditions and rights of women in Islam and Islamic states which has dealt with women's issues on the Islamic nations and beyond. On the theoretical level it has been demonstrated that Islam as a faith and way of life promotes human rights. However, the practical application of Islamic principles entails complications and difficulties. Amidst hostile propaganda and a negative overall global attitude towards religion, the Islamic Republic of Iran has embarked on an experience of government by religion.

Several factors should be studied in order to throw light on the condition and status of women in Iranian society. The parameters that have been proposed, by international organizations and the UN, are superficial and restricted, in the sense that they cannot convey qualitative and essential cultural changes and developments in a society. The current indicators of human and social development can reflect to some extent the economic and social status of a society, while the cultural and political situation needs more assertion and an in-depth consideration of the moral discourses in human aspects of development.

Changing Perspectives

If we choose an overall perspective on the contemporary condition and status of Iranian women, the first matter that would attract our attention is the different attitude of society towards women. This attitude is intrinsically different from the conventional consumerist and sexist stance which sees women as sex objects serving the purpose of entertaining men and satisfying their lust. This difference is quite evident at first sight; a visitor to Iran will never encounter even a single case of propaganda or advertisement employing women as a means to enhance the sales of a particular product. Whether in the cinema or in the streets, posters or billboards, books, journals, magazines or television films and advertisments, women are not portrayed as objects of sexual attraction, nor are they employed by any means to expose their beauty for the sale or promotion of goods.

This difference is actually the manifestation of a unique and unprecedented conceptualization on gender issues and the status of women. Rooted in the principles of Islam are contemporary interpretations of religious authorities such as those of Imam Khomeini, who perceived Islam as a religion and motivating force that could intervene with practical agendas for the socio-economic dilemmas of contemporary societies and provide solutions to the most intricate problems of the human race.

In Islamic society, therefore, the woman perceives herself, from her early years, not as a mere sex object but as the purveyor of other, more elevated and sublime values. The opposite sex also perceives women in this way. This non-discriminatory, non-sexist attitude forms the basis for gender perspectives and roles in the Islamic state, and one can speculate that all policies and methods stem from this perspective.

Legal Status

Since the basis of the legal system in Iran is the Islamic *Shari'ah*, all legal and legislative matters should be considered in that context. In the introduction of the Constitution of the Islamic Republic of Iran, the role of the woman has been defined in terms of her prominent role in the family as the educator of human beings and as a major contributer to the process of social development.

The 3rd Article of the Constitution states that 'the rights of all citizens, men and women, shall be safeguarded and legal security shall be provided for all, while all persons are equal before the law'. The 21st Article of the Constitution states that 'the government is responsible for the guarantee of rights of women in all aspects, in adherence to Islamic principles.' The issues of support for mothers, legal support for the family, insurance opportunities for vulnerable women, and rights of guardianship for mothers have been considered in the law. In addition, in all economic laws and legislation Iranian women enjoy equal rights, as well as certain maternity benefits.

On the issue of dissolution of the marriage contract, the woman has been given the right to divorce under specific circumstances. Divorce is possible only under strict and specific conditions for both parties. This is contrary to the naive attitude contending that women in Iran do not have equal rights in the marriage contract. This attitude, prevailing among contemporary feminist viewpoints, regards any discrepancies in basic rights between the sexes to be a source of gender discrimination and inequality. Equality in its essential definition, however, does not necessarily imply sameness, particularly when dealing with gender issues that entail different personal and social roles. In other words, in the case of gender issues, equality and justice do not necessarily entail sameness in rights or the non-existence of discrepancies. Considering the particular role and responsibilities of a woman in the diverse aspects of her personal and social life, if we assume those roles to be identical to those of the opposite sex, we would be depriving the woman of her basic rights as a daughter, a wife, a mother or a human being.

On the other hand, critics and contemporary opponents of Islam lack a collective and comprehensive viewpoint on Islamic edicts; they also tend, when evaluating particular laws, to rip them out of context and to judge them according to their standards of development and modernization. Many amendments and modifications have been added to the civil, penal and judicial code of the Islamic Republic during the past years, enhancing the rights of the woman according to the principles of Islam. Educational programmes have also been undertaken by various media; however, much remains to be done in all aspects of the legal status of women. As in other contemporary societies, a major dilemma encountered today in Iran is the existence of negative social mores and derogatory attitudes towards women, which are promoted falsely in the name of religion, itself proven to transcend all conceivable standards of human values.

Access to Decision Making

Social justice and equality can be achieved only if women, like men, enjoy the human right to determine and decide their own lives. The principle of free will, unquestionably one of the most prominent principles contained in the Holy Qur'an, maintains this principle irrespective of race or gender. While the Almighty has guaranteed and decreed our freedom of choice in life, how could any Islamic system be established without an effective mechanism to reconcile the legitimate aspirations of the people with the rulings of contemporary religious authorities? As this mechanism evolved in the last decade with the establishment of an Islamic ¡ 'republic' led by the *velayat-e faqih*, women were integrated from the very first referendum and ensuing decision-making processes of the Republic. This was largely a consequence of the crucial role of women in promoting the unity and struggle of the nation during the years of resistance and revolution against the shah.

The past decade has witnessed an increasing number of women voters, women candidates and women parliamentarians. The present Consultative Assembly contains nine women; it is a small percentage, but the increasing trend is promising. The highest political position presently held by a woman is the Advisor to the president on Women's Affairs. She is also the head of the Bureau of Women's Affairs and the National Committee. Currently, all ministries dealing with women's issues directly or indirectly have appointed an advisor for women, and women hold positions as heads of departments or sectors in many ministries and governmental as well as non-governmental administrations. Many improvements have also been made in the role of women in the judicial system, where they are presently active as lawyers, legal experts and advisors.

Several other organizations have been devoted to women, including the socio-cultural Committee of Women, which takes part in major policy making and planning for women's educational and cultural advancement. The Ministry of the Interior has established a Commission for Women's Affairs which has active branches in even the most remote provinces of the country, addressing their problems at the executive level. Apart from such official national institutions in the government sector, favourable socio-political conditions have laid grounds for the formation of grassroots-based non-governmental organizations (NGOs) serving the purpose of enhancing the status of women and the family.

Stemming from a highly religious society, most of these organizations developed on the basis of religious incentives. Considering the inherent value of attending to the moral and material needs of fellow human beings in Islam, charity organizations usually follow cultural rejuvenation strategies alongside their financial assistance programmes for needy families and women. Minority women such as the Armenians, Jews, Zoroastrians and Assyrians are also actively involved in such activities and have major NGOs. Many of these women-focused NGOs grew out of the era of the war, during which women provided crucial support by forming logistical backup centres in mosques in each district in cities and villages. The moral support women provided by encouraging their sons and husbands to engage in the holy defence of Islam and their homeland also laid the groundwork for the establishment of grassroots organizations – this era in our history served to realize the sublime and paramount role of the woman in defending human values and spiritualism. In a world torn apart by capitalist, consumerist-driven incentives and secular materialistic attitudes, the people of Iran stood up to revive and reintroduce spiritual values.

The years of revolution and war were instrumental in changing social mores and attitudes towards women in both traditionalist and modernist sectors of Iranian society. Imam Khomeini, as a charismatic leader and an indisputable authority, played an active role in establishing the cultural foundations of a progressive religious attitude towards women, as he had in other dynamic matters related to contemporary society.

Economic Conditions and Employment

Despite the economic pressures of the war and its aftermath, Iranian women have persisted in economic activities such as agriculture and industry. In terms of distribution of the female labour force across occupational groups, the 1986 census gives the following information on women's employment:

Professional, technical and related occupations: 35 per cent of employed women
Agriculture, animal husbandry, forestry, fishing: 26.6 per cent of employed women
Production and transport: 23.4 per cent of employed women.

In the villages, women account for production of approximately 40 per cent of national agricultural products. While they have equal access to credit, income, and the right of ownership, in both rural and urban areas, women usually have less access to the means of production due to several factors, including their own unawareness and the biased social mores that surround them. By 1991, the Ministry of Agriculture established agricultural training centres for women, recognizing their key role in agriculture; an Office for the Development of Rural Women has also been very active in promoting the advancement of rural women.

Since 1990, new incentives have been taken which include training and vocational education schemes in national education planning. In the industrial sector, women now constitute a major work force receiving equal pay and insurance benefits. Since 1990, labour legislation has given women the right to three months' maternity leave with no loss of priviliges and their jobs guaranteed. In the past years, many women in the private sector have embarked on economic ventures in business-related sectors.

The past decade has witnessed a decline in the percentage of officially employed women (1981–91). This trend is largely attributable to the difficult war time and post-war economic conditions, which, among other things, created an unfavourable climate of competition for work between men and women in the services and industrial sectors.

This decline can also be attributed to the significant increase in the percentage of women in the field of education. In different sectors, however, the employment trends are interesting. While in industry there is a decrease, in the services sector statistics indicate an increase in the percentage of women. It is worth mentioning that specialists attribute the increase in government services and specialized employment for women to a trend in women's attitudes giving preference to qualitatively higher occupations.

Overall, it is evident that today there are no legal or judicial obstacles to the employment of women. While work in itself, apart from its economic merits or social benefits, is considered to be an indispensable part of a Muslim's life, the particular form it takes depends on many factors. The government has undertaken responsibility to provide job opportunities for women, with due consideration to the fact that employment conditions should not endanger the woman's family roles and motherhood. In fact, maintaining this delicate balance between social and family roles has always been a subject of discussion amongst female intellectuals, who prefer not to totally sacrifice one for the other.

Education and Health

As mentioned before, changing social mores and attitudes during and after the Islamic revolution paved the way for the integration of women into the social sphere, particularly in the area of education. During the past decade, the illiteracy rate in Iran has declined significantly; the gender gap still exists in the latest census, but the rate at which women are closing in is promising. The integration of religious incentives with the educational process, which was effectively promoted by Imam Khomeini, has accelerated the pace considerably, and even among remote villagers, girls are sent to school alongside boys. The number of girls in the elementary stage has tripled during the past 15 years, while the number of boys has not increased at a comparable pace. This is indicative of the fact that obstacles to girls' education have diminished. Higher education is a venue with broad vistas for women; the greatest upward trends have been observed in medicine, the sciences, the humanities and teacher training.

Presently, a significant percentage of women are active as faculty members and instructors in academic institutions. They perceive their work as a precious service to society, and they usually have lofty ideals and objectives in mind. Since 1992 a number of significant obstacles to women's education in all fields of higher education (particularly certain engineering and agriculture fields) have been removed. Women have equal opportunities and equal access to all fields and all levels of higher education.

Health is currently one of the important indicators of social development, and women should be considered as both providers and beneficiaries of health services. Since health is an issue interrelated with various socio-economic factors, any effective programme in this area should take into consideration comprehensive planning. Women have specific health needs and successful planning in this field must take gender perspectives into account. This has been appreciated by policy makers and the importance of integration of women's special concerns into the mainstream of development programmes is well-accepted.

Presently, more than 75 per cent of the rural and 60 per cent of the urban population in Iran is covered by health care services of the government; by the end of the second Five-Year Plan there will be health care for all of Iran's population. Women's life expectancy has increased from 56.3 in 1979 to 69 in 1985; due to serious investment in mother-and-child health care services life expectancy is set to increase further. In addition, implementation of serious family planning schemes has helped to reduce the maternal mortality rate from 245 to 54.

Gender discrepancies in infant mortality, life expectancy, malnutrition and disabilities still exist, but effective policy making will ultimately remove the gap. One should mention, however, the importance of religious belief on people's health practices and attitudes to health. Religious convictions have been channelled successfully to serve the interest of the people's well-being, health and personal hygiene, which are all strongly documented in Islamic texts. A successful experience reflecting the people's readiness to sacrifice in the way of God (*fi sabil-il-lah*), took place in the city of Shiraz during the Iraq war. Thousands of volunteer housewives were recruited in a health project where each woman undertook the responsibility of monitoring 50 households in the vicinity of her home on the following matters: Mother-and-child health care, immunization, nutrition, and family planning. During 1993, through proper planning and policy-making, popular forces were mobilized to implement a large-scale immunization scheme for the eradication of polio among all children under five.

In Iranian society, as in other developing societies, objectives like 'health for all' can be envisaged only if proper gender perspectives are integrated into planning schemes taking into account people's particular cultural and religious convictions. Iran has embarked on a wide-scale campaign to attain the ambitious objectives of development in both its economic and cultural dimensions.

The conventional paradigms of economic and social development, which promote the capitalist consumerist policies of the West, or encourage moral decadence, instability of social institutions such as the family, or deny the importance of social justice, cannot be adopted by any progressive nation.

Development must be redefined to include the spiritual and moral dimensions of the human being. The post-modernist discourses of the eighties endeavoured to keep religion and spirituality off the agenda despite the great social difficulties and distress that these societies faced.

However secular theories of politics and social order have failed explicitly to cope with the dilemmas and deep-rooted problems of contemporary societies. Social attitudes have changed and theoreticians and scholars alike have re-embarked on a campaign to reconsider spiritualism as a major and indispensable aspect of human nature and thus social institutions.

Feminism, which had originated with the women's liberation movements of the sixties, took secular overtones from the start, perceiving religion as an obstacle to women's advancement. Considering the fact that this trend began in Christian societies, and notwithstanding some of the basic and interpretive gender perspectives of Catholicism in particular, this attitude was not surprising.

The movement for the advancement of women has clearly surpassed the limits of a particular 'ism' and has become a national and global trend which nations regard mandatory for their social development. This trend, which still carries secular and anti-religious overtones, has re-established itself on the agenda of the United Nations.

However, in recent years the global attention that religion, especially Islam, has received is changing attitudes and positions. Islam is now being regarded increasingly as a religion that can encourage moral and spiritual development, as well as social and economic justice, and achieve modernization and scientific as well as technological advancement. The Islamic Republic of Iran should enhance its efforts through the enlightenment and mobilization of its people, despite its obstacles and difficulties, to provide an example of Islamic governance and a model of the application of these sublime principles for generations to come.

Sources

*Faculty Member, Tarbiat Modarres University, Tehran, and the Centre for Women's Studies and Research, Tehran, Iran.

Amargiri-ye Jari-ye Jami'at, 1370. Natayej-e Omumi-ye Kol-e Keshvar (Population Census, 1991).
Bassiri, Sussan, 'Women and Health: A Global and National Overview', *Farzaneh, Journal of Women's Studies* (Tehran), vol. 1, no. 4, 1995.
Bureau of Women's Affairs, *Draft National Report of Women in the Islamic Republic of Iran.*
Iran, Ministry of Health and Medical Education, *National Report on Health, 1993.*
Iran, Statistical Centre of Iran, Planning and Budget Organization, *Statistical Yearbook, 1370* (1991).
Moghadam, Valentine, *Women's Employment Issues in Contemporary Iran*, [n.p.]: Middle East Association of North America, 1994.

UNICEF Tehran and Women's Bureau of the President's Office, UNICEF Tehran, 1993: *'Gender Analysis Workshop, Proceedings'*, Tehran.
Woman and Development, 1994, *A Report on Important Measures Taken for Women since the Victory of the Islamic Revolution*, Tehran.

12

The Status of Women in the Arab World

MARIAM SELIM

As I will be dealing in my presentation with the Arab woman, it is unreasonable to address this matter without a survey of the reports prepared by Arab national committees participating in the Fourth World Conference on Women, held in Beijing in September 1995. Here I would like to say, from the outset, that what I shall present in my paper draws on these reports and on works undertaken in seminars, conferences and studies over the last year or two.

The status of the Arab woman remains an open question, claiming the attention of researchers and authors. Despite Arab women's obtainment of some gains, she remains unable to stand alongside the man as much as she should. Perhaps one of the most prominent reasons for the injustice done to her follows from, or is tied to, the degree of cultural advancement of the society in which she lives.

But the disparity between the sexes is a global problem, according to UN statements on the status of women world-wide; for despite some improvement, the disparity between the sexes has remained significant over the past 20 years. I would like here to point briefly to the status of women at the global level, so that we can see where the Arab woman stands. The investigation undertaken by a number of specialized UN agencies, including the UN World Population Fund, UNICEF, the UN Development Fund for Women, and the International Labour Organization, confirms that the economic discrepancies between countries are intensifying the discrepancy between men and women.

In order to assess the situation this study will look at five factors: the developments that have occurred in family life, leadership and decision-making in the structure of society; health; fertility; education, and economic life. In the advanced countries (Europe, the former Soviet Union, North America, Australia, New Zealand and Japan), women's health has improved during the past 20 years and birth rates have declined. But the participation of women in economic life has varied.

This participation is particularly high in north and eastern Europe (including the former Soviet Union) and North America, but it was much lower in Australia, Japan, New Zealand and west and southern Europe. Discrepancies in income between men and women remains wide. Women, who number only slightly less than men (2.6 billion out of a population of 5.3 billion), receive less attention in health and education from governments than men do. In 1985, the illiteracy figure for women was 597 million, compared with 342 million for men.

Women receive a lower income than the international average for men by 30–40 per cent. Furthermore they work longer hours than men, sometimes with a difference of 13 hours per week in Africa and Asia. We must also draw attention to practices that render women victims of harmful traditions. The General Assembly of the World Health Organization passed a resolution banning 'harmful traditional practices' that each year victimize 80 million young and elderly women, namely the partial or complete amputation of female sexual organs.

The WHO affirmed that these traditions, which also involve stitching sexual organs to prevent sexual contact, are the cause of half the mortality rate among women during pregnancy or childbirth, principally due to bleeding. This amounts to 500 thousand deaths per year quite apart from the death of four million newborn every year from the same cause. The amputations are undertaken on infants in the first months after birth, or on young girls from seven to eight and up to 17 years of age, in nearly 30 countries. Among the Arab countries engaging in this practice are Mauritania, Somalia, Sudan and Egypt, with the most vicious practices involving the elimination of prominent sexual organs and sewing up the wounds, sometimes with thorns when string is not available. The head of the mother-and-child programme in the WHO affirmed that deterrence laws are not sufficient, because these laws remain ink on paper. The detention of women who practise these operations has been met with popular protest.

These traditions are practised for social and not religious reasons. They were originally meant to impose chastity and also provide protection for women from rape. The WHO argues that these practices are tied to poverty, illiteracy and women's subjugation. In some communities, men refuse to marry a woman who has not undergone this operation. The irony is that the victims of such practices are among their biggest defenders, starting with the traditional midwife who administers them. The best approach to curb these practices is to improve the status of women in these communities, culturally and socially.

Furthermore, the practice indirectly contributes to the spread of malnutrition, because the women know the difficulties that await them at childbirth. So they eat little during pregnancy in order not to gain weight and thus fall victim to anaemia. From this introduction we shall proceed to show the link between international, regional and national developments. The importance of this connection has increased with advances in communications and visual information technology, which have turned the world into a large city in which states form side streets and residential areas.

This advancement was the net outcome of an intellectual and scientific diversity affecting the whole of humanity. In parallel with this, peoples and states are living under intellectually and politically diverse conditions, competing with each other for the realization of their aspirations.

International relations based on respect for sovereignty, right of self-determination and non-interference in the internal affairs of states have yielded a number of important international documents. The United Nations Organization during the sixties and seventies issued the International Agreement for the Elimination of Racial Discrimination on 21 December 1965, the Two Decades on Human Rights on 16 December 1966, the Declaration of Elimination of All Forms of Discrimination against Women on 7 November 1967, and the Agreement to Eliminate All Forms of Discrimination against Arab Women on 18 December 1979.

As for equality between the sexes, the UN announced on 11 November 1972 that the year 1975 shall be regarded as International Women's Year. A conference was held in Mexico, then a second conference, then a third in Nairobi in 1985, which adopted the Nairobi Strategy for the Year 2000 on Equality, Development and Peace. A review of the Arab reports presented at the Fourth World Conference on Women in Beijing, reflects the deterioration in the special status of women in the nineties. This could be attributable to the wars that the region has witnessed, from the war in Lebanon that persisted for 17 years to the Iraq–Iran war that ended in 1988, then the Gulf war that bled the resources of the region and constrained development. We know that in every crisis a country suffers it is the women who pay the highest price for the difficulties, and recent studies have begun to talk about the 'feminization of poverty'.

Changes in the Status of Arab Women, from the 1980s

The national reports of Arab countries on women's participation in positions of authority and decision-making, at all levels, reveals the following:

1. A disparity in women's participation in parliaments and vacillation over her participation, either because of (a) the amendments that have occurred in legislation and laws, or (b) the adoption by some countries of the approach of appointment of women to parliament, to ensure their political participation.
2. The limited impact of the political role of women, for objective reasons

in the case of some countries, relating to the nature and distinctiveness of political challenges and problems in these countries.
3. The paucity of financial resources for backing women's entry into election battles.
4. The weak political experience of women and lack of independence in political choice, and their following sometimes the political choice of the man.
5. Women's participation as being merely symbolic or for appearance's sake.
6. The inability of women in some Arab countries to exercise their political rights.

In considering the status of women in political participation, one may mention that despite the constitutions of some Arab countries and their legislation in making a point to give women political rights, without discrimination between women and men on rights and obligations, the degree and weight of women's participation in authority and in decision-making vary from country to country, according to UN indicators, as follows:

Participation in Parliaments and National Assemblies

(a) Egypt

When discussing the reality of women's participation in parliamentary life, we find that Egyptian women are ahead of their counterparts in other Arab countries, in terms of entry into parliamentary institutions. In 1957, the first two women parliamentarians were elected. The number increased fourfold by 1967. The early emergence of party life in Egypt (the Wafd, Nasserite, National Congress parties) had a significant effect in accelerating the entry of the Egyptian woman into the arena of parliamentary life. With the development of economic, social, cultural and educational conditions, and the subsequent increase in the role of women, Law 1979 was issued, whereby 33 seats were allocated in the Egyptian National Assembly for women; every governorate acquired a woman representative and they made up 9.8 per cent of total membership in the National Assembly. The number of female members increased to 36 by the year 1982.

It appears that the gains achieved by Egyptian women, at the level of parliamentary participation, did not last long, because of the objection of men to this rapid advance in female participation. In 1986, the National Assembly cancelled the law allocating seats for women, on the pretext that it contravenes the law of equality on the basis of sex. This led to a fall in the number of female National Assembly members in the elections of 1987 which amounted to 18 or 3.9 per cent of total membership. In the elections of 1992 the number of women decreased to 10 members, three of them appointed by the President of the Republic; this reduced the percentage further to 2 per cent of total membership.

The trends outlined above suggest that the growing role of women in the Egyptian National Assembly is not the result of any increased awareness or concerted effort by the women, but rather the brainchild of a process of appropriating for them a certain share or percentage of Assembly seats, which in turn confirms the weak level of confidence in the political role of the woman. On the other hand, to complete the picture of Egyptian women's participation in parliamentary life, the number of women participants in the Egyptian National Assembly in 1980 was 7, or 3.3 per cent of the total membership. This figure increased to 12 in 1992, making the ratio 9.4 per cent of total membership.

(b) Syria

In Syria, from the start of the social revolution until now, women have won significant political rights. During the 1986 elections, they won 16 seats in the Chamber of Deputies, or 8.2 per cent of the total number of seats at that time. In the 1990 elections, the number of seats held by women became 22, rising in 1994 to 24 or 6.9 per cent of the total seats in the Chamber of Deputies. However, the Syrian study confirms that women did not reach the Chamber of Deputies by independent nomination but rather by their enlistment in political parties.

(c) Lebanon

The first Lebanese woman to enter the Chamber of Deputies entered by default in 1963 while the second did not enter until 1991, and by appointment. The first real entry of a Lebanese woman into the Chamber of Deputies was in 1992, when three women acquired seats. However the nomination of women and their winning of seats in the Chamber of Deputies was not tied to a political line or social system, but was effectively a positive reaction to the positions of men whom these women were associated with. It has also been shown that women's votes, which form half of Lebanese society's votes, had not yet become a source of pressure on political decision-making.

(d) Palestine

The Palestinian paper mentioned that 1964 witnessed the formation of the Palestine National Council, in which women's participation consisted of a limited number of women selected by the political leadership not exceeding 2 per cent of the total membership of the Council; that percentage doubled during the seventies to 4 per cent. In 1980, the efforts of the General Union of Palestinian Women were rewarded with success, when they were able to raise female membership in the Council to 25 or 9 per cent of the total Council membership of 250. The number of female members continued to rise reaching 43 in 1992 or 10 per cent of the total. When the Central Council was formed as an intermediary authority between the Central Committee of the PLO and the Palestine National Council, five women out of a total membership of 180 were elected as members of the Central Council. This represented 4.6 per cent of the total number of seats in the Central Council.

(e) Jordan

The Jordanian study noted that participation of women in parliamentary life goes back to 1978 when three women were appointed out of 75 members. The number of women members rose to four in 1984.

When the first parliamentary elections took place in Jordan in 1989 12 women, none of whom succeeded, were nominated. In 1993, one woman, out of three candidates, succeeded in winning a seat. Women's participation in the Senate began in 1989 and was followed by the appointment of two women to the Senate formed in 1993.

The Jordanian study attributes the failure of women to occupy additional seats in the parliament to several factors, most prominent being: (a) the long absence of democracy in Jordan, (b) the low level of awareness among women of the importance of having representatives in parliament, and (c) shortage of funds needed to finance advertising campaigns for women candidates.

(f) Yemen

Since the forties Yemeni women have participated in political demonstrations and demanded entry into public life. But participation in parliament came relatively late. The first parliament appointed in Aden in 1978 included ten women out of a total of 301 members in the ruling party list. In the northern governorates women were not permitted to nominate themselves for elections to the National Assembly (1987), even if they were permitted the right to vote.

When the unification of North and South Yemen took place in 1990, the women who were members of Aden's parliament were the participants in the united parliament of the north and south. In the general elections that took place in 1993, which included the governorates of the north and south, two women won out of 300 Assembly members. One should mention in this regard that the question of Yemeni women's participation in parliamentary life remains minimal, with no expectation of increased participation ratio for the foreseeable future. The percentage of women voters also remains low, only 16 per cent of all women eligible to vote turned up at the polls, despite the issue of several religious edicts (*fatwah*) affirming the need for women to participate in voting for righteous men???.

(g) The Gulf States

The national reports from the Gulf showed no opposition by some Gulf states to women sharing in political life. The Kuwait report indicated that Kuwait's Constitution does not differ from other constitutions in terms of affirming the principle of equality between the sexes in rights and obligations. Article (29) stipulates that 'people are equal in human dignity and are equal before the law in rights and obligations, with no discrimination between them according to sex, origin, language or religion'. The United Arab Emirates (UAE) report mentioned frankly that women do not, so far, engage in politics. The report of the Sultanate of Oman enunciated that there is no parliamentary system in the Sultanate, but there is an Advisory Council whose members include men and women.

(h) Iraq

In Iraq the National Assembly Law guarantees the principle of equality in nomination and election. The percentage of women in the Assembly in 1980 was about 6 per cent of the total Assembly members. Women's representation rose in 1985 to 13.2 per cent, then declined to 10.8 per cent in 1990. As for the autonomous Kurdish province, women's representation in membership of the Legislative Council of 1988 was about 4 per cent.

(i) Sudan

In the Sudan, it is clear that women's political participation has increased through representation in Parliament, which rose from 11 women to 25, compared with 300 men, during the interval 1992 to 1994. In Somalia there was one woman member compared with 76 men.

Participation in Government

From reading the national reports of the Arab countries, the following points are evident:

1. The relative weakness or complete absence of women's representation in top leadership positions.
2. Women's limited effectiveness in taking top decisions.
3. The concentration of the highest percentage of leadership positions that are held by women in the fields of education, culture and social affairs.
4. The reaching by some women in some Arab countries to the post of

minister, or deputy minister or under-secretaries of ministries, but only in financial terms, as a result of promotion, with no sharing in the decision-making process.
5. The difficulty in obtaining accurate statistical data on the status of women in high positions, for reasons of obscurity or lack of a single definition over the highest positions of state.

We turn now to surveying the status of Arab women in the area of participation in government. In Egypt, the first woman minister was appointed in 1960. Two women ministers were also appointed in 1993. Women's representation in top leadership posts is meagre, constituting 11.8 per cent of the top positions, such as first under-secretary, under-secretary, and director general.

In Syria, the first woman minister was appointed in 1976 as Minister of Culture. The Jordanian woman obtained this position in 1979 and then was granted the Ministry of Social Development, then returned again to that post in 1984 with the position of Minister of Information. The nineties has witnessed a twofold increase of Egyptian and Jordanian women holding ministerial positions: a second woman minister was appointed in Egypt in 1993 and in Jordan in 1995.

The decade also witnessed the appointment of one woman minister in South Yemen's Executive State Authority in 1990 and the appointment of one woman in the Palestinian Authority Council which is equivalent to a ministerial post.

There remains no mention of Lebanese woman, who have yet to acquire any ministerial post. No politician, party or social association, including women's associations, have called for a Cabinet position for women. However, one woman was appointed for the first time as Director General of the Ministry of Social Affairs, in 1993.

We do not find in the Kuwait report any reference to slating women for inclusion in areas of leadership or authority. But women have participated in social and development issues, rising in stature and occupying all positions culminating with the appointment of a woman, in 1994, to the post of under-secretary and director general. In the UAE, the national report indicates that women were able, during the period 1971–1993, to reach about 27.1 per cent of top administrative posts.

In Oman, the national report indicates that in 1990, one woman was appointed as Under-Secretary of the Ministry of Development and Census Affairs. The number of women who held the position of director rose from 22 during the years 1980–85 to 266 by 1990. In Iraq the national report reveals a contradiction in the statistical figures expressing occupational ratios for women in top administrative positions of government. This may be due to the absence of a unified definition across countries of top positions of government. Be that as it may, the statistical data show that the percentage of women occupying such top positions reached 10 per cent in 1992 with the highest participation by women in leadership and supervisory positions occurring in the Ministry of Industry and Minerals, in which they held 38 per cent of total posts. This is followed by the Ministry of Housing and Construction at around 25 per cent of total posts.

Participation in Foreign Affairs and International Relations

Woman have penetrated the diplomatic corps in those Arab countries that went through developmental experiences, such as Egypt, Iraq, Jordan, Lebanon and Palestine. In these countries women's participation has increased, and in some of these countries women have served as ambassadors and taken part in other diplomatic positions.

The reports of the Gulf states do not refer to women occupying any posts in the diplomatic corps except for a reference in the Kuwait national report to a Kuwaiti woman holding the position of ambassador. One should note here that six Gulf women from Bahrain, Oman and Saudi Arabia work within the 'Technicians' category of the UN and hold positions within their states' quotas.

Women diplomats in Egypt's Foreign Ministry comprise 14 per cent of the total number of diplomats. In Lebanon the proportion of women in the diplomatic corps rose to 10 per cent in recent years. Legal statutes impose special conditions on women working in this sector as married women are not permitted to sit for examinations in the foreign corps. Jordanian women did not enjoy the right to become ambassadors until 1980, when the first woman Jordanian ambassador was appointed.

In Iraq women hold high positions in the diplomatic corps. Official statistics show that the number of women occupying the post of advisor or those of first, second and third secretary, chargé d'affaires and director reached 29 per cent in 1980, rising in 1985 to 30 women, one of whom aspired for the post of minister plenipotentiary. By 1993, the number reached 54. In the Sudan statistics show a weakening in women's representation in official diplomacy, despite women occupying positions of leadership at all levels of decision-making.

Participation in the Domestic National Scene

The national reports present the most important indicators of women's participation in national domestic life as follows:

1.   No Arab women have to date achieved the position of governor.

2.   Women's participation varies between Arab societies, due either to the cancellation by certain states of stipulations that had supported women's participation or to the inability in practice of women to take advantage of the rights awarded to her.

3.   There has been a fall in women's participation in village councils in recent years.

4.   Some countries have resorted to direct appointment of women to roles in their affairs as a way of ensuring participation.

The following was also apparent:

1.   Some countries have confused the meaning of participation in the management of domestic affairs with participation in party activity, 'whether as government or as opposition'.

2.   Certain countries have made a point of providing information on women's performance as managers of public affairs while others have ignored this matter.

3.   Palestinian society has emerged as a special case of women's participation in the management of public affairs and one in which this function has merged with participation in military and political affairs.

Leading Businesswomen with their own Capital

Syrian studies show that women registered in the Chamber of Commerce and Industry for the cities of Damascus and Aleppo number 985, a number that does not exceed 2.37 per cent of total persons registered. In statistics of the Iraqi Chamber of Commerce and Industry, the proportion of women contributing to business activity dropped from 27.5 per cent to 16.5 per cent. The national report affirms a continuing decline, for reasons relating to conditions resulting from the sanctions suffered by the country.

As for Palestine, the proportion of businesswomen with their own capital amounted to 1.28 per cent of the total listed in the Chamber of Commerce of the city of Nablus; while in Jerusalem, the proportion is 65 per cent of total shareholders in the Jerusalem Medicaments Company. For the Gulf states, the UAE report on women who are self-employed and have their own capital says that statistics show that, in 1980, the proportion of these women out of the total population who are self-employed amounted to 0.4 per cent; in 1985 this figure declined to 0.3 per cent and then to 0.2 per cent. In Qatar 1986 statistics show that only one woman was self-employed out of 499 Qataris of the same category. Nine women from other nationalities were self-employed in comparison with 1422 non-Qatari men.

In Oman official statistics show that, in 1993, the proportion of leading businesswomen with their own capital amounted to 27 per cent of the overall total.

Leading Businesswomen in Management

National reports indicate unavailability of detailed figures on the status of Arab women in the category of top management. However we know that there are no Gulf women in this category. It is very difficult to obtain accurate statistics on the status of Palestinian women, due to their special situation. In Egypt, the proportion of leading businesswomen working in management fields amounted to 19.9 per cent. In Syria the number of women managers in the public sector is one out of 5053. In Kuwait, the ratio of women holding top management positions rose from 3.2 per cent in 1980 to 7.6 per cent in 1993. In Iraq, women hold 10 per cent of such positions.

Employers and Owners of Business Establishments

Among the most important findings of the national reports were the following:

1. The vague meaning of 'owners and employers of business establishments'. Some reports lumped them all together, without differentiating the sectors of economic activity, others were inclined to excessive detail and enumeration of figures on women in the industrial, agricultural and service sectors while others regarded women's work as marginal, like 'travelling saleswomen' among businessmen. Finally, some reports did not to refer to women at all.
2. The relationship between women's participation and the economic policies of the state. In Egypt, for example, the rise in the ratio of businesswomen was linked to the application of policies of liberalization and economic reform.
3. The linkage of the businesswoman's nationality with the social structure of society and prevailing value system. It was evident that in Qatar, for example, the overwhelming majority of businesswomen, sparse as they are, are non-Qatari.
4. The special case of the Palestinian people led to difficulty in identifying the status of Palestinian businesswomen who reside in the Arab states. Poor statistical material also made it difficult to clarify the status of Palestinian woman within the Occupied Territories.

It is apparent from Kuwait's statistics that the number of businesswomen increased 2.5-fold between 1980 and 1993. However the figure remains relatively low when compared with the number of males in this field. This returns to the special conditions of Kuwaiti society, in terms of customs and habits, which hold the head of the household accountable for the care of the family, with women receiving their own financial security and private accounts in banks, as per the tenets of Islamic *Shari'ah*.

In the UAE a small but increasing number of women own business establishments. It should be noted however that despite the increase in the number of these businesswomen, the ratio of businessmen to women did not change between 1980 and 1985 and even decreased from 0.4 per cent to 0.3 per cent in 1993. It is expected that increased economic activity in the state and expansion of the scope of economic sectors will lead to the entry of larger numbers of women into this field.

Modalities and Programmes supporting Women's Progress

Within the framework of projected strategies, one can point to the following conclusions derived from the national reports:

1. Most of the national reports discussed the role of government in supporting modalities for the advancement of women, whether by underscoring the mechanisms of ministries concerned with women's affairs or the role of government in supporting women's federations and societies. It was evident that government support for women's NGOs helped stimulate the women's federation as one mechanism for their advancement, within the frame of hegemonial political organizations in which the woman's role was pre-set. But this sometimes leads to exhibitionism and to proposals that defy the structure of Arab society and the prevailing value system.
2. Most proposals contained in the national reports came in the form of disjointed ideas that have no connection with the reality of Arab women. Furthermore they failed to state clearly the following: programmes and projects, policies pursued, human and financial resources, the needs of women from different backgrounds, needs and numbers, the ignored role of media and environmental mechanisms, and, finally, no clear indication of the apparent shortage in modalities and programmes.
3. They revealed the vagueness of a hegemonial and coordinated policy for supporting modalities for the advancement of women, and the dissonance of the modalities utilized; this in addition to the employment of these modalities to support the role and place of some privileged women,

to the exclusion of large sectors of women in society.

4. They noted the use of the institutions of civil society and women's NGOs as alternative legal mechanisms to political and union activity, leading in certain cases to the focus of these women's organizations on political movement work at the expense of women's societal issues, or to focus on women's welfare activities at the expense of political participation.

5. The awareness by some NGOs in recent years of the ineffectiveness of the social welfare approach when confronting the challenges besetting women, and their independent judgement that they should emulate an approach to improving and supporting women's conditions as a fundamental means for implementing her programmes.

6. The crystallization of the special case of Palestinian women in their dual role, for the Israeli occupation has impelled the employment of women's programmes, politically and militarily, in the interest of the Palestinian cause.

Awareness of Nationally and Internationally Recognized Rights of Women

In the context of the national reports as proposing that legislative means and basic measures followed by the Arab countries in recent years be utilized to increase the awareness between men and women as to women's rights, one may present the following indicators and details:

Legislative Tools

Most constitutions stipulate equality between the sexes in rights and obligations. They also stipulate equality of opportunity between them. Basic legislation regulates public rights and social, financial and personal relations on the basis of absolute equality in rights and obligations, with due consideration to the distinctiveness of the woman's role. Legislation sets aside special rights for the protection of motherhood and childhood, reconciling women's duties to her family with her work in society, and rendering her equal with men in the political, economic, social and cultural fields.

Despite the Arab woman's enjoyment of a large measure of social rights, by power of constitution and law, especially in the exercise of her political and economic rights and her right to financial security, and despite certain amendments in the texts of laws and measures followed in personal statutes – Arab women continue to suffer from the following:

1. Legal exception in the basic groundwork of constitutions and laws,

forbidding the wife to travel except with the approval of the husband and the neglect of legislative texts on expenditures and child-rearing to address the problems faced by the divorced woman or when child-raising.

2. The ineffectiveness in general of legal texts, and laxity in their implementation, embodied in the failure of women in most Arab countries to reach a position in the judiciary or advance to leadership positions in domestic affairs, such as governess or mayor.

3. The inability of the woman who is married to a foreigner to obtain citizenship for her husband and children, whereas the man who marries a foreign woman can obtain citizenship for his children and her.

The exceptions in the legislative stipulations concerning women are embodied in the gap between the stipulated and the implemented in most Arab countries, with regard to the Agreement on the Elimination of All Forms of Discrimination against Women, the failure of some countries to endorse it, and its qualified endorsement by others with their provisos on certain articles relating to personal statutes, because they are inconsistent with the principles of Islamic *Shari'ah*.

It remains to draw attention to the special situation of the Palestinian woman, who suffers subjection to Arab, foreign and Israeli legislation in addition to enduring the problem of nationality. The Palestinian woman carries up to this day a travel document or the nationality of the country in which she took refuge.

The national reports indicate that most Arab countries suffer from their failure to raise awareness of women's rights. This may be due to the absence of a clear strategy consistent with the needs of women as a socio-economic force. The urban woman has benefited from these measures, the middle-class woman in particular, but not her colleague in rural areas or other strata of society, who represent the majority of women in Arab countries. Perhaps the reason for this is the failure to enforce legislation addressing the conditions of most Arab women. One should stress the great difficulty in exercising political rights that are granted 'from above', in the context of village culture codified by traditions that regulate relations and roles between individuals and dictate the subordination of the woman to the man.

Poverty

According to the World Health Organization the people most vulnerable to harm are women and children and the working population who live under serious conditions of high risk. Furthermore, World Bank figures for the Middle East and North Africa show that the poverty rate rose during the second half of the eighties – and poverty is clearly something that is qualitatively distinct – a large proportion of poor families are headed by women. Very often the situation of women as an individual within the family is worse than that of men, given the discrepancies arising from the qualitative division of food allocation and other realities within the family. The following are some of the indicators of poverty in the domain of women in the Arab region:

Women who are Breadwinners for their Families

There has been an increase in the number of families headed by women, with a concentration of most of these families in urban areas.

1. Widowhood is considered the principal reason behind women supporting their families in most Arab countries that suffer from poverty. In Lebanon it was found that most women who support their families are widows. In Somalia, research results show that, among the most important causes of poverty in the domain of women, is widowhood resulting from war. These researches show plainly that 71 per cent of families in rural areas are supported by women, because of the death of the husband in war in Somalia, in addition to other reasons, including departure of the husband to work in Arab countries that import labour.
2. Gulf states are distinguished by an objective condition that has led to a description of these states as societies of prosperity and plenty. The state in these societies plays an important role in preventing the burgeoning of the phenomenon of women in charge of families, a role embodied in the state's material support for this category.
3. As for Palestine, it is a special case, because of the demographic changes, continuous war and permanent emigration and displacement that have led to women becoming the breadwinners of their families; this in addition to the death, detention and exile of their men.
4. Somalia is also considered a special case. The results of some studies show plainly that women who live below the poverty line represent 49 per cent of the population in nomadic areas, 47 per cent of the population in rural sedentary areas and 42 per cent in urban areas. The principal factor underlying the poverty is war and its consequences: hunger, exile and violence.
5. Most families supported by women fall within the category of the poor. In the Arab Republic of Egypt, the average income of families supported by women is 37 per cent less than the average of families supported by men. In Jordan, most families headed by women are in the lowest income brackets, against 19.3 per cent of total families in this income

bracket.

6. As for the Gulf states with their special situation, the UAE national report shows that per capita GNP averaged about $17,600 in 1993. One notes an increase in the ratio of women supporting their own families, from 1.6 per cent to 2.6 per cent of total families. The state takes care of these families through financial allowances needed to provide a standard of living appropriate to the social situation of the state.

The state in Kuwait has an important role in preventing the aggravation of the crisis of women responsible for their families; the Kuwaiti woman does not suffer from this problem because of the application of the Public Assistance Act. In Oman, despite the small rise in the ratio of women supporting their families, the state is careful to increase financial allocations for them.

Unemployment

National reports show the following:

1. Unemployment among women is linked with poverty and illiteracy.
2. The rate of unemployment as a whole is generally lower in the Gulf states. The reason for this decline may be due to these states seeking to make available employment for all their citizens, while not permitting expatriate labour to enter except on condition of contract for actual work.
3. The rates of unemployment increased in some Arab countries, because of the return of expatriate labour to their countries of origin.
4. The condition of occupation in Palestine, the hostilities in Lebanon, and the Gulf war led to a decline in the proportion of Palestinian women in the labour force.

It is certain that, during economic crises, the unemployment rate among women exceeds that of men. The general trend in situations of high unemployment is to give preference, when hiring, to men, when labour is in surplus. This is confirmed by the statistics on the Arab countries.

Public Day-Care Centres for Children

National reports show that despite the noticeable increase in the number of public centres in recent years, the proportion of children enrolled in them is small in comparison with the total number of children who fall within the same age category and are in need of enrolment in these centres. In addition, some researchers have shown plainly that these centres are marginal and ineffective in reducing the burdens on the working woman.

Vocational Training

National reports show the following:

1. Vocational training is regarded as among the most important means of assisting in the upgrading of skills required for the labour market.
2. The indicators on the presentation of vocational training in the Arab countries differ. Some countries, such as Egypt, adopted in the characterization of vocational training the indicators of vocational and technical systems training. Other countries, such as Jordan and Palestine, turn to characterization of the role of official and private training institutes in this regard.
3. Despite the increase in women trainees during recent years, their number remains small compared to their male counterparts.
4. Interest in training increased in the Gulf states after the 1990 war in response to the policy of substituting national manpower for expatriate manpower.

Women in Education, Health and Labour

We turn here to the basic starting points in the study of educational, health services and labour issues, which may be briefly summarized as follows.

The basic challenge to equipping women for education, health and labour is the increase in the population rate of some Arab countries. The rate of population growth is high in Arab countries, compared with other developing countries. Moreover, the comparative increase in fertility ratios is considered the principal cause behind the increasing rate of population growth. This means an increase in the ratio of younger age groups to total population, which to some extent leads to a narrowing of material capacities in the provision of health, education and labour services.

Among the most important time periods in which women endured factors of change and transformation were the sixties, seventies and eighties. The most important of the factors were laws that changed and determined the framework and context of Arab society during these decades. The decades were characterized by an increase in school enrolment ratios, a commitment by most Arab countries to individual health and social care, a commitment to provide job opportunities for every man and woman, and the adoption of much legislation for increasing women's participation in labour and rendering women equal to men in rights and obligations.

Despite the development of social legislation, in practice it did not provide an opportunity for employing the capabilities and energies of women. Arab women suffer the consequences of traditions that fetter the philosophy of advanced legislation in a world characterized by rapid motion and change. This impels some Arab societies to issue special laws for women designed to support and help them exercise their rights.

Illiteracy

National reports indicate the following:

1. The endeavour by the Arab countries to implement illiteracy eradication programmes in the domains of both men and women.
2. Despite a relative decline in the illiteracy ratio between men and women, Arab society continues to suffer the consequences of the problem of illiteracy in general, and the problem of illiteracy among women in particular.
3. Illiteracy ratios among women vary from one country to another. In Yemen, the illiteracy ratio among women is 85 per cent, followed by Somalia at 79 per cent, Egypt around 59.2 per cent, Kuwait 38.4 per cent, Syria 31.6 per cent, Iraq 25.2 per cent, Jordan 25 per cent, and Palestine 21.2 per cent. The reasons for the continuing high rate of illiteracy among the Arab countries are as follows:

    i   Traditions, especially in rural and nomadic areas.

    ii   Increase in the rate of illiteracy among women, which may be due in part to an increase in illiteracy for age groups over 40, who did not have an opportunity to learn.

    iii Failure to adhere to the policy of compulsory education.

    iv Population density in some countries.

    v   Paucity of material and human resources in some Arab countries.

    vi Some Gulf states are distinguished by the establishment of programmes for illiteracy eradication, with a noticeable comparative drop in the illiteracy ratio, compared with some other Arab countries. This may be explained by the financial capability of these states, in addition to their smaller populations.

    vii The positive role of NGOs and their effectiveness in illiteracy eradication programmes, and the active cooperation between these NGOs and governments in this regard.

    viii It is also clear that illiteracy eradication programmes do not bear fruit. They are confined to providing simplified sessions for teaching the basics of reading and writing in general. When the sessions come to an end, the woman student gradually loses what she had gained because of the absence of follow-up.

Education

One may summarize the indicators of education at the level of the Arab countries as follows:

1. All laws and constitutions of the Arab countries stipulate the right of women to education, and to equal opportunities with men in this right.
2. The Arab countries achieved over the past two decades noticeable progress in the field of education generally, and the education of women in particular. The size of female enrolment in all stages of education increased in comparison with previous decades, and in many Arab countries female education ratios equalled male ratios at the various stages of education. One can even say that in most Arab countries the ratios of female graduates matched the enrolment ratios at the various stages of education.
3. Female enrolment ratios are affected by geographic location. The ratios in rural and remote areas are lower than in urban areas.
4. Though compulsory education in the Gulf states is something recent, some states were distinguished by a rise in the ratio of female education, sometimes even exceeding the ratio of their male counterpart. This could be attributed to the fact that Gulf women regard education as a source of social mobility and entry into society.

Going beyond the figures, one can infer that education as a social system came to adapt to society's traditional culture. That is to say, the evaluational perception of the variable of education is not tied to the quantitative indicator only. Arab women's superiority in scholastic achievement, for example, even if regarded as a positive indicator suggesting a distinction of women from men, could also be considered as indicative of the continued disparity in the equalization of opportunity in society. For the diversification of opportunities for the young man and his activities prompt him to distribute his energies and activities between the various opportunities available to him, rendering him unable to concentrate on scholastic achievement, whereas the young girl does not have the opportunities available to the man, and so she has no choice but to concentrate on scholastic achievement.

This last point is underlined by the fact that, despite the comparative increase in the rate of female graduates from secondary education, most of them are enrolled in arts faculties and very few of them (where the educational system permits) are enrolled in practical and technical faculties.

Within the framework of Palestine's exceptional case, in terms of confronting educational processes, especially during the time of the *intifadah* and the current transitional phase, Palestinian women share with their Arab sisters the comparative inequality in opportunity for education, for reasons already cited above.

Health

Despite a noticeable improvement in the level of public health in Arab countries, as per the indicators of human resources development, there is some variation between the Arab countries in the level of public health. Most Arab countries continue to suffer from:

1. A relative decline in average life expectancy at birth, in comparison with some developing countries and also with all the states of the advanced world.
2. Increase in the mortality rate of mothers during pregnancy and childbirth.
3. Increase in infant mortality accompanying the previous increase.
4. Increase in fertility ratios, multiple pregnancies and childbirth, and large families, leading to less care for each child.
5. Deterioration in the health situation of Arab women by repeated pregnancies and childbirth under difficult social and economic conditions.
6. Deterioration in the level of nutrition revealed an increase in the ratio of women working in agriculture, whether paid or unpaid. There are historical reasons for this, relating to the woman assuming the burden of farm work, or to factors proceeding from social changes at the level of the last era, when the husband departed to work in the Gulf states.

Discussion of the increase in the rate of women's work requires a redefinition of 'the roles of the woman' in a correct manner that accords with the actual needs of society and its challenges. The role is rights that are gained and obligations that are met, within the contextual social framework. The multiple roles of the woman, both within and outside the home, have led to a misunderstanding of these roles. She was obliged to work outside the home according to new standards, and she had to work within the home according to old standards. The multiple roles of wife/mother have exhausted her psychologically and physically, and this has affected her role as producer and as caretaker. Le gislation contributed to creating new social systems and new intellectual visions that did not effect a fundamental change in individual inclinations or in the culture of the family, including the woman herself.

There are certain technical statistical attempts that emerged in the new system of national accounts prepared by the UN, which regard the housework of the woman as production and calculate it within economic activity. But this concept is still in the research stage and has not been absorbed socially or culturally.

Violence against Women

The current period is characterized by concern in international organizations, women's movements and human rights organizations over violence against women. Given the prevalence in Arab society of values and customs that proceed from Islamic teachings, which urge respect, generosity and care for women, society's institutions do not recognize the existence of this problem and try as much as possible to suppress signs of violence against women. This may be due to the widely held view that any problem that besets a member of a family is an internal problem that should be resolved within the family, especially if that person is the woman. Violence against women in some countries, such as Lebanon, Iraq and Palestine, is regarded as of secondary importance, a product of the suffering by every man and woman of the consequences of war or occupation.

Serious Forms of Violence against the Arab Woman

These include being obliged to leave school, being forced sometimes into marriage, early marriage, the beating of girls by parents, and occasionally forcing the woman to relinquish her personal or civil rights by force of customs and wonts. Some hold that polygamy in certain Arab countries is a form of violence against women. It is very difficult to give a quantitative measure to violence waged against women, because of the absence of data on this, or the holding of the issue of such violence as a family matter, or the failure of the woman to see some of these acts as forms of violence.

Methods Applied for the Protection of Women from Exploitation

There are in some Arab countries laws that protect the woman from exploitation, while others lack such legislations that forbid abuse of the rights of women and female minors. Some NGOs seek to make women aware of their legal rights by arranging workshops, issuing newsletters and monthly publications, organizing training seminars and providing legal counsel for women.

The Impact of Disputes and Wars on Women

The Arab region has witnessed nearly six wars resulting from the Arab–Israeli conflict, the Iraq–Iran war, the Gulf war in 1991, and the strife in Lebanon, Yemen and Somalia. The populations of Arab countries suffered all forms of expulsion, displacement and dispersion, and this has led to an increase in the number of refugees, the greater part of whom are women and children. Lebanon suffered the consequences of civil strife, and Israeli invasion and occupation of parts of its territories. Lebanese women did not surrender to the harsh suffering but confronted and resisted it forcefully. Detention, kidnapping, martyrdom, displacement, crippling – all increased her determination and resolve. She supported the family. The Lebanese woman suffered the impact of direct and indirect displacement. She suffered the tragedies of war and occupation embodied in the deterioration of her livelihood and situation.

Algerian their country also suffer from the deterioration of the situation in Algeria and are vulnerable to being butchered and killed, and to all forms of violence. Jordan received a third exodus of Jordanians and Palestinians, returning from the Gulf as a result of the Gulf war. It is worth mentioning that women made up half of the refugees, displaced and returnees. Woman has borne the greater economic burden of this wave of displacement, which included, among other things, greater family responsibility and household burdens, a reduction in the level of available services, a rise in unemployment among returnees, which in turn led to a rise in unemployment among women.

In Yemen, the southern provinces witnessed the hostilities of January 1986. The war had its impact on women and children. Women bore their responsibilities and those of their children where their fathers were killed or imprisoned. In the internal strife that broke out in 1994, Yemeni women suffered as well, because the armed conflicts and decision-making involved a male issue. In the war between Iraq and Iran, women in both countries were the first victims of war. The same was the case in the Gulf war. The sanctions imposed have also had their impact on women and their families; the conditions of the sanctions added to their tasks and responsibilities within the family and outside it.

In the Somalia war, some 20,000 Somali families took refuge in Yemen. Somali women worked as servants in homes, and many diseases spread among them and their families.

There is no woman in the world who has suffered the effects of armed conflict and perpetual wars as much as the Palestinian woman. During half a century of Arab–Israeli conflict and the suffering of the Palestinian people from the impact of war and aggression, starting from the year 1948, hundreds of thousands of Palestinian families have been dispersed, the displacement of males has grown, the ratio of females to males in the West Bank and Gaza has increased, as did celibacy among women, which in turn increased polygamy and divorce. Palestinian camps in Lebanon witnessed destructive wars, increasing the suffering of Palestinian women even more.

Women and the Environment

The role of Arab women in preserving the environment is embodied in indicators to be found in the national reports. These include:

1. The enlistment of women in some Arab countries in the Ministry of the Environment. Their ratio in Syria constituted 60 per cent of the total staff of the Ministry of State for Environmental Affairs.
2. Increase in the proportion of women working in environmental research centres, participating in studies and setting technical standards for the protection of the environment from pollution.
3. Organization of seminars on the role of women in protecting their families from pollution.
4. The endeavour by NGOs to protect the environment. In Lebanon, according to available statistics, there are 30 institutions concerned specifically with the environment, and these include a large number of women.

Many women representatives of women's, NGO and professional societies participate actively in environmental protection committees, committees for water rationalization and consumption, parks and floral societies, and health and protection societies. Women implement many programmes and actions aimed at enhancing society's awareness and how to safeguard the environment in all its forms, including rationalizing energy, water and electricity use, maintaining cleanliness, arranging in-door gardens, raising birds and animals, and entrenching sound values and habits in children and families through lectures and educational and counselling seminars.

Women and the Media

In the context of the communications and technological revolution, as mechanisms to be relied on in economic, social, cultural and scientific transformation, the world is heading today towards supporting the role of women in the media, whether at a practical level in media institutions or improving and developing information programmes addressing women's causes.

Arab countries apply the international approach in supporting the role of women in this sphere. The distinctiveness of Arab society, however, means that there are specific ways in which this is done:

1. Most Arab media continue to project the image of the traditional woman and focus on the traditional role of wife, housewife and mother. Her traditional image is projected at the expense of her other roles as worker and contributor to decision-making and as human being equal to the man in rights and obligations. When women emerge in their new roles, they seem cold, unmoved, emotionless and inhuman, which prompts others to turn against them.
2. Media sources need to address modern women's causes, such as the environment, peace, and equality in opportunity and human rights.
3. There is widespread commercial exploitation in advertising of the image of woman to promote commodities.
4. In some Arab countries suffering the consequences of war, the media image of woman is distorted.

Note

* Faculty of Education, Lebanese University, Unesco, Beirut, Lebanon.

Seven

Border and Territorial Disputes between Arabs and Iranians

13

The Dispute Between the United Arab Emirates and Iran over Three Islands

SHIMLAN EL-ISSA*

Introduction

The case of the dispute between the United Arab Emirates (UAE) and the Islamic Republic of Iran over the islands of Abu Musa and Greater and Lesser Tunb is regarded as another phase of tension in the Arabian Gulf region, which has not known stability for over two decades. The cause of tension between Iran and the states of the Arabian Gulf is due to the fact that Iran rejects, up to the present, discussing the islands it occupied in 1971, or examining the matter. A number of sessions were held to attempt to resolve the problem peacefully between the two sides, but all ended in failure.

The issue of the Arab islands has once again surfaced in Gulf and Arab politics. It was discussed at the last Gulf summit meeting held in Bahrain in December 1994, and it held a prominent place in the 49th session of the UN General Assembly in New York. This study examines the dispute between the UAE and the Islamic Republic of Iran in a bid to understand Arab–Iranian relations in the forthcoming phase.

Geographic Location of the Three Islands

The importance of the three Arab islands, Abu Musa, Greater Tunb and Lesser Tunb, is in their geographic location. They are situated near the entrance of the Strait of Hormuz in the Arabian Gulf, which is regarded as among the most important passageways in the world. The state that controls it can easily control the entire Arabian Gulf region.[1]

It should be emphasized here, before talking about the geographic loca-

237

tion of the islands, that sources differ over how far the islands are from the Arabian and Iranian coastlines. The Arab side sees them as closer to its coastline, the Iranian as closer to its own.

i. Abu Musa Island

Abu Musa Island lies 94 miles from the entrance to the Arabian Gulf at the Hormuz Strait, about 75 km from the Iranian coast and nearly 48 km from the Omani coast off the Sharqah emirate. Its area is 20 km². The island is rectangular in shape and its topography is flat and sandy, devoid of trees except for a small patch near fresh water wells.

Before the Iranian occupation, an Arab population of some 1000 persons resided on the island, which has an elementary school, a customhouse, mosque and palace for the deputy governor of Sharqah. The inhabitants of the island used to work as fishermen and shepherds. The island has important minerals, such as iron oxide and oil.

ii. Greater Tunb Island

Greater Tunb Island lies 59 km southwest of Qeshm Island and 78 km northwest of Hamra' Island. It is circular in shape, with a diameter of about 3.5 km and an area of about 9 km². Its residents, numbering 200–700, work as shepherds and fishermen. There are two schools, a lighthouse for guiding ships, and it has oil. It is under the suzerainty of the emirate of Ras al-Khaimah.

iii. Lesser Tunb Island

This island is about 90 km distance from the Arabian coast and 13 km away from Greater Tunb Island. It is triangular in shape, 2 km long and about 1 km wide at its southern tip. The island is comprised of three hills, dark in colouration, and inhabited by sea birds. There are no people on the island, which is under the suzerainty of Ras al-Khaimah.[2]

Historical Background of the Arab Islands

After the fall of *elayet* administration in Oman, the Qasimis flourished, ruling over the Omani coast and becoming extant in some parts of southern Iran during the 18th century, through a branch of their tribe, who proceeded from Ras al-Khaimah to the Iranian coast.[3] Iranian historians admitted Qasimi activity and control over southern Iran and the Arab islands. *Kaihan al-Arabi* journal wrote that before going into the causes of conflict over ownership of the three islands, one must return to the mid-18th century. After the death of Nader Shah in 1747, Iranian influence was constrained in the Persian Gulf. This created a situation favourable for the start of [Qasimi] penetration in the area. The Qasimis, or 'Joasmees', are an Arab tribe who lived in Sharqah and Ras al-Khaimah. A branch of this tribe moved to Iran and settled in Bandar, but, according to an Iranian historical source, the chief of this branch, named Sheikh Said bin Qadib, was able to take control of this port against a subsidy of 2000 Iranian Riyals. This was during the rule of the Zands. After that, his sons assumed by turn command of the port, repaying part of the monthly subsidies. As Abu Musa and Greater and Lesser Tunb belonged to Bandar Lengeh, the Qasimis remained in charge during that period.[4]

It is very clear that the Iranian sources recognize the preponderance of the Qasimis over the Arab islands and others. But they sought to undermine Arab ownership of these islands by saying that their rulers used to be paid wages from Iran in return for taking care of the Arab port of Lengeh before Iran seized it. The Qasimis' influence spread in the 18th century to the northern coast, where some settled in the Lengeh area and brought the three islands and coast along the Gulf under their control. This occurred in 1835 during the traditional apportioning between the Qasimis – the current rulers in Sharqah and Ras al-Khaimah – over ownership of the Gulf islands, whereby Serri and Henqam went to the Lengeh Qasimis, and Abu Musa, Greater and Lesser Tunb and Seer Abu Nu'ayr to the Qasimis of the Oman coast, that is, Ras al-Khaimah and Sharqah.[5]

Among the definitive evidence of the Arab identity of these islands is the affirmation of the British Agent in Bushehr, who confirmed in 1879 that the two islands of Tunb and Lengeh were under Qasimi suzerainty.[6] In 1887, Iran occupied the emirate of Arab Lengeh and extended its influence and control to the two islands of Serri and Henqam, Arab islands belonging to the Qasimis, situated west of Abu Musa Island and directly before it. Also in 1887, Iran began demanding the two islands of Serri and Abu Musa, but Britain, through its minister plenipotentiary in Tehran, replied to Iran that the islands are Arab, owned by Arab sheikhs attached to Britain by special treaties under British protection. Britain, he stated, was responsible for their foreign affairs.[7]

As for the recent Iranian demand for the Arab islands, in 1923, when the Wadi Dhahabi Company discovered quantities of hematite in Hormuz Island and wanted to extend its activities to Abu Musa Island, Tehran proceeded to occupy the island and hoist the Iranian flag. In 1925, Iran sent a geological mission to inspect the quantity of hematite available on the island. Britain, however, opposed Iran's exploitation of the islands and once again announced that they were Arab islands. Iran made several more attempts at the beginning of this century to occupy the islands, but was prevented by Britain.[8]

Iran took advantage of the withdrawal of British troops from the Gulf and the UAE's declaration of independence. It occupied the three Arab islands on 30 November 1971. The Shah's troops invaded the Emirates' islands a few hours after the UAE's declaration of independence on the pretext of returning them to the Iranian motherland.[9] It should be emphasized here that the Shah of Iran had announced on 16 February 1971 his country's intention to occupy these islands, by force if necessary, in case of failure to hand them over peacefully to Iran before the final date of withdrawal of British troops from the Arabian Gulf at the end of that year. By a strange irony, Britain had promised to hand over to Iran Greater Tunb and Lesser Tunb Islands in case of its withdrawal from the Gulf. The Iranian Court Minister, Asadollah Alam, mentioned in his memoirs this dialogue with the British Ambassador in Tehran: 'I met the British Ambassador in the afternoon; we discussed the subject of Bahrain and the Gulf islands, which he was keen on presenting as two prominent matters. He said: Tunb will be easy for us, but Abu Musa no, being very close to the Arabian Peninsula. I replied that this is not considered among Iran's rights, or giving the Arabs a right, and they should not keep a grip on an Iranian area, an area that His Majesty will not abandon. The Ambassador proposed that solving the problem of Bahrain will encourage formation of a union of Arab emirates, whereby Iran can occupy Abu Musa as in the interest of joint security of the Gulf, and we may depend on British support if this happens'.[10] As a result of mediation by Britain, the power protecting the Gulf emirates then, and the talks that took place in Tehran in mid-November between the last British political agent in the Gulf, William Loess, on behalf of the ruler of Sharqah, and the Shah of Iran, a final agreement was reached, described as a memorandum of understanding dated 29 November 1971. Immediately thereafter, the ruler of Sharqah, Sheikh Khalid bin Muhammad al-Qasimi, announced that he reluctantly accepted a final agreement with Iran reached in mid-November to resolve the long-standing dispute between the two sides, through joint administration of Abu Musa Island, in the face of an Iranian threat to use force if he did not accept this measure. The preamble to the 'memorandum of understanding' included a reminder that neither Iran nor Sharqah will abandon their demand over Abu Musa and neither recognizes the demands of the other party. Given this preamble, the following measures and arrangements were arrived at:

1. The landing of Iranian troops on the island and the occupation of areas

agreed upon on the map attached to the memorandum.

2. Iran will exercise full sovereignty within the areas agreed upon for occupation by Iranian troops and hoisting of the Iranian flag over them.

3. Sharqah will retain full sovereignty over the remainder of the island, and the flag of Sharqah shall remain hoisted over the Sharqah police station, based on the same tenets in force with regard to the hoisting of the Iranian flag over Iranian military locations.

4. Iran and Sharqah each recognize the extension of the island's territorial waters – a distance of 12 miles into the sea.

5. Butez Gas and Oil Company will undertake to exploit the oil reserves of Abu Musa Island and the sea bed, based on the agreement in effect and which Iran must accept. The Company will pay half the revenues of the said reserves directly to Iran and the other half shall be paid to Sharqah.

6. Iran's and Sharqah's citizens will enjoy equal rights in the territorial waters of Abu Musa Island.

7. An agreement for financial assistance will be signed between Iran and Sharqah.[11]

Although the landing of Iranian troops on Abu Musa Island took place in implementation of the text of this agreement, the UAE and some other Arab states condemned it as an act of aggression. The UAE issued a statement with this wording on 3 December 1971. It criticized the Iranian occupation, condemned the use of force in occupying part of Arab lands, and defended respect for legal rights and the need to discuss any disputes between states and resolve them by peaceful means.

It is noteworthy that the signing of this forced settlement between the ruler of Sharqah and rulers of Iran took place under pressure and the threat of occupation of these islands by force if a solution favouring Iran was not reached. One may therefore regard this agreement as void since that threat was in violation of international law, incorporated in the charter of the United Nations, based on Article (52) of the Convention on the Law of Treaties. The ruler of Ras al-Khaimah refused to respond to Iranian demands over the two islands of Greater and Lesser Tunb, which Iran occupied by force on the same day.

The Illegality of Regional Changes resulting from the Use of Force under recent International Law

Recent international law came to cancel the principle of 'law in the service of force', which traditional international law tolerated, to become based for us on 'force in the service of law'. It prohibited those who address its provisions to resort to a show of force, in whatever form.

Recent international law, in contrast with its predecessor, is distinguished by the numerical increase of its persons, expansion of its functions and diversification of its topics. States are no longer in themselves regarded as the sole legal persons of international law. There are other entities that play an active and influential part in the traffic of international relations, and are legally competent to bear rights and fulfill obligations, such as, for example, national liberation movements, international organizations and non-national companies, or even the individual in certain cases, whenever his functions widen. International law is no longer the law of sovereignty, coexistence, trade; it performs today wider and more comprehensive functions. It is a 'law of cooperation', 'law of harmony', etc.[12]

Finally, political or consular relations, the law of the seas or of wars, are no longer the core of recent international law. Rather its subjects have diversified to include all fields, such as the international economy, international trade, environment and development. Rare are the human activities today that are outside the scope of international law.[13] The most important development witnessed by recent international law is represented by the invalidation of legitimacy in regional changes originating or arising from the use of force, with total prohibition of its use in international relations. Here, the international community exerted considerable effort to establish the norm 'prohibition of the use of force in international relations'. These efforts were expressed in the promulgation of a number of international conventions and protocols that sought to gradually divest any regional change emanating from the use of force of legitimacy.

The efforts culminated with the declaration of the United Nations Charter issued on 26 June 1945, wherein Article (2), paragraph (4), stipulated: 'All members shall refrain in their international relations from the threat or use of force against the territorial integrity or political independence of any state, or in any other manner inconsistent with the purpose of the United Nations'.[14]

Iranian Infringements on the Memorandum of Understanding over Abu Musa

In March 1992, the President of the Islamic Republic of Iran, Mr Hashemi Rafsanjani, paid a surprise visit to the island of Abu Musa. This is regarded as the first undertaken by an Iranian head of state to the island since its occupation, and that of neighbouring Greater and Lesser Tunb Islands, by Iran in 1971. After this visit, Iranian authorities began to take a series of administrative measures by which Iran sought to affirm its control and impose its hegemony over the entire island and its residents, in a move towards annexation by fait accompli. They forbade the nationals of the

UAE on the island, who are the original inhabitants, as well as Arabs and foreign residents, from movement in the island except within one kilometre of the geographic area containing the Arab population and UAE's government services facilities in Abu Dhabi. The Iranian military authorities in the island also imposed a series of security and administrative measures on fishing vessels belonging to UAE nationals, in particular those owned by inhabitants of the island, such as forbidding fishing in the island's territorial waters, except by permits issued by them, renewable every five days.[15]

As part of the provocative measures directed to constricting the local population's means of livelihood, Iranian military authorities in the island closed down all shops, which numbered 18, with only one still open – the cooperative – and it cannot meet the whole population's needs.

Completing the constriction of livelihood, the Iranian military authorities forbade entry of anything into the island, however small, except by permission of the Iranian military commander there. They also tightened searches of incoming persons from the island's own residents, those of the UAE or anyone working there, and under conditions that, to say the least, are inhuman and arbitrarily imposed, having no military urgency or serious security grounds, and difficult climatic conditions as well, whether in summer or winter. (Historical facts show that Iranian authorities resorted more than once to harassing the population of the island over their livelihood, on the pretext that they use the island as a centre for smuggling certain commodities the Iranian state has a monopoly on, such as sugar, tea and tobacco).

The Iranian authorities did not stop there, however, but proceeded to forbid citizens from building new homes or facilities, or even renovate their old homes, except on a very limited scale. They also refused to permit the extension of telephone lines to the island, where the area inhabited by the Arabs has only two telephones, one in the police station and the other in the home of the wali of the island, appointed by the ruler of Sharqah. Nor did they permit the establishment of clinics or transporting patients by air to hospitals in the UAE, whatever the condition of the patient.

In a bid to impose Iranian sovereignty as a fait accompli, the Iranian military authorities forbade entry of cars carrying UAE licence plates. They also forbade the hoisting of the Emirates flag over the island, in violation of the memorandum of understanding between the governments of Sharqah (UAE) and Iran in 1971.

The Iranian military authorities also went beyond the limits of their area of military jurisdiction in the island (whose total area is approximately 22 km^2). In the context of this expansion, they built a prototype Iranian village, erected military posts in the western part of the island, and occupied locations in the vicinity of the hematite mines (Mughr) in the eastern part, known as the 'khulwa' area. Diplomatic sources in Abu Dhabi indicate that Iran brought military reinforcements to the island and increased the number of its troops from 120 to 500 soldiers and set up Chinese-made Silkworm missile batteries.[16]

The Political Causes of Iranian Infringements

Why did Iran escalate its infringements in Abu Musa Island at this particular time? It is a question posed by more than one observer and person concerned with Iranian relations. The question was raised many times, but the answers were so variable as to suggest that the political behaviour of a state is rarely the result of one factor alone, but rather many interrelated factors eventually leading to the state's specific political behaviour in its international relations at a given point in time.

In presenting an answer to the above question, answers and opinions have differed. Some saw Iran's attachment to the islands of Greater Tunb and Lesser Tunb and completion of its occupation of Abu Musa Island as effectively a 'message of warning' to the nationalities comprising the Iranian state, which are looking to separatism from the motherland and the announcement of a national state along the lines of what is happening now in central Asia, Iran's neighbour, or as is happening in Iraq and Afghanistan, or the demands of the Kurds in Turkey, etc.

The gist of this message is that the Iranian state is not prepared to forfeit any part of its territories, even if this were to be a few small islands whose total area does not exceed a hundred square kilometres. Commentators do not conceal their apprehension on the reality of such separatism, as the Iranian state is composed of various nationalities, such as Persians, Baluchis, Kurds, Turcomens, Azeris and Arabs, particularly as the separatist drive has begun among Iran's Kurds, while US and Turkish harassment of Iran in Azerbeijan worries Iran and rocks its boat.

A second opinion attributes Iranian infringements on Abu Musa Island to the deterioration of the economic situation in Iran. The economic crisis Iran is currently going through impels it to pursue a course defusing this crisis, even if it means sparking an oil crisis with its neighbours in a bid to increase oil revenues or its oil reserves. Those holding this opinion see Iran burdened by weakening oil reserves. By imposing its control on Abu Musa and the two Tunbs, it affirms its ownership of these islands. It will declare its territorial waters, estimated at 12 miles offshore, as beginning with the end of the land limit of these islands in the direction of the UAE; with that, all oil wells and oil reserves in these waters become its own. The demands of the Iranian negotiating team in Abu Dhabi apparently reflected this crisis, for the Iranian delegation requested from the UAE financial indemnities, claiming they are entitled to them because of losses incurred by Iran in the war with Iraq.

The Iranian delegation expressed their dissatisfaction with the quota Iran received from the Mubarak oil field and accused the UAE of extracting more oil than it is entitled to. Others of this opinion see flawed economic policies pursued by the Iranian government as leading to the deterioration of economic and social conditions, the spread of unemployment, and the increasing inflation and prices of basic commodities.[17] These have provoked popular resentment that turned into hooliganism and demonstrations in Iran's major cities, threatening to bring down the government, even the entire regime. This prompted the Iranian government to tighten its measures in Abu Musa Island and speak of uncovering a vast plot being hatched in this island to undermine the safety and security of the country, in a bid to distract the Iranian public's attention from the problems they are enduring and rally them to the greater national cause. Such remarks – discovering conspiracies – may preoccupy the people for a while, and lighten their campaigns against the government, or cause them to drop hooliganism or disturbances they might undertake in protest over the extremely difficult conditions the country is going through.

A third opinion goes on to describe Iranian infringements on the island as a veritable 'Iranian warning' directed at the Gulf Cooperation Council (GCC), the states of the Damascus declaration and the US, in that any security arrangements in the Gulf cannot exclude Iran. What Iran wants to say to the states of the GCC and their allies is that, by its historic weight and civilizational and cultural record, and human, economic and military strength, as well as political and strategic interests in the Gulf and the world, it cannot accept a marginal role that does not obtain for it national objectives on the matter of Gulf security. Those who back this view dismiss such a position on the grounds that the second Gulf war showed the fragility of the Gulf's security system and ineffectiveness and incapacity to confront alone any external challenge. GCC states concluded security and defence pacts with states within the Arab orb, and bilateral security arrangements with states outside it. It is noteworthy that these agreements excluded Iran from security arrangements, or at best gave it a marginal role, at a time when the statements by officials in Iran left the impression that what was intended was the establishment of a security system with Iran as the hub, and this is what caused the disappointment of Iranian officials with the behaviour of their Arab neighbours in the Gulf.

Opinion-holders close with the feeling that Iran, by its measures in Abu Musa Island, is drawing the attention of the GCC and their allies, particularly the US, and it is presumptuous to draw up a formula for the region's security that gives no weight to Iran's nearby presence. The fact of Iran's infringements on the memorandum of understanding is not something new. It began in the era of Muhammad Reza Shah Pahlavi, with the circulation of the memorandum, and continued to burgeon since the advent of the

Iranian revolution and until the end of the second Gulf war, with Iran completing its infringements by declaring takeover of the island by fait accompli in the first quarter of 1992.

Domestically, Iran's deteriorating economic and social conditions and growing conflict between the moderate line and the hard line within the ruling institution, and the emergence of separatist disputes among some nationalities comprising the Iranian state, are undoubtedly other factors that threaten the ruling regime in Iran, in terms of the legitimacy of its continuation. There is no better issue than Iranian sovereignty over the islands in dispute between Iran and the UAE to bring the Iranian people under the government's fold.

Conclusion: Towards a Peaceful Settlement to the Islands Issue

Since the outbreak of the crisis between the Arabs and Iran over the three islands, a number of attempts were made to resolve the crisis peacefully. Direct negotiations were held between Abu Dhabi and the Islamic Republic during 27–9 September 1992 across three working sessions, but the two sides did not reach an amicable solution; Iran refused to address its occupation of the Arab islands or even discuss it. Iranian officials affirmed their total refusal to discuss this issue; Sheikh Natiq Nouri, the chairman of the Consultative Council, declared in a response to the GCC communique: 'The leaders of the Gulf Arab states have perhaps forgotten history, for even before they gained their existence from British imperialism, these islands were, are and will remain Iranian'.[18]

The Iranian President Ali Akbar Hashemi Rafsanjani warned against encroachment on the islands, and threatened by saying that the Emirates will cross a sea of blood before reaching them. He affirmed that Iran will not relinquish the three strategic islands in the Gulf, whatever the cost.[19] The UAE continued to invite pursuit of solutions by peaceful means, despite Iran's insistence and refusal to negotiate over the islands. The UAE intensified its movements at the regional level with the GCC states and those of the Damascus declaration, and with the Arab states through the Arab League. It also took the issue of the Arab islands to the UN. Iran responded to the UAE calls by affirming its position, namely:

1. The two islands of Greater and Lesser Tunb are Iranian islands and are an integral part of Iranian territory, and Iran's sovereignty over them is not open for discussion with others in any way.
2. Negotiations over Abu Musa Island must be within the framework of the memorandum of understanding, and in a way that serves Iran's security, economic and strategic interests in the Gulf.

3. Great power intervention, under whatever guise, should be avoided and an end brought to the raising of regional demands in international gatherings.

Because of Iran's absence and unresponsiveness to peaceful efforts and initiatives for solving the problem, the UAE announced its full readiness for arbitration by the International Court of Justice as the foremost instrument for resolving disputes between states, and pledged to accept all results that may proceed from the judgement of the International Court, being based on legal evidence and documentation. The truth everyone knows is that we Arabs cannot ignore Iran as an important Islamic state in the region, particularly as it is the largest Gulf state, in area and in important strategic location, and in its population of nearly 60 million. Imperialist powers played a major role in fuelling and deepening the conflict between the Arabs and Iran; Britain played a strange role in supporting the Arabs at times, the Shah of Iran at other times, in order to sustain its interests in the region.

In the past, Iran was an ally of the US in the Gulf. In the sixties and seventies, it became the biggest and strongest, financially and militarily, due to US support, and the Shah of Iran played an active role as policeman of the Gulf. Today, things have changed after the Islamic revolution in Iran, and the collapse of the Soviet Union recently. The new world order is under the leadership of a US seriously seeking to limit the role of Iran, due to its revolutionary positions over Israel and the security of the region as a whole.

Arabs and Iranians need one another for many reasons – political, economic, social – and so must cooperate and consolidate their joint interests. The Arab region is on the threshold of many changes because of the peace process with Israel. It is irrational and unacceptable that Arab–Israeli relations expand and the major Islamic neighbour, Iran, be ignored ... Thus, it is our view that Arabs and Iranians should concentrate on issues that serve their mutual interests, and try to resolve their problems and border differences by peaceful means.

Notes

* Department of Political Sciences, Faculty of Commerce, Economics and Political Sciences, University of Kuwait, Kuwait.

1.   Abdel Malik Khalaf al-Tamimi, 'Iranian Occupation of Arab Islands in the Gulf: A Study in the History of Arab–Iranian Relations, 1787–1971', *Journal of Gulf and Arabian Peninsula Studies*, vol. 14, no. 75 (July 1988), p. 131.

2. See *Ibid.*, and Muhammad Hasan Eiderous, *Political Developments in the State of the United Arab Emirates* (Kuwait: Dar al-Salasil, 1983), p. 165.

3. Al-Tamimi, op. cit., p. 132.

4. 'The Three Islands between the Historical Evidence and the Plotting of the West', *Kaihan al-Arabi* (Iran), 8 October 1994.

5. Saleh al-Tayyar, 'The Arab Identity of the Three Islands is Confirmed by Historical and Legal Facts', *Ukaz* daily (Saudi Arabia), 24 December 1994.

6. Al-Tamimi, 'Iranian Occupation of Arab Islands in the Gulf: A Study in the History of Arab–Iranian Relations, 1787–1971', op. cit., p. 132.

7. Eiderous, *Political Developments in the United Arab Emirates*, op. cit., p. 162.

8. Ibid., p. 166.

9. *The International Journal*, 20 April 1994.

10. Asad Alam, *The Shah and I: Secret Memoirs of the Iranian Court Minister*, prepared by Ali Naqhi Khani, translated by a team of Arab experts (Cairo: Madbouli Press, 1993), p. 92.

11. *The International Journal*, 20 April 1994. See also headline on Iran, London, November 1992.

12. Sultan Hamed, Aisheh Rateb and Salaheddine Amer, *Public International Law* (Cairo: Dar al-Nahda al-Arabiyyah; Kuwait University Press, 1987), p. 42.

13. Muhammad Aziz Shukri, *Public International Law during Times of Peace*, pp. 30–1.

14. I. L. Claude, *International Organization and World Peace* (Cairo: Dar al-Nahda al-Arabiyyah, 1964), p. 656.

15. *The International Journal*, 20 April 1994.

16. *Arab Weekly*, 28 September 1992.

17. Nazli Muawwad Ahmed, 'Turkey and Iran and the Second Gulf Crisis: A Comparative Analysis', *Social Sciences Journal*, vol. 19, nos. 1–2 (Summer 1991), p. 19.

18. Natiq Nouri calls on the GCC not to follow the lead of the jealousies of the ambitious, in *Kaihan al-Arabi*, 28 December 1992.

19. Hashemi Rafsanjani, 'The Emirates Shall Cross a Sea of Blood to Reach the Islands', *Jaridat al-Arab* (London), 8 June 1994.

14

Iraqi–Iranian Boundary and Territorial Disputes

SAYYAR AL-JAMIL*

Introduction

The greatness of man, society and civilization rests in the opportunity and effort to identify what can destroy them, that barriers may be laid before accelerating events and violence, until freedom and love of man remain ever victorious over the inevitability of things.[1]

Boundary and territorial disputes between Iraq and Iran were and remain among the most dangerous and vital of geo-political issues in the Middle East, particularly in the 20th century, when the residues of four centuries of chronic historical conflict between Iranians and Ottomans still remain.

This paper is an attempt to analyse the geographic dimension, dismantle the historical structure and determine a future vision, so as to reveal frankly for our future generations the controversies of the subject, its complexities and dilemmas, the generations for whom we have absolutely no wish to stand on a dormant volcano that may erupt again to kill thousands. This must be done through the formulation of living intellectual dimensions, embodying effective policy alternatives, planting future understandings that are conscious and are represented by the spirit of the age, progress and freedom.

Boundary, territorial and political disputes all over the world have been settled, yet the 'differences' that are the subject of this study have not been decided. It is true that there exist similar regional and international problems, but their history goes back no more than two centuries. They were the product of colonies and their wane in the 19th and 20th centuries, whereas Iraqi–Iranian boundary and territorial disputes span nearly five centuries. These have had a considerable impact on the recent and contemporary historical shaping of the Middle East, aside from their forthcoming impact on its future generations.

Accordingly, this subject is in dire need of further analysis, comparative study and research, in addition to stability in the intellectual, political, sociological and psychological understanding of Arabs, Iranians and Turks – the most prominent peoples of the Islamic Middle East and most versed in Islamic history, impact, civilization and culture, as well as regional partnership and geographic contiguity. But there are intellectual and ideological dimensions, with differences in thought, mentality, understanding, terms of reference and actions, creating dilemmas that make and oblige them today to reconsider. For they are at the crossroads of a new historical formation and the approach of a new century. This research paper of mine is perhaps a visionary contribution along those lines.

The Issues: The Geographic Dimension and the Historical Foundation

The Regional Dimension

Nature designed Iraq's and Iran's geographic boundaries, frontiers, outlets and tracts far back in time. The strategic nature of their territorial centres, urban and rural suburbs, land, riverine and marine areas, served to link East with West, despite the world's shifts and changes, whether during the classical, medieval or modern periods.[2]

Each side had its own territory affecting the relations of the other, whether at the level of political entities or social links or economic diversities or religious concentrations. If Iraq and the lands of Syria were a basic link, with mountains in the highlands and deserts in the lowlands, between Iran and the Mediterranean and Europe, Iran and its diverse, extensive provinces is a basic land link between Iraq and the Far East.[3]

Accordingly, the Iraq–Iran border, with all its territorial frontiers, geographic divisions, natural barriers and geopolitical lines, has been of foremost importance since earliest times, due to its strategic nature, rich heritage and diverse legacy across history. And yet? We can say that the features of the territorial dimension were clearly determined between the two sides through recent turbulent historical interactions, especially those resulting from the Ottoman–Iranian conflict across four full centuries, since the early 16th and until the early 20th century.[4] The residues of this conflict had a serious impact on the historical events generated by the 20th century, given that the Iraqi territorial dimension became a real geographic ground on which events were played out. Indeed, Iraq's location and strategic significance were among the principal causes in the burgeoning of this chronic conflict and its difficult consequences.[5]

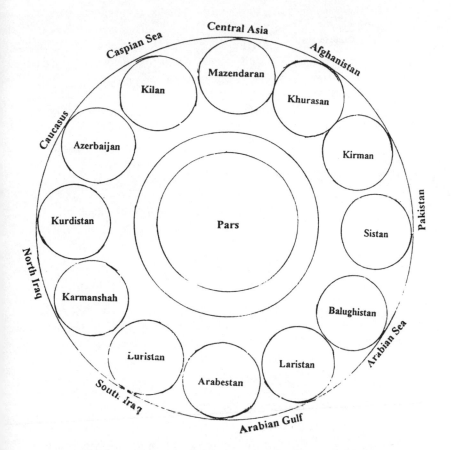

Figure. Geographic sketch of the Iranian provinces and surrounding domains (provincial expanses).

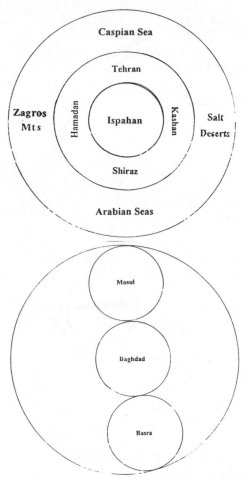

Figure. Iran (the territorial domain)
Figure. Iraq (the territorial domain)

(a) The Territorial Scope of Iraq

Modern Iraq, according to John M. Kinneir, extends from northwest Iran, longitudinally from the outlet of Shatt al-Arab to the south until the Merdin Rocks to the north, latitudinally from the edge of the Zagros Mountains to the east until the banks of the Khabor to the west. This means that its boundaries generally extend from the upper Euphrates River and north-west Mesopotamia to the Nejd highlands southwards. To the east, the Zagros chain extends to Arabestan (Khuzastan), and in the north, to the vilayet of Diyarbekr, at the frontiers of eastern Anatolia, containing Armenia and the Kurdish provinces in the northeast.[6] Iraq, since olden times, was known for its three famous places: Mosul, Baghdad and Basra.

The Territorial Divisions between Arabs and Persian Lands
Between these two worlds extend several regions that are geographically diverse, in mountains, contours, plateaux and waters (lakes, rivers, seas), from the north to the south, beginning with the highlands of the Zagros, down to Karand, Zuhab, Mandali and Zurbatiyah, through the marsh lakes, ending in the Shatt al-Arab, the Arabian Gulf, and then the Gulf of Oman and the Arabian Sea. As for population, national and anthropological divi-sions between the two worlds, they are many and diverse, governed by the ethnographic divisions of the past. Among the ancient peoples that settled the arduous territories of west Iran, becoming among the most prominent barriers between the Arabs and Persians, were the Azaris, Turcomen, Kurds, Kashgars, Bakhtiyaris, Luris (north and centre), Arabestanis, Laris, Sistanis and Baluchis (south).[7]

(b) The Territorial Scope of Iran

We can say that the huge area of Iran, estimated at 1,640,000 km², is three-quarters barren steppe or arid desert, comprised of red sand and patches of petrified salt (or salt deserts). Thus, sources of fresh water and agricultural land, and demographic concentrations, were all dispersed along the north and west of Iran.[8] The territorial domain with its dual frontiers between Iran and Iraq is crowded with tens of rivers that flow throughout the year.[9] They are a natural 'resource' not to be found in other geographic boundary and territorial zones. Perhaps the Zagros Mountains, with their long chains, are the most prominent natural divides.

Iran was formed from several important provinces and obtained its di-verse spaces entirely with time. Perhaps the most famous of these provinces adjoining the geographically wide and historically significant central

province, located in the heartland and becoming the hub of its extensions
from olden times to the present, is the province of Persia (Fars) and its
capital Shiraz (south) – Isfahan (north). As for the surrounding circle of
provinces that combine to form Iran, these are: Azerbeijan, Kurdistan,
Karmanshah, Luristan, Arabestan/Khuzestan and the Bakhtiarian Mountains, Laristan, Sistan, Karman, Khurasan, Mazendaran, Qizwin, Kilan, etc.[10]
All these provinces were Persianized across history. What concerns us here
is the region between Iraq and Iran; this includes Azerbeijan, Kurdistan,
Kermanshah, Luristan, Arabestan, and the Arabian Gulf – regarded as
among the richest of Iran's provinces in natural resources, from water to oil.

The population of the two worlds, the Iraqi and Iranian, is an important
source of border divides in contemporary history. The people of border
villages, across the generations, were well aware of the limits of their lands,
pastures, water sources, mountain peaks, steppes and villages. The Ottoman state used to always rely on them to confirm Iraq's territorial rights.
Maps and sketches were unknown. Boundaries were not seen as 'lines', but
as 'zones' – meaning that some lands were left as geographic leeway for
purposes of contact; they were termed 'gaps' in the medieval histories (especially in the Islamic geographic expanse), just as they are termed 'trucial
zones' in modern histories.[11]

(c) Boundaries and Frontiers: The Semantic Meaning and the Understood Meaning

The actual meaning of the concept 'boundary' of the old empire is, like
other 'terms', determined by the emergence of the modern state in its three
complete elements: people, territory, sovereignty. If the extent of the 'province' was, in olden times, shaped solely by internal laws recognized by the
parties concerned, or the forms of rule, the criterion of the new international boundary enjoys the care and protection of national/regional laws
and constitutions, in addition to international law, the charters of the international community, the UN and international organizations, and
recognition by governments.[12] This means that 'boundary' is determined
by agreement between the states concerned through treaties, agreements,
arbitration decisions, population inclinations, geographic factors, historical
legacies, or national assets. It becomes more stable if subjected to planning
by international working groups in the field, specializing in territorial de-
marcations of the state, its exercise of sovereignty and the extension of legal
authority over it.[13]

Thus, the two terms *geographic frontiers* and *international boundaries*
should be separated. And yet? There are certain key factors that affect boundary disputes and territorial problems; among them are legal factors, such as

customs, security, and residency; social factors, such as family concerns, sectarian differences, and religious disputes; economic factors, in trade, agriculture, oil; political, intellectual, ideological, propaganda factors; cultural factors such as identity, language, etc. The geopolitical boundary must necessarily overlap into the geographic boundary of countries. International boundaries and regional disputes over them have stabilized in most continents, especially Asia, which holds very old and complex legacies – even apart from the boundary disputes between China and Russia, India and Pakistan over Kashmir, and Iraq and Iran.[14] The Iraqi–Iranian boundary and territorial disputes are regarded today as among the oldest and most dangerous complex disputes of the pre-colonial age. They should have stabilized and calmed down from the start of the 20th century, which witnessed the longest and most violent war between these two neighbouring states. Their boundaries had been determined geographically, and the dividing line between them was completed, through an international boundary demarcation commission in 1914, following the signing of the most important historical document in 1913, entitled the Astaneh Protocol. As the agreements between the two parties did not prevail, nor the state of peace and stability, due to Iran's continuous demands and vacillations throughout the 20th century, we must address bilateral historical ties and analyse their components, structure and contents in the treaties, agreements and protocols on boundaries and territories, which have extended over long tracts of time, from the early 16th century to the end of the 20th.

The Historical Foundation of Modern Iran

This perspective is regarded as one of the basic approaches to examining historical formations, elements and meanings, the foundation of which is a collection of treaties, agreement stipulations, commission records and protocols, so as to understand clearly the disparity in policies, trends, aspirations and regional interactions, with an understanding of the process of development and sharpening of bilateral differences and disputes. The question now is: what is the nature of the 'relations' between the two countries through the course of historical formations?

These discordant 'relations' went through two sets of formations, ruled by a number of aspirations and extensions drawn from states and from the political, dynastic and shahanshahi systems that ruled Iran in its ten historical models, and which had a far-reaching impact on extensions and interventions or the eruption of conflicts and wars in the direction of Iraq. They are shown chronologically in Table 1.[15]

Dismantling the Historical Structure

The historical structure of the three regional parties – Iran, Iraq and Turkey – teaches us that Iraq, since the fall of Baghdad at the hands of Hulagu and the end of the Abbasid caliphate in 656 AH/1258 CE, was the scene of intervention, conflict and dispute between the Iranian and Turkish worlds. If the Turks remained since the start of the 14th century CE and left the world with a historical sultanic entity represented by the Ottomans since, Iran from the same date experienced ten forms of political rule.[16] The relations of both with Iraq are represented in the table opposite.

1. Five Iranian administrations survived across two full centuries; historically they intervened in large parts of Iraq; these administrations were purely Turcomen.
2. The modern history of Iran began with the emergence of the Safavid state, which occupied Iraq at the start of the 16th century. It was a basic source of the Ottoman–Iranian conflict, a conflict inherited by successive political administrations over four centuries and until the early 20th century. This historic Ottoman–Iranian conflict was over Iraq, which experienced extended Ottoman rule from the Chaldiran regional war of 1514 until the allied victory of the First World War in 1918.[17]
3. The 20th century inherited the residues of these volatile regional and international conflicts, especially the pattern of relations that exacerbated the differences between Iran and Iraq.

1. The Historical Perspective on Regional Ties between Iraq and Iran

The historical perspective is held as a methodological base for examining components, meanings and residues (including treaties and stipulations in agreements), followed by understanding the vision, policies and inclinations, when describing the historical structure of the regional system between the central states (by which I mean Iraq, Turkey and Iran). As the subject of this study is the Iraqi–Iranian boundary and territorial disputes, the tabulation of the historical structure will depict the nature of the differences that the bilateral ties between the two countries served produced during this century, regarded as an extension of all that transpired before, and the legacies left by the Ottoman–Iranian conflict as internal political, psychological and sociological residues;[18] or it will depict those interactions that were brought into relief by various causes and effects: a regional strategy toward international and colonialist powers' moves, beginning with interest and control over trade routes and land, river and maritime lines of communication, whether Iraqi or Iranian, and ending with the strategic and increasingly huge oil reserves over the days and years.

Table 1

Iranian States	Toward Iraq	The Ottomans
		1281 Establishment
1. Muzaffarids 1314–93		
2. Jalayirids 1336–1432		
3. Timurids 1370–1506	Historical	
4. Kara-Koyunlu 1380–1468	interpenetration	
5. Ak-Koyunlu 1378–1508		
6. Safavids 1501–1786		1516–34
7. Afshars 1736–95	Regional conflict	Ottoman
8. Zands 1750–94		domination
9. Qajars 1779–1924		1914–18
10. Pahlavis 1924–79	The State of Iraq	British occupation

The historical perspective to the structure of regional relations between Iran and Iraq in particular, with their resultant treaties and agreements, will show us the extent of the historical dangers besetting the region, its cities, suburbs and populations. These treaties, agreements and protocols did not materialize without campaigns, events, wars, battles, sieges and attacks. They had a profound impact on the mentalities, thought and psychology of societies in the region. Iraq and Iran each carry a very heavy legacy of militarist and treaty inheritances across the span of modern history. Their situation may well be, by this inheritance of relations, so rare and particular as to be unknown among other peoples.

Articulation and Periodization

We can set the historical divisions for the contents of bilateral disputes by drawing on political treaties, which are regarded as basic dividers between the two sides since the 16th century and until today. A close and full examination of the texts of the 'treaties' shown below, and our comparative analysis of them, reveal some to be distinctive in historical weight. We can regard four of these as basic treaties. The Amasiya Treaty of 1555 remained the historical basis of relations between the two ancient adversaries for 85 years, i.e., until the Treaty of Zuhab (1639), which became a focus to 208

Table 2

Historical Structure of Boundary Treaties, Agreements and Protocols

---

1514   Chaldiran War

1555 Amasiya Treaty (basic)	16th century = 2 treaties
1590 Farhad Pasha Treaty	(Safavid–Ottoman conflict)

1613 The Bilateral Agreement	
1618 Treaty of Sarv	17th century = 3 treaties
1639 Treaty of Zuhab (basic)	

1727 Amir Ashraf Treaty	18th century = 3 treaties
1731 Ahmad Pasha Treaty	(Safavid–Ottoman conflict)
1746 Bilateral Treaty	(Safavid/Naderi–Ottoman conflict)

1823 First Erzerum Treaty	
1847 Second Erzerum Treaty (basic)	19th century = 2 treaties
1850 (Demarcation Commission)	(Qajar–Ottoman conflict)

1913 Astaneh Protocol (basic)	
1914 (Demarcation Commission)	
1937 Iraq–Iran Treaty	20th century = 3 treaties
1938 (Demarcation Commission)	(Iran–Iraq conflict)
1975 The Algiers Agreement	
The Boundary Treaty	

Total Number of Treaties   13

Annexes   2

Total Treaties to Iraq–Iran War 1980–88   15

---

years of relations. This remained the case until the Treaty of Erzerum (1837), a historical basis for 66 years of relations, until the signing of the Astaneh Protocol in 1913, whose stipulations drew up the contemporary relations between the two new parties (Iraq and Iran) for 62 years, i.e., until the signing of the Algiers Agreement in 1975.

Residues of Territorial and Boundary Conflicts

The consolidation of the Iraq–Iran boundary took ages. It began concurrently with the Ottoman–Iranian conflict, following Safavid encroachments into Iraq and east Anatolia. With the interaction and sharpening of strategic, economic, political, religious and hegemonial factors, exploding the regional conflict between the above two sides, Iraq's combined regional/international strategy, by land, river and sea, emerged as among the most prominent of Ottoman provinces, in its inner and outer lands.[19] The 'Iraqi border' and 'regional lines of communication' were fundamentals in the Amasiya Treaty for the two parties (Ottoman and Iranian) in 1555.[20] Then Iran ceded in the Treaty of 1590 to the Ottoman state the provinces of Luristan and Shahr-i-Zur, which became Iraqi land, as they had been viewed in the past.[21] In the Treaty of Sarv (1618), the Ottoman state ceded Darnah and Dartank, both under Baghdad's tutelage, to Safavid Iran in return for ceding the provinces of east Anatolia to the Ottomans.[22]

The Zuhab Treaty of 1639 is regarded as among the more significant for the two sides. It was concluded after the Ottoman victory over the Safavids, following the former's recovery of Baghdad and its surroundings, which had been under Safavid control for 15 years. The treaty's basic stipulations provided that the boundaries of Jassan, Badran, Mandalgin (i.e., Mandali), Darnah and Dartank belong to the *vilayet* of Baghdad, and all villages to the west of Zinjir Castle belong to the Ottomans, in addition to Shahr-e Zur, Awkali Crossing and Banjawin village.[23] Thus, the Zuhab Treaty was a historical pivot consolidating the original territorial boundaries between Iraq and Iran, especially in the geo-historical mechanics of the succession of treaties that followed it.

Analysis of the Nature of the Differences: Treaties in the Contemporary Historical Context

Ottoman–Iranian conflict in the Iraqi arena intensified during the 18th century. Its tragic and bitter events were sufficient to elicit large-scale boundary and territorial changes,[24] especially during the interventions of Afsharid rule in Safavid government, with the Zuhab Treaty (1639) remaining as reference in the articulation of the territorial boundary, despite the signing of the Amir Ashraf Treaty in 1727, which incorporated Hoveyzeh in the Ottoman state, for purposes of ensuring Basra's safety; it was also decided within this treaty to retain the lands and forts controlled by the Ottomans.[25] Iraqi forces penetrated Iranian territory in defence; they took control of Hamadan, Kermanshah, Ardalan, Luristan and Sultaniyeh. All of them fell under Ottoman influence, but the Ottomans ceded them and Hovayzeh to Iran in the Treaty of 1731, signed by Ahmad Pasha, the famous wali of Baghdad.[26]

The fuse of conflict between the two sides (Iraqi–Iranian) was lit, continuing for over ten years (1732–43). It came between two serious historical events. The first was the siege of Baghdad, 1732–33, a tragic and bitter siege of six months, under Nader Qawli Khan, who would put an end to Safavid rule in 1736, establish the Afshari dynasty and suicidal military state, lead his great campaign against Iraq in 1743 and lay a vicious siege to Mosul. But he failed in the last, returning to his country disappointed, after hasty local negotiations. The Treaty of 1746 was signed between the Ottomans and Iranians; it stipulated that the boundary set by the Zuhab Treaty (1639) serve as its basis.[27]

2. Regional Disputes and International Intervention: the 19th Century

Conflict between the two sides resumed during the 19th century, but it took on an international character, with the influences of the British and Russians clearly apparent. After the Iraqis repulsed the Iranian forces marching on Baghdad, during the Qajari era, before the two negotiated what became the First Erzerum Treaty of 1823, which was not sufficiently detailed or comprehensive to resolve the complex problems leading to the series of endemic wars between the two states,[28] and with Iran seizing the opportunity to rid itself of the stipulations of the Zuhab Treaty of 1639, the root differences remained, hidden deeply in it, and international interventions in the region's affairs escalated. The second Ottoman–Iranian war erupted in 1840, at the northern and southern borders of Iraq, by Iran's brief takeover of Iraq's Suleimaniyah town.[29]

Thus, there were no solutions except through resort to renewed negotiations. The Ottoman–Iranian Boundary Demarcation Commission began its work at its headquarters in Erzerum in 1934.[30] The Ottomans demanded the return of Khorramshahr and territories west of the Karin River, the reactivation of Zuhab and the need to implement the stipulations of the First Erzerum Treaty. International interventions by Britain and Tsarist Russia were manifest in pressures exerted by their Ambassadors, over the issues of Khorramshahr and the Shatt al-Arab in particular.[31] Here we can pause for a moment to note some of the stipulations of the Second Erzerum Treaty of 1847, which became a basic treaty in determining the framework of bilateral territorial relations for more than half a century. What is pertinent to Iraq in these stipulations?

Iran was to relinquish the 'plains' west of Iraqi Zuhab, in return for the mountains of Wadi Karnad east of the area. The Ottoman Porte would officially recognize Iran's absolute sovereignty over Khorramshahr, its port, Khidr Island, the dock and territories east of Shatt al-Arab, and Iran's navigational right in it from the sea up to the border point of the two states.

The remainder of the stipulations considered good neighbour policy and preservation of the security and stability of the border.[32]

To implement what came in the treaty, an international commission was formed in 1848, comprised of representatives of Russia, England, Iran and the Ottoman Porte, for determining boundaries.[33] The commission began work in 1850 at Khorramshahr, to decide on the city's fate in a final way. The commission confronted international problems and complications, such as the outbreak of the Crimean War 1853–1856 between the Ottoman state and Russia, with England entering the war on the side of the Ottomans; then the outbreak of war between Britain and Iran in 1856. The commission's work was suspended. Then came the Russo-Ottoman war of 1877 and the holding of the Berlin Conference of 1878.

After the Crimean War, representatives of England and Russia drew up a detailed and precise map for the common Ottoman–Iranian borders, completed in 1869 after considerable and arduous effort. The two states were provided with it in 1870, and they were requested to consolidate their boundaries according to it, bearing in mind that a boundary treaty was concluded in 1869 which stipulated 'maintaining the status quo at the borders until a negotiated settlement is reached between them by the Quadripartite Commission on Boundary Demarcation'.[34]

When the Shah of Iran, Naser al-Din, visited Baghdad and the holy threshold at the end of 1870, he proposed to the wali, Medhat Pasha, negotiations with the First Secretary of Iran. The negotiations were long and strenuous, but they did not reach any results – except to renew the boundary difficulties and problems with greater violence and intensity![35]

3. The New Constants: the Astaneh Protocol of 1913

Problems and differences between the two sides complicated considerably at the turn of the 19th century, which witnessed major changes in positions along with transformations in political ideas and standards – in addition to an increase in the influence of England and Russia in the two states, Ottoman and Iranian. The problems of the Iraqi border were posed. On 21 January 1911, the Tehran Protocol was signed, stipulating appointment of another joint technical commission, with headquarters in the Ottoman capital of Istanbul, to be entrusted with the task of once again establishing the boundary between the two states, on condition that another, technical subcommittee be entrusted with establishing the borderline in the field and endorse the stipulations of the Second Erzerum Treaty (1847) as the basis for this.[36] As the two sides did not reach the stage of designating a joint work plan, Britain and Tsarist Russia intervened in the matter, to conclude the famous Astaneh Protocol on 4 November 1913.[37] It was signed by representatives of Russia and Britain as mediating states, and by the Ottoman Foreign Ministry and the Iranian Ambassador at Istanbul on behalf of their states.

What did this Protocol establish?

(a) Article (2) stipulated: 'the boundary line shall be determined on the ground by a demarcation commission comprised of the commissariats of four governments'.
(b) Article (5) stipulated: 'in the event of a part of the boundary left undetermined, that part shall be considered as finally demarcated and is not subject to any inspection or amendment thereafter ... '
(c) Article (6) stipulated that both the Ottoman and Iranian governments 'during the course of the demarcation work shall establish police stations at the boundaries'.[38]

The commission finalized the coordinates of the boundary markers on the maps, and on the ground, from the far north to the far south, in 1914; this was confirmed in the procès-verbal of 1914. With that, the boundary disputes between the two ancient states were decided, in deference to a new century, and Britain and France, along with their allies, worked to establish a new world order after the First World War came to an end, and to decide how the geo-political map of the world should look following the peace conferences of Paris (1919) and San Remo (1920).[39]

Important strategic factors materialized at the turn of the 19th century, entering the historical domain of Iraqi–Iranian boundary and territorial disputes. Among the most prominent was the discovery of oil and its reserves, then the process of excavating it from Iraq and Iran. Oil played a basic and vital role between 1901 and the thirties; then its strategic importance increased considerably across this century.[40] As the division of modern states and their formation occurred in the pre-Cold War period, or during difficult interventions or in the wake of their horrifying consequences, subsequent regional developments, especially between Iraq and Iran, followed a different path than might otherwise have occurred. Until the outbreak of the First World War, there was continuous rivalry between the oil companies to obtain concessions from the Ottoman Porte, whether German, French, English or American companies.[41] It is very evident that the drawing up of the Iraqi–Iranian border in the Astaneh Protocol of 1913, and the work of the Iraq–Iran boundary commission of 1914, were affected by these international factors and ther ole of the ambitious oil companies, for the Middle East fell under the aegis of the global oil economy.

Let us now analyse what was decided during the work of the mixed committee on the Iraq–Iran boundary, in desk as in field studies, at the start of January 1914, beginning from Khorramshahr, and ending its work on the peak of Mt Ararat, where the last boundary post between Iraq and Iran was implanted. The commission's work ended on 26 October 1914. Detailed records of its sessions were recorded, totaling 87 of some of the rarest international documents; 18 detailed boundary maps between the two states were also drawn up, and 223 boundary markers were implanted between the Ottoman and Iranian sides. The demarcation line came to cross through the middle of Shatt al-Arab for a length of 4 miles (7 km). The commission was empowered to revise and supplement when planning the boundary.[42]

The Astaneh Protocol of 1913 is regarded as more precise and clear than the Second Erzerum Treaty of 1847. It was established on new principles in both boundary determination and planning, which was not the case in previous treaties. Accordingly, the governments of contemporary Iraq, from 1921 onwards, endorsed the texts of the 1847 Treaty, the Protocol of 1913 and the boundary demarcation memoranda of 1914 in verifying Iraq's inherited boundary and territorial rights.[43] The 1913 Protocol contained eight articles that included land and river boundaries,[44] in accordance with precise geometric determinations and prevailing geographic divides based on identity, allegiance and the nationality principle. Iran realized a gain in the 1913 Protocol: the relinquishing by the Ottoman state of part of its territory facing the port of Khorramshahr and its dock, to a distance of four miles; the borderline passes through this area in the middle of Shatt al-Arab to the distance mentioned, then returns to follow the left (east) bank of the Shatt al-Arab until the outlet of the Arabian Gulf.[45]

4. The Two New Kingdoms: Iraq and Iran

A new historical page was turned in bilateral relations (Iraqi–Iranian) with the 20th century, following the birth of the two new regional states after the Paris Peace Conference of 1919: the Kingdom of Iraq (Hashemite) in 1921 and the Kingdom of Iran (Pahlavi) in 1925. But the disputes, agreements and differences in views between the two parties continued, along with the difference in the regional and national/patriotic orientations of both. In addition to this came international political/economic predilections and alliances,[46] the alterations in the map of the Middle East, and the birth of national, regional or religious powers and states (or racialist ones, like the Zionist entity).

Iraq was placed under the British Mandate; then its political entity was established with the monarchical government of 1921. The country inherited all the obligations borne by the Ottoman state before the First World

War (1914–1918), and it inherited all the international rights enjoyed by the Ottoman state by virtue of Article 50 of the Lausanne Treaty of 1923.[47] Accordingly, Iraq inherited the legacy of previous historical treaties between the Ottoman and Iranian states, including the boundary and territorial disputes with Iran, the same disputes that continued across the 20th century, in addition to what its situation acquired in the way of new formulas, additional elements and geo-political developments arising from the world order after the Paris Peace Conference of 1919 and the San Remo Conference of 1920.[48] This is apparent from the appearance of new political, ideological and intellectual precepts hitherto unknown, such as national identification documents, ethnocentrism, political consciousness, sectarian discrimination, colonialist hegemony, minority positions and foreign concessions in light of political treaties, citizenship laws, the problem of expatriates, travel, transfer and residency instructions, etc.

Thus, the disturbances and tensions found their way into the relations between the two new states, Iraq and Iran, from the start of the twenties. Iran initiated this 'phase' after the end of the First World War, in what it presented to the Paris Peace Conference of 1919, asking for its own annexation of large tracts of Iraqi land, including the Iraqi Kurdistan province in the north. Its demands reached up to the city of Mosul and territories still further in, some of them at the Euphrates.[49] Iran ignored the Iraqi monarchy established in 1921; perhaps it was preoccupied with putting its own internal affairs in order, for recognition was delayed until 1929.[50] But it called for granting its expatriates in Iraq foreigner privileges, the same 'privileges' enjoyed by expatriates from some European, American and Asian (Japan) states. The problem remained until the cancellation of foreigner privileges in Iraq in 1929.

Iraq was granted a time limit of four years (1924–28) following the issuing of the Iraqi citizenship law to Iranians residing in Iraq, for them to decide on whether to choose nationality or not. The government of Iraq refused Iran's request for an extension, knowing that this would pave the way for Iranian consulates in Iraq to persuade Iranians to choose Iraqi citizenship, especially in the Basra area.[51]

Iran, for its part, continued to pursue a policy of territorial and sectarian dissension. From its side, border incidents recurred because of some refugees, and then Iranian acts of aggression on the Iraqi border occurred. There was no cooperation between the two governments, Iraqi and Iranian, over the Kurds. Iran's moves extended to Iraqi tribes in contiguous border areas between the two countries, for naturalizing them as Iranian citizens. This was regarded as blatant interference in Iraq's internal affairs, and the Iraqi government submitted a letter of protest to the British High Commissioner, clarifying that it will be obliged to lift diplomatic immunity on Iranian consulates in Iraq.[52] As a result of the border incidents, backed by armed Kurdish elements, Iranian armed incursions across the border were frequent, in violation of the principle of good neighbourliness.[53]

5. The British Position on the Political Disputes

Britain's position on Iraqi–Iranian boundary and territorial disputes clearly reflected its strategic interests in the lands of both parties. At times it would respond to Iran's claims and attempt to persuade Iraq; at other times it would protest Iranian infringements and ask Iraq to take firm stands towards Iranian expansionism and intransigence,[54] whether over the border incidents or the issue of common rivers and Iran's cut-off of the waters of some – which caused considerable loss and damage to the local border population, forcing them to migrate and depopulate the areas.[55] Britain sought to convince Iran to recognize the Iraqi monarchy. The 'recognition' arrived in April 1929, after six years of postponement; memoranda and diplomatic representation were exchanged, in accordance with diplomatic procedure.[56] All this occurred after the problem of Mosul was decided in favour of Iraq, the motherland, for Iran had kept a close watch on developments and placed considerable store by the conclusion the League of Nations was to reach regarding Mosul province. The intent was there, were it not for the decision taken in favour of Iraq, to demand the incorporation of borderlands and revise the boundary in Shatt al-Arab. It should be borne in mind that this shatt is a national river, not an international one such as the Danube. For the Shatt al-Arab River flows within the territory of one state, which it owns by virtue of eternal possession.

6. The Burgeoning of Territorial, Boundary and Water Disputes

With the recognition by Iran of the state of Iraq and its government in 1929, King Faisal I sent his senior adviser Rustum Haidar to Iran, to meet Shah Reza Pahlavi and to receive official recognition, strengthen ties, and reduce border incidents somewhat. An exchange of diplomatic memoranda and enquiries were made as per established procedures. An interim agreement was concluded between the two states, of one year duration, renewable every six months by the two governments. After its recognition of Iraq, Iran did not recognize the legitimacy of the previous agreements; it denied the previous documents that had been concluded, and it announced its refusal to abide by them. It saw the Second Erzerum Treaty of 1847 and the Astaneh Protocol of 1913, and thus the determination of the Demarcation Commission in 1914, as without power of execution of the boundary report. The most important 'problems' the Shah posed were the land boundary, the common boundary rivers, which number 25, and after these, the problem of the Shatt al-Arab.[57] The differences grew until they became dangerous, especially after the signing of the Anglo-Iraqi Treaty of 30 June 1930, in which the independence of Iraq and its membership in the League of Nations were endorsed.

Early in 1931, diplomatic relations between the two states were established. Tawfiq Sweidi was appointed first Minister Plenipotentiary to Iran. The man was to play an outstanding role in enhancing bilateral relations and building confidence measures with Iran's politicians in the days he spent in Tehran, between 1931 and 1934. Among the most prominent entries of Sweidi's memoirs during his stay in Iran were the following important impressions, information and positions:

1. Iranian delay and stalling in addressing the Iraqi political memoranda.
2. Iranian border violations against Iraq.
3. The cut-off of water flows from the Iranian mountains to Zerbatiyah, Mandali and other Iraqi areas.
4. The Kurdish question; investigations at the border and the recalling of the outlaws.
5. Iraq's extensive preoccupations with the situation of its Arab brethren in the province of Arabestan (Khuzestan).
6. The Shatt al-Arab and Iraq's preoccupation with its right to the whole of it, both the Iraqi and Iranian banks.[58]

The problem of the Shatt al-Arab is regarded as among the most dangerous of bilateral problems started by Iran, which always took the theory of Teimurtash, Iran's Minister of Court in the late 1920s and early 1930s, as the basis for its claims. The 'theory', as Tawfiq Sweidi wrote, can be summarized as follows:

His theory on the issue of the Shatt al-Arab is that the demarcation of boundaries, for all nations, is according to the fixed principles that they follow. A river, valley, mountain or otherwise is taken as a natural divider. The prominent coordinates in the contours of the land are identitified, to make them into a boundary between two countries. However, no international convention has been made to render a river so important as the Shatt al-Arab a divide between the two countries, and it was handed over entirely to one [of them].[59] The Iranians' excuse is that they were forced to agree to what was decided by the boundary demarcation commission because of foreign interventions and British designs on the important provinces of the Ottoman Empire.

7. Bilateral Negotiations and the Treaty of 1937

Relations between the two countries improved after the entry of Iraq as a member of the League of Nations in 1932. The Shah of Iran, Reza Pahlavi, directed an invitation to Iraq's King Faisal I to visit Iran. The visit took place in April 1932. The issue of the boundary in Shatt al-Arab was the focus of discussion between the two sides. The Iranian government expressed its desire for there to be a *thalweg* line,[60] the deep water part of the river as a dividing line between the two sides. Iraq rejected this. Tensions and disagreements escalated. Thus, once again, a series of Iranian aggressions ensued against Iraq, and pressures were applied through:

1. Irregularities by Iranian vessels in the Shatt al-Arab by their disregard of instructions from Iraq's Basra port.
2. Iranian infringements on Iraqi rights in common boundary rivers.
3. The construction of border police stations, with sentries posted inside Iraqi territory, until 1934.
4. Tribal forays on the border from both sides.[61]

Iraq decided to bring up the 'subject' before the League of Nations Council, as per Paragraph 2 of Article 11, in 1935. After extensive discussions, the League decided on 21 January 1935 that direct negotiations be opened between Iraq and Iran. Iraq's Foreign Minister, Nuri Said, and accompanying delegation met in Tehran on 5 August 1935 Shah Reza Pahlavi, who recognized the legality of the Erzerum Treaty of 1847. He said: 'Iraq holds me accountable for every cent and fraction of a cent. I do not want more than two miles (3 km) in Shatt al-Arab before Abadan'.[62] Iraq's Council of Ministers did not agree to the Shah's request, because the Iraqi Constitution does not permit relinquishing any part of State land.[63] But the Council agreed to lease the said area on condition that Iran respond to Iraq's legitimate rights. On 17 December 1935, the Iranian delegation arrived in Baghdad to negotiate on the boundary problems.[64]

The negotiations between the two sides continued for some two years, during which important events occurred. Mustapha Kemal Ataturk took the initiative to mediate between Iraq and Iran, for the sake of building a regional military coalition in the Middle East to face the dangers of the international situation then. All this was embodied, later, in the Kariz [Saadabad] Pact, on 8 July 1937. As for Iraq and Iran, their negotiations had finally succeeded with the initialling of the texts of the Boundary Treaty on 26 June 1937 in Baghdad, as a prelude to a final signing in Tehran on 4 July 1937. What did this new treaty contain?

Iran recognized the legality of the Astaneh Protocol of 1913 and the minutes of the sessions of the Boundary Demarcation Commission in 1914.

Iraq conceded the *thalweg* line before Abadan to a distance of about four miles. The two sides signed two agreements: the first on 18 July 1937 and the second on the 24th of the same; both included security and diplomatic issues.[65]

8. The Peak of Alliances: from the Kariz Pact of 1937 to the Baghdad Pact of 1955

The signing of the Treaty of 1937 by Iraq and Iran, on 4 July 1937, and the conclusion of the Kariz Pact on 8 July 1937 by the four neighbouring states – Iraq, Iran, Turkey and Afghanistan – as a regional Middle Eastern alliance, was a real beginning to an important and new historical phase in regional relations (especially between Iraq and Iran). It prevailed for a long time; tensions were reduced and joint interests were strengthened. The Second World War broke out in 1939; Shah Reza Pahlavi relinquished the throne to his son Mohammed in September.[66] Iraq's policy was split between the two warring camps, leading to the famous Meiss uprising in May, which triggered the Iraqi–British war, while Turkey remained safe and sound as a neutral. And yet?

Iraqi–Iranian relations developed considerably during the forties and fifties, or rather in the period 1937–1958. Boundary disputes died down and regional ties were enhanced as a result of signing the two most prominent regional pacts connected with the West and its colonial domains, especially Britain and the US, who gave much attention to the Middle East and showed exceptional interest in Iraq, Turkey and Iran as a regional barrier to the Soviet Union. The two pacts are the Kariz Pact of 1937, during the reigns of King Ghazi and Shah Reza Pahlavi, and the Baghdad Pact of 1955, during the reigns of their sons, King Faisal II and Shah Mohammed Reza.

The question now is: how did these relations develop over time?
It should be said that the development of regional relations between Iraq and Iran was subject in the post-Second World War period to their ties with the West, whether Britain or the US, in the decade of the fifties. These ties developed both regionally and internationally during that decade to include Turkey and Pakistan, culminating in the Baghdad Pact of 1955, comprised of Iraq and Turkey, then Britain, Iran and Pakistan. Later, the United States also joined.[67] Although the idea and the plan were devised by Nuri Said, Iraq's Prime Minister, implementation of the 'project' and its transformation from a regional coalition into an international association became, for national and Arab regional public opinion, 'an imperialist

association shackling the Middle East to the West', although the man was a political official who was contributing to tranquillity in the region. But he was one of the prominent factors behind the explosion of the state of affairs at the levels of collective struggle and the masses.

9. Ten Years of Tension and Shifts: 1958–1968

Sure enough, it was not long before the situation changed. After three years, the revolution of 14 July 1958 broke out in Baghdad, toppling the monarchy in Iraq, the strong ally of Iran and Turkey. Accordingly, Iraq broke away from the regional and international alliance that Baghdad was the source and seat of, and went on to witness wide-scale changes and shifts in its modern history. Tensions and disagreements returned between the two states, as Shah Mohammed Reza Pahlavi declared on 28 November 1958 that the Treaty of 1937 is 'intolerable and unprecedented in history' and announced his desire to cancel it. This 'statement' was effectively an eruption of latent positions. Iran led a diplomatic and propaganda campaign against Iraq; it massed its troops on the southwest border and east banks of the Shatt al-Arab, placed all its forces on alert, deployed artillery and tanks in Abadan's fortifications, despatched squadrons of warplanes to its base in Dezful, and massed three divisions in Khorramshahr port.[68] Iraqi–Iranian relations thus became extremely strained, threatening to explode at any moment.

Iran announced on 7 May 1959 that Khosrowabad is an extension of Khorramshahr port. What this means is the acquisition of a new dock for Khorramshahr, along the lines of what it acquired previously in Abadan in 1937. Iraq rejected the Iranian declaration and notified Iran on 9 June 1959 that all the waters of the Shatt al-Arab fall under Iraqi sovereignty, in accordance with previous boundary agreements and treaties, except for a limited area before the two ports of Khorramshahr and Abadan. Iranian infringements on Iraqi sovereignty increased in the Shatt al-Arab, and border incidents resumed at the scale they were before 1937. Iraq was unsuccessful in its peaceful methods to repel these infringements, through the United Nations and the International Court of Justice. The two sides did not reach a clear finish, despite the holding of negotiations during the period 1960–1966. Though there was a slight improvement in relations, and visits by senior Iraqi officials to Tehran between 1965 and 1968 were made during the term of the two brothers Abdel Salam and Abdel Rahman Aref, these did not culminate in any conclusion of a treaty between the two sides on the boundary disputes and territorial problems.[69]

10. Burgeoning Disputes and the Algiers Treaty of 1975

With the revolution of 17–30 July 1968 in Iraq and major political developments that came to the fore, attempts were made to settle the outstanding
disputes with Iran. An official Iranian delegation arrived in Baghdad in
February 1969 for negotiations, presenting a new protocol for an alternative treaty to that of 1937, and a protocol annexe stipulating administration
of the Shatt al-Arab, whereby navigation would be conducted jointly by
the two sides. The Iraqi side, for its part, proposed agreements for the regulation and maintenance of navigation. When the Iranian delegates found
the Iraqis unreceptive to concluding a new and alternate treaty, they broke
off the meetings and returned to their country. Iranian infringements resumed with intensity in the Shatt al-Arab. The Iranian Ambassador in
Baghdad was summoned to the Iraqi Foreign Ministry on 15 April 1969
and was handed a strongly worded letter of protest, which the Ambassador
regarded as a threat and insult to his country's honour and sovereignty. The
Deputy Foreign Minister of Iran announced to the Iranian Senate on 19
April 1969 the unilateral cancellation by the Iranian government of the
Boundary Treaty of 1937.[70] Iran's government adopted provocative measures and began to amass troops along the length of the entire boundary
with Iraq, especially at Shatt al-Arab, while Iranian vessels began to move
in Shatt al-Arab under escort by Iranian gunboats, with warplanes flying
overhead,[71] in violation of established laws, as they were in Iraqi waters.
Relations between the two states reached crisis proportions, and the situation was close to breaking point, with both on the brink of war as the
information and propaganda war between them intensified. Iraq, through
its permanent ambassador to the UN, submitted a report that drew the
attention of the Security Council, and notified them of the dangerous situation prevailing all along the boundary between the two states.[72] Iraq
expressed its desire for a negotiated peaceful settlement to the disputes, as
conveyed in the statement of its Foreign Minister at the UN, on 3 October
1969, and accepted the Jordanian government's efforts to resolve the conflict, to which Iran did not respond, maintaining silence.

Tensions and disturbances in Iraqi–Iranian relations continued in the
following years, and other factors emerged to add to the tensions, especially Iraq's strong stand over Iranian occupation of the three Arabian Gulf
islands at the end of 1971. The Iraqi government severed diplomatic relations with Iran and filed, along with Libya, Algeria and South Yemen, a
joint complaint to the UN Security Council against Iran's expansionist operations in the Arabian Gulf. The situation remained volatile between the
two sides. Border clashes occurred in 1974 after Iraq announced in February 1974 its rejection of US interventions, following the Ramadhan (October
1973) war, to sign a peace between the Arabs and the Zionist entity.[73] When

Iraq participated in that war, it called on Iran to halt its propaganda campaigns, border operations and support for quislings operating in the north.

Iraq was preoccupied by Iran for many years, trying to recover security and stability from mutinies in the north financed by the Shah. During the OPEC member states summit conference in Algiers in March 1975, Algerian President Hawari Boumeddien initiated a successful historical initiative for resolving Iraqi–Iranian disputes. On 6 March he brought together Saddam Hussein (then Vice-President of Iraq's Revolutionary Council) with Shah Mohammed Reza Pahlavi in his presence, and the Algiers Agreement was signed, deriving from the principle of good neighbourliness and implementation of the principles of the inviolability of national soil, common borders and non-interference in the internal affairs of both sides.

The agreement reached between them was on the following:

1. To conduct a final mapping of their land boundary, based on the Constantiniyyah (Astaneh) Protocol of 1913 and minutes of the Boundary Demarcation Commission (mapping) of 1914.
2. Demarcation of the river boundary according to the *thalweg* line.
3. The two sides will reactivate mutual security and confidence all along their common borders and pledge to conduct firm and effective control over them, in order to put a final end to all incursions of a terrorist nature, wherever they come from.
4. The two sides agree on the said arrangements as being part and parcel of a comprehensive solution and thus any infringement against one of the components will naturally conflict with the spirit of the Algiers agreement. The two sides shall remain in constant contact with President Boumeddien, who will provide, when necessary, Algeria's brotherly assistance for the implementation of these decisions.[74]

Thus, and in accordance with the Algiers Treaty, the traditional ties between the two states of Iraq and Iran were resumed. Both formally announced the need to keep the region far from any foreign intervention. On 15 March 1975, the Foreign Ministers of Iraq, Iran and Algeria met in Tehran; it was agreed to form three subcommittees. The first will map the land boundary, as per the Astaneh Protocol of 1913 and minutes of the Demarcation Commission of 1914; the second will determine water boundaries between the two states on the basis of the *thalweg* line; the third will monitor the borders and prevent any incursions and terrorist acts.[75]

On 13 June 1975, the boundary and good neighbourliness treaty, as well as the three accompanying protocols relating to the above three subcommittees' work, was signed in Baghdad. And yet?

Despite a beginning by both sides to apply the Algiers Agreement, Iran began to witness volatile internal developments that buffeted the situation of the state during 1977–1979, concluding with the fall of Shah Mohammed Reza Pahlavi in 1979 and proclamation of the Islamic Republic of Iran. This serious situation had a far-reaching impact; it led to suspending implementation of the Algiers Agreement's stipulations and start of a new and contemporary historical phase in Iraqi–Iranian relations.

11. The Three Protocols and Factors to the Outbreak of War[76]

The Algiers Treaty of 1975 between Iraq and Iran would certainly have been a genuine historical step towards ending the prevailing problems and ancient disputes between the two neighbours; it would have allowed for an atmosphere of cooperation and understanding to pervade bilateral relations, and neighbourly relations would have been built on solid foundations. Many negotiations and contacts took place between the two sides in order to apply the stipulations of the Agreement, and several technical issues. In March 1975 three protocols were signed that derived from the Algiers Agreement, namely:

1. A protocol determining the river boundary
2. A protocol remapping the land boundary
3. A security protocol for the common borders.

Iran implemented application of the first protocol and made the boundary in Shatt al-Arab follow the *thalweg* navigation line, after it had followed the left bank of the river. Meanwhile, more time was required for remapping the land boundary, by the Constantiniyyah (Astaneh) Protocol of 1913 and the minutes of the Boundary Demarcation Commission of 1914, in view of the great length of the boundary and the measures required for the process of setting up border markers.

It was assumed that Iran would hand over to Iraq the latter's lands, the Iraqi identity of which was affirmed in most of the treaties. But it delayed in implementation of this because of the difficult conditions that Iran was going through during the last years of the reign of Shah Mohammed Reza Pahlavi, 1978–79. The bitter bloody security and political events climaxed with the outbreak of widespread revolution against the Pahlavi regime. All Iranian political factions participated in the 'revolution', and the new regime led by Imam Khomeini took the place of the old regime of the Shah; it assumed power in Iran on 11 February 1979. Iraq despatched its recognition of the new Iranian regime and wished it well, through proper channels, expressing hope of cooperation according to the principles of good neighbourliness and the implementation of the obligations implied therein in lieu of the Agreement, in particular that relating to the hand over of Iraqi territories to Iraq's authorities.

I think that this 'point' registered the actual start of a crisis of confidence for Iraqis towards the new Iranian regime, which did not stop at its stances over implementation of the stipulations of the Algiers Treaty of 1975, but took to disrupting the principles of good neighbourliness by issuing and repeating a series of statements to not abide by the Agreement or return the Iraqi land to full Iraqi sovereignty. The Iranian regime stepped up its propaganda war by making announcements attributed to its leaders, to the effect that Iraq is part of the possessions of the Persian State, calling for export of the revolution, blatantly interfering in internal affairs, and engaging in repeated attacks on the Iraqi Embassy in Tehran and Iraqi consulates in Iran.

All this caused ample legal grounds for terminating the Algiers Agreement of 1975, the stipulations of which the new Iranian regime should have treated with much respect, as it was an international agreement that commanded considerable sanctity as a basis of international law between two states whose joint history is filled with complex historical boundary and territorial disputes. The agreement's exclusion from the principle of impermissibility of termination of treaty or unilateral drafting of it by one of the parties is acceptable in *two situations:* when one of the parties to the treaty breaches his obligations (i) fundamentally, (ii) when conditions undergo a fundamental change.

The Iraqi government relied on a basic legal principle when treating the Algiers Treaty as effectively terminated, and announced that termination for the following [direct] reasons:

1. The failure of the Iranian side to hand over Iraqi lands to Iraq, in lieu of the protocol remapping the land boundary, and Iran's continued infringements on the borders and seeking to take over new territory.
2. The emergence of hostile stances by both parties towards one another. The historian can confirm this through an inspection and tally of the official Iraqi memoranda deploring Iran's breach of good neighbourliness, threatening the security of Iraq and its national unity, and the increase in aggressions and excesses by Iranian forces on land, sea and air, including shelling of Iraqi cities.
3. The sharp, strong and repeated statements issued by Iranian officials of Iran's non-adherence to implementation of the stipulations of the Agreement that the Shah had signed with Iraq, which had for many years given shelter to Imam Khomeini against the Shah. This means that the new Iranian leadership had no intention of implementing the stipulations of an 'agreement' such as this, in addition to the 'stances' adopted towards Iraq specifically!
4. The Iraqi feeling, and Arab awareness, of the dangers of the notion of

'exporting the revolution', a 'notion' that is unprecedented in history. It is known that the principles of revolutions that inspire people are freedom and progress, not, by any means, export! What does this mean, strategically, for the Iraqis in particular, and the Arabs in general? It not only means the toppling of the political system, but the fragmentation of Iraqi social structure and tearing apart of Iraq's national unity ... and penetration of the fabric of the Arab nation!

All these reasons called for Iraq's termination of the Algiers Agreement on 17 September 1980, placing on Iran the international responsibility of what will result from this!

12. The Iraq–Iran War: the Peak of Conflicts and Foulest of Battles 1980–1988[77]

The dangers burgeoned, events moved quickly, opportunities for dialogue and understanding disappeared, and the malice of the propaganda cold war intensified to bring on a political war, after all channels were closed to the tide of collision sweeping the two adversaries. The outbreak of the Iraq–Iran war is regarded as a very difficult moment of history, accumulating all the negative historical residues and gathering all the legacies of Iraqi–Iranian border and territorial disputes, in addition to the cleaving of all complex and latent psychological obsessions, all of them surfacing after long centuries of containment and isolation.

Iraqi sources indicate that the Iranian armed forces shelled Iraqi cities (strangling Mandali and Naft Khaneh) and some border police stations, starting 4 September 1980. Iran occupied parts of Iraqi territory at Zein Qaws and Sheikh Saad. That day promised to be the actual start of the outbreak of war, within a narrow stretch of land between the border markers 46 and 51. The Iraqi sources continued their protest through Iraq becoming obliged to liberate them by force on 10–11 September 1980. It is noteworthy that Iran had recognized the return of this 'coordinate' to Iraq in the treaties of 1937 and 1975, but it did not return it to Iraqi sovereignty, compelling Iraq to recover it by force, after heavy fighting. But Iraq had despatched through its Foreign Ministry more memoranda on Iran's un-called-for infringements, summoning the Iranian Chargé d'Affaires in Baghdad on 8 September. Iraq referred to the right of self-defence in an Iraqi Foreign Ministry memorandum submitted to the UN Secretary General on 14 September.

When all efforts to contain the crisis failed – as the Iraqi diplomatic sources state – Iraq decided on 17 September 1980 to terminate the Algiers Agreement and reassert full legal and active sovereignty over Shatt al-Arab. Accordingly, Law No. 69, dated 1976, regarding endorsement of the international border treaty on good neighbourliness, and the three protocols annexed to it, with their four supplements of letters and joint minutes of meetings, was cancelled. In response to all that has been said, the Iraqi armed forces began their attack and battle, by land, sea and air, against Iranian positions. They advanced towards pre-designated targets in Qasr Shirin, Mehran and Sirbil Zahab. They also advanced towards Ahwaz, Khorramshahr, Dezful and a number of other cities on a battle front that burned with destruction and ferocity. At the same time, Iraq called on Iran to recognize legally and frankly 'Iraq's legitimate historical rights' to its land and waters, adhere to the policy of good neighbourliness and abandon its expansionist policies (through export of revolution) and interference in internal affairs. All this was on 28 September 1980. Iraq notified the UN Secretary General on the same day of its decision to halt the fighting with Iran if it adheres to these, and to resort to direct negotiations in light of Security Council resolution 479 dated 28 September 1980.

But Iran refused to accept the resolution. The 5th of October 1980 was set as the date for a ceasefire, but the Iranian side would not commit itself to it. The destructive, harsh, complicated and interlocking war continued for eight very difficult years. Its contrived and diverse historical phases witnessed destructive battles on land, sea and air, using the most powerful, vicious and expensive advanced weaponry, all along a 1200-km front with its varied geography in land, seas between mountains, lowlands and highlands, plains and rivers, lakes, seas and coasts, islands, cities and citadels. Its four phases included difficult shifts from skirmishes to offensive lightning wars, to counter-offensives, to defences that were fixed, then mobile, to economic war, war on economic and oil installations, to urban warfare, the shelling of east Basra and cities and islands, to attacks in 'human waves', and to missile warfare.

It was a destructive and unprecedented war, in ferocity and duration, in the strangeness of its woes and reasons, in the secrecy of its folds and backrooms, in the profiting of the 'world' for its continuation and the insanity of its expenditures, with the stupidity of Iran in sending 'human waves' and the corrupting effect of its events on Iraqi and Iranian societies and their generations and economies. The world was repelled by its tragedies and ignored it, and it came to be called the 'forgotten war'. Iran failed to reach its objectives announced in the years it called the 'decisive years'. Iraq succeeded in a series of successive wars that culminated in the liberation of Fao Island. A cease-fire was reached between the two sides on 8 August 1988. The situation remains stable until today, but without a treaty between the two sides to this very day!

The Boundary of the Future: a View of the Options

1. For the Sake of New Principles

After this survey investigation of the nature of Iraqi–Iranian boundary and territorial disputes across history, it is necessary to derive a future vision in order to determine the possible courses from the various 'options' apparent. We are on the threshold of a new century, in a 'region' that is vital and will increase in strategic importance over time. It is in no way possible to ascertain future frameworks and options between the two sides in the region; decisiveness in addressing the chronic disputes extant between them will remain subject to difficult and complex historical turnings, the same for the very process of finding a future boundary. A scientific vision of the interconnections of the present and formulations of the future courses are necessarily embodied in the factors of attraction and power, in all their components and core issues, both regionally and internationally.

Yes, drawing up joint plans for the future is a necessary and vital need, for Arabs, Turks and Iranians together, in light of the fundamental transformations the modern world is witnessing today, especially after the collapse of the Soviet Union and the Socialist camp and fall of international will into the hands of the United States alone. This is apart from the sharpening of discrepancies in the positions, policies and courses of action for the interim period until the start of the next century, leading all to an age of capitalist economics, with its Western values and new mechanisms. We have learned from the experience of 'Middle East dilemmas' that complex boundary and territorial problems between Iraq and Iran were, since the start of this century, useful opportunities for foreign interventions in the region.[78]

Thus, maintaining the conflict between the two sides hot or cold, will very much favour the Zionist movement and state of Israel, by putting in sharp relief a new perspective it is seeking to realize under the title 'The Middle East in 2000'.[79] Israel is also seeking to play on the weakness of political positions, distort nationalist values, shatter basic assumptions, ignite regional strife and maintain Arab fragmentation, even dissociate the Arab Near East from the Arab Maghreb and bring the entire Middle East under a new sphere of influence by force. The process of 'dismantling' for the new Near East begins with Turkey, Israel, Egypt and the countries within their orb, as a first security-economic matrix; North Africa by way of the Mediterranean, with south Europe, constitutes a second security-economic matrix. The role of Iraq and Iran is reduced to the Asian gateway,[80] a prospect for the later phase.

The question now is: what tasks fall to the central states of the region?
Its need is necessary and urgent, before adversaries can become aware of it, or before it is too late to build new conditions, joint interests and security horizons pervaded by peace, respect for patriotic and nationalist will, with non-interference in internal affairs. Otherwise the boundary problems and disputes between the two sides (Iraq and Iran) will remain a stumbling block to building the future boundary, especially as they have a very long and complex legacy of sharp disagreements, heated deferrals, and treaties and agreements. Perhaps it would really be useful to draw a future vision of the legacy of their bilateral relations in the 20th century. But what else? It is necessary to make a distinction when dealing with international laws and political regimes. The former, with its charters, treaties and agreements, are fixed, as they embody the historical and geo-historical interests of the two sides. The latter, however, with all that they reflect in referral authorities, messages, statements, claims and ideas, are subject to replacement or change with time.

There are basic principles that demand advancing hand-in-hand with into the future; among these are:

1. Respecting commitments, treaties and historical pacts concluded.
2. The need to dissociate, here, between international laws and political and religious slogans.
3. Faith in the geographic boundary deriving from the geo-historical fron tiers between the two sides.
4. The inviolability of non-interference in internal affairs of any party by the other.
5. Participation of all concerned and neighbouring/regional parties in Ara bian Gulf security.
6. Work towards averting foreign interventions and their possible man ipulations in the region.
7. Determination of a vision for a regional strategy towards the new in ternational developments.
8. Developing Arab ties with regional parties (particularly the Islamic) and giving them favoured treatment in the framework of joint mutual interests.
9. Rising above every form of intransigence and historical animosity and eliminating them, and becoming conscious of historic destiny by halt ing racial, religious, sectarian and other negative tendencies.
10. Working for cancellation of remaining historical residues in political thought, lodged in the mind of society and appended to cultural art iculation.

2. We, the West, and the Future

We have learned from bitter historical experience that the great powers hope for regional war between the two belligerents (Iraq and Iran) more than being disturbed by it,[81] not to mention encouraging such wars and revelling in their tragedies and pains. The difficult experience also shows us that, the more protracted a war the more others can profit from it, internationally, regionally and locally.[82] Similarly, additional long historical experiences on regional relations in the Middle East have shown that joint and mutual dialogue took place between the West and the countries of the Middle East, but it has changed into a mute dialogue since the fifties, a change that has begun to have a counter-effect on the nature of regional and international relations for the states of the area. These began to encounter severe jolts across nearly half a century since the Second World War, due to the division of the world between the two camps or coalitions, capitalist and socialist, and what they introduced in the way of impacts, policies, alliances, stances, awareness, feelings and sentiments, which, in turn, provoked angry political and ideological reactions among divergent social forces.[83] All of these were a basic and very real matter for the West, which proceeded to acquire a closer understanding of the area, playing upon its rampant contradictions, advancing at the expense of its oil/primary raw materials, not to mention what it designed, and continues to design, for the future of the world in terms of a 'market economy' and capitalist schemes. As for Middle Eastern peoples specifically, whether at the level of social classes, or the elites concerned, or the many and various political groups and parties and leaders in authority, whatever their leaning and organization, across half a century all have been, remain and will continue to be, undiscovered for the ultimate purpose of the West or the understanding of its tactics, thought, or replacement of dialogue with that same logic it used from a position of strength, efficiency and cleverness. This is apart from the testing of its plans, what it banks its moves on, and its futures, as per the type of historical phase and colour of the political climate. The English and French in the inter-war period did not have what the Americans and Soviets had in the Cold War period and during detente, and both are different from what the US has today, drawing up for the whole world a burdensome and dangerous design for the next century, entitled 'the new world order'.[84] The question is: of what concern is all this to us?

We are on the threshold of a new century, a new history and a new formation. The future vision must necessarily be broad in scope, for Arabs, Turks and Iranians, who constitute the core of the Middle East. It is also necessary to derigidify traditional and inflexible 'axioms', criticize their shortcomings, and put an end to their dangerous progress and anti-future. Liberating our societies from Islamism, its repressions, rifts, contradictions, conflicts and painful history, is a key task for any future formation and structuring of our histories, that we may keep up with the dynamics of events and repulse the approaching dangers.

3. The Global Vision and Matrix: Future Interactions

A vision of this type, deriving its future perspective from a complex historical content – and I have sought to be neutral on this – is among the most important that can possibly determine the global–existential vision for opening a new chapter of history, endowing the active political and social forces in it with the way to the future and closing the book of the past so saturated with disputes, dispersions, contradictions, conflicts and negotiations.

The final question: is a global–existential vision on the subject attainable? On this, I would say the following. Without Iraq as an existential–strategic and regional dimension, with all its geographic length and breadth, it is impossible to put in order or develop Arab–Iranian relations. Iraq represents in its centrality in the Middle East and Arab historical geography, a basic depth in the modality of development and future interaction, as gateway to Asia or eastern front to the Arab nation. Putting in order Iraqi–Iranian relations on the premises of sovereignty and joint interests would help build a regional and Arab strategy towards the Asian world, in addition to a global and historical centrality for Iraq in the Islamic corner.[85] Does not all this require, when we are in the midst of a changing world, a gathering of regional, Arab and Islamic cards in order to find an ending to the problems outstanding between the two countries?

Once again, let us turn in our statements and enquiries to the question: where do we stand, with our geo-historical balance sheet and 'static' or scholastic legacies and current intra-regional rifts, before the kinds of development that are being witnessed by large parts of the modern world on the advent of a new century?

A systemic vision of the transformations in the Middle East, for the short- and medium-term, and for the foreseeable and far future,[86] teaches us that Iraq is without doubt the gateway of the Arabs to the world of Asia, which will witness in all, or at least some, of its systems, serious and wide-scale transformations in the next century. Just as Egypt was the Arabs' gateway to the European world in past centuries, Iraq will be an important gateway, for it falls between the vital domain of the Middle East and the square of its coming crisis.[87] Richard Nixon, in his last book, *Seize the Moment*, published in 1993, hinted that the new challenge facing the United States for the future is to create a 'new axis of power' that extends between China and Iraq, passing through the central Asian republics to the north and India to the south, reaching to Iran and the Arabian Gulf.[88] Iran must necessarily focus its attention on this continental 'issue', which would greatly affect its place in the Middle Eastern. What is the theory of 'dual containment' but one of many new methods in confronting challenges by the method of 'seize the moment'?

Thus, Iraq would be the future Arab gateway towards the 'new Asia system', with all its transformations and configurations. It is necessary to rise above the wounds and the tragedies, and it is necessary to recover regional cohesiveness, modernize the Islamic vision, and re-programme Arab nationalism. The return of peace, stability and reconciliation between Iraq and Iran would open the main gates and channels to the rising new Asia; without these, the two will become, along with the Arabian Gulf countries, 'buffer zones': blocking the meeting of nationalisms in the new circumstances of globalization.[89]

Visionary Inferences

Finally, I would say that intellectual and historical awareness, by virtue of the nature of the topic and analyses of its components, and elaboration on its controversies, clearly reveals to us the two hegemonial systems – the colonialist of the 19th century and the imperialist of the 20th – and their dangerous influences in arranging the affairs of Iraqi–Iranian relations. The threat of the first system was in the Second Erzerum Treaty of 1847 and the Boundary Demarcation Commission of 1850, up to the Constantiniyyah [Astaneh] Protocol of 1913 and the Boundary Demarcation Commission of 1914. The threat of the second system was in the Treaty of 1937 and Boundary Demarcation Commission of 1938, up to the Baghdad Pact of 1955 and the Anglo-American role in arranging regional reconciliations. That is, in both these systems Britain had a prominent role in arranging the affairs of the two countries' relations.

What we truly need is a *conscious futurist vision*, given the thrust of this terrifying legacy of historical residues and psychological after-shocks, which continue to dominate in these relations. We also need a global vision towards this difficult legacy of disputes. Our future generations and our regional future will undoubtedly demand of us an 'investigation' into fundamentals when building the coming age, when all wounds, pains, hatreds, ambitions and aggressions disappear, and with them disavowal of agreements and violations of treaties too. Foremost among these fundamentals are the following:

1. *Complete faith in modern life, its historical formations, international and regional charters*, and working through laws, conventions and living customs that coincide in perception and application with other nations' situations.

2. It is in no way possible to cancel prevailing realities in the 20th century by skipping over a long and diverse history, to a very remote past that cannot possibly find today *a realistic backdrop for dealings, thought and destiny*.

3. Addressing all the offences of this painful reality through respect for laws, charters and treaty stipulations issued by the parties concerned, recognizing legitimate historical and geographic rights, and *genuinely rising above all contradictions that fill this reality, for the sake of building joint and sustainable interests. Confronting the new challenges* generated at the end of this century, or those encroaching on our coming generations. As the historian Albert Hourani put it: 'Do not be gladdened by the fall of the Socialist system; rather beware of encountering the vacuum, privation and the *racial wars* ... '90

4. The world, and the Middle East with it, awaits the birth of a *new world order* represented by a new capitalist force and led, with disturbances, by the United States, for an estimated period of 50 years. What will the Middle East and its geopolitics look like? What is Israel's role in the so-called *'new Middle East order'*? What is the place of Iraqi–Iranian boundary and territorial disputes in it, and then the political, security and programming of new challenges? What is our regional, Arab and Islamic capacity to respond to all these? The future will tell.

Notes

* Department of History, Faculty of Arts, University of Mosul, Mosul, Iraq.

1. Gaston Bouthoul, Rene Carrere and Lous Annequin, *Wars and Civilizations*, preface by Jean Guitton (Paris: [n. pb.], 1978), p. 3.

2. Sayyar Al-Jamil, 'Iraq's Strategy and Its Impact on the Emergence of Ottoman–Iranian Conflict', *Arab Futures*, vol. 6, no. 10 (June 1980), p. 14.

3. See article on 'Iran' in *Encyclopedia Italiana*, 'Dis. M. Il Red' Italia (Rome: [n.pb.], 1933), vol. 11, pp. 523–8.

4. Among the most prominent books dealing with these histories is Stephen Hemsley Longrigg, *Four Centuries of Modern Iraq*, London: Oxford University Press, 1925.

5. See Robert W. Olson, *The Siege of Mosul and Ottoman–Persian Relations, 1718–1743* (Indiana: Indiana University Press, 1975), pp. 11–30.

6. See geographic details, updated and old, since 1813 in John Macdonald Kinneir, *A Geographic Memoir of the Persian Empire* (London: John Murray, 1813), p. 236.

7. John Gaisford, ed., *Atlas of Man*, foreword by HRH Prince Charles (London: Marshal Cavendish, 1978), pp. 132–3. Compare geographic/historical data on Iran in: Peter Jackson and L. Lockhart, eds., *The Cambridge History of Iran* (Cambridge: Cambridge University Press, 1986), p. 116.

8.   Donald Newton Wiber, *Contemporary Iran* (London: Thames and Hudson, [1963]), pp. 5–6.

9.   The two best documentary studies in Arabic on these 'rivers' (25) and their banks between Iran and Iraq are Falah Shakker Aswad, *The Iraqi–Iranian Border: A Study on Prevailing Problems between the Two Countries* (Baghdad: Al-'Ani Press, 1970), pp. 31–93 and Rashad Qazanji, *Iraqi–Iranian Border Report and Shared Border River Waters* (Baghdad: Directorate of Public Irrigation, 1969), pp. 12–19.

10.   For more geographic details, see Kinneir, *A Geographical Memoir of the Persian Empire*, op. cit., pp. 54, 81, 85, 147–8, 159, 161, 168–9 and 189.

11.   André Miquel, *La Géographie humaine du monde musulman jusqu'au milieu du 11ème siècle* (Paris: Mouton, 1973), p. 18.

12.   Details in A. O. Cukwurah, *The Settlement of Boundary Disputes in International Law* (Manchester: Manchester University Press; Dobbs Ferry, New York: Oceana Publications, 1967), p. 10.

13.   J. R. V. Prescott, *Geography of Frontiers and Boundaries*, Hutchinson University Library, Geography (London: Hutchinson, 1967), pp. 30–9.

14.   See Muhammad Abdel Fadeel, 'The Crisis in Arab Strategic Thinking: A Future Perspective', *Arab Futures*, vol. 17, no. 192 (February 1995), p. 25.

16.   Sayyar Al-Jamil, *The Emergence of the Modern Arabs 1516–1916* (Mosul University: Dar al-Kitab Institute, 1991), p. 59.

17.   Ibid., pp. 60f.

18.   Sayyar Al-Jamil, *The Siege of Mosul: The Regional Struggle and the Routing of Nader Shah* (Mosul: Beit Mosul, 1990), pp. 23–9.

19.   For approaches and details on the theory of 'inner and outer lands', see: Sayyar Al-Jamil, *The Ottomans and the Formation of the Modern Arabs: A Contemporary Vision* (Beirut: Arab Research Institute, 1989), pp. 356–86.

20.   On 'Amasiya', see Shakker Saber Al-Zabit, *International Relations and Border Treaties between Iraq and Iran* (Baghdad: Dar al-Basri, 1966), pp. 18–19.

21.   Ibid., p. 21.

22.   Ibid., p. 24.

23.   For old details on the Zuhab Treaty, see *The History of Mustapha Na'mah* (Istanbul: [n.pb.], 1281 AH), part 3, pp. 394–5.

24.   Regarding these major geographic changes, see historical maps drawn by Donald E. Pitcher, *An Historical Geography of the Ottoman Empire from Earliest Times to the End of the Sixteenth Century*, Leiden: E. J. Brill, 1972.

25.   Al-Zabit, *International Relations and Border Treaties between Iraq and Iran*, p. 41. (From: *General Treaties, Collection C*).

26.   Shakker Sami Sobhi, *Sobhi's History* (Istanbul: [n.pb.], 1198 AH/1783 CE), p. 50.

27.   Historical details in Olson, *The Siege of Mosul and Ottoman–Persian Relations, 1718–1743*, op. cit., p. 187. See also analysis in Al-Jamil, *The Siege of Mosul: The Regional Struggle and the Routing of Nader Shah*, op. cit., pp. 213–15.

28.   Jacob Coleman Hurewitz, ed., *Diplomacy in the Near East: A Documentary Record, 1535–1914*, 2 vols. (Princeton: Van Nostrand, 1956), pp. 90–2.

29.   Longrigg, *Four Centuries of Modern Iraq*, op. cit., p. 287.

30.   See details available on this conference in Abdel Aziz Nawwar, *Iraqi–Iranian Relations, a Study in Conference Diplomacy: The Erzerum Conference, 1843–1844* (Cairo: Dar al-Fikr al-Arabi, 1974), pp. 145–6 and other pages.

31. Gabriel Noradounghian, *Recueil d'actes internationaux de l'ottoman, tome 2: 1789–1856*, no. 2 (Paris: F. Pichon, 1897), p. 92.

32. For the text of the stipulations see Hurewitz, ed., *Diplomacy in the Near and Middle East: A Documentary Record, 1535–1914*, op. cit., pp. 91ff.

33. The Ottoman Porte assigned one of its prominent engineers, Darwish Pasha, as member of the said commission. He submitted a report on the Persian–Ottoman border (the Iraqi Foreign Ministry translated it to Arabic in 1913), after he visited the area. See Darwish Pasha, *Report on the Demarcation of the Iranian–Ottoman Border*, trans. by the Iraqi Foreign Ministry, Iraq: [Ministry], 1953. The report highlighted Ottoman possession of the Arab city of Khorramshahr, along with the aide-mémoires of commission members on the common borders.

34. Mustapha Abdel Qader Al-Najjar, *The Political History of the Eastern Boundaries of the Arab Land in Shatt al-Arab: A Documentary Study* (Basra: Association for the Defence of the Arabism of the Arabian Gulf, 1974), pp. 84–9.

35. Yaseen Abdel Karim, 'Eastern Boundary Agreements until the Nineteenth Century' in *The Eastern Boundaries of the Arab Land: A Historical Study*, various authors (Baghdad: Dar al-Hurriyya Publishing, 1981), pp. 220–1.

36. Tariq Y. Ismail, *Iraq and Iran: Roots of Conflict* (Syracuse, N.Y.: Syracuse University Press, 1982), pp. 230–6.

37. See text of the Protocol in Jaber Al-Rawi, *Iraqi–Iranian Border Troubles and Military Conflict* (Baghdad: Dar al-Shu'un al-Thaqafiyah, 1989), pp. 40–17.

38. The texts are in ibid., p. 416. For details, see Hurewitz, ed., *Diplomacy in the Near and Middle East*, vol. 2, op. cit., p. 316.

39. Hisham Sharabi, *Governments and Politics in the Middle East in the Twentieth Century*, Van Nostrand Political Science Series (Princeton, N.J.: Van Nostrand, 1962), pp. 61 and 87.

40. See H. Bush, 'Oil in the Middle East' in *German Geographic Studies on the Middle East*, investigation by Eugen Kerth, translated and edited by Fouad Ibrahim et al. (Beirut: Arab Institute for Research and Publications, 1983), p. 31.

41. Ibid., p. 31. Compare William Stivers, *Supremacy and Oil: Iraq, Turkey and the Anglo–American World Order, 1918–1930* (Chicago, Ill.: Chicago University Press, 1982), pp. 150–9.

42. Details in C. H. D. Ryder, 'The Demarcation of the Turco–Persian Boundary in 1913–1914', *Geographical Journal*, vol. 66 (1925), pp. 22–42.

43. See full texts in *Proceedings of the Sessions of the Commission for Demarcation of the Turkish–Persian Border for the Year 1913–1914* (Baghdad: Government Press, 1948), pp. 8–12.

44. See consecutive Iraq–Iran boundary markers from north to south in Ibid. Compare Iraq, Council of Ministers, *Republic of Iraq Directory for 1960*, supervised by the Ministry of Guidance, Mahmoud Fahmi Darwish and Kamal and Ahmad Susa eds. (Baghdad: Dar al-Tamaddun, 1961), pp. 99–100.

45. On the complex problems of the Shatt al-Arab, see Abdelkader Benabdallah, *La Question du Chatt el-Arabe* (Montréal: Editions Canada-Monde Arabe, 1982), pp. 116–32. For more details, see Elihu Lauterpacht, 'River Boundaries: Legal Aspects of Frontiers', *International and Comparative Law Quarterly*, vol. 9 (1960), pp. 208–35, despite my reservations over certain views and ideas expressed in his passages.

46. Sayyar Al-Jamil, 'Intellectual and Political Options before the Arabs and Turks', *Arab Futures*, vol. 17, no. 185 (July 1994), pp. 113–14.

47. See by way of comparison Stephen Hemsley Longrigg, *Iraq: 1900–1950: A Political, Social and Economic History* (London, New York: Oxford University Press, 1953), p. 16, and Philip Willard Ireland, *Iraq: A Study in Political Development* (London: Jonathan Cape, 1937), pp. 21–37.

48. Hanna Batatu, *The Old Social Classes and the Revolutionary Movements of Iraq: A Study of Iraq's Old Landed and Commercial Classes and of Its Communists, Ba'thists and Free Officers*, Princeton Studies on the Near East (Princeton, N.J.: Princeton University Press, 1978), p. 201.

49. See Kamal Mazhar Ahmad, *Kurdistan in the First World War Years* (Baghdad: Kurdish Scientific Academy Press, 1977), p. 332.

50. Muhammad Kamel Abdel Rahman, *Iran's Domestic Policy during the Reign of Reza Shah, 1921–1941*, reviewed by Kamal Mazhar Ahmad (Basra: Basra University Centre for Iranian Studies, 1988), pp. 140–1.

51. Ibid., pp. 141–2, relying on Iraq's royal archives.

52. Khalil Ali Murad, 'Iran' in Khalil Ali Murad et al., *Turkey and Iran: A Modern and Contemporary Historical Account* (Mosul: [n.pb.], 1992), p. 159.

53. C. W. Baxter, *Memorandum on Relations between Persia and Iraq*, (n.p.: [n.pb.], 1928), pp. 10–15.

54. This is clarified by an in-depth study of Anglo-Iraqi treaties in 1922, 1926 and 1930, compared with the stipulations of paragraph 2 of Article 3 in the Lausanne Treaty of 1923. This in addition to the actual positions of the British as revealed in documents F.O. 371/13778 E. 613/58/84: Persia (1929).

55. Khalid Al-Azzi, *The Problem of Boundary Rivers between Iraq and Iran* (Baghdad: [n.pb.], n.d.), pp. 33–6.

56. F.O. 371/13779 (Persia) E. 2708/58/34 (1929), and F.O. 371/18970 (Persia) E. 171/32/34 (1934).

57. Aswad, *The Iraqi–Iranian Border: A Study on Prevailing Problems between the Two Countries*, pp. 18–19.

58. Tawfiq Al-Sweidi, *My Memoirs: Half a Century of the History of Iraq and the Arab Cause* (Beirut: Dar al-Kitab al-'Arabi, 1969), pp. 193–240.

59. Ibid., pp. 221–2.

60. The term *thalweg* refers to the imaginary line marking the deepest navigable part of the river, i.e., where the river's waters are deepest.

61. See Iraq, Foreign Ministry, *The Iraqi–Iranian Border Issue*, Baghdad: [The Ministry], 1934), and Iraqi government memoranda of 13 May, 13 June and 11 July, 1933. To complete the information, see Iraq, Foreign Ministry, *The Iraqi–Iranian Border Issue (1934)*, Annex B.

62. Iraq, Foreign Ministry, *The Iraqi–Iranian Border Issue* (Baghdad: [the Ministry], 1935), p. 16.

63. Ibid., pp. 16f.

64. Abdel Razzaq Al-Husseini, *The Political History of Modern Iraq*, part 3 (Saida: 'Urfan Press, 1948), p. 327.

65. Iraq, Foreign Ministry, *The Iraqi–Iranian Border Issue (1935)*, p. 23.

66. For details, see Rouhollah K. Ramazani, *The Foreign Policy of Iran: A Developing Nation in World Affairs, 1500–1941* (Charlottesville: University of Virginia, 1966), p. 290.

67. Majid Khadduri, *Independent Iraq, 1932–1958: A Study in Iraqi Politics*, Royal Institute of International Affairs (London, New York: Oxford University Press, 1958), p. 165.

68.   *New York Times*, 24 December 1959.

69.   Al-Najjar, *The Political History of the Problem of the Eastern Boundaries of the Arab Land in Shatt al-Arab: A Documentary Study*, op. cit., pp. 310–13.

70.   Memorandum issued by the Iraqi Foreign Ministry (Baghdad), no. 6614/4, dated 21 April 1969.

71.   Iraq, Foreign Ministry, *Remark on the Iranian Claims and Allegations Regarding the Iraq–Iran Boundary Treaty of 1937: The Legal Status of the Borders between the Two Countries in Shatt al-Arab* (Baghdad: The Ministry, 1969), p. 19.

72.   Majid Khadduri, *Republican Iraq: A Study in Iraqi Politics Since the Revolution of 1958* (London, New York: Oxford University Press, 1969), p. 169.

73.   Mohammed Hasanein Heikal, *The Ayatollah's Guns: The Story of Iran and the Revolution* (Beirut: Dar al-Shurouq, 1982), p. 137.

74.   Iraq, Foreign Ministry, *The Iraqi–Iranian Border Issue* (Baghdad: [the Ministry], 1975). See documentary texts published in the dailies *Al-Jamhouriyyah* (Baghdad), 7 March 1975 and *Al Thawra* (Baghdad), 11 March 1975.

75.   Jaber Al-Rawi, *Iraqi–Iranian Border Troubles and Military Conflict*, op. cit., p. 308.

76.   The writing of this 'investigation' relied on a number of Iraqi diplomatic papers and memoranda, with several writings that discussed the factors behind the outbreak of war.

77.   I limited this 'investigation' to Iraqi diplomatic sources, with follow-up of the hostilities from some of the known dailies.

78.   Jacob Coleman Hurewitz, *Middle East Dilemmas: The Background of United States Policy* (New York: Harper, Russell and Russell, 1973), p. 6.

79.   See proposals and projections presented by Shimon Peres in his book, *The New Middle East*, Muhammad Hilmi Abdel Hafiz trans. (Amman: Al-Ahlia Publishing and Distributors, 1994), p. 6.

80.   Details in Marvin C. Feuerwerger, 'Iraq: An Opportunity for the West?', *Middle East Review*, vol. 14, nos. 1–2 (Fall 1981 – Winter 1981–82), p. 27.

81.   Pierre Beylau, 'Irak–Iran: Le Jeu des grands', *Cahiers de l'orient*, no. 1 (1986), p. 126.

82.   Such as Israel's discovery that these 'disputes' are among the foremost methods for bolstering its position and enhancing its interests. See Nadav Safran, *The Embattled Ally* (Cambridge, Mass.: Harvard University Press, 1978), p. 339.

83.   Simon Jargy, *L'Orient déchiré: entre l'est et Ouest* (Paris: Labor et Fides, Publications orientalistes de France, 1984), p. 51.

84.   For further analyses, see Sayyar Al-Jamil, 'The Vital Domain of the Middle East towards the Coming World Order/From the Triangle of Crises to the Square of Crises: Future Challenges', *Arab Futures*, vol. 17, no. 184 (June 1994).

85.   See introduction to analyses in Claudia Wright, 'Religion and Strategy in the Iraq–Iran War', *Third World Quarterly*, vol. 7, no. 4 (October 1985), p. 849.

86.   Regarding these transformations in the so-called 'new Middle East order' within the forthcoming world order, see Haifa Jawad, ed., *The Middle East in the New World Order* (New York: St Martin's Press, 1994), pp. 51–6 and 77–9.

87.   Regarding the world order scenarios for arranging Middle East futures, see Dru C. Gladrey, 'Sino-Middle Eastern Perspective and Relations Since the Gulf War: Views from Below', *International Journal of Middle East Studies*, vol. 26, no. 4 (November 1994), p. 680.

88.   Abed al-Fadeel, 'On the Crisis in Arab Strategic Thinking: A Future View', p. 31.

89.   The contemporary intellectual Samir Amin has set new perceptions of 'globalization' in a document on his new and private programme 'Towards the Future', with the help of a team of well-known 'Third World' scholars.

90.   See interview with Albert Hourani in *Al-Qabas* daily (Kuwait), 24 April 1990.

15

Arab–Iranian Territorial Disputes: Cooperation in the Region, not Confrontation

PIROUZ MOJTAHED-ZADEH*

Introduction

With the ending of an ideologically oriented Cold War as a result of the collapse of the Soviet Union and breakup of the Warsaw Pact, the changing world order began to display new trends of moving towards an economically oriented multi-polar international structure.

This end of the Cold War coincided with increased economic competition between North America, Europe and Southeast Asia. Economic successes of the European Union encouraged other powers to form economic associations of their own. The United States joined forces with Canada and Mexico and created the 'North American Free Trade Area' (NAFTA), while 17 economies of Southeast Asia created the 'Association of Southeast Asian Nations' (ASEAN), with Japan as its potentially leading partner in future. Although Russia's 'Commonwealth of Independent States' (CIS), with the Slavic and Islamic nations of the former Soviet Union, may not succeed eventually in its present form, it nevertheless represents a new form of association in that part of the world. This changing world order of the 1990s has deeply influenced the global system, and in spite of endeavours in Washington for the creation of the concept of 'new world order' with a uni-polar system in which the United States tops the pyramid of the global hierarchical system of power, the world is rapidly heading towards an unprecedented geo-political order of economic competition in a multi-polar system that could, in time, lead to a kind of economic cold war between associations of economic giants.

The survival of other nations in this emerging geo-political order will undoubtedly depend on their grasp of this situation and their ability to create economic associations of their own in their particular regions.

Formation of new economic associations depends, above all, on defining a spatial arena based on the geographic concept of 'region'. Nations of such an arena are normally partners in some aspects of a common cultural, historical and economic life. In short, a 'region' is a geographical arena with some homogeneity of environments – the objects that constitute geo-political regions.

The region of the Persian Gulf has for some decades been wrongly considered by some as a sub-region of the so-called region of the 'Middle East'. The term 'Middle East' (or 'Near East' or 'Near and Middle East') has been used with great variation in terms of territories. It has extended variously from North Africa to the Indian subcontinent, and from the Caucasus to the Red Sea and beyond. This vast area, with its obvious lack of homogeneity in environment, cannot be considered a 'geo-political region'. The area known as the 'Middle East' is, in fact, an amalgam of several different environments such as 'The Persian Gulf', 'The Levant', 'The Maghreb', etc., each of which is a region on the merit of its own special characteristics. The question to be addressed here is whether it is necessary to consider this whole area of such great diversity as one region. The answer to this cannot but be in the negative.

The term 'Middle East' has been used for convenience, referring to a political environment shaped mainly by Arab–Israeli relationships, and such a usage of the term is harmless. Of the regions identifiable within the limits of the so-called 'Middle East', the Persian Gulf presents a unique model for a geo-political region. While the southern half of the Persian Gulf could conveniently be considered as a sub-region of the wider 'Arab world', the geo-political region of the Persian Gulf represents a homogeneous environment in itself. This region includes nations varying in some cultural aspects, but with similarities in political, strategic and economic preoccupations. It includes Iran, Iraq, Saudi Arabia, Oman, Kuwait, the United Arab Emirates, Qatar and Bahrain.

With the migration of Arab tribes to the coasts of the Persian Gulf over the two centuries immediately preceding the advent of Islam, there began a great mixture of Arab–Iranian populations in the coastal areas of this sea. As the new faith, Islam, overwhelmed various religions, the process of the emergence of a community particular to the Persian Gulf, north and south, began. Although Arabs and Iranians are of different ethnic backgrounds, and notwithstanding the fact that the Iranians succeeded within two or three centuries of the Islamic era in reviving their national language and national identity and independence, the two continued their intermingled cultural activities in the cradle of Islam and, in that respect, they have become almost inseparable in the region of the Persian Gulf.

The increased trade exchange between the two shores created a situation in which the process of cultural conglomeration and language mixture reinforced the distinctiveness of the Persian Gulf, while continued migration from both Iran and the Arabian Peninsula to the region and their mixture, made it quite difficult, even now, to say who in the Persian Gulf is of true Iranian stock and who is of true Arab stock.

Geographical location, on the other hand, brought the Persian Gulf to the heart of the old world, as the great routes of the old world had to pass through this region; this factor has given the region its importance since time immemorial. An added factor that strengthened this region's character as a separate geo-political region has been its strategic importance since the end of the 15th century to rival outside powers. The Portuguese, the Dutch, the French, the British and the Russians each found their domination of this region crucial to their colonial policies in the East. With the defeat of the French in the Napoleonic wars, the British, the Russians, the Ottomans, the Iranians and the Wahhabis became the main contestants in the region. The political environment created by each power, especially by the British, which lasted throughout most of the 19th and 20th centuries, together with the economic life flourishing around pearl diving and trade – replaced in the first half of the 20th century by oil economy – have all become objects of a distinct environment that can be referred to, with confidence, as the 'geo-political region of the Persian Gulf'.[1]

This distinct region, with its common environment, provides the best opportunity for the littoral nations to cooperate towards the creation of an economic association that is urgently needed for the economic survival of the regional countries in the emerging economically oriented, multi-polar world of geo-politics. Similarities of economic concern and related strategic issues, together with the global significance of the region for its enormous capacity of oil and gas production, its vast trade links with all the economic associations of the world, provide a unique opportunity for the creation of such an economic association.

While the involvement of extra-regional powers in the affairs of this region will inevitably add unnecessary complications to its political life, the inclusion of a regional nation like Iraq would inevitably make it more responsible for preservation of peace and maintenance of the status quo in the region. Here it is worth examining the question of whether Iraq would behave so irresponsibly towards its two neighbours, Iran and Kuwait, should it be a member of a collective regional configuration for security and cooperation.

Iraq's invasion and occupation of Kuwait, from this particular point of view, seems to be the fulfillment of Iran's prophecy of the early 1970s, that the creation of an incomplete region configuration would be considered a threat to the regional itself or the countries left out. This warning came in the wake of the expression by Saudi Arabia of a desire for the formation of a cooperation arrangement in the Persian Gulf, without the participation of Iran and Iraq.[2] It is a desire that was fulfilled in 1981 in the form of the Gulf Cooperation Council.

An important component of a regional arrangement for economic association is, however, recognition of the oil-consuming world's natural and legitimate interests in the region, which cannot but guarantee continued and safe supplies of oil and gas from the region, dialogue on which is to be channelled through the international energy markets. Peaceful settlement of territorial and boundary disputes, on the other hand, is an essential element in preparing for the creation of an economic association in the region, for unwarranted arguments aimed at reviving settled territorial and boundary disputes will gravely harm the prospect of regional cooperation.

Arab–Iranian Territorial Differences

There are a number of territorial disputes in the region of the Persian Gulf that, in general terms, can be classified into two categories: inter-Arab territorial disputes, and Arab–Iranian territorial differences. Of the first category, the following instances are noteworthy: territorial disputes between Iraq and Kuwait, which are now supposed to be resolved; Kuwait and Saudi Arabia over Qaruh and Umm el-Maradem Islands; Saudi Arabia and Qatar over their border areas; Qatar and Bahrain over the Hawar archipelago; Saudi Arabia and the United Arab Emirates (UAE) over the Bureimi and Liwa regions, and the UAE's unsettled territorial problems with Oman over areas around the Diba region.

Although Bahrain, Kuwait, Oman, Qatar, Saudi Arabia and the UAE have created the Gulf Cooperation Council (GCC) between themselves, real and effective cooperation between them is sometimes thwarted by these instances of territorial dispute. Cases in point in recent years were the Qatar–Saudi Arabia border clashes, and the disputes between Bahrain and Qatar under consideration at the International Court of Justice. Of the second category, there are two major areas of territorial dispute between Iran and the Arab states of the region: the Iraq–Iran border disputes, and the issue of the UAE's claims to Abu Musa and the Tunb islands.

The Iran–Iraq Territorial Disputes

The Iran–Iraq territorial and border disputes began several centuries ago and ended in the eight-year war of the 1980s. These disputes have been repeatedly exploited for political purposes by both parties. While Iran used the issue of Iraqi Kurd movements (a peripheral issue in the two countries' disputes) in the 1970s to establish its hegemony in the region, Iraq had been using the actual border disputes during the 1960s, 1970s and 1980s to forge a regional leadership role in the Arab world. It was in this context that Iraq planned and financed belligerent propaganda campaigns in the Arab world against Iran over the past thirty years or so. Viewing itself as the most eligible candidate for rivalries for Arab leadership in that period (when hostility with Israel was the determining factor in reaching a position of leadership in the Arab world), Iraqi leaders found their ambitions frustrated by countries situated on the front-line with Israel, such as Egypt. To turn this 'geographical disadvantage' into a geographical advantage exclusive to Iraq in the Arab world, Iraqi leaders concluded they needed a new common enemy for the Arabs with whom Iraq would be the sole front-line Arab state. Not only was Iran the natural choice, it was the only choice: a country with a long history of rivalries with the Arabs; a country suspected at the time by some Arabs of political or economic collaboration with Israel, and a country with which Iraq's territorial and boundary disputes provided the best instrument or pretext for conflict. These disputes were presented to the Arabs as the symbol of Iran's ill intentions towards 'Arab lands'. Extensive planning of a propaganda campaign against Iran, which was allocated huge sums of money over the past three decades, included attempts to change historical names of geographical features,[3] whereas Iran refused to seriously consider similar undertakings. The river separating Iran from Iraq is still referred to in Iran as 'Shatt el-Arab'.

With the success of the Islamic revolution of Iran in February 1979, relations deteriorated initially with the Arab neighbours. This was mainly because of a perceived threat to the security of the region, arising either from a direct initiative by the revolutionary government of Iran in the form of 'exporting the revolution' to neighbouring countries, or as a result of Islamic uprising in the countries of the region taking inspiration from Iranian revolutionaries.[4] These developments, together with encouragement from the West, enticed Iraq to unilaterally abrogate the Algiers border agreements of 1975 with Iran, and to champion the slogan of defending the Gulf Arabs from Iran's alleged revolutionary threats.

Hoping for a quick victory over the Iranian army, which was largely dislodged by the revolution, Iraq waged a war of attrition against Iran that dragged on from 1980 to 1988. Not only did Iraq fail to achieve its declared war aims, but Iraqi President Saddam Hussein wrote on 14 August 1990 to President Hashemi Rafsanjani of the Islamic Republic of Iran, confirming that Iraq was prepared to negotiate a border and territorial settlement with Iran on the basis of the Algiers accord of 1975. Most of the land held by the Iraqis in Kurdistan and Khuzistan was also released to the Iranians as a result of the withdrawal of all Iraqi troops to the boundary predating September 1980.[5]

Quite apart from the fact that territorial and boundary differences with

Iran have always been used by Baghdad as instruments of political ma-
noeuvring for Arab leadership, geographic and historical implications of
these differences have been studied extensively,[6] and so there is no need to
go through them again here.

The Islands of Abu Musa and the Tunbs

Although attempts have been made in the past two years to politicize and
internationalize the question of UAE claims to the islands of Tunb and
Abu Musa, probably hoping to use the issue as an instrument of exerting
pressure on the Islamic Republic of Iran, the nature of the claims could still
be viewed as genuine, motivated by misunderstanding on the part of both
sides of the 1992 incidents.

The 1992 Incidents

The Iranian authorities were reported in April 1992 to have prevented a
group of non-national employees of Sharjah from entering Abu Musa Island. These were Pakistani, Indian and Filipino labourers and technicians
and Egyptian teachers. Iran denied reports that its officials in Abu Musa
had expelled UAE nationals. The High Council of the UAE met on May
12 to discuss 'the issue' of Abu Musa Island. It was reportedly agreed at the
end of the meeting that commitments by any member of the Union were to
be treated as commitments by the Union as a whole.[7]

A representative of the UAE visiting Tehran prior to this meeting had
suggested that a joint commission of representatives of Iran and the UAE
should be formed to study the issue, but authorities of the Islamic Republic
of Iran rejected the suggestion on the grounds that there is no such thing as
the issue of Abu Musa.[8] Furthermore, it was reported on 24 August 1992
that Iranian authorities refused entry into Abu Musa Island of a large party
of over one hundred different nationalities (mainly Egyptian), who were
also refused entry to the island in April of that year.[9]

Having proved to the Iranians that they were teachers and their families
were going to Abu Musa to complete school examinations – indigenous
inhabitants of Abu Musa village are under Sharjah suzerainty, according to
the 1971 Memorandum of Understanding – they were allowed by the Iranians in November 1992 to enter the island. Reporting the incident, the
Times of London claimed that ' ... Iran unilaterally reneged on that [Memo-
randum of Understanding] deal, convincing many Western observers that
it planned to use the island in the shipping lane that carries half the world's
oil as a base for three submarines that it is now purchasing from Russia'.

The newspaper, furthermore, repeated allegations made in Abu Dhabi and Cairo that Iran had asserted its full sovereignty over the whole of Abu Musa.[10] Tehran denied all these charges and sent representatives to Abu Dhabi to find a peaceful end to the problem. This talk was brought to an abrupt end because of the UAE's unexpected demand for the two islands of Greater and Lesser Tunb to be ceded to it, in addition to Abu Musa.

The UAE government distributed in October 1992 a position paper to permanent representatives at the United Nations, highlighting what it deemed as facts of history about these islands. Iranian sources, meanwhile, made it clear that the reason for their action was that 'in recent months, suspicious activities were noted in the Arab part of Abu Musa Island'.[11] What had prompted Iran to take these actions, according to Iranian sources, was suspicious activities taking place in the Sharjah-controlled section of the island in the preceding months, involving a number of third-country nationals including individuals from Western countries:

Observers believe Iranian guards and agents were watching the comings and goings of foreigners in the island for some time. Reports from military sources in Tehran say that without the permission of the Iranian Government, the United Arab Emirates was building new establishments in the non-military part of the island. It seems that with the agreement of certain Arab countries, a number of non-native Arabs are to become residents on the island ... Iran's worst fears were realized when the GCC foreign ministers at the end of their Jeddah meeting declared that they will support the UAE in regaining sovereignty over the three islands belonging to Iran (September 10, 1992).[12]

Iran had in November 1971 warned Sharjah, through the Office of the British Foreign Secretary,[13] that it would take any measure in the island of Abu Musa it deems necessary to safeguard the security of the island and/or of the Iranian forces therein. This warning was conveyed to the Ruler of Sharjah by the British Foreign Office on the understanding that no reply to it would amount to its acceptance.[14]

President Rafsanjani of the Islamic Republic of Iran announced in his Friday prayer of 18 September 1992, that the Iranian authorities had arrested a number of 'armed third-party nationals' who were trying to enter Abu Musa illegally, of whom a Dutch national was in prison in Tehran. He then added: 'Iran's policy in the Persian Gulf is not the creation of enemies and conflicts, but defence of its territorial integrity, and we will act seriously to ensure this'.[15]

The UAE, on the other hand, without officially denying these serious charges of breach of the spirit and letter of the 1971 Memorandum of Understanding, accused Iran of preventing UAE nationals from entering Abu Musa, demanding visas from them. The UAE also accused Iran of gradual encroachment in Abu Musa, by building roads and an airstrip, and of intending to expand its military presence in the island.[16]

Media campaigns intensified after the failure of Iran's attempts at direct negotiations with the UAE in September 1992. There were unconfirmed reports that Iran and Sharjah were prepared to reaffirm the provisions of the 1971 Memorandum in their entirety before the leaders of the UAE intervened and the UAE foreign minister decided to tie any agreement on Abu Musa to a demand for the 'return' of the two Tunbs to UAE sovereignty.[17]

With the flare-up of border conflict between Qatar and Saudi Arabia, together with the outcome of a frank and academic exchange in a round-table discussion among academics of the two countries, arranged in London on 18 November 1992, which coincided with the defeat of George Bush (perceived defender of UAE claims) in the US Presidential elections, and with the admission to Abu Musa by the Iranian authorities of the Arab teachers, tensions between the two sides eased towards the end of 1992. But the announcement in Abu Dhabi in late December 1992 of the closing statements of the 13th GCC summit rekindled tensions between Iran and the UAE. This statement called on the Islamic Republic of Iran to 'terminate its occupation of Greater and Lesser Tunb Islands, which belong to the United Arab Emirates ... '[18]

This naked attack, from the Iranian point of view, on the arrangement arrived at between Iran and Great Britain on behalf of the Emirates some 21 years earlier, and upheld by the UAE since its creation in 1971 and by the GCC since its creation in 1981, provoked a strong reaction from Tehran. President Hashemi Rafsanjani made a statement on 25 December of that year, warning the GCC that ' ... to reach these islands one has to cross a sea of blood'.[19] He then dismissed this claim as totally invalid. Yet, the GCC reaffirmed the claim in the closing statements of its subsequent summits and thus prolonged the disputes between Iran and the UAE.

The UAE Arguments

The outstanding point in the arguments put forward by the British in the past, and adopted by the UAE, is the argument of priority in occupation.

The British Minister in Tehran wrote to the Iranian Foreign Ministry in 1904, arguing: 'What he [the Sheikh of Sharjah] had done was only to hoist his flag in the islands still not occupied by any one of the governments ... '[20]

This claim is vague and ignores the following facts:

1. That Iran was the only government in the vicinity of these islands at the time, and the expression 'had not been occupied by any one of the governments' makes little sense.
2. That the Sheikh of Sharjah was not, at the time, a 'state' or 'one of the

governments' in the Persian Gulf. He was a tribal chief (probably of Iranian descent) under British protection, with a tribal dominion still without territorial dimension. This is confirmed by all official British documents relevant to the affairs of the emirates, including assertions by a number of former British political representatives in the Persian Gulf,[21] and by authoritative British academics.[22]

3. That Iran had lease arrangements in the 19th century with Oman, according to which the Sultan of Oman was accorded by Fath-Ali Shah in 1811 and by Naser ad-Din Shah of Iran in 1856, lease title of Bandar Abbas, Minab and southern Gulf coastal regions from east to west as far as Bahrain. If all these areas belonged to Iran, the islands of Abu Musa and the two Tunbs, situated in its geographical centre, could not have been unoccupied.

4. That marking occupation or ownership of territories by hoisting flags was a new concept introduced to the region of the Persian Gulf by European powers, whereas Iran's sovereignty and suzerainty over these islands, as well as all other territories offshore and inland areas of the region of the Persian Gulf, were traditionally established without the display of flags of identity.

5. That Iran had in 1887 hoisted its flag in Sirri and Abu Musa Islands to mark its suzerainty over these islands, in the wake of the dismissal of the Qasimi deputy-governorship of Bandar Lengeh. (See Abbas Eqbal Ashtiani, *Ettelaati dar bereh-e Bahrain va Jazayer-e Khalij-e Fars* (Tehran: [n.pb.], 1328 AH [1949 CE]), p. 144).

6. That all works of geography and history of Arab and Islamic geographers/historians of post-Islamic era writing on the region of the Persian Gulf, confirm that all islands of that sea belong to Iran. The British had only to look at *Nezhat al-Qolub* of Hamdollah Mostowfi, for instance, to find assertions of the following nature: 'Islands situated between Sind and Oman and in the Persian Sea belong to Persia, the largest of which are Qis [Qeshm] and Bahrain ... '[23] Confirmation of Iran's control of all areas of the Persian Gulf in later periods can be found in European documents. Quoting documents of Portuguese–Safavid periods in his 'Notes', Captain Robert Taylor of British India, for instance, remarks: ' ... Since the Arabs have retaken Muskat (1620s), and the Portuguese have no strength in the Gulf, every man that goes a fishing pays to the King of Persia five Abbasees* only (the Portuguese used to extract 15), whether his success be good or bad. The merchant also pays some small trifle to the king, on every thousand oysters.'[24]

7. That the Iranian prime minister, Haji Mirza Aqasi, officially asserted in 1840 Iran's suzerainty over all the islands in the Persian Gulf.[25] This proclamation was not officially challenged by Britain or any other government at the time, or at any time thereafter.

8. That numerous official British maps of the 18th and 19th centuries confirm Iran's suzerainty over the islands of Abu Musa and the two Tunbs.[26]

The British maintained in their disputes with Iran over the islands that: 'Qasimi control of the southern Gulf and the islands had been established long before the Persian coast was settled'.[27]

Such suggestions defy the facts of history of the region, mainly because of the lack of clarity as to which branch of the Qasimi family is meant to have established control over the two Tunbs, Abu Musa and Sirri islands 'long before the Persian coast (the 1887 settlement of affairs of Lengeh) was settled'. If the suggestion refers to the Qasimis of Lengeh, no doubt they governed Lengeh Governorate and its dependent ports and islands as Iranian subjects and officials long before they were dismissed in 1887. But, if otherwise, the suggestion implies that the main branch of the family had established their control over these islands before 1887, or after that. Firm evidence is needed to clarify in what manner this 'control' was established, and to which country the islands belonged before being brought under their control.

Here, other official British documents assist in a better understanding of the situation. There are a number of British, French and Russian official maps, dating back to the 18th and 19th centuries, confirming that these islands belonged to Iran. Another official British government document verifies that these islands were occupied by the Qasimi family after the establishment of one branch of that family at Lengeh or thereabouts, without clarifying whether that branch or the main branch of the family occupied these Iranian islands:

In the second half of the 18th century the Arabs of the pirate (later called the Trucial) coast of Arabia occupied the islands of Tanb (also called Tunb, Tamb and Tomb), its dependency Nabiyu Tanb, Abu Musa and Sirr; it seems probable that they did so in the very confused period subsequent to the death of Nadir Shah. These Arabs also settled on the Persian littoral, in the same way as the Huwala Arabs had done; it is not recorded when these Arabs actually reached the mainland, but it seems logical to assume that they did so after they or some of their fellows had established themselves on the islands.[28]

This story, if true, is only another admission that the islands of the Tunbs, Abu Musa and Sirri were under Iranian suzerainty and were occupied illegally by the Qasimis at a time when Iran was leaderless and deeply sunk in confusion. Nevertheless, the main branch of Qasimi family's presumed occupation of these islands was not recognized by the British until 1903, when they advised the main branch of the Qasimis (of Sharjah) to plant their flag on these islands.

The phraseology of correspondence: Apart from resorting to these old and long exhausted arguments put forward by the British of India during the colonial era, the UAE bases its claims over the islands of Tunb and Abu Musa on a number of letters exchanged between the Sheikhs of Sharjah and Ras al-Khaimah on the one hand, and British political agents and rulers of various tribes of the southern coasts of the Persian Gulf and the Qasimi Sheikhs of Bandar Lengeh on the other. Some of these letters date as far back as 1864. These documents contain many inconsistencies and contradictions, with an amazing set of fanciful claims on various localities up and down the region. The validity of the claims contained in these letters was not even confirmed by the Sheikhs of Dubai, who did not, in most cases, even find them worthy of reply. The most important of the letters is the one written by Sheikh Yusuf al-Qasimi of Bandar Lengeh to the Sheikh of Ras al-Khaimah, which states:

I have received your letter.

Haji Abul Qasim, the Residency Agent, came to me and informed me about your complaint about the island of Tomb. The island of Tunb is actually an island for you o' the Jawasims of Oman, and I have kept my hand over it, considering that you are agreeable to my doing so, and that our relations with you are intimate and friendly. But now when you do not wish my planting date offsets there, and the going across of the Busmaithis to cut gross there, I shall prohibit them for our mutual relations to remain friendly.[29]

Quoting this letter in isolation is misleading. Examination of this document in the proper context of circumstance in which it was written will clarify the true nature of its contents. When in 1873 disputes erupted between the Qasimi Sheikhs of Lengeh and Ras al-Khaimah over the issue of grazing of local livestock in Greater Tunb, the arbitration of British political agents was sought.[30] Sheikh Hamid al-Qasimi of Ras al-Khaimah complained on 10 February 1873 to Haji Abul Qasim, British political Agent in Lengeh, that Bu-Samaith tribesmen of the Iranian ports of Aslaviyeh, Charak and Lengeh, encouraged by Sheikh Khalifah al-Qasimi of Lengeh, prevented his subjects from entering Tunb Island for grazing their domestic animals. Haji Abul Qasim ruled that Tunb Island belonged to Lengeh (Iran) and the Bu-Samaiths had traditional rights to the grazing there. As further enquiries into the dispute became necessary, the Political Resident in Bushehr, Edward C. Ross, empowered Haji Abdel Rahman, Political Agent in Sharjah, to carry out more extensive enquiries. Having visited the island and interviewed Sheikh Qasimi of Ras al-Khaimah and Sheikh Qasimi of Lengeh, Haji Abdel Rahman concluded his report by asserting that the Tunb Island belonged to the *eyalet* of Fars (Iran) and administered by the governorship of Lengeh. Based on this report, Mr Ross wrote to Sheikh Qasimi of Ras al-Khaimah on 19 April 1873, stating that Tunb Island belonged to Lengeh and the inhabitants of Ras al-Khaimah should refrain from annoying Iranian livestock breeders there, and should take their horses out of Tunb Island.[31] Ten years later, when relations were normalized and with encouragement to establish friendly relations with the Qasimi Sheikhs of Ras al-Khaimah, Sheikh Yusuf al-Qasimi of Lengeh wrote a letter of compliment (reproduced opposite) to the Qasimi Sheikh of Ras al-Khaimah.

The expression 'the island of Tunb actually or in reality is for you' leaves little doubt about the standard Oriental courtesy or complimentary nature of the correspondence, which was conditional on relations remaining friendly. Furthermore, a few lines below this statement, Sheikh Yusuf leaves little doubt as to the Oriental complimentary nature of the letter. There he states: 'And the town of Lengeh is your town' (see section marked 2 on the original document). No one has ever been under any illusion, then or at any other time, that Port Lengeh belonged to any country but it has always been and still is an indivisible Iranian territory. The question here is: while this courteous or complimentary reference to Lengeh as 'belonging' to the Sheikh of Ras al-Khaimah has never been and cannot be taken literally, how could the same reference to the Tunb Island have been and is still taken literally? Certainly the expression *mi casa es su casa* ought not to be.

When in 1929 Abdel Aziz Al Saud, King of the new Saudi state in Arabia, wrote to Sheikh Hamad al-Khalifah of Bahrain complaining about the treatment of his subjects in Bahrain, he received a letter of compliments from the Sheikh, who said that 'Bahrain, Qatif, Hasa and Nejd are all one and belong to Your Majesty'[32] (Document No. 53 of *Selection of Persian Gulf Documents*, 1989, Vol. I, pp. 168–9). Certainly inclusion of Bahrain in that list could not been anything but a compliment.

British sources, on the other hand, have been insinuating that Iran claimed the islands of Greater and Lesser Tunb in 1877 and the island of Abu Musa in 1887 or 1888. What these sources conveniently neglect is the fact that Iran reminded the British in 1877, and 1887 or 1888, of Iranian suzerainty over these islands and that the insinuation of Sharjah or Ras al-Khaimah suzerainty was irrelevant.

Dual legal status: As for the British claim that these islands had been ruled by the Arab governors of Lengeh, in their capacity as Qasimi Sheikhs rather than Iranian officials, it is incomprehensible how this dual legal status of the Qasimi governors of Lengeh could have been arranged. How the governor of Lengeh could rule dependent islands of the governorate, not as governor but as holder of another official and legal title, is an abstraction.

To try and give this argument some form of legal validity, the British government asked Sir Edward Beckett, the legal expert of that government at the Foreign Office (who later served as a member of the International

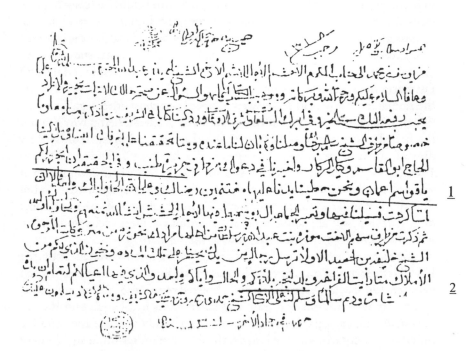

Copy of original letter of 1 Jamad II 1301 AH (1882 CE), from
Sheikh Yusuf al-Qasimi of Bandar Lengeh to Sheikh Hamid al-
Qasimi of Ras al-Khaimah. Where marked <u>1</u>, the author of this letter
refers to the Tunb Island, and where marked <u>2</u>, the author speaks of
Bandar Lengeh.

Court of Justice at The Hague), to evaluate legally this claim of dual legal
status for the Lengeh Qasimis vis-à-vis the issue of ownership of the three
islands. He ruled in 1932 that: 'My conclusion is that, unless further evidence is forthcoming that it can be proved that during the period 1880–1887
the [Qasimi] Sheikh at Lingah ruled the islands under some title different
from that under which he ruled the mainland (I doubt if it will be easy to
show this), the Persians did possess sovereignty over Tamb and Abu-Musa
during those years'.[33]

Apart from masses of official British and Iranian documents confirming the legal status of the Qasimis of Lengeh as 'Iranian officials of Lengeh governorship and loyal subjects of the Iranian government', the British appear not to have taken all the facts into consideration when making this suggestion. It is not known what their explanation would be to such questions as, when individual Qasimi governors of Lengeh were changed, dismissed or appointed by the Iranian authorities, would it affect the changed or dismissed governor's other mysterious legal or traditional status as 'hereditary Qasimi ruler' *vis-à-vis* Lengeh and its dependent islands? Furthermore, when the Qasimi governorship of Lengeh was abolished by the Iranian authorities in 1887, what happened to their other legal or traditional status *vis-à-vis* Lengeh and its dependent islands? And why did not the British protest against continuation of Lengeh and these islands under direct Iranian suzerainty for so long as it did, between 1887 and 1903 and 1908 (Lesser Tunb was occupied in 1908)? It is also worth noting that it was not the first time the British claimed dual legal status for the Qasimi Sheikhs of Bandar Lengeh. They had once before done the same in respect of Sirri Island, but abandoned that futile argument after exchanging a few notes of claims and counter-claims with the Iranians.[34]

The factor of prescription. One of the legal arguments hinted at by the UAE is the factor of prescription. That is to say, since about 68 years elapsed between 1903, when Sharjah's flag was hoisted over these islands, and 1971, when they were returned to Iran; and since rulers of Sharjah and Ras al-Khaimah had, during this period, constructed buildings there and installed official representatives on the islands, the factor of prescription should have overcome any Iranian claim of suzerainty.

It is noteworthy that the factor of prescription stands, according to international regulations, when occupation of a territory is continued 'uninterrupted', 'undisturbed' and 'unchallenged'. As has been discussed above, the government of Iran began protesting against, and challenging, occupation of the Tunbs and Abu Musa less than a year after their occupation by the emirates in 1903. Not only did Iran repeat its protests and challenges every year since 1904, and not only did Iran exhort Britain on several occasions to negotiate with its ways of recognizing Iran's rights to these islands, but it physically interrupted their occupation on several occasions, even succeeding in regaining Great Tunb at the end of 1934, albeit for a brief period. There is no doubt that Iran's consistent and vigorous campaign during the 68 years of the occupation of these islands by the emirates allows little room for the argument of prescription.

Also noteworthy is a point asserted by some UAE sources in this respect: that the facts of history must be ignored in such discussions, because if a historical approach is followed 'with which we [the UAE] disagree in international relations, a number of Middle Eastern countries will disappear, will cease to exist … '[35] This argument has no relevance to the case of the islands of Tunb and Abu Musa, because the Tunbs and Abu Musa are not countries.

Territories ceded from the Persian or Ottoman Empires in the past and appearing as new countries were sizeable and populous areas, which opted for or achieved independence one way or another. They were not occupied and annexed by other states, as was the case of the islands in question, whereas Tunb and Abu Musa Islands were almost uninhabited when seized from Iran at the turn of the 20th century and annexed by Sharjah.[36] Greater Tunb and Lesser Tunb had been and still are completely uninhabited. These were chunks of Iranian territory seized by Great Britain at the turn of the 19th century for reasons of perceived security needs at the time. Furthermore, at least two articles of the Memorandum of Understanding of 29 November 1971 between Iran and Sharjah explicitly confirm Iran's suzerainty over Abu Musa Island. Article (2) of the Memorandum allows Iran to maintain military units in the northern parts of Abu Musa, with full suzerainty. Military units with full suzerainty over the areas concerned can only be established in a country's own territory. Article (3) of the Memorandum recognizes the Iranian law of territorial waters for Abu Musa, whereas the breadth of Sharjah's territorial sea was, at the time, three nautical miles, in accordance with the British law of territorial waters.[37]

The current UAE claims are that the Memorandum of Understanding was accepted at the time (1971) under duress, and they had accepted the new status of Abu Musa in the form of 'de facto' recognition. Iran was not negotiating with Sharjah to impose upon it anything under duress. The above claim is made in clear contravention of the fact that Sharjah was, at the time of the agreement, a British protectorate, and her foreign affairs were, according to the 1864 and 1892 agreements, the responsibility of the British government, with which Iran had arrived at that Memorandum of Understanding arrangement. Great Britain was, at the time, still a major power in the world, much stronger than Iran, and would in no way accept such an arrangement from Iran under duress.

In fact, the reverse argument would sound more plausible. Iranians could argue that, by imposing on Iran an agreement on shared suzerainty over Abu Musa, Britain, a major power acting for the emirates, prevented implementation of Iran's full suzerainty over the whole of the island of Abu Musa. Under duress, Iran had to give the new status of the island 'de facto' recognition. Moreover, while arguing, in its position paper of 27 October 1992, that the Memorandum of Understanding was imposed upon Sharjah under duress, the UAE demanded in the same document that Iran remain committed and bound to that 1971 Memorandum. This demand clearly contradicts the UAE's argument of imposition of the Memorandum under duress, and renders it null and void.

The UAE officials also chose to ignore the fact that, when arriving in Abu Musa Island on 30 November 1971, the Iranian military forces and their commanders were personally greeted and welcomed by H.H. Sheikh Saqar bin Muhammad al-Qasimi, brother of the present ruler of Sharjah, who represented his brother, H.H. Sheikh Khalid bin Muhammad al-Qasimi, the late ruler of Sharjah. This high level of welcome extended to the Iranian forces in Abu Musa can hardly suggest acceptance under duress of the Memorandum of Understanding by Sharjah.

Conclusion

In a rational analysis, it is almost obvious that the question of Iran's suzerainty over the islands of Tunb and Abu Musa was settled through negotiations in 1970 and 1971 between Iran and Britain. This was the outcome of about 68 years of Iran's protests and demands for the return of these islands to it. Otherwise, Britain, still in charge of territorial and boundary interests and foreign relations of the emirates in November 1971, would at least have issued a statement of protest against the signing of the Memorandum of Understanding between Iran and Sharjah concerning the status of Abu Musa Island and against Iran's seizure of the two Tunbs.

This conclusion, however, is not designed to reaffirm Iranian suzerainty over the islands of Tunb and Abu Musa. Documented facts are demonstrated, as clearly as possible, in the main text of the papers, and I leave the final conclusion to the readers. What I would like to argue here is that revival of an issue settled through negotiations between Iran and Great Britain cannot but harm all prospects of cooperation in the Persian Gulf for peace and the possible creation of a regional economic association. Considering the vital significance of a move for the creation of such an association in the region for survival in the emerging geo-political order of an economically oriented, multi-polar world, one is bound to question the wisdom of attempts for the revival of these settled disputes.

The UAE High Council declared on 17 May 1992 that international commitments of each emirate in the pre-1971 period were commitments of the United Arab Emirates. Considering that Iran and Sharjah were preparing, at that time, to negotiate their differences, this UAE undertaking was clearly aimed at preparing the grounds for politicizing and internationalizing the legally arranged shared Iran–Sharjah suzerainty over Abu Musa Island. Such an undertaking is hardly conducive to a spirit of friendship necessary for overcoming differences by peaceful means. The UAE's intentions became pronouncedly known when other members of the GCC were goaded into repeatedly issuing communiques supporting the UAE's bid to internationalize the issue. Otherwise, no treaty between two states creates rights and responsibilities for a third country, according to the accepted legal principle of *pacta tertiis nec nocent nec prosunt*. The UAE's cooperation with other members of the GCC can hardly set aside this principle.[38]

King Fahd of Saudi Arabia asked Iran, in his message to the 1994 Hajj pilgrims, to give the islands of Tunb and Abu Musa to the UAE. This was unprecedented. For the first time in history, a leader of one country asks another country to give parts of territories under its suzerainty to a third country. The uproar resulting from this episode overshadowed the international opinion arising against Saudi Arabia's 'interference' in the domestic affairs of the Republic of Yemen and the resultant civil war in that country.

This treatment of Iran–UAE differences reached its climax when the GCC foreign ministers meeting issued a communique in Saudi Arabia on Monday, 5 June 1994, expressing regret that Iran did not comply with their earlier instruction to 'evacuate' the three islands.

The repeated expression of support for the UAE territorial claims against Iran by the GCC annual summit and ministerial conferences, on the other hand, will not help the prospects for peace and cooperation in the Persian Gulf; albeit, to some, these annual expressions of support may seem no more serious than those made by some Arab leaders in Baghdad during the years of the Iran–Iraq war, in support of Iraq's territorial and boundary claims against Iran, which were eventually discredited by Iraqi President Saddam Hussein himself, in his letter of 14 August 1990 to President Hashemi Rafsanjani of the Islamic Republic of Iran.

Given the location of Abu Musa and the two Tunb islands in the strategically sensitive Strait of Hormuz, and given that both the regional countries of the Persian Gulf and the oil-consuming countries of the industrial world depend heavily on peace and security in the Strait of Hormuz, it is important to note that supporting any one of the two sides in this argument against the other can easily lead to conflict, potentially as explosive as that of the Kuwait crisis of 1990–91. Political leaders of the US and Europe have been warned by the Iranians of the danger of their hints of one-sided support in this issue. The message of President Hashemi Rafsanjani of the Islamic Republic of Iran, on 21 February 1993, to Prime Minister John Major of Great Britain (then head of the European Union), contained the following points:

I find it necessary to criticise the double standard employed by the West in approaching the long-standing territorial claims that create instability and insecurity in the region. We can see such a double standard in your attitude towards Iraq's claims over Kuwait and Iran *vis-à-vis* the unfounded claims of some of our southern neighbours. If such an approach is right, then Iran can make many historical and documented claims with regard to its neighbours.[39]

It is true that territorial and boundary disputes in the Persian Gulf have prevented proper and lasting Arab–Iranian cooperation in the region. However, it is also true that whenever there was a situation of emergency involving the overall interests of both sides, cooperation between Iran and its Arab neighbours materialized. The best example of this is the seven-year period (1968–1975) of Arab–Iranian cooperation in the region.

This period of Arab–Iranian cooperation was prompted by a sense of emergency arising from the announcement in January 1968 of the British Government's decision to withdraw its forces from east of Suez and thus leave the issue of security in the Persian Gulf to its littoral powers. This announcement coincided with the declaration of US President Nixon's doctrine of non-interference in regional conflicts, leaving regional security around the world to friendly regional players. This situation precipitated a sense of urgency for regional cooperation in the Persian Gulf, to maintain peace and security in that region. An added impetus in the emergence of this situation was the 1965 meeting between the Shah of Iran and King Faisal of Saudi Arabia, during which they agreed on extensive cooperation among Muslim nations. These agreements not only put a final end to years of Shi'a–Sunni conflicts in the region, but paved the way for the creation of the Islamic Conference.[40]

Iran and its Arab neighbours promptly realized that settlement of geographical differences was to be seriously considered as a necessary precondition for the promotion of cooperation amongst them in the region. It was under the influence of this state of strategic urgency that many complex border issues were settled. Two of the most complicated border issues settled in this period were those of the continental-shelf boundary settlement of late 1968, between Iran and Saudi Arabia, and the 1971 understanding between Iran and Sharjah on Abu Musa Island. These were followed by a number of other settlements, such as: the continental-shelf boundary settlements of 1970 between Iran and Qatar, 1972 between Iran and Bahrain, 1975 between Iran and Oman, and the river and inland boundary settlement between Iran and Iraq in that same year.[41] Maritime boundaries between Iran and Kuwait, at the head of the Gulf, were covered by a draft agreement between the two sides, but it is not in force because of continued territorial and boundary disputes between Iraq and Kuwait. Also, Iran delimited its maritime boundaries with Dubai in 1972, but official ratification of this agreement is prevented by uncertainties arising from the unclear terms of the 1971 arrangements between Iran and Sharjah over Abu Musa Island. A draft agreement also came into being between Iran and Abu Dhabi in that period, but it too is rendered inoperative by the situation concerning Abu Musa Island.[42]

Other manifestations of Arab–Iranian cooperation in the period 1968–1975 include Iran's internationally praised withdrawal of historical claims to Bahrain, and its swift and highly effective response in 1973 to Oman's call for assistance in defusing a Marxist separatist conspiracy against its territorial integrity. This swift and extensive military assistance eradicated the 12-year-old armed struggle of Communist separatists in Dhofar province of Oman in a short period of under three years. It is noteworthy that, while Iran was busy defending Oman's territorial integrity, almost all Arabs accused it of having territorial designs on Oman. These attacks reflected on a wider scale of growing mistrust between Arabs and Iranians in the region, the flame of which was being fanned by dubious sources in the West, especially after it became clear that Arab–Iranian cooperation in other fields, such as OPEC international oil policies, effectively tipped the balance of power in the international geo-political system in favour of the regional states of the Persian Gulf.

Some Western accusations that Iran had territorial ambitions against Arab states of the region successfully impressed some Arabs, despite the fact that Iran had withdrawn territorial claims to Bahrain and defended the territorial integrity of Oman. These accusations reached their climax in 1977 with the publication of Paul Erdman's inflammatory novel, *The Crash of 79*. Such intrigue and propaganda, clearly aimed at destroying all prospects of Arab–Iranian cooperation, eventually resulted in the collapse of Iran's proposal for the creation of 'a collective security pact in the region with the participation of all states littoral to the Persian Gulf',[43] and put a final end to that short period of Arab–Iranian cooperation in the region.

Today, it is not impossible to envisage a repeat of history and reanimation of the spirit of collective cooperation in the region. A major step in this direction would be to satisfactorily settle remaining Arab–Iranian territorial differences. Of these, Iran's differences with Iraq can only be settled if and when Iraq sincerely separates geographical issues with Iran from its inter-Arab politics. Alternatively, the only interim solution left for the rest of the region for cooperation is to go ahead without an active participation from Iraq, until it is able to give immediate geographical interests priority over old and long-exhausted inter-Arab geo-political ambitions and is able to identify its regional and global interests with those of the rest of the region.

The issue of Abu Musa and Tunb Islands can be settled if both parties genuinely feel the need for serious cooperation in the region. Let me expand on this. Given that the changing world order necessitates rethinking in all regions for preparing to face the challenges of the new global geo-political realities, through creation of regional political-economic structures for cooperation, continued Arab–Iranian territorial and other disputes would only benefit outside interests – the potential future rivals of the region. In other words, cooperation between Iran and the Arab states of the region is possible primarily if national interests were to be put before the geo-political interests of the great powers. Materialization of such cooperation will, then, depend on amicable and just settlement of the issue of UAE claims to Abu Musa Island, in which context the following recommendations may prove to be of some assistance:

1. Complete de-politicization of the issue of these claims, by preventing third-party interests from interfering in the matter.
2. Undertaking by Iran ways and means of reassuring Arab states of the region of their sincerity and of in there being no ill intentions towards the territorial and sovereignty status quo of the region.
3. Undertaking by the UAE to reduce its territorial claims to a more realistic proportion. That is to say, the UAE should show good intentions by abandoning unrealistic claims to the two Tunb islands, which are recognized by all informed independent observers as being Iranian, by virtue of documented geographical and historical verification.
4. Acceptance by both sides that the 1971 Memorandum of Understanding lacks clarity in various aspects of application of separate Iranian and Sharjah suzerainty over the island. The terms of the Memorandum of Understanding need to be improved in areas related to the extent of the activities of the two sides in the island and visits of third-party nationals to the island.
5. Completion of maritime boundary delimitation between Iran and the UAE on the basis of new and improved arrangements in Abu Musa Island, which would remove all boundary differences between the two sides.

Notes

* Researcher at the School of Oriental and African Studies, University of London; Chairman, Urosevic Research Foundation, London; Consultant, United Nations University.

1. See Pirouz Mojtahed-Zadeh, *The Changing World Order and the Geo-political Regions of Caspian Central Asia and the Persian Gulf*, London: Urosevic Foundation, 1992.

2. See Pirouz Mojtahed-Zadeh, *Political Geography of the Strait of Hormuz*, Joint Geography Department/Middle East Centre Publication, SOAS, London: University of London, 1990.

3. See statements made by Pirouz Mojtahed-Zadeh in A. M. Farid et al., *Round Table Discussion on the Dispute over the Gulf Islands* (London: Arab Research Centre, 1993), p. 47.

4. Pirouz Mojtahed-Zadeh, 'A Geo-political Triangle in the Persian Gulf: Actions and Reactions among Iran, Bahrain and Saudi Arabia', *Iranian Journal of International Affairs*, IPIS, vol. 6, nos. 1 and 2, Spring/Summer 1994, pp. 47–59.

5. K. S. McLachlan, 'Iranian Policies in the Northwest Persian Gulf',

paper presented to GRC Seminar on the Kuwait–Iraq Boundary Issue, SOAS, February 1994, p. 10.

6.   There are numerous publications on Iran–Iraq border disputes, but for an introduction to the historical background of the disputes, see Chapters 6 and 7 by Richard Schofield and Pirouz Mojtahed-Zadeh, respectively, in K. S. McLachlan, *Sovereignty, Territoriality and International Boundaries in South Asia, Southwest Asia and the Mediterranean Basin*, London: GRC, SOAS, London University, 1990.

7.   *Echo of Iran*, vol. 40, no. 5 (52 London), 13 May 1992, p. 9.

8.   *Echo of Iran*, quoting the daily *Abrar* (Tehran), 13 May 1992; *Echo of Iran*, op. cit., p. 9.

9.   BBC Radio, Persian Service News Bulletin, Tuesday, 25 August 1992.

10.   *The Times* (London), Tuesday, 22 September 1992, p. 11.

11.   *Echo of Iran*, August/September 1992, vol. 30, nos. 8 and 9 (55 and 56), p. 3.

12.   *Echo of Iran*, ibid., p. 4.

13.   For the original text, see No. 6 of Appendix III in Pirouz Mojtahed-Zadeh, *The Islands of Tunb and Abu Musa*, London: Middle East Centre, SOAS, University of London, 1995.

14.   See No. 7 of Appendix III, Ibid.

15.   *Echo of Iran*, op. cit., p. 4.

16.   Presentation by Dr Hassan al-Alkim's presentation to the *Round Table Discussion on the Dispute over the Gulf Islands*, op. cit., p. 32.

17.   Embassy of the United Arab Emirates, press release, London, October 1992.

18.   BBC summary of world broadcast, the Middle East ME/1573/A/7, 29 December 1992.

19.   *Middle East Economic Survey*, CR, 11 January 1993.

20.   Extract from the Persian text of letter of 26 Rabee II 1322 AH (1904 CE) from the British Minister in Tehran to the Iranian Ministry of Foreign Affairs, document 84, in *A Selection of Persian Gulf Documents* (Tehran: Foreign Ministry of the Islamic Republic of Iran, 1989), p. 268.

21.   See, for example, J. B. Kelly, 'Eastern Arabian Frontiers', and R. Hay 'The Persian Gulf States', Ibid.

22.   See, for example, J. C. Wilkinson, 'Water and Tribal … ', Ibid.

23.   Hamdollah Ahmad bin Abi-Bakr Mowstofi, *Nezhat al-Qolub*, ancient text dating back to ca. 730 AH, n.c.: [n.pb.], 1307 AH (1928 CE).

* Abbasee was the currency unit of Safavid Iran, introduced by and named after Shah Abbas the Great, the most famous of the Safavid shahs in whose memory Port Gombrun was named 'Bandar Abbas'.

24.   R. Taylor, *Brief Notes of Captain R. Taylor*, Bombay: Bombay New Series No. XXIV, 1856/27.

25.   See above.

26.   See Appendix II in Pirouz Mojtahed-Zadeh, *The Islands of Tunb and Abu Musa*, op. cit.

27.   India Office Library and Record, Memorandum of 24 August 1928, File No. L/P and S/18/B397, pp. 4512–28.

28.   Extract from the Confidential Document (17188) of His Britannic Majesty's Government, 'Persian Frontiers', 31 January 1947, section 1, E10136/4029/34, FO 371/45507 171546, Paragraph 72, p. 13.

29.   Extract from a letter from Sheikh Yusuf al-Qasimi, Chief of Lengeh, to Sheikh Hamid bin Abdullah al-Qasimi, Chief of Ras al-Khaimah, dated

1 Jamad II 1301 AH (1883 CE). See Dr Hassan al-Alkim's presentation to the *Round Table Discussion on the Dispute over the Gulf Islands*, op. cit., p. 35.

30.   See D. H. Bavand, *Barrasi-ye Mabani-ye Tarikhi va Hoquqi-e Jazayer-e Irani-ye Tunb va Abu Musa* ('Examination of the Legal and Historical Backgrounds of the Iranian Islands of Tunb and Abu Musa'), *Jameh-e Salem* monthly (Tehran), vol. 2, no. 7, December 1992–January 1993, p. 15.

31.   'Mr Reilly's Correspondence and Memoranda', *Persia and Arab States, Order in Councillor Jurisdiction 1857 to 1882*, part II, 'Further Correspondence Respecting Consular Jurisdiction in Persia 1874–76', FO 60/451, p. 19.

32.   Document No. 53, *Selections of Persian Gulf Documents*, Vol. I (Tehran: IPIS, 1989), pp. 168–9.

33   Extract from Sir Edward Beckett's Memorandum, dated 12 March 1932, FO 371/18901.

34.   For more information on this subject, see Pirouz Mojtahed-Zadeh, *The Islands of Tunb and Abu Musa*, London: Middle East Centre/SOAS, London University, 1995.

35.   Statement of Dr Hassan al-Alkim, *Round Table Discussion on the Dispute over the Gulf Islands*, op. cit., p. 41.

36.   Abu Musa and Greater Tunb had 300 and 250 inhabitants, respectively, in November 1971, when returned to Iran.

37.   The UAE expanded its territorial sea to 12 miles in 1993.

38.   Muhammad Reza Dabiri, 'Abu Musa Island: A Binding Understanding or a Misunderstanding?', *Iranian Journal of International Affairs*, vol. 5, nos. 3 and 4, Fall/Winter 1993/94, p. 583.

39.   *Etelaat* daily, 21 February 1993.

40.   For more information, see Pirouz Mojtahed-Zadeh, 'Iran's Maritime Boundaries in the Persian Gulf' in K. S. McLachlan, *The Boundaries of Modern Iran* (London: GRC/SOAS-UCL Press, 1944), pp. 101–27.

41.   For more details on maritime boundary delimitations in the Persian Gulf, see Pirouz Mojtahed-Zadeh, *Keshvarha va Marzha dar Mantaqeh-e Jeopolitik-e Khalij-e Fars* ('Countries and Boundaries in the Geo-political Region of the Persian Gulf'), translated into Persian by Hamid-Reza Malek-Muhammadi Nouri, Tehran: IPIS Publication, 1993.

42.   For more information, see Pirouz Mojtahed-Zadeh, 'Iran's Maritime Boundaries in the Persian Gulf' in K. S. McLachlan, *The Boundaries of Modern Iran*, op. cit., pp. 101–27.

43.   Pirouz Mojtahed-Zadeh, *Political Geography of the Strait of Hormuz*, op. cit., pp. 5 and 46.

Eight

The Kurdish Question

16

Arab and Iranian Positions on the Kurdish Question

SAAD NAJI JAWAD*

The Arab and Iranian Understanding of Minority Issues in General

Until the First World War and emergence of the nation-state, Arab and Iranian attitudes on minorities in the region derived mainly from Islamic doctrine, which was flexible and did not discriminate according to nationality but rather on the basis of faith. Although the Holy Qur'an did give precedence to the Arabs, as per the verse 'you are the best of peoples evolved for mankind',[1] that preference was immediately rendered conditional on "enjoining what is right, forbidding what is wrong",[2] while other verses of the Holy Qur'an, as well as prescripts of Prophetic *hadith*, affirmed the absence of preference except on the basis of faith: for example, the verse "verily the most honoured of you in the sight of God is [he who is] the most righteous of you",[3] and the *hadith*, "there is no difference between Arab or Iranian except in faith", among other sayings. The Islamic Faith and the exercise of political authority by Muslim leaders, even for non-Muslims and those who preferred to remain apart, continued to respect difference. Such persons were subjected to a tax that exempted them from restrictions: namely, serving in the Muslim army and the Islamic state. As a result, no ethnic minority problem emerged in Islam or the Islamic Empire, whether that minority embraced the Faith or not. Islam remained the principal uniter and the sole protector in this regard. This fraternity deepened as non-Arab Muslims discovered that their being non-Arab was no obstacle to their enjoyment of all rights and privileges accorded the Arabs in Islamic states. Indeed, there are many examples of minority figures dominating in government and dislodging its Arab elements. There are even stronger examples of Arab and non-Arab rivalries for control of government or for steering the course of the empire. What needs to be said is that the victory of non-Arab elements in such struggles did not mean the end of the Arab Islamic Empire (with the exception of Ottoman undertakings in

311

the later phase) but rather a continuity in the pursuit of Islamic ends; a classic example of this was Salaheddine al-Ayyubi.

Thus, one can say that conflict continued to occur within the bounds of Islam, the bounds of the political authority of the Muslim empire, and one cannot possibly view events then in terms of minorities aspiring for national rights.

At the end of the 19th century, nationalist ideas were clearly beginning to influence more than a few peoples of the region. Calls for national rights became commonplace. Although the Kurds did not form, in their history, an independent state of their own, as others within the region had done, and thus their sense of nationhood was somewhat belated, this does not mean that such sentiment did not appear among them. It was an aim of the central empires that ruled then (Ottoman and Safavid) to curb growing nationalist sentiment and nationalist attempts to consolidate the national rights of those the empires ruled over. Indeed, the various nationalities co-operated to confront the Ottoman Empire's Turkification efforts. On the other hand, the Ottoman-Safavid conflict involved the Kurds directly, as they inhabited the territories separating both empires. The Kurds were exploited as fighters to protect the borders of the empires to which they belonged, against certain gains, such as the establishment of some emirates. This situation involved the Kurds of both sides border militias, fighting one another for the interests of their powers. Perhaps this explains the perpetual readiness of the Kurds to fight instead of cooperate with one another.

The start of the 20th century, specifically the First World War and post-War period, led to the emergence of new states from the remains of the old empires. Minorities began to see themselves in a different light. In small new states, dominant nationalities were permitted statehood and exclusive control of government, while smaller minorities were disregarded. If the actions of European colonial administrations can be interpreted as successful bids to lay the seeds of dissension and discord between the peoples of this region, it is unfortunate that dominant ruling nationalities followed their lead and forgot what they endured under the assimilationist measures of previous governments (the Arabs under the Turks, for example), oppressing lesser nationalities or, at best, viewing minorities with doubt and suspicion. This problem was particularly evident in Iraq, which is one of the more diverse and pluralistic of the Arab countries as far as minorities are concerned. The proportion of those accusing the Kurds of collusion with the British was much higher than those calling for an understanding of their true sentiments and the meeting of their national aspirations, or to preserving their national distinctiveness. The same occurred in Syria, where the Kurds were accused of collaborating with French colonialism against the national movement.

In Iran the situation did not differ significantly. It was evident that the prevailing nationalism (Persian) was unwilling to accept the demands of other minorities or even discuss minority presence, because, in the Persians' view, such would threaten the very existence of the Iranian state. A similar situation to that in Iraq and Syria appeared as the Iranian state began to accuse the Kurds (and other, neighbouring minorities) of collaboration and collusion with the former Soviet Union against the interests of the Iranian state. The establishment of the republic of Mahabad in 1946, with Soviet support, seemed to confirm and increase these fears.

Against a growth in the Kurds' dream of national rights, a dream justified by the fact that they, like other peoples of the region, are entitled to their own state, the larger ruling nationalities worked harder at establishing more centralized states, so that minorities became vulnerable to losing what little independence or decentralization they enjoyed under the Ottomans and Safavids, or even under direct colonial rule. The Kurds were thus obliged to accept the new situation and work with it even as it was based on an unfair equation, positing the states they live in as national states (Arab, Persian, Turkish), with their having to accept whatever the ruling nationality gives them.

The experience of Mahabad and the establishment of the Zionist entity in the heart of Palestine increased the suffering of the Kurds, for they are oppressed in Iran because of the government's fear of their undertaking a similar venture; and they are oppressed in the Arab nation on the pretext that they are working towards another "Israel" in north Iraq. No consideration is given to historical and geographical realities, such as that the Kurds are from this region, not passing visitors.

The Emergence of the Kurdish Problem in Iraq and Iran

The Kurds in Iraq inhabit the northern and northeastern part of the country. Neighbouring them, in the northwestern part of Iran, are the Kurds of Iran, who exceed them in number: 5.5–6.5 million, according to one census, compared with 1.5–3.5 million in Iraq.[4] However, the number of Kurds in proportion to total population, is higher for Iraq than for Iran, amounting to 15–20 per cent in Iraq compared with 9–11 per cent in Iran.

The Kurdish problem did not appear as an ethnic problem or a minority confronting a devious majority in the countries of the Middle East (Turkey, Iran, Iraq, Syria) until after the beginning of this century, and in particular after the First World War. It became clear that the Allies' intention was to establish new states over the remains of the defeated Ottoman Empire. This intent was confirmed by the resolutions of the Paris Peace Conference in 1919. Although the Kurds undertook to send representatives on their own behalf to this conference, as Arabs and Armenians had done, in order to affirm their right to independence based on Wilson's Fourteen Points, their effort failed, while the Arabs succeeded in achieving various states. On the other hand, in 1920, the Kurds received a promise of statehood for themselves through the Treaty of Sèvres, in which Articles 62, 63 and 64 provided that the Kurds inhabiting Turkey have the right to establish a state enjoying autonomy that may develop into an independent state. But this treaty was not implemented and was replaced, as a result of Turkish pressure, by the Treaty of Lausanne (1923), which divided up the region as we find it now. Thus was the international pledge to the Kurds nullified.

In Iraq, the region of Kurdistan saw the emergence of more than one movement, each representing a different trend of thought. At first, armed tribal uprisings occurred against British encroachments, securing victories for the Muslim Ottoman army. Then the situation changed and a movement emerged calling for an independent state like the Iraqi state. After this movement was crushed, many tribal movements emerged to oppose the extension of government administration and authority to the remote parts of Kurdistan, an extension that would have meant an end to the [independent tribal] influence enjoyed by the tribes for a long time. These movements remained extant from 1918 until 1933, then suppressed through British assistance and Kurdish tribes loyal to the central government in Iraq. During 1941–46, different kinds of movements emerged, and sources differ in their evaluation of them. Some sources describe them as British-inspired revolts, made to spite the Iraqi army, which had, briefly, expelled the pro-British government (1941). Others described them as the result of Nazi propaganda. Still others blamed the Communists and [former] Soviet Union for provoking such movements. Certainly all these elements, in addition to the role of Kurdish parties and political associations at that time, contributed to the emergence of those movements, which were originally led by Mustapha al-Barazani, and then came to an end with his expulsion, and his aides, from Iraq to Iran at the end of the Second World War.

The move of Barazani and his aides to Iran was not only to flee from the Iraqi army; it was also to gain support for the Kurdish movement or enlist in it, for it had succeeded, with Soviet support, in establishing a Kurdish republic (autonomous) for the first time, named the Republic of Mahabad.

There were two reasons behind the establishment of a republic in Mahabad: *first*, the presence of an active national cultural movement in that area that Soviet forces in north Iran sought to exploit; and *second*, the Soviet Union's desire to establish more Soviet-type republics along its southern borders.

The Kurds of Iran saw their wish come true. They were the ones who, until then, looked to the Kurds of Iraq as their guide in establishing a vanguard party to represent them under the leadership of Qadi Muhammad, a magistrate and notable. That party formed a ministry of republic administrations during its formation 1945–46. On the other hand, the Kurds of Iraq, especially the Communists and those with leftist leanings, followed the example of the Iranian Kurdish experience and formed in 1946 an Iraqi democratic Kurdish party along the lines of the party in Iran.

Also during this period (1939–46), the two areas of Kurdistan, in Iraq and in Iran, saw much political and cultural activity that resulted in the formation of several political parties and cultural associations extending across the political spectrum, from the Right to the Left. The period also witnessed several schisms and disputes, a consequence of the personalities of the leaders who had surfaced into political life.

In such a situation (the emergence of armed movements in north Iraq, the Republic of Mahabad in Iran's Kurdistan), the two monarchical governments of Iran and Iraq could see no other solution but force. Even when calls for a truce were raised within these governments, such as in the attempts by the well-known Iraqi Premier Nuri Said to find a political solution to the problem in 1944, through some concessions and reforms, the ruling majority rejected these attempts and stressed the military option.

On the other hand, the formation of national Iraqi and Iranian states coincided with the increasing influence of nationalism in both countries. In fact, the first understanding of the national movement for Arabs, Persians and Kurds alike, was progressive, not exclusivist. Very soon, however, the pluralistic nature of the states concerned was ignored, and attention was focused on elevating the image of the dominant nationality. Despite the danger implicit in this thought for national unity in both countries, the trend continued, reaching a point where it was transformed into a melting pot principle aimed at assimilating the minorities into the larger nationalism. Writings, theorization and researches began to appear in this regard. For example, Arab writings focused on the origin of the Kurds and regarded them as of Arab descent, traceable to the historical figure Kurd bin Murad bin Amer, and so they became Arabs who were displaced to remote regions and acquired ignoble habits. Thus, according to that theory, the Kurds do not possess a national or ethnic identity, and are called on to join the dominant Arab nationality. Regarding the other current of Arab opinion, they should emigrate from the Arab lands they live in and move to Turkey and Iran. Some writings focused on the fact that the word *kurd* in Persian means "brave" or "courageous fighter", so that this mountain people (the Kurds) acquired their name because of their qualities, and this quality does not have any national connotation. Abdel Karim Qasim adopted this second view, while Abdel Salam Aref adopted the first. Helping to promote such beliefs were certain Kurdish tribes who insisted on tracing their lineage back to the household of the Prophet .

On the other hand, the Syrian understanding of the problem was very

different. Modern Syrian patriots refused to discuss the Kurdish problem
in Syria, relying on the fact that the great majority of Kurds in Syria were
originally refugees from Turkey who came in at various times. This fact
kept the Syrian patriotic movement from giving serious thought to this
issue or its possible development, bearing in mind that the small number of
Kurds in Syria was another contributing factor to the Syrian position.

A similar trend developed in Iran, whose Persian nationalist advocates
saw the Kurds as part of the Persian people, possessing no particularly identity and, historically, occupying the lands of ancient Medea or the kingdom
of Korsh that formed the ancient Iranian state. This view was stretched to
the point where all parts of Kurdistan were demanded (in Turkey, Iraq,
Syria and Azerbaijan) on the grounds that they are integral parts of Iranian
territory. Two factors were important in promoting this thought: (1) the
Kurdish language, which originated from a branch of the Indo–European,
to which the Persian language also belongs; (2) the affirmation by many
authors that the Kurds as a people are of Medean or Aryan origin, which is
also the origin of the Persian people. The title the former Shah of Iran gave
himself, *Arya Mehr* or 'light of the Aryan people', is not far from this thinking, for he sought to make himself the custodian or defender of the entire
Aryan people in Iran, which includes the Kurdish people.

The Kurdish Understanding of the Problem

As to the Kurds' own understanding of the problem, it was, in the beginning, very vague. It is noteworthy that the understanding and position of
the Kurdish patriots at the beginning of the 20th century was more developed than at mid-century or after. During the First World War, when the
national movement emerged in Iraq, Syria and Iran, Kurdish intellectuals
cooperated with the Arab and Iranian in confronting colonialism. Educated Kurds were active elements in Iraqi, Syrian and Iranian national parties
that frequently rose up against government associated with colonialism. In
short, Kurdish elements gave precedence to the wider and more comprehensive national goals, not the parochial. Even the enthusiastic among them
found it difficult to express their opinion or oppose the tide of national
union.

But this sentiment could not prevail, for two reasons: *First*, the majority,
securing part of their national goals, proceeded to ignore minority issues
and dealt with the Kurdish parties and movement generally from a position
of superiority combined with considerable distrust; *second*, the entry of the
foreign element, or foreign intervention, was an important factor in provoking minority matters, as some saw cooperation with foreign parties more
useful materially and politically.

Ultimately, the Kurds' own understanding of their problem revolved about two goals: (i) in the long term, independence; (ii) in the short term an extended autonomy. Though all knew the first goal to be unattainable, they remained insistent on the need to preserve their distinctiveness through autonomy or, more recently, federation. A more complicated problem was that the Kurdish parties kept changing their objectives and demands, sometimes to the point of impossibility, especially when the governments concerned were weak. Meanwhile, these same governments would neglect promises to the Kurds when they found themselves in a position of strength and could apply the military solution.

Deepening the problem further was the sharp division within Kurdish society: some were always ready to cooperate with the central government, and some were always ready to oppose it. The two never agreed, neither then nor now.

A new development that characterized the actions of Kurdish opposition groups in Iraq and Iran was their impotence, not only in the uniting of Kurdish society but even in their dealing with governments and national movements. For these reasons, as well as the multiplicity of Kurdish centres, the vagueness in their objectives, and their occasional lack of realism, all efforts to achieve a negotiated peaceful settlement of their problem failed. Moreover, all negotiated government solutions were confined to dealing with the problem from above, without expanding the needed democratic base; in Iran, dealing with the problem remained in terms of no right for the Kurds to preserve their ethnic and cultural distinctiveness.

The Arab and Iranian Solutions to the Problem

Although the problem of minorities among the Arabs and Iranians was apparent from the very start of the formation of national states for the two peoples, what is noteworthy is that both parties were clearly incapable of achieving the solution that would end the problem – i.e. they were incapable of developing a solution commensurate with the continuance and growth of the problem.

It can be argued that the two monarchies of Iraq and Iran, whatever their limitations, were able to establish some sound principles for reassuring the Kurds. For example, leaders would frequently select well-known Kurdish personalities for ministers (e.g. ministers of defence or interior). Kurdish functionaries, civilian and military, who were loyal to the regime or administratively competent, always found themselves in important military and civilian posts in the state. These governments pursued a policy of creating a new identity applicable to all, and spoke of an Iraqi identity, Iranian identity and so on.

On the other hand, patriotic Kurdish opposition figures always found themselves at the front-line of secret national parties. This did not mean, of course, that the regimes were always conciliatory when dealing with the problem; on the contrary, the most brutal military means were applied to wipe out any militant Kurdish movement in the area. Very often the brutality would encompass entire clans or tribes. Even so, this did not affect the policy of truce followed by these regimes towards loyal Kurds accepting the new identity.

The success of the national movement in ending monarchical rule in Iraq, then in Iran, placed that movement in a very awkward position on the minorities issue. On the one hand, the success of the revolutions heartened Arabs, Iranians and Kurds considerably. On the other, they failed to meet the very patriotic and national expectations and sentiments they bolstered in the Kurds. (There are some who say, in truth, that these revolutions also failed in satisfying the sentiments of most Arab and Iranian patriots. But this failure was concealed by the patriots' freedom to express their opinions without being accused of chauvinism or separatism, which was not the case for those who called for Kurdish national rights).

The successive governments in Iraq failed to find a peaceful political solution to the Kurdish problem until 1970. The monarchy, which had crushed the Kurdish tribal movements and uprisings in the 1920s and 1930s up to 1946, found in the extension of the Iraqi identity a concept sufficient to resolve the problem and allay Kurdish fears. This regime, as we noted before, adopted the approach of appointing loyal Kurds to sensitive posts. With the Hashemite union between Iraq and Jordan in April 1958, a prominent Kurd was appointed as Iraqi Prime Minister, to assuage possible Kurdish fears over the numerical superiority of the Arabs in the new state. Although these measures were more far-reaching than the ones to follow, such a sensitivity to the Kurdish reality did not reach the roots of the problem. During the monarchy, no Kurdish party was permitted, despite the Kurds' efforts to achieve one; though many Iraqi–Arab parties were allowed. The same case was true in Iran. When the monarchy in Iraq fell and was replaced by a republic in 1958, Abdel Karim Qasim thought that, to win over and reassure the Kurds, it would be sufficient to reject the idea of unity with the United Arab Republic (Egypt and Syria), permit Mustapha Barazani and his followers to return to Iraq, accommodate the activism of the Kurdistan Democratic Party and emphasize Arab–Kurdish brotherhood. Qasim did not realize the fact that the Kurds' aspirations and demands in the new regime were much broader than such personal measures, while the nationalist trend that succeeded Qasim, focusing on the idea of Arab unity, failed to get through to the Kurds that the idea of Arab unity does not mean assimilation for the Kurds. The Kurds at that time aspired to a better status, to the point of requesting autonomy; neither Qasim nor his successors were about to let this happen. Until 1970, the solution remained one of improvised steps and measures far from the roots of the problem.

It was the same in Iran. After the destruction of the Republic of Mahabad, the Shah of Iran dealt with the Kurds on the basis of allegiance to the throne. Every loyalist had a good chance of reaching a high position, while the fate of those calling for improvements in economic, social, cultural or political life was a very different matter. When the national movement succeeded in overthrowing the Shah, the new regime thought that this would be a great victory for all and all patriots should follow the regime and set aside their differences.

There was also a similarity of approach over the Kurdish question, whenever governments felt the need to reduce pressure or provide some concessions, until such time as the opportunity availed to make the Kurds submit by force. This occurred, for example, in Iran on 14 July 1958 and in Iraq during the dispute with the Shah of Iran or during the Iraq–Iran war.

Thus, the problem continued to grow, and with it the national rift in both countries. In Iraq, the situation reached a point where the militant Kurdish movement was becoming a formidable force and an undeclared government. When the Baath party assumed power for the second time in Iraq in 1968, there was a need to solve the problem in a very different way from that during its first rule (1963), i.e. by military force. And indeed, the party pursued a conciliatory policy towards the problem, with occasional understanding of the very core of the problem. Thus, the admission of Kurdish national rights reached the point of enjoying autonomy. It included the more important admission of the right of the Kurdish people to unification and liberation, all for the sake of a peaceful solution to the problem. This peaceful solution was indeed realized and prevailed for four years (1970–74). But it kept two basic problems unresolved: *First*, the problem of mutual distrust, and *second*, the problem of the wide gap in understanding between those who issue fundamental, deep and important decisions to solve the problem, and the narrow-minded administrators whose job is to implement the decisions. In addition to this, there was foreign intervention (Iranian and Israeli) that kept working on undermining the agreement, and the absence of the needed democratic atmosphere and institutions able to bring about the peaceful solution and develop it. Thus, despite the scope of the agreement, the two sides continued to drift further apart, each of them thinking he had sufficient military power to tip the scales in his favour if need be. And so events moved towards war. They remained that way until the resort to arms became much easier than resorting to dialogue between the two parties. Although Iraq made some good qualitative progress in the areas of constitutional legislation and law, guaranteeing the Kurds their rights, the problem remains.

The situation was much the same in Iran at first. The Kurds participated in the popular uprising that overthrew the Shah. After that, the new regime showed no interest in Kurdish demands, feeling that the success of the revolution was sufficient to satisfy anyone opposed to the Shah, while any secondary demands meant opposition to the revolution and the new regime. As for the Iranian Kurds, they felt that their role in the national uprising should entitle them to their national rights. When they expressed this desire, it was viewed as a major problem and their behaviour was held as a challenge to the new regime, to be crushed by force so as to preserve the success and continuity of the revolution. The violence in Sanandaj and Mahabad that followed the fall of the Shah, and the disturbances happening now in the Kurdistan of Iran and the continuous assassinations of Iranian Kurdish leaders – all attest to current Iranian policy towards the cause. Thus, the two sides headed towards armed military confrontation, and this remains the approach followed in Iran today.

On the other hand, at no time did the Iranian regime feel a need for legislation or laws protecting the Kurdish minority or any other ethnic minority (in contrast to Iraq). On the contrary, the new regime in Iran revised the constitution to the neglect of ethnic plurality in the state. It tried to make the Kurds feel that they are accepted in the new configuration as Muslims. In other words, the Islamic solution was adopted to absorb the problem. At a time when this solution might have reduced tensions, if only the wider, flexible Islamic understanding were adopted, what was proposed and applied was the reverse. The Islamic understanding was narrowed and transformed into a sectarian one: making the Ja'fari Twelver doctrine the official religion of the state and its leader, according to the constitution. As most of the Kurds adhered to a different doctrine, this indirectly meant that they were second-class citizens. Outside of this solution, no project was proposed in Iran to address the Kurds' national aspirations.

In summary, the problem remained and continued to be expressed as a military one in both Iraq and Iran. The situation was one of ebb and flow. Whenever Kurdish elements achieved some successes, their positions hardened and increased the rift with central authority. Whenever the government of Iraq, or that of Iran, felt it could – or had a chance to – subdue Kurdish areas, it did not hesitate to do so. Each party continued to await an opportunity against the other. In every case and on every occasion, the Kurds received support from a state neighbouring the one they belonged to, to spite the regime they were at odds with. In such situations, peaceful solutions and enlightened thought are pushed aside.

Concluding Remarks

It is evident from all that has been said that the Kurdish problem has evolved and grown to a point where a comprehensive solution is due, one involving foresight and time, so that the gap in the national fabric may be bridged. The complexity of the problem derives essentially from the short-sightedness of all parties. There is a prevailing view among many that lays much of the blame on the external or foreign element, in provoking or maintaining the problem. Even if this were true, surely it cannot succeed unless there are already internal factors and elements conducive to that. Re-tracing this problem and its evolution reveals a need for considerable change in the prevailing perceptions; these needed changes are in:

1. The belief that it is still possible to impose a solution by force, or from above. Any solution to the problem must be by democratic means, permitting the minority the right to express themselves freely in accordance with protecting freedom of expression and the opinion of the other. It was the absence of democracy that led to absence of the dialogue and public participation needed for the solution. On the other hand, experience has shown that this process (the democratic) proved successful in building a national unity that all are prepared to defend and uphold. In addition, this approach is sufficient to guarantee the particularity of the lesser within the great and guarantee, as well, that no mutual harm is inflicted. Put differently, the democratic solution enables peoples to participate in it, and this is both much needed and very important.

2. The prevailing and erroneous belief that has long thwarted reaching a peaceful solution: the dominant nationality's belief that autonomy or federation means, in the final analysis, separatism, if not immediately so. But the application of this type of solution in a sound and democratic way has shown that it does not lead to minority separatism. Rather, it is oppression that has always bred intransigence, greater opposition and the desire to separate.

3. The conviction of the ruling elites in Iraq and Iran: namely, that the international political situation does not permit the emergence of a Kurdish state; so there is no need to fear such a result, and the fate of the Kurds will remain tied to the fate of the countries they live in. If this conviction is the case now, there is nothing to suggest it will be the case tomorrow. Thus, the ruling elites and national movements in both countries are called on to establish formulae for understanding, before being compelled by the international community, on the pretext of human rights or democracy, to accept a very different situation.

4. The false belief or misunderstanding among all the parties, Arab, Iranian and Kurd, that cooperating with the foreigner is easy and more

profitable than joint cooperation between Arabs and Kurds, or Iranians and Kurds. Such cooperation may solve the problem more quickly. Arabs and Iranians have expressed clearly their readiness to cooperate among themselves, or with outside forces, against the Kurds, at a time when the Kurds found it easy and more profitable to cooperate with the foreigner against the people they live with, even when they have felt that the foreigner does not believe in their goals or rights. It is time that everyone began to feel that the patriotic solution is the only sound solution and that dependence on the outside does not serve the national interest.

The international experience has repeatedly shown that the policy of assimilation and absorption cannot succeed, no matter how long it prevails. Quite the contrary, respecting the distinctiveness of minorities is always sufficient to enrich the cultural and national heritage of all. There remains the dire need for constitutional and institutional measures ensuring the democracy of the solution and its maintenance far from the influence of individuals.

Last but not least, continued pursuit of the military solution may pacify the situation briefly, but in the end will only widen the distance between the Kurds and the peoples they live amongst. Arabs, Iranians and Kurds are called upon to work toward that which will ensure for them a better life in the future.

Notes

* Faculty of Political Science, University of Baghdad, Baghdad, Iraq.

1. *Surat Al-i-Umran, ayah* 110.
2. *Ibid.*
3. *Surat al-Hujurat, ayah* 13.
4. According to the 1993 survey, the total population of Iran is 61,183,138, while that of Iraq (for the same year) is 18,445,487.

Select Bibliography

Ghassemlou, A. R. et al. *People without a Country: The Kurds and Kurdistan*, edited by Gérard Chaliand, translated from the French by Michael Pallis. London: Zed Press,1980.
Jawad, Saad, "The Kurdish Revolt in Iraq: An Assessment of its Failure", *Inter State*, (UCW-Aberystwyth, UK), vol. 1, no. 2, 1981.
Kutschera, Chris, *Le Mouvement national Kurde*. Paris: [n.pb.], 1979.

17

The Kurdish People:
from Confrontation to Coexistence

SAIDEH LOTFIAN*

The focus of this paper is the link between ethnicity, national cohesion and human development in general, and the future of the Kurdish people in the Middle East, in particular. Although a broad consensus has emerged on the need for stable socio-economic development, few Middle Eastern countries have achieved dramatic and uninterrupted improvements in the standards of living. The decisive question is, why? And the most logical answer is political instability. A careful examination of the most serious impediments to economic development in this region suggests that the extent to which slow economic progress remains a problem has been influenced significantly by political as well as economic factors. Among the most notable political factors, one must pay attention to the causes of political unrest in these societies. Central to the goal of achieving higher levels of economic development is a recognition that these states must seek solutions to the problem of instability and an end to all types of conflict. However, a number of obstacles stand in the way of obtaining the objective of ending sub-national conflicts. The regional governments are keenly aware of the vulnerability of their societies, and have been trying to make themselves more secure against acts of sabotage, armed attack by rebel forces and subversion from outside, which are considered major consequences or phases of ethnic violence. We shall begin with the assumption that improvement in overall aspects of development and welfare will decrease political instability, as manifested by ethnic conflicts such as the Kurdish rebellion in several Middle Eastern countries. Important questions to be answered include: In what direction is this minority-majority (or centre-periphery) relationship moving in the post-Cold War regional system? Why are Iraq, Iran and Turkey anxious about their future security in the context of the Kurdish demands for more autonomy? Apart from security-related issues, what are their reasons for concerns about the future status of their Kurdish-inhabited provinces? Is there a greater chance of peace with granting local autonomy to the Kurdish minority or a lesser one? Is there a hope that by prompt action we can stress the ethical dimension of the living conditions of less fortunate peoples?

Introduction

Political disorder and conflicts at sub-national levels have been ongoing in most states in the new Middle East, an area stretching from Afghanistan and Iran to the Red Sea region in the west, and the Central Asian republics of the former superpower, the USSR, to the north. Why have conflicts, and most specifically the ethnic uprisings among the Kurds, occurred? Before answering this question, let us present some definitions for a few major concepts (e.g., ethnicity, nationality, nation-state), which are used repeatedly in this study.

The concept of *nationality* describes the relation of a person to a particular state. The term *ethnicity* refers to the so-called minorities who are not yet assimilated, and can cause a problem for central governments.[1] An *ethnic group* is a distinct people with a different culture living in a state. The members of an ethnic group are bound together by common ties of culture, race or nationality. The origin of the term *nation* is the Latin verb *nasci*, 'to be born', and initially defined a group of people born in the same place. Subsequently, two distinct sets of characteristics of nationhood have been identified: (1) The objective characteristics such as geography, history, economic structure; (2) the subjective characteristics such as consciousness, loyalty, will.[2] Thus, a nation is made up of communities of people who see themselves as one people on the basis of common ancestry, history, society, ideology, language, territory, and religion. Today, there are thousands of ethnic groups in the world. Some are very small in population and area, while others are large. Consider the case of Oromo in Ethiopia. The dominant race of Ethiopia is the Amahara. Others are Tigreans, Afars, Somalis, Oromo (Galla) and other races. The Oromo comprise about 40 per cent of the entire population of 46 million Ethiopians (or over 18 million people).

States range in size from larger political units such as India, which stretches across 3,165,596 km², with a multinational and multilingual population of 845 million, and 17 regional official languages as well as hundreds of unofficial languages,[3] to small and micro-states such as Monaco, which covers an area equal to 2 km², with a population of about 30,000, and Bahrain with its total area of 688 km² forming an archipelago of about 33 small islands in the Persian Gulf and an indigenous population of about 331,000.[4] The majority of nation-states have not achieved a high degree of homogenization.[5] Hobsbawm asserts that 'in a world in which probably not much more than a dozen states out of some 180 can plausibly claim that their citizens coincide in any real sense with a single ethnic or linguistic group, nationalism based on the establishment of such homogeneity is not only undesirable, but also largely self-destructive'.[6]

Even some of the oldest nation-states (e.g. Great Britain and France) have a multinational or multilingual or multiethnic character. More than 95 per cent of the world's 180 states are multinational, that is, composed of many nations. These 180 states assert sovereignty over the world's 5000 or so nations and peoples. A truly homogeneous nation-state is very uncommon in the contemporary international system. There are many ethnic, linguistic groups and nationalities that have had a troubled relationship with states. These groups include Ossetians (in Georgia), Basques and Catalans (in Spain), Corsicans (organized as the Front de la Liberation Nationale de Corse in France), Finnish (or Lapp in Sweden), Kanaks (or Melanesians in the New Caledonia in the South Pacific Ocean), Mayans (in Guatemala), Mestizos (in Belize), Miskitos (in Nicaragua and Honduras), Berbers (in Algeria and Morocco), Oromo (in Ethiopia), Afars of Ethiopian origin (in Djibouti), Tutsis (in Burundi and Rawanda in Central Africa), Tibetans (in China), Tamils (in Sri Lanka), Kurds (in Syria, Iran, Iraq and Turkey), Baluchis and Pathans (in Pakistan), and hundreds more. The history of international relations is replete with accounts of colonial rulers who managed repeatedly to play the representatives of the rival communities in their dependent territories against each other. British colonial policy as a rule discouraged ethnic integration in the territories of the British Empire, and made it increasingly difficult for some communities to compromise. The incompatibility of the minority-majority positions led to heightened tensions that exploded in deadly and protracted ethnic conflicts. Now, we turn our attention to the status of the Kurds as a minority group in Iran.

The Kurdish People of Iran

Iran is composed of several sub-national ethnic, religious and tribal communities, of whom the Kurds are but one group among many other ethnic communities. About 9 per cent of Iranians are Kurds; most of the rest of the population identify themselves as Persian (51 per cent), Azerbaijani (25 per cent), or Baluch, Lur, Arab and other groups (15 per cent). The Kurds are also a minority in Iraq (20 per cent), Turkey (17 per cent), Lebanon (1 per cent), Azerbaijan and Syria, where they number less than three million. As these figures demonstrate, the Kurds are one of the main ethnic minority groups in the Middle East region which have the potential to cause trouble for regional states in the coming century. An oft-mentioned security risk is that if ethnic minorities reside in more than one state, they can be used as a 'fifth column' by a neighbouring state intending to destabilize an adversary regime from within.[7] In Iran, some members of these ethnic groups live in relatively homogeneous communities in various parts of the country. Yet, many members of various minority groups have moved from place to place, and settled in the traditional territories of other groups. It is common to observe cohabitation and coexistence of Persians, Azeris, Kurds and others in different parts of Iran.

Kurdistan Province in Iran covers an area of approximately 28,203 km², almost ten times the size of Luxembourg and makes up 1.7 per cent of the total geographic area of Iran. Less than 1.5 million live in Kurdistan, or about 2.1 per cent of Iran's population in 1992.[8] The population density is 43.6 persons per square kilometer, and ranks 12 among the 24 provinces of Iran. This area includes the central city of Sanandaj, where 38.8 per cent of the population lived in 1992, and the major cities of Saqqez, Baneh, Marivan, Gharveh, and Bijar. Discrepancies in official and unofficial figures are largely due to political reasons. The Kurdish leadership intentionally overestimate the population of the Kurds in Iraq, Iran and Turkey. Most statistical sources put the population of the Iranian Kurds at 5.4 million (or about 9 per cent of the total population).[9]

Parts of Kurdistan are fertile, while others, especially the northern mountainous areas, are largely uninhabitable. The land along the numerous rivers and in the valleys can be extremely fertile and rich in forest. In order to meet demand for energy sources, large portions of Kurdistan have been deforested, leading to higher probability of floods in the area. If the present deforestation trend, because of the need to expand the area under cultivation and cattle grazing, were to continue indefinitely, the 320,000 ha of natural forests will be completely destroyed and cleared in less than 20 years. The artificially planted forests for fuel wood production, commercial timber production and environmental protection, are planned and promoted by the Tehran government. Increasing attention has been paid in recent years to forest plantations in Kurdistan and other provinces. In 1992, a total of 670 ha of new land came under rehabilitation projects, involving tree planting (mostly native species of oak, walnut, spruce pine), and fence enclosures to stimulate natural regeneration of degraded lands in Kurdistan by the Office of Natural Resources of the Reconstruction Jihad Organization. The mineral resources of Kurdistan have not been fully exploited, and in fact high production and transport costs may still discourage large-scale investment in mineral industries.

Some official estimates put the population of the province of Kurdistan in 1992 at below 1.25 million. Over half of Kurdistan's inhabitants are estimated to be in rural areas. They live in the largely forested northern highlands, where Iran's mountain ranges of the Zagros provide grazing grounds for nomadic and tribal communities. The rivers of the region have

considerable potential for irrigation, and historically there has been cultivation in the valleys. More than 47 per cent of the population of Kurdistan
currently live in urban areas. Within the region, there are important differences. Sanandaj is nearly 61 per cent urban, reflecting the city's stage of
development and the special features of its urban structure and history. At
present, most of the Kurdistan population live in the ten cities, and 76
villages of this western province. Despite migration to the cities, the rural
population in some areas has remained relatively large. Rural population
density is not very high compared to many parts of the country. The standard of living, while improving, remains low. It is not clear whether added
demographic pressure will benefit agricultural development or, on the contrary, jeopardize the development of rural areas. Although the fertility rate
in urban Kurdistan is lower than rural fertility, it is still higher than in other
Iranian provinces. There is a view that urbanization and migration to the
cities is a burden. Rural surplus population becomes an urban surplus, and
creates an inefficient and unproductive 'informal sector' consisting of street
vendors, and other marginal occupations. The Tehran government and foreign aid donors initiated modest agricultural development projects in the
1960s. Their proximity to Iran's border with Iraq, inaccessibility and lack of
readily exploitable natural resources, gave them low priority for economic
development.

As shown in Table (1) below, in Kurdistan, 59.4 per cent of the population are literate, ranking it 23 among the 24 Ostans. Only southeast Ostan
of Sistan and Baluchistan has a lower literacy rate (50 per cent).[10] Infant
mortality in Kurdistan was 18 in 1000 births in 1992, ranking fifth in the
country. The number of doctors per 1000 population was 0.19 in 1992,
ranking 22 in the country, and the number of hospital beds was 1 per 1000
population in 1992, ranking 15 among the 24 Ostans.[11] The statistics tell
part of the story, but by no means all, where education, health and general
living standards of the Kurdish-inhabited region of Iran is concerned. These
figures do not describe the personal traits of the Kurds, who are mostly
religious, resilient and industrious people, known for their courage and
strength in the region. Similarly, the dedication of government employees
who are sent to Kurdistan to help the local peoples are never shown in the
statistical handbooks. The physicians, nurses, soldiers, educators and officials who are involved directly in providing services to the inhabitants of
Kurdistan have often become easy targets of attack by the rebels, across the
border with Iraq.

Nevertheless, part of the reason for the Kurdish problem of Iran is
political circumstances. It is true that insurgency would have been less likely
had it not been for the Iran-Iraq war. Though a sense of grievance among
the Kurds gradually increased, their interest lay in avoiding being ignored
by the policy-makers and in more involvement in their own affairs, not

Table 1

Absolute and Relative Indicators of Development, in the Kurdistan Province of Iran, 1991

Indicators	Whole Country	Kurdistan Region	Rank
Area (km²)	1,633,	18928,203	16
Total pop. (millions)	58,110227	1,230560	16
Average annual pop. growth rate	3.28	2.67	20
Population density	35.6	43.6	12
Urban population (%)	57	47.7	15
Average annual growth rate of urban pop.	4.3	6.51	3
Rural population (%)	43	52.3	10
Average annual growth rate of rural pop.	2.02	-0.2	23
Infant mortality rate (in 1000 births)*	14.3	18.0	5
Physicians (per 1000 pop.)	0.31	0.19	22
Hospital beds (per 1000 pop.)	1.48	1.00	15
No. of clinics and health centres (per 1000 pop.)	8.1	9.00	13
Literacy rate (%, +6)**	74.3	59.4	23
Primary & secondary school enrollment (av. no.)	30.79	28.62	7
Agricultural land area (1000 ha)	16,872	1,197	3
No. of tractors (per 1000 ha)	11	7.3	21
Fertilizer consumption***	86.5	12.3	24

:*   These figures are for 1992
** Literacy rates for individuals of population over 6 years of age
*** Number of kilograms of plant nutrient per hectare of arable land
Source: Jomhori-e Islami Iran, *Sazeman Barnameh*, and *Budgeh-e Ostan-e Kurdistan. Amarnameh-e Ostan-e Kurdistan, 1371*, (Tehran: Markaz-e Amar-e Iran, Khordad, 1373), various pages.

separatism. The problem of clashes between central and provincial administrations is age-old and has its parallels in many Third World countries.
The reason why similar situations have not produced rebellion and insurgency in other provinces in Iran was that it was not in the interest of any
neighbouring country to organize, finance and arm them. It becomes clear
that the motives of foreign interference, though in part economic in nature,
have primarily been political and strategic, since control over the mountainous region in Kurdistan not only provides an effective buffer to protect
friendly regimes, it also gives the foreign forces a commanding position in
the region providing direct access to the oil-rich province of Khuzistan.
The problem of regional strife that flared up in the early eighties in Iran
would have been of little consequence without foreign support. As part of a
programme for destabilizing Iran and gaining a foothold in the region,
insurgents are likely to be tacitly encouraged in the Ootan of Kurdistan and
elsewhere inside Iranian territory.

Great Power Rivalry and the Kurdish Predicament

Turning now to a short discussion of overall foreign policies of the great
powers towards the Kurdish quandary, and the impact of these policies on
specific regional developments, one notes that Kurdistan had a pivotal place
in the secret negotiations of the major powers during the First World War.
In April 1916, in a secret message sent by Russia's Foreign Minister Sazanov
to the French Ambassador in St Petersburg, two major points were specifically made: (i) That Russia shall annex the regions of Erzerum, Trabzon,
Van and Bitlis, up to a point subsequently to be determined on the littoral
of the Black Sea to the west of Trabzon. (ii) That the region of Kurdistan to
the west of Van and Bitlis, between Mush, Sert, the course of the Tigris,
Jezira-ben-Omar island, the crest-line of the mountains which dominate
Amadiya, and the region of Merga Var, shall be ceded to Russia. In return,
it [Russia] shall recognize the right of France to the areas lying between
Alma Dagh, Kaisari and Kharput.[12]

It is also noted that French government officials contemplated extending France's influence to the Kurdish areas of Serdesht inside Iran:

Russia was initially firmly opposed to giving any Kurdish parts to France,
because it wanted the whole of Ottoman Armenia and Kurdistan for itself.
However, it agreed at last, after lengthy bargaining and coaxing, to let large
Kurdish regions fall within the zone of French influence. Britain, on the
other hand, had well-known claims to Mosul province and tried to establish its foothold there in every way, as part of its plan for the control of all
oilfields and necessary outlets in the Middle East. The same motive drove
it to consider acquiring part of Iranian Kurdistan in view of its importance

in this respect, ignoring the fact that Iran had remained neutral throughout the war years.[13]

In spite of these secret plans, the great powers could not establish a protectorate in Kurdistan. However, political unrest and terrorism directed against governmental armed forces grew rapidly in Iran every time the Tehran government grew weak. In 1925, Reza Khan obtained special powers from the Iranian Majlis and moved to ruthlessly remove his opponents, including tribal chiefs, religious authorities and others. Rebel Kurdish chiefs who advocated separatism were among the tribal opponents whose lands were captured by the central government. Concerned over the growth of ethnic nationalism within Iranian territory, the Shah ordered the imperial forces to capture the rebel forces, who were outnumbered and poorly equipped.

Perhaps the most significant event in the history of the pro-independence movement of the Kurds in Iran occurred after World War II, when Iranian Kurds, supported by the USSR, established a puppet Kurdish state in Mahabad, formerly known as Sauj Bulagh. The USSR clearly intended to annex the northwestern parts of Iran. The Mahabad Republic lasted from 22 January to December 1946, and finally collapsed after the Soviet Union withdrew its forces from the Iranian territory.[14] The Iranian Kurdish movement has not been able to present itself as a unified and powerful force to Tehran. Apparently, the Shah never trusted the Kurds and was ready to deal with any ethnic uprising. Efforts were made by the Shah's regime to 'Persianize' the Kurdish provinces. The Shah's development projects for Kurdistan, similar to his other programmes, failed to make dramatic changes in the quality of life of the people of Kurdistan. At any rate, direct encouragement by Iraq might have contributed to the renewal of sporadic Kurdish fighting with the Iranian government. Despite the fact that the leaders of the movement were pursued by the *Savak* (Iran's state security agency), Iraqi-backed Kurdish forces conducted an insurgency against the Shah's regime.

Although the contest between the government and the minority groups has often grown out of internal power struggles, yet, one must take into account exogenous factors that might dramatically intensify the problem of disintegration of a multi-ethnic society. The case of Kurdish struggle for autonomy in the Middle East is a good example of why foreign governments provide support for a sub-national group. The foreign policy behaviour of the great powers in Kurdistan cannot be understood simply within the framework of regional relations. The most decisive factor for the involvement of the great powers has been international competition over access to strategic bases in the Persian Gulf and the Indian Ocean. Not surprisingly, various great powers in the post-World War II international system have shown an interest in the ambitious plan of formation of an independent Kurdistan and have taken the side of the separatists. For instance, when the decision-makers in the former Soviet Union found that their foreign policy goal of establishing a pro-Soviet Kurdistan was unattainable, they discontinued their support for the Kurdish separatist movement. It is clear that the Russian leaders would be very careful in re-establishing close ties with the Kurdish rebel groups. At the moment, Russia has to face serious internal ethnic conflicts of its own. Other problems, such as the slowdown of economic growth, and lack of resources needed for national investment in both civilian and military sectors, will also dissuade Moscow from pursuing adventurist political policies in the Middle East.

From a Western viewpoint, the most critical strategic implications of the creation of an independent Kurdistan is its impact on the future security of the Strait of Hormuz, through which the Gulf states export their oil. Other issues of concern include its impact on the expansion of their influence in the region and its impact on the future availability of military bases in the region. Because of the strategic geographic location of Kurdistan, particularly its closeness to former Soviet republics and Persian Gulf ports, access to Kurdish military facilities is viewed as a major security asset.

The Kurdish People of Iraq and Turkey

The most significant event in the history of the pro-independence struggle of Iraqi Kurds occurred when Mulla Mustapha al-Barzani, the leader of the Iraqi Kurdish movement, and Saddam Hussein signed an agreement that was officially announced by Iraq's President Bakr on 11 March 1970. To solve the Kurdish problem, Baghdad had promised to recognize Kurdish as the official language in Kurdish-dominated provinces, and to allow increased political participation of Kurds, notably to permit the appointment of a Kurdish Vice-President and creation of Kurdish political organizations.[15] The 1970 agreement between Baghdad and the Kurdish leadership reflected the power balance of the contracting parties. The government of President Bakr acquiesced to the official recognition of Kurdish identity and guaranteed its complete internal autonomy, but secured political rights to control the Kurd-inhabited provinces of Iraq. However, oppression, corruption and maladministration engendered Kurdish resentment towards the Iraqi government.[16] This resentment seems at times to have turned into opposition to the central authority of Baghdad. Signs of trouble surfaced in 1980. A new cycle of terror and killings began when the Iraqi President ordered the invasion of Iran in the summer of 1980, and diverted most troops to the Iranian borders adjacent to Khuzistan and the Kurdish provinces. This provided the Iraqi Kurds with an opportunity to intensify their insurgency inside Iraq, and in Turkish border areas. The renewed violence that erupted in the aftermath of the first and second Persian Gulf wars was a later and more intense phase of the ethnic conflict that emerged in the late eighties.[17] It not only underlined the fact that sub-national conflicts (if not settled amicably) tend to be of long duration and to persist indefinitely despite intervals of uneasy peace, but it also showed the failure of external powers to contribute to the conflict resolution.

In Turkey, the Kurds have been accused of sabotage and destruction of infrastructure, such as roads, oil pipelines, dams, electricity lines, and disrupting economic life of the country. Armenians from bases in the Syrian-controlled Beqaa Valley are accused of cooperating with the Kurds in launching guerrilla war against Turkey. Activities relating to political movements among the Kurds in Turkey took a new form following the cease-fire between Iran and Iraq. As noted earlier, the end of the Persian Gulf war provided Baghdad with an opportunity to concentrate on disturbances in its Kurdish provinces. Iraq's ruthless policies forced the Kurds to cross the borders and settle in refugee camps inside Turkey. Over 100,000 Kurds fled across the borders to Iran and Turkey, where most of them live as refugees to this day.[18] Statistics compiled by international human rights organizations show that thousands of Kurdish people died as a direct result of Iraqi armed forces attacks.[19] Turkey's crushing of the Kurdish movement and the flight of the Kurds opened a new chapter in Kurdistan's history. The Turkish government has recently intensified its efforts to destroy the rebellion against Ankara's policy of refusing to recognize the Kurds as a distinct ethnic group.[20]

Despite the mounting concern over the suffering of innocent Iraqi civilians as a result of the continuation of the UN-imposed sanctions on this country, many policy-makers say economic pressures on the Baath regime in Baghdad must not be abandoned. These observers fear that Saddam Hussein may become unrestrained in oppressing the Kurdish people, and commit further acts of aggression against Iraq's neighbours. With no military victory in sight for the Kurds, the leaders of various Kurdish groups (as shown in Table 2) should push for a lasting negotiated solution of their confrontation with central governments. However, the obstacles are intimidating in a country where the warring sides tend not to change their steadfast positions. As long as Arabs, Kurds, Turks, Azaris and Persians in Kurdistan are locked together geographically, economically and politically, not in trust but in suspicion and hate, endlessly terrorizing one another, we shall witness human tragedy of bloody fights.

Table 2

Kurdish Groups in Iran and Iraq

Iran
Kurdish Democratic Party (Hezb-e Democrat Kurdistan) is a party
supporting the interests of the Kurdish minority, and was led by
Abdel Rahman Qassemlo. It was outlawed in 1979.
Kurdish Socialist Party (BASSOK).
Party of Toilers (Hezb-e-Kumelah): a major Kurdish party led by
Sheikh Azedin Husseini.

Iraq
Kurdish Democratic Party (KDP), (al-Hizb al-Dimuqruuti al-Kurd) was
founded by Mulla Mustapha al-Barzani in 1946. It experienced a
number of cleavages, both before and after the cease-fire of March
1975. Thus, the group that joined the National Front in 1974 was
essentially a Marxist rump of the original party. In September 1978,
it affirmed its support of the Front and of the Baath Party's
'revolutionary struggle'. It is led by 'Aziz Hashem Aqrawi.

Kurdish Democratic Party (Provisional Leadership), (KDP) was formed
in 1975 following the March Algiers agreement between Iran and
Iraq and the collateral termination of aid to the Kurds by Iran and
the United States. With Mulla Barzani having withdrawn from the
insurgency, thereby completing dismemberment of the original KDP,
the Provisional Leadership declared itself the legitimate successor to
Barzani's party. Having refused to cooperate with either the National
Front or the Communists, it undertook renewed guerrilla activity
through what had been the military wing of the old party, the
Peshmergas. Since then, the Provisional Leadership has consistently
opposed the government's efforts to resettle Kurds in southern Iraq
and has engaged in clashes with both the Iraqi army and the rival
PUK. Mulla Barzani died in Washington in March 1979, while in
mid-July, several hundred party members returned to Iraq from Iran,
where they had resided since 1975. A late 1979 congress failed,
however, to resolve differences between the party's so-called
'traditionals' (led by Barzani's sons, Massud and Idris) and
'intellectuals' (led by 'Abd al-Rahman) factions.

Kurdish Revolutionary Party (KRP) originated as a secessionist
offshoot of the original KDP and in 1974 joined the National
Progressive Front along with the neo-KDP and another offshoot, the
Progressive Kurdistan Movement. At a conference in January 1978,

KRP members remaining in Baghdad reiterated their support of the National Front.

Patriotic Union of Kurdistan (PUK) is based in Damascus. It has received support from the Syrian Baath. It resulted from the 1977 merger of Jalal Talabani's Kurdish National Union (KNU) with the Socialist Movement of Kurdistan and the Association of Marxist-Leninists of Kurdistan. The KNU was formed in mid-1975 when Talabani, a left-wing member of the original KDP, refused to accept Mulla Barzani's claim that the Kurdish rebellion had come to an end.

Those Who Face Death (Peshmergas): guerrillas of the KDP.

Unified Socialist Party of Kurdistan (PSUK) is led by Dr Mahmoud Osman.
Source: Alex P. Schmidt, *Political Terrorism: A Research Guide*, Amsterdam: North-Holland Publishing Co., 1985; also, Europe, *The Europe World Yearbook, 1993*, London: Europa, 1993.

Conclusion

My conclusion is tentative, since my primary goal here was not to provide a definitive answer to the empirical questions, but to suggest what kind of evidence would be needed to examine the relationship between the Kurds as a significant minority group and the Middle Eastern states. More emphasis was placed on the status of Kurdish people of Iran, and the attitude of the Tehran government towards them. It is quite clear that assessment of policies needs to be conducted in the context of the interests and goals of both the state and the sub-national ethnic groups, and decisions must be framed in terms of what is feasible as well as needed.

As for the hypothesis that there is a direct link between economic development and political instability, it is clear that no government in the Middle East can afford to ignore domestic ethnic problems, if it is proven that the creation of a stable political environment is a necessary condition of economic development.[21] A key to understanding ethnic conflicts is the superior-inferior relations between the dominant ethnic group and other sub-national groups. In most cases, the dissatisfied minority groups are worse off than the other inhabitants of the states. The major demands of minorities are generally more equal distribution of power and wealth and preservation of ethnic cultures. When these demands are not met, ethnic minorities become disillusioned and even militant. Under these circumstances, it would seem all the more critical for the governments to address the difficult task of negotiating with the leaders of the ethnic movements, because people do not forget their old grievances but wait for a favourable circumstance to renew their struggle for a better economic and political life. This explains why rioting and widespread political unrest occur when the central government weakens and loses its total control over peripheral areas of the country.[22] There is nothing very new about this minority-majority confrontation situation, for the Kurdish people – like other ethnically distinct groups – have historically wished for a measure of self-determination and an end to being totally controlled by others. However, the pursuit of a better life rather than the creation of a state of 'Kurdistan', is the most cherished goal of the majority of the Kurds.

As to the situation of the Iranian Kurds, it could be concluded that economic improvement since the end of the long war with Iraq has been evident in Kurdistan, but much more needs to be done. In Iranian society, ethnic and cultural groups do not form the basis of a system of social stratification. Many such groups have begun to lose their sense of ethnic separateness since various groups are linked together economically, politically, and in marriage alliances. It is clear that access to economic or political power does not depend on ethnic origins of individuals. Therefore, it has been possible for the Kurds to enter into civil service, the armed forces and the political arena. It would be unwise to attach too much significance to the ethnic factor in the society and politics of Iran at the expense of other factors that have maintained regional differences. In Iraq and Turkey, respect for the Kurdish people's fundamental rights and democratic freedoms, and the protection of Kurdistan's natural environment and commencement of earnest negotiations on the relations between the central governments and the Kurdish minorities must be emphasized. The advantage of such a scheme would be that it would bring order to the present uncertain future of the Kurdish minorities in these states. Yet, in the final analysis the success of this scheme will depend on bringing together all sides. Fundamental disagreement exists between the involved parties on what degree of sovereignty and autonomy should be given to the Kurds in the three Middle Eastern states. There is also disagreement between various Kurdish leaders on such questions as whether a united Kurdistan should be created, and what should be the formal status of Kurdistan. It can of course be suggested that political and administrative centralization, rather than ethnicity, is the real cause of instability. We must leave it to future research to address this question. What is evident is that the problem will not resolve itself, nor can it be resolved by foreign actions, whether by force or diplomatic means. It will require agreement between the Kurds and the individual governments involved. A willingness to compromise in the interest of peace and security is needed. There can be no enduring gain for anyone unless there are gains for all.

The evidence from the consequences of Baghdad's policies towards the Kurdish minorities inside its territories supports the view that the use of political repression and lack of political freedom lead to national and regional instability. Most importantly, the Kurdish case sheds light on the interaction between economic well-being of indigenous people and civil strife. We know that not all ethnic people demand total autonomy, and that suppression of these groups has failed to bring an end to their confrontation with the central governments. Finding solutions is of extreme importance for the stability, and economic prosperity of the region, with major implications for global economic and political life. As long as economic causes of intense dissatisfaction prevailing among ethnic groups are not removed, one could expect the Middle Eastern nationality problems to continue. In fact, many other non-ethnic minorities (e.g., the underprivileged socio-economic groups) may indicate their commitment to self-determination. As a distinct group, no ethnic group should be forced to lose its ethnic identification and cultural heritage.[23] In bilingual communities, both the dominant language and the regional languages could be taught in the schools and universities. It is useful to even overemphasize the point that the main reasons for these movements and their struggles against central governments are only slightly ideological/political, and mostly economic in nature. For the Middle Eastern states to use repressive and coercive tactics means essentially future ethnic conflicts at even higher levels of intensity. Ending these conflicts requires fundamental changes involving alterations in political and economic structures at both national and international levels. At the national level, denial of the very existence of ethnic problems (notably in Turkey), or opting for military instruments to handle the situation (most brutally in Iraq) only encourages the growth of separatist movements.[24]

There is a possibility of confrontation along ethnic and regional lines, if the central government's policy of developing backward provinces is not earnestly followed, and new opportunities for the advancement of young people are not opened up. One problem that continues to concern Middle Eastern countries (and almost all other developing states) is the fact that their economies must operate in international and domestic environments of severe stress, making development more difficult. It cannot be denied that many Middle Eastern countries are faced with tremendous obstacles (such as inadequate resources, limited infrastructure, weak administrative capacity). Even if these states overcome their economic problems, most of them cannot or will not distribute the benefits of better economic performance equally among all people. Those who benefit more from the economic policies of the regime, tend to support it more. If the governments do not discharge their responsibilities of improving the standards of living of all of the citizens and rewarding them equitably, they will be laying the foundation of widespread feelings of frustration and discontent. To solve the problem of political instability, the governments have no choice but to invest in people by emphasizing education, health, population control and environmental protection reform policies. In spite of these problems, in the context of the policy of socio-economic equalization, the traditional regional gaps between the central and peripheral areas of the country must be gradually narrowed in order to minimize the probability of the eruption of violent insurrection. It is plausible to assume that by redressing the inequalities in the levels of economic development of various provinces, the states will be able to remove the major underlying structural sources of conflict. There is certainly no doubt that, in accordance with the principle of equality and mutual security, the security of one side is the prerequisite of the security of the other. Conversely, without radical political transformation and improvement of economic life of the disadvantaged groups, such as the Kurds, ethnic conflicts will continue to plague the regional states. Cooperation between the bordering states and a willingness to compromise on issues that are vital to their security must characterize their relations. All countries want to be able to assert their national interests independently of outside interference, particularly in such important issues as territorial integrity and control of their people's future. Although nationalism remained a divisive force during the Cold War, there was a remarkable move towards international forms of cooperation and political organization. In the mid-1980s, the European Community members initiated a historic attempt to conclude the formation of a single and integrated market. The 12 European states plan to become the largest global trading bloc, and even remove internal frontiers. Western Europe is only one example of a group of nations moving consciously and voluntarily to form a closer association. Another trading bloc (NAFTA) is forming in North America, including Canada, Mexico, the United States, and nations of the Caribbean Basin. Without doubt, the regional states in a more united Middle East would find it easier to solve their economic and political problems through cooperation with one another.[25]

Whenever armed hostilities by ethnic groups break out, using force, the central governments may manage to control but not to eliminate ethnic conflict, especially when these conflicts are exacerbated by externally planned interventions in the political affairs of the states. Powerful exogenous factors may arrest the possible development of a pattern of coexistence. Certainly at the roots of the ethnically-based political disintegration of Iraq lies the legacy of British colonial policy, which tended to harden ethnic divisions by means of the separate organization of communal groups in the colonial territories. By encouraging factionalization and attempting to play one ethnic group against another (based on the principle of 'divide and rule', which the British Empire had mastered), the great powers sought to strengthen their own positions in many Middle Eastern societies.

The only effective way of coping with internal instability problems of this type is to treat negotiations with minority groups seriously, and to be willing to compromise. It may be advisable to create at least a partial geographic basis for a political federation of the country, to replace the unitary system of government. The leaders of the ethnic minorities must be satisfied with shared control over their destiny. Given the history of the rebellion, one cannot help wondering whether the leaders of the Kurdish movements have other goals in mind. There is no need for a separate state of 'Kurdistan' to ensure the safety and well-being of the Kurds. On the contrary, a landlocked and newly independent Kurdistan will not have the resources needed to raise the standard of living of its people, The Kurds will be unable to establish a sustainable economy independent of massive foreign economic and technical aid. The last thing that the Middle East needs is more weak and externally-dependent states. The newly established states may extend strategic facilities to a great power for intelligence and military purposes. This may lead to intense foreign competition for bases in the area, and eventually add to the level of tension.[26]

Western efforts to 'solve' the problem have been constant and, unfortunately, a failure. There must be a guarantee of an equitable distribution of power between local, regional and national government. In the Third World, there is a tendency towards centralization, and a suspect federalism. Arguments that multinational states should move towards federalism because of ethnic diversity of different regions of the country, are weakened by the danger of disintegration and partition of these states. This is not to say weakened by the danger of disintegration and partition of these states. This is not to say that the local governments must be left out of the decision-making process. In fact, additional opportunities to influence national decisions must be granted to local units. A political system in which many people feel unheard is not robust and stable. The objectives of the government should be the assertion of national sovereignty and the preservation of domestic harmony. If the key to economic development is political stability, in the political as well as the economic sphere, central government must inspire confidence and direct the whole nation with a long-term plan for development. In the case of Iran, bearing in mind the range of the interests of social groups, as well as the needs and objectives of Islamic rule, we should realize that carrying out gigantic transformation in a country such as Iran is in itself a most difficult undertaking. Yet without doubt, the country has at its disposal extensive resources for further accelerating the pace of nationwide development.

Notes

* Associate Professor of Political Science, Department of Political Science, Tehran University, Tehran, Iran.

1. Theodore Shanin, 'Ethnicity in the Soviet Union: Analytical Perceptions and Political Strategies', *Comparative Studies in Society and History*, vol. 31, no. 3 (July 1989), pp. 409–11.

2. David Sills, ed., *International Encyclopedia of the Social Sciences*, 17 vols., (New York: Macmillan, Free Press, 1968), vol. 5.

3. The Constitution of India recognizes Hindu as the official language, and also specifies 17 regional languages (e.g., Telugu, Bengali, Tamil, Urdu, Marathi, Gujarati, and so forth). Many other local languages are also used by the Indians.

4. Saideh Lotfian, 'The Relative Position of Micro-states and Dependent Territory in the International System in the 1990s', *Journal of the Faculty of Law and Political Science*, no. 31 (April 1994), pp. 183–226.

5. For a development of this theme, see: Milton Esman, 'Ethnic Politics: How Unique is the Middle East?' in: Milton Esman and Itamar Rabinovich, eds., *Ethnicity, Pluralism, and the State in the Middle East*, (Ithaca, N.Y.; London: Cornell University Press, 1988), pp. 271–88.

6. Eric Hobsbawm, *Nations and Nationalism Since 1780: Programme, Myth and Reality*, (Cambridge: Cambridge University Press, 1993), pp. 186–7.

7. This follows the suggestions of John Anderson, 'Ethnic Dilemmas in Pakistan, Iran and Afghanistan as Security Problems', in: Hafeez Malik, ed., *Soviet-American Relations with Pakistan, Iran and Afghanistan*, New York: St Martin's Press, 1979.

8. Jomhori-e Islami Iran, *Sazeman Barnameh and Budgeh-e Ostan-e Kurdistan. Amarnameh-e Ostan-e Kurdistan, 1371*, Tehran: Markaz-e Amar-e Iran, Khordad, 1373. [Islamic Republic of Iran, *The Programme and Budget Organization of the Kurdistan Province, and the Statistical Yearbook for the Kurdistan Province, 1992*, Tehran: The Centre for Statistics of Iran, 1994].

9. Different figures are given by the Kurdish sources. Refer to: A. R. Ghassemlou, 'Kurdistan in Iran', in: Gerard Chaliand, ed., *A People without a Country*, translated by Michael Pallis, (New York: Olive Branch Press, 1993), pp. 95-121.

10. Islamic Republic of Iran, *The Programme and Budget Organization of the Kurdistan Province*, and *The Statistical Yearbook for the Kurdistan Province, 1992*, *op. cit.*, p. 552.

11. Ibid., p. 553.

12. See the instructive historical account of great power rivalries over Kurdish areas by: Kamal Mahdar Ahmed, *Kurdistan during the First World War*, (London: Al-Saqi Books, 1994), p. 187.

13. Ibid.

14. For a discussion of the events preceding the establishment of the Mahabad Republic, beside older works, attention should be paid to: Gerard Chaliand, *The Kurdish Tragedy*, (London, New Jersey: Zed Books, 1994), pp. 5 and 74. An American official who had been in Iran at the time writes that, 'In the absence of effective Iranian authority, the Soviets maintained direct relations with the tribes–the Jalali in the north, the Shikak in the mountains west of Shahpur, and the Herki west of Rezaieh. The chiefs of these tribes were allowed to manage their own

affairs by the Soviets, who only required that they maintain security and provide grain for the Red Army'. See: Archie Roosevelt (Jr), 'The Kurdish Republic of Mahabad', in: Gerard Chaliand, *A People without a Country*, op. cit., pp. 122–38.

15. For details of the 1970 March Manifesto, see: Martin Van Bruinessen, 'The Kurds between Iran and Iraq', *Middle East Report*, vol. 16 (July–August 1986), pp. 14-27; Nader Entessar, 'The Kurds in Post-revolutionary Iran and Iraq', *Third World Quarterly*, vol. 6, no. 4 (October 1984), pp. 911–33; William Hazen, 'Minorities in Revolt: The Kurds of Iran, Iraq, Syria and Turkey', in: Ronald de McLaurin, ed., *The Political Role of Minority Groups in the Middle East*, New York: Praeger, 1980; Edmund Ghareeb, *The Kurdish Question in Iraq*, Syracuse, N.Y.: Syracuse University Press, 1981; Arthur Turner, 'Kurdish Nationalism', in: Chelkowski and Robert Pranger, eds, *Ideology and Power in the Middle East*, Durham, London: Duke University Press, 1988, and W. Workman, *The Social Origins of the Iran-Iraq War*, (Boulder, Colo.: Lynne Rienner, 1994), pp. 71–4.

16. In reviewing the constitutions of the countries in the region, one must come to the initial conclusion that liberties and human rights of citizens, including minorities, are protected by the central governments. Only three states (Israel, Oman and Saudi Arabia) have no formal and written constitutions. In the other states, the principles of equality and justice are recognized in constitutional clauses such as 'citizens are equal before the law, without discrimination because of sex, blood, language, social origin or religion' (Iraq), and 'all individuals are equal without any discrimination before the law, irrespective of language, race, colour, gender, political opinion, philosophical belief, religion and sect, or any such considerations' (Turkey). In reality, liberties and human rights of the people have frequently been curtailed. A full range of coercive measures have been employed, including restricting access to certain areas, monitoring movement of people, mass transfer of populations, deportation, destroying homes and entire villages, invoking martial law, imprisonment, torture, summary execution, and even genocide. Most recently, these tactics have been used against the Kurdish citizens of Iraq and Turkey. For a survey of this discussion and an analysis of its results, see: Saideh Lotfian, 'Human Rights and the Challenge of Ethnic Separatist Movements in the Middle East', *The Iranian Journal of International Affairs*, vol. 6, nos. 1-2 (Spring-Summer 1994), pp. 91–118.

17. For a more general statement of this argument, see: Edgar O'Ballance, 'The Kurdish Factor in the Gulf War', *Military Review*, vol. 61 (June 1981), pp. 13–20.

18. Amir Hassanpour, 'The Kurdish Experience', *Middle East Reporter*, vol. 24, no. 4 (July-August 1994), p. 5.

19. Andrew Whitley and Susan Meiselas, 'The Remains of Anfal', *Middle East Report*, vol. 24, no. 4 (July-August 1994), pp. 8–11. For a detailed discussion of Iraq's chemical bombardment of the Kurdish villages, and interviews with those who survived the attacks, see: Middle East Watch, *Human Rights in Iraq*, (New Haven, Conn.: Yale University Press, 1990), pp. 75-96, and Peter Sluglett, 'The Kurds', in: *Saddam's Iraq: Revolution or Reaction*, London: Zed Books, 1986.

20. For the Kurdish struggles in Turkey, see: Michael Gunter, 'The Kurdish Problem in Turkey', *Middle East Journal*, vol. 42, no. 3 (Summer 1980), pp. 389-406; Joane Nagel, 'The Conditions of Ethnic Separatism: The Kurds in Turkey, Iran, and Iraq', *Ethnicity*, vol. 7 (1980), pp. 279–97; Ali-Fuat Borovali, 'Kurdish Insurgencies, the Gulf War, and Turkey's Changing Role', *Conflict Quarterly*, vol. 7 (1987),

pp. 29–45, and Robert Olson, 'The Kurdish Question Four Years on: The Politics of Turkey, Syria, Iran and Iraq', *Middle East Policy*, vol. 3, no. 3 (1994), pp. 136–44.

21.   Cynthia Enloe, *Ethnic Conflict and Political Development*, Boston: Little, Brown and Co., 1973; Lewis Snider, 'Minorities and Political Power in the Middle East', in: Ronald de McLaurin, ed., *The Political Role of Minority Groups in the Middle East*, op. cit., and Dennis Thompson and Dov Ronen, eds, *Ethnicity, Politics, and Development*, Boulder, Colo.: Lynne Rienner, 1986.

22.   Saideh Lotfian, 'Human Rights and the Challenge of Ethnic Separatist Movements in the Middle East', *The Iranian Journal of International Affairs*, vol. 6, nos. 1 and 2 (Spring-Summer 1994), pp. 91–118.

23.   For an analysis from this frame of reference, see: Paul Brass, 'Ethnicity 24. Saideh Lotfian, 'Human Rights and the Challenge of Ethnic Separatist Movements in the Middle East', *The Iranian Journal of International Affairs, op. cit.*

25.   For a discussion of the decline in territoriality, nation-states and nationalism in the new international order, and new ways of thinking about the relationship between individuals and communities, see: Matthew Horsman and Andrew Marshall, *After the Nation-State: Citizens, Tribalism and the New World Disorder*, London: Harper Collins, 1994.

26.   Many authors suggest that foreign interference is an important factor. See, for example, Saideh Lotfian, 'Human Rights and the Challenge of Ethnic Separatist Movements in the Middle East', *The Iranian Journal of International Affairs*, op. cit.; also, Edward Chaszer, 'International Protection of Minorities in the Middle East: A Status Report', *Middle East Review*, vol. 18 (Spring 1986), pp. 37-48.

Nine

The Palestine Question in Arab-Iranian Relations

18

The Palestine Question In Arab–Iranian Relations

AHMAD SUDKI EL-DAJANI*

Introduction

Since it began more than a century ago, the Palestine Question has occupied an important place in Arab–Iranian relations, as an expression of the Zionist colonialist invasion of Palestine in 'the heartland of the Arab and Islamic worlds' and the challenge this posed to the peoples of the dominated Islamic civilization, including the Arab and Iranian. This challenge entered a new phase after the quake that shook the Gulf in 1991, the holding of the 'Middle East peace conference' in Madrid on 30 October 1991, and the US bid to impose a regional order in the 'dominion of Islam' under the name of a 'Middle East order' led by the Israeli Zionist entity.

This study deals with the Palestine Question in Arab–Iranian relations within the framework of the present Seminar on Arab–Iranian Relations. It attempts to treat, within that framework 'the place of the Palestine Question and extent of its centrality for the Arab and Iranian peoples', its place in relation to the national security of each, and the impact on Arab–Iranian relations of current attempts to resolve the Arab–Israeli conflict.

When we speak of Arab–Iranian relations, what comes to mind is an Arab dominion and an Iranian dominion, both contiguous to one another within an 'Islamic world' where Islamic civilized life flourished for fourteen centuries, after it carried the Message of Islam and embraced the civilizations of the region. What also comes to mind is that the term 'Islamic world' incorporating these two dominions, is a recent usage by Western authors, dating to the 19th century and applied to *diyar al-Muslimin* ('the domains of the Muslims'), which extended from the western edge of the Maghreb on the Atlantic Ocean to the eastern rim of Sinkiang Province in China, from central Asia to the north to equatorial Africa in the south. The term came into use in Islamic circles after publication of *The Contemporary Islamic World* in the 1920s, which included the comments of Emir Shakeeb Arslan on the writings of the American Withrop Stoddard in his book *The New World of Islam*, translated by 'Ajaj Nuwayhid. Another point that comes to mind is the still more recent Western term 'Middle East', which today is commonly used by Westerners to denote the greater part of *diyar al-Muslimin*. It appears that the evolution of the meaning of this term, which was first used in 1902, derived from 'two concerns, oil and Palestine', according to Mu'een Haddad in his article 'The Meaning of the Middle East'. It was linked to British strategic thinking, as clarified by Jalal Mu'awwad in his article 'Middle East: The Evidence', and after that with US strategic thinking. The author of this study explains these terms in his two books *On the Future* and *Confronting the Middle East Order*.

Geographic proximity is one important factor controlling Arab–Iranian relations and the place of the Palestine Question in these relations. This bound some Arabs working in the political sciences to incorporate Iran in the term 'countries that neighbour' the Arab world. But there are other determining factors in Arab–Iranian relations; on these I prepared a working paper for this seminar, entitled 'Historical and Geo-strategic Ties and the Common Interests and Challenges of Contemporary Advancement'. The summation of these factors reduces to one: The sense of belonging to a single civilization. This is what binds other Arabs working in the political sciences to underscore cultural belonging and to speak of a 'dominion of Islamic civilization', which they also called 'the dominion of Arab Islamic civilization', in deference to the Arabic tongue, which became the dominant medium of communication because of its being the language of the Holy Qur'an. The term was shortened to 'dominion of Islam', which is the term used by Gamal Abdel Nasser in his book *Philosophy of the Revolution*. These persons are careful to avoid using the term 'Middle East' for this dominion. It is noteworthy that the 5th Arab Nationalist Conference endorsed in its communique the term 'civilization dominion', while noting 'the relative stability of relations between the Arab states and Iran and Turkey in the framework of the Arabs' outlook towards their wider civilization', and while affirming 'the need to develop the positive aspects alongside this civilization that embraces at the same time a strategic thrust for the Arab nation incorporating the joint interests of both parties and maintaining the deep spiritual and cultural ties between them'.

It is this fact of belonging by the Arab nation and Iran to the dominion of Islamic civilization, which Muslims, Christians and other believers helped build, that forms our understanding of Arab–Iranian relations. They are ties between Arab and Iranian peoples at the popular level, pointing up the cultural experience of each in all its aims, aims that basically embrace a singular cultural identity, similarity of conditions prevailing during its formation, liberation of the land from foreign domination, the unity of nation and territory, *shura* (Islamic legal counsel) and democracy, and a threshold of development, social justice and cultural revival. It also embraces formal ties between the Iranian state and the Arab states, individuall and collectively, in the framework of an Arab order embodied in the League of Arab States and in regional Arab associations.

The Place of the Palestine Question for the Arabs and the Iranians

The Palestine Question occupies a special place for both Arabs and Iranians. This was manifest in their great concern over it ever since its inception more than a century ago, through its successive phases, one after the other, and in the formulation of the objective of liberating Palestine, a major objective that they underscored, dreamt of realizing and sought. It appears that the attachment of our Arab and Iranian brethren to the Palestine Question is a strong one, with deep historical roots lodged in historical memory and popular conscience. There is no better demonstration of the strength of this attachment and its deep roots than that the changes that encompassed the Arab and Iranian nations, and the Palestine Question, for over a century, did not affect the fixed objective of liberating Palestine, though at times it did affect the degree of interest in the Palestine Question, more or less.

As for the reasons for the Palestine Question's occupation of such a special place among the Arabs and Iranians, two stand out, one relating to Palestine and the other to its case. Palestine in the popular conscience of every Arab and Iranian is a land blessed by God; it contains the Aqsa Mosque, associated for every Muslim with the Prophet's ascension to heaven, and containing the Church of the Holy Sepulchre, to which Christians make pilgrimage, and the Mosque of Abraham and birthplace of the prophet (*marabi' al-anbiya'*), whom Muslims, Christians and Jews believe in. Visiting it is thus a dream to be sought. In Arab and Iranian annals it is associated with events dating to olden times, causing hearts to throb, and preserved in the stories of the prophets ever since the Flood. It is also associated with events since the emergence of Islam, a part of its living history of victories, defeats, glories and setbacks. The Frankish invasion of Jerusalem and its surrounding territories, and resistance to it through holy war, occupies a special place in the historical annals, pointing to the 'biography of Al-Malik Al-Zahir', which the general public of the domains of Islam (*diyar al-Islam*) continued to listen to generation after generation until recent times. Among the things that stand out in this biography is the *fidawis*, those who roamed between Iran and the Arab nation and helped play a prominent role in the struggle against the Frankish aggressors. In it also emerged the exchange of articles between Palestine and other Arab countries, between Iran and Transoxiana, through the story of Al-Malik Al-Zahir Baybars himself. Palestine exists in the daily life of every Arab, and Iran is part of his civilizational dominion, which maintains his interests and

livelihood. How many merchants have travelled all quarters of this dominion, following the Silk Road and other trade routes from olden times, and
how many travellers there have been!

The Palestine Question emerged during the last quarter of the 19th
century, as a result of the Zionist colonialist settlement of Palestine, at a
time when the Arab nation and Iran, and other countries of *diyar al-Islam*
and the dominion of its civilization, faced the challenge of European colonialism during its second great wave. Iran endured Czarist Russian
aggression from the north and British provocations in the south. Persia had
lost Georgia and Armenia (Yerevan and Lenkoran) after two wars in three
decades at the turn of the 19th century. The Islamic khanates were liqui-
dated and the local culture and national sentiment suppressed with terror,
wrote Jamal Hamdan in his *Strategy of Colonialism and Liberation*. Russia
began to look toward occupying the Gulf, which Peter the Great described
with the phrase, 'who controls the Gulf controls the world'. Russia struck
at Iran from three directions, and Russian colonialist policy regarded any
areas south of the Caucasus as vital and a sphere of influence; it saw in Iran
a 'Russian Suez Canal' and sought to open a corridor for itself to the Gulf.
Iran also suffered much from British intervention in the Gulf, led since
1763 by the British resident political officer in Bushehr's harbour, who had
become 'effectively the crown king of the Gulf'. The intensity of this intervention increased after Bonaparte invaded Egypt in 1798, as did the intensity
of Persia's resistance to British intervention. British residents repeatedly
accused the government of Iran of seeking to weaken British influence in
the Gulf and other Islamic countries; among these was William Jones, who
wrote of this to Ambassador Henry Rawlinson in Tehran in 1860, as
Mustapha 'Aqeel reports in his book *Iran's Policy in the Gulf 1848–1896*.

The Arab nation, for its part, was suffering the French colonialist invasion of Egypt in 1798, and succeeded in resisting Bonaparte's campaign.
However, not long after, it faced the major colonialist onslaught of 1830, in
which France focused on Algeria and Britain on Aden and the coastal areas
of the Arabian Peninsula and the Gulf. Even as it confronted these, the
second colonialist wave struck in 1881, starting with the French invasion of
Tunisia and British occupation of Egypt.

It was not difficult for Arabs and Iranians to see a connection, when the
Palestine Question and Zionist colonialist settlement of Jerusalem and its
surroundings emerged, between colonialist schemes in Palestine and what
colonialism was plotting for each of them in all parts of 'the Islamic dominion'. Their notables could see, through careful observation and thought,
what most others intuitively sensed and knew from historical memory, that
this Zionist entity European imperialism is trying to implant in Palestine
is in fact a front-line European colonialist base, thrust into the Islamic
heartland, through which the European invaders seek to reinforce their

domination over all countries of the Islamic world in Asia and Africa. Notables and public together were also aware of the targeting of Muslim and Christian holy places by a Europe intent on encroaching against Islam and Islamic civilization and on destroying the morale of their adherents. Thus did the Palestine Question, from its very inception, appear to our Arab and Iranian brethren as their own, each and every one of them. It has a spiritual dimension for the Muslim, being an Islamic issue, and for the Christian attached to Islamic civilization, who helped build it; it also has geographic, political, economic and cultural dimensions, in view of the destruction and threats to all these dimensions following the Zionist invasion of Palestine.

This fact was confirmed and reinforced by the course of the Palestine Question across a century and in the phases of the Zionist invasion–infiltration (1882–1917), penetration (1917–48), invasion (1948–67), expansion (1967–82) and regional dominance on behalf of the forces of international hegemony (1982–). This four-fold description was adopted by Jamal Hamdan, whose study on the establishment of Israel, *Strategy of Colonialism and Liberation*, ended with eight conclusions governed by geo-politics: Israel is a colonialist state par excellence; its colonialism is sectarian; and also racialist; it is a part of overseas European colonialism; it is also a settler-state first and foremost; but still the embodiment of a multi-purpose colonialism (colonialist, strategic, economic); it originated as an expansionist colonialism with its Zionist slogan of 'your land Israel is from the Nile to the Euphrates'; and finally, it is a colonialism that is directly and indirectly working for world Zionism and world imperialism.

Confirmation of the special place of the Palestine Question for Arabs and Iranians can be found by tracing its past, though here we note some distinguishing features between the Arab nation and Iran. The 1919 Paris Peace Conference at the end of the First World War (1914–1918) entrenched European colonialism in most of the Arab world, after it was carved up into political boundaries and spheres of influence between Britain and France, and even Italy; the Conference also rejected Iran's pleas and permitted England, in the name of a mandate over Palestine, to work on implementing the Balfour Declaration, issued on 2 November 1917, for the purpose of establishing a Jewish state in Palestine. England confronted Iran with this through a treaty aimed at subjecting it entirely to British control, according to Donald Leber in his book *Iran: Past and Present*. Although the Shah and government were prepared to accept this, popular unrest resisted and prevented its ratification.

One distinguishing feature was the holding of the General Islamic Conference in Jerusalem, 7–17 December 1931. It was held at a time when the peoples of the Arab world and Iran were preoccupied with country struggles for independence and expulsion of the colonialist, following the forced fragmentation of the Arab nation and divisions between the parts of the Islamic world. It was clear from the activities of this conference, the calls for its holding and the publicity surrounding it, just how special the Palestine Question was for all peoples of the Islamic dominion. Its resolutions included a decision on the holy places and dome of the [Prophet's] ascension, alongside five stipulations relating to the Palestine Question, and it called for confronting the Zionist danger, just as it deplored every form of colonialism in any country, within the framework of one of the objectives of the conference–'the search for disseminating forms of Islàmic cooperation'. What is noteworthy is the public acclaim received by this conference, despite the persistence of European colonialist forces and those ensnared by them from among 'immersers' in country zeal, who feigned national superiority so as to undermine the original sense of national belonging. Shakeeb Arslan, in his comments on 'The Present Islamic World', pointed to these attempts at inflaming 'unwholesome enthusiasm' between nations against the Islamic fraternity and drawing a group from among the Persians to pursue the same, 'as well as others of the Islamic nation'. He said: 'But this is still limited when compared to the great majority under Islam, and more than one aversion they had to the Sunnites has faded now, because of the overall decay of political Islam's power and the Persians' need for solidarity with all other Muslims'. Arslan spoke of his vision to link the Persian brethren with Muslim issues in general, and the Palestine Question in particular, during the inter-war period of Zionist penetration; he said: 'The Persian state is still an Islamic state and protector of Shiite activity in Islam; everyone who has visited the land of the Persians, even from among Europeans, has noted that the Persian nation feels what the Islamic world in its entirety feels; its concern for Turkey, the land of the Arabs, Egypt, the Maghreb and all countries of Islam is a very real concern; what troubles the Muslims troubles it and what pleases them pleases it.' He gave as an example what happened at the General Islamic Conference: 'At the end of last year, when the Islamic Conference was held, a group of prominent Shiites attended, such as Seyyed Tabataba'i, Seyyed Hussein Al-i-Kashef al-Ghata' and Shiite religious scholars ('ulema) in Iraq. The conferees representing the entire Islamic world were twice led in prayer by the prominent legist of ijtihad (independent rational judgment in interpretation of the Law), Seyyed Hussein Al-i-Kashef al-Ghata', who overwhelmed all the Muslims, and a prominent member of Syria's proud youth, Riyadh al-Solh, declared that 'this day marks the dawn of Islamic unity'. These remarks, which return to 1932, and the place the Palestine Question held for Arabs and Iranians, show how they subordinated minor contradictions between Muslims, both Sunnite and Shiite, and between all those belonging to Islamic civilization, nations and creeds, to the overriding contradiction – that between them and European colonialism and its

Zionist ally. Salaheddine al-Tabataba'i of Iran was designated Secretary General of the General Islamic Conference.

Another distinguishing feature is the reaction to the Palestine tragedy of 1948 and emergence of Israel as the state of the Zionist entity; this was clearly and strongly felt throughout the Arab nation and Iran. We recall the demonstrations in Tehran in 1948, denouncing the rape of Palestine, precisely as had occurred in Arab capitals, and how Ayatollah Kashani led the popular movement demanding resistance to Zionism, and how the response to the challenge expressed itself in the movement to nationalize oil, which Kashani supported Musaddiq on, precisely as it expressed itself in the 23 July 1952 revolution in Egypt and the outbreak of the Arab revolution. Iran witnessed, just as Arab countries and other Islamic countries witnessed, popular campaigns during the Palestine war to gather funds and send volunteers.

The special place of the Palestine Question for Iran underwent a test in 1960 when the Shah recognized 'Israel' and permitted it political and commercial representation. Large sectors of the Iranian nation became angry with the Shah's regime and many regarded his cooperation with Israel as 'a veritable stab to their dignity and pride in their Faith – their strength and their vessel', as Fahmy Howeidy described it in his book *Iran from Within*. When the Palestinian struggle began with the establishment of the Palestine Liberation Organization in 1964, and a new episode of the Palestinian revolution began, we saw a strong response from Iranian youth in support of this revolution. This responsiveness grew after the 1967 war and Israel's occupation of east Jerusalem. A similar test occurred in Arab Egypt in 1977, when its President visited the Knesset in occupied Jerusalem, after which he concluded with it the 1979 treaty under US patronage, which witnessed the Camp David accord of 1978. The results of these two tests were one in essence, even if differing in details, and reactions were identical in Iran and the Arab nation to one of our dominion's states recognizing the Zionist entity.

The beginning of the Zionist phase of expansion in 1967 was a decisive factor in deepening the attachment of most Iranians and Arabs to the Palestine Question, and, simultaneously, to the capitulation of a few to the West under US leadership, accepting the status quo and abandoning the Palestine Question. It is noteworthy just how deep the attachment to the Palestine Question is this majority's, nurtured by both the spiritual and national dimensions of the issue; it became clearer for the Arabs as an Islamic Arab question, and for the Iranians as an Iranian Islamic question, or perhaps to be more precise, an 'Islamic Iranian question'. The majority view among students of the consequences of the 1967 war and making peace with 'Israel', is that both were among the most important factors leading to the emergence of the Islamic revival movement in Islamic countries. This movement places the liberation of Palestine and its holy places from Zionist occupation among its top objectives.

Clearly the trend in the conflict with the Zionist–imperialist alliance in our region, shifted attachment to the Palestine Question from one of mere sympathy to rational awareness by the Arab and Iranian publics. This explains their capacity to remain steadfast before a psychological warfare aimed at separating them from the Palestine Question; some of the weapons applied are highly invasive, especially those exploiting contradictions between the brethren and changes in positions to a point that exceeds the red limit. The events of the eighties confirmed that our Iranian brethren's attachment to the Palestine Question remained steadfast under the most difficult of conditions, whether during the Iraq–Iran war or when the position of the Palestinian leadership towards Iran changed. When the Arab people of Egypt endured the same psychological warfare to separate them from the Palestine Question, during the same period, they in turn confirmed the depth of their attachment to it. The same applied to other Arab peoples.

This rational awareness of the Palestine Question enabled Arabs and Iranians to understand the nature of their struggle against Zionism. The writings of the Islamic revolution in Iran expressed the view of the majority towards this conflict, as did the writings of the Arab and Islamic currents in the Arab nation. It is a conflict of destiny, in which they face the states of Western imperialism and world Zionism, and the purpose of this imperialist Zionist alliance is not only the occupation of Palestine but completing the domination of the Arab nation and the other states of the Islamic world. We find this detailed in the book by Rifaat Seyyed Ahmad on *Islamic Movements in Egypt and Iran*.

'Israel' and the National Security of Iran and the Arab Nation

The place of 'Israel' in relation to the national security of Iran and the Arab nation follows from its being 'essentially a colonialist settler-state and instrument of world Zionism and imperialism', according to Jamal Hamdan. Iran and the Arab nation fall within the Islamic dominion and belong to Islamic civilization. Israel raped Palestine, which occupies an important place in the Islamic dominion, and after it became a colonialist settler-state, it proceeded to work for itself and the forces of Western hegemony for control of the region.

While this paper was being written, at the start of 1995, an event was was reported by news agencies on 7 January 1995: 'Israeli threats to strike at Iran's nuclear facilities'. Simultaneously, the agencies carried statements by the Israeli Prime Minister, who threatened Egypt and the Arab countries and spoke of war. These threats came during the visit of US Defence

Secretary Perry to the region. 'Israel' had proceeded in the second half of 1994 to accuse Iran of supporting terrorism, and accused Arab states and forces of being terrorists, echoing US accusations of the same towards these states and forces. If we recall Israel's strike at Iraq's nuclear installations in June 1981, in implementation of a US–Israeli aim, we see how serious these Israeli threats are when it is a question of implementing US policy, and how clear the danger posed by Israel is to the national security of both Iran and the Arab nation.

It is noteworthy that, despite this obvious threat to the security of both our Iranian and Arab brethren, we find Israel succeeding in establishing 'contacts' with some states of the region, secretly for the most part, then more openly since the Madrid conference in 30 October 1991. These contacts always appeared when disputes broke out between friendly states in the Arab nation or the Islamic world. On the one hand, they served to inflate the conflicts that broke out, so as to weaken their parties and bleed their energies; on the other hand, they penetrated the region so as to give Israel a position of regional leadership. It is clear that this ultimately involved an Israeli threat to the national security of both Iran and the Arab nation. At the same time, it revealed the 'complexity' of national security, given the prevailing regional situation and the political map of its states and the borders which the imperialist powers played a major role in drawing up.

The crux of the complexity of 'national security', for both Iran and the Arab nation, is the presence of a serious external danger threatening both and the whole dominion of Islamic civilization that contains them. This danger is most prominent over the 'Gulf', which is located between them, with 'Israel' as the spearhead of foreign hegemony. Moreover, there are contradictions between Iran and some of its friendly Arab neighbours over borders and policy; these rendered probable the outbreak of the Iraq–Iran war in 1980, which continued for eight years, and soured relations between Iran and some other Arabian Gulf countries. Inter-Arab contradictions also emerged and intensified because of the prevalence of the country perspective. It thus became necessary, when discussing Arab national security, to 'specify what this means, to clarify its connection with country security, and with the security of the region and regional associations, to recall the sources of threat and how to deal with them, and what security policies may be formulated and drafted to support and preserve security'. A number of researchers, including Abdel Mon'im al-Mashshat, posed the question: 'Is it possible under present conditions to talk about Arab national security, with all that this entails in country choices that may disagree with collective security?'[1] The communique of the 5th Arab Nationalist Conference, issued in May 1994, observed that 'eliminating the nationalist reference of Arab national security resulted in a country security that has slipped away from the dominion of regional security, in pursuit of attachments to foreign centres'. Perhaps the greatest difficulty in determining certain states' understanding of security, whether country-wide or regional, is that, as one former Arab defence minister put it, 'there is considerable mixing among leaderships between state security and their own personal security'.

Among the most dangerous consequences of 'country' contradictions, ruled by the 'state country' approach and its political boundaries, is the impression it gave that the Israeli threat to the national security of Iran and the Arab nation is not the only threat. The situation reached a point where there was talk of a brotherly country's threat to the security of another, sometimes placed prior to the Israeli threat. It has become commonplace in some studies to mention 'Israel' alongside Iran and one or more Arab states, as threatening other Arab states; indeed, we have even begun to see pledges of silence over external proposals for a convergence of the security interests of one country of our region with Israel's security interests, only to be followed by a call for cooperation in all fields. But then the Arab nation witnessed a retreat from these proposals, once the US settlement process in the wake of the quake in the Gulf showed its true face, thanks to the emergence of Arab-nationalist–Islamist thought and the facts of the situation.

We have said that the Israeli threat to the national security of Iran and the Arab nation proceeds from the strategic ties between the Zionist entity and the US, and the latter's policies toward the Islamic world generally and the 'Gulf' in particular. William Quant wrote on this policy after 'Operation Desert Storm', saying: 'Let us remind ourselves of American interests in the Middle East, and ask what will actually be the situation in the post-Cold War era. We still have two sets of specific political and economic interests that draw us to that part of the world, and they are, quite simply, oil and Israel. The US is the largest importer of oil in the world; as a great power, it cannot afford to be oblivious to Gulf oil. The US commitment to Israel, even if its roots do not extend to tangible economic or political interests, is at least as absolute as our interests in the Gulf, for domestic US considerations basically. We ask whether either of the two interests complements the other. The answer is a definite no. Hence the importance of peace in the Middle East'.[2]

What is noteworthy in Quant's discussion on Israel is that he adopts the view that Israel does not constitute a tangible political or economic interest for the US and that the commitment returns to domestic US policy. The circle has widened among those in the US who speak of a decline in the strategic importance of Israel after the collapse of the Soviet Union, whereas it climaxed in the eighties during the term of President Reagan, in conformity with his policy of confronting the Soviet Union, which in turn led to the conclusion of a US–Israeli strategic alliance; this is explained in Yousef El-Hassan's book, *Merger: A Study in the Special Relationship between the US and Israel in Light of the Strategic Cooperation between Them*. Be that as it may, US policy soon returned to commissioning Israel with specific tasks in the region. Les Aspen, the former US Defence Secretary, specified in his statement on 16 June 1993, before the Israeli–US Public Affairs Committee (IUPAC) in Washington, six objectives agreed upon with Israeli Prime Minister Rabin in the framework of what he called 'adjusting our strategic thinking in light of the changes that have occurred in the world'. All of these objectives threaten the national security of Iran and the Arab nation to the core. They are: 'Guaranteeing that institutions of national security in the US and Israel work in parallel; determining the kinds of dangers facing Israel today and confronting them; maintaining US security assistance to Israel and aiding it; maintaining its qualitative military edge; preserving close contact between the two militaries; optimizing utilization of the military-industrial base in both countries; maintaining a strong American military presence in the region, and working with Israel to prevent the proliferation of nuclear, biological and chemical weapons'.

We acquire a better understanding of these joint objectives when we recall US policy for control of Gulf oil. Michel Jobert clarified, in his discussion of this policy, that 'controlling oil, in terms of quantity produced and price, remains the sole permanent dominant concern for the United States, all else being peripheral and supplementary'. He called for focusing on the more important issue of 'US tutelage in every time and place, for economic and strategic reasons'. Our understanding is furthered by the last objective on preventing the proliferation of nuclear weapons, the intent here being Iran and several Arab states. One recalls how Ariel Sharon, the former Israeli War Minister, boasted early in 1982, after the conclusion of a strategic agreement between Israel and the US, that Israel will be moving in five domains, the widest falling between Pakistan to the east and the Maghreb to the west, within which is a domain including Iran and Turkey, and within that the Arab oil states and then the Arab states neighbouring Palestine, and finally Palestine itself.

The Israeli threat to the security of Iran and the Arab nation intensified with the US decision to harass 'states rejecting' the settlement process that the US is leading in the region and the plan it has begun to implement for the establishment of a Middle East order. We see this presented blatantly and frankly in an article by the US national security adviser, Anthony Lake, published in *Foreign Affairs* (Spring 1994) under the title 'Confronting Backlash States'. In this article he describes some of these states as 'beyond the law, choosing not only to be outside the family but attacking its basic values as well'.[3] The phrase reveals the extent of US determination to impose the world order it wants, and to strangle whoever continues to resist it. It placed Iran on the list of those states that the US should confront. Thus, the US and Israel quickly initiated systematic propaganda campaigns against Iran, reaching a climax at the start of 1995 when a White House official announced on 5 January 1995 that the US is 'deeply concerned' over Iran's determination to acquire nuclear weapons despite its signing of the non-proliferation treaty, and considers that Iran's successful acquisition of nuclear weapons 'would constitute a threat to our vital interests in the Gulf'. A US Defence Secretary spokesman did not conceal that the issue will be a topic of discussion between the Secretary of Defence and Israeli officials during his visit to the region, but 'it will not be the principal basis for the talks'.

It is clear today that 'Israel' escalated its propaganda campaign against Iran to the point where some researchers asked: is a new Israeli approach toward Iran under way? Hooshang Amirahmadi answers this question in his study, 'Iran and the Islamic Threat: The New Israeli Approach',[4] noting that Israel accused Iran of being behind the Buenos Aires blast last summer and that there was an Israeli call to pursue Iranians and attack Iran, for strategic and tactical reasons. He clarified that 'Israel is concerned over Iran's backing of movements rejecting the settlement, and links this backing and the Iranian rejection of the settlement to soliciting support from the US and certain Arab regimes. Hence the Israelis' recent talk of an Iranian danger instead of an Islamic danger'. The national security of both Iran and the Arab nation falls within the security of the 'Islamic world', which the forces of international hegemony saw as a single dominion that should be dismembered and relations between some of its countries shattered. We saw how Zionist thinking played a special role in fabricating the idea of 'the Islamic threat', after the collapse of the Soviet Union, and spread that notion in the West. Thus, Bernard Lewis writes in 1990 about 'The Roots of Islamic Anger', and then in 1992 'A New Middle East', in which he announces the death of Arab nationalism. We have also seen how the Israeli leadership spread the idea of 'the Islamic peril' through their official trips to many states following the Gulf war.

The leaderships of Iran and the Arab nation were aware of the position of Israel in relation to the security of the Islamic world in general and the national security of the Arab nation and Iran in particular. Thus we see the revolution of 23 July speaking of the danger posed by Israel to the Islamic dominion, and we see the Islamic revolution in Iran also speaking of this danger: 'The aim of the imperialist powers in creating Israel was not only the occupation of Palestine but also that every Arab state will suffer the fate of Palestine if Israel is given the opportunity', thus related the Imam in support of the Palestine cause.[5] Official Iranian and Arab announcements repeatedly warn 'that Israel seeks to exploit divisions apparent in the Arab world to achieve its hegemonial ends', as brought out in the statement issued recently by the Iranian Presidency on the occasion of the visit of the Syrian Foreign Minister (7 January 1995). Our region today is witnessing a near unanimous sense of danger over 'Israeli nuclear militarization' and the need to mobilize the diplomatic capabilities of the region to force Israel to destroy its nuclear arsenal. The meeting between Egypt and Iran on this issue is noteworthy, despite their differences on other matters, and it confirms the growing awareness of Israel's place in relation to the national security of both and the threat it poses to the security of the entire Islamic world.

The Impact of Current Attempts to Resolve the Arab–Israeli Conflict on Arab–Iranian Relations

Efforts are currently under way to settle the Arab–Israeli conflict according to a US–Zionist plan for building a 'Middle East order' in our Islamic civilization dominion. Implicit in this plan are adverse consequences for Arab–Iranian relations. To grasp these adverse consequences we must trace the plan of the order. A number of serious works on it have been issued in our Arab nation, including one issued by the Centre for Arab Unity Studies; we consider here some of its points, detailed in my two books *Confronting the Middle East Order* and *No to the Racialist Solution in Palestine*.

The first of these points is that the order is directed against the Islamic dominion as a location, so as to entrench the Zionist entity in it and therefore control its affairs. It is closely tied up with the US plan to form a 'new world order', promoted by George Bush during the Gulf crisis, and which involves aspects relating to market considerations. Sato, the Director General of the International Peace Institute in Tokyo, confirmed in an interview with *Al-Hayat* daily (31 May 1994), after a visit to the region, that 'there must be cooperation between the states of the region, because if you look at its history, you will find that the present borders have no meaning and economic ties between its states are always positive.'

A second point is that this order will take into account the international parties, as these will be active in the region. This is what motivated the settlement scheme to adopt two lines: bilateral negotiations between Israel and the Arab parties, and multilateral negotiations in which more than 30 states will participate and hold discussions within the six working groups.

The holding of the Casablanca economic summit at the end of October 1994 was within the framework of pursuing a Middle East order. It is to be noted that Iran, Iraq and Libya were not invited, being states the US regards as 'backlash'. Syria did not attend the conference either, nor did Lebanon. When Shimon Peres was asked about the possibility of initiating a new Middle East order without them, he said 'it is not possible', but he stressed that Israel supports US policy towards the 'backlash states'. Noteworthy here is a clarification by Sato, within his previously mentioned statement: 'Japan and the West view with interest the opportunities for peace in the region, but are worried that the problem of Iran will grow in view of the discrepancy in positions regarding how to contain this state and its present policy'. This remark reveals the intent of the West and its clients over this new order, just as it reveals how implementation of the scheme affects Arab–Iranian relations. Syria became aware early on of the aim of the multilateral negotiations, which were boycotted by Syria and and Lebanon. The call for boycotting them is growing in Arab strategic circles; these include Amin Huweidi, who appealed in an article in *Al-Ahram* daily (31 January 1995) for the 'boycott of the multilaterals' working groups, through which Israel is seeking to 'pickpocket' Arab capacities, from water to manpower to capital to large markets to energy'.

It is clear that the current settlement process, for the 'designers' who laid down plan of the Middle Eastern order, has imperialist aims including, among other things, the damaging of Arab–Iranian relations so as to facilitate the influence of Israel in the region and that of Western hegemonial forces led by the US. The *Tehran Times*, on the occasion of the holding of the Arab economic summit, warned against opening markets to Israel and regarded the Israeli role in Arab markets as serving only Israel.

It is also clear that the current settlement process had unforeseen consequences and considerations for the 'designers'. But they were anticipated by the thought proceeding from this region. It is noteworthy that external schemes always contain loopholes that result in reversals upon implementation. This is not strange; those who prepared them are from outside the region, do not truly understand it and wish it harm: 'And [the unbelievers] plotted and planned, and God too planned, and the best of planners is God.'[6] How many times such plotters admitted this fact after it was too late! An example of this is found in Anthony Lake's article in *Foreign Affairs*, where he described US strategy towards Iran and Iraq, twice in the seventies and then in the eighties, as destructive.

Martin Endyk repeated this description before the US Senate in February 1994. It is known how our dominion has suffered from this destructive strategy and from the fall by some of us into the trap of inflaming contradictions between us. When we recall the consequences and considerations of the settlement process, we find among them an escalation of Israeli state terrorism and expansionist ambitions, with a view at this stage towards 'economic hegemony', or what some of our Arab intellectuals call 'greater Israel' in the Zionist imagination, just as we see an escalation in the Resistance, its structure and the qualitative improvement of its operations due to the bounty of its faith, embodied in its activism in south Lebanon and Palestine. We see setbacks in the settlement process on all tracks – those which the forces of international hegemony were able to impose 'dictated agreements' on the Arab parties in, and those which they could not.

Some in the West expected this setback early. Michel Jobert said in the study mentioned earlier: 'Perhaps an opportunity is available for a lame peace between Israelis and Palestinians, depriving the barter in the Arab states of its favoured marketplace, but one cannot bank on that, if this tenuous tranquility were to prevail, inter-Arab conflict would not resume with even greater ferocity, thus simultaneously justifying and facilitating US presence.' What holds true of the Arabs between themselves holds true of Arab–Iranian relations between some bedouin Arab states and Iran, after having been cajoled into inflating secondary contradictions and forgetting the principal contradiction of an external enemy poised against them all.

There is one blatant example of inflated secondary contradictions, which both the people of the pen and people of the sword have contributed to in the dominion of our civilization, resulting in adverse effects on Arab–Iranian relations: what they write and announce about the 'Gulf'. Whereas the facts of place, time and persons present the 'Gulf' as the connecting link between Arabs and Iranians, as I showed in my book *Unity of Diversity and Arab Islamic Civilization in an Interconnected World* (the chapter on 'Union Inspired from the Gulf'), we find some dabbling with the idea of 'Gulf' as a divider between the brethren and as 'raw material' for conflict over it, starting with its name. Political scientists have been goaded into arbitrary readings of history. One of them has said, 'for thousands of years, the Gulf remained under the domination of ... the Egyptians', and then mentioned the name of a state, while another responded to him with the very same statement, mentioning another state. History confirms that both these states and all 'states' bordering the Gulf fell within a single state – the Islamic caliphate – and for many centuries.

The quake in the Gulf early in 1991 led to increased foreign presence in the Gulf, thanks to the inflating of secondary contradictions. It is clear that the forces of international hegemony are continuing to exploit the current settlement process to preserve their concentrated presence there, for the purpose of plundering the wealth of the oil region. This plunder employs several means, including depressed oil prices and depletion of the oil-producing countries' wealth through weapons sales. It is also clear that these forces are exploiting the current settlement process, in addition to poisoning Arab–Iranian relations, by singling out states that resist this hegemony in the Islamic dominion, one after the other. Now we see them imposing a meeting with Israel by the parties that signed 'the peace agreements', as occurred in 2 February 1995, and forming an institution from this meeting, as the US Secretary of State announced, to confront those states that refuse to sign. We have seen how some of these parties continued to declare their non-acceptance of this, worked to keep this meeting small and sought to remain attached to the Arab order.

Perhaps among the most important manifestations in our 'Islamic dominion' today is response to the challenge of the settlement process that the forces of hegemony are trying to impose on us, and the consequent revival of thought in our area within the framework of this response. Among the most important proposals is the need to work towards establishing a regional order originating from us and for the whole of the Islamic dominion. Jamal Hamdan spoke in his book *Strategy of Colonialism and Liberation* of a regional 'power triangle' encompassing Turkey, Iran and Egypt. Mohammad El-Sayed Selim adopted this term in his study for *Mediterranean Affairs*.[7] We see in Iran now talk of 'a new cultural revolutionary Middle East devoted to Islam and incorporating Islamic peoples from central Asia and north Africa within the framework of a revolutionary understanding that approximates the Iranian understanding of international relations', as Ibrahim Arafat put it. The writer of these words addressed the subject of 'Islamic solidarity and the ability to establish a regional order in the Islamic world' for the benefit of the Seminar on the Islamic World and the Future, held in Cairo during October 1991. He published it in his book *The Future through a Pious Muslim's Eyes*; then he broached the subject at the beginning of 1992 in an article on 'A Regional Order for Our Area', which was included in his book *Prosperity, Not Oppression*. He finds that the best conclusion to that study is what was brought out in the article, and so we present it below, with the reader's indulgence, word for word.

Annex

A Regional Order for Our Area

We are in the first days of the year 1992 CE. The moment prompts Arab opinion to reflect and yearn over the future, to determine the most important issues still in abeyance for the present and future of this nation, which our political thought should consider, then arrange according to priority and then develop a future perspective on and propose ideas for their treatment.

This reflection and yearning stage abruptly ended when it became evident that several issues were competing for first place. I found the most urgent of these to be the issue of establishing a 'regional order for our area'.

I asked myself: Why is this issue urgent today? And how do we address it, given the existence of a 'League of Arab States' as a regional Arab order and the existence of the 'Islamic Conference Organization' as a regional order for the Islamic world.

The first thing that comes to mind, in urgent justification of this issue today, is that all states of the region, including the Arab and Islamic dominions, will be confronting it in the 'multilateral negotiations' not long from now, within the 'settlement conference' relating to the Arab–Zionist conference. These negotiations, according to those who have adopted the decision of the conference, must focus on the region's various issues, such as 'arms limitation, regional security, water, refugee affairs, the environment, economic development and other topics of joint concern', as brought out in the letters of invitation by Presidents Bush and Gorbachev to attend the conference in October 1991. It is clear that all these issues fall within a 'regional order for our area'. And surely we Arabs have our own views on these and on the subject as a whole.

Another reason for the urgency of this issue follows from who the caller is for these negotiations. The US, in its bid to establish what President Bush called a 'new world order', claims to seek to defuse 'regional trouble spots' and 'end conflicts' resulting from them and to organize 'regional orders' that accord with its perception of that new world order.

Thus we, the Arabs, find ourselves before an 'international process' aimed at drawing up our region from ideas developed by the US with its Western allies, with 'Western Jewry' playing a special part in that development. One can assume, then, that this process will give first priority to 'Israeli security' and opportunity to the 'Zionist entity' in the region. The worst is yet to come for us, unless we respond with ideas of our own regarding the regional order for our area.

This US–Western desire to arrange our area coincides with a trend to arrange other parts of our world, between whose peoples and ours are ties and connections linked by joint interests, such as black Africa, which did not enter the dominion of Arab Islamic civilization, the states of Eastern Europe, and the states of Southeast Asia. What is required is that our political thought yields a vision of the ties that may be established between the regional order in our area and the regional orders in those areas, within the framework of 'cooperation' called for by the spirit of our civilization, and not from the standpoint of 'conflict'. This is a third reason for the urgency of the issue.

It is clear today, after the two earthquakes in eastern Europe and the Gulf, that the prevailing view of political thinkers and political scientists in our world, especially in the US, regarding collective security within a world order framework, is that this order should rest on firm 'regional orders' that achieve solutions for regional disputes and formulas for cooperation. This conviction is tied up with a new stage that the United Nations has entered after 18 months of changes, between the fall of 1989 and spring of 1991. It is a stage different from the preceding four decades. The Academy of the Kingdom of Morocco was the first to examine this stage in its seminars on 'The United Nations after the Gulf War', held in Casablanca in April 1991. The conviction also takes into consideration the potential threats arising from disputes within the US and the other powers over intervention in the internal affairs of other states–the temptation of the 'arrogance of power' so often talked about by the late US Senator J. William Fulbright in his famous book, though under different names and excuses. The latest seminar by the Academy of the Kingdom of Morocco, on 'The Principle of Intervention: Does It Give a New Legitimacy to Imperialism?', held in Rabat in October 1991, revealed the magnitude of these dangers. We draw here for evidence on the clarifications of Charles William Mainz, the editor-in-chief of *Foreign Policy* magazine: 'The UN will not ultimately become a policeman, irrespective of the consequences of the Gulf crisis. What needs to be obtained over the long run, then, is a solution at the regional level'.[8] Mainz expected that the US, as a great power, and other great powers would be aware in future of the 'high costs of intervention, in spilt blood and money down the drain first and foremost. The world order must rest, then, on something greater than the shoulders of US military might. Those who bank on something else cannot expect the US to exhaust itself to the same degree in a subsequent crisis.'

We draw also on what Shahram Chubin said in *Survival* magazine: 'It has become a commonplace that regional constructs must themselves be the cornerstones for building security in all parts of the world. This reflects in part the political and logistical difficulties in intervention and its costs. The same for the popular view that regional arrangements are a legitimate reflection of local policies. It is usually held that such associations reflect the spirit of the areas, and build accord in opinion and contribute to general security.'[9] Thus we find ourselves with a fourth reason for the urgency of the 'regional order for our area'; we are responsible for this area, and whoever is under the illusion that others will bear this responsibility for us is wrong.

When we consider how to address this vital issue we must examine several matters involving the following:

1. That the time is appropriate today, following the two earthquakes, to proceed with addressing these matters. There is a sense of need for this regional order for ourselves, and for others. This was said frankly during the Gulf crisis when a regional solution to the crisis was contemplated. It was confirmed then that suffering exists because of the non-existence of an effective regional order.

2. There is no complete understanding as yet of what this regional order should rest on, for the US and its Western allies, if on anything. The West, which put its house in order by the Treaty of Paris at the end of 1991, still has thoughts about how other houses in our world should look. One example here is the proposal in Western circles to establish a 'Gulf security order', where we note a certain perplexity in determining the dominion of that order and its place in its region, besides the contra-

dictions within the elements proposed.

3. The US and UK announced early in 1991 that 'there is a need for a kind of structure for regional security in the Gulf that Western states should support, if asked to do so; the situation calls for establishing an order for arms limitation, economic assistance within the region should have a role, and the Arab–Israeli problem should be resisted with renewed vigour'. The UK affirmed, reluctantly, that 'the idea of security should develop from the region and not be imposed on it from the outside'. Shahram Shubin noted, while presenting these elements, that 'the West needs to concentrate on the causes of possible instability, and acknowledge that the influences of outside forces on it is limited'.

4. The third matter is that we, the people of the area, have not developed a vision of this regional order, even if some ideas on it have been circulated. Some of the ideas circulating in official circles are in the Damascus declaration and some in the latest GCC summit's communique on Gulf security. A number of books have been published on Arab political thought that also include ideas circulating in unofficial circles. What we wish to affirm here is that we can come up with such a vision. Over the past four decades, broad lines have been drawn, and had they been adopted, we would have averted the horrors that befell us. But the problem has always been the absence of a cohesive mechanism linking political thought and decision-making. Yet how much we remain in need of a cure to this malady!

The first step to take in addressing this vital issue, after a consideration of the above three points, is to determine the dominion of the 'region' in which the order will be established, according to agreed upon criteria, and thus to determine the angle of vision. The difficulty here is the diversity of dominions of loyalty from which to begin the treatment. Is a 'region' a number of countries which adopt a common interest, or is it the dominion of the entire nation? Or is it a dominion of wider civilizational activity? We have seen the West rely, in the Treaty of Paris, on this latter dominion, to reach a 'Western order' where eastern Europe joined western Europe, Canada and the US. There is a big difference between adopting this comprehensive dominion and the economy that rested on a partial dominion within it, incorporating 'Western laissez-faire capitalism', which carried the name of the West, in contradistinction to an east 'western Europe' in its midst that carried a different doctrine, until the quake that shook it to its foundations.

We never tired of affirming, for three decades, that what determines our region is an active cultural belonging to an Arab Islamic civilization, built by Arabs, Muslims and Christians, with the help of other nations and creeds. This affirmation implies a tacit warning against making the mistake Europe did when it embraced the dominion of the nation, rendering it a reason for conflict between nations, especially as this form imposed on us during colonialist domination also served to fragment the dominion of the single nation into smaller country dominions, each with its own national identity. How misled were those who sought to achieve security for themselves by falling hostage to this smaller country dominion or by pursuing expansionism. How often have we borne witness to the words of Arnold Toynbee on this subject, when he explained the disastrous consequences of the Western model in Europe itself, 'and how nevertheless it is as nothing compared to the havoc reeked by this same principle when it emerged in other countries'. We recall what he advocated in his study of history, when he rendered 'civilization' as the unit of the study. It is noteworthy that schools of thought in the West have witnessed a return to adopting this dominion, after having concentrated for a time on 'the global world dominion' as a 'global village'. We drew on a study written recently on 'the intellectual unit', based on the study by Michael Vlabos, 'Culture and Foreign Policy', where it is argued that 'the greater truth for international tribes is their cultural area, not global village', cultural area being the dominion of civilized activity. The author concludes his research by saying that 'the sense of self among peoples is formed basically at the level of the cultural area and not the community or national dominion'.[10]

Ignoring this dominion of civilized activity in the quest to establish a regional order results in disastrous consequences. We have seen how this omission in a phase of modern history led to a conflict between us and our brethren, who represent the depth of our Arab nation, until we and they fell into the trap of 'response'. Residues of this continue to appear in theoretical political studies, making the 'conflict' that occurred the basis of research instead of 'cooperation' as that basis and starting point. We have repeatedly warned of the need to be rid of these residues. Another disastrous consequence of studying a partial dominion apart from the wider civilizational dominion is the slip into arbitrariness when dealing with the reality. An example of this can be seen in Western studies on 'Gulf security', which try unsuccessfully to override the fact of location in dealing with this state or that.

When we adopt the 'civilized activity dominion' as a basis for designating our angle of vision to address the issues, this does not mean that we ignore the existence of dominions within it whose basis is loyalty to a direct interest or party or nation. It is possible for the 'regional civilization order' to have branches within it. We have seen how the 'eighties witnessed, at their start and end, the emergence of secondary orders within the Arab order.

The other step in the treatment of this vital issue, after determining the dominion of the area, is confronting the fact that a colonialist settler entity occupies a central position in it. It is one of two Western colonial settlements that have remained from the old world; the other is the apartheid regime of South Africa. The implantation by the West of a Zionist racialist entity in the heart of Palestine, the heart of the Arab nation and Islamic world, created a conflict that, as soon as it subsides, erupts anew. This conflict, says Charles Mainz, has its influential international side, and it is sufficient for us to note that this international dimension is what made the West arm the entity with nuclear weapons, exactly as it did with its counterpart in South Africa, thus confronting the West with bids by the countries of the region to own nuclear weapons. It is clear that the West sought, since the emergence of the Zionist entity, to place it in a special position within the regional order of the area drawn up according to its present interests. It is, today, mindful of this capacity even more than at any time in the past, and is prepared for it through 'multilateral negotiations'. So how shall we deal with this new development?

There is no alternative to the matter of principle whose core is that a colonialist settler base in the region cannot be part of its regional order. Even if this were to be imposed by force, its permanence is doubtful, because this base will always be drawn to its own benefactors and their regional order; there are historical precedents dominating the ties connected with its existence, the connection between it and its founder, and between them both and the people victimized by it and the region that has been victimized as well.

A regional order for our area, in view of the above, is indeed a vital and urgent issue. It warrants our full attention during this period. If only the secretariats of the Arab League and Islamic Conference Organization could have formed a 'think tank' comprised of the cream of our intellectuals in the Arab and Islamic dominions, so that each could formulate a working paper on either and discuss them in a joint meeting to formulate ideas and a vision, for discussion and then endorsement by all those concerned.

Notes

* Chairman, Chief Council for Education, Culture and Sciences, Heliopolis, Cairo, Egypt.

1. Abdel Mon'im al-Mashshat, 'Arab National Security: There is Still a Chance', *The Middle East*, 36 (December 1994).
2. Michel Jobert *et al.* 'After Desert Storm: A Global View for the Future of the Middle East', preface by Ibrahim Nafe', Cairo: Al-Ahram Centre for Translation and Publishing, 1992.
3. Anthony Lake, 'Confronting Backlash States', *Foreign Affairs*, 73:2 (March–April 1994).
4. Hooshang Amirahmadi, 'Iran and the Islamic Threat: The New Israeli

Approach', *Mediterranean Affairs*, 34 (October 1994).

5. *Confronting Zionism*, translated by Khadr Nureddine and Rifaat Seyyed Ahmad.

6. The Holy Qur'an, *Surat Al-i-Umran, ayah* 54.

7. Mohammad El-Sayed Selim, 'Interaction in a 'Power Triangle' Intellectual and Institutional Framework', paper presented to the Seminar for Integrative Tripartite Dialogue between the Arabs, Iran and Turkey, *Mediterranean Affairs*, 33 (September 1994).

8. Charles Mainz, 'Dateline Washington: A Necessary War?', *Foreign Policy*, no. 82 (Spring 1991).

9. *Survival*, 33:2 (Spring 1991).

10. Michael Vlabos, 'Culture and Foreign Policy', *Foreign Policy*, no. 82 (Spring 1991).

19

The Palestine Question in Arab–Iranian Relations

It is a pleasure for me to take up, in this paper, an issue which, more than any other, has been of great concern for politicians in the aftermath of World War II. It has also caused some of the major developments in the Middle East, making this region the focus of attention for international politicians for over five decades. I am referring, of course, to the Palestinian issue, which is the main bone of contention in the Middle East.

As the title indicates, the focus is on one aspect of the Palestinian issue: the link between the Palestinian issue on the one hand, and the relationship between the Arabs and Iran on the other, and its repercussions on these relations. I tried, as best as I can, to find the similarities and dissimilarities between the way with which both Arabs and Iranians dealt with the Palestinian issue. I thought that I would, at the end of the day, be able to show to the world that the similarities are far greater than the dissimilarities. This finding will reinforce our hope that a better future awaits us; yes, a future where any issue similar to the Palestinian issue will unite the Islamic *ummah* (nation) so as to protect its rights and defend its interests.

Where Does the Palestinian Issue Stand in the Arab World?

When talking about the importance of the Palestinian issue in the Arab world, I thought it would be good to divide the repercussions of this issue into 'positive' and 'negative'. In this endeavour, I will rely on my analysis and on direct experience.

Positive Repercussions

(a) Unity of the Arabs

Arab unity and the slogan 'a united Arab *ummah* with an eternal mission from the Atlantic Ocean to the Persian Gulf', were rousing slogans for

many decades in the 20th century. This unity was the core of most liberation movements in the Arab world in the not too distant past. Moreover,
the Arabs relied on this very unity to confront local nationalist tendencies,
such as the Copts in Egypt, Syrian nationalism in Damascus. However, the
story does not end there. Many people voiced their desire to establish a big
federal Arab country comprising the whole Arab world. This very idea was
proposed during the conference held in Beirut in the 1980s[1] under the title:
'The Future of the Arab *Ummah*'.

The Palestinian issue has always been the backbone of the case for unity.
A number of those advocating unity said in this regard: 'The call for unity
and Nasserism is due to the loathing of the defeated regimes. This call
raised the awareness of people without stopping at national borders'.[2]

While the Arab League is a symbol of Arab unity, it has been concerned
with the Palestinian issue more than any other issue since the occupation of
Palestine, which coincided with the birth of the Arab League. For instance,
in its meeting held on 14 December 1947, the Council approved 17 resolutions, 11 of which were about the Palestinian issue.[3] Since its founding, the
Arab League has made it its duty to discuss the Palestinian issue in international fora.

As the years went by, the Palestinian issue became ingrained in the conscience of the Arab *ummah*, especially following the 1967 setback. 'Following
1967, the Palestinian issue, along with the Palestinian struggle and the com-
mandos, became the focus of attention and a source of hope; they became a
means of communication between countries; thus, Arabism was equated
with the Palestinian issue; the issue became the glue that held the Arabs
together; its success meant they had succeeded, its failure meant they had
failed'.[4]

(b) Correcting the Concept of Arab Nationalism

Much ink has flowed on the issue of Arab nationalism. Some people believe it to be a racist movement, advocating the superiority of the Arabs. In
that case, Arab nationalism is contradictory to Islam and the Qur'an. As
you know, Islam rejects any racial discrimination and grants superiority to
the most pious: 'Verily the most honoured of you in the sight of God is [he
who is] the most righteous of you'.[5] Others said that Arab nationalism is
only a reaction to the Ottoman Empire, which ruled the Arab world until
World War I. In this case, once again, Arab nationalism is contradictory to
Islam.

Although Arab nationalism has a European flavour, since it was imported from Europe, it remains different in that it is not secular, whereas
European nationalism is a secular nationalism par excellence, since it calls

for the separation of state and religion.[6] Arab nationalism does not advocate the elimination of Islam in Arab societies, because it is well aware that Islam is etched in the conscience of the Arabs. Hence, we notice that those who advocate Arab nationalism consider Islam to be a capital element in the formation of the Arab identity as well as Arab nationalism. This is, indeed, the positive element of Arab nationalism, in the view of non-Arab Muslim communities. This very idea refutes the allegations that Arab nationalism was created to confront the Ottoman Empire and Caliphs.

It is obvious that the confrontation was between the Ottomans and the Arabs, not between Arabism and Islam. Turning to the real causes behind the emergence of Arab nationalism, we see that the 'will to fight off the colonial powers was the backbone of Arab nationalism'. Furthermore, the increasing Zionist pressure in Palestine reinforced nationalist feelings in the Arab world'.[7] Muslims of non-Arab groups are more than ready to embrace Arab nationalism, because it is a move in the right direction; i.e., to help the Palestinian cause, since it concerns all Muslims. So, when we say that the Palestinian cause has reinforced nationalist feelings in Arab communities, one should consider these words – which are true and tangible – as a correction to the concept of Arab nationalism. The credit, in this respect, goes to the Palestinian cause itself.

(c) Maturing the National Goals of Arab Countries

Since the occupation of Palestine in 1948, the Palestinian cause has inflamed the feelings of the Arabs. The citizens of the Arab world have been seeing first-hand the shortcomings of the colonial powers' rule, such as their refusal to recognize the rights of the Arabs in Palestine, seeking to divide the Arab world through the creation of a foreign entity on Palestinian soil. All of these factors have outraged the Arab citizen. They have also incited every Arab citizen, whether in the Arabian Peninsula or North Africa, to seek freedom and aspire for independence. So, as you can see, anti-colonial feeling had a positive effect, in that it fueled the flames of independence. The results were fabulous, since most Arab countries succeeded in achieving independence in the fifties and sixties. One should not forget that the rallying around the Palestinians had some positive results on every Arab country, because 'in today's world, neither security nor independence can be achieved in countries lacking elements conducive to progress.'[8]

Some Arab thinkers consider the Palestinian cause to be the pillar of the pan-Arab movement in Egypt; indeed, the Palestinian issue drew the attention of the Egyptians even before Egypt was threatened by Zionism.[9]

In that respect, Dr Anis Sayegh says: 'The Palestinian cause played a major role in the elaboration and development of Arabism in Egypt.'[10]

(d) Bestowing Legitimacy on Arab Regimes

Every regime must rely on its people so as to be able to resist, if threatened by outside powers or forces. This popular support must be tangible, even if those in power are not elected. Indeed, every regime tries to woo its subjects by advocating what the people advocate and by taking interest in matters deemed by the people to be of utmost importance. The Palestinian issue is indeed one of those issues. A number of Arab authors have said that 'the legitimacy of Arab regimes stems from their commitment to defend the issues of interest to the Arab communities. Prominent among those issues is the Palestinian one'.

As the years passed, we have been hearing slogans and resounding songs pledging loyalty and love for Palestine. However, these were meant, in reality, to distract people and to dispel the idea that the Arab regimes are not doing enough and that they are squandering the holiest cause in the Arab world, this century. Some Arab regimes, which sided with the Palestinians, have gained popularity overseas, in other Arab countries, and at times, their popularity exceeded that enjoyed by national regimes. This is a clear testimonial to the legitimacy bestowed by the Palestinian cause on the Arab regimes.

Negative Repercussions

Those were the four positive results stemming from the Palestinian issue. However, as I stated at the beginning, there were negative ones as well. These are:

(a) Divisions in the Arab World

Undoubtedly, the occupation of Palestine was a premeditated plot containing all the elements of conspiracy, a conspiracy not only directed at the Palestinian people but also at the Arabs and the Muslims. A quick glance at the map shows how important Palestine is. You can also see that, with Palestine occupied, the link between east, west, north and south is severed. Now there is a foreign element at the doorstep of many Arab countries. This foreign element not only threatens the borders of those countries, but aspires to relocate Jewish communities to them. The associated regional developments were not coincidental; they were the result of studies conducted by the colonial powers that ruled the world at that time. These studies span a century, from 1850 until 1950. The solutions that were given were the following: either give the Jews in the 'diaspora' a home in Latin America (Argentina, for instance) or in Uganda in Africa. However, the colonial powers chose, at the end of the day, Palestine, because the location of Palestine is of utmost importance, very sensitive, very dangerous, both economically and politically. It is very well known how important the Middle East is. Is it not enough that the region contains about 70 per cent of the world's reserves of oil?[11]

The occupation of Palestine left the region of the Middle East hanging by a thread, awash with events and developments, some of which affected inter-Arab relations. Accusations of betrayal, due to the wasting away of the cause or neglecting it, became the hallmark of inter-Arab relations. This created divisions in the Arab world, not only geographical – because of the occupation of Palestine – but political as well. The Palestinian cause has divided the Arab world into blocks and groups, some progressive and others reactionary. The positions of the various groups collided at times, while at other times they maintained a truce; so much so that the most radical countries were the most competitive and aggressive.[12]

(b) Increased Antagonism between Arab Governments

When the plot to divide Palestine was hatched, according to a United Nations resolution (no. 181) adopted by the General Assembly on 29 November 1947, the Arab world of seven independent countries then (Egypt, Yemen, Saudi Arabia, Jordan, Iraq, Syria and Lebanon) was the scene of cutthroat competition, even outright enmity between the seven countries.

The inter-Arab war had already started in 1943, when Nuri Said proposed in his book the unification of Syria, Lebanon, Jordan and Iraq. The English Commissioner got hold of the book. The proposal caused a storm of protest in Egypt and Saudi Arabia. There was, as well, disagreement on the establishment of the Arab League,[13] on whether to name it 'The Arab League' or 'The League of Arab States'. Was the League to represent the people and unite them, or was it a league of Arab governments?

In addition to that, Egypt was trying to hold the reins of initiative in the Arab world. Nuri Said was pursuing the same aim with the support of Britain. On the other side, family disputes between royal families in the Arabian Peninsula, Iraq, Jordan and Syria, were adding fuel to the fire already raging between them.[14]

The competition became even fiercer with the founding of blocks. Following the fall of Palestine, rivalry turned into enmity. This deeply-rooted enmity soon degenerated into fighting, with the Arabs destroying each other. Let us not forget what occurred in Yemen in the 1960s, and what befell the Palestinians in Jordan and Lebanon afterwards.

A number of Arab thinkers said that 'the disappointment following the loss of Palestine and the helplessness of the Arab world as of 1948 undermined the Arab region. Furthermore, old enmities reared their ugly head again, pitting one country against another, sometimes even one leader against another. Thus, the Middle East drifted into a cycle of military coup d'etat, political assassination, plots and skirmishes. New regimes came to power chanting revolutionary slogans. Various opposing ideologies surfaced along with new leaderships. Some countries sided with one block against the other, during the Cold War that pitted the US against the former Soviet Union. Then came the Baghdad pact alliance, which was brought down by Nasser.[15]

So, the Palestine issue was present in the minds of the people and affected the situation as a whole in the Arab world. It became an element of discord and enmity among Arab states. However, the blame does not lie on the Palestinians, because they did not cause this tension; rather, the tension was prevalent in spite of them. In all fairness, it could be said that the Palestinians were among the victims.

(c) The Arab World Lagged Behind

The 50-year-old struggle and ongoing war between the Israelis and the Arabs affected Arab societies deeply. The war and the Palestinian issue were used as the pretext for every adverse result stemming from this conflict. For example, the Palestinian issue was blamed for the stagnation of social and economic development in the Arab world, or at least in the countries directly concerned by the conflict.

Some Arab thinkers said: 'For a long time, Arab unity has been a scapegoat for many Arab regimes, which failed to achieve security, development and stability for their peoples; these regimes sought to hide their own failure by blaming it on the pro-unity regional movements'.[16] In fact, the Palestinian issue was the excuse given for every failure and backwardness plaguing the Arab world, even the development of the idea of democracy. Indeed, the successive wars impeded the advancement of democracy in many Arab countries. Here one should note the bitter fact that the industrially and economically advanced states, which held the reins of world economic development and called the shots, stood for the most part on the side of the Zionist entity. Hence the lack of serious cooperation with most of the Arab countries and the denial of prerequisites for economic advancement and progress.

Once again the Palestinian issue is presented as though it is a factor of backwardness in the Arab world. But it is not, of course, to blame for this sorry situation; rather, as I said before, it is its victim.

The Place of the Palestinian Cause in Iran

In order to do justice to this issue , one should divide it into two parts: before and after the Islamic revolution that triumphed on 11 February 1979.

Before the Revolution

Before the Islamic revolution in Iran, the people and the government held diametrically opposed views. The Iranian people were one hundred per cent behind the Palestinians, because they were confident that the Palestinians were within their rights. They also believed that it was their duty to rally to the defence of Muslims under attack by non-Muslim forces. The government, however, pursued a wholly different line, a policy in line with the West. We all know that the regime headed by the Shah was one of the main regimes giving the West a foothold in the region, with a strategic importance at the height of the Cold War comparable to that of the Zionist entity. Needless to say, the Zionist entity was the counter-weight to the Arab states during the Cold War.

The Iranian people were totally opposed to this policy pursued by the government. Indeed, the monarchy was out of touch with its people, so much so that it collapsed under the weight of the revolution, which adopted the slogan of liberation of Palestine and Jerusalem even before it triumphed. The Iranian people have been repeating what Imam Khomeini said: 'Today we liberate Iran; tomorrow, we will liberate Palestine.'

The uprising that took place in Iran in the year 1342 (5 June 1963) resulted in the death of thousands of people and the deportation of Imam Khomeini to Turkey, from where he went to Najaf. This uprising was an angry reaction to the regime, which was cooperating with Israel. The cooperation of the Iranian government with Israel went against the wishes of the Iranian people and the public interest. Indeed, the Iranian people were baffled by government support for a foreign entity occupying an Islamic territory.

Iranians remember the various attempts that were made before the revolution to normalize relations with Israel, to no avail. These attempts were met with outrage and wrath. When an Israeli football team was invited to play a match in Iran, people took to the streets and riot police were called in to disperse the crowds. Given the Iranians' strong rejection of normalization of relations, the monarchy had no alternative but to keep its relations with Israel secret.

So, as you can see, even before the revolution, the Palestinian issue was ever present in the conscience of the Iranian people. The position of the government, however, was to yield to foreign will. Thus, the government kept its relations with Israel in the dark, fearful of the wrath of the people.

At times, the monarchy tried to woo a number of Arab regimes, in order to defuse the anger of the Iranian people, which rejected its policy.

The Islamic Revolution and the Palestinian Issue

Revolutionary Islamic Iran always believed that the Palestinian cause was a just one. It realized, long before its triumph, the injustice done to the Palestinian people, and it appreciated the danger posed by the Zionist onslaught. Thus, following the triumph of the Islamic revolution, defending Palestine became a priority for Iran. One of the first decisions taken by the revolutionary government, was to replace the Israeli Embassy with a Palestinian one.

When relations were severed with Israel, some analysts said: 'It is the first political measure to resound in the region. The former regime used to supply Israel with 60 per cent of its oil needs. In fact, the Zionists, along with the Shah, spearheaded anti-Soviet policy in the Middle East.'[17]

However, a number of Palestinians failed to understand the position advocated by the Iranian revolution. The Iraq–Iran war unveiled a bitter and sorry situation: nationalist, racist considerations were given priority at the expense of Islamic ideals. For Islamic considerations do not stop at national borders; they include Muslims wherever they are. Many Iranians were thus frustrated, but they kept their frustration in check. Indeed, it did not undermine the convictions of the Iranian Muslim people that the Palestinian cause was a just one, and so should be defended. Palestine was an Islamic territory that had been occupied and subjected to aggression. Finally, needless to say, the Palestinian issue was of utmost importance to the Islamic *ummah* as a whole.

Following the triumph of the Islamic revolution, people and government began seeing eye to eye on the Palestinian issue, which was not the case before. With that in mind, and mindful that the Palestinian issue was a matter of principle for the whole of the Islamic *ummah*, Iran took a decisive stand about the conflict and the solutions being proposed and attempts being made to solve it. The Iranian stand was based on the following: 'There will be no debating of the basics'. While the Iranian government supported any discussion of the details, it opposed any debate on the core of the matter or the principles. Among the principles was the need to repel the enemy from the Islamic holy land, redress the injuries and establish what was right.

So, the Iranian position on this issue was to oppose any proposal in conflict with these principles. However, a clarification is in order here: Iran did not reject any attempt to achieve true peace, but it did reject any act of surrender, of giving in. After assessing the latest developments, Iran held that the peace being proposed was not a true peace, one that would redress the injuries and safeguard the dignity of the Islamic *ummah*, which must also be secured.

Imperialist powers have been seeking, through massive propaganda campaigns, to confront the Muslims. Not only did they occupy their land and plunder their wealth, but they also portrayed the Muslims as terrorists, though these powers were responsible for organized terrorist acts throughout the world. These same powers are still trying to mislead public opinion by portraying Islam and what they call 'Islamic fundamentalism and extremism' as the real threat to the West, after the fall of Communism.

But these fabricated lies are only an attempt to harm the Muslims wherever they are, and force them to accept unjust solutions. Moreover, these same powers are doing their utmost to drive a wedge between Arab and Islamic countries. By doing so, they will make sure that these countries will become isolated and outraged. Every country will see no point whatsoever of establishing relations with its neighbours. Let me remind you of what an American university professor said about the situation in North Africa in 1955. He spoke about a possible Libyan or Algerian occupation of northern Tunisia and referred to the dangerous situation this could entail. Northern Tunisia is close to southern Europe. So the professor thought that American troops must remain in the region to prevent Libya and Algeria from occupying northern Tunisia – to protect Europe, not Tunisia. This was only a pretext to justify the continued presence of a huge fleet in the region and air bases in Europe.

Such scenarios are common in the West because the West only thinks of safeguarding its own interests, sparing no effort to secure them. The huge Middle East market is but another scenario. The aim is to plunder Arab wealth – or what is left of it – following the disastrous Kuwait episode. Another aim is to marginalize Egypt, even though Egypt was the first country to sign a peace accord with Israel, when Sadat visited occupied Palestine on 19 November 1977.

Palestine Unites the Arabs and the Iranians

The Palestinian issue began as a national issue, then, over the last two decades, it has turned into a cause close to the hearts of all Muslims, wherever they are. The spirit of *jihad* or 'struggle' became more ingrained, and the dedication to this just cause, more potent. The Palestinian issue became an Islamic issue, and all Muslims, be they Arab or not, rushed to its defence. As you can see, the Palestinian issue has become an element of unity, bringing together the whole Islamic community. Therefore, it goes without saying that it brought the Arabs and Iranians together, since they are Muslims. I present the following arguments to support this thesis:

1. The Arabs considered the Palestinian issue as a national issue, while the Muslims have given it priority. Indeed, no one will ever condone the occupation of Palestine. But when the reason is one and the vision is one, all parties concerned belong to the same camp.
2. Iranians, along with the Arabs and Muslims in general, face the same dangers. A quick glance at the situation around the world shows that the threat posed by Zionism and its guardians is great. Consider, for instance, the massive propaganda campaign launched against the Islamic Republic of Iran, and the accusations concerning our alleged attempt to acquire nuclear weapons. Moreover, we have been threatened on several occasions, and have heard plenty of talk about bombing our nuclear facilities, which are earmarked for peaceful ends. These threats were levelled in the past against Pakistan, along with allegations that Islamic countries were a threat to the Zionist entity and its hegemony over Palestine. Moreover, the pressure being brought to bear on Egypt as regards the nuclear non-proliferation treaty is only one link in the chain of dangers hanging over the Arab and Islamic peoples.
3. The 'singular target': What is meant by this expression is that all Arab and Islamic countries are targeted by Western powers, which are plundering the region. For instance, Iran is accused of terrorism and the development of nuclear weapons. It is, furthermore, threatened for one simple reason: to dissuade it from opposing the unjust solution the West wants to impose on the Palestinians. On the other hand, the West threatens to withhold or reduce any financial aid to Egypt. They even discuss imposing sanctions on Egypt and forcing it to give up its share of the Nile, only because Egypt insists that the Zionist entity sign the Nuclear Non-proliferation Treaty, if Arab countries are to sign it.
4. The imperialist powers are not only targeting Iran and the Arabs directly. They are also trying to undermine Arab–Iranian relations, by exploiting the issue of Palestine. They are using the so-called peace process to strain these relations. To this end, they portray Iran as the main impediment to the so-called peace process. The plan is to alienate the Arabs from Iran, the true Muslim country.

Indeed, the same scenario occurred eight years ago (1980–88), during the war that was imposed on Iran.

Conclusion

I conclude with the following observations:

1. The Palestinian cause concerns the Arabs as much as the Muslims. Hence, it concerns all Muslims who refuse to forfeit Islamic land and rights.
2. The Palestinian issue can bring the Arabs together, as well as Arabs and Muslims.
3. Peace should not entail a surrender and submission to a de facto situation.
4. The Muslims have not used their full potential to find a fair solution to the Palestinian issue.
5. The same perils arising from the occupation of Palestine threaten Arab countries, Iran and other Islamic countries. These countries, therefore, should unit. Unity will allow them to safeguard their national and regional security and will allow them, as well, to defend the holiest symbols of principles and values, among the most prominent of which are Palestine and Jerusalem.

Notes

* Institute of Political Studies, Tehran, Iran.

1.   Khair El-Din Haseeb et al., *The Future of the Islamic Ummah: The Challenges, The Alternatives: Final Report of the Future Prospects of the Arab Nation Project*, project on 'The Future Prospects of the Arab Nation', the final report, (Beirut: Centre for Arab Unity Studies, 1988), p. 43.
2.   Ghassan Tweini, *A Second Reading of Arab Nationalism*, (Beirut: Nahar Publishing House, 1991), p. 17.
3.   Hasan Nafi'ah, 'The Political Role of the Arab League in the Independence of Some Arab Countries and in the Palestine Question', paper submitted to the 'Seminar on the Arab League: The Reality and the Ambition', (Beirut: Centre for Arab Unity Studies, 1992), p. 143.
4.   Tweini, op. cit., p. 18.
5.   The Holy Qur'an, *Surat al-Hujurat, ayah* 13.
6.   Majid Khadduri, *Political Trends in the Arab World: The Role of Ideas and High Ideals in Politics*, (Beirut: United Publishing House, 1985), p. 187.
7.   Fahmia Sharafeddine, *Arab Socialism: Limits, Dimensions, Philosophical Background*, (Beirut: Arab Development Institute, 1987), p. 35.
8.   Ali El-Din Hilal, *'Arab League Charter'*, paper submitted to the Arab League, in: *Reality and Ambition*, op. cit., pp. 77-92.
9.   Muhammad El Arabi Moussa, *History of Egypt*, (Beirut: Arab Publishing Institute, 1982), p. 236.
10.   Anis Sayegh, *The Idea of Arab Nationalism in Egypt*, (Beirut: Heikal Ghareeb, 1959), p. 239.

11.   Bishara Khidr, 'The Arab Republican System: Geo-political Realities', in: *The Fire of the Gulf and the Arab System*, (Tunis: International Studies Association, 1992), p. 72.

12.   Marwan bin Al-Arabi, 'Thoughts on the Arab System Across Half a Century', in: ibid., p. 45.

13.   Abdel Hamid Al-Muwafi, 'The Founding of the Arab League', *Arab Affairs*, no. 1 (March 1981), p. 10.

14.   Barry Rubin, *The Arab States and the Palestine Conflict*, (Syracuse, N.Y.: Syracuse University Press, 1981), p. 151.

15.   Marwan bin Al-Arabi, 'Thoughts on the Arab System Across Half a Century', op. cit., pp. 44–5.

16.   Abdel Ilah Balqaziz, 'Who Will Rescue Arab Regional Unions?', *Ash-Shurouq*, 18 February 1993, p. 28.

17.   Rouhollah Ramazani, *Revolutionary Iran*, (Baltimore, Md.: Johns Hopkins University Press, 1986), pp. 148 and 152.

Ten

Comparative Study of Civil Society in Iran and the Arab Union

20

Arabs and Iran: State, Islam and Civil Society

RIDWAN EL-SAYYED*

Governance and religion are inseparable twins; one cannot survive without the other, because religion is the cornerstone of governance and governance is the guardian of religion. However, a religious and a secular king cannot possibly rule over one kingdom. Indeed, the religious king will have the upper hand, because religion is the basis and governance is a pillar, and the basis has precedence over the pillar.

'The Era of Ardashir', researched and presented by Ihsan Abbas, (Beirut: Sader Publishing House, 1967), pp. 53–4.

When the religious charisma is more potent than the political regime, it tries to subdue it or even control it. Since the state itself pretends to have its own charisma, then the religious party may consider it as devilish.

Max Weber, 'Economy and Society', (Berkeley, Calif.: University of California Press, 1978), vol. 3, p. 1163.

I

In a recently published article, a researcher of Iranian descent wrote:[1] Why were Iranians in a hurry to draft a constitution, publish it, and implement it a year after the 1979 Islamic revolution? Does an 'Islamic state' need a constitution? He gave the following answer: 'Undoubtedly, the constitution is not one of the priorities in the Islamic world and in particular, it is not one of the priorities of those who hold the view that the *Shari'ah* (Islamic Law) and the Qur'an are the constitution. Moreover, the word constitution does not have the same meaning in Iran as in the Western world. However, the Iranians, who were the first to have launched a revolution in Asia in 1906, advocating the establishment of a constitution, are obsessed by it and cannot conceive of life without a constitution, including Khomeini himself'.

Indeed, since the beginning of the 20th century, ever since the middle of

381

the 19th century, the concepts of constitution, law, reforms, regulations and the state have figured in the writings and the activities of the Islamic elite in the Islamic world.[2] Needless to say, the priorities differed according to the circumstances prevailing in each country. It is sufficient to mention the examples of Egypt, the Ottoman Empire, Tunisia, India and Syria here.

The elite in Iran focused in the last 95 years of the 19th century on the following: a strong national state, getting rid of Western influence, orderly and clean administration, constitutional rule and parliamentary democracy.[3] The elite discovered later on that, the first two goals (a strong national state and the elimination of foreign influence) cannot be achieved unless constitutional rule is implemented along with the establishment of a parliament. It might be important to wonder what is the background to the concept of the constitution. Do we mean by constitution what the Ottoman reformists meant about the constitution of 1876: the power of the people or its sovereignty, determining in the constitution the powers of the ruler, with the consultative council (*showra*), or the parliament as it had been called in the constitution of 1906, or 'The Two Delegates' as it was called in the Ottoman Empire, undertaking to monitor the operation of government, its implementation of the constitution and its running of the affairs of the state? One can deduce from the name of the Ottoman parliament ('The Two Delegates') that the concept of delegation of powers and representation was the basis of the power of people, its sovereignty[4] and its right to establish its power and monitor its implementation – this concept was clearer in the minds of Ottoman constitutional reformers than it was in the minds of the non-reformers. However, the goals were similar: to define the powers of the ruler, strip him of procedural and executive powers, and transfer these powers to the executive authority, which should be accountable to the parliament. Apart from that, any differences between the two as to distant motives and indirect goals can be ascribed to the different circumstances prevailing in Iran, in the Ottoman Empire, and in Egypt, which had been run by an accountable government before Iran and even before the Ottoman Empire.[5]

The Ottoman experience was originally an attempt to bring modernization. It began at the start of the 19th century, after a deterioration in the situation of the army following successive defeats at the hands of the European forces, and national movements that sprang up in the regions controlled by the Ottoman Empire. Infusing the army and the state with new blood and opening up to the modern European experiences, led to the emergence of a new bureaucracy and a new elite of officers, employees, merchants and cultivated people spread throughout the Ottoman Empire. Soon, this new elite wanted to play a part in political life and called for decentralization or outright independence. Therefore, the constitution and the parliament in the Ottoman Empire were a response to needs or demands that the

Empire could not do without: To preserve the unity of the Empire through equality of all before the law and participation of all peoples and communities living in the Ottoman Empire in the administration and parliament; and through granting the vilayets and surroundings a share in executive power, giving them acceptable effectiveness and freedom within the broad framework of the historical Ottoman entity.[6] Hence, Ottoman representation within 'The Two Delegates' was representation for communities and peoples within the compartments of the vilayets, legalized by the Vilayet Law of 1864, after the Humayuni line issued in 1856 had stipulated equality and comprehensive Ottoman citizenship.[7]

Iran did not face the problems faced by the political elite in the Ottoman Empire. Indeed, Iran was very similar to a national entity, as we understand it today. It is true that it was home to some minorities, such as the Turcomen, Kurds, Arabs, etc. But the majority were, and still are, Iranian and Shiite. The Russians and the British wielded great influence in the palace and at the borders. However, they were never a threat to the Iranian entity. On the contrary, the challenge they posed played a big part in strengthening national and patriotic sentiments among the elite.[8]

Moreover, the Iranian Shah Naser al-Din (1848–96) was corrupt and an extravagant spend thrift. This led to an increase in Iran's foreign debt and an increase in the influence wielded by foreign businessmen and European governments, as was the case in Egypt during the era of the Khedive Ismail. Therefore, the Iranian elite demanded the adoption of a constitution and the establishment of a parliament, so as to limit the powers of the Shah, define them and make financial reforms. The strong national state's main demand was to unify the scattered regions, eradicate tribal influence in the army and state, and to confront any Russian meddling in northern Iran. Hence, the issue of the constitution and the nation state in Iran were national issues, as was the case in Egypt on the eve of the Urabi revolution and the British occupation in 1882.[9]

The Iranians called their constitution *mashruteh*. Tahtawi first translated the French word *la Charte* as 'Carte or La Carta'. Indeed, the Iranian constitution was modeled on the Belgian, so it is probable that the two words have the same origin. However, the events that took place in 1905 and 1906 gave a new meaning to the word, the meaning of conditions or limits, in other words, to place conditions on the Shah and limit his powers. A number of researchers[10] said that the concept of the constitution was first greeted with a lot of enthusiasm, but later on gradually lost a lot of its appeal after it became obvious that outside pressure was behind it. However, this did not apply to the constitution of 1906 in Iran, nor to the constitution of 1923 in Egypt, and, strictly speaking, nor did it apply to the Ottoman constitution promulgated in 1876. However, the letters sent by the British Ambassador (Canning) to the British Foreign Office say otherwise regarding the 1856 Hamayuni Law and the decrees and regulations that preceded it.[11] But little credence is given to these allegations. In Iran, the situation was crystal clear. In the last quarter the 19th century, Iranian merchants, along with some employees and a number of intellectuals, founded secret associations like their counterparts in Istanbul and Egypt.[12] The influence wielded by the Baha'is and the Freemasons was blown out of proportion. Indeed, the assessment of the role played by these latter two groups is influenced by events that occurred towards the middle of the 20th century. The elite was constantly complaining about the foreign running of the customs administration (by the Belgian Naus), the disorderly army, the outrageous number of trips by the Shah, the huge debt he had incurred, and the injustices and measures taken by the governor of Tehran. The elite realized that it was possible to pressure the regime and to reap great benefits, as was the case during the 1880s with the monopoly on tobacco when the Shah was compelled to back down under the weight of religious pressure, Indeed, the clergy issued a *fatwah* (edict) prohibiting the use of tobacco.[13] On 26 April 1905 a number of merchants, clergymen and intellectuals decided to gather around the Shrine of Shah Abdol Azim, close to Tehran. They demanded that the Belgian director of the customs department and the governor of Tehran be removed. The Shah rejected their demand. For months, the situation remained unchanged, until mid-December 1905, when a larger number of people gathered around the shrine to protest, demanding, in addition to the removal of the Belgian director of customs, the establishment of a 'house of justice'. The Ottoman Ambassador to Tehran carried their message to the Shah, who agreed to their demand in January 1906 but did very little to implement it.

The protesters became bolder and increased in number, clamouring for a constitution or *mashruteh* This demand was drafted by the politician Sani al-Dawleh and the cultivated Yahya Dawlatabadi drafted the first demand regarding the council of justice and its panel. On 5 August 1906, the Shah agreed to the new demand and he issued a decree ordering his prime minister to establish a parliament (*Majles Showra-ye Melli*) with the following task: 'to discuss the matters deemed important to the Empire and to protect public interests'. The parliament was elected in Tehran; municipal and regional elections were also held. The parliament opened its first session in October 1906.[14]

The parliament was very active between 1906 and 1913. It issued a variety of annexes to the Constitution; it established regional panels with specific powers and who were, in part, popularly elected. It also founded the national police and reorganized the army. It made various attempts to reform the finances of the government. Moreover, it promulgated a law to organize land tenure. Thanks to popular support, it was able to foil the two attempts that were made by the Muhammad Ali Shah to regain power.

Finally, it defeated him militarily and forced him for leave to Russia.[15]

However, the main achievements of the constitutional era were: the establishment of an executive authority accountable to parliament and the promotion of parties. In 1907, two parties were formed whose founding members were members of the Consultative Council: the moderates and the democrats. The moderates represented some of the clergy and merchants, along with some aristocrats close to the palace. It is believed that the moderates were pro-Russian. The democrats were pro-British and they were a minority in the parliament; however, they were more efficient. They had in their ranks, journalists, writers and some members of the newly-formed middle class. They controlled most of the papers that were published in Tehran and in the region.

Their platform was very bold, consisting of eight points: separation of state and religion, compulsory military service, distribution of land to farmers, to limit the powers of the executive authority, the establishment of an agricultural credit bank, the imposition of indirect taxes rather than direct ones, and the elimination of the council of notables. The alliance between Britain and Russia during World War I brought the two parties together and infused the democrats with additional strength. However, the triumph of Britain at the end of the war, the emergence of the Soviet Union and temporary marginalization of Russia in Iran, caused a change in the map of parties in Iran; the Socialist (Marxist) Party was founded and the rest of the parties adhered to the Reform Party, the party that won a majority in Parliament in 1923.[16]

II

Parliamentary life in Iran was dealt a severe blow with the arrival of Reza Shah to power in 1925. The Shah did not undermine the Constitution of 1906; however, parliamentary life became marginalized, as was the case during World War I. The conservative forces that pulled together in the early 1920s were looking for a strong man to hold the reins of power. They justified the support they gave the Shah by saying that the council and constitutional governments were unable to contain violence, curb the chaotic situation or limit the adverse effect this situation was having on the lives of the people. In reality, the Council was unable to deliver on one of its main promises, for different reasons. It had promised to create a national central state that could put a halt to the chaos prevailing among the tribes; it failed, as well, to confront foreign influence and attacks. On the eve of World War I, the Russians in the north occupied Tabriz, and the British were interfering in the affairs of the state, imposing their views on the government and the Consultative Council.[17]

Reza Shah succeeded in disarming and disbanding the tribes. He also built a modern army devoid, for the first time, of any foreign elements. He also linked the regions to the central authority and imposed a comprehensive educational programme that greatly limited the influence of the clergy. These steps were taken between the years 1922 and 1941. They were implemented in a violent and despotic way, influenced by Mustapha Kemal in Turkey. Indeed, the Shah made a visit to Turkey in 1934, and he was very impressed by the 'Kemalist' experience; he became more hostile to the clergy, that same clergy who hadplayed a big role in his rise to power. However, the Shah, unlike Mustapha Kemal, did not fight foreign presence on Iranian soil, and was not keen on respecting the constitution and parliament, as Kemal was.

The British removed Reza Shah in 1941, accusing him of being pro-German. His young son, Mohammed Reza, succeeded him. He was weak and inexperienced. This allowed the Parliament to regain its former power, and parties flourished again. (One of the main features of this era was the emergence of the Marxist Party and the National Front headed by Muhammad Musaddiq). The then prime minister, Muhammad Sudki, tried to turn the Shah into a constitutional monarch and strip him of his powers and to nationalize Iranian oil. At first glance, it seemed that the national forces had won. However, the fear of the army and the refusal of the clergy to back the radical programmes of Musaddiq enabled the American CIA and the army to wage a coup d'etat in August 1953, toppling the constitutional cabinet and the elected parliament. The Shah regained power and remained at the helm until the Islamic revolution in 1979.[18]

Pluralism and parliamentary life came to an end in Iran, coinciding with the end of pluralism in Egypt as well (1953). The reaction of civil society to these sudden events was as expected in those Islamic countries. The excuses for it varied from support for the foreign element (backing of the US, as a strong superpower, in the Cold War) to internal reasons (the weak pro-Constitution parties, the influence wielded by foreign powers over parties and Parliament, the latter's failure to achieve national goals, corruption in political life, a chaotic situation that scared away the conservatives, belief of the masses in a strong and potent country, etc.).[19] The pro-Constitution 'new forces' were not strong enough, although they had a great impact on the people and considerable political clout. One thing must be said: that the Egyptian experience is at one and the same time similar, yet different, from the Iranian experience.

In 1866, Ismail of Egypt instituted a limited parliamentary system, calling it the Consultative Council of the Deputies. It had its by-laws and abided by certain regulations. Its powers were limited, at first, to discussing the issues submitted to it by the government. However, during the dispute with foreign consultants, Ismail agreed to extend its powers, hoping that it would support him against the European creditors who were most influential. Although the British in conjunction with the Turks – who controlled Egypt nominally – removed Ismail in 1879 and named Tewfiq to replace him, the Council supported the powers vested in him and imposed a constitution, in 1882.[20] But when the British occupied Egypt in 1882, the parliamentary and constitutional life came to an end. Councils and commissions were formed under the occupation; they did not have real powers or representation until the conflict between Abbas II and the British Commissioner worsened at the beginning of the 20th century. In fact, this had given Mustapha Kemal some political leeway to declare the formation of the National Party in 1907. This was followed by the establishment of the 'party of the nation', the 'constitutional reforms' party and other smaller parties that same year.[21]

In Iran, in the same year, public, overt pluralism began to flourish while the country was experiencing its first constitutional revolution, Just like Iran, the 'party of the nation' was considered to be the party of big landowners and pro-British employees. The National Party, on the other hand, comprised the new radical intellectuals and small employees. The Reformist Party was considered to be pro-Ismail, although Mustapha Kemal had a good relationship with Ismail. However, these parties quickly lost any clout they had after Ismail struck a deal with the new British Commission. The National Party came under intense pressure following the death of its first leader, and the forced departure of its second leader, in 1910.[22]

As was the case in Iran, World War I was followed by the imposition of an emergency state, while the British kept a firm grip on the situation. But in 1919, Saad Zaghlul launched his movement, which compelled the British to recognize the independence of Egypt formally (1921) and the Constitution was promulgated in 1923.[23] The parliamentary experience in Egypt differed from that of Iran until the middle of the 20th century. Despite the pressure applied by the British and interference of the palace, the undermining of the constitution and the artificial founding of pro-British parties, the parliamentary and constitutional experience lasted in Egypt until 1953, when it came to an end following the July revolution of 1952. So, the Egyptian experience came to an end the same year that the Iranian experience was halted by the US-backed military coup d'etat.

However, the differences between the two are not limited to the fact that the Egyptian experience lasted a little longer. There were other features unique to the Egyptian experience. *First*: the elite in Egypt comprising the intellectuals, lawyers, journalists and entrepreneurs, were more numerous and influential than those in Iran at the beginning of the century. Moreover, the elite played a bigger role in Egypt than their counterparts in Iran. *Second*: the Egyptian religious elite did not play as capital a role in the Egyptian national movement as Iran's religious elite. Of course, we cannot deny the indirect impact of the reforms of Jamaleddin al-Afghani and Mohammed Abduh and their followers. Nor can we deny the role played by the Azhar and its adherence to the general course of the national movement in 1919. However, these elements should not be compared to the Iranian national movement and its senior activists: The dismantling of the monopoly of tobacco (1891), the active participation in the movement of the year 1905, the divisions over the constitution (1907–1909), the emergence of Sheikh Nouri, who was opposed to the Constitution, the support given to Reza Shah (1923–1925), the support given to Musaddiq followed by a withdrawal of the support (1952–1953). I will, later on, study the specifications of Islamic entities in Egypt and Iran. *Third*: the emergence of popular movements with party backing in Egypt, which was lacking in Iran. In Iran, there was no party like the Wafd Party in Egypt, nor was there any Islamic party similar to the Muslim Brotherhood, as far as its continuity and the number of its followers were concerned. *Fourth*: the double role and task of the Egyptian national movement was to struggle for independence and to apply pressure so as to achieve democracy. In Iran, only in the second half of the 1940s did Iranian parliamentary life experience a similar duality of purpose, during the struggle launched against the Soviets in Iran (1945–1947), the nationalization of oil (a move directed against the British and Americans) and the extension of constitutional and democratic life[24] (a move directed against the Shah, Mohammed Reza).

III

The Mongols swept across the Islamic world to Baghdad in no more than 40 years. They overran the capital of the Abbasid Empire in the year 656 AH (1258 CE). They also killed the last caliph, Al-Musta'sim Billah.[25] Hence, they controlled the eastern regions of the Islamic world, reaching Iraq and the Euphrates. It was not long beforehand that the descendants of Genghiz Khan (the grandchildren and children of Hulagu) established their own kingdom in Iran. The kingdom was called in the writings of palace employees in Iran, Iran Zamin. (Iran had been called Iran Shahr in the past. The word has the same meaning as Iran Zamin: the country of the Aryans). This represented a renewed consciousness by the Iranian elite of their particular identity and distinctiveness, and they have sustained a sense of continuity since pre-Islamic times, put in writing in the *Shahameh* of Ferdowsi in the year 1010 CE.

The Mongols were not Iranians, but they thought it was in their best interests to encourage the pre-Islamic Iranian identity. Thus, they sought to keep Iranians apart from the Muslims of Egypt and Damascus, who were ruled by the Mamluks, all the more so as the Mamluks reinstated the

Abbasid caliphate in Cairo.[26] When a number of the Ilkhanid sultans converted to Islam, 30 years after the establishment of their dynasty, they saw it appropriate to convert to Twelfth Imamate Shi'ism, so as to remain different from the Mamluks, who were Sunni. Thus, Shi'ism became the motto of Iran Zamin.[27] This motto did not last for long, because most Iranians were Sunni. But it did secure for them the support of a strong Iranian Shiite elite. This elite encouraged conversion to Shi'ism, to a point where Shi'ism became part and parcel of the Iranian 'nationalism' or *'asabiyah* or identity in the 16th century, at which time the Safavids consolidated their grip over Iran.

The Safavids, the first dynasty to rule over the whole of Iran, declared Imamate Shi'ism as the religion of the realm and the nation.[28] According to Iranian lore, the 'Turan' (the Turkic peoples of central Asia) are the principal enemy of Iran. Needless to say, the Ottomans used conversion to Sunnism as a weapon to fight the Safavids and Qajars. The sultans of the two dynasties, likewise, used Iranian territorial *'asabiyah* (Iran versus Turan) and conversion to Shi'ism (the Imamate versus Sunnism) as their defence of the sultan in the face of Ottoman incursion.[29]

The conflict between the two empires stopped in the 17th century, when the Turks managed to take Iraq. However, national or neo-national awareness in Iran was thriving. So the dispute became over borders (with Russia, not the Ottomans) rather than identity. And so Western cultural and military intervention after the 18th century did not constitute as much of a problem or difficulty in the identity of the nation or state for Iranians as it did for the Ottomans, and all other parts of the Sunni realm as well, with its many ethnic groups and different races and cultures.

The reactions in Iran to the European penetration were different from the Ottomans', as regards the impact of this penetration on the public identity. The domestic balances were different for the two configurations. The European penetration into the region made the Turks and the people under their control tighten their attachment to what held them together: the caliphate, which embraced, controlled and organized the plurality within the Empire. In this respect, the Sunni religious institution, whose seat was in Istanbul, operated within the bounds set by the Ottoman Empire; it is part and parcel of that Empire and abides by its rules.[30] In Iran, it was not possible to absorb the religious institution or make it abide by the state. Many scholars endorsed the policy pursued by the potent Shahenshah under the reign of the Safavids. However, because of the doctrine of Twelfth Imamate Shi'ism (the disappearance of the twelfth Imam, the only legitimate ruler, whose return or re-appearance is awaited), they could not follow their Sunni counterparts in terms of recognition of the sultans and recognition of the legitimacy of the Shahenshah; the more so as Shi'ism delegates to the scholars the running of the affairs of the community in the absence

of the Imam.[31] The Shiite community delegates to their scholars the running of the affairs of the community during the period of absence. The
scholars enjoy an independent authority and direct link with the community, tighter than the temporal authority. Senior scholars do not dabble in
politics, since there is an absence of legitimacy during the absence of the
Imam. However, they cannot remain idle when a threat looms over the
community, such as with the Ottoman incursions, Russian conquests,
European monopolies to which the authorities are subjected, injustices meted
out at the hands of the Shahanshah, or emergence of divisive forces such as
Baha'ism. Intervening on these particular grounds became a fait accompli
at the beginning of the 19th century, when Shiite jurisprudence matured
after the triumph of fundamentalists over communicators. Indeed, there
was one authority in Najaf, Qom and Mashhad.[32]

In the meantime, Fath Ali Shah Qajar (1797–1834) and his successor,
Muhammad Shah (1834–1848), implemented reforms in the ranks of the
army and in the state administration favouring modernization and centralization. Those steps were met with scepticism by the religious institutions,
which considered them harmful to large sections of society.[33]

Meanwhile, Baha'ism was considered to be a departure from mainstream
Shi'ism. The scholars applied pressure on the state to quell it, and the state
was happy to oblige. Indeed, it was fearful that a revolution led by the
scholars might ensue if it did not comply with their demand.[34] During
1891–1892, the scholars spearheaded a protest wave against the monopoly
on tobacco conceded by Naser al-Din Shah (1848–1896) to a British company. He was forced to retract his concession later on.[35] In 1905, the reformist
scholars, with the help of the intelligensia and the merchants of the Bazaar,
forced the Shah Muzaffar al-Din (1896–1907) to adopt the constitution
and establish a parliament in 1906. However, the involvement of right-
wing liberals in the parliament and the constitutional movement frightened
away the religious elite. So, it became torn between supporting the constitution or withdrawing this support. Sheikh Fazlollah Nouri (d. 1909) led
an anti-constitution movement along with the liberal movement. He was
executed after the escape of the new Shah Mohammad Ali Qajar (1907–
1909), who was supported by the sheikh against the advocates of the
constitution.[36] When it appeared that things were getting out of hand in
1923, because of the wrangling between the parties, and foreign intervention, the religious authorities in Najaf, Qom and Tehran (Behbehani and
Na'ini – Modarres was still hesitant) supported Reza Shah as future king
and not as president of the republic (because Islam is against the establishment of republics, many scholars came to hold after the atrocities perpetrated
by Mustapha Kemal against Islam and the clergy) in 1925.[37]

IV

In his well-known study *Religion and Politics in Contemporary Iran*, Shahrokh Akhavi said that Iranian religious institutions did not experience the reformist wave experienced by Egypt and Turkey.[38] This view cannot be true. The Shiite scholars were deeply interested in modernization and all that was new in Iran and Iraq, even if the approach or the method was different. Indeed, the triumph of the fundamentalists in the second half of the 18th century is a living proof that modern methods gained the upper hand. Here one can mention Behbehani and Hujjat al-Islam Shafati (d. 1844) and finally Sheikh Ansari (d. 1864).[39] Ansari was not content with implementing the new methods; he added another dimension – contracts and transactions. This suggests a deeper understanding of the era and its needs.

Ever since then, all new writings on contracts and transactions of the scholars were the only way to success, making them among the most prominent scholars and authorities.[40] It is true that at the time, Ansari played a very important role in the history of jurisprudence, as he was the first who had a majority that recognized his abilities. However, Shirazi (1815–1896), a follower of Ansari, played a special role in the religious Iranian institution, because he was one of the most prominent figures of Shi'ism and author of the famous edict banning the use of tobacco, when Naser al-Din Shah gave the concession for a tobacco monopoly to a British company (1891–1892).[41] The edict by Shirazi was made at the behest of Jamal al-Din, who sent a letter to Shirazi from the Shrine of Shah Abdol Azim, where he was staying, close to Tehran. In the letter, he warned Shirazi of the gravity of the step and the threat it represented to the independence and economy of the country. In other words, Shirazi was aware of the colonial plans being hatched for Iran.

It also means that Shirazi knew Jamal al-Din and was aware of his opinions, and of the consequences resulting from any decision that would antagonize the Shah. Since the start of the 20th century, a large number of Iranian clerics have spearheaded the pro-constitution wave.

These were about 50 sheikhs and scholars who became members of the first parliament elected in 1907. This generation of clerics had ideas and opinions similar to those held by Jamaleddin, Mohammed Abdo, Al-Kawakibi and Muhammad Rashid Rida. We note among the aforementioned two prominent figures. The first was a member of parliament and took part in policy-making between 1905 and 1925. The second published a theoretical study advocating constitutions and the holding of consultations. The first was none other than Sheikh Hasan Modarres (d. 1938), the Tehran religious scholar noted for his honesty and belief in the constitution and parliament; he continued to run for elections until 1925 when he, along with Musaddiq, opposed termination of Qajar rule.

However, he later turned a blind eye to this so as to avoid chaos.[42] The second prominent figure was Hossein Khan Na'ini (1850–1936), a follower of Shirazi and one of the scholars residing in Najaf. In 1909, when Sheikh Nuri (d. 1909) struggled against the constitution and the Consultative Council, Na'ini published his famous book, *A Warning to the Nation and Deontology of the Milleh in Support of Constitution and Democracy*. When Na'ini spoke about despotism, one sensed that he had read the book by Kawakibi (1845–1902) on *Forms of Despotism*, printed in Cairo in 1905. He went on to profess the preference of constitutional government in the absence of the Imam, and that Qur'anic consultation stipulates that such a government should be formed.[43]

Khorasani and Mazandarani lauded Na'ini's book. But Khorasani (d. 1911) perceived the constitution and democracy differently, as is evident from his letter from Najaf (1907) to the Iranian MPs, drawing on his support for the constitution. In his letter, he endorsed the view of Sheikh Nouri, calling for the establishment of a Consultative Council that would implement the [Qur'anic] tenet of 'enjoining what is right and forbidding what is wrong'.[44] In reality, Shiite clerical leaders were unable to grasp the intricacies surrounding the constitution and the parliament; unlike their followers – be they young or middle-aged – who were members of the parliament. The bottom line for senior scholars revolved around the ethics, about the identity of the community, its unity and its loyalty to Islam. Thus, a Shi'ism emerged between the young and old, and between the young and the old on the one hand, and the members of the secular intelligensia on the other. The situation was prevalent in Egypt and Turkey, pitting traditionalists against the advocates of modernization. However, the reformists and advocates of modernization gained the upper hand, because they became part of the state's plan to implement modernization. However, the unexpected developments in the 20th century brought, once again, the clergy in Egypt and Iran together.

The Sunni Islamic reformist drive appeared in Egypt and other Islamic countries in 1840, and remained very influential until 1930. The advocates of reform made an alliance with statesmen in the Ottoman era during the reorganization. This reorganization was aimed at establishing a new system that could absorb the shock of the international changes caused by the West in the Islamic world. The final result was, first, to establish a new political system, and second, to revive the Message of Islam and its laws.[45] The advocates of reform submitted two theses in this respect: the thesis of 'public benefits' by Tahtawi (1801–1873) and the thesis of 'the reorganization' by Khaireddin Tunisi (1810–1890). The reformist movement secured major achievements in all areas of interest to it, the social, political, economic and ethical. Regarding the renewed call for Islam, its culture and doctrine, the reformers in Egypt and the Arab Maghreb unearthed the old doctrine of 'The Aims of the *Shari'ah*', using two books written by the great Maliki scholar Ibn Ishaq al-Shatibi (d. 798 AH, 1395 CE), entitled: *The Agreements* and *The Standing Firm*. Other scholars and Shatibi, including Juwayni (d. 478 AH, 1085 CE), Ghazzali (d. 505 AH, 1111 CE) and Izz al-Din bin Abdel Salam (d. 644 AH, 1265 CE), perceived that the *Shari'ah* has one aim, and that is protecting the interests of the worshippers regarding five basic necessities: the rights of soul, religion, mind, descendants, and ownership of property.[46] The reformers embraced these ideas as matured in the thinking of Shatibi. At that time, historical and cultural events had isolated Islam and its doctrine in certain specific domains. The Western onslaught came close to eliminating them entirely from society and state. Thus, the reformers' attention and effort focused on attempting to bring about a comprehensive renewal, which rendered of no use the old and traditional mechanisms of the doctrine that had been stunted by the gradual dissociation of politics from *Shari'ah* in Islam's political and cultural history and the embrace of Aristotelian logic in the applications of measurement.[47]

So, in line with the legitimate necessities regarded by Shatibi as innate or related to the mind (similar to 'natural law'),[48] the reformers defined the issues concerning public life of the state and people ('public interests', as Tahtawi put it): the political establishment and its institutions, the army, the educational system, public services. The doctrine of 'human interests' included: 'the concepts of patriotism, the constitution, freedom for women, the fact that Islam is open since it is a universal religion. As a result, the old belief in the *Dar al-Islam* and *Dar al-harb* was undermined. The reformers regarded Western civilization as the civilization of the world and this century, and they were convinced that we should benefit from it and become part of it, because such a policy served the best interests of Muslims and Islam.[49] They felt no qualms about calling the political groups that were spreading in the Islamic world under Islamic names as, in reality, Western groups with Western concepts and ideas. In his reply to a letter 'from a reader' in *Manar* magazine in 1907, Rashid Rida said:[50] 'Muslims, do not think that the statements based on consultation stem from Islamic law. We have benefited from the Holy Book, from the biographies of the Caliphs. We did not benefit from the Europeans. Indeed, had we not imitated our Muslim forefathers, you would have sworn that we have stayed away from Islam.'

The anti-caliphate measures taken by Mustapha Kemal in Turkey stirred fear in the hearts of the Sunni and Shiite scholars. The Turkish parliament abolished the caliphate in March 1924. It declared the establishment of a Parliamentary Republic and elected Mustapha Kemal as President. The parliament paved the way for such an announcement, enacted laws and implemented measures directed against Islam, its institutions and its representatives. It seemed, at that time, that hostility to Islam as a religion and an institution had become a litany. On the 1st of November 1922 the Turkish parliament separated the caliphate from the empire; in other words, it separated the state from religion indirectly. The abolition of the caliphate in March 1924 was followed by the closing down of religious schools and religious courts, and the abolition of the office of *Sheikh al-Islam*. Law No. 163, enacted in 1926, banned religious parties. In 1927, Islamic property (*waqf*) was nationalized and placed at the disposal of the State. Finally, the Constitution was issued in 1928, devoid of any reference to Islam.[51]

In Egypt, it seemed that the marginalization of Islam was not as marked as in Turkey. Indeed, it became obvious that all new entities that emerged in the Levant following World War I, and following the dominance of the British and French, no longer needed the Islamic reformers, their edicts or their jurisprudence. Britain and France were the trustees of these new entities (officially mandated by the international body, the League of Nations, trusteeship over these new entities). Hence, Britain and France were, in reality, calling the shots in these new entities, and controlled their elites. The national opposition parties rejected foreign influence, but they did not want a return to the old or even reformed Islam; they were demanding, under the banner of Western values, the establishment of national entities, parliaments, independence, recognition of the authority of the people, and their right to self-determination. In the 1920s, Turkish hostility to Islam surpassed the hostility of secular elites to Islam in Egypt and Iran. However, Egyptian and Iranian elites seemed too independent and determined to let bygones be bygones (Kasravi in Iran, Ali Abdel Razek in Egypt, for example) and to forget colonialism (Mohammad Mosaddiq in Iran and Saad Zaghlul in Egypt, for example).

These new manifestations surprised the Islamic elite in the 1920s. Indeed, they served to eliminate what little support remained for the parliament in Iran and any republican longings by the clergy, paving the way for Reza Shah to rise to power. In Egypt, the new manifestations sapped Islamic reforms, prompting the advocates of reform to become introverted and overly protective of Islam and the identity of the community. In such an environment, religious associations keen on preserving the Islamic identity began to emerge. These associations were extremely interested in religious rituals and symbols, while they showed little interest in public issues, except where these issues involved a confrontation with the foreign forces and influence provided that the confrontation revolved around human need or ethics, not politics. Among these associations were: The Young Muslims, Muslim Brotherhood and Juridical Society in Egypt, The *Fedaiyan Islam* and others in Iran, the Muslim Scouts Association in Syria.[52]

Reza Shah was keen on pleasing the senior Shiite clergy in Najaf, Qom and Mashhad, between 1923 and 1925. They responded positively to the

Shah's overtures, and asked for a number of reforms relating to the religious identity of the country and the community: opposition to increasing British influence, preserving the Islamic character of the Constitution (the religion of the state as Islam, the Ja'fari sect, and the need for accord between religious legislation and state laws, and to form a council of religious lawyers in *ijtihad* to look into the extent of this accord and the edicts of the *Shari'ah*), and opposition to Baha'ism.[53] However, the Shah soon enough ignored his promises and proceeded to build modern institutions, limiting the influence of the clerics and the Shiite *marja'* in the administration, in education, *in the waqf* institution, the courts and the judicial system. The reforms went beyond the symbolic: the veil was forbidden, employment of persons in religious dress was forbidden, and emphasis was placed on Iran's pre-Islamic past.[54]

Religious elites were shocked by the Kemalist streak in Reza Shah. No sooner were they able to organize their ranks against him, than the Shah was pushed aside by the British and Soviets in 1941. Just as Ayatollah Abdol Karim Ha'eri supported or tolerated Reza Shah, so Ayatollah Borujerdi (1961) supported Mohammed Reza Shah or did not in general object directly to him, especially during the first part of his reign (1942–1953), when the country was apparently threatened with Soviet occupation in the north and British domination everywhere. However, many of the Ja'fari sect emerged from the state of fear and shock that overcame them during the days of Reza Shah, and they returned to the arena of conflict over Iran's identity in the days of comparative party activism during the first period of Mohammed Reza's rule. These were led by Ayatollah Tabtaba'i of Qom, then Ayatollah Kashani; both were able, with their supporters, to compel the Shah and his government into stalling many of Reza Shah's laws and measures relating to the clergy and to the identity of the country.[55] It was common knowledge that the *Fedaiyan Islam* organization, led by Nawab Safavi, always had the support of Tabtaba'i and Kashani, with its Shu'ubiyyah overtones and the assassination of those politicians and intellectuals who posed a threat – in their view – to the Islamic identity of the country.[56]

While fear of Communism and the strength of the Tudeh party prompted Kashani to abandon Musaddiq and make a truce with Shah Mohammed Reza, a third party of religious scholars, led by Ayatollah Khomeini, continued to regard the monarchy as a danger to the constitution and the Islamic nature of the country, pointing to what Reza Shah did when his power increased after 1925, with US and Baha'i support.[57] Ayatollah Borujerdi died in 1961, and with that, the Shah lost the last of the chief ayatollahs who continued to support his authority.

Mohammed Reza proceeded in the 1960s, after striking at all political parties, to renew his legitimacy through measures for modernization and reform. He considered them to be agreeable to the US Administration, to the peasants and to the rising urban bourgeoisie. There was a new electoral law that granted women the right to vote. Then came the 'white revolution' to eradicate feudalism to the benefit of small farmers and landowners. In 1971 and 1972, the Shah spoke of the need to separate state and religion, and establish state-run religious schools that would train pro-regime clerics.[58] Meanwhile, the number of US consultants in the army increased, and in the administration and internal security. Iran also recognized the state of Israel.[59] These various regulations and decrees angered various groups of people, such as the new National Front, a party focusing on national issues, the Bazaar merchants, and men of religion.[60]

However, pluralism along with political life had already been undermined. And so these groups failed to make a difference, except for the older clerics and their students. Prominent among these was Khomeini, who regarded the Shah as an American, Israeli and Baha'i lackey. In March 1963, Khomeini took to the streets, carrying the Qur'an in one hand and the 1906 Constitution in the other, declaring that the Shah has betrayed Islam and the Constitution. The demonstrations were violently suppressed in June 1963. Khomeini was arrested and then exiled to Turkey in November 1964. He then went to Iraq, to the Najaf, in 1965.[61] There he elaborated on the reasons behind his insistence that the Pahlevi family should be ousted from power and an Islamic state established: (i)the despotism of the Shah and the fact that he strayed from Islam, as was obvious during the 1971 celebrations that glorified ancient pagan Iran; (ii) the Shah's strong links with anti-Arab and anti-Islamic forces (the US and Israel). He also opposed the Shah's flouting of Islamic ethics in his life and conduct and as regards the laws he enacted.[62]In 1971, Khomeini published his book, *The Islamic Government*, which detailed the Islamic state alternative to the ruling regime in Iran: *velayat-i faqih* during the age of absence of the Imam.[63]

In Egypt, the Muslim Brotherhood movement had increased in popularity during the 1940s. Its focus was on identity and ethics. Its members carried out a number of political assassinations similar to those carried out by the *Fedaiyan-e Islam* organization in Iran. Backbiting against the regime turned into boycott in 1954, when the movement fought with the regime of the July 1952 revolution for authority; they were routed and later ordered to disband.[64] It is noteworthy that the confrontation between the Iranian regime and the clergy served to gradually unite the clergy, bazaar merchants and the National Front around Khomeini. This did not occur in Egypt because the regime of the July revolution enjoyed wide popular support for driving out the British, for confrontation with Israel, France and Britain and, subsequently, even the US, and the regime's position on issues such as national wealth, independence, Arab national demands, and carrying out reforms for the benefit of the needy. So the state's crackdown on pluralism did not affect its popularity. Moreover, the Islamic opposition parties in Egypt did not enjoy the support of the Azhar, which backed the regime even when the latter was fighting the Muslim Brotherhood.

But the position of the Azhar changed in the mid-1960s. There are undeniable facts indicating that the Iranian opposition used the writings of Muslim Brotherhood members (especially Sayyed Qotob and Abdel Qader Audeh) during its struggle against the Shah. The Brotherhood, acquainted with Nawab Safavi and his movement since the end of the 1940s, was not aware of the importance of the opposition waged by the Iranian clergy, perhaps because its leaders were scattered in exile in the Gulf and Europe. They had made alliances foreign to their political and intellectual world, the one they had known in the 1940s and early 1950s.[65] Noteworthy was the change in rhetoric of both parties: They became advocates of severing relations with the West and the regimes that came to power with the help of the West, be they capitalist or socialist. Khomeini went into exile in 1964. With his departure, the chances of negotiations between him and the Iranian regime were nil. The book written by Sayyed Qotb, entitled *Landmarks on the Road*, published in 1964, was the precursor to a break with all new regimes. As Ayatollah Khomeini declared his Islamic alternative to the Shah's rule, Sheikh Yusuf Qardhawi began issuing his series, as of 1974, on *The Inevitability of the Islamic Solution*.[66]

V

Medieval Islamic societies in the Islamic Near East and the Maghreb were home to many political, social, economic and artisan organizations.[67] The first three Islamic centuries were very prosperous,[63]with much cross-culturation, like a tree with branches and sub-branches. Religious and political organizations used different means to oppose the state. As to the social, economic and artisan organizations, they had codes of conduct or specific customs that used to govern their relations with the state. These customs or codes were developed over time. In the *Book of Al-Medinah* laid down by the Prophet there is a reference to the categories of society after his departure to Yathrib (the main categories being the Emigrants, the tribes of Yathrib, and the Jews), followed by another on the contractual nature of political gathering in Islam.[68] However, the conquests created a big empire; customs and traditions specific to this empire assured, and led to, protracted conflicts about the identity of society, or authority, or political gathering. These conflicts created two political traditions: (i) The *shura* or consultations tradition. Its hey-day was in the 8th century CE, especially in the city of Kufa. Its underlying concept is that consultation is the right of the overwhelming majority of the *ummah*; (ii)The tradition of empire, which considers political contract as divinely sanctioned, between God and Caliph, with the latter giving himself the title the 'Caliph of God'.[69]

However, by the 19th century, a kind of reconciliation and balance between traditionalists and those who later came to be called *ahl al-hal wa'l 'iqd*, the specialists in *shura*. Although the latter did not have a clearly defined structure or terminology, scholars in legal policy and theories of state viewed them as the cream of society – scholars, princes, tribal chiefs, high officials of state and the military. With the inclusion of this formula in decision-making and administration, a line was drawn between Islamic law and politics, but not between religion and state.[70] Affinities continued on the religious, political and social levels, without causing any significant disruptions, except during the occasional internal crises (power struggles or famine or turmoil) or external crises (foreign invasion, particularly Crusader, Mongol and Tartar, war to re-conquer lost territories, European incursions into the Islamic world). Large Islamic cities (especially the locales of strong central government or those governed by weak central states) were home to local administrations governed by prominent figures (the presidents in Iran and the Levant) and by sheikhs, notables or magistrates (in Syria, Egypt and the Maghreb).[71]

Regarding social associations (youth movements, Sufi societies, tribes, clans, shopkeepers, schools, inns, rest houses, mosques) and trade and artisan unions, they were governed by the codes of conduct of their professions or by the customs prevailing in the city. As for the specialists in *shura*, their domain was consultation and the associated terminologies, concessions and consensus.[72]

In the 18th century, the Islamic world witnessed, prior to direct European economic and military intrusion into the Islamic heartland, a comprehensive revivalist movement with multifaceted aspects, after bottlenecks emerged in the basics of control, linkage and traditional openness.[73] However, the European intrusion created a new situation that impelled the *shura* to give way to new concepts, such as 'public benefits' and the *Tanzimat* of the reformers, as expressed by Tahtawi and Khaireddine Tunisi. The political reformers, along with the scholars and the intellectuals, thought that modernizing institutions, the administration and the army would be sufficient to withstand the test.[74] But the nation-state, in its European form, was still a dream in the minds of many; thus, the call for greater national integration gained momentum.

Gradually, a comprehensive Arab culture took shape that refused to accept the reality, in national and Islamic elites. The national elite considered European entities as the sole model to emulate and imagined that these entities were highly unified and integrated. The Islamic elite was appalled by the abolition of the caliphate and devoted itself to re-establishing it, with the image of the first caliph in mind. However, the reality was, and still is, different. Numerous, scattered and divided 'country entities' remained, and they seemed to have no clear connection with either the nationalist or the Islamic message; indeed, they could not deliver on promises or on the hopes pinned on them in these messages. Perhaps this glaring contrast between the cultural ideal and the political reality was behind the lack of enthusiasm for the first democratic experience in the Arab world. That experience faded away by the end of the 1940s, allowing for the emergence of 'pure' national regimes. Indeed, the Syrian–Egyptian experiment at the end of the 1950s came close to the national ideal of an integrated state. But since the beginning of the 1960s, the gap between the actual and the ideal returned and became dominant. Added to this was the corporate nature of country regimes having a nationalist outlook, a corporate nature that stifled political pluralism by hitting at political parties, and also went on to deny all non-governmental institutions and agencies, except those that were its own creation. This implied the gradual loss of functional legal representation, through trade unions, youth and student associations, lawyers' and journalists' syndicates, student clubs and associations of professors and magistrates.

These developments took place in the 1960s in all Arab countries that experienced pluralism. Even in those countries where political plurality was not abolished, parliamentary life was disrupted. In Morocco, the disruption had internal political causes; in Lebanon, the disruption resulted from civil strife, and parliamentary elections were not held between 1972 and 1992. Across that period spanning two decades (the 1960s and 1970s), the *Islamic Phenomenon* exploded in most Arab countries.[75] On the one hand, the national/nationalist state proved incapable of delivering on its promises. On the other hand, that state controlled all, blocking any attempt at the expression of interests, aspirations or ambitions. Radical Islam was the expression of disillusionment and protest; it was the means to counter what was happening on the political and cultural fronts. Islam exploded into revolution or struggle because it lacked the means or channels by which it could play a role in the decision-making process peacefully. Revolutionary Islam and its legitimacy were not far from the ideas and activism prevailing in the 1960s and 1970s. Indeed, where could these young people be introduced to other thought or another interpretation of Islam and the functions of the state? Where they were exiled in the remote corners of the Gulf? In their original countries? The brief moment of liberalism they knew during the Islamic reform era was gone forever. What remained in their countries were 'absolutes' (or what the media called 'constants'), the 'absolutes' of nationalism and socialism. So they cried out the Islamic 'absolute'. But the dominant feature was a point of faith. They were, by origin, revivalist groups, concerned over identity, its purity, symbols and slogans. So all their declared slogans and even programmes were basically a function of need. Indeed, rebellious movements in Islam are offspring of the ideal nation state. Because of this, they are something very new. This explains why they departed from traditional and reformist Islam. Indeed, traditional Islam amounts to a lifestyle, while reformist Islam is an attempt to bestow legitimacy on a different understanding of the religion. The new Islam is a call for a new, hard-line and pure democracy. Justice is one of the highest values of Islam, as religion and as culture. The *Shari'ah* is the symbol of that value, in a world wallowing in illegitimacy and despotism!

In Iran, the events of 1953 and what followed, considerably disrupted political life. However, the National Front attempted to reorganize itself towards the end of the 1950s. It started or made an attempt to act in the beginning of the 1960s. Student unions and teachers' syndicates played a big role in organizing demonstrations, protests and strikes.[76] However, since the mid-1960s, they have gone underground, while radical movements have increased (Tudeh Party and various left-wing splinter groups).

But the religious explosion led by Khomeini came early in 1963. (Is it possible that the Muslim Brotherhood were planning a revolution in Egypt in 1964 or 1967?) This can be interpreted as the response to the regime's reign of terror against the people and its total dependence on the US. On the other hand, the clergy in Iran are well-organized in the seats of the Ayatollahs in Qom and in the major cities, which are home to large religious schools whose teachers are some of the most senior clerics. This unique feature enabled the clerics of Iran to act quickly and efficiently, which was not the case for other political parties or the unions, who were constantly watched by the security forces.

The explosion that occurred can be attributed to two causes: *first*, the Iranian psyche; *second*, conversion to Shi'ism. As is known, paganism in Iran stressed the ongoing conflict between the good (Ahura Mazda) and the evil (Aharman), and the conflict of this dualism can only end with the triumph of the good.[77] Shiite Islam, on the other hand, stresses the principle of justice. For both Shi'ism and Zoroastrianism, compromise is out of the question, because that would mean that evil wins. Furthermore, belief in the *unknown* carries Mahdist and missionary connotations, curbed in times of tranquillity by the principle of *taqwah*, which in turn is quickly lost during crises or violent change, paving the way for waiting for that moment when the two explode anew in a total struggle to the finish. Khomeini's genius lay in his capacity to combine the *charismatic dimension* of the Shiite Imam (hence his title by Iranians, *Imam*) and the *practical dimension*, manifested in his writings on *velayat al-faqih* in 1971. If it were not for these two features, it would have been impossible to turn the movement of the masses into a revolution that led to the creation of an authority and establishment of a state in 1979.

In the eighties, the Islamic revolution headed by Khomeini was able to establish a corporate system similar to the one established by Nasser. However, the Iranian Islamic regime was more conservative in economic and agricultural policies,[78] and tougher with the opposition. Nasser was ruthless with the Islamists; Khomeini was unforgiving with the Tudeh Party and other left-wing groups.[79] Reports compiled by regional or international human rights organizations are full of condemnations of the violations perpetrated in the Arab nation. The same applies to Iran, which has been under fire since 1981.

The eighties came to an end in the Arab nation with a coup d'etat in Sudan, establishing a regime based on the *Shari'ah*. Following the death of Khomeini, moderate and radical voices together began to be heard. Indeed, both are now locked in a power struggle. There are a few independent newspapers, and there are some intellectuals who are making their cases heard. However, one of the main developments since the death of Khomeini has been the return to a multitude of authorities. Needless to say, while Khomeini lived, he was the only authority and was the leader and spiritual guide of Iran. His successor, Khamene'i, was unable to combine the two qualities, despite official insistence to the contrary. This means that the religious institution governing Iran is no longer in power, at least not all of its members. In fact, many senior scholars are considering retirement from political life, turning to teaching, for instance. The senior authority will be chosen from among the retired. And if that is out of the question, because of the pressure to recognize Khamene'i as the authority, then the Ayatollah would rather keep a multitude of authorities, as was the case for most of the last two centuries.[80]

In the Arab nation, the 1980s witnessed many important developments regarding the return of institutions of civil society to do efficient work. Plurality has been restored on a regular basis. However, most parties, with few exceptions (Morocco and Yemen), have not been very effective, being constantly pressured by the governments, lacking representation, with most of the elected tied to the regime or ruling party which dominates the administration of the state and vital facilities of concern to the public.[81] The main Islamist groups have turned into a strong and legal political team (Jordan, Yemen), or illegal ones (Egypt and the rest of the Arab countries). Islamists participated in the elections of the eighties and entered parliament (Jordan, Yemen, Lebanon, Algeria), or were represented by one of the legal parties (Egypt). However, this limited democracy did not lead to any changes in the policies pursued by the governments, or to a peaceful transition of power, or to a change of leader or regime in any Arab country.

Non-governmental organizations were more efficient and wielded more influence and clout. These NGOs include trade unions, syndicates (lawyers, journalists, engineers, doctors, chambers of commerce), women's unions, human rights associations. Perhaps their greater effectiveness is due to the fact that they carry out specific tasks; hence, their members are keen on preserving and protecting them. The number of NGOs in the Arab world is estimated at around 60,000, but they vary greatly in degree of efficacy, strength and efficiency.[82]

It seems that, with the continuation of privatization and moves towards a market economy in many Arab countries, most NGOs and political parties will see their efficiency and power increase. A study conducted on the Arab lawyers' syndicate and the human rights organization shows that these organizations were relatively successful, despite outside pressure and the difficult conditions under which they operate.[83]

VI

This study has been plagued, from the outset, by practical and methodological difficulties.

I was asked to undertake a study of civil society in the Arab nations and Iran in the modern era. Iran has been an independent, unified country for five centuries, whereas this is not the case for the Arabs. Moreover, political and social circumstances differ for Arabs and Iranians. Pretending that these difficulties do not exist because of the two belonging to the same region, the Middle East, would be a delusion. After some thinking, I decided to compare Iran and Egypt and to make some references to the Ottoman Empire in the 19th century, and to other Arab entities. I chose to make an historical comparison, although history does not clarify all that needs to be clarified. Since the state and political society have played a major role in bringing about this comparison, I focused on the political experience of both sides: the regimes and the political parties, along with the constitutions, without overlooking other social forces. The point of such a method lies in showing that the difficulties encountered by pluralism have had a negative impact on NGOs, such as trade unions and civic associations. Indeed, the regime that appeared to be consolidating its abilities to serve society, during the 1950s and 1960s, looks now to be working against the people, against institutions, NGOs and civic associations.

If the main weak point of this approach was to consider the Arabs as 'a single unity', in comparison with Iran, another problem relates to the Islamist factor, which has become decisive on both levels, the political and social, since the 1970s, and more so in Iran than the Arab nation. The study has shown that Iran is unique in this respect, but we cannot deny the increasing strength of Islamists in the Arab countries. Researchers have always considered the Islamists a major obstacle to the emergence of 'civil society'.[84] It has been said that Islamists do not recognize plurality, because of circumstances that surrounded the emergence of Islam itself.[85] It has also been said that, irrespective of the circumstances and differences between Islam and civil society, the experience of an Islamic state in Iran,

Sudan and Algeria shows how hard it is for Muslims to recognize plurality.

In reality, the corporate state is a cultural and political phenomenon, which is not only limited to Islamic societies. The aforementioned experiences have other aspects as well; some of these were mentioned and should not be overlooked in the analysis. I am not being apologetic or defensive here. But it must be said that it is hard, in the best of circumstances, to understand the relations between groups on the basis of the discourse they profess, and the same applies to the relations between society and the state and its bureaucracy.

The problem does not lie in the fact that there is democracy without there being democrats[87] along the lines of Muhammad Abdo, who said 'Islam exists even without Muslims'! The problem lies in the *Tanzimat* considered by Khaireddine Tunisi as the criteria for modernization. It has become certain today that they will not become so except if based on, even proceeding from, the 'public benefits' or the public domain called for by Tahtawi. The public domain is teeming, in both Iran and the Arab nation, with motion, change, expansion and the opening of horizons and looking to the future. This can herald the emergence of new conceptions of the *Tanzimat*, the state and political society,[88] in Iran as in the Arab nation.

Notes

* Editor-in-Chief, *Al-Ijtihad* magazine; Professor of Islamic Studies, Lebanese University, Beirut, Lebanon.

1. Roy Mottahedeh, 'The Islamic Movement: The Case for Democratic Inclusion', *Contention*, vol. 4, no. 3 (Spring 1995), pp. 111–12. See the critical study of the new Iranian constitution, as compared to the one published in 1906, in: Asghar Shirazi, 'Die Widersprüche in der Verfanung der Islamischen Republik', *Occasional Papers* (Berlin), no. 32 (1992).

2. Compare, for example: C. W. Findley, *Bureaucratic Reforms in the Ottoman Empire: The Sublime Porte, 1789–1922*, Princeton, N.J.: [n.pb.], 1980; Uriel Heyd, *Foundations of Turkish Nationalism*, London: Luzac, 1950; Roderic Davison, *Reform in the Ottoman Empire, 1856–1876*, Princeton, N.J.: Princeton University Press, 1963, and Albert Hourani, *Arabic Thought in the Liberal Age, 1789–1939*, Oxford: Oxford University Press, 1979.

3. See Amin Banani, *The Modernization of Iran*, (Stanford, Calif.: [n.pb.], 1961), pp. 5–27.

4. Roderic Davison, 'The Advent of the Principle of Representation in the Government of the Ottoman Empire', in: William Polk and Richard Chambers, eds, *Beginnings of Modernization in the Middle East*, publication of the Centre for Middle Eastern Studies, 1, (Chicago, Ill.: University of Chicago Press, 1968), pp. 93–108.

5. Compare: Ali Din Hilal, *Politics and Governance in Egypt: The Era of the Parliament, 1923–1952*, (Cairo: Library of the Renaissance of the Levant, 1977),

pp. 26–43, and I. Gershoni and James Jankowski, *Egypt, Islam and the Arabs*, (Oxford: [n.pb.], 1986), pp. 3–20.

6.   Roderic Davison, *Reform in the Ottoman Empire, 1856–1876*, op. cit., pp. 52–80; ibid., pp. 93–7, and Hasan Kayali, 'Elections and the Electoral Process in the Ottoman Empire, 1876–1919', *IJMES*, vol. 27 (1995), pp. 265–86.

7.   Roderic Davison, *Reform in the Ottoman Empire, 1856–1876*, op. cit., pp. 52–80 and 358–408.

8.   Mansour Moaddel, 'Shi'i Political Discourse and Class Mobilization in the Tobacco Movement of 1890–1892', in: John Foran, ed., *A Century of Revolution: Social Movements in Iran*, (Minneapolis: [n.pb.], 1994), pp. 1–20.

9.   Janet Afary, 'Social Democracy and the Iranian Constitutional Revolution of 1906–1911', in: John Foran, ed., ibid., pp. 21–43.

10.   Compare, for example: Ghassan Salamé, *Towards a New Arab Social Contract: A Study in Constitutional Legitimacy*, National Culture, 10, (Beirut: Centre for Arab Unity Studies, 1987), pp. 61–3, 68; Haidar Ibrahim Ali, 'Civil Society in Egypt and Sudan', pp. 509–10, and Abdallah Saef, 'Civil Society in Legal Arab Thought', pp. 223–4, two papers presented at the Seminar on Civil Society in the Arab World and its Role in Achieving Democracy: Discussions and Researches of the Seminar, Beirut: Centre for Arab Unity Studies, 1992.

11.   A. Cunningham, 'Stratford Cunning and the Tanzimat', in: William Polk and Richard Chambers, eds, *Beginnings of Modernization in the Middle East*, op. cit., pp. 245–66.

12.   Ervand Abrahamian, *Iran between Two Revolutions*, (Princeton, N.J.: Princeton University Press, 1982), pp. 57–9; Said Amir Arjomand, *The Turban for the Crown: The Islamic Revolution in Iran*, (Oxford: [n.pb.], 1988), pp. 35–6; Ann Lambton, 'Secret Societies and the Persian Revolution', *Middle Eastern Affairs*, vol. 4, no. 1 (1958), and *Middle Eastern Affairs*, vol. 16 (1963).

13.   Ann Lambton, 'The Tobacco Régie: Prelude to Revolution', *Studia Islamica*, vol. 22 (1965), pp. 36–62, and Nikki Keddie, *Religion and Rebellion in Iran: The Tobacco Protests of 1891–1892*, London: Cass, 1966.

14.   The classic study of the constitutional Iranian revolution is the study conducted by E. G. Browne, published in 1910 (2nd ed. printed in 1966). There is another classic study in Persian, by Ahmad Kasravi (1951). I have referred here to: Vanessa Martin, *Islam and Modernism: The Iranian Revolution of 1906*, London: I. B. Tauris, 1989; and Afary, 'Social Democracy and the Iranian Constitutional Revolution of 1906–1911', in: John Foran, ed., *op. cit.*, pp. 21–43.

15.   Said Amir Arjomand, *The Turban for the Crown: The Islamic Revolution in Iran*, op. cit., pp. 40–57; Janet Afary, 'Social Democracy and the Iranian Constitutional Revolution of 1906–1911', in: John Foran, ed. op. cit., pp. 41–63; Ervand Abrahamian, *Iran between the Two Revolutions, op. cit.*, pp. 86–99.

16.   Ann Lambton, 'Iranian Political Societies', op. cit., pp. 88–9; Banani, *The Modernization of Iran*, op. cit., pp. 20–1.

17.   M. Zirinsky, 'The Rise of Reza Khan', in: John Foran, ed., *A Century of Revolution: Social Movements in Iran*, op. cit., pp. 47–77; also, Nikki Keddie, *Roots of Revolution: An Interpretive History of Modern Iran*, (New York: [n.pb.], 1965), pp. 111–42.

18.   Ervand Abrahamian, *Iran between Two Revolutions*, op. cit., pp. 267–80; Susan Siavoshi, 'The Oil Nationalization Movement', in: John Foran, ed., op. cit., pp. 78–105; also, Said Amir Arjomand, *The Turban for the Crown: The Islamic*

Revolution in Iran, op. cit., pp. 71–2. There is an amusing story about Musaddiq's life, struggle and reformist ideas in: Roy Mottahedeh, *The Mantle of the Prophet: Religion and Politics in Iran*, (New York: Simon and Schuster, 1985), pp. 115–33.

19.   Compare: Taher Labib, 'Is Democracy a Social Demand? The Relation between Democracy and Arab Civil Society', paper presented to the Seminar on Civil Society in the Arab World and its Role in Achieving Democracy: Discussions and Researches of the Seminar, (Beirut: Centre for Arab Unity Studies, 1992), pp. 339–67; Ghassan Salamé, *Towards a New Arab Social Contract: A Study in Constitutional Legitimacy*, op. cit., p. 68; John Waterbury, 'Democracy without Democrats in the Middle East: The Potential for Political Liberalization', in: Ghassan Salamé, ed., *Democracy without Democrats? The Renewal of Politics in the Muslim World*, (London: I. B. Tauris, 1994), pp. 23–47, and Roger Owen, 'The Practice of Electoral Democracy in the Arab East and North Africa: Some Lessons from Nearly a Century's Experience', in: E. Goldberg, R. Kasaba and J. Migdal, eds, *Rules and Rights in the Middle East: Democracy, Law and Society*, (Washington, D.C.: [n.pb.], 1993), pp. 17–42, especially 20–1, 35 and 40.

20.   Jacob Landau, *Parliaments and Parties in Egypt*, (New York: Praeger, 1954), pp. 73–5; Ali Din Hillal, *Politics and Governance in Egypt: The Era of the Parliament, 1923–1952*, op. cit., pp. 30–40; and Yunan Labib Rizk, *The History of Egyptian Cabinets*, (Cairo: Centre for Political and Strategic Studies, 1975), pp. 76–82.

21.   Yunab Labib Rizk, *Pluralism in Egypt under the British Occupation, 1882–1914*, (Cairo: Egyptian–British Library, 1970), pp. 3–20; Mahmoud Metwali, *Egypt and Pluralism and the Parliament before 1952*, (Cairo: Culture Publishing House, 1980), pp. 18–32; Ali Din Hillal, *Politics and Governance in Egypt: The Era of the Parliament, 1923–1952*, op. cit., pp. 58–89.

22.   Ali Din Hillal, ibid., pp. 78–82; Issam Diyae El-Dine, *The National Party and the Secret Struggle*, (Cairo: The Egyptian Public Book Panel, 1987), pp. 68–73.

23.   Compare: Abdel Aziz Rifai, *The Revolution of Egypt in 1919: A Historical Analytical Study, 1914*–1923, Cairo: Arab Book Publishing House, 1966; Abdel Khaliq Muhammad Lashine, *Saad Zaghlul: His Role in Egyptian Politics, 1914–1927*, (Cairo: [n.pb.], 1975), pp. 170–86. See also: Marius Deeb, *Party Politics in Egypt: The Wafd and its Rivals, 1919–1939*, London: Ithaca Press, 1979.

24.   Compare: Ervand Abrahamian, *Iran between Two Revolutions*, op. cit., pp. 86–92; Said Amir Arjomand, *The Turban for the Crown: The Islamic Revolution in Iran*, op. cit., pp. 72–5; and Sussan Siavoshi, 'The Oil Nationalization Movement', in: John Foran, ed., op. cit., pp. 131–3.

25.   J. A. Boyle, 'Dynastic and Political History of the Ilkhanids', in: *The Cambridge History of Iran*, vol. 5, (Cambridge: Cambridge University Press, 1991), pp. 365–90.

26.   Dorothya Kravolski, 'The Term of National Iran and its Revival in the Era of the Mongols', in: Dorothya Kravolski, *Iran and the Arabs*, (Beirut: [n.pb.], 1993), pp. 17789.

27.   A. Bausani, 'Religion under the Mongols', in: *The Cambridge History of Iran*, vol. 6, *op. cit.*, pp. 540–73; also, Dorothya Kravolski, 'The Authority and the Legitimacy: A Study of the Mongol Pitfall', in: Dorothya Kravolski, *op. cit.*, pp. 190–215, especially pp. 205–7.

28.   R. Savory, *Iran under the Safavids*, Cambridge: Cambridge University Press, 1980.

For comparison and contrast between the Ottomans, Safavids and Qajaris, and the relation between the spiritual and temporal, see: Wajih Kawtharani, *The Scholar and the Sultan: A Study of Two Historical Experiences: Ottoman, Safavid, Qajari*, Beirut: Rached Publication House, 1989. Compare with *Jurisprudence (Ijtihad)*, vol. 1, no. 4 (Summer 1989), pp. 281–5.

29.   Compare: Adel Alouch, *The Origins and Development of the Ottoman–Safavid Conflict (906–962 AH / 1500–1555 CE)*, Berlin: Klaus Schwarz Verlag, 1983; also, Elke Eberhard, *Osmanische Polemik gegen die Safaviden im 16 Jahrhundert nach arabischen Handschriften*, Freiburg: Schwarz Verlag, 1970.

30.   Compare: Richard Repp, *The Mufti of Istanbul: A Study in the Development of the Ottoman Learned Hierarchy*, (London: Ithaca Press, 1986), pp. 238–46. Compare with my review of the book, in: *Jurisprudence (Ijtihad)*, vol. 1, no. 3 (Summer 1989), pp. 28, and with my book: *The Nation, the Community and Power: A Study in Arab Islamic Political Thought*, Beirut: Arab Elector Publishing House, 1984, 1987.

31.   Compare: Ibn Moutahar Al-Hilli, *The 11th Door*, (Tehran: [n.pb.], 1986, pp. 211–216; Sheikh Tusi, *The End in Edicts and Jursprudence*, (Beirut: [n.pb.], 1981), pp. 131–48; J. Eliash, 'The *Ithna 'Ashari* Juristic Theory of Political and Legal Authority', *Studia Islamica*, vol. 29 (1969), pp. 25–8; and W. Madelung, 'Authority in Twelver Shi'ism in the Absence of the Imam', in: W. Madelung, *Religious Schools and Sects in Medieval Islam*, (London: [n.pb.], 1985), pp. 170–93.

32.   About relations between the clergy and the Qajaris and fundamentalists, compare: Hamid Algar, 'Religious Forces in 18th and 19th Century Iran', *The Cambridge History of Iran*, vol. 7, op. cit., pp. 705–51.

33.   Hamid Algar, *Religion and State in Iran, 1785–1906*, (Berkeley, Calif.: [n.pb.], 1969), pp. 126–33; Ann Lambton, *Qajar Persia*, (London: I. B. Tauris, 1987), pp. 194–222; and Shaul Bakhash, *Iran: Monarchy, Bureaucracy and Reform under the Qajars*, London: Ithaca Press, 1978.

34.   Hamid Algar, 'Religious Forces in 18th and 19th Century Iran', *The Cambridge History of Iran, op. cit.*, pp. 726–9.

35.   Ann Lambton, 'The Tobacco Régie: Prelude to Revolution', *Studia Islamica*, vol. 22 (1965), pp. 46–52; Nikki Keddie, *Religion and Rebellion in Iran: The Tobacco Protests of 1891–1892*, op. cit., pp. 111–36.

36.   Compare: Said Amir Arjomand, 'The *'Ulema's* Traditionalist Opposition to Parliamentarianism, 1907–1909', *Middle Eastern Studies*, vol. 17, no. 2 (1981), pp. 38–56; Abdul-Hadi Hairi, 'Shaykh Fazl Allah Nuri's Refutation of the Idea of Constitutionalism', *Middle Eastern Studies*, vol. 13, no. 3 (1977), pp. 331–46, and *Shi'ism and Constitutionalism in Iran*, (Leiden: Brill, 1977), pp. 72–108; M. Milani, *The Making of Iran's Islamic Revolution*, Westview Special Studies on the Middle East (Boulder, Colo.: Westview Press, 1988), pp. 29–30; and Shahrough Akhavi, *Religion and Politics in Contemporary Iran: Clergy-State Relations in the Pahlavi Period*, (New York: [n.pb.], 1980), pp. 25–6.

37.   Shahrough Akhavi, ibid., pp. 18 and 28–32.

38.   *Ibid.*, pp. 21–2. See also a review of the book in: Fadl Chalak, 'Religion and Politics in Contemporary Iran', *Jurisprudence (Ijtihad)*, vol. 2, no. 5 (Autumn 1989), pp. 223–34.

39.   Hamid Algar, *Religion and State in Iran, 1785–1906*, op. cit., pp. 126–33; Roy Mottahedeh, *The Mantle of the Prophet: Religion and Politics in Iran*, op. cit., pp. 210–19.

40.   Roy Mottahedeh, ibid., pp. 221–2.

41.   Ann Lambton, 'The Tobacco Régie: Prelude to Revolution', op. cit., pp.36–62.

42.   Shahrough Akhavi, *Religion and Politics in Contemporary Iran: Clergy–State Relations in the Pahlavi Period*, op. cit., pp. 30–1; also, Roy Mottahedeh, *The Mantle of the Prophet: Religion and Politics in Iran*, op. cit., pp. 224–5.

43.   Fereshteh Nouraie, 'The Constitutional Ideas of a Shiite Mujtahid: Muhammad Hussain Na'ini', *Iranian Studies*, vol. 8, no. 4 (1975), pp. 234–47; Abdul-Hadi Hairi, *Shi'ism and Constitutionalism in Iran*, op. cit., pp. 101–51; and Wajih Kawtharani, 'The Issues of Reform, *Shari'ah* and the Constitution in Modern Islamic Thought', *Jurisprudence (Ijtihad)*, vol. 1, no. 3 (Spring 1989), pp. 247–63.

44.   Amir Arjomand, *The Turban for the Crown: The Islamic Revolution in Iran*, op. cit., p. 52. The opinion held by Na'ini changed after the execution of Sheikh Nouri and the Russian/British occupations of Iran. Compare: Abdul-Hadi Hairi, *Shi'ism and Constitutionalism in Iran*, op. cit., p. 114 ff.

45.   Compare: Fahmi Jedaan, *The Basis of Progress in Islamic Thought in the Modern Arab Nation*, 2nd ed., (Beirut: Arab Institute for Studies and Publishing, 1981), pp. 114–86; Ridwan El-Sayyed, 'The Strands of Modern Islamic Thought: Its Principles, Trends and Goals', in: Ridwan El-Sayyed, *The Policies of Modern Islam* (in press).

46.   Compare: Ridwan El-Sayyed, 'The Issue of Human Rights', *University Papers* (Beirut), no. 2 (Winter 1993), pp. 81–99.

47.   Compare: Ridwan El-Sayyed, 'Roots and Modernization in Contemporary Islamic Thought', in: El-Sayyed, *The Policies of Modern Islam*, op. cit. See also Ibn Taimiyyah, *Against the Greek Logicians*, translated with an introduction and notes by Wael Hallaq, (Oxford: Clarendon Press, 1993), pp. 131–74.

48.   He says about the necessities: 'They are every religion'. Compare: Abdel Magid Turkey, 'Shatibi and Modern Legislative Jurisprudence', *Jurisprudence (Ijtihad)*, vol. 2, no. 8 (Summer 1990), pp. 237–55.

49.   Fahmi Jedaan, *The Basis of Progress in Islamic Thought in the Modern Arab Nation*, op. cit., pp. 116, 183, 192, and other pages.

50.   Muhammad Rashid Ridha, *Political Excerpts from the Magazine 'Manar'*, introduction and study by Wajih Kawtharani, (Beirut: Dar Tali'ah Publishing House, 1980), p. 97. Compare: Khaireddine Tunisi, *The Best Means to Delve into the State of the Kingdoms*, researched by Maan Ziadeh, (Beirut: Dar Tali'ah, 1972), p. 195.

51.   Bernard Lewis, *The Emergence of Modern Turkey*, (London: Oxford University Press, 1968), pp. 242–81; Jacob Landau, *The Politics of Pan-Islam: Ideology and Organization*, (Oxford: Clarendon Press; New York: Oxford University Press, 1990), pp. 176–82.

52.   Compare: C. D. Smith, 'The Crisis of Orientation: The Shift of Egyptian Intellectuals to Islamic Subjects in the 1930s', *IJMES*, vol. 4 (1973), pp. 382–410; Shahrough Akhavi, *Religion and Politics in Contemporary Iran: Clergy–State Relations in the Pahlavi Period*, op. cit., p. 66.

53.   Akhavi, ibid., pp. 26–32; also, Abdul-Hadi Hairi, *Shi'ism and Constitutionalism in Iran*, op. cit., pp. 144–9.

54.   Akhavi, ibid., pp. 32–59.

55.   Ibid., pp. 61–3; also, Amir Arjomand, *The Turban for the Crown: The Islamic Revolution in Iran*, op. cit., pp. 84–6.

56. Akhavi, ibid., pp. 61–3, and Arjomand, ibid., pp. 84–6.

57. Akhavi, ibid., pp.95–105; M. Milani, *The Making of Iran's Islamic Revolution*, Westview Special Studies on the Middle East, op. cit., pp. 41–6; and Arjomand, ibid., pp. 91–3.

58. Akhavi, ibid., pp. 105–8.

59. Arjomand, op. cit., pp. 100–1.

60. Ibid., pp. 94–6, and Akhavi, op. cit., pp. 120–3.

61. Misagh Parsa, 'Mosque of Last Resort: State Reforms and Social Conflict in the Early 1960s', in: John Foran, ed., *A Century of Revolution: Social Movements in Iran*, op. cit., pp. 135–59.

62. Amir Arjomand, *The Turban for the Crown: The Islamic Revolution in Iran*, op. cit., pp. 98–105; Shahrough Akhavi, *Religion and Politics in Contemporary Iran: Clergy–State Relations in the Pahlavi Period*, op. cit., p. 166–8.

63. The book was published in Arabic twice, under the titles *The Islamic Government* and *Walayat Al-Faqeeh*. See the demands made by religious officials before Khomeini's book in the book by Fehmi Houwaidi, entitled *Iran from Within*, pp. 52–4.

64. The classic study on the Muslim Brotherhood is the one compiled by Richard P. Mitchell (1969). It was twice translated into Arabic.

65. Amir Arjomand, *The Turban and the Crown: The Islamic Revolution in Iran*, op. cit., pp. 97–8.

66. Many volumes were published under various titles, such as: *The Islamic Solution: Its Means, Its Alternatives*, and *The Islamic Solution: A Necessity, an Imperative*.

67. Compare: Ridwan El-Sayyed, *The Concepts of Communities in Islam*, Beirut: Arab Selection Publishing House, 1984, 1992; Wajih Kawtharani, 'Civil Society and State in Arab History', paper presented at the Seminar on Civil Society in the Arab World and its Role in Achieving Democracy, organized by the Centre for Arab Unity Studies, pp. 119–31; Khaled Ziadeh, *The Traditional Image of Civil Society: A Methodical Reading of the Records of the Religious Court in Tripoli in the 17th Century and the Beginning of the 18th*, Tripoli: Lebanese University, 1984.

68. Compare: Ridwan El-Sayyed, 'The Issue of the *Shura* and the Imperial Streak in Light of the Historical Experience of the Ummah', *Jurisprudence (Ijtihad)*, vol. 6, no. 25 (Fall 1994), pp. 41–62.

69. Compare *ibid.*, pp. 41–62, and Ridwan El-Sayyed, 'The *Shura* between Text and Historical Experience of the Ummah', in: El-Sayyed, *The Politics of Modern Islam* (in press).

70. Compare: El-Sayyed, 'The Issue of *Shura* and the Imperial Streak in Light of the Historical Experience of the Ummah', in: El-Sayyed, 'The Court of Injustice Pleas: An Aspect of Relations between State and Religion in Islam', *Studies* (University of Jordan), no. 12 (1985), pp. 5–36.

71. Compare: Richard Bulliet, *The Patricians of Nishapur: A Study in Medieval Islamic Social History*, Harvard Middle Eastern Studies, 16, (Cambridge, Mass.: Harvard University Press, 1972), pp. 126–48; Ridwan El-Sayyed, 'State and City in Islam: A Study in the Visions of Mawardi and Ibn Khaldun', *Forum for Dialogue (Al-Abhath)*, no. 10 (Summer 1988), pp. 6–30, especially p. 29.

72. Compare: Roy Mottahedeh, 'Towards an Islamic Theology of Tolerance', in: T. Lindholm and K. Vogt, eds, *Islamic Law Reforms and Human Rights*, (Oslo: [n.pb.], 1993), pp. 25–36.

73. Compare: Peter Gran, *Islamic Roots of Capitalism: Egypt, 1760–1840*, fore-

word by Afaf Lutfi As-Sayed Marsot, Modern Middle East Series, no. 4, Austin: University of Texas Press, 1979.

74. Compare: Maan Ziadeh, 'Civil Society and State in Contemporary Arab Revivalist Thought', paper presented at the Seminar on Civil Society in the Arab World and its Role in Achieving Democracy, organized by the Centre for Arab Unity Studies, pp. 153–72.

75. Concerning the 'Islamic phenomenon', compare: Nazih Ayubi, *Political Islam: Religion and Politics in the Arab World*, London, New York: Routledge, 1991; and John Ruedy, ed., *Islamism and Secularism in North Africa*, New York: St Martin's Press, 1994.

76. Compare: John Foran, 'The Iranian Revolution', in: John Foran, ed., *A Century of Revolution: Social Movements in Iran*, op. cit., pp. 160–88.

77. Compare: R. N. Frye, *The Heritage of Persia*, (London: Weidenfeld and Nicolson, [1962]), pp. 3–28; and A. E. Christensen, *L'Iran sous les Sassanides*, (Osnabruck: O. Zeller, 1971), pp. 286–94.

78. Compare: Shaul Bakhash, 'The Politics of Land, Law and Social Justice in Iran', *Middle East Journal*, vol. 43, no. 2 (1989), pp. 186–201; Mehrdad Haghayeghi, 'Politics and Ideology in the Islamic Republic of Iran', *Middle Eastern Studies*, vol. 29, no. 1 (January 1993), pp. 36–52; and Fehmi Houwaidi, *Iran from Within*, pp. 156–60.

79. Compare: Ervand Abrahamian, 'Khomeinism' (1993), and 'Public Confessions in the Islamic Republic of Iran', in: E. Goldberg, R. Kasaba and J. Migdal, eds, *Rules and Rights in the Middle East: Democracy, Law and Society*, op. cit., pp. 191–223; Haggay Ram, 'Crushing the Opposition', *Middle East Journal*, vol. 46, no. 3 (1992), pp. 226–39; Mansoor Moaddel, *Class, Politics and Ideology in the Iranian Revolution*, (New York: Columbia University Press, 1993), pp. 199–264; and Ali Banuazizi, 'Iran's Revolutionary Impasse: Political Factionalism and Societal Resistance', *Middle East Report* (November–December 1994), pp. 2–8.

80. Roy Mottahedeh, 'The Islamic Movement: The Case for Democratic Inclusion', *Contention*, vol. 4, no. 3 (Spring 1995), pp. 116–18; R. Cottam, 'Inside Revolutionary Iran', *Middle East Journal*, vol. 43, no. 2 (1989), pp. 168–85; and Shahrough Akhavi, 'Elite Factionalism in the Islamic Republic of Iran', *Middle East Journal*, vol. 41, no. 2 (1987), pp. 181–201.
The famous disagreement about the term of the scholar remains. The public term is advocated by the regime. However, many scholars disagree. One of the most famous books written in that respect is the one by Ayatollah Montaziri, *The Term of the Scholar*. Compare: Fehmi Houwaidi, *Iran from Within*, pp. 141–8.

81. See Saad Eddin Ibrahim, 'Civil Society and Prospects for Democratization in the Arab World', in: A. R. Norton, ed., *Civil Society in the Middle East*, (Leiden: Brill, 1995), pp. 39–44; and Roger Owen, 'The Practice of Electoral Democracy in the Arab East and North Africa: Some Lessons from Nearly a Century's Experience', in: E. Goldberg, R. Kasaba and J. Migdal, eds, *Rules and Rights in the Middle East: Democracy, Law* 82. Saad Eddin Ibrahim, op. cit., pp. 51–4. Ibrahim cited two Arab countries as examples, Lebanon and Somalia, where civil war had erupted. In Somalia, all social and political structures were broken up because of the limited role of NGOs; whereas in Lebanon, the basic structures were not destroyed, despite protracted war, because of the strength of its NGOs.

83. Mustapha Kamel Al-Sayed, 'Civil Institutions at the National Level', paper presented at the Seminar on Civil Society in the Arab World and its Role in Achieving Democracy, organized by the Centre for Arab Unity Studies, p. 652 ff.

84. Compare concepts of civil society in: Z. A. Pelezynski, ed., *The State and Civil Society: Studies in Hegel's Political Philosophy*, Cambridge, New York: Cambridge University Press, 1984; and Ernest Gellner, 'Civil Society in Historical Context', *International Social Science Journal*, no. 129 (1991), pp. 495–501.

Today, many people consider the state as opposed to society. Others think that the state is one of society's institutions, as for any other lobbying group. Compare: E. Shils, 'The Venture of Civil Society', *Government and Opposition*, vol. 26, no. 1 (1992), pp. 3–20; M. Walzer, 'The Idea of Civil Society', *Dissent* (Spring 1990), pp. 293–304; and C. Taylor, 'Modes of Civil Society', *Public Culture*, vol. 3, no. 1 (1990), pp. 95–132.

85. Compare: B. Turner, 'Orientalism and the Problem of Civil Society in Islam', in: Asaf Hussein, Robert Olson and Jamil Qureishi, eds, *Orientalism, Islam and Islamicists*, (Brattleboro: Amana Books, 1984), pp. 23–42; Yahya Sadowski, 'The New Orientalism and the Democracy Debate', *Middle East Report*, no. 183 (1993), pp. 14–21; and John Waterbury, 'Democracy without Democrats?', in: Ghassan Salamé, ed., *Democracy without Democrats? The Renewal of Politics in the Muslim World*, op. cit., pp. 23–47.

86. Compare: Ahmad Moussalli, 'Modern Islamic Fundamentalist Discourses in Civil Society, Pluralism and Democracy', in: A. R. Norton, ed., *Civil Society in the Middle East*, op. cit., pp. 79–119; E. Goldberg, 'Private Goods, Public Wrongs, and Civil Society in Some Medieval Arab Theory and Practice', in: E. Goldberg, R. Kasaba and J. Migdal, eds, *Rules and Rights in the Middle East: Democracy, Law and Society*, op. cit., pp. 248–71; and Seif Ed-Dine Abdel Fattah Ismail, 'Civil Society and the State in Islamic Thought and Practice (A Mathematical Review)', paper presented at the Seminar on Civil Society in the Arab World and its Role in Achieving Democracy, organized by the Centre for Arab Unity Studies, pp. 279–311.

87. The title of the book that was edited by Ghassan Salamé (1994), and included in an article by John Waterbury under the same title. This issue was the issue tackled during the seminar held by the Centre in Cyprus, under the title 'Democracy Crisis in the Arab World: The Proceedings of the Seminar Organized by the Centre for Arab Unity Studies', Beirut: CAUS, 1984. Also, the paper by Samir Amin, under the title 'Remarks on the Method of Analysing the Democracy Crisis in the Arab Nation', pp. 307–24, along with the comments.

88. Compare, with a pessimistic view: Mustapha Kamel Al-Sayyed, 'A Civil Society in Egypt?', in: A. R. Norton, ed., *Civil Society in the Middle East*, op. cit., pp. 269–93.

21

Civil Society in Iran: Continuity and Change

MOHAMMAD HADI SEMATI*

Introduction

The concept of civil society, along with its corollary democracy, appears to have become fashionable nowadays. Leading periodicals, numerous books and a variety of conferences have taken an interest in the idea of civil society. At first glance, this may sound reasonable , considering the profound transformation in the former Soviet Union and the onset of velvet revolutions across Eastern Europe. These popular upheavals have indeed expanded the outlets for political participation and resulted, for the first time since World War II, in the birth of new institutions accommodating such participation. But underneath the euphoria, there is confusion over what exactly civil society is. This confusion remains. Indeed, recent developments in both societies that are undergoing massive change and in industrialized democracies have compounded the debate over the nature and functions of civil society.

The purpose of this paper is not a full treatment of the theoretical problematic of civil society. After briefly illustrating some of the difficulties of conceptualization, I will try to explain the peculiar nature of the Iranian state, its relation to civil society and the prospects for the development of an autonomous civil society. Particular attention will be paid to the dilemmas facing a religiously constituted polity in a post-revolutionary society.

Civil Society

The notion of civil society, notwithstanding its origin in European political thought, has become a conceptual tool in analyzing societies as diverse as former East Germany, Colombia and Somalia, which are not only geographically a continent apart, but culturally belong to three different worlds. Historical development of the term and the mutations it has experienced throughout the years, make an assessment of the utility of the concept even more difficult. Some may argue that the incorporation of the notion into contemporary political discourse and its acceptance by academia have given it the status of a universal construct.

The modern idea of civil society as a relatively homogeneous whole, separate from or antagonistic to the state, is a product of the late 18th and early 19th centuries. The genesis of the concept and the disputes surrounding it before the Enlightenment, though helpful to our discussion, are not critical for the arguments being advanced in this paper. It is more appropriate to draw on the more prevalent conceptions of civil society that have been formulated since the Enlightenment.

For some, civil society is primarily an arena of associational life that cements together a variety of socio-political forces and makes them a homogeneous entity *vis-à-vis* the state.[1] This broad conceptualization focuses on individual and collective interests that are promoted in a public sphere immune from state control. Others view civil society as an independent arena in which interests are organized in more or less formal structures that can exert pressure on the state and remain free from its tutelage.

Gramsci defined civil society as the realm in which the state rules, not through naked force, but rather through its cultural hegemony and the creation of an entrenched moral order. For Gramsci, therefore, the state dominates civil society through 'ever more conspicuous elements of regulated society'.[2] Poulantzas abandoned the concept of civil society altogether and proclaimed that it masks the true nature and function of the state.[3] The omnipresent state permeates society through the economic structure, hence rendering the concept useless.

The evolution of the concept from a mere collection of social groups freed from absolutist states in early modern Europe, to more modern and sophisticated neo-Marxist conceptions, demonstrates the theoretical divide in the literature. The gulf between these conceptualizations is not easy to bridge. It seems that the mainstream definition of the concept emphasizes the creation of a public space between the state and private life where a plethora of associations, organizations, and social movements defend themselves against possible state encroachment. This particular definition presupposes a set of rights and privileges whose maintenance and assertion in the public space reveal the need for autonomy from the state. Autonomous mobilization of groups cannot take place in a vacuum. It is absolutely essential to have the state set the boundaries within which individuals and organizations can operate and exert pressures on the state. Thus, one cannot comprehend the development of civil society in a given historical context without scrutinizing the nature of the state and its trajectory in that particular society. This is more so in under-developed and developing societies where the experience of state-building manifests internal contradictions and uneven development, and where the state has left its mark on the social formation and the mosaic of social forces. In order to understand the history and the state of civil society in Iran, let us begin with an anatomy of the state.

Rentier State Capitalism: 1963–1978

This is perhaps the most critical period of a complex development process in Iran, for the state has assumed an important role and molded the social formation in significant ways. The first priority was given to land reform, which had both economic and political objectives. On the political side, the state was interested in: (1) uprooting the power base of the traditional landlord class in the countryside; and (2) defusing potential peasant uprisings by meeting some of their demands. The state, insofar as the first political objective was concerned, scored major points and substantially disorganized and fractured the landholding class.[4]

On the economic front, the underlying objective was to integrate the agricultural sector into the national market, which was becoming an institution of the new capitalist mode of production. This objective could not be achieved by automatic or voluntary actions on the part of the autonomous peasantry. The state therefore intervened to assure the integration of the agrarian economy with the national market.[5] Although the state built large and complex bureaucracies to commercialize agriculture, or introduce capitalist farming, its attempt to integrate agriculture into the national economy was not quite successful. It also scored high on the expansion of the role of the state.[6]

The oil revenue provided a 'safe' source of capital for the state throughout the 1960s and 1970s. In 1967, oil accounted for 13.8 per cent of GDP. This figure increased to 19.5 per cent in 1972 and 48.7 per cent in 1977.[7] Furthermore, oil income increased from 45.6 per cent of total government revenue in 1963 to 49.2 per cent in 1970, 67 per cent in 1973, and 73.6 per cent in 1977. The substantial surge in oil revenue gave a considerable boost to the state's aggressive industrialization programme. The role of the state massively increased in various sectors. At its peak, the state's share of investment grew to 58.5 per cent under the Fifth Plan (1973–77).[8]

The coercive apparatus of the state experienced unparalleled growth, both quantitative and qualitative.[9] Rapid industrialization, social welfare expenditure, and the development of the armed forces meant the establishment of large bureaucratic structures to carry out regulatory and coordinating functions. This further fueled the urbanization trend of the 1970s. In many provinces, over 50 per cent of employment was provided by the state. The village structure, which had mainly been changed by land reform, now had to face agents of the state who represented various bureaucratic outfits.

In the 1960s and 1970s, one could make a good case that the state in Iran became a strong and over-expanded bureaucratic structure that penetrated every aspect of social organization. Its strength, paradoxically, turned out to be its weakness. For it was a 'rentier state' whose plentiful source of income from oil, and its omnipresent bureaucracy and police apparatus, delinked it from major social classes.[10] The main medium through which the state-society nexus was connected was coercive institutions. Thus, by the mid-1970s the state was a highly autonomous organization *vis-à-vis* civil society. The pervasive presence of the state had serious implications for building institutions that could enhance citizen involvement. It effectively dwarfed the development of civil society and provided the state with a structural advantage that would be difficult to overcome for years to come.

Post-Revolutionary Trends

It is not easy to write about the outcomes of a great social revolution that is still in progress, and the life span of at least one generation has not yet passed since its occurrence. Social revolutions have usually resulted in the building of stronger and more bureaucratized states, accompanied by mass mobilization in favour of the new regime.[11] The Islamic revolution of Iran seems to be no exception. Following the transfer of power, the state was reconstructed and new institutional frameworks to foster revolutionary mobilization were formed. Indeed, the new elites managed to reconstitute state power within a new ideological framework that was in sharp contrast to that of the old regime.[12] The ethos of social justice rooted in Islam, combined with revolutionary fervor and ideals, forced the post-revolutionary state to be more responsive to the downtrodden. This would mean more state involvement in redistribution and social spending. A variety of revolutionary organizations and bureaucratic structures were the fruits of this process.

The ideology of statism and over-extended state machinery seems to be a continuous theme in the contemporary history of Iran. For many, this legacy from the pre-revolutionary period, along with post-revolutionary state-building, are structural impediments to the formation of institutions within civil society. Secure petrodollars, albeit with proclaimed awareness of the dangers, still feed the political economy of Iran, thereby accommodating traditional clientelism rampant in rentier economies.

The rentier nature of the Iranian state does not seem to be conducive to the 'civilization' of society. As Luciani has succinctly argued:

Implicitly, I assume that the state will expand to the limit of its economic capabilities. If it has the means to do so, the state will do everything, and there will be nothing that civil society (the private sector) can do except in support of the state. If the state does not have the means, and must obtain them from society (the private sector), then there is a chance for the latter to limit the power of the state.[13]

Therefore, one cannot be optimistic unless there is a change in the underlying economic structure.*

The imperatives of development in peripheral formations, as cases in Asia and Latin America reveal, demand strong state action. These societies usually take detours in industrialization and infrastructure development. To provide a favourable climate for investment, the state must intervene to create order and stability and forge an alliance among competing interests. State intervention in the development process thus becomes a necessity, resulting in a diffused social structure. Such a diffused social formation in which spheres of civil society and state are intertwined, is incapable of accommodation among divergent interests. Coercion then becomes a tool for resolving paradoxes embedded in the social structure. One may argue that this depends on the choices being made by elites in the developing world; if one chooses the right development strategy, one would not need coercion in the course of development. However, empirical records are not so promising when it comes to state intervention in the development process.[14]

Is there an optimum level of state intervention at which both socio-economic development and the autonomy of civil society could be balanced? And if there is such a point, how could an equilibrium be achieved? It is extremely difficult, if not impossible, to maintain such a balance in Iran, where a combination of populist pressures, serious international constraints, and a war-shattered economy pulls the state in many directions. Despite the problems of development imperatives, the Islamic Republic of Iran has shown amazing resiliency in the face of unbearable crises. The state, however, still has the commanding role in the economy, and it is doubtful that any substantial and steady reduction of that role could be reached in the near future. Moreover, intra-elite discord over the proper course of action, insofar as state intervention is concerned, has engendered indecisive actions on the part of the government. Fragility of policies and elite incoherence on development issues severely compound the already unfavourable conditions at the domestic and international levels.

What seems to be taking place in Iran is indicative of certain fundamental changes that will have a profound impact on the social structure in the long term. Although identifiable changes underneath the surface could be observed, yet all are in a dynamic, fluid and quite possibly reversible phase. First of all, the state is gradually shrinking and thus opening the way for other players to obtain a share of its functions. The retreat of the state will not be restricted to the economic domain but will more likely pave the way for private concerns in other areas to challenge the state. The present liberalization programmes embarked upon by President Rafsanjani are already de-politicizing part of everyday economic life, hence making it unnecessary for the state to get involved and defend itself. In other words, any contradiction in or failure of an economic policy is not going to be turned into a political issue that may incapacitate the state. In addition, the state's withdrawal will dramatically reduce possible social conflicts, since the structure of the relationship would be less amenable to collision. This is particularly true in the case of Iran, where state executives now recognize the dilemmas of policy-making in a crisis environment.

Secondly, continuous crisis, financial or otherwise, besetting the state compelled elites to take coalition building and consensus formation seriously. Moreover, the realities of power politics appear to have demonstrated that factional politics requires strategy, resources and, above all, allies. This could be a prelude to a politics of which compromise is an important element. The experience through which Iran is going may not be exactly similar to what some of the North African countries have experienced, but the underlying logic seems to be the same. 'In countries such as Algeria, Jordan, Tunisia, and Morocco, by the late 1980s the acute financial crisis of the state put the politics of consensus and coalition-building on the political agenda, albeit in limited and manipulated forms'.[15] As the development plans proceed and international pressures headed by US sanctions start biting, post-revolutionary state-builders in Iran will be even more attentive to the need for bargaining in the field of domestic politics. Lacking consensus for unified action is no longer attractive. Coherent state policy in times of acute crisis dictates a tacit political agreement on the basis of which different factions could accommodate each other. The parameters of consensus-building and cooperation are changing in the context of an evolving discourse of compromise, and under tremendous pressure from within and from the international system.

Thirdly, a change in the class structure of Iran is rapidly under way. The middle class composition of the population is widening, and the demographic structure of Iranian society, similar to many Muslim countries, clearly underscores the potential significance of this class.[16] The importance of this change stems from the fact that, along with sheer quantitative enlargement, greater educational opportunity offers the middle class an opportunity for self-expression, while growth in this educated stratum of society creates severe constraints on the financial and other resources of the state, increasing the chances of potential clashes between state and society and possibly inducing the state to further domination over society through coercive measures. Nonetheless, the trend seems to be unavoidable, and the avalanche of new demands could be retarded for a short while, but not indefinitely. The class structure then may prove to be fertile ground for nourishing social forces that could limit state intrusions. As the level of demands increases, and they become more articulated, the state would not be able to retain its unyielding power, at least as efficiently as it used to, vis-à-vis society.

Let us now turn to more tangible and immediate changes that have set the stage for the germination of a civic sphere in Iran. These changes, though still unfolding in a dynamic context, represent the struggle of a nation undergoing a revolutionary transformation and trying to resolve internal contradictions based on its history and encounters with the outside world. *First* and foremost, there was the creation of a parliamentary structure after the revolution. Lively and open debates covering a range of issues, from economic policy to foreign policy to cultural policy, have fostered a discourse of legislation and relative autonomy of the legislature. Although Iran has had experience with parliamentarism and constitutionalism, this time around it has surpassed all expectations, given the pattern of post-revolutionary state-building.[17] Despite the presumed rigidity of the *Shari'ah*, the Islamic Consultative Assembly has been flexible enough to respond to changing circumstances over the last 17 years.

Needless to say, the parliament has to operate within a unique constitutional framework that subordinates its legislative activity to an appointed higher structure, the Council of Guardians. However, the idea of legislation and the dissemination of information about the political in-fightings within the parliament have sensitized the discussion over the proper role of a modern legislative body that is guided by a tradition of Shiite jurisprudence. A fully developed legislative structure to which citizens and groups can have access, emerges from an interaction among different socio-political forces. These forces are indeed defining themselves in contemporary Iran, and one cannot but be hopeful that the end result will be further institutionalization of parliamentarism and the emergence of more articulated and refined political platforms.

Second, over the last few years, the public has benefited greatly from the publication of numerous periodicals representing diverse political and philosophical persuasions. The titles and fields of interest include art, architecture, philosophy, religion, communication, theology, and ethics. Indeed, new journals and magazines are still mushrooming at national as well as local levels. The prolific marketplace of ideas has created a vibrant intellectual atmosphere that has been very rare in the contemporary history of Iran. The discursive field of intellectual discourse is seen as enriching experience from which fundamental questions pertaining to the future of Iranian society are being raised. The current soul-searching climate emanating from the exchanges between these publications is a vital step towards authenticity. The quest for authenticity, self-destructive as it may sometimes be, is providing a sense of self-confidence in elites, which is believed to be a pre-condition for strengthening civil society. Thus, this is an arena where civil society is being further consolidated. Of course, this is not to say that limitations and state control do not exist. On the contrary, one cannot say or write whatever he or she deems desirable.

The present debates signify a discernible shift in the outlook of the intellectual community as compared to the previous generations. First there has been a departure from simplistic categorizations of the world and human experience. Secondly, the new generation has moved away from the developmentalist paradigm of modernization, which had been imprisoned by the Parsonian dichotomous scheme for decades. Third, the current intellectual community is well-versed in Western social theory and cutting-edge research in social sciences and humanities. Last but not least, the existing generation seems to reflect on the past while looking to the future. In other words, from secular to religious publications, an inclination to be attentive to the force of tradition is undoubtedly present.

Thirdly, the mobilization of groups whose bearing on major socio-political changes has not been noticeable in the past. Women are increasingly finding themselves in public life and are faced with increasing opportunities for social mobility. The revolution has helped to lift many restrictions barring women from engaging in social and political affairs. The space provided for women is definitely generating group consciousness, thereby activating a major proportion of the population. Major indicators show considerable improvements in women's condition.* Altered divorce laws, educational advancement, improved labour laws, and many other subtle changes are bringing issues of women's rights to the forefront. The changing nature of gender relations are signs of the evolving maturity of a civic sphere. Women are going to be a strong force to be reckoned with, and their solidarity structure, though still very weak, is adding another layer to the already established networks of civil society. I by no means contend that women as a group suffering from centuries of oppression are suddenly freed from subjugation. All I suggest is that women as a whole, and relative to their historical role, are more than ever occupying the public space, and this is indeed critical for a society whose female population is a little more than 50 per cent.

Fourthly, parties and partisan competition do not seem to have a strong tradition in Iran. The few instances of the formation of parties proved to be short-lived. The post-revolutionary experience has not been a success either. After the last few years of factional politics, the political landscape despite its complexity, is much less confusing. Factions, groups, and cliques are more recognizable and adherents to them seem to be more able to identify with their respective factions. Although still fluid and constantly changing, party identification is incrementally affecting the mass nature of politics. Due to sharper distinctions between groups and their enunciated ideological and political differences, the debate about parties has started again. The discussion about parties and their functional utility is very much tied to the need for consensus regarding development policies. Despite the lack of formal party structures, informal networks and pressure groups are openly performing their tasks, and with relative freedom. These informal structures are more and more defining themselves and becoming outspoken in agenda setting. To the extent that civil society's cardinal institution is the party, any move in the direction of the development of a culture of party competition should be welcomed.

All of the subtle changes mentioned above are taking place in the context of an emerging theoretical dissonance regarding the nature of the state and political authority in Shiite Islam. The debate is about sources of legitimacy, rights and responsibilities of both the state and citizens, and justificatory systems for defining the boundaries, if there is one, of the state and society. In a nutshell, it is about the political philosophy that gave rise to the Islamic state. This is a very familiar debate in the Arab world, particularly in Egypt.[18] Iran is therefore reviving, albeit in very different national and international circumstances, the discourse of religious authenticity. As for the notion of civil society, the two very familiar schools are engaged in an exchange, the result of which is not definitive.

The school that follows a strict interpretation of the text, rejects outright the concept of civil society.[19] It maintains that the mere acceptance of the term is contrary to the absolute guardianship of the jurist. In other words, 'no man-made and legal institution has the right to supervise him, and he is solely responsible before God'.[20] Since the authority is bestowed on him by divine ordinance, institutional structures within society cannot undermine his legitimacy. This interpretation thus leaves no room for an autonomous civic sphere vis-à-vis the state.

The other interpretation approaches the text more hermeneutically and allows for the institutional supervision of political authority and its accountability to citizens.[21] The resolution of this theoretical quarrel is indeed significant for the future of civil society in Iran.

Conclusion

Fundamental, albeit subtle, changes are under way all across the Middle East. From North Africa to the southern part of the Persian Gulf, one can detect new movements, original ideas, and a different breed of discourse about modernizing tradition. Certain structural shifts in the nature and function of the state are common in both Iran and the Arab world. The state is in retreat across the region. Disillusionment, despair, and failure to reach the imagined authentic self in the face of massive international pressure, have ignited the search for social reconstruction and self-definition.

In Iran the discussion about a 'home-grown' pathway to civility has started from the 'bottom up'. In the Arab world similar discussions, though advanced in a different configuration of social forces, have started anew. The debate about institutional arrangements that could curtail state power is widespread. Despite the shortsighted and ahistorical view of many, we have not reached the 'end of ideology'; rather, the era of political reconstruction anchored in a domestic soul-searching has begun. I believe it is a crucial juncture at which the entire Muslim world must make strategic decisions. It is a rocky terrain where the Arabs and Iranians would be better off travelling together.

Notes

* Professor, Faculty of Law and Political Science, University of Tehran, Tehran, Iran.

1.   August R. Norton, 'The Future of Civil Society in the Middle East', *Middle East Journal*, vol. 47, no. 2 (1993), p. 211.

2.   Antonio Gramsci, *Selections from the Prison Notebooks*, translated and edited by Quintin Hoare and Geoffrey Nowell Smith, (London: Lawrence & Wishart, 1971), p. 263.

3.   Nicos Poulantzas, *Political Power and Social Classes*, translated by Timothy O'Hagan, (London: New Left Books, 1973), p. 124.

4.   Farhad Kazemi, *Poverty and Revolution in Iran: The Migrant Poor, Urban Marginality, and Politics*, (New York: New York University Press, 1980), pp. 35–6.

5.   Afsaneh Najmabadi, *Land Reform and Social Change in Iran*, (Salt Lake City: University of Utah Press, 1987), p. 169.

6.   Ibid., p. 168; also, Eric Hoogland, *Land and Revolution in Iran*, (Austin: University of Texas Press, 1982), chap. 5.

7.   PBO, 1978, p. 37. For an examination of the oil industry and its impact on the national economy, see Fereidun Fesharaki, *Development of the Iranian Oil Industry*, New York: Praeger, 1976.

8.   Data and analysis concerning the development plans are available in: Ervand Abrahamian, *Iran between Two Revolutions*, (Princeton, N.J.: Princeton University Press, 1982), pp. 425–35.

9.   Ibid., and Mark J. Gasiorowski, *U.S. Foreign Policy and the State: The Building of a Client State*, Ithaca and London: Cornell University Press, 1991.

10.   Hossein Mahdavi, 'The Pattern and Problems of Economic Development in Rentier States: The Case of Iran', in: Michael Cook, ed., *Studies in the Economic History of the Middle East*, London: Oxford University Press, 1970. Also, Theda Skocpol, 'Rentier State and Shi'i Islam in the Iranian Revolution', *Theory and Society*, vol. 11, no. 3 (1982), pp. 265–84.

11.   Theda Skocpol, 'Social Revolution and Mass Military Mobilization', *World Politics*, vol. 40, no. 2 (1988), pp. 147–68.

12.   Farideh Farhi, *States and Urban-based Revolutions: Iran and Nicaragua*, (Urbana and Chicago: University of Illinois Press, 1990), chap. 5.

13.   Giacomo Luciani, 'The Oil Rent, the Fiscal Crisis of the State and Democratization', in Ghassan Salamé, ed., *Democracy without Democrats? The Renewal of Politics in the Muslim World*, (London: I. B. Tauris, 1994), p. 135.
14.   For an interesting study concerning human rights trade-offs in the course of development, see Jack Donnelly, 'Human Rights and Development: Complementary or Competing Concerns?', *World Politics*, 36 (1984), pp. 225–83.
15.   Manochehr Dorraj, 'State Petroleum and Democratization in the Middle East and North Africa', in: Manochehr Dorraj, ed., *The Changing Political Economy of the Third World*, (Boulder, Colo.: Lynne Reinner Publishers, 1995), p. 136.
16.   Philippe Fargues, 'Demographic Explosion or Social Upheaval', in: Ghassan Salamé, ed., *Democracy without Democrats? The Renewal of Politics in the Muslim World*, op. cit., p. 157.
17.   For a superb account of constitution-making and parliamentary tradition in Iran, see Said Amir Arjomand, 'Constitutions and the Struggle for Political Order: A Study in the Modernization of Political Tradition', in: Serif Mardin, ed., *Cultural Transitions in the Middle East*, New York: E. J. Brill, 1994. In this essay, Arjomand examines the interplay of international and national political traditions in the making of constitutions and, by implication, parliamentary structures.
18.   For an analysis of the ideas of leading Islamic thinkers who walked this familiar terrain, such as Seyyed Qotob and Hasan al-Banna, see Ahmad S. Moussalli, 'Modern Islamic Fundamentalist Discourses on Civil Society, Pluralism and Democracy', in: A. R. Norton, ed., *Civil Society in the Middle East*, vol. 1, Leiden: E. J. Brill, 1995.
19.   Ernest Gellner purports that the idea of civil society could not easily be justified by Islamic texts. Because politics and religion are so inseparable, it is hard to conceive of the separation between state and society. See Ernest Gellner, 'Civil Society in Historical Context', *International Social Science Journal*, 43 (1991), pp. 495–510.
20.   Mohsen Kadivar, 'State Theories in Shiite Jurisprudence', *Rahbord*, no. 4 (1994), pp. 1–41.
21.   *Ibid.*, p. 30.

Eleven

International Relations in the Arab and Iranian
Corners, and Sensitivity of International Interests
to their Ties

22

Arab-Iranian Rapprochement: the Regional and International Impediments

MAHMOOD SARIOLGHALAM*

This paper attempts to explore the international aspects of Arab-Iranian relations, with an emphasis on the aftermath of the Iranian revolution in 1979. Compared to many other regions in the international system, the Middle East as a sub-system is one salient internationalized region. Though from a political economy perspective, all regions are now internationalized, there is a peculiar distinction between the Middle East and all other similarly viable developing regions (Pacific, West Asia and Latin America): of these four regions, the Middle East is the most politically-dependent.

The assumptions and hypotheses of this paper stem from the above premise. This paper rests on two interrelated assumptions: (1) the Middle East is the most internationalized region among developing areas; and (2) Arab-Iranian relations are strongly overshadowed by this fact. This state of affairs is, largely, a result of two factors: *first*, the weak structure of the state in the Middle East and, *second*, Middle Eastern regional dynamics, most notably the Arab-Israeli conflict and the political and security ramifications of the oil industry. The conclusion drawn is that the two fundamental reasons why Arab-Iranian relations have not entered into an efficiently developing status are the weak Arab state structure and the highly internationalized Middle Eastern political structure.

The Middle East and the Theory of Internal Integration

Perhaps no region has been so disturbed as the Middle East as a consequence of the rise of the modern world. The Middle East, due to its cultural traits and various politico-historical peculiaraties, was not prepared to absorb or learn from the ramifications of modernization.[1] In return, during the twentieth century, perhaps no region has been used and misused as much as the Middle East. Although, in this process of colonization and neo-colonialism, the West can be blamed for much of Middle Eastern ills, it is the belief of this author that the incompetence of the elite groups in the region is also a significant causal factor. The Arab world accommodated the West in a negative way – i.e., it was not a form of accommodation that nurtured sustained economic development or political adaptation. Iran, due to its internal deficiencies, elite incongruencies and societal stratification, while oscillating between confrontation and consent, could not accommodate tradition and modernity in a model-like process of societal and political development.[2]

Pacific-region history demonstrates the possibility of such positive engagement and absorption. These states have demonstrated an apparent ability to absorb those technological and institutional aspects of European modernity that are conducive to material success,[3] whilst maintaining, albeit in various uniquely 'modern' forms, some continuity with their perceived cultural and historical legacies.[4] Borrowing a third world specialist's terminology, the NICs (newly industrialized countries) of East Asia have 'domesticated'[5] new norms of international economic and political conduct. The keys to these countries' success, in the belief of this author, are certain modes of learning, change and adaptation on the one hand, and elite-level consensus-building processes on the other. There are, of course, economic and international factors contributing to the Asia-Pacific region's development. But these less tangible variables have also proved remarkably paramount in the unfolding of economic and social development.[6]

It is the argument of this essay that the marginalization and decay that characterize Middle Eastern societies is largely due to structural factors. The main blame must lie with the elites of the region, who have tended to lean toward sweeping and inflexible ideological responses to the problems of development. Middle Eastern elites have largely failed to develop flexible – and 'pragmatic' – styles of rhetoric, leadership and problem solving. The result has clearly been misconduct, waste, malaise, frustration, despair and most important of all, dependence.[7]

In development literature, this essay emphasises domestic indicators rather than external ones. Towards this end, the author has developed the *theory of internal integration* as an explanation for the rise of NICs, and also as a prescription for developmental strategies of countries like Iran and other Middle Eastern states.[8] In this context, it is the belief of this author that it is analytically and theoretically much more appropriate to look into domestic and regional variables than to trace the causality of underdevelopment and dependence in the Middle East. Let us now apply these various approaches.

The State Structure and Arab-Iranian Relations

This section attempts to draw correlations between the structure of the state in the Middle East, and international influence in the region. As to the nature of the Iranian state, it is evident that two different sets of arguments can be presented in the pre- and post-revolutionary stages. Since this paper focuses on the post-revolutionary period, a preliminary conceptualization of the state in Iran is analyzed below.

Although the domestic orientation of the Iranian revolution in 1979 for the most part decreased foreign control and externally-directed agenda-setting, Iranian foreign policy initiatives – due to the weakness of Middle Eastern polities – actually contributed to greater internationalization of the region. Domestically, Iran spoke and acted with much greater freedom and sovereignty, which may be attributed to the nature of the Iranian revolution. Historically, Iran had always been sensitive to its authenticity. This sensitivity was heightened in the aftermath of the revolution.[9] The post-revolutionary concept of authenticity in Iran concentrated on Islamic foundations. The perception of Iranian statesmen was directed towards obtaining greater Islamic authenticity. Middle Eastern states were encouraged to look inward instead of expanding their interdependencies. The ideological pressures of the Iranian revolutionary state on the Arab states were to act independently of foreign influence, to decrease external penetration of Muslim affairs and to move towards 'Islamic unity' among Muslim countries. Moreover, the Islamic state in Iran encouraged Arab polities to return to Islam, safeguard Muslims from 'Westoxication' and avoid mixing with alien cultures. Iranian foreign policy pursued the de-Americanization of Middle Eastern politics, since it perceived American influence as a major obstacle to its most profound political ideal: bringing about greater Muslim sovereignty and authenticity.[10]

The basic reaction of the Arab states was a widespread feeling of being threatened. This feeling of threat caused a chain of reactions by Arab states that actually resulted in opposition to Iran's initial intentions. Arab states tended to maintain greater political distance between Iran and themselves, develop closer relations with the West – and especially the United States – replace the Israeli threat with the 'Iranian threat', and internally portray greater 'Islamic posturing'.[11]

The nature of the Arab state from Oman to Morocco, let alone Iraq and Saudi Arabia with their much closer geo-political proximity to Iran, could not accommodate these environmental demands. These demands stem from a foreign policy that carried an orientation founded upon the political idealism of Iran's Islamic revolution.

These foreign policy outlooks and demands, though well-intended and original, were unrealistic and lacked strategic substance. They disregarded the deep dependencies of the Arab world and the historically-accumulated misperceptions between Iran and the Arab state system. In their historical interactions, Iran and the Arab world have not experienced long durations of peace and constructive relations. Major Arab states and Iran have generally faced each other as competitors in trade, territory, religious assertiveness,

political power and regional status. Therefore, in an already tense and dis-
trustful environment, the influence of international players has only
intensified the political and cultural interactions. It is no coincidence, then,
that Iran's major trading partners and frequent political allies, have historically been extra-regional.

The argument here is that a stronger Arab state system could have contributed to heightened stability and dialogue between Iran and the Arab
world, as one could find historical interactive and reinforcing relationships
between, for example, France, Germany and England in Europe. The presence of dialogue and mutual-reinforcement between these European
countries is largely attributable to the internal strength of their states.[12]
The Middle Eastern dilemma of weak states seeking foreign mechanisms
for regime security and false legitimization processes is not unique to this
region. Many African, Latin American, and now Central Asian countries,
also suffer from this weakness.

It would be difficult to argue against the fact that the Iranian state became much stronger after the revolution, arguing for the causes it believed
in and defending its interests, regardless of the actual nature of these causes
and interests. It is also a fact that the Iranian state was able to hold back
well-armed Iraqi forces and prevent the loss of Iranian territory, despite a
global and regional consensus to defeat Iran. This was the first war Iran
had engaged in for 160 years where territorial integrity was not lost.

It should be pointed out that a strong state is a reflection of domestic
homogeneity. Iranian social homogeneity was maintained through the war
until at least 1988. In a strong state, state-society relations are such that the
ruling elite is able to gain at least a minimum of bargaining chips in its
interactions with representatives of global economic enterprises – and/or
of other governments – where it can uphold foreign interests and gain a
better national position vis-a-vis external interests and influences. It is clear
that most Arab states do not tend to benefit from such a status.

To substantiate this point, I would like to draw upon a careful study
conducted by the Centre for Arab Unity Studies. Concerning the status of
state-society relations, it asserts that, 'a certain incongruity [exists] in the
vertical sequence or horizontal distribution of social formations in the Arab
world'.[13] Moreover, it contends that Arab societies are in a state of transition from a traditional stage, governed by hereditary criteria, to a stage
conducted according to the criteria of achievement and functionalism.[14]
The occasional appearance of modern social formations in some Arab countries does not mark the disappearance of the traditional and kinship
formation and mentality. There exists 'a persistent individual attachment
and loyalty to the traditional formations'.[15] The authors of this interesting
study further state that 'one of the inconsistencies of the Arab social system
since political independence lies in the fact that, during periods of social

unrest or conflict, some of the modern social formations have themselves sought to profit from these traditional loyalties in their struggles'.[16]

As to the economic standpoint of the Arab state system, the most notable examples concern the OPEC and OAPEC countries. As the above study points out, the OPEC experience now symbolizes an era of unfulfilled hopes, and the rapidly worsening deterioration of Arab economic bargaining power. Contrary to expectation, the flow of oil income into some Arab countries did not produce Arab solidarity and/or strong Arab states vis-à-vis the external environment. To compensate the current deficit in their balance of payments, the non-oil producing Arab countries have had to rely extensively on foreign loans. Presently, Arab states' external debt amounts to more than $100 billion compared to $4.7 billion in 1970.[17]

The substantial increase in Arab exports and imports has not led to greater Arab solidarity or a stronger Arab state system. 'Tens of billions of dollars have been spent on projects in the contracting and civil engineering market, the lion's share of which has gone to foreign companies, foreign contractors and foreign consulting firms'.[18] Data also indicate that a large portion of worldwide contracts awarded to the 400 largest US contractors consisted of Arab construction contracts. Despite vast amounts of income earned during the last third of the 20th century by the Arab world, the study points out that Arab states have become more dependent on the outside world for loans, products, food supplies, arms and [political] *fait accomplis*. Furthermore, it is generally evident that the Arab world has become more dependent on the increased export of petroleum, on foreign imports, foreign loans, foreign technological expertise and foreign food. In some senses, the cultural dependence of the Arab states has also increased. The net result may be summarized as political dependence.[19]

Although Iran has not produced tangible results in its drive towards economic self-sufficiency, and subsequent post-war strategy of economic privatization, it does enjoy more political independence than any Arab country. Elite sovereignty is a function of the ideological outlook and material interests of the ruling coalitions.[20] Ruling coalitions in Iran and much of the Arab world are rather distinct. The post-revolutionary Iranian elite have very little international exposure, have risen to power through revolutionary processes, and, generally speaking, are not characterized by middle-class social roots. The cleric network in Iran has allowed the state to remain politically indigenous while learning the methods and mechanisms of statecraft in a difficult process. Most Arab elites depend heavily on international power coalitions and global power networking.[21]

One can even contend that many Arab states have been formed and given birth by exogenous factors. The political matrix that included Iran and much of the Arab world – as far as the state formation processes are concerned – carries numerous contradictions. Indigenously-based, legitimized and elected elite groups in the Arab state system are, to be fair, nil. Where international or extra-regional interests form the nature and scope of the relationships between competing and rival neighbouring states, vulnerabilities on both sides of the regional matrix will prevail. The fragile nature of Arab-Iranian relations, especially in the post-revolutionary period, is a result of the region's political map, which is organized and directed by extra-regional interests. This is due to the region's political weakness and lack of well-developed, indigenous national interests.

The Regional Structure and Arab-Iranian Relations

No region in the post-World War II era has experienced as intense an environment of conflict and confrontation as the Middle East. Given the great potential of this region for growth and development, it is the least developed region in the Third World compared to Asia-Pacific and Latin American regions. In this context, the Middle East has also been the least peaceful region of all. In Spinoza's outlook on war and ways to contain it, 'peace among as well as within states [is] essential to the development of uniquely human capacities'.[22] Moreover, Rousseau observed that ' ... the difficulty is not only in the actors but also in the situations they face.' While by no means ignoring the part that avarice and ambition play in the birth and growth of conflict, Rousseau's analysis makes clear the extent to which conflict appears inevitably in the social affairs of men.[23] In *The Wealth of Nations*, Adam Smith also placed a great value on peace as a significant prerequisite for growth and opulence.[24] The conflictual atmosphere of the Middle East is pivotal to its continued political marginalization. The outcome of this situation – and the central theme of this paper – is the deepening of Middle Eastern internationalization.

In tracing the causal chain for this second process of internationalization, one can cite the Arab-Israeli conflict and the complex network of the oil industry, arms sales and Arab dependency. No other issue has absorbed so many Arab resources – particularly energy and time – as the Arab-Israeli conflict. The opportunity lost in this regard is enormous. Undoubtedly, as a result of this conflict, the region has become further internationalized. Of course, one objective approach to the analysis of this relationship would be to tabulate statistics, historic events and elite statements foreshadowing the impact of Arab-Israeli wars on the internationalization of the region. But the issue is beyond quantitative analysis, for the intangible variables in the calculus of power have a more powerful determining role than the tangible ones. The weaknesses of the Arab order, especially in the areas of conceptual and strategic cohesion, commitment, mobilization of moral resources, and conviction over the future, are mostly responsible for Arab permeability to external influences.

It is probable that the 1967 Arab-Israeli war furthered the internation-alization of the Middle East. By allowing the Soviets to participate in Middle Eastern diplomacy, Egypt broke the Western political monopoly in the region. 'The entry of the Soviets into the area freed the Arabs from their dependence on the West, gave them more room to manoeuvre in world affairs, and made the superpowers compete for their favours. Local actors would not have been able to shape their relationship with the superpowers without the structural context of the Cold War. This context bestowed on smaller states considerable freedom of action, but it had some drawbacks as well'.[25] The competition between the USSR and the US over the Middle East, which was mainly brought about by the dynamics of the Arab-Israeli conflict, made Arab countries' diplomacy and intra-regional relations sus-ceptible to the global calculations of Moscow and Washington, thus further complicating Arab dependency on the outside world.

Israel's credibility and efficiency lay in its sophistication of organization, strategic outlook, group morale and conviction. Certain political traits in the Middle East, in both the Arab and non-Arab areas, are responsible for much of the decay, defeat and malaise. Personalized styles of decision-mak-ing, a non-instrumental outlook on state, society and politics, the prevalence of idealism, realities being obscured by elite rhetoric and national interests being subordinated to mass excitements, are some of the fundamental and substantive shortcomings of statesmanship in the Middle East. The 1970s were characterized by despair and indecisiveness in the Arab world. The Camp David Accords, in particular, further divided Arab states. When, in 1982, the Israelis invaded Lebanon, there was a remarkable silence in Arab capitals. In the 1980s, with heightened internal vulnerabilities – particu-larly after the end of the Cold War – the Arab world looked increasingly to Washington to finalize issues and policies. So, the Israeli issue not only drained Arab resources, it also demoralized Arab politics. As Israel gained an upper hand in agenda-setting and negotiations, Arab states – both indi-vidually and collectively – looked to external powers to gain bargaining chips vis-a-vis Israel.[26]

For the OAPEC sector of the Arab world, the dichotomy of depend-ency and internationalization has emerged through the petroleum industry. Since the statehood of most of the OAPEC countries is rather recent, formed by external legal and political considerations, the institutional setting within which the oil industry in these countries is developed, is closely intertwined with external political interests. The remarkable political influence of the Seven Sisters in the oil industries of the Arabian Peninsula cannot be dis-counted or underestimated.[27]

The complex triangle of oil companies, Arab states' security, and the sale of weapons, is the most influential force for internationalization in the Arabian Peninsula. The arms race in the Persian Gulf, that reached its peak in the aftermath of the Iran-Iraq war, is a reflection of superfluous and artificial threat perceptions fueled by extra-regional interests. The late and still developing statehood of some Arab countries, and the immediate dependence of these states on the complicated network of international petroleum industries, have created forces and interests that cannot be dealt with on an exclusively regional basis. There are vast international interests intertwined with regional dynamics. Lack of domestic institutional settings and constituency-based national coalitions have obviously intensified this process of internationalization.[28]

In this regard, one author points out that

> ... the trend since the beginning of the 1970s has been towards more authoritarian rule. Spontaneous demonstrations and protests have declined; dynasties and regimes once thought to be unlikely to survive are still with us; genuinely independent opposition parties, movements, and groupings have declined in importance and political freedoms are more or less repressed in what has become almost a state of permanent 'state of emergency' ... Traditional legitimizing formulas like hereditary kingship have been insufficient in themselves to provide security. Rulers have had to resort to three ... strategies: ideologies and symbols that both mobilize and pacify the 'masses'; reliance on externally located potential political 'assets' such as big power security and diplomatic assistance and Western commercial and financial linkages to accommodate the interests of important strata and elites, and the growth of loyal constituencies.[29]

The availability of large sums of petrodollars, essentially processed by foreign technology and management, coupled with crises of authority and legitimacy, has created a situation where instabilities arise, which are only resolved and contained by structural military and political dependencies. Therefore oil revenues, though useful in the development of a semi-infrastructure in some OAPEC countries, have resulted in political drawbacks that may not be reconciled in the medium, let alone the short, term.[30] The existence of numerous small states with a short history of statehood is another obstacle in the path of growth, security and cooperation in the Persian Gulf. Inviting external governments to provide security and deterrence automatically puts an end to meaningful bilateralism, and to regional economic and political multilateralism and integration. In other words, the structure of the state system that includes Iran and its closest Arab neighbours mirrors such a diversity of institutions, political experiences, historical mind sets and perceptual dispositions, that the spectrum of coordination, collaboration, cooperation, union and integration is rendered intractable, to say the least. The political consequences of oil dynamics, security dynamics and intrinsic disparities among states in the Middle East have heightened the internationalization of the region.

Conclusion: The International Matrix of Arab-Iranian Relations

The above analyses are not meant to be criticisms or pessimistic expressions. They are realities to be dealt with sequentially. They are realities that post-revolutionary Iran has not realized. This has had extremely negative results for Iran's foreign policy. The purpose of this paper was to explain why Iran and the Arab world have not been able to develop sustained and integrative bilateralism and multilateralism. The roots of the historical split between the Persians and the Arabs should not be underestimated. As we contemplate in retrospect, we can consider ethnic and religious differences to account for the discord. But in modern times, the ethno-religious differentiation is not sufficient to explain the unwillingness and uncertainties involved in cooperation and interdependency.

The 20th century international system displays an environment permeated by diversity and the tolerance to deal with diversity. In this context, therefore, what are the possible explanatory themes for the enduring conflict between Iran and its Arab neighbours? For the post-revolutionary period, a two-pillar argument has been suggested: The weaknesses of the Arab state system and the increasing internationalization of the Middle East. From a political standpoint, the Iranian post-revolutionary state has become stronger, while state control in the Arab world has been upgraded. Yet the degree of external dependency of these states has increased. Iranian foreign policy in the 1980s and 1990s was dominated by the politics of the Arab and Islamic worlds. It was perhaps ill-advised for Iran to pursue a policy of demanding greater Arab sovereignty and authenticity. As a result, both the ideological and national interests of Iran have been undermined, since greater sovereignty is guaranteed through national cohesion and greater accountability in the state, not through foreign policy directives which rely on the policies of other nations for their implementation.

In the post-revolutionary period, for very clear ideological reasons, Iran, did not recognize the intrinsic structural weaknesses of Arab states and underestimated the salience of international interests in the region. Therefore, Iran set a national policy of encouraging Arab leaders to decrease their reliance on external forces. Iran probably meant well for its neighbours, but it did not recognize the fragile nature of authority and legitimization in these states. Such a foreign policy was received with suspicion and feelings of inferiority. Most Arab countries reacted by maintaining their distance from Iran, and even by bridging gaps between themselves and the Western powers. The Arab world had not experienced a revolution in its structural sense and did not attempt to understand the immediate political consequences of revolution. The Iraqi invasion of Iran, and the subsequent Arab consensus to contain the Iranian revolution, only served to enhance the traditional emnity between Iran and its Arab neighbours.

The solution for gradual progress in Arab-Iranian relations may be grounded in the *Theory of Internal Integration* that I have advanced elsewhere.[31] Basically, this theory advocates the domestic structure argument. It suggests that greater institutionalization should be encouraged and de-personalized national leadership advanced. Eras of ethnic superiority are over now. Comparative advantage, educational creativity, political credibility and solid national political and economic institutions are indicators of rationality, and reliable measures in statecraft and statesmanship. Iran and the Arab world need further communication to settle differences. Both sides should proceed exclusively with economic and cultural interests. Greater regional interdependencies will enhance positive perceptions and create mechanisms for the avoidance of conflict. If the Arab world continues to learn about Iran through Western eyes, it will delay the possibility of enforcing confidence-building measures. Only through greater domestic processes of political and institutional strengthening can both sides hope for rational bilateralism and multilateralism. Even if the de-internationalization of the Middle East is an objective for both sides, strengthening of domestic forces is the best policy. This problem-solving approach is not directed towards the short term. Rather, it presupposes long, arduous and energetic bids by both sides to change, adapt, learn and accommodate.

Notes

* Director General, Centre for Scientific Research and Middle East Strategic Studies, Tehran, Iran.

1.   See Bernard Lewis, *The Shaping of the Modern Middle East*, (New York: Oxford University Press, 1994), pp. 24-44, and William Cleveland, *A History of the Modern Middle East*, (Boulder, Col.: Westview Press, 1994), pp. 61–79 & 113–25.
2.   Bernard Lewis, ibid., pp. 89-90 and 144-5.
3.   Gary Hawes and Hong Liu, 'Explaining the Dynamics of the Southeast Asian Political Economy', *World Politics* (July 1993), pp. 634-647.
4.   Doh Chull Shin, 'On the Third Wave of Democratization: A Synthesis and Evaluation of Recent Theory and Research', *World Politics* (October 1994), pp. 135–70.
5.   Ali Mazrui, 'Exit Visa from the World System: Dilemmas of Cultural and Economic Disengagement', in: *Third World Strategy*, ed. Altaf Gauhar, (New York: Praeger, 1983), p. 144.
6.   See Alasdair Bowie, *Crossing the Industrial Divide: State, Society and the Politics of Economic Transformation in Malaysia*, New York: Columbia University Press, 1991.
7.   For classic writings on this, see: Kenneth W. Thompson, *Masters of International Thought*, (Baton Rouge: Louisiana State University Press, 1980), pp. 67-92.
8.   Mahmood Sariolghalam, 'Theory of Internal Integration', *Nameh Farhang* (a cultural quarterly in Farsi), no. 13 (Spring 1994), pp. 100–10.

9.   Mahmood Sariolghalam, 'Conceptual Sources of Iranian Foreign Policy', Occasional Papers of the UAE's Centre for Strategic Studies and Research, Abu Dhabi, January 1995.

10.   Mahmood Sariolghalam, 'Conceptual Sources of Post-revolutionary Iranian Behaviour towards the Arab World', in *Iran and the Arab World*, ed. Hooshang Amirahmadi and Nader Entessar, (New York: St Martin's Press, 1993), pp. 22–6.

11.   Fouad Ajami, 'The Summer of Arab Discontent', *Foreign Affairs* (Winter 1990-1991), pp. 7–16.

12.   Peter Katzenstein, ed., *Between Power and Plenty*, (Madison: University of Wisconsin Press, 1978), pp. 3-23.

13.   Khair El-Din Haseeb, Saad El-Din Ibrahim, Ali Nasser et al., *The Future of the Arab Nation*, (London: Routledge,1991), p. 107.

14.   Ibid., p. 108.

15.   Ibid.

16.   Ibid.

17.   Ibid., pp. 117–28.

18,   Ibid , p. 130.

19.   Ibid., pp. 131–2.

20.   Peter Katzenstein, op. cit., p. 306.

21.   Michael Hudson, 'State, Society and Legitimacy: An Essay on Arab Political Prospects in the 1990s', in:*The New Arab Decade*, (Boulder, Col.: Westview Press, 1988), pp. 22–8.

22.   Kenneth Waltz, *Man, the State and War*, (New York: Columbia University Press, 1954), p. 163.

23.   Ibid., p. 170.

24.   Adam Smith, *The Wealth of Nations*, ed. Andrew Skinner, (London: Penguin Books, 1970), pp. 77-82.

25.   Fawaz Gerges, *The Superpowers and the Middle East*, (Boulder, Colo.: Westview Press, 1994), p. 246.

26.   Richard Parker, *The Politics of Miscalculation in the Middle East*, (Bloomington: Indiana University Press, 1993), pp. 167-212.

27.   John Blair, *The Control of Oil*, (New York: Vantage, 1976), pp. 98-121.

28.   Michael Hudson, op. cit., pp. 35-37; also, Charles Butterworth, 'State and Authority in Arab Political Thought', and Fahmi Jedaan, *The Foundations of the Arab State*, ed. Ghassan Salamé, (London: Croom Helm, 1987), pp. 91-149.

29.   Michael Hudson, ibid., p. 23.

30.   F. Gregory Gause, 'The Political Economy of National Security in the GCC States', a paper presented to a conference in Abu Dhabi on [Persian] 'Gulf 2000', 27-29 March 1995, pp. 3-7.

31.   Mahmood Sariolghalam, 'The Theory of Internal Integration', op. cit.

23

Arabs and Iranians in the 'New World Order'

NIVEEN ABDULMONEM MASAAD*

Introduction

One of the views commonly held in the literature on the so-called 'new world order' is the bias of this order against Muslims in general, and Arabs in particular.[1] This idea, it should be noted, was endorsed by various groups. In fact, the post-war world has witnessed multiple thinkers such as Jironovski in Russia, and Huntington in the United States, who have expressed certain prejudices concerning Arabs and Muslims. For example, they portray Islam as an emerging danger and a unique threat to the 'civilized world'. This following study attempts to investigate and revise this view. It also seeks to analyse the conditions of both Arabs and Iranians in the shadow of the 'new world order', on the basis of some basic assumptions:

1. That there has been an actual and tangible regression in the status of both Arabs and Iranians, within the framework of this new system.
2. That this deterioration in international status, similar to any other phenomenon, cannot be explained with reference to a single factor, but to a combination of interrelated socio-economic and ideological determinants. In this respect, the unsatisfactory economic performance of both Arabs and Iranians at the international level comes at the top of these causes.
3. That, as long as some states preserve their monopoly over vital strategic items such as oil or gas, it is valid to presume not only a relative retreat, but also variable interactions with the major powers. Naturally, if the concerned states are polarized either to the Left or the Right, the analysis acquires new dimensions.
4. That issues such as democracy, arms control, the internationalization of markets, in particular those of a Middle Eastern orientation, are considered as the best examples illustrating, simultaneously, the retreat in importance and the relativity of this retreat.

In light of what has ben presented, this study can be divided into three

436

main parts. The first covers the different approaches which are currently used in the analysis of international conflict and cooperation. The second explores a number of cases revealing the types of interactions between Arabs and Iranians on the one hand, and the active superpowers on the other. The third part focuses on Middle Eastern projects and investigates the Arabs' and Iranians' stances *vis-à-vis* such proposals.

International Relations in the Post-Cold War World: Attempts at Understanding

Following the precedent of the Soviet collapse, the different interpretations of international conflict and cooperation revolved, mainly, around the civilizational, national and economic axes.

The Civilizational Axis

In the summer of 1993, Samuel Huntington published an article in *Foreign Affairs* carrying an interrogatory title: 'The Clash of Civilizations?' This article triggered wide debates, which remain unresolved. It has been considered a turning point in the development of American political thought, as has been George Kennan's article in the fifties, which used to be considered the chronicle of the containment concept. Huntington took off from a basic assumption alleging the prominence of the Catholic–Christian–Western civilization economically, politically and militarily. With the disappearance of the Soviet opponent from the world map, West–West military conflict is unlikely since, argues the author, democracies are not prone to fighting each other. Effectively, with the exception of Japan, there is no sharp economic challenge confronting the West. Thus, the concepts of 'free world' and 'international society' become two faces of the same coin.

While Western civilization witnesses such development, the other civilizations become more self-conscious (the Confucian, Japanese, Hindu, Slav, Orthodox, Latin– American and, possibly, the African civilizations). This rising self-consciousness rests on several factors, the most important of which is the impact of modernization. In fact, the huge revolution in communications sweeping the world increased the different civilizations' awareness of their boundaries. Such frontiers exclude the other; they are crossed with great difficulty, in contrast to the economic, ideological, or even national boundaries.

In this respect, it is necessary to note Huntington's definition of civilization as a combination of language, culture, and religion. The last element, it should be noted, is rather permanent in nature. Accordingly, Huntington suggests three possible types of interaction between the Catholic–Christian–Western civilization – 'the West' – on the one hand, and the other world civilizations – 'the Rest' – on the other. The first mode is isolationist in character and is not easily propagated, for it requires a withdrawal from the Western dominated international arena. Analysts remain sceptical about its stability in light of the traditional models of this mode: Burma and North Korea. The second mode is 'band wagoning', by means of adapting the subjective civilizational values to those pertinent to the West. Such a type is, in its turn, unattainable, for with the exception of the successful Japanese experiment, all the attempts launched in this direction by culturally fragmented states, such as Turkey, have ended in failure. As for the third type, it is self-constructive, geared to balance the power of the West over the short run, with the aim of challenging it in the long run. On the basis of this last type, a military–economic cooperation is supposed to take place between two or more civilizations, while each preserves its own independent character. Huntington maintains that this type shall form the essence of international interactions in the post-Cold War era. Within this framework, he thinks a dual cooperation between the Islamic and Confucian civilizations quite likely. This is due to a number of principles shared by the two concerned civilizations which clash, however, with Western democracy. Such principles are exemplified in: emphasizing duties at the expense of rights, favouring collective behaviour over individualism (Confucianism), connecting religion and politics, and believing in the unity and jurisdiction of God (Islam). Huntington seeks to provide readers with various examples illustrating the readiness of both civilizations, the Confucian and Islamic, to confront the West. According to Huntington, they both amass weapons, upgrade and exchange them (China's arming of Libya and Iraq and North Korea providing Iran and Syria with armaments are cases in point). Evidently, the lesson of the second Gulf war was clear; the victorious struggling against the United States depends on the ownership of nuclear weaponry.

On the basis of the preceding points, Huntington expects post-Cold War conflicts to be neither ideological, nor national in character, but civilizational. He goes as far as to claim that the first spark of a Third World War might occur in the Balkans or the Caucasus. Identifying himself as a Western, Catholic Christian, Huntington concludes by explaining what he perceives to be the responsibility of the West *vis-à-vis* this situation.

Accordingly, he asserts that the immediate tasks before the West are: to preserve its unity, recruit supporters from among the other civilizations, and develop cooperation with Russia while kindling discord between the Islamic and Confucian civilizations. However, over the long run, the West has the duty of luring the non-Western civilizations whose power is almost equivalent to its own, but whose values and interests differ from it.

Huntington suggests that this end is best served by developing a better understanding of the other religions, and forging common grounds with them. In this last instance Huntington seems to be destroying the essence of his article, which was originally based on the impossibility of reconciling the different civilizations.

Huntington's article was subject to a number of criticisms, impelling the author to defend himself while remaining sceptical about the credibility of any alternative theoretical framework. The most significant criticism leveled against Huntington's hypotheses, can be summarized as follow:

1. Regarding Huntington's denial of the impact of modernization in lessening the intensity of civilizational fanaticism. A country like India, in Fouad Ajami's assessment, did not achieve its current status except by struggling against this fanaticism, and by adopting secularism. Islamic fundamentalism, despite all allegations, is represented by youths taught by Westerners. These young people searched for their freedom in Western countries. As for the revival of Confucianism, it is, as Liu Binyan mentioned, an illusion existing only in Huntington's mind; for China is currently confronting an ethical disintegration following 47 years of continuous Communist rule. Actually, what applies to the analysis of a single civilization, also applies to the analysis of interactions between the different civilizations. Besides, the lines distinguishing civilizations are flimsier than Huntington imagines. Regarding the Western and Islamic civilizations, they are, in spite of their bloody legacy inside and outside Europe, closer to each other than to the Confucian civilization. Moreover, in its important investigation concerning 'Islam and the West', *The Economist* acknowledged three civilizations only – Islam, Christianity and Confucianism – as opposed to the eight listed by Huntington. As for the other civilizations, they are considered to be of the same fabric, or at least from similar ones (the Latin American, the Orthodox-Slav, and Japanese civilizations). Others were essentially fabrications (the African civilization). In all cases, the coexistence of the three civilizations is a reality, a possibility and a necessity. This logic was pushed a step further by al Sayed Yassin, who prophesied the creation of a new international conciliatory system, balancing opposites; such as substance versus spirit, centralization versus decentralization, the relativity of thought versus the expression of ideologies.

2. Huntington mocked the idea of 'the end of history', endorsed by Fukuyama, following the defeat of Communist ideology. Yet, he fell prey to the same trap in his assertions about the pre-eminence of Western civilization, and his presumption that it will inherit the earth. In this context, 'Abdul Wahab al-Missiry reduced the difference between Fukuyama and Huntington to the time span anticipated by each one of

them for the realization of Western civilization's final victory. The former believes this victory has already been achieved with the end of the bipolar system: Capitalism/Communism, while the second affirms that the world has to live for some time with the dichotomy Confucianism–Islam/Christianity. Moreover, al-Missiry puts the general post-modern philosophy in the same trench with the hypotheses on the end of history and the clash of civilizations. For him, all three spring from an attempted ban on man's right to make free cultural choices.

3. The debate about the Islamic–Confucian coalition reiterates the cultural determinism of Huntington's book *The Third Wave*, where he argues that only certain civilizations are qualified to carry democratic values. Bertrand Badie had previously refuted these assumptions by insinuating that the anti-democratic systems of government which Huntington currently associates with 'the rest' had flourished for a long time in Catholic, Christian and Western societies in the form of the divine right of kings. Huntington did not clarify how he would reconcile his cultural determinism with his confidence in the West's ability to impose its democratic culture on the other states, entities and civilizations.

4. The national states were, and still are, the most important active international parties – since the different civilizations function within national frameworks and not vice versa. Huntington's overstepping this reality has inaccurately led to diminishing the impact that realpolitik considerations play in orienting states' policies. Interests, not religions, are the factors that determine international positions, whether in the second Gulf war or in Bosnia–Herzegovina. Moreover, Ajami informs us that Iran has supported Armenia in its struggle against Azerbaijan, a fact that cannot be accommodated into Huntington's thesis. Within the same context, Kishore Mahbubani points out that the interests of the West impel it to be open to the world, and militate against any substantial culturalism. American prosperity, for instance, depends on invading the markets of the developing countries.[2]

The National Axis

If Huntington bets on the diminishing role of nationalism in shaping international affairs, other thinkers such as James Kellas value the impact of the national factor in both the internal and external realms. In his book *Politics of Nationalism and Ethnicity* (1991) Kellas focuses heavily on the renascence of primordial loyalties in nationalist forms. He signals that such revivals represent the sixth chain in nationalist evolution, which started prior to the 19th century with the foundation of nations and has continued till the present day with the collapse of the Soviet Union. In the course of his analysis of current nationalist revivals, Kellas distinguishes between so-called ethno-nationalism – revolving around a particular race (the Kurds and Tamils); social-nationalism – based on a single culture whose social interactions have been stabilized for a period of time (Catalonia); and offi-cial-nationalism – whose conditions are determined by the Constitution regardless of the racial or cultural origins of the citizens.

However, national differences are one thing and nationalist proclivities another. Kellas justifies nationalist motions on the domestic level as the result of socio-economic and cultural injustices. Repressed nationalities rebel within their countries in an attempt to change this unjust status quo. It is to be noticed that Kellas does not exclude the advanced countries from his analysis, for the nationalist revival is, in his opinion, sweeping all states, albeit in different degrees. On the other hand, among the different symp-toms of injustice, Kellas emphasizes the cultural. In this respect, Kellas agrees with a number of analysts who tend to exaggerate the impact of the cultural determinant, whether in shaping nationalism or in instigating it. In this category is Benedict Anderson, who stresses religion as a factor, and uses terms carrying special connotations, such as 'pilgrimage', to illustrate the way each nationality takes benediction from its religious symbols. Re-garding the external arena, Kellas affirms that the degree of national homogeneity determines the type of foreign relations a state has. It is very common for the multinational state to breed nationalist conflicts with other states, or at least get involved in these conflicts. It does that when the posi-tion of a particular nationality existing within its territories is threatened, or simply to divert attention from its domestic conditions (the Kurds in the Turkish–Iranian–Iraqi relationships). But, if this is the general rule, it does not negate the fact that nationalities might instigate or facilitate integra-tion within wider regional entities for the sake of proving their particularity in a more favourable atmosphere (the Basques in Spain and their support for the European Union). Finally, Kellas suggests a consolational democ-racy stipulating constitutional interference in the interest of weaker nationalities, in order to decrease the drawbacks of nationalist revivals. However, Kellas does not clarify whether or not he generally favours the democratic solution with respect to transnational nationalist struggles.[3]

Kellas' thought provokes a number of necessary comments, the most important of which are:

1. The mixing between ethnicity and nationalism: Kellas seems sometimes cognizant of the difference between the two concepts. He considers ethnicity a biological phenomenon that might pave the way for the emer-gence of nationalism as a phenomenon having multiple cultural, economic and political dimensions. However, in other instances, Kellas combines the two concepts under the label: ethno-nationalism, meaning race, as

exemplified by the Kurds. Yet, this example is inaccurate, for the Kurds possess all the nationalist qualifications and pillars. It should be noted that this confusion is a common error among analysts of nationalist phenomena, whether in tackling the state level or its minorities. In 1993, for example, Alain Gresh published a book on *Nationalism in the East*, in which he defined ethnicity as a religio-linguistic racial compound. Hence, he broadened the concept and rendered it similar to that of nationalism. Gresh believed that, with the exception of the Russian and Ukrainian models, the revival of primordial feelings in eastern and central Europe took ethnic, rather than nationalist, forms. If we add Kellas' definition of official-nationalism to Gresh's analysis, the picture becomes more complicated, since nationalism, according to the former's definition, is synonymous with the nationality carried by citizens regardless of whether or not they are natives of the state.[4]

2. Some analysts consider Western Europe to be immune from nationalist revivals, both in intra-European relations and within each state. Mattei Dogan wrote an article supporting this viewpoint, in which he tried to prove that the Germans, French, Dutch or Italians' opportunistic feelings of belonging to the European community overshadow their nationalist feelings towards their respective states. He substantiates his argument by offering a number of case studies illustrating the retreat of Westerners' pride in their countries, their weakening confidence in their armies, and their defeatist feelings, in return for the high esteem in which they hold each other and their rising loyalty towards the European community. A noteworthy point mentioned in Dogan's article is the role played by national fanaticism in motivating the policies of Western countries *vis-à-vis* the other nationalities, whether in Africa, South Asia, or Eastern Europe.[5]

3. One of the principal theses in Kellas' work is the decisive role played by nationalities in multinational states, leading either to divisiveness and external conflicts, or to regional coordination and integration. This thesis is refuted by the existence of several African countries that have not been pushed to either side despite their extreme heterogeneity, but were confined to a kind of masochism or collective suicide through civil wars.

4. Emphasizing the real nationalist consciousness, rather than the false consciousness, in the shaping of international relations: among the important causes of this falsification is that economically exploiting states (or classes) need to make the exploited states (or classes) imagine their having a specific nationalist character. The goal of the dominant classes or states is to consecrate the divisive elements and prevent the unification of these states (or classes) against them. The Yugoslavian scene was Chris Harman's testing arena for the previous Marxist hypothesis. In his opinion, the essence of the Yugoslavian struggle is economic and not

nationalist. The state bureaucracy has persisted in exploiting the working class for the achievement of capitalist accumulation and the acceleration of gain. However, the bureaucracy's refusal to make any economic sacrifice coloured the struggle with a deceitful nationalist trait.[6] It is obvious, therefore, that Harman's opinion differs from Alain Gresh's opinion concerning the ethnic nature of the East European conflicts.

The Economic Axis

Dr Boutros Boutros Ghali, former secretary general of the United Nations, is the most prominent analyst to adopt the economic adjustment approach to the study of international relations following the fall of the bipolar system. In an inaugural article published by *Al-Siyasah Al-Dawliyyah* ('International Politics') in the summer of 1991, entitled 'Dialogue and Conflict between the North and South', Dr Ghali mentions that, following the fall of the ideological curtain between East and West, another curtain of a different intensity was formed to separate North and South. In the Pacific Ocean, a new curtain shall fall between the Soviet Union (which had not collapsed yet) and China, or between Australia and Indonesia. As for the Mediterranean, a similar curtain shall be drawn between its rich and poor shores; whereas a third one shall be drawn between North and South America in the Caribbean.

In comparison to the Pacific and Caribbean curtains, Dr Ghali thought that the strongest and most difficult curtain to penetrate would be the one separating the two shores of the Mediterranean. Why is this? Dr Ghali offers two principal reasons in answering this question. The first one is geo-political. It is exemplified in the fact that the northern Mediterranean states will be impelled to defend themselves against the waves of southern immigrants fleeing economic and political crises. This impression is backed up by the progressive increase in fertility rates amongst the populations of southern Mediterranean nations, whose percentage will soon reach 67 per cent in four Arab states (Egypt, Tunisia, Algeria, Morocco), increasing the current population size from 120 million souls, to 200 million in the first quarter of the 21st century. If Western Europe shuts its doors before the waves of Turkish, Iranian, African and Arab immigrations, the north Caribbean will do the same *vis-à-vis* its south, albeit with more tolerance. Effectively, the south Caribbean is ready to negotiate with its north by virtue of its crystallized political consciousness, its Christian civilization and the multiplicity of alternatives open before its citizens, particularly in countries such as Argentina or Mexico. Hence, it will allow the potential emigrants either to remain, voluntarily, where they are, or to move north. As for the second reason, it is connected to the ensemble of current international variables that have increased Western Europe's ethnocentrism, brought eastern and central Europe back to the big European house, trivialized the importance of the South and turned it into a heavy burden. The imperatives impelling the United States to construct military bases, those stirring France's generosity, or motivating the [ex-] Soviet Union to contribute in financing a giant project such as the High Dam, have vanished. The ideological struggle between East and West has ended. In addition to that, the countries of the South that have mismanaged their shares of economic assistance are duly punished. The orientation towards decreasing the financial facilities granted to the South and the lack of enthusiasm in summoning an international conference to study the debt cases, is one type of punishment presented by Dr Ghali.[7]

Without neglecting the impact of the civilizational and nationalist variables in the shaping of international relations in general, this study contends that the economic approach is more appropriate for interpreting the deterioration of the status of Arabs and Iranians within the so-called 'new world order'. But, on the other hand, despite the author's agreement with the general orientation of Dr Ghali's thesis, this study argues for the existence of more than a single curtain separating the north of the Pacific Ocean from its south and the north of the Caribbean from its south, as well as the north Mediterranean from its south. The southern shores of these seas and oceans are not homogeneous entities. Economic criteria, in particular, distinguish one southern state from another. It should be mentioned that the discrepancy in the economic potential and importance of the southern states is related to the third technological revolution that started 20 years ago, approximately, and led to an essential change in the world economic structure. In fact, in addition to uncovering the deterioration in the relative power of the [ex-] Soviet Union, which led the latter to its collapse, this revolution created standards differentiating and distinguishing between the southern states, enabling us to divide them into four major categories:

1. The newly industrialized states such as Hong Kong, South Korea, Singapore, Malaysia and (to a lesser extent) Mexico and Argentina. These states have realized important economic achievements in the course of the last two decades. This has been despite the problems they have confronted in their relationships with the states of the North (viz. access to international markets). They are now enjoying a position of increased bargaining power .

2. The oil rich countries such as the Gulf states, Libya before Lockerbie, and some Latin American countries. These countries grew into a distinctive group with peculiar conditions, interests and aims, by virtue of their oil surpluses and the escalation in prices following the October 1973 war.

3. The intermediately advanced countries, enjoying multiple productive structures and imports, yet simultaneously indebted. Egypt, Syria, the three Maghreb countries, Turkey, Iraq and Iran all belong to this category. Even though the last two states are oil rich countries, their economic status was deeply hurt as a result of the first and second Gulf wars.

4. Last, there are the marginalized countries that rely on exporting raw materials, such as Sudan, Yemen, Somalia, Mozambique and Mali.[8]

Each of the groups listed above occupies a different position on the international arena by virtue of its economic performance. For example, in contrast to the 4.1 per cent share of the 50 marginalized African countries in the international domestic product in 1990, four newly industrialized countries accounted for more than half the previous percentage in the same year, i.e., 2.4 per cent.[9] Concerning the size of exports, we find that Malaysia exported the equivalent of $40.705 billions in 1992, in contrast to $41.833 billion for Saudi Arabia, $4.040 billion for Tunisia, and $412 million for Sudan. As for Iran, it exported the equivalent of $18.235 billion.* However, the analysis of these countries' exports in terms of equipment and transportation machines – which are considered to be indicators of economic development – provides a different picture. In this respect, statistics tell us that between 1970 and 1992, the percentage of Malaysian oil exports and primary items to its total exports, decreased from 30 per cent to 17 per cent, and from 63 per cent to 22 per cent, respectively. On the other hand, its sales of equipment and transportation machines increased from 2 per cent to 38 per cent of its total exports; the percentage of the other manufactured items increased from 6 per cent to 23 per cent, while the exports of textiles and ready-made clothes leaped from 1 per cent to 6 per cent of the total exports. As for the percentage of primary products, other manufactured items, textiles and ready-made clothes in Saudi trade, they were equal to 0 per cent of its total exports. Yet, the percentage of machines and transportation equipment increased from 0 per cent, to 1 per cent, while the percentage of oil decreased slightly from 100 per cent to 99 per cent of the total Saudi exports. Concerning Tunisia, the proportion of its fuel and primary products exports deteriorated from 46 per cent and 35 per cent to 16 per cent and 11 per cent, consecutively. But the proportion of its other manufactured products, textiles and ready-made clothes increased remarkably from 19 per cent and 2 per cent to 64 per cent and 40 per cent. As for Sudan, the percentage of its fuel exports was raised from 1 per cent to 3 per cent of its total exports; in addition, the percentage of the other manufactured goods, textiles and ready-made clothes, increased from 0 for both items to 1 per cent of the total exports. The percentage of primary products decreased from 99 per cent to 96 per cent, of the total exports, while the share of equipment and machines remained at 0 per cent. In the Iranian case, fuel occupied 90 per cent of total exports in the period between 1970 and 1992. The percentage of primary products, machines, transportation equipment, textiles and ready-made clothes was stabilized at the level of 6 per cent, 0 per cent, and 3 per cent respectively, while the proportion of other manufactured products decreased from 4 per cent to 3 per cent of Iran's total exports.[10]

Moreover, if we took into consideration the impact of economic power relationships on the comprehensive relations of power, the picture becomes more complex. The revolution in communications benefited certain countries such as Dubai and Bahrain, which entered the international network of stock exchanges and financial centres. In contrast, countries like Saudi Arabia, Iran or Kuwait, though they remain economically important, remain financially limited by the interaction between two sets of factors. The first set is the international demand of oil – which will increase by 1.5 per cent annually, to reach 74.5 million barrels by the end of the century (in contrast to approximately 60 million barrels daily at the present time). It points out that the OPEC countries, and the three states mentioned in particular, in addition to Iraq – after the lifting of the embargo – will cover between 30–31 million barrels of the new daily international demand, that will be accruing essentially from east Asia and the Pacific Ocean.[11]

The second set of factors include negative reflections on the pricing policies, particularly the increase in the production of non-OPEC members, the OPEC internal disagreements over their production shares and, most importantly, their rejection of the carbon tax. It is worth noting that the issue of taxation on fuel combustion was instigated on a wide scale, three years ago, in the Rio De Janeiro conference on the environment. The idea relates to the European countries' need to reduce their consumption of oil, in view of the probability that carbon dioxide emissions contribute to raising the temperature of the atmosphere. Until now, some members of the European community opposed the suggestion. In addition, the United States and, naturally, the oil rich countries, doubt the ability of the suggested tax to cut off consumption at the needed rate and favour the development of 'clean' technology. However, the tax on carbon is still raised on different occasions; sometimes it is justified by the claim that oil is concentrated in unstable areas, at other times it is invoked for the sake of financing the process designed to cut back the costs of the European labour force (and hence, European exports).[12] Finally, the marginalized group was negatively affected by the change in the conditions of international commerce in favour of manufactured goods, especially high-tech products. It should be noted that the sub-Saharan African states are still exporting a number of basic raw materials, though genetic engineering enabled the North states (such as Canada, France and the United States) to control the international food trade, while the resource-saving technology contributed in the production of the same items with less primary materials. But if demand for these items is on the decrease, the African states' need for hard currency urges them to double their supply; thus, further weakening their statuses.

Arabs, Iranians and the Cases of the 'New World Order'

If the previous section answered the question, why have Arabs' and Iranians' importance diminished in the so-called 'new world order', this part treats another question: How did such a retreat occur, and what are its symptoms? A thorough review of the international agenda following the collapse of the bipolar system reveals that the most important subjects in this area are democracy, human rights, arms control and the internationality of markets.

Democracy and Human Rights

There is a consensus among the northern states that it is no longer possible to disregard 'the way other governments treat their citizens', according to the expression of the American President Bill Clinton.[13] Nevertheless, these countries differ over the extent to which the democratic and human rights principles should guide the course of their foreign policies. Some argue that the northern states should support democratic experiments and benefit from the huge international developments in this respect. 'International legitimacy' in whose name the allied forces launched a deadly war against Iraq created a model for emulation, namely, the imperative of respecting the law domestically. The communications revolution has raised the common citizen's awareness of the dimensions of democratic development in the world and potentially strengthened his independence from the state. Some would also argue that the end of the struggle between East and West put the individual's health, his liberty and prosperity at the core of international interest regardless of his geographical belonging.[14] Some analysts push this logical further by their talk about 'sympathy' becoming the only motive for military intervention in the immediate post-Cold War era. They argue that, in contrast to the old, economic (the US invasion of Haiti in the 20th century), missionary / civilizational (the European colonization of African and Asian states), or national security (Soviet interference in Afghanistan) precedents for intervention, the Somalian, Bosnian and north Iraqi models are of a different brand. They are human interventions to save people from starving to death.[15] Since the most important trait distinguishing the United States as a people and nation is 'its commitment to political and economic freedom, liberalization, pluralism, democracy and the rule of law', it becomes natural for it to conduct successive international campaigns to spread peace and restore hope.[16]

On the other hand, some analysts caution against a foreign policy carried away by the slogans of democracy and human rights. They reject the adoption of these slogans as criteria for dealing with ruling regimes, through rejection or punishment. Actually, such policy would leave only a small number of regimes (mainly in western Europe and Japan) for the United States to acknowledge, since 80 per cent of the world states suffer from one form or another of arbitrary government. In order to make its point, this second group of analysts uses the Salman Rushdie affair as an example in the framework of relationships between the West and Iran. They question the significance of human rights violations in the case of an author who trespassed certain perceived borders of respect by criticising the Islamic sanctities. They also question the wisdom of the Western countries, which allows their relationships with the Islamic world to deteriorate to the point of no return because of some irresponsible words uttered by a writer.[17] By the same token, they wonder about the possibility of ignoring the relativity of democratic practices. A single state might impose constraints on public and private freedoms, yet possess the appropriate seed for a potential democratic development, namely an elected parliament.[18] In this respect, a survey of the Arab arena reveals the following phenomena:

1. The records of the Arab states in the fields of democracy and human rights, following the end of the Cold War, is a very modest one, but insufficient to motivate an international opposition or the imposition of strict sanctions on the violators. Saudi Arabia, for example, has witnessed successive rounds of arbitrary arrests covering all types of political opposition (women, university professors, ulema). The last of these occurred in the month of September 1994, when – according to official Saudi statistics – 110 Saudis were imprisoned.[19] The ex-American secretary of defence Dick Cheney clearly expressed the position of his country *vis-à-vis* the Saudi conditions, when he answered a question concerning the United States' determination to change the Saudi institutions along more democratic lines. He stated that, 'The short answer is no, for throughout the years we have sought to preserve these institutions despite the suppression of democratic forces in the area'.[20] Outside the confines of the Arabian Peninsula, the violations of human rights in Egypt and Tunisia do not get any special attention. When the European Parliament decided to punish Morocco and Syria financially, by decreasing assistance offered to them in the period between 1992 and 1996, it soon revised its decision. In Jordan, the democratic advance is looked at

suspiciously, for fear of leading to the election of 'Hamas' supporters. As for Algeria, it is interesting to note that the year it witnessed the formation of a non-constitutional presidential council, i.e. 1992, is also the year it received a flow of international loans, in addition to the different forms of military and political support offered to the new system.

It would be useful to compare the international response *vis-à-vis* the Algerian experiment to its Haitian and Peruvian counterparts. In the case of Haiti, the American States Organization was convened following the September 1991 events, to condemn General Cedras' coup d'etat, reject his military regime and support the imposition of an economic embargo against Haiti. Effectively, Venezuela suspended its oil exports to Haiti. The United States, the biggest trade partner to Haiti, froze Haitian credits in its banks. Finally, in 1994, the American military invasion of the island took place to restore the deposed President Jean Bertrand Aristide. As for Peru, the economic sanctions succeeded in forcing Alberto Fujomori's regime to hold legislative elections, under the supervision of the American States Organization, in November 1992. It should be noted that the United States, Spain, Germany and Japan had stopped their economic assistance to Peru, and \$1.4 billion of IMF reconstruction and development aid to the country was frozen.[21]

2. One of the results deduced from analyzing variations in international responses from Chechenya to Kurdistan and from Saudi Arabia to Iran, is that the North interferes militarily when Muslims are murdered and not when they are murdered at the hands of Christians. Also, northern states, as a general rule, do not pressure for establishing democracy in a Muslim state, except, maybe, to embarrass the fundamentalist ruling regime.[22]

However, the previous reading of the different models and cases is not the only possible one. Alternative readings based on the calculation of gains and losses are valid as well. To illustrate, the obstruction of democracy in the Gulf area stemmed from the uncertainty of the North as to what will happen to economically important states such as Saudi Arabia, the Emirates or Kuwait (oil, markets, deposits) on the eve of a democratic takeover.[23] This point, in particular, lies behind some analysts' criticism of the US role in encouraging the subversive activities of Iraqi regional unity, but most alarmingly, they fear the probable destabilization of the Gulf area.[24] From a different perspective, the case of East Timor in Indonesia (a Muslim state) struggling for self-determination is a very significant example illustrating the way interests affect the North's stance on democracy, either positively or negatively. This case was instigated by Portugal in November 1991, following the demonstrations sweeping the region and the concomitant arrests and trials. But when it vetoed the new agreement between the European community and the ASEAN for this reason, the community ignored the Portuguese point of view and resumed its normal economic relationships with the ASEAN. Its rationale being that the problem was a bilateral one between Indonesia and Portugal only.[25] As for the allegation concerning the propagation of democracy outside the Islamic world, it is refuted too. It is in fact argued that the United States raised the special case of prisoners and children's exploitation in China, and that of children under the legal working age in Thailand, due to the highly competitive cheap products produced by these states.[26] Moreover, some maintain that the American interference in Haiti was not for re-establishing democracy, but to stem the tide of human emigrations from the Caribbean area. This is illustrated, not only by the supportive American position towards the military coup against the nascent Haitian democracy in 1988, but also by the contemptuous American attitude to President Aristide himself on the eve of the coup which reversed him.[27]

Arms Control

Although the idea of arms control in the Middle East area was originally related to the beginnings of the Arab–Israeli conflict,[28] its importance has escalated by virtue of a number of considerations. One of these is the declining confidence the United States has in its ability to control the influx of arms to the area following the collapse of the Soviet Union. In addition, the North's reading of the previous wars in the area made it connect the arms race of these states to the triggering of their political conflicts. Also, the progression of arms control – particularly in the area of nuclear weapons – between the United States and Russia, and elsewhere (South America, the Korean peninsula, South Africa, China, some of the ex-Soviet Union republics, etc.) raised hopes for generalizations.[29] But in reality, a similar advance cannot occur smoothly in the Middle East area, where the case of arms control is complicated by the fact that atomic weapons are not confined to two principal regional states only, such as Brazil and Argentina, or the two Koreas, or even India and Pakistan.[30] Furthermore, the Israeli presence as a strategic ally to the North makes it difficult to strike a balance between it, the Arabs, and Iranians. These factors influence efforts at arms control in the area, whether in the framework of international initiatives or multilateral negotiations.

On the first level, the different initiatives – the American (May 1991, July 1992), French (June 1991), that of the five major powers (July 1991), or that of the Security Council (October 1991) – approved an incremental policy in dealing with armament in the area, from elimination, to freezing, to controlling, thereby consecrating the existing strategic imbalance in favour of Israel.[31] As for the elimination, it focused on chemical and biological weapons in the hands of Arabs and Iranians. The different initiatives stipulated total abidance by the two international agreements concerning these two types of weapons. Accordingly, a succession of measures took place with the aim of eliminating the Iraqi weapons of mass destruction in implementation of the Security Council resolution number 678, clause (C).[32] The related Iranian efforts were subject to strict supervision, as represented in the obstruction and searching of the Chinese ship Yin He in the Saudi harbour Dammam, which was suspected of transporting chemical weapons to the Islamic Republic.[33]

Regarding freezing, it centered on the ownership, production and development of all nuclear weapons and surface-to-surface missiles, with a commitment to destroying the latter. It is to be noted that this clause stabilizes the current technological gap between those owning nuclear arms, i.e. Israel (between 100 and 200 nuclear bombs)[34] and those who do not. Besides, by including the destruction of missiles, it attempts to put an end to the relative advantage of Arabs and Iranians in this respect. In this context, one analyst notices that though the range of the Israeli surface-to-surface missiles varies between 130 km and 1500 km, putting it in a better position in comparison to its Arab and Iranian counterparts, whose range varies between 70 km and 600 km (with the exception of Saudi Arabia, which owns missiles with a range of 3000 km), yet the Israeli missiles remain less accurate in hitting their targets. This is illustrated by comparing the Israeli Lance missiles and the SS-21 missiles owned by the Arab states. The medium range ballistic missiles owned by the confrontational Arab states are capable of hitting deep into Israeli territory, hence counterbalancing the superiority enjoyed by the Israeli air defence.[35] In the course of implementing the previous clause, the United States exerted strong pressures on China, Russia and North Korea to stop the exportation of arms to the area. This reached the extent of threatening China to deprive it from the status of most favoured nation in protest at its selling M-11 missiles to Syria[36] and its determination to construct the Iranian nuclear plant in cooperation with Russia. Concerning Iraq, the post-second Gulf war occurrences managed to pave the way for destroying the largest part of its static and mobile missile launchers (around 200 platforms).[37]

Regarding the limiting, it focused on traditional weapons by means of adjuring the five major powers and the major global exporters to regulate the inflow of these weapons to the area. But if the basis of this previous text is restrictive, conditioning the restrain on highly flexible criteria such as the extent to which the defensive needs of the state were fulfilled without injuring its economy, the degree to which a state propagates regional stability and fights international terrorism, etc., permitted a flexible interpretation of the text. A serious study brought attention to the danger of spreading

traditional weapons in the different areas of the world, amidst preoccupation with atomic weaponry. The study focused on the case of Rwanda in
particular, which received flows of traditional weapons from Russia, France,
the United States, South Africa, and even from Egypt (through French
mediation) leading to the escalation of its tribal conflict.[38]

A close scrutiny of the Middle East shows that the oil countries were
the principal beneficiaries from the selling of traditional weapons, side by
side with Israel; not because they fulfill the necessary conditions or criteria,
but because they are capable of spending lavishly and compensate the deficits in the major states' balances of trade, amidst the shift from military to
civilian production. Thus, only one day after the initiative of the ex-American President George Bush on the 29th of May 1991, the United States
concluded a $700 million deal with Israel for the purchase of ten F-15
aircraft and the financing of 70 per cent of the expenses for developing an
anti surface-to-surface Israeli missile. Besides, less than a few months later,
the United States announced its intention to sell 28 H-64 helicopters to
the Emirates and Bahrain.[39] On the whole, the Gulf states account for the
largest share of American, French and British sales to the area, assessed by
some sources at $50 billion in the period between 1990 and 1993.[40] In
contrast, the armament efforts of countries categorized as 'Rogue'[41] or 'Backlash'[42] states by the North – namely, Syria, Sudan, Libya, Iran and Iraq –
have been severely curtailed. Evidently, the United States' interference succeeded in aborting the T-72 tanks deal (300 tanks) worth $200 million
between Syria and [ex-] Czechoslovakia in May 1991. Russia has also abstained from signing new deals to provide Syria with traditional weapons.[43]
By the same token, the European Parliament imposed a ban on the supply
of weapons to Sudan, and stretched the prohibition to cover even the military and security equipment essential for domestic security.[44]

Though Iran strives to compensate for the strategic imbalance it faces in
regard to its neighbouring Gulf states – 206 planes for Iran, including only
40 advanced MIG-29 planes, in contrast to 624 planes for the Cooperation
Council states including Mirage 2000 and Toronado-15 planes (Saudi Arabia owns 150 planes of the last category) – Iran remains at a disadvantage
in comparison to these states with the respect to its rates of defence expenditure (less than $3 billion annually, while Saudi Arabia spent in 1990
around $13 billion).[45] It also needs a long time to absorb the technology of
some traditional weapons such as submarines.[46] Nevertheless, the United
States led a campaign calling for a prohibition on the supply of traditional
weapons to Iran. Forty-nine eminent American personalities pertaining to
different intellectual trends and specializations signed a statement protesting against the sale of German technology and weapons to Iran through
Czech mediation.[47]

In a different area, the Arms Control and Regional Committee Working Group – stemming from the Moscow conference in 1992 – clashed with Israel regarding two main questions. The first one was Israel's refusal to subject its weapons of mass destruction (nuclear, chemical and biological) to the supervision of the International Agency for Atomic Energy. It considered this issue as being beyond the interests of the committee.[48] It is to be noted that while the United States tended to accept the previous Israeli position, it did not comment on Israel's threat to destroy the Iranian nuclear efforts; but proceeded in pressuring Egypt and the other Arab states to ratify the nuclear proliferation treaty. The commitment of non-nuclear states to abstain from possessing nuclear weapons (articles 2 and 4 of the 1995 conference on nuclear non-proliferation) and the efficiency of the guarantees extended by the International Agency for Atomic Energy (article 3 of the same conference) remain as key points of impasse in this area.[49]

The second question, concerns Israel's sticking to bilateral agreements as the framework for dealing with the Arab states regarding the weapons of mass destruction. It is obvious that the previous tactic exploits certain disagreements in the Arabs' points of view to dispense with any commitment. For while Egypt requests the elimination of all weapons of mass destruction from the area, Syria (boycotting the committee's sessions) is committed only to constrain their usage. If we add the official Iranian position, the picture becomes even more complex. In spite of the fact that Iran is not invited to participate in the Arms Control and Regional Security Committee, it crystallized a vision based on rejecting the United States' claims about the dual usage of technology for military purposes. The Iranian foreign ministry issued a statement defending the right of the Islamic Republic to possess the technology for nuclear, biological and chemical weapons in order to benefit from their investments, which go back to the Shah's age, or most importantly, to exploit their hoped for fruits in the fields of agriculture, industry and health (i.e., the peaceful usage of weapons of mass destruction). It pointed out that the dual usage claim applies to those who did not join the nuclear non-proliferation treaty (i.e., Israel) and not to its members (including Iran).[50] But outside this frame, some Iranian voices do not object to the use of the weapons of mass destruction in defensive purposes, and consider this usage a necessity for preserving the national security of the state.[51]

In general, the different alternative futures of the weapons of mass destruction could be summarized in: overt deterrence, controlled proliferation, a nuclear weapon free-zone, or opaqueness. By surveying these alternatives, one realizes, in the final analysis, that the Middle East will exemplify, until further notice, the last alternative – involving imbalance at the expense of both Arabs and Iranians. Opaqueness seems to be the best term for describing the future of the Middle East for several reasons. First, there is complete uncertainty as to Israel's nuclear capabilities. Secondly, Israel refuses to commit itself to mutual and comprehensive guarantees with the states of the area. Thirdly, Israel not only threatens to use force (its ultimatum in 1995 to strike against the Iranian nuclear efforts), but uses it effectively to prevent others from possessing atomic weapons (the precedent of destroying the Iraqi nuclear plant in 1981 is a case in point). Finally, international pressures and temptations are comparatively weak in the presence of a local environment (parties, military institutions, public opinion, etc.) which values the nuclear alternative and praises its gains.[52]

The International Markets

To what extent have the Arabs and Iranians benefited from the internationalization of markets resulting from the third stage of the technological revolution? To what extent are northern technology and investments freely flowing to the area, or to what degree are workers allowed to take off to the North whenever it occurs to them? These two questions open the way for surveying the movement in the capital and workers market from the North to the Arab states and Iran and vice versa. As for the market of technology, it was covered in the course of the discussion on the North's position *vis-à-vis* arms control.

To start with capital flows, it is noticeable that neither the Arab states nor Iran have benefited much from the big increase in the flows of direct foreign investments since the mid-eighties, which currently represents one-fifth of capital flows. Even though the benefit to the states in the South from foreign investments jumped from 12 per cent in 1987 to 22 per cent in 1992, the bulk of this percentage went to East Asia, to the Pacific Ocean, Latin America and the Caribbean. This was due to the availability of a more suitable atmosphere for investment (education, roads, electricity, etc.) in these areas. Such countries espouse an externally oriented developmental mode (the exporting economy), while adopting policies preserving justice between foreign and native investors. In addition to this, the focus of foreign investments has effectively shifted from the extractive sector to areas that flourish naturally in these states, such as high-tech industrialization, transportation and banking.[53]

A more detailed analysis on the state level shows that Egypt's share of direct foreign investment diminished from $547 million in 1980 to $459 million in 1992, despite its place at the head of Arabs' recipients. Tunisia occupied the second rank in this respect with a diminishing share of $235 million, in comparison with $379 million. The share of the Sultanate of Oman was reduced from $98 million to $59 million in the same period. Syria's share, hoever, increased from 0 to $67 million. As for Sudan, its share was stabilized at the level of 0, while Iran's shifted from 0, in 1980, to

$170 million, in 1992. The previous numbers give rise to two comments. The first is the huge disparity in the shares of states belonging to the same South group, as between Egypt and Tunisia, on the one hand, and Syria and Iran, on the other. These findings could be explained by weak absorbing potential, or the stumbling of the economic liberalization policies in certain cases. The second remark concerns the relatively low total share of the Arab countries and Iran, in comparison with that of Mexico, which has more than doubled throughout the same period, from $2.156 billion to $5.366 billion, or Malaysia and Argentina's share, which leaped from $934 million and $678 billion to $4.118 billion and $4.179 billion respectively.[54] The danger of this condition for the Arab states and Iran stems from the acute need for foreign investment to stimulate developmental efforts in view of the limited local investments and their modest efficiency (less than 10 per cent of the gross domestic product).[55] In contrast, Arab capital does not move freely; it is constrained by a ceiling that it cannot surpass even if it tried to. For instance, when the Gulf states aspired to increase their shares in the International Monetary Fund and the International Bank for Reconstruction and Development, their demands were turned down, for Arab capital is not allowed to compete with northern hegemony over internationally sovereign institutions.

Regarding short and long term financial stocks and bonds, they, in their turn, recorded a remarkable increase, especially between 1989 and 1992, from $8 billion to more than $34 billion. Similarly for direct foreign investment, the largest part of this increase fed East Asia, the Pacific Ocean, Latin America and the Caribbean. While the share of Arab states and Iran remained null from 1980 till 1992, Brazil's increased from 0 to $119 million and Mexico's share shifted from 0 to $5.213 billion.[56] These states have all taken off from the 0 point, but a 12 years lapse steered each of them to a different path.

Concerning loans, they were affected by the need to reconstruct the east European states, by the rise in the size of southern debt, and the availability of other sources of finance. These factors had, in general, limited the flow of loans to the South between 1980 and 1992. southern states with disparate economic performances have been subject to this decrease. Tanzania, for example, witnessed a drop from $710 million to $165 million. Loans granted to Argentina fell from $3.023 billion to $2.477 billion, while loans to Malaysia and Indonesia increased from $1.423 billion and $4.277 billion to $1.680 billion and $6.197 billion respectively. On the Arab arena, the general decrease in the total flow of loans varies in degree between states. On the one hand, Egypt recorded a sharp decline in loans from $2.558 billion to $1.416 billion, the Somalian drop was from $188 million to 0, and Syria's share fell from $11.168 billion to $350 million. On the other hand, however, the decrease was moderate in Oman, from $454 million to $144 million, and in Morocco, from $1.686 billion to $1.274 billion, Only loans extended to Tunisia and Algeria witnessed a rise, from $777 million and $3.538 billion to $1.157 billion and $8.538 billion respectively. However, if Tunisia's improving economic performance explains the increase in the loans granted to it, fear of worsening conditions and the succession of emigrants' waves towards the North following the cancellation of legislative elections, explain the increase in the Algerian case.[57] The third exceptional model, illustrating an increase in the flow of loans from 0 in 1980, to $4.314 billion in 1992, is Iran.[58] This is the result of two main factors: the opening of Rafsanjani's system to the external world in order to finance reconstruction following the war with Iraq, and the willingness of the international community to reward Iran for its stance towards the invasion of Kuwait.

The increasing loans might also be looked at from another angle, as an attempt to get the Arab states and Iran entangled in a web of debt (cf. the Egyptian model). However, from a different perspective, the rise in loans might be considered as consolidating developmental efforts. In this respect, Dr Henry 'Azam cites the two cases of Libya and Iraq, which illustrate the previously mentioned complexities, in addition to being subject to harsh international sanctions hindering them from borrowing for the sake of promoting their oil industries. This situation should be compared to that in the oil rich states, which do not face any difficulties in borrowing from foreign countries. In fact, their national oil companies enable them to manage the monetary needs for such development.[59]

Regarding the labour market, this is another confrontational arena between North and South. The essence of this conflict is, specifically, emigration to the North. Statistical figures reveal that southern emigrants increased from 5.7 million in 1979, to 18.2 in 1992, i.e. they have almost tripled.[60] The demographic problem in the South has been pointed out as a determining factor. But it is also possible to add the stalled nature of democratic and economic development in many southern countries. These three critical issues stimulating South emigration are known as 'the 3 Ds'.[61]

The case of immigrants is generally raised concerning southerners, whether Arabs, Muslims, non Arabs or non Muslims. In the United States, there is an unabated debate around the negative impact of immigrants on the American national economy. The decrease in work opportunities, the lowering of salaries and the pressure exerted on the infrastructure which far exceeds the tax revenues are but some of these negative effects. It is worth noting that the percentage of Asians, the principal category of immigrants in the U.S., increased from 6 per cent of the total number of immigrants in the fifties, to 45 per cent in the eighties, to be followed by the Latin Americans, whose percentage has stabilized at 40 per cent since the sixties; as for the percentage of Europeans, it shrank from two-thirds in the decade of the fifties to its current level of about 15 per cent .[62]

In Europe, on the other hand, the case is more pressing, because of sharper economic competition. While the American economy was capable of providing 21 million jobs between 1975 and 1985, European job openings had simultaneously shrunk by approximately one million . When a slight improvement occurred between 1985 and 1989, enabling the community to provide 4.8 million work opportunities, about 40 per cent of them were part time jobs.[63]

The general outline presented above does not cover all the difficulties encountered by the Arab, Iranian and Turkish labour force that succeeded in penetrating the northern fences. This work force, despite its variability, was affiliated to an area inflamed by domestic, transnational, and regional conflicts, as shown. Consequently, the West tried to avoid close ties with this spot, for fear of being turned into an arena where the people from the area could confront each other to settle their accounts (the bombing of the World Trade Centre, the assassination of the Jewish Rabbi Kahane, the attack on Jewish interests in Europe and the US, the elimination of the Iranian or Kurdish opposition, etc.).[64] Naturally, the northern fears are closely linked to the rise in the percentage of Arabs, Iranians, or Turks in the total number of immigrants. In a state like France, the immigrants from Africa had not increased by more than 1 per cent of the total number on the eve of the Algerian war of liberation. Then, gradually, their relative weight increased to reach 24.5 per cent in 1968 and 43 per cent in the early eighties. The majority of them (90 per cent) are natives of the Arab Maghreb (38.1 per cent of total immigrants).* Some sources claim that Maghreb expatriates, specifically, are responsible for half the increase in the number of foreigners in France between 1975 and 1982, because of their youthfulness and high fertility rates. It is also estimated that the total remittances of Moroccan immigrants amounted, in 1985, to the huge sum of 22 billion FF approximately.[65] The intricacies of circumstances in the three Maghreb states (the relationship of the Renaissance 'Al-Nahda' with the FIS 'Jabhat al-Inqadh al-Islamiyyah', and the activities of the Salvationists in Morocco, etc.) and the involvement of some Algerian immigrants in France in these activities[66] lie behind the rising appeal of the nascent fanatical French Right's discourse.

In general, the North has resorted to two approaches in handling the immigrants' problem. The first is a long-term regulation designed to dry up the sources of emigrants by endorsing population control in the South, legalizing abortion, and encouraging sexual relationships outside wedlock. These were, in fact, the topics around which the 3rd UN Conference on Population and Development was convened, in Cairo. As for the second tactic, it is a short-term one, dealing with the present situation and attempting to lessen its drawbacks as much as possible, Within this category, one could mention the strictness in granting visas, the ease with which they can subsequently be withdrawn, restraining the movement of immigrants between the states of the European Union – even if the association with which the immigrant is affiliated transferred its activities to another European country – and the arbitrary implementation of the 'family reunification' policy (placing harsh conditions on reunification, such as strict tests on the father's revenue, and deportation of the wife in the event of divorce). This short-term approach generally works to encourage the unemployed immigrants to return to their native homes. With the acceleration of steps towards European union, some express their fears concerning the unification of special immigration legislations, to the extreme detriment of the Arab work force in Europe.[67]

The previous remark brings us to discuss the two final points related to the internationality of markets, and, specifically, the freedom of commercial exchange and the extent to which the Arab states and Iran were affected by it. The first point concerns the international economic blocs and their impact on trade and investment with the states falling outside their boundaries. The widening of the European Union, in 1986, to encompass both Portugal and Spain, created problems for the Tunisian and Moroccan export of citrus fruits. It is interesting to note that the European Union was, in 1991, the first trade partner of both Tunisia and Morocco, accounting for 68 per cent and 72 per cent respectively, of their imports and absorbing 74 per cent and 68 per cent respectively of their exports. Besides, the United Tariffs Agreement between the European Union and Cyprus, in 1988, affected the Egyptian exports of potatoes which used to compete with their Cypriot counterparts. With the coming of 1992, the total value of Egyptian exports to the members of the Union decreased to $104 million, in contrast to $127 million in 1989. The oil rich countries were not immune to these problems. For example, the Saudi balance of trade with the European Union witnessed a deficit amounting to $2.5 billion, due to the Union's decreasing purchase of oil (in contrast to Japan and the newly industrialized countries), in addition to the custom exemptions enjoyed by the Union's exports (in contrast to the Saudi and Gulf petrochemical exports in general).[68] The foundation of a free trade zone in East Asia and the Pacific Ocean area by the ASEAN countries (Singapore, Philippines, Thailand, Brunei, Malaysia, Indonesia)* contributed in activating their sub-regional trade, currently representing 30 per cent of their total foreign trade. The joining of the ASEAN states to the APEC organization (the NAFTA states + others, the most important of which are Japan, China and South Korea) is expected to diversify their sources of direct foreign investment.[69]

For its part, Iran tried to keep up at this level of development by opening up the membership in the Economic Cooperation Organization to include the Islamic republics of the [ex-] Soviet Union, in addition to Afghanistan, Turkey and Pakistan. However, this bloc remained only moderately effective because of the domestic problems of its member states (the Afghani war and the Tajik conflict) and their conflicting relations (the Iranian–Turkish competition over the Islamic republics).

As for the second point, it is related to the emergence of the International Trade Organization since 2 January 1995 to supervise for a complete decade (until the year 2005) the implementation of the Uruguay round's decision to liberate international trade. The probable opinion is that the ending of 'historical preferences' enjoyed by the southern products, and the release of free competition in the international realm will be very costly for the Arab states** and Iran if their economic performance does not improve. States such as Egypt or Sudan, whose food imports represent 29 per cent and 22 per cent, respectively, of their total imports, will be directly affected by liberalizing the trade of agricultural items by a percentage ranging between 10 per cent and 25 per cent. Simultaneously, the commitment to decrease the subsidy offered to farmers in both states might impel them to change the nature of their activities, hence widening the present food gap. On the other hand, the liberalization of the commerce of manufactured goods will deprive the free zones in states such as Iran (Qeshm and Kish) of their importance, because foreign companies will not be obliged to invest in these areas to evade the quantitative restrictions imposed on their exports. Stopping the implementation of the artificial fibres treaty will strengthen the position of the newly industrialized states, at the expense of countries such as Morocco, Tunisia or Egypt, especially since the exports of ready-made clothes from the newly industrialized states enjoy a relative advantage because of the workers' low wages. It is worth mentioning that the three Arab states listed above invest huge sums in the manufacture of textiles. Yet the textile industries of these countries remain technologically modest and extremely labour intensive. Moreover, the opening of the marginalized states' markets (Mauritania and Somalia's, for instance) before the advanced electronic and electrical appliances will deprive such countries of the chance to produce this technology, let alone develop it. Although the oil states will be affected by the factors listed above with respect to liberalizing their services (construction, banking and transportation, etc.) because of their weak competitive power, yet the anti-dumping policy will alleviate the pressure on national products in comparison to the pre-International Trade Organization era. In addition to which, the liberalization of agricultural trade will rationalize the Saudi production of high-cost wheat; hence, putting an end to the kingdom's attempt at achieving sufficiency.[70]

The internationality of markets is an incrementally shaped phenomenon. While keeping a minimum predominance for the North, the international circle is increasingly broadened to include strata from the southern states. However, the Arabs and Iranians seem to remain, for the foreseeable future, outside the historical cycle, which seems to be working against their short and medium term interests.

The Middle Eastern System: what's in it for the Arabs and Iranians?

The legitimacy of the Middle Eastern system, according to its supporters, stems from its contribution to the reinforcement and 'consolidation of the new world order' from various angles. First, it secures the flow of oil to the industrialized countries, and protects them from price fluctuations. Secondly, it prevents the outbreak of regional wars due to the unhindered behaviour of ambitious forces – namely Iraq or Iran – or due to the persistence of the Arab–Israeli conflict for an indefinite period. Thirdly, it frees the northern states from direct and regular involvement in the problems of the Arab area, without disturbing their strategic interests.[71] With regard to future developments, the post-second Gulf war era witnessed a flow of Middle Eastern projects, the most significant of which were initiated by states that do not belong to the area, but have certain interests there. The less important projects were initiated by countries of the region, though conditioned upon their compatibility with the northern initiatives, in appearance and content. Without jumping to conclusions, it is necessary first to sum up the suggested Middle Eastern projects as follows:

The American project, essentially, is composed of two main parts. The first is the selection of Arab heartland states (Egypt and the Arab Mashriq states with the exception of Iraq) and the Gulf countries (with the exception of Iran). The project then seeks to tie them by strategic relations with both Israel and Turkey. The second part is the dual containment of both Iraq and Iran.[72] It is valid to say that, while the first part of the American project aims at preserving the balance – or rather the imbalance – between the Arabs and Israel, the second part prepares the appropriate environment for that through a strict surveillance of any shift in Arab–Arab, or Arab–Iranian relations of power.[73] This explains the duality of the American conduct towards Syria whose efforts to develop its military capabilities have been curtailed by the US, similarly to Iran and Iraq. Evidently, these countries share, in the American logic, all the characteristics of backlash states which encompass: the hegemony of particular trends on authority, the rejection of popular participation, the inability to form external alliances even with countries sharing the same ideological orientation, the tendency towards external expansion and the usual subjection of these states to international sanctions.[74] Yet, unlike Iraq, Syria whose role is decisive in determining the success of the Arab–Israeli peace process, has been integrated in the framework of the suggested American Middle Eastern system.

Though the previous American project enjoys high credibility in light of the new international variables, it is not immune from criticisms, especially regarding its second phase. It seems that the dual containment policy is destined to trigger wide debates, whether in the middle of the century, or at its end. In the 1950s, George Kennan (head of the Political Planning Department in the American State Department) wrote an article entitled 'Sources of Soviet Conduct'. In this article, Kennan argued that the animosity of the Soviet Union to the external world is a reflection of its internal political system, where the Soviet political party monopolizes power and organization, while chaos pervades the rest of the Union's structures. Because this system did not and shall not respond to Western conciliatory policies, the solution rests in blockading Russians wherever they are, and whenever they start attacking 'the interests of a secure and stable world'. The criticisms advanced by Winston Churchill, Henry Wallace and Walter Lippmann against Kennan's thesis focused on the exhausting of the United States resources, by dragging it into conflicts between parties that do not even enjoy the status of states (in the modern sense of the term). This policy, according to the critics, denies the legitimate Soviet influence on its immediate environment (central and eastern Europe) and wastes the chance of the West to make international peace, at a moment when it could negotiate from a power standpoint.[75]

In the 1990s, Martin Indyk (former head of Far East and South Asian Affairs in the American National Security Council) renewed the call for the 'dual containment' approach, albeit in a different political context. The principal point in Indyk's vision is that the United States no longer needs to back Iran at the expense of Iraq, or vice versa, for two reasons. The most important of them is the drawbacks of historical precedents in this respect. In fact, the harvest of support extended by the successive American administrations to the Shah's regime, then to Saddam Hussein's system, has seen the breakout of an Islamic revolution, followed by two regional wars. As for the second reason, it concerns the collapse of the Soviet Union, which has deprived Iraq of its pressuring card, the way a peaceful settlement in southern Lebanon should deprive Iran of its 'ace'. Besides, the first and second Gulf wars secured a balance of power between the two states, at the minimum level of their military capabilities. Finally, the Iraqi invasion of Kuwait contributed to placating the opposition of the Gulf 'friends' to entering a network of security arrangements with the United States, through which they would recuperate their independence.[76] Nevertheless, Martin Indyk was careful in distinguishing between the dual containment policy *vis-à-vis* Iraq, on the one hand, and Iran, on the other. The United States' containment of Iraq aims at ousting the present system, while its containment of Iran is confined to changing the conduct of the Islamic Republic *vis-à-vis* the United States. Effectively, the disagreement with Iran 'should not be wrongly depicted as a clash of civilizations', but as a conflict of interests. In the final analysis, the United States does not object to undertaking an authoritative dialogue with President Hashemi Rafsanjani's regime.[77]

It is possible to characterize most of the critiques raised against the vision of Martin Indyk, whether stemming from the Western camp, or from within the United States, as involving either a scepticism concerning the efficiency of containment and opposition to the legitimacy of containing either party. On the one hand, there were those who doubted the success of dual containment on the basis that it is impossible to contain the two states simultaneously. If the containment of Iran requires a strong Iraq that is not left prey to Iran's attempt at freeing itself from its regional isolation, the containment of Iraq requires Iranian cooperation, without which international sanctions become obsolete. Moreover, containing the two states simultaneously will forge bridges of understanding between them, in place of Rafsanjani's original policy *vis-à-vis* Iraq, which used to be based on blockading it and picturing its actions as the most serious danger threatening the oil rich kingdoms.[78]

On the other hand, there are analysts who challenge the legitimacy of disciplining Iran and to a lesser extent Iraq. Regarding Iran, Graham Fuller determined 12 differences between it and Iraq to illustrate his point. The most crucial difference advanced by Fuller is Iraq's launching of two wars against its neighbours throughout the last 15 years, whereas Iran renounced its previous confrontations in the Gulf. Iraq, with its present authoritative system, does not represent an optimistic picture for political development, since all depends on the figure of the president. As for Iran, it is a relatively open system, and has the potential for further evolution if the West were to change its attitude towards it. According to Fuller, the allegations about Iran's role in obstructing the peace process or in supporting the Islamists are products of imagination, rather than reality. Fuller expressed this view by asserting that the overnight disappearance of Iran from the world map would not change Egypt or Algeria's problems with the Islamists.[79] The legitimacy of blockading Iran is also challenged by economic interests. States like Germany (the number one European trade partner with Iran), Japan and Italy are not enthusiastic about isolating the Islamic Republic, even if it were only to ensure that the latter will pay back its current debts, in order to involve it in more.[80] There are, thus, limitations on the ability of these countries to apply economic pressures on Iran. Therefore, in 1994, the above countries participated with nine other European states in rescheduling $8.028 billion of the Iranian debt, turning them from short-term into medium-range debts (to be reimbursed over a six years period).[81] Moreover, a number of American businessmen have an interest in trading with the Islamic Republic. In 1992, profits from Iranian-US trade amounted to $750 million.[82] If we add the private accounts of some Gulf states, Syria,

Sudan and maybe Turkey and Pakistan, to the previous figures, the picture becomes even more complex.[83]

In so far as it concerns Iraq, the real problem stems from the present contradiction between the legal basis upon which the international sanctions against Saddam's regime rest, namely, its repression of Iraqis, and the fact that the persistence of these sanctions lies behind the suffering of the Iraqi populace. It is noteworthy that the embargo imposed on Iraq for the sixth consecutive year led to a number of drawbacks, the most important of which are: the diminishing value of Iraqi domestic products in 1993 to $3.3 billion – i.e. 39 per cent of its value before the invasion of Kuwait in 1990; the increase in the rate of inflation throughout the same period, from 40 per cent to more than 100 per cent, and the decrease in the average per capita income from $335 annually, to $65 in 1991, then to $44 in 1992. The last rate falls short of the determined international poverty line by $100. The burden of these sanctions is heavier on children and the elderly. This could be illustrated by the increase in child (under 5) mortality from its natural rate by 100,000 cases between 1991 and 1993 and the doubling in the mortality rate for elders (over 50) in comparison to 1989. In addition to this, the Iraqi population suffers from many diseases and epidemics due to the shortage in medicines, medical apparatus, spare parts, potable water, etc.[84] From a different perspective, the legitimacy of the international position *vis-à-vis* Iraq's conduct towards the UN Commission on Elimination of Weapons of Mass Destruction is controversial. For whereas the United States denies any real cooperation having taken place between the Iraqi side and the concerned Commission, China, Russia and France hold a different opinion, paving the way for the gradual lifting of international sanctions.[85] 'The Western alliance in the Persian Gulf has turned into an alliance where every partner does whatever it wishes'; this sentence uttered by one of the Western commentators indicates very well the level of confusion in the international position *vis-à-vis* Iraq.[86]

The Italian project adopts a different approach from its American counterpart in terms of the criteria for the inclusion and exclusion of the Arab states in the suggested Middle Eastern system. On the basis of this project, all the Mediterranean states, whether Arab or non Arab (with the exception of France) are to be involved in a structure approaching that of the Cooperation Council and the European Security Council. In return, all Arab states overlooking the Red Sea shall be excluded. Both policies are justifiable. The Mediterranean character of the new system is derived from the common difficulties shared by these countries, particularly their security problems, which have been exposed by the two Gulf crises and wars. Geographical proximity and the huge development of weapons of mass destruction transformed the north of the Mediterranean into the natural extension of the conflicts existing in the south. In addition, the non Mediterranean states, especially the Gulf countries, are not included in the project because of the different alternatives open to them, which tend to favour a reliance on the United States for security purposes. Lutfy al-Khuly argues that in both the first and second cases, the Italian initiative caters to the European and Arab partners' need to shake off their feelings of inferiority and prove themselves: The Europeans by trying to break the joint German–French hegemony over the European community (the Spaniards, Greeks, Italians, Cypriots, etc.) and the Arabs (the peoples of the Arab Maghreb in particular) by exploiting the project to cooperate with their immediate geographical neighbour, instead of a broader Middle Eastern system, where their role would be almost nil.

In light of these arguments, it is possible to say that the Italian initiative represents an upgrading of the Middle East concept by adding a European dimension to its traditional African and Asian aspects. But, this, in itself, raises doubts about its applicability. In fact, we have already realized that the evolution in the direction of European unity will intensify sub-regional interactions among its members, at the expense of their external commitments. Besides, the disparity in the levels of technological and economic development of the members might motivate the European states to apply the same policy of subjugation – to which they were subject in the framework of the European group – over the Arab states south of the Mediterranean.[87] The Moroccan kingdom expressed its awareness of this reality (i.e. the possibility of marginalizing its role) on the eve of the Casablanca summit on 2 November 1994. Hence, while suggesting a number of economic projects linking it to Spain, it concomitantly sought to open its doors to sub-Saharan Africa and offered to link it to Europe by means of a network of railways going through the Strait of Gibraltar. The situation seems to be moving in the direction of a three level hierarchical system: Israeli–European, Middle Eastern–Arab, and Arab–African under the label of a single system.[88]

The Israeli project is prominent among the initiatives adopted by the regional countries. Second in prominence to it are the Turkish and Iranian projects. The former, as advanced by Shimon Peres in his book *The New Middle East*, stems from the idea that poverty is the principal challenge to the countries of the area. He relates this poverty directly to the flourishing of the radical and 'fundamentalist' religious trends in the region. Within this framework, Peres calls for what he labels the economic regional system or the joint Middle Eastern market, which is inspired by its European counterpart, for the sake of mobilizing the potential capabilities of the area and investing them in the interests of their populaces. Work on this project is to start immediately – even before 'consolidating a permanent peace' – through Arab–Israeli cooperation in fields involving the exploitation of the desert and water desalination. The second stage starts more ambitiously, by encompassing international consortiums to achieve huge regional projects – such as the digging of a canal to connect the Red Sea to the Dead Sea and creating a Saudi–Jordanian–Israeli harbour. As for the third and last stage, it shifts to the consolidation of the political dimensions of the suggested regime, by forming a network of official transnational institutions consecrating democracy and venerating human rights.[89]

It is obvious that the signaled Middle Eastern market falls short of the idealist picture drawn by Peres, whether substantively, or with respect to its geographical boundaries. A close observation of projects selected for developing 'regional' cooperation discloses the real aim for which the mobilization of the area's resources takes place. Such mobilization, claimed to be for the benefit of the people of the region does not serve anyone, in practice, but Israel. Certain types of projects are definitely neglected (roads, electricity, and commerce) since they do not necessarily revolve around the Israeli pivot. Dr Ghassan Salamé maintains that Jordan and Palestine, specifically, will be the first to lose out from the inauguration of the suggested Middle Eastern market. For, in contrast to the anticipated rise in the value of Israeli exports to the total Arab parties from $11 billion and $20 billion annually, harsh restrictions will be imposed on the entry of merchandise (particularly agricultural products) and workers (especially technocrats) to Israel.*[90] From a different perspective, despite the fact that Peres' project gives, at first glance, the impression of encompassing all Arab states, its being directed against what the Israeli Foreign Minister calls 'Islamic fundamentalism' will cause it to spontaneously exclude countries such as Sudan and Iran.

If we move to Turkey, we shall discover that, like Iran, it believes economic cooperation to be an appropriate basis for a new Middle Eastern system, after being extended south to include the oil rich countries. Turkey had already adopted a project to serve this end prior to the end of the second Gulf war. Accordingly, it suggested a semblance of an economic security alliance among the member states, taking Ankara as the headquarters of its general secretariat.[91] However, the Turkish and Iranian projects disagree over the Israeli role in their frameworks. If Israel exemplifies a basic pillar of the Turkish Middle Eastern project, its relationship with the Islamic Republic is based on a kind of mutual rejection. Less important is the stance *vis-à-vis* Syrian and Egyptian participation in the suggested systems. In reality, Turkey does not object to involving Egypt and Syria (to a lesser degree) in a number of inherited problems. As for the position of these states in the Iranian project, it remains controversial, particularly regarding Egypt, and especially if this system is being linked to the performance of a special security project in the framework of the Gulf area. The response of both states, the Turkish and Iranian, to the Damascus declaration illustrates some of these conflicting positions. On a second level, and in view of the prevalent international and regional variables, the competitive abilities of Turkey and Iran vary, as do their abilities at influencing the suggested Middle Eastern system. Turkey is a NATO member, and is exempted from controlling traditional weaponry according to Bush's first initiative in this domain. It also presents itself as the castle of democracy and political freedom in the region, and expresses its willingness to solve one side of the economic problems of the new order, namely water scarcity. Iran, on the other hand, does not possess any of these qualifications. Concerning the Arab states, which are meant to participate in the Middle Eastern organization, they face dangers from both the Iranian and Turkish projects, which threaten to entangle them in an area rich in problems and poor in resources (central Asia, and the Caucasus); and hence make them bear part of the burden of its reconstruction.

Conclusion

The civilizational approach is insufficient to explain the distinctions in international positions among Muslims. It is evident that some Muslim states represent an attractive magnet to the interest of the international community. These states are already involved with some major powers in transnational organizations, and undertake negotiations from a power standpoint. These considerations support the assumptions of analysis based on economic and realpolitik interests. The Middle Eastern projects prove the accuracy of the previous statement, despite the diversity of their proponents. All of these projects stem from the crucial role played by the economy in spreading peace among the states of the region. They have all adopted the economy as a criterion for including certain states and excluding others. Most importantly, all of them have bet on the Arabs' inability to form an Arab economic market, or to mobilize their goods for their own benefit. Therefore, it was not by coincidence that the Gulf states formed the major common denominator in all the Middle Eastern projects (with the exception of the Italian project). It was also no coincidence that they were emphatically connected to Turkey, Iran, Israel, or central Asia and the Caucasus, while being uprooted from a segment or all of their Arab context. In light of this, one could confidently assert that the 21st century looks set to be the century of giant economic corporations. Without reviving the economic integration treaties signed in the framework of the Arab League and its specialized organizations, the Arabs' international status will further retreat. Their destiny would be to act forever as the financiers of North and South ambitions.

Notes

* Assistant Professor, Faculty of Economic and Political Sciences, University of Cairo, Cairo, Egypt.

1. Niveen Abdulmonem Masaad, *'Athar al-Mutaghayirat al-'Alamiyyah al-Jadidah 'ala al-Siyasah al-Kharijiyya al-Iraniyyah tijah al-Mantiqah al-'Arabiyyah: 1989–1993'* ('The Impact of the New International Variables on Iranian External Relations towards the Arab Region: 1989–1993'), in: Jamal Z. Qassim and Yunan L. Rizq, eds., *Al-'Ilaqat al-'Arabiyyah al-Iraniyyah (Arab–Iranian Relations)*, (Cairo: Ma'had al-Buhuth wal Dirasat al-'Arabiyyah, 1993), pp. 369–70. See also: Muhammad Atrash, *'Tatawur al-Nizam al-Dawly'* ('Development of the International System', *Al-Mustaqbal Al-'Araby*, vol. 16, no. 171 (May 1993), pp. 25–6, and Seif 'Abdul Fattah, *'Hawl al-Tahayuz fi Mafhum al-Nizam al-'Alamy al-Jadid'* ('Concerning Prejudice in the Concept of the New International Order'), *Mustaqbal al-'Alam al-Islamy*, vol. 2, no. 8 (Fall 1992), pp. 7–8.

2. See Huntington's article, the criticisms leveled against it and his defence in: Samuel P. Huntington, 'The Clash of Civilizations?', *Foreign Affairs*, vol. 72, no. 3 (Summer 1993), pp. 22–49; Fouad 'Ajami, 'But They Said, We Will Not Hearken', *Foreign Affairs*, vol. 72, no. 4 (September–October 1993), pp. 2–9; Kishore Mahbubani, 'The Dangers of Decadence', ibid., pp. 10–14; Liu Binyan, 'Civilization Grafting', ibid., pp. 19–21; Samuel P. Huntington, 'If Not Civilizations, What? Paradigms of the Post-Cold War World', *Foreign Affairs*, vol. 72, no. 5 (November–December 1993), pp. 186 ff; Salah al-Din Hafez, *'Hiwar al-Adyan wa Tahadiyyat al-Salam'* ('Dialogue of Religions and the Challenges of Peace'), *Al-Hayat* daily, part 1, 21 December 1994; Al Sayed Yassin, *Al-Taghayyurat al-'Alamiyyah wa Hiwar al-Hadarat fi 'Alam Mutaghayyir'* ('International Changes and Dialogue of Civilizations in a Changing World'), Strategic Monographs 14, (Cairo: Markaz al-Dirasat al-Siyasiyyah wal Stratijiyyah bil Ahram, 1993), p. 12; Jamil Matar, *'Harb Hadarat'* ('War of Civilizations'), *Al-Hayat* daily, 20 September 1993; 'Abdul Wahab al-Missiry, *'Al-Nizam al-'Alamy al-Jadid'* ('The New World Order'), *Manbar al-Sharq*, vol. 3, no. 14 (July 1994), pp. 10–12; and 'Islam and the West' (Survey), *The Economist*, vol. 332, no. 7875, pp. 3–5. Concerning Huntington's opinion on the relationship between culture and democracy, and Badie's response, see: Samuel P. Huntington, *The Third Wave* (Norman and London: University of Oklahoma Press, 1991), pp. 298–316, and Bertrand Badie, 'Democracy and Religion: Logic of Culture and Logics of Action', *International Social Science Journal*, no. 128 (August 1991), pp. 511–21.

3. James Kellas, *The Politics of Nationalism and Ethnicity* (London: Macmillan, 1991).

4. Alain Gresh et al., *A l'Est: Les Nationalismes Contre la Democratie?* ('To the East: Nationalisms Against Democracy?'), Bruxelles: Editions Complexe, 1993.

5. Mattei Dogan, 'The Decline of Nationalism within Western Europe', *Comparative Politics*, vol. 26, no. 3 (April 1994), pp. 281–303.

6. Chris Horman, 'The Return of the National Question', *International Socialism*, no. 56 (Autumn 1992), p. 361. Regarding the same economic-pragmatic perspective on ethnic conflicts in Africa, see: Ocwad Panoley, *Racial Conflict in Africa* (Cairo: Arab Research Centre, 1991). See also the critical remarks on the analysis

of Kellas's book in: Nevine Munir Tewfiq, 'Nationalist Awakening: A Comparative Analysis' (unpublished paper, 1994), pp. 22–9.

7. Boutros Boutros Ghali, *Al-Hiwar wal Sira' bayn Al-Janub wal Shimal'* ('Dialogue and Conflict between South and North'), *Al-Siyasah Al-Dawliyyah*, no. 105 (July 1991), pp. 155–60.

8. Discourse with Taha 'Abdul 'Alim, head of the economic section at the Centre for Political and Strategic Studies, Cairo, in *Al-Ahram* daily, 29 November 1994.

9. The World Bank, *World Development Report 1994*, (Oxford: Oxford University Press, 1994), pp. 186–7 and 190–1.

* It should be noted that Saudi Arabia, Tunisia and Sudan are the biggest Arab states in their respective groups (the oil rich, the multi-structured, and the marginalized). Iran is also one of the biggest states in the third group; hence, the significance of surveying their economic performances. Malaysia is tackled in this context specifically because it is a Muslim country, though not the biggest newly industrialized country.

10. *World Economic Outlook 1993*, (Washington, D.C.: International Monetary Fund, 1993), pp. 124–5.

11. Al-Bahy 'Issawy, *Al-Mutaghayyirat al-'Alamiyyah fil Siyasat al-Petroliyyah'* ('International Variables in Oil Policies', *Al-Ahram* daily, 2 September 1994.

12. See the discussion with Gilbert Pertel, General Secretary of the Oil Manufacturing Association, in: *Al-Hayat* daily, 29 September 1994.

13. Ahmad Shakara, *Al-Fikr al-Istratijy al-Amriky wal Sharq al-Awsat fil Nizam al-Dawly al-Jadid'* ('American Strategic Thought and the Middle East in the New World Order'), *Al-Mustaqbal al-'Araby*, vol. 16, no. 170 (April 1993), p. 55.

14. 'Abdul Mon'im Sa'id, *Al-Dimoqratiyyah wal Nizam al-'Alamy al-Jadid'* ('Democracy and the New World Order'), *Mijalat al-Dimoqratiyyah*, kitab 4 (August 1992), pp. 12 – 14.

15. Michael Mandelbaum, 'The Reluctance to Intervene', *Foreign Policy*, no. 95 (Summer 1994), pp. 13–16.

16. Larry Diamond, 'Promoting Democracy', *Foreign Policy*, no. 87 (Summer 1992), p. 29.

17. George Lenczowski, 'Iran: The Big Debate', *Middle East Policy*, vol. 3, no. 2 (1994), p. 61.

18. James A. Bill, 'The United States and Iran: Mutual Mythologies', *Middle East Policy*, vol. 2, no. 3 (1993), p. 100. Concerning human rights violations, see: Mahmud Monshipouri and Christopher G. Kukla, 'Islam, Democracy and Human Rights, the Continuing Debate in the West', *Middle East Policy*, vol. 3, no. 2 (1994), p. 33.

19. *Al-Hayat* daily, 27 September 1994.

20. Mehdi Noorbaksh, 'The Middle East, Islam and the United States', *Middle East Policy*, vol. 2, no. 3 (1993), p. 91.

21. Morton H. Halperin, 'Guaranteeing Democracy', *Foreign Policy*, no. 91 (Summer 1993), pp. 112–15. Concerning the European Parliament's position vis-à-vis human rights in Morocco and Syria, see: Gema Martin Monuoz, *Huquq al-Insan wal Tahawullat nahw al-Dimoqratiyyah fil Buldan al-'Arabiyyah'* ('Human Rights and the Democratic Transformations in the Arab Countries'), unpublished paper submitted to the conference on *Azmat al-Khalij wal Nizam al-Siyasi fil Sharq al-Awsat'* ('The Gulf Crisis and the Political System in the Middle East'), Aix en Provence, 23–5 January 1992, p. 20.

22.   About the Islamists' reading of the West's position on democracy, see: Ghassan Salamé, 'Islam and the West', *Foreign Policy*, no. 90 (Spring 1993), pp. 28–32.

23.   Mehdi Noorbaksh, 'The Middle East, Islam and the United States', op. cit., p. 91. See the same view in: Burhan Ghaliyun, *Al-Dimoqratiyyah al-'Arabiyyah: Juzur al-Azma wa Afaq al-Numuw* ('Arab Democracy: Roots of the Crisis and Horizons of Development'), in: Burhan Ghaliyun, ed., *Hawl al-Khiyar al-Dimoqraty: Dirasat Naqdiyyah (Concerning the Democratic Option: Critical Studies)*, (Beirut: Centre for Arab Unity Studies, 1994), pp. 116–18.

24.   Richard Falk, 'Can U.S. Policy toward the Middle East Change Course?', *Middle East Journal*, vol. 47, no. 1 (Winter 1993), p. 17.

25.   Bilabari Kausikan, 'Asia's Different Standard', *Foreign Policy*, no. 92 (Fall 1993), p. 29.

26.   *Ibid.*, p. 28. About the impact of the economic factor on the issue of democracy and human rights in Sino–American relations, see: Robert A. Manning, 'Clinton and China: Beyond Human Rights', *Orbis*, vol. 38, no. 2 (Spring 1994), pp. 197–99, and Meriam Daftari, 'Sino–American Relations: From Hostility to Friendship and from Friendship to … ?', *Iranian Journal of International Affairs*, vol. 3, no. 182 (Spring–Summer 1994), pp. 188–197.

27.   Nabil Shabib, *'Haiti: 'Asr al-Harb 'ala al-Hijrat al'Bashariyyah?'* ('Haiti: The Age of Wars Against Human Emigrations?', *Al-Hayat* daily, 28 September 1994. Also, David C. Hendrickson, 'The Renovation of American Foreign Policy', *Foreign Affairs*, vol. 71, no. 1 (1992), p. 62.

28.   Regarding the early efforts of Egypt in this respect, see: 'Abdul Mon'eim Sa'id and Muhammad Qadry Sa'id, *'Dhabt al-Tasalluh Janub al-Bahr al-Abyad al-Mutawassit: Wijhit Nazar 'Arabiyyah'* ('Arms Control South of the Mediterranean: An Arab Perspective', *Al-Siyasah Al-Dawliyyah*, no. 109 (July 1992), pp. 33–7.

29.   Concerning the details of these developments, see: Barry R. Schneider, 'Nuclear Proliferation and Counter Proliferation: Policy Issues and Debates', *Mershan International Review*, vol. 38, supplement 2 (October 1994), p. 212; Stephen J. Cimbala, 'Nuclear Weapons in the New World Order', *Strategic Studies*, vol. 16, no. 3 (June 1993), pp. 173–99, and Ted Galen Carpenter, 'Closing the Nuclear Umbrella', *Foreign Affairs*, vol. 73, no. 2 (March–April 1994), pp. 8–13.

30.   Gerald M. Steinberg, 'Non Proliferation: Time for Regional Approaches?', *Orbis*, vol. 38, no. 2 (Spring 1994), p. 418.

31.   For a detailed presentation and critique of these initiatives, see: Muhammad 'Abdul Salam, *'Siyasat al-Dhabt al-Dawly li Tasalluh al-Sharq al-Awsat'* ('International Arms Control Policies towards Middle East Armament'), *Al-Siyasah Al-Dawliyyah*, no. 109 (July 1993), pp. 243–6; Ahmad Ibrahim Mahmud, *'Al-Amn wal Taswiyah, Ittijahat Dhabt al-Tasalluh fil Sharq al-Awsat'* ('Security and Settlement, the Orientations of Middle East Arms Control'), *Al-'Araby*, 16 August 1993; and Mohammad El-Sayed Selim, 'The Arms Control Dimension in the Middle East Peace Process: Approaches and Prospects', *Studies in Security and Strategy*, vol. 2, no. 8 (July 1994), pp. 8–19.

32.   For the text of the decision, see: *Al-Siyasah Al-Dawliyyah*, no. 105 (July 1991), p. 135.

33.   Robert Manning, 'Clinton and China: Beyond Human Rights', op. cit., p. 196.

34.   For more details about the Israeli nuclear weapons, see: Tarek Ziyada, *'Ta'ziz al-Tasalluh al-Nawawy al-Israily fi Zaman al-Mufawadhat'* ('Consolidating the

Israeli Nuclear Weaponry in the Era of Negotiations'), *Al-Hayat* daily, 4 July 1994.

35.   Mahmud 'Azmi, *'Tahdid al-Tasalluh fil Sharq al-Awsat: Bayn Iqtisam al-Aswaq wa Tahdid al-Amn al-'Araby'* ('Arms Control in the Middle East: Between the Division of Markets and the Threat to Arab Security'), *Shu'un al-Awsat*, no. 3 (September 1991), p. 29.

36.   *Ibid.*, p. 34.

37.   *Ibid.*, p. 34.

38.   Stephen D. Goose and Frank Smyth, 'Arming Genocide in Rwanda', *Foreign Affairs*, vol. 73, no. 5 (September–October 1994), p. 89.

39.   Mahmud Azmi, op. cit., p. 31.

40.   *Al-Sharq Al-Awsat*, 17 August 1993.

41.   This expression was used by Huntington as mentioned in: John Sigler, 'Pax Americana in the Gulf: Old Reflexes and Assumptions Revisited', *International Journal*, vol. 41 (Spring 1994), p. 289.

42.   This expression has been used as a title for Anthony Lake's article: 'Confronting Backlash States', *Foreign Affairs*, vol. 73, no. 2 (March–April 1994).

43.   Yahya Sadowski, 'Scuds Versus Butter: The Political Economy of Arms Control in the Arab World', *Middle East Report*, vol. 22, no. 177 (July–August 1992), p. 7.

44.   *Al-Hayat* daily, 18 December 1994.

45.   James A. Bill, 'The United States and Iran: Mutual Mythologies', op. cit., pp. 103–4.

46.   Dore Gold, 'The US and Gulf Security', in Schlomo Gazit, ed., *The Middle East Military Balance, 92–93*, (Tel Aviv: Jaffee Center for Strategic Studies, 1993), p. 81.

47.   Lenczowski, 'Iran: The Big Debate', op. cit., pp. 57–8.

48.   See the declaration of David Every, head of the Israeli delegation at the Arms Control Committee in Tunisia in: *Al-Hayat* daily, 16 December 1994.

49.   John Simpson, 'Nuclear Non-proliferation in the Post Cold War Ear', *International Affairs*, vol. 70, no. 1 (January 1994), pp. 30–5.

50.   *Iranian Journal of International Affairs*, vol. 6 (1994), pp. 242–5.

51.   Daniel Pipes and Patrick Clawson, 'Ambitious Iran, Troubled Neighbours', *Foreign Affairs*, vol. 72, no. 1 (1992–1993), p. 127.

52.   Etel Solingen, 'The Domestic Sources of Regional Regimes: The Evolution of Nuclear Ambiguity in the Middle East', *International Studies Quarterly*, vol. 38, no. 2 (June 1994), pp. 306–7 and 311–29. Concerning the conditions of arms control in the Middle East, see Amin Huwaidi, *'Al-Had min al-Tasalluh fil Sharq al-Awsat bayn al-Misdaqiyyah wal Wahm, Mustaqbal al-'Alam al-Islamy'* ('Arms Control in the Middle East between Credibility and Illusion, the Future of the Islamic World'), op. cit., p. 184.

53.   *World Economic Outlook 1993*, pp. 74–5.

54.   The World Bank, *World Development Report, 1994*, pp. 204–5.

55.   The World Bank, *'Al-Taqrir al-Sanawy lil Bank al-Dawly li 'Am 1994'* (*Annual Report, 1994*), p. 154.

56.   The World Bank, *World Development Report, 1994*, pp. 204–5.

57.   *Ibid.*, pp. 208–9.

58.   *Ibid.*, pp. 208–9.

59.   Henry 'Azam, *'Tabi'at al-Munafasah 'ala Ijtizab Ru'us al-Amwal al-'Alamiyyah'*

('The Nature of the Competition over Foreign Capitals', *Al-Hayat* daily, Part 2, 17 November 1994.

60. Jamil Matar, *'Asr al-Hijrah ila al-Shimal'* ('The Age of Emigration to the North'), *Al-Hayat* daily, Part 1, 20 August 1994.

61. Bichara Khader, 'L'immigration Maghrebienne face à l'Europe' ('The Maghribian Immigration Facing Europe'), (n.c.: [n.pb.], 1992), p. 22.

62. Jeffrey S. Passel and Michael Fix, 'Myths about Immigrants',*Foreign Policy*, no. 95 (Summer 1994), pp. 152–4.

63. Ibid., p. 157.

64. About the Islamists' activities in the West specifically, see: Michael C. Dunn, 'Islamic Activists in the West: A New Issue Produces Backlash', *Middle East Policy*, vol. 3, no. 1 (1994), pp. 137–145.

* It is noteworthy that there are very few Mauritanians or Libyans in France.

65. Robert Escalier, 'Les Chiffres de l'immigration Maghrebienne en France' ('Number of Maghreb Immigrants in France'), in: *L'Etat du Maghreb (The Maghreb States)*, sous la direction de Camille et Yves Lacoste, (Paris: La Decouverte, 1991), pp. 95 and 97.

66. For more details about the activities of the Islamic Salvation Front's supporters in France, see: Niveen Abdulmonem Masaad, 'The Case of Jabhat al-Inqadh in Algeria', in: 'Ola Abu Zeid, ed., *The Islamic Movements in a Changing World*, forthcoming from Markaz al-Buhuth wal Dirasat al-Siyasiyyah, in cooperation with Friedrich Ebert.

67. Bichara Khader, 'L'Immigration Maghrebienne face à l'Europe', op. cit., pp. 4–17.

68. Rodney Wilson, 'The Economic Relations of the Middle East: toward Europe or within the Region?', *Middle East Journal*, vol. 48, no. 2 (Spring 1994), pp. 270–5.

* It is to be noted that one-third of the Islamic states are members in this organization.

69. 'Abdul Wahab Sabry, *'Al-Su'ud al-Iqtisady li Sharq Asia: Al-Ittijahat wal Muhaddidat'* ('The Economic Ascendance of East Asia: Trends and Determinants'), *Al-Siyasah Al-Dawliyyah*, no. 116 (April 1994), pp. 135–6, and Ahmad Muhammad Farag, *'Al ASEAN wal APEC: Khiyarat al-Iqlimiyyah wal 'Alamiyyah fi Sharq Asia'* ('The ASEAN and APEC: The Regional and International Choices in East Asia', ibid., no. 116 (April 1994), pp. 141–2.

** The Arab states that have already signed the GATT treaty are Egypt, Algeria, Tunisia, Morocco, Mauritania, Qatar and Bahrain. However, the other Arab states are expected to join the treaty, particularly after ending the Arab economic embargo on Israeli merchandise.

70. Ibrahim Nawwar, *'Ittifaqiyat al-GATT wal Iqtisadat al-'Arabiyyah'* ('GATT Agreements and the Arab Economies'), *Kurrasat Istratijiyyah*, vol. 4, no. 22 (Cairo: Markaz al-Dirasat al-Siyasiyyah wal Istratijiyyah in *Al-Ahram*, 1994), pp. 12, 18–27; 'Abdul Fattah Al-Jibaly, *'Dawrat Urugway wal 'Alam al-Thalith: Hisabat al-Maksam wal Khusarah'* ('The Uruguay Round and the Third World: Calculations of Gains and Losses'), *Al-Siyasah Al-Dawliyyah*, no. 118 (October 1994), p. 200; 'Ali 'Abdul 'Aziz Suliman, *'Ittifaqiyat al-GATT: Al-Makasib wal Makhawif'* ('The GATT Agreements: Gains and Fears'), *Al-Siyasah Al-Dawliyyah*, no. 116 (April 1994), pp. 102–3, 105; 'Umar 'Abdullah Kamel, *'Al-Iqtisadiyyat al-'Arabiyyah wa*

Haqiqat Khasa'ir ma ba'd al-GATT' ('The Arab Economies and the Reality of the Post-GATT Losses'), *Al-Ahram Al-Iqtisady*, no. 1352 (5 December 1994), pp. 68–9; UNDP, *'Taqrir al-Tanmiyyah al-Bashariyyah li 'Am 1994'* (*Human Resources Report, 1994*), (Beirut: Centre for Arab Unity Studies, 1994), p. 16.

71.   Jamil Matar, *'Nahw Nihayat al-Nizam al-Iqlimy al-'Araby kama 'Arifnah'* ('Toward the End of the Arab Regional System We are Accustomed to'), *Al-Hayat* daily, 9 August 1990, and Nassif Y. Hitti, *'Al-Tahawwulat fil Nizam al-'Alamy wa Minakh al-Fikry al-Jadid wa In'ikasatahu 'ala al-Nizam al-Iqlimy al-'Araby'* ('The Shifts in the International System, the Intellectual Environment and its Reflection on the Arab Regional System', *Al-Mustaqbal Al-'Araby*, vol. 15, no. 165 (October–November 1992), pp. 51–2.

72.   Taha Majdub, *'Adhwa' al-Tahawwulat al-Istratijiyyah fil Siyasah al-Kharijiyyah al-Amrikiyyah'* ('Lights on the Strategic Transformations in the American Foreign Policy', *Al-Ahram* daily, 11 May 1994.

73.   See the review of Marwan Bishara's book, 'Bill Clinton: The Campaign, the Administration, the Foreign Policy', *Al-Hayat* daily, Part 1, 1 May 1993.

74.   Anthony Lake, 'Confronting Backlash States', op. cit., p. 46.

75.   Henry Kissinger, 'Reflections on Containment', *Foreign Affairs*, vol. 73, no. 3 (May–June 1994), pp. 113–30.

76.   Richard Falk, 'Can US Policy toward the Middle East Change Course?', op. cit., p. 12.

77.   Martin Indyk et al., 'Symposium on Dual Containment: US Policy toward Iran and Iraq', *Middle East Policy*, vol. 3, no. 1 (1994), pp. 1–5.

78.   Mohsen M. Milani, 'Iran's Post Cold War Policy', *International Journal*, vol. 41 (Spring 1994), p. 338, and F. Gregory Gause III, 'The Illogic of Dual Containment', *Foreign Affairs*, vol. 73, no. 2 (March–April 1994), pp. 60–1.

79.   Indyk et al., 'Symposi' on Dual Containment: US Policy toward Iran and Iraq', op. cit., pp. 7–10.

80.   Edward G. Shirley, 'The Iran Policy Trap', *Foreign Policy*, no. 96 (Fall 1994), p. 78.

81.   Vahe Petrossian, 'Iran Puts Its Finances in Order', *MEED*, vol. 38, no. 33 (19 August 1994), pp. 2–3.

82.   Phoebe Marr, 'The United States, Europe and the Middle East in the Post-Cold War Era', *Middle East Journal*, vol. 48, no. 2 (Spring 1994), p. 222.

83.   George Lenczowski, op. cit., 'Iran: The Big Debate', p. 55.

84.   Thomas R. Mattair and Stephen Brannon, 'U.N. Sanctions Against Iraq: Issues Influencing Continuation or Removal', *Middle East Policy*, vol. 3, no. 1 (1994), pp. 36–9.

85.   *Al-Hayat* daily, 21 December 1994.

86.   Mohammad Ali Emami, 'Perspectives on the Security of the Persian Gulf', *Iranian Journal of International Affairs*, vol. 5, nos. 3–4 (Fall–Winter 1994), p. 677.

87.   Lutfy Al-Khuly, *'Arab Na'am! Wa Sharq Awsatiyun Aydan* ('Arabs Yes, but also Middle Easterners?'), (Cairo: Markaz al-Ahram lil Tarjama wal Nashr, 1994), pp. 69–85.

88.   'Abdul Mon'eim al-Mashat, *'Qiraat Isti'adiyyah li Mu'tamar al Dar al-Bayda' wa Masa'il Salam wal Inma' al-Iqlimy'* ('Recapitulative Readings of the Casablanca Conference, the Peace Issues and the Regional Development'), *Al-Hayat* daily, 13 November 1994.

89.   Shimon Peres, *'Al-Sharq al-Awsat al-Jadid'* (*The New Middle East*), translated by Muhammad Helmy 'Abdul Hafiz, (Amman: Al-Ahlia lil Nashr wal Tawzi', 1994), pp. 69–85.

* It should be noted that the total value of Israeli exports witnessed an incremental increase in the past few years, from $7.839 billion in 1986 to $12.133 billion in 1990, to $13.282 billion in 1992. The electronic and electrical equipment specifically represented a high percentage of these exports (27.7 per cent in 1990). The previous increases are due to Israel's success in signing a free trade agreement with the USA and a commercial agreement with the European group; hence, giving Israeli merchandise access to the markets of these states under low custom duties.

90.   See Ghassan Salamé, *'Afkar Awaliyyah 'an al-Suq al-Awsatiyyah'* ('Preliminary Ideas about the Middle East Market'), *Al-Mustaqbal Al-'Araby*, vol. 16, no. 179 (January 1994), pp. 67–74. For more details concerning Israel's economic performance, see: Nazira al-Ifendi, *'Al-Iqtisad al-Israili: Muhaddidat al Ada' wa In'ikasat al-Salam'* (*Israeli Economy: Determinants of Performance and Repercussions of Peace*), *Kurrasat Istratijiyyah*, no. 19 (Cairo: Markaz al-Dirasat al-Siyasiyyah wal Istratijiyyah in *Al-Ahram*, 1994), pp. 9 and 26–7.

91.   Jalal Mu'awad, *'Al-Tasawwur al-Turky li Amn al-Khalij ba'd al-Harb'* ('The Turkish Vision of the Gulf Security in the Post War Era'), in: Mustapha 'Ilwy, ed., *'Misr wa Amn al-Khalij ba'd al-Harb'* (*Egypt and Gulf Security in the Post War Era*), (Cairo: University of Cairo, Faculty of Economics and Political Science, Markaz al-Buhuth wal Dirasat al-Siyasiyyah, 1994), p. 228.

Twelve

The Middle East Order

24

Arab and Iranian Policies Towards Middle Easternism and Gulf Security

MOHAMMAD EL-SAYED SELIM*

Introduction

This paper begins from certain assumptions and raises certain policy-oriented questions. It may be appropriate to clarify these assumptions and state these questions before dealing with the substance of the paper. First of all, we assume that images and visions, regardless of their level of conformity with reality, shape political behaviour. Consequently, an understanding of the content and structure of these images is crucial for understanding political interactions between individuals and states. If such images are held as crucial, the images of political and cultural elites are even more crucial for comprehending foreign policies and the possibilities of inter-state conflict and cooperation.

Elite images influence and shape national enterprise, as well as the external behaviour of states. In his widely quoted study, written in 1979, Ole Holsti explained the crisis of American foreign policy, at that time, as stemming from the lack of consensus within the American political elite on future trends in US foreign policy. He likened the US to a three-headed eagle, each head looking in a different direction. As a result, the eagle is unable to move.[1] We may add that comprehending the images of political elites towards certain issues is crucial for understanding the dynamics of their relationships. The relative distance between the images of two elites regarding a certain issue influences the possibilities of rapprochement between their states. Here I should add that the concept of political elites refers to both official and non-official political elites.

Finally, this essay assumes that the issues of Middle Easternism and Gulf security are among the most central in Arab–Iranian relations at the moment, and that the images of the Arab and Iranian elites concerning these issues will influence the future course of Arab-Iranian relations to a great extent, and will also influence the fortunes of some of the policies pursued by other powers – such as America's 'dual containment' or Israel's regional penetration strategies.

If these assumptions are accepted, then this chapter raises certain questions that we believe are of central importance to Arab-Iranian relations. It aspires to assess the extent to which Arab and Iranian elites are united or divided on strategies of dealing with the crisis of Middle Easternism and Gulf security. What are the main areas and elements of agreement and/or disagreement within each elite, and between Arab and Iranian elites? Are there any cross-cutting connections and similarities between the images of each elite? In other words, are the Arab elites united against the Iranian elite? How did the Arabs and the Iranians debate their images of these issues? To what extent has there been an open and democratic dialogue between the Arabs and the Iranians on the issues of Middle Easternism and Gulf security? And what are the outcomes of the Arab and Iranian images, as far as the future fortunes of the issues under consideration are concerned?

The chapter is divided into two parts. The first will deal with Arab policies and visions towards Middle Easternism and its implications for Arab-Iranian relationships. The second treats Arab policies and visions towards Gulf security and their corresponding implications for these same relationships. This organization is based on a conceptualization holding that the dynamics of influence in the Middle Eastern case on the Arab and Iranian relationships differ from those influencing the same relationships with respect to the Gulf security issue.

The Arabs, the Iranians and Middle Easternism

Despite the fact that the Middle Eastern project appeared on the political scene as early as the 1950s – as an alternative to the Arab project – it did not crystallize as the subject of debates and implementation until the early 1990s, after the Madrid Peace Conference of 1991 gave rise to 'multilateral negotiations' in the domains of economic cooperation, refugees, water, arms control, etc. This project gained a strong momentum with the Palestinian-Israeli declaration of principles in September 1993, as well as with the convocation of the Casablanca summit in October-November 1994, inaugurating the launching of the Middle Eastern project. In this respect, it should be noted that the 'Casablanca declaration' stipulated that 'the establishment of pillars for an economic group in the Middle East and North Africa would at a certain stage, necessitate the inflow of items, capital and labour in the area, as well as the creation of a development bank.' The conference created a self-steering committee and an executive secretariat, and received hundreds of economic projects inaugurating the concept of constructing 'a Middle Eastern framework'.

The Arabs and Middle Easternism

The visions and policies of the Arab parties with regard to the Middle Eastern project varied between supporters or rejectionists, and conditional supporters or conditional rejectionists. The supporters proceed from 'an opportunistic' vision for international transformations. The essence of this vision is that, since these transformations push in the direction of rebuilding the Oriental regional system, there is an imperative to work 'in accordance with', not 'against', these transformations, in order to exploit them. Moreover, the group's vision stems from a conceptualization which maintains that Middle Easternism is not a zero sum game, but involves reciprocal benefits for all parties. Thus, what the Arabs have failed to achieve throughout the last half century, they could realize by Middle Easternism. Lastly, the supporters emphasize the wide range for movement and manoeuvres in the framework of the new project. They do not believe any party can 'dictate' special policies to the Arab partner. Hence, the Arabs can use whatever fits their interests from this project.

As for the opposers, they base their stance on a 'historical' vision of the Middle East project as an extension of the colonial hegemonial projects presented by the West in the early fifties. Accordingly, it is part of an extended grand Western strategy for controlling the Arabs. Consequently, such a project is but 'a zero sum game', where the Arabs lose for the benefit of Israel and the West. Through this project, Arabs lose their integration, their identity and their culture, and are dissolved within a larger geographical framework. Lastly, the opposers affirm that the project is under Western auspices; hence, a 'dictated game', where manoeuvres are out of the question. In fact, the Middle Eastern project is, according to this group, a complete package, where the Arabs' losses will definitely exceed their benefits, and where there would be no freedom of choice.

Yet, between these two poles, other trends emerged, expressing their conditional support or rejection. Such conditions include the conclusion of the Arab-Israeli settlement first (according to the reserved supporters), or achieving Arab integration first, then moving to the Middle Eastern project as a later stage (according to the reserved rejectionists).[2]

In the framework of all these trends, it is possible to distinguish governmental policies and visions, and non-governmental visions and conceptualizations endorsed by Arab and Islamic businessmen, intellectuals and political parties.

Arab Visions and Policies Supporting Middle Easternism

A number of Arab economic and political trends, and governments, are rallying under the banner of the group backing the Middle Eastern project, either unreservedly or on conditional terms. These proceeded from a number of intellectual premises, the most important of which are:[3]

1. The intellectual shifts occurring in the early nineties, calling for an historical compromise with the non-Arab parties in the Middle East area,

especially with Israel, following the realization that even a major super-power (the ex-Soviet Union) could not withstand the Western attack.
2. The Middle Eastern market realizes a number of benefits for the Arab states, *viz* providing a big market, achieving an intermarriage between technology and resources, assisting in economic specialization and real-locating the money from military expenditures to development.
3. Israel cannot dominate the Arab nation, because it relies on foreign aid. By the same token, its importance for its allies will diminish with the achievement of the Middle Eastern project.
4. There is no contradiction between Middle Easternism and Arabism; the first being an economic project and the second a civilizational one; hence their possible coexistence.
5. It is possible to avoid the anticipated negative effects of the Middle Eastern project through a number of Arab arrangements.

In the framework of this group, one could distinguish between official sup-porters, non-official supporters, official conditional backing and non-official conditional backing (the conciliatory trends). We shall present these poli-cies and trends consecutively:

Official Support Policies

The Moroccan and Jordanian governments head this group. Hence, it is not strange for the first Middle Eastern conference to be held in the former, while the next conference shall be convened in the latter. The Moroccan government's position stems from its belief in the close association existing between the political settlement and Middle Easternism, whereby each leads to the other. It also rests on its visualization of the final goal as 'drawing a map for a new Arab world directing its interests to development, evolution, and shunning any confrontational or isolationist policy'. Accordingly, the Moroccan policy looks at the Israeli Western peace as an irreversible stra-tegic line, and considers the Arab boycott of Israel as practically terminated. For the Moroccan government, this approach is capable of preparing a suit-able atmosphere for the political settlement.[4]

As for the Jordanian government, it approves of a comprehensive visu-alization for the Middle Eastern project, in the sense of relying on a number of economic and security arrangements in the framework of the Middle Eastern conference for cooperation and security, to be established along the same lines as the Conference on Security and Cooperation in Europe. The goal, according to the Jordan conceptualization, is 'the establishment of a free trade zone Middle East'.[5]

Even though both Morocco and Jordan point to the importance of the peace settlement, the totality of their officially declared policies rests on the final goal of the Middle Eastern project, and the comprehensive content (economic and security) of this project. They do not seem to draw any direct organic link between this settlement and Middle Easternism.

Non-official Supporting Trends

This group encompasses most Arab businessmen, and some intellectuals closely associated with supporting governments. In view of the economic gains that businessmen will probably reap from the Middle Eastern project, they are its stoutest defenders. Dr Mahmoud Wahba is a case in point. He has published a book entitled *Israel, Arabs and the Middle Eastern Market*, in which he affirms that 'the Middle Eastern market is a new economic reality that cannot be ignored. Thus, there is no leeway for a choice, since this economic situation would impose itself with the passage of time. Hence, we cannot but get ready for it'. Wahba's advice is to follow an incremental building up of the Middle Eastern market for the sake of achieving 'the economic integration of the Middle Eastern countries', whereby Arabs will achieve a comparative advantage in confronting Israeli competition. Moreover, this market will create obstacles for Israel, the most important of which is its decreasing ability for external reliance.[6]

Besides, some Egyptian and Jordanian intellectuals confirmed the importance of the Middle Eastern project as being part of the 'new world order', and as being necessarily beneficial for the Arabs. In this respect, Dr Fahd Al-Fank argues – in a study about 'the economic dimensions of the peaceful settlement' – that the Israeli economic danger is quite exaggerated and that Israel, in the framework of the new Middle East, will turn into a normal foreign state dealing with Arab countries.[7] Ali Shafiq Mahana also argues that Arab participation in the Middle Eastern project is a duty, as it is 'inevitably existent'.[8] Dr Abdul Mon'eim Sa'id, in his turn, affirms that the fear of the Middle Eastern market 'is unfounded'. For the Arab partner owns natural and human resources. Israel's scientific technology has to compete with the whole world, including its allies. Besides, the Israeli intellectual invasion is unjustifiable because of the deep-rootedness of Arab culture, in comparison with Israeli cultural pluralism. Accordingly, Sa'id calls for an Arab League overlapping with the Middle Eastern framework.[9]

Official Conditional Supporting Policies

Egypt, the Gulf Cooperation Council states and the Arab League raise the banner of this group. The policies of these parties *vis-a-vis* the Middle Eastern project revolve around approving it in the framework of a set of conditions and reservations that should precede its implementation. Accordingly, this group is for 'constraining' the concept of this project, so as to confine it to the regional economic cooperation arrangements, without including any commitments for a joint market. The first of the conditions stipulated by this group's members is 'for the Middle Eastern regional project to be preceded by a comprehensive agreement between the Arab states and Israel in the differnt arenas'. These agreements should, therein, stipulate arrangements, either for the Israeli withdrawal from the occupied Arab lands or for regional security. Hence, the achievement of economic cooperation depends on achieving a comprehensive peace and total withdrawal.[10] This policy differs from the Moroccan and Jordanian policies for the stress it puts on 'the priority' to be given to the political and security settlement over the Middle Eastern project, whereas the latter stresses their 'simultaneity', in the best assessments.

As for the second condition, it is for the Middle Eastern project to be preceded by an Arab project, so as to prevent the first from being a substitute for the second.[11] Finally, the Middle Eastern project should be put in its proper frame, for it is not a new regional system, but merely an arrangement for a regional economic cooperation that does not aspire to the level of a regional project. These arrangements should not be the source of fear for the Arabs, because 'the peace with Israel will not result in any economic advantage for it'.[12]

The Conciliatory Trends

By this we mean the unofficial trends that proceed from the acceptance of the Middle Eastern idea, while yet requiring a number of policies guaranteeing protection against its negative repercussions and enhancing its positive impact. Saad El-Din Ibrahim, Sa'id Al-Naggar, Ghassan Salamé, Abdul Raouf Al-Ridy and Lutfy al-Khuly are the most prominent advocates of this trend. Ibrahim has, in fact, affirmed that any fear of the Middle Eastern project is out of place. According to him, such a project will not materialize in the medium term; besides, it would not represent a danger for the Arabs if they knew how to deal with it.[13] By the same token, Al-Naggar presents a comprehensive conciliatory approach encompassing a strategy for dealing with the Middle Eastern project. This strategy could be summarized in a number of elements, the most important of which is: working for the success of the Palestinian–Israeli agreement in reaching a just and comprehensive peace between the Arabs and Israel, conditioning an end to the Arab boycott upon the conclusion of a political settlement between the Arabs and Israel by means of a conventional, collective decision. This is to be followed by an Arab–Israeli peace permitting the conclusion of diplomatic relations and normal economic relationships with

Israel; and hence accepting it fully as part of the Middle East. This, in its turn, is to be followed by the normal commercial exchange, based on treating Israel and other foreign countries on an equal footing and coordinating between the five Arab confrontation states – Egypt, Palestine, Jordan, Syria and Lebanon – during the negotiations period. Moreover, it is illegal to construct any Middle Eastern projects or institutions at the expense of Arab projects or institutions.[14]

As for Ghassan Salamé, he believes, in spite of his awareness of the dangers accruing from Middle Easternism, that the decision determining the positions on the Middle Eastern project should be left to Israel's neighbouring countries and should follow an approach based on 'economic rationality', in the sense of giving priority to economic calculations over the ideological slogans.[15]

Similarly, Abdul Raouf Al-Ridy suggests the crystallization of an Arab strategy to deal with Middle Easternism, the establishment of a balanced security system prior to the economic cooperation within the Middle Eastern framework, and the creation of an Arab council for businessmen and foreign affairs thinkers, whose task would be to crystallize a unified Arab policy.[16]

Lutfy Al-Khuly offers a similar vision, based on reconciling the Arab and Middle Eastern systems. Al-Khuly's logic rests on the fact that the Arab system does not only exist in an Arabist setting, but also in a geographical location: the Middle East, where non-Arab states are present as well. Thus, Arabism has to be opened to all civilizations, cultures and markets within this region, in which its interests naturally lie. The Arab system is, effectively, required to turn into a partner in a broader regional system. The latter should not be seen as a substitute for the Arab system. Besides, the Arab system is no longer capable of operating on its own, what with new variables such as water scarcity, environmental pollution, etc., because these issues are connected to the Middle East as a whole. Consequently, it needs to enter into a relationship of interdependence with its broader Middle Eastern context. Finally, Al-Khuly affirms that 'there is no alternative before the nationalist and religious fundamentalisms in the Middle East but to conclude a kind of security, political and economic reconciliation through realistic bargains on common interests. There is no alternative but for the national security of every Arab state to operate in overlapping circles encompassing the Middle Eastern circle.[17]

The Rejectionist Arab Visions and Policies Concerning Middle Easternism

The position of Arab rejectionists, whether states or multiple and varied political currents, stems from a number of basic intellectual assumptions:[18]

1. The Middle Eastern project is a Zionist–Western project aimed at integrating Israel into the Arab area and conferring a distinctive status on it, or eradicating Arabism culturally and civilizationally.
2. The Middle Eastern project will benefit no one but Israel. The Arab party will not reap any rewards from this project, in view of the unsuitability of Israeli technology for the Arab world.
3. The Middle Eastern project deprives the Arab area of its Arab–Islamic particularity, and turns it into a mere geographical trend devoid of any cultural or civilizational content.
4. The Middle Eastern project will not materialize for its being linked to temporary variables.

Within this group, it is possible to distinguish between two currents – namely, the official Arab rejectionist trend and the unofficial one. We will tackle the most important policies and visions of both trends consecutively.

The Official Rejectionist Policies

Libya and Syria represent an official trend within the framework of the Arab group rejecting, in principle, the Middle Eastern project, though the Syrian rejection is conditioned by specific reservations, as we shall see. The Libyan policy, on the other hand, stems from its rejection of the Zionist project as a whole, and its holding to the impossibility of an Arab cohabitation with it. The Libyan policy affirms that the Arabs will eventually be victorious over the Jews in Palestine. This historical ideological vision is based on rejecting the peace settlement with Israel as an act impeding the historical process. As for Middle Easternism, Libya affirms that it is not an inevitable question, but one that is linked to specific regional and international circumstances that shall, necessarily, change. The Middle Eastern project is, in fact, according to this vision, an old renewed American–Zionist project resting on the strategic coalition between the US and Israel. Its existence depends on the 'new world older'. It is, put simply, 'a project for a comprehensive regional system aimed at disembodying the Arab regional system and impeding its Arab political and civilizational entity'.[19] Thus, Libya rejects the whole Middle Eastern project.

Syria, too, rejects it. Abdel Halim Khaddam, the Syrian Vice-President, points to the fact that the Middle Eastern market is an Israeli attempt to extend its hegemony over the Arab world, with the aim of dividing it.[20] Mohammad Zakariyya Isma'il, ex-Secretary General of the Syrian Foreign Ministry, holds that the essence of the Middle Eastern project is 'tearing the Arab identity apart and creating a new Middle Eastern system where Israel occupies the leadership role under the American umbrella'.[21]

Therefore, Syria abstained from taking part in all projects and negotiations concerning Middle Eastern economic cooperation following the Madrid Peace Conference, including the multilateral negotiations stemming from the Madrid and Casablanca conferences.

Yet, it seems that the Syrian rejectionism does not extend to a fundamental rejection of the Middle Eastern project. For the Syrian declarations indicate that if the political settlement is first clearly achieved, Syria would be ready to negotiate forms of economic cooperation. Some sources have even suggested that a delegation of Syrian businessmen participated in the Casablanca summit conference.[22]

The Unofficial Rejectionist Trend

This trend might be the dominant one among the non-ruling cultural and political elites in the Arab world. It encompasses in general the pan-Arab, Islamist and leftist political opposition forces. These currents reject the Middle Eastern project for various reasons.

The two nationalist and Islamist currents have effectively expressed this rejection during the nationalist–Islamist dialogue in Beirut in October 1994. In this respect, the nationalists stressed the Zionist–Western coalition as a threat to national and Arab independence. They also emphasized the importance of foiling what they perceive as attempts to normalize Zionist colonial settlements on Arab land. The Islamist paper stressed bolstering the Palestinian resistance, rejecting any interaction with the Israeli enemy, and 'keeping the spark of hatred and rejection alive in the spirits of the new generation'.[23]

Even though neither of these trends dealt directly with the Middle Eastern project, they are both taken as references for refutation of its intellectual justifications. Thus, it might be appropriate for us to survey some of the ideas propagated by the nationalist and Islamist trends, together with those of the leftist trend's symbols.

On the nationalist level, we can refer to Mohammed Hassanein Heikal, Ahmad Sudki El-Dajani, Siyar Al-Jumayil, Samir Al-Tiqi, Mahmoud Abdel Fadil, Ahmad Yussuf Ahmad and Saad El-Din Wahba. Heikal, for his part, views Middle Easternism as a penetration of the Arab world from all sides. Accordingly, he thinks it difficult to imagine a Middle Eastern market achieving for the Arabs in the morrow what the past was incapable of.[24] El-Dajani argues emphatically that the process of preparation for the imposition of the Middle Eastern system is based on accepting the status quo that came into existence in June 1967. For Dajani, this new system focuses on the economic and social dimensions at the expense of the other elements in the human community, and disregards completely the Arab masses.[25] Siyar Al-Jumayil points to the fact that the Middle Eastern project rests on pillars, the most important of which being: the US hegemony, the creation of a regional order for cooperation between the Middle Eastern countries, separating the Arab east from its west, and igniting racial and communal strife.[26] It is noteworthy that Al-Jumayil does not point to Israel's status in the project, or what he labels as the Middle Eastern Marshall Plan consecrating the US–Israeli hegemony.[27]

Following the same line, Mahmoud Abdel Fadil launched the most virulent critique of the Middle Eastern system, warning that it would abort the changes for independent and integrative development of the Arab economy, due to Israeli infiltration, let alone dissolving and fragmenting the Arab system itself. Abdel Fadil suggests an alternative view based on intensifying Arab economic cooperation. On the other hand, he inadvertently talks about ending the Arab boycott of Israel on condition of this being concomitant with the comprehensive political settlement.[28]

Ahmad Yussuf Ahmad adds, in the same context, that the chances for the existence and continuation of the Middle Eastern system are dim, since the system is based on injustice. He adds that the system is incompatible withthe actual relationships of power in the Middle East, since it neglects the integration of Iraq and Iran, and is overly reliant on a temporary international balance of power, namely the US hegemony.[29]

In addition, Saad El-Din Wahba affirms that the Middle Eastern project is imposed by the US in order to alienate the Arabs from their real identity.[30] On the level of the Islamist trend, Magdy Ahmad Hussein asserts the rejection of Israel as a racist country 'whose legitimacy is unacceptable. This system will inevitably collapse, the way the South African and Russian systems did. The solution does not lie, therefore, in the Middle Eastern project, but in the establishment of a democratic, non-racial state in Palestine'. Nevine Mustapha, for her part, affirms that 'the Israeli dealings with the Arab parties, under the auspices of the Middle Eastern market project, will not be on an equal basis ... Israel will succeed in penetrating the Arab economies and cutting the thin thread linking them. It would restructure these economies in the framework of a new type of division of labour ... that would consecrate a kind of economic dependency and hegemony', she argues.[31]

The intellectual justifications for the rejection of Middle Easternism made by the leftist current do not differ much from those of the nationalist and Islamist groupings. The head of the Nationalist Progressive Unionist Party (NPUP) in Egypt, Khalid Mohy al-Din, maintains that the Middle Eastern market aims at 'providing Israel with the means for an affluent life by exploiting Arab resources and imposing a new colonial system preserving US imperial interests, Israel's role as the pillar of these interests, substituting the Arab regional system and the joint Arab action institutions and putting an end to the idea of Arab nationalism'.[32]

Hussein Abdel Raziq, editor-in-chief of *Al-Yassar* ('The Left') magazine adds that 'the Middle Eastern market is an old US–Israeli idea aimed at creating a non-Arab regional system whose security is linked to the US'.[33] Middle Easternism, from the perspective of the leftist group, is no market (because such a market will not materialize since it contradicts Israel's interest), but a project for US–Israeli political hegemony.[34]

As for Mohammad Sid Ahmad, he focuses on a strategy for treating the deficiency resulting from the establishment of the Middle Eastern project. He offers two strategies, which are: 'erecting a network of supranational institutions corresponding to the Arab states that would enjoy sovereign powers similar to them, for the purpose of providing a mechanism capable of crystallizing the common Arab interest, or resorting to Japan and other East Asian states in order to contribute with projects competing with Israel's.'[35]

Finally, it is clear that the national, Islamist and leftist currents agree on fighting the Middle Eastern project, though the intellectual frameworks and philosophical assumptions underlying this resistance occasionally differ from one current to the other. This agreement was firmed up in the unified statement of February 1995, signed by the Egyptian NPUP, Labour and Nasserite Party. In this statement, the three parties condemned in one voice the Middle Eastern project specifically.[36]

The Iranians and Middle Easternism

Iranian policy towards the Middle Eastern case is distinguished by a higher level of harmony in comparison with the Arab policies. This could be understood in light of the multiplicity of Arab parties on the one hand, and their direct involvement in the Middle Eastern project on the other. Iran, however, is not directly entangled in this project. In general, Iranian policy tends to consider the Middle Eastern project as a premature issue, which, at best, should be preceded by the complete recovery of the Palestinians' rights. Hence, participation in the Middle Eastern project at the present stage threatens to liquidate the Palestinian case. In fact, Iranian opposition to the Middle Eastern project does not merely stem from ideological imperatives related to the Islamic revolution, but is also linked to the impact of this project on Iranian interests as such. For this project, in the event of its success, will connect the Arab Gulf states to the Middle East, thus jeopardizing the relative status of Iran in the Gulf. The project will also boost the Israeli and Turkish roles in the Gulf, at the expense of Iran. In addition, Iran is not sure whether it will be included in this project.[37]

The truth of the matter is that Iranian policy *vis-a-vis* the Middle Eastern project springs from a realistic view of the international transformations, based on an accurate reading of these shifts and on the necessity of accommodating itself to them. Hence, Iran affirms that its regional role will focus on economic reconstruction, and the prevention and containment of regional crises.

Moreover, the Gulf area and central Asia represent the central arena where Iranian foreign policy is active.[38] In the framework of this understanding, the Middle East is not considered an important geo-political arena for Iran. Iran does not oppose a process of peaceful settlement in the Middle East. It looks at the Palestinian case as important for both the Islamic world and itself, but as an issue that primarily concerns the Palestinian people themselves. In this context, the Iranian President Rafsanjani accepted the possibility of establishing Palestinian rule next to the Israeli government, as a step towards achievement of the final goal. He considered the establishment of this rule as 'a positive step'. By the same token, the Iranian Ambassador in Germany affirmed that his country does not oppose peace in the Middle East and is not anti-Jew. We only want Palestinians to return back to the lands from which they were expelled and to live there once again, maintains the Iranian Ambassador.[39]

Accordingly, the official Iranian policy could be classified as in the same category as Egyptian policy. Yet the Iranian policy is more strict with respect to the absolute priority it grants to the settlement of the Palestinian case. This policy is echoed by a current of Iranian intellectuals. In spite of their opposition to the political process inaugurated by the Palestinian–Israeli agreement, and their preference for the Syrian policy rejecting Middle Easternism, these intellectuals are ready to acknowledge the factors impelling the Palestinians to accept this agreement, and ask them to improve the terms of the settlement. This current expressed its ideas at a conference organized by the Centre for Scientific Research and Middle East Strategic Studies in Tehran in 1994, attended by Prof. Farhang Rajaee, Dr Mahmood Sariolghalam, Mr Ahmad Naaghibzadeh and Mr Mohammad Ali Muhtadi.[40]

We also notice, however, another political current in Iran, represented by the leadership of the Iranian revolution. These reject both the political settlement and the Middle Eastern project. For when the Gulf Cooperation Council states announced the termination of some forms of boycott against Israel, in the framework of the new Middle Eastern arrangements, Ayatollah Al-Khamene'i declared his condemnation of the decision as a 'major treason of Islam, the Arabs and Palestinians'. Mohsen Redha'y, general leader of the Revolutionary Guard army, had announced on the eve of the Madrid Peace Conference that the only solution is not merely the recovery of the territories occupied in 1967, but the liberation of Palestine from the Zionist claws, and its annexation to Islam. In the journal *Jumhuryi-ye Islami* ('The Islamic Republic'), mouthpiece of the Iranian revolution,

Ali Burhan expressed his disapproval of the declarations uttered by the Iranian Ambassador in Germany – to which we have previously referred – maintaining that the Foreign Ministry's silence about these declarations contradicts Iranian long-term policy towards Zionism.[41]

This non-official trend finds its echo among another sector of Iranian intellectuals. This group rejects the Middle Eastern project for the same reasons offered by the Arab official and non-official rejectionist lines. Ali Shukuhy wrote an article entitled 'The New Israeli Policy from the Nile to the Euphrates', in which he warns about the creation of a common market with Israel as a party, since this would guarantee its survival and control over the economies of the area; hence, the Israeli extension into this area would become economic instead of military in nature.[42] Jalal Khoshen Shuhra has also written an article, entitled 'Analyzing the Economic Circumstances of the Middle East', wherein he attacks the Middle Eastern project on the grounds that it will make the Zionist system the sole ruler of the economy of the area. This project will also incur heavy losses on Egypt, the most important of which are wasting some of the Suez Canal revenues, due to transferring Gulf oil through Israel, and digging the Jordanian–Israeli canal from the 'Aqaba Gulf to the Mediterranean Sea'. Shuhra also claims that it will deprive Egypt of the privileges it enjoys in the Arab market.[43]

As a result, Iran adopts a specific policy towards the Middle Eastern case, based on opposition to the project unless preceded by a settlement of Arab political and security cases. The Iranian policy is also characterized by its variable non-official political visions, ranging from an intellectual one based on conditional acceptance to one that rejects the project in its entirety.

Reflections of Arab/Iranian Policies and Views Concerning Middle Easternism and Relations between the Arabs and Iranians

Observation of Arab and Iranian policies and views concerning Gulf security uncovers the fact that such policies are characterized by a high degree of diversity, whether on the Arab or Iranian levels. There is no singular Arab or Iranian view about the identity of the Middle Eastern project and the way to deal with it; rather, there are multiple policies and visualizations concerning this case in both the Arab and Iranian worlds. This could be attributed to a number of variables, the first being the political and cultural elites' intellectual and ideological frames. The nationalists and Islamists reject this Middle Easternism on the basis of the impact they visualize on Arabism or Islam. The liberals, on the other hand, support it in various ways, because it corresponds to their ideological conceptualization of a new world where open markets play the central role. The diversity is also due to the different visualizations of interests that might be affected by Middle Easternism, or by the benefits that would accrue from it. For the conditional Iranian view rests on imagining the possible effects of Middle Easternism on the relative status of Iran in the Gulf, whereas it is possible to understand the Moroccan support in light of the benefits it anticipates from its linkage to this project. Finally, the intellectual variability of the Arab and Iranian views of Middle Easternism goes back to the social transformations witnessed by both the Arab and Iranian worlds, represented in new influential social forces enjoying transnational interests and linkages. Such forces could express views and policies differing from those offered officially.

The variability and multiplicity in the Arab policies and visions surpasses that of their Iranian counterparts. The Arab world is actually oscillating between multiple and conflicting official policies and non-official visions. Within each group there exist trends completely rejecting, conditionally supporting, or opposing. This diversity is understood in light of the multiplicity of Arab actors, their various connections to the influential international forces, and the degree to which they could be affected by the Middle Eastern project. Because Arabs represent, at least at the present moment, one of the principal 'issues' in the Middle Eastern project, they tend to express more policies and visions concerning this project. This explains, for us, the relative 'richness' of Arab policies and visions, compared to their Iranian counterparts. Thus, whereas the Iranian visions and policies were confined to rejecting the Middle Eastern project and launching warnings against its dangers, it did not offer an alternative conceptualization or particular mechanisms for dealing with this project (or at least avoiding its negative effects). Accordingly, the Iranian perspective was limited to rejection of the project and determining the required 'goals'.

On the other hand, the Arab visions and policies are distinguished by a higher degree of sophistication and complexity. In fact, the Arab paradigm on Middle Easternism instigates a number of cases, the most prominent being:

1. What is specifically offered to the Arab world? Are these arrangements for economic cooperation? Or for a Middle Eastern market? Or rather a new Middle Eastern regional system?
2. Would the Middle Eastern project materialize, whatever form it took? Or is it an inapplicable dream?
3. If the Middle Eastern project is implemented, would it succeed in achieving its goals, or is it doomed to failure for various considerations?
4. What are the mechanisms through which we can deal with the Middle Eastern project so as to achieve the Arab interest?

These are some of the cases that arise by the Arab paradigm, none of which is clearly crystallized in the Iranian perspective. As we previously suggested, this relative disparity in the richness of the two paradigms is due, to a large extent, to the difference 'in the relative political distance between Arabs and Iranians towards the Middle Eastern project'.

Most important is the phenomenon of 'overlap' between the Iranian and Arab policies and visions regarding the project. We have actually witnessed an Iranian current rejecting the Middle Easternism in principle, on the basis of a logic that does not differ much from that of some Arab rejectionists. Moreover, the expressions of Iranian policy resemble some Arab policies, especially Arab policies that acquiesce to Middle Easternism on condition of being preceded by a political settlement and the recovery of Palestinian rights. Hence, the Arab world does not clash with the Iranian world with respect to this project; rather they overlap on the level of policies and visions, creating, therein, forms of entanglement, linkage and even balance in the relationships between them. Accordingly, Arab–Iranian relations concerning the Middle Eastern project are characterized by horizontal overlappings – by virtue of similar policies, visions, trends and social strata – rather than vertical separations and discrepancies.

Arabs, Iranians and Gulf Security

The Gulf security issue differs from the Middle Eastern issue in various respects. The first difference is that the interactions concerning Gulf security are in essence military-security in nature and, to a lesser extent, socio-economic. For Gulf security focuses mainly, at least at the present moment, on a number of arrangements related to confronting military threats and the possibility of certain militant groups resorting to violence against the Gulf states. Though this concept has started to gradually widen to encompass arrangements concerning securing the Gulf against environmental hazards and how to exploit its resources, it is not yet sufficiently entrenched to become part of the general concept of Gulf security, at least for some of its states.

The second angle looks at the case of Gulf security as an Arab–Iranian issue, where the superpowers play the role of external effectors, at least with respect to a number of its states. As with Middle Easternism, it is primarily concerned with economic cooperation arrangements among the 'Middle East' states, and avoids the military-security arrangements on the grounds that the economic approach will pave the way for security cooperation – at least in the conceptualization of Middle Eastern project planners. It is also a case related to the Western–Israeli project geared to the establishment of a new economic arrangement which the local forces – the Arab at least – would be 'compelled to respect' under different forms of pressure. In other words, Gulf security is basically regional. On the other hand, the Middle Eastern case is an issue related to the 'new world order' seeking to re-structure the Oriental regional system. However, this does not mean that the 'new world order' is not an influential factor in the case of Gulf security. What we mean is that the subject of the Gulf issue is Arab–Iranian, whereas the matter is quite different in the Middle Eastern case.

From a third perspective, Gulf security is characterized by the hegemony of official policies and the limitedness of non-official visions (even their absence). By virtue of its being basically a security-military matter, governments determine what should be done on this issue. In contrast, Middle Easternism is full of a number of non-official visions and civil pressure groups.

Finally, the Gulf security case is distinguished by a fourth phenomenon, namely, that Arab–Iranian interaction towards it is fragmented and vertical in nature, whereas their relationships in Middle Easternism are characterized by overlapping horizontal interactions. Disagreements seem to be almost complete on most of the issues derived from the Gulf security case; namely: what is meant by Gulf security? What are the sources of threat to Gulf security? How is Gulf security ensured? and other issues. Nevertheless, this does not negate the existence of some, extremely limited, symptoms of Arab–Iranian interactions concerning Gulf security.

These modes of disparity affect the nature of Arab–Iranian policies towards the two cases. For instance, security-military issues instigate distinct types of sensitivities, and an array of policies differing from those instigated by the economic and social issues. In general, it is difficult for the states espousing different intellectual orientations to agree on the former type of cases, while it is possible to reach a kind of agreement on the latter. This is exactly what we witness in the Arab–Iranian interactions over Gulf security.

It is beyond the scope of this paper to survey and analyze all Arab and Iranian policies towards the Gulf security case. This issue lacks, effectively, a unified Arab stance towards it, since policies vary even among the Gulf Cooperation Council states themselves. Therefore, we shall focus on the policies of some principal players, namely; Saudi Arabia, Kuwait, Iraq, Oman, Qatar, Egypt and Iran.

However, before tackling these policies, we should mention the conflicting issues between the Arabs and Iranians on the Gulf, or the problematic of naming it. For while the Iranians are determined to add the expression 'Persian' to the name Gulf, some Arabs ignore this label completely and call it 'Arabian' Gulf, since Arabs occupy about half of the Gulf shores. In spite of the fact that the appellation is quite a superficial symbolic matter, it triggers many sensitivities for both Iranians and Arabs. It is crucial to settle this issue with the agreement of the two parties, by means of an Arab–Iranian joint research team of historians and geographers, to study the origins of this case, offer their opinions concerning the historical roots of the name, and suggest a suitable designation that would win the consensus of all concerned parties.

The Arabs and Gulf Security

Similar to Arab policy towards Middle Easternism, there is no unified Arab policy with respect to Gulf security. In this section, we shall try to observe and compare the policies of some Gulf Arab states, as well as Egypt, towards Gulf security.

Saudi Policy towards Gulf Security[44]

Throughout the decade of the eighties, Saudi Arabia considered the main source of threat to Gulf security as Iran, Israel, domestic saboteurs in the Gulf Arab states and, to a lesser extent, the Cold War between the two superpowers. Thus, Saudi policy towards Gulf security focused on the security of the Arabian Gulf states similar to it, since Gulf security was considered a primarily Gulf issue and since the 'Gulf Cooperation Council' states were capable of achieving this security, in the Saudi perspective. Saudi policy on Gulf security rested on this specification of the sources of threat, those benefiting from Gulf security and the strategic foundations of security. This policy revolved around the following imperatives:

1. Neutralizing the Gulf area in the framework of an American relationship. What was meant by this was keeping the area away from the arena of Cold War conflict, in the framework of an implicit 'special relationship' with the US.
2. Creating a Saudi deterrent force resting on efficient naval and air forces.
3. Crystallizing Arab Gulf integration, with the exclusion of Iraq. The Gulf Cooperation Council and the Dar' al-Jazirah ('Peninsula Shield') were formed in this context, while preventing Gulf coordination from exceeding a certain ceiling.
4. Focusing on the internal dimensions of Gulf security, as a premium condition for achieving Gulf collective security in the framework of bilateral treaties among the Gulf Cooperation Council states for the exchange of information, training and the hand-over of criminals.
5. Balancing the Iranian threat by supporting Iraq in its war against Iran. For this purpose, Saudi Arabia offered $26 billion to Iraq in order to assist it in its war against Iran.

6. Settling the Gulf border conflicts on the basis of 'middle-of-the-road solutions'.

Following the Iraqi invasion of Kuwait, however, Saudi policy underwent a radical shift in its intellectual foundations and strategic orientations. On the level of awareness, Saudi Arabia began to consider Iraq as the principal source of threat to Gulf security. In the Saudi vision, Iran's position as a potential source of threat to Gulf security regressed in importance. Yet, Saudi Arabia persisted in emphasizing that the Gulf Cooperation Council is the sole beneficiary from Gulf security, i.e., that Gulf security means primarily the security of these states. Accordingly, it is possible to detect the following components of Saudi policy towards Gulf security in the post-Iraqi invasion of Kuwait:

1. *Reducing the Iraqi military force* through Iraq's total commitment to execute all UN Security Council resolutions, especially those relating to Iraqi weapons of mass destruction, as a first step towards the establishment of Gulf security.
2. *Taming the Iranian role*: the Iraqi invasion of Kuwait led to an upset of the Gulf balance of power in favour of Iran. One stable indicator of Saudi policy in Gulf security was the establishment of an Iranian–Iraqi balance, in such a way as to prevent either country from dominating the Gulf area. However, the fact that the Gulf Cooperation Council states entered a confrontation with Iraq, and cannot afford to enter into a second confrontation with Iran, impelled Saudi Arabia to focus on containing and stabilizing the Iranian role through the resumption of diplomatic relations with it. Hence, it seeks to prevent the escalation of the Iranian–Emirates conflict, and froze the Damascus declaration (which Iran opposes). Saudi Arabia has sought, in fact, to 'secure' the coming danger from the Iranian front by 'absorbing' Iranian impetuosity in the Gulf, at least in the current stage.
3. *Developing Saudi deterrence capability* through the creation of a huge land force reaching the same level of efficiency as the air force, after having realized that the threat to Gulf security may be terrestrial, coming from the neighbouring lands.
4. *Creating an Arab Gulf deterrent force*: Saudi Arabia relinquished its previous policy, which used to call for a merely symbolic Gulf force. Instead, there arose a new policy based on the creation of an efficient deterrent Arab Gulf force, through the gradual development of the Peninsula Shield force, on condition that it does not turn into a unified Gulf army, as suggested by the Sultanate of Oman.
5. *The limited Arab participation in the construction of Gulf security*: Following the Iraqi invasion of Kuwait, Saudi Arabia became more receptive to

accepting the Western contribution to Gulf security, though this tendency did not reach the level of Kuwait's policy – based on the formation of a network of alliances with the superpowers. Hence, Saudi Arabia adopts a mean between the complete rejection of Western presence and the creation of security alliances with the superpowers. This policy revolves around the accumulation of a limited amount of Western armaments (US) –mainly on Saudi land – and the intensification of military security cooperation with the US in the form of joint military exercises, training and granting the US some facilities in Saudi military airports, and acquiescing to the security arrangements concluded by certain Gulf Cooperation Council states with some superpowers.

6. *Excluding the Egyptian and Syrian role in Gulf security*: Saudi policy does not admit of any collective Arab role in Gulf security. Its alternative to it is bilateral cooperation between the Gulf Cooperation Council states, on the one hand, and the Arab states on the other, especially Egypt and Syria, who took part in the Kuwait liberation war. Thus, Saudi Arabia soon turned away from the formula of the Damascus declaration, stipulating a security arrangement between Egypt and Syria on the one hand, and the Gulf Cooperation Council on the other. It opposes the Egyptian project suggesting the signing of collective protocols for security cooperation between the eight countries, and insists instead on the second formula. Accordingly, Saudi policy does not visualize the creation of official structures for Gulf security, whether foreign in nature (the US vision expressed by former US Secretary of State James Baker) or regional (the Egyptian project). On the other hand, Saudi Arabia believes that Gulf security in confronting the Iraqi threat could be achieved on three related levels: Saudi deterrence power, the security integration of the Gulf Cooperation Council states, and developing the Peninsula's deterring power into a credible rapid deployment force, but not into a 'supra' force dominating the Gulf armies.

Finally, Saudi Arabia opts for coordination with the Western states. This policy reflects, accurately, the Saudi desire to emerge as a regional leader in the Gulf area, while simultaneously neutralizing the Iraqi and Iranian roles and preserving the West as a relatively close, tacit reserve, to which it could resort on the eve of crises.

Kuwaiti Policy towards Gulf Security[45]

Prior to the Iraqi invasion, Kuwaiti policy was characterized by its attempt to preserve the relative independence of Kuwait *vis-à-vis* the three major regional forces: Iraq, Iran, and Saudi Arabia. It sought to establish a trilateral balance between these forces on the basis of avoiding entanglement in broad regional commitments. It offered its undeclared support for Iraq in its war against Iran, especially after the war shifted in favour of the latter. In addition, Kuwait did not link itself to any superpowers. So, it did not resort to them except in emergency cases, represented in the Iranian threat to Kuwaiti tankers by the end of the Iraq–Iran war.

Yet, the Iraqi invasion of Kuwait led to a radical change in Kuwaiti policy, whose essence was a shift from the policy of balance to the 'military deterrence' of the principal threat to the security of Kuwait and the Gulf, namely Iraq. This policy revolves around the following four tenets:

1. Excluding Iraq from the strategic balance formula by isolating it diplomatically, boycotting it economically and weakening it militarily, in addition to insisting on the complete and literal interpretation of UN Security Council resolutions relating to it. This goal is also achieved by subjecting Iraq to stern international supervision, to prevent it from acuiring any reliable military capabilities.
2. Reinforcing Kuwaiti defence capability through developing the Kuwaiti armed forces and the 'Peninsula Shield', in cooperation with the Gulf Cooperation Council states. This means Kuwait's turning into a country enjoying military capabilities and a credible deterrence against any possible Iraqi invasion.
3. Relying on external guarantees for the security of Kuwait: this is to be achieved through a network of security alliances with the superpowers of the 'new world order', especially with the US. It is also done by granting these forces facilities on Kuwaiti land, so as to enable them to return rapidly to Kuwait in the event of an Iraqi threat. In this respect, Kuwaiti policy differs from Saudi policy, which had some reservations concerning the extent to which Kuwait is linked to foreign forces.
4. Excluding direct Egyptian, Syrian and Iranian roles in Gulf security: This means confining the Egyptian and Syrian role to a symbolic political support for Kuwait in normal times and military support when requested in times of crisis. The Iranian front is to be 'stabilized' through a political rapprochement with Iran, while concomitantly excluding it from Gulf security military arrangements. For, since Gulf security relies – in the Kuwaiti conceptualization – on US guarantees, and since the US, the principal ally, pursues the 'dual containment' strategy against Iraq and Iran, it is quite logical to exclude the Iranian military role from the security arrangements.

Iraqi Policy towards Gulf Security[46]

It is difficult for Iraq to develop a clear policy towards Gulf security, in view of its exceptional situation at the present time. It is logical, however, for Iraqi policy to confront the US–European–Gulf bloc rallied against it in an attempt to systematically exhaust and weaken it. Yet, it is possible to detect some elements of an Iraqi policy, or more accurately, an Iraqi concept for the Gulf security case. This conceptualization stems from viewing the US and Iran as the principal sources of threat to Gulf security. For Iraq, Gulf security signifies the security of the Arab states in the Gulf. This security could be achieved by means of an Arab framework linked to Arab collective arrangements. This is compatible with the Iraqi vision that believes Gulf security begins with the termination of Western foreign presence in it, whether in the form of coalitions with some Gulf states or in the Gulf waters. This presence, in fact, represents the first source of threat to Gulf security, in addition to Iran.

Some studies published lately, and written by prominent officials in Iraq ,persist in considering Iran a source of threat to Gulf security.[47] Accordingly, Gulf security arrangements rest solely on the Gulf Arab states, i.e. the Gulf Cooperation Council and Iraq. It is highly probable that Iraq favours a collective Arab framework to reinforce the security of the Arab states. In this respect, Iraq focuses on improving its relations with the Gulf Arab states, especially Oman, Qatar, Bahrain and Saudi Arabia, as a prelude to discussing Gulf security arrangements in connection to the Arab system.

Oman and Qatar's Policies towards Gulf Security[48]

Oman's and Qatar's policies towards Gulf security are distinguished by their special nature, overlapping in some respects with Iranian policy. For, whereas the Saudi, Kuwait, Iraqi and Egyptian policies (as we will see later) exclude the Iranian role, to the extent of regarding it as a source of threat to Gulf security, Oman and Qatar emphasize the centrality of the Iranian role in laying the foundations of Gulf security. They insist on involving Iran in the security arrangements. Besides, the two states do not, in principle, exclude Iraq, as do Saudi Arabia and Kuwait. Qatar has, in fact, called for ending the breach between the Gulf Cooperation Council and Iraq, for the sake of the Arab national interest. However, like the general policy of the Gulf Cooperation Council states, these two countries have reservations concerning the Egyptian, Syrian and even Arab participation in Gulf security arrangements. They prefer this participation to take place on the basis of bilateral treaties.

Qatar and Oman argue for security arrangements concluded in cooperation with the major Western powers. But it is noticeable that such a policy does not determine the sources of threat against which the security arrangements are to be directed. There is, besides, a contradiction between the stress put on the Iranian role, on the one hand, and the linkage to Western powers and – intensification of Western presence in the Gulf – on the other.

In concluding our survey of the Gulf Cooperation Council states' policies, it is worth noting that both the United Arab Emirates and Bahrain follow policies that agree with most of the general orientations of Saudi and Kuwaiti policies.

Egyptian Policy towards Gulf Security[49]

Egyptian policy towards Gulf security stems from viewing Iran, mainly, and Iraq, to a lesser extent, as the sources of threat to Gulf security. Accordingly, Egypt believes that Iran has expansionist goals towards the Arab Gulf states. Thus, the security arrangements should focus on providing security for these states, hence necessitating the exclusion of the Iranian role at the current stage. The Egyptian emphasis on this conceptualization was, to a large extent, a reflection of Iran's insistence on excluding the Egyptian role, through the thesis maintaining the 'Gulf identity of security', a thesis accepted by all the Gulf Arab states notwithstanding their disparate conceptualizations.

Egyptian policy concentrated, following the Kuwait liberation war, on establishing arrangements for collective security between the Gulf Cooperation Council, Egypt and Syria – in the framework of the Damascus declaration formula issued in March 1991. This declaration is, in the eyes of the Egyptian policy-makers, the ideal formula, creating an arrangement encompassing the six Gulf states, in addition to Egypt and Syria, with a Western support to deter the threat directed against these states on the part of Iran and Iraq. Consequently, Egypt did not welcome the military treaties that some Gulf states concluded with some Western powers, on the grounds that the security arrangements should rest, from the start, with the eight states. In this context, Egypt offered another formula for cooperation between the eight states, through the signing of protocols for comprehensive military cooperation. But the Gulf states did not approve of this formulation.

Egypt also maintains it has a role in Gulf security despite the fact that it does not belong to the area. For Egyptian politics sees a direct link between Gulf security and Arab national security. It also justifies its vision by virtue of the Egyptian economic interests in the Gulf, and the role undertaken by

Egypt in the Iraq–Iran war and the Kuwait liberation war, on the invitation of the Gulf states. However, according to the Egyptian vision, the Egyptian role does not necessarily mean a direct military role, but could extend to encompass other forms of cooperation. On the other hand, Egyptian policy does not exclude permanently the Iranian role from Gulf security. Egypt, as a matter of fact, believes in the possibility of integrating Iran into arrangements for Gulf security at a later stage, when acceptable foundations would have been laid for the Arab–Israeli relationship, and when the Gulf Cooperation Council would have ensured their security.

Iranians and Gulf Security[50]

In contrast to the Gulf Cooperation Council states and Egypt, Iran considers a foreign presence in the Gulf as the principal source of threat to the security of the area. The foreign presence signifies, in this context, the strategic presence of any non-Gulf power, or any power that does not belong to the Gulf. The Gulf means, in the Iranian conceptualization, all the Gulf states, since the body of water linking Iran and the six Gulf states is not a purely Arab water, but a common water. Likewise, the Gulf states have common interests in investing the Gulf's physical resources for their mutual benefit. Hence, the security of the area should be essentially a Gulf regional security ensured in the framework of the collective security conceptualization adopted by the Gulf states. Any security arrangements permitting the influential presence of a non-Gulf power will not achieve the security of the Gulf, but rather link it to foreign interests. Therefore, Iran offered its participation in the defensive arrangements of the Gulf Cooperation Council.

Nowadays Iran admits, according to the declarations of the Iranian President on 19 December 1994, the re-introduction of Iraq into the Gulf regional order. Accordingly, Iran objected to the defensive alliances concluded between some of the Gulf Cooperation Council states and the Western powers. It opposed the formula of the Damascus declaration for its exclusion of Iran, while giving two non-Gulf states (Egypt and Syria) a role in ensuring Gulf security.

Some Arab states concerned about Gulf security feel that – with the current absence of an Arab Gulf–Iranian strategic balance – Iranian policy towards this issue is a prelude for Iranian hegemony over the Gulf. This Arab perception is reinforced by Iran's tendency to increase its conventional and unconventional military forces. But whereas Iran looks at these forces as the guarantee of Gulf security, others fear the intermarriage between Iranian military power and its ideological goals.

Reflections of Arab/Iranian Policies Concerning Gulf Security on Relations between the Arabs and Iranians

Observation of Arab and Iranian policies towards the issue of Gulf security reveals a limited overlap between the two sets of policies. For, with the exception of the Iranian-Arab Gulf vision's emphasis on the Gulf identity of this issue, and the Iranian-Iraqi vision focusing on the Western threat to Gulf security, the Arab and Iranian policies towards Gulf security remain contradictory in essence. This is negatively reflected in overall Arab–Iranian relations. Effectively, Arab nationalist thought argues persistently that Iran's desire is to 'smash the Arab security ring in the Gulf', while Iranian thought concentrates on the Arab Gulf's attempt to 'deny Iranian interests in the Gulf'.

And yet, concomitant with such disparate views, both Arabs and Iranians confront similar problems and challenges in the Gulf. The most important of these are the challenges of environmental degradation, the socio-political struggles, and the role of opposition social movements. These elements require a new Arab-Iranian perspective on Gulf security. In our opinion, the starting point in this perspective is the agreement of Arabs and Iranians on general principles to govern Arab-Iranian relations with respect to Gulf security. The most crucial of these principles may be:

1. The principle of non-interference in the internal affairs of other states,
2. Respecting the sovereignty and independence of the territories of the existing states in the Gulf,
3. Settling disagreements between these states by peaceful means.
4. Respecting the legitimate interests of each state.
5. Achieving political change by peaceful means.

The respect paid to these principles as a group of general political conventions represents the necessary approach for the formulation of a Gulf security perspective based on the interdependence of Arabs and Iranians in this area. This interdependence means, in this context:

1. A group of linkages connecting the Arabs and Iranians at the governmental and non-governmental levels;
2. A group of cases on the Arab-Iranian agenda, including security, economic issues, etc.;
3. Abstaining from the use of force in the settlement of disputes.

Is it possible, then, for Arab-Iranian relations to take this form? Even though the task is enormous, it is not impossible. The international and regional challenges are incentives for reaching a new starting point based on a recognition of the mutual interests of all parties in the area. On the other hand, the second element for the Arab-Iranian paradigm on Gulf security should revolve around the creation of 'cooperative security'. This signifies a security system where all parties' security strategies would be integrated and complement each other, and where the security concept widens to encompass the comprehensive strategic dimensions, especially the non-military dimension of security. The establishment of this system requires agreement over a group of common arrangements, including a series of rules and measures organizing the conduct of Arab and Iranian security.

There is a variety of types of cooperative security that the East Asian states, Latin American, South Africa and other states have established, such as conflict management and pre-emption. Likewise, systems for arms control, conflict resolution, confidence building, etc. have been adopted in different parts of the world. If these systems have been established in other regions of the developing world, there is nothing, in principle, preventing their incremental adoption in the Gulf area.[51]

There is no doubt that the intensification of intellectual meetings between Arab and Iranian scholars in the forthcoming stage will be a crucial step on the path to discovering constructive alternatives in this respect.

Conclusion

The Middle Eastern and Gulf security cases are considered to be the most critical issues in current Arab-Iranian relations. They represent a model illustrating both cooperative dimensions and conflicting aspects. Both Arabs and Iranians face similar challenges from the 'new world order' leadership. The most significant of these challenges might be the attempt exerted by such leaderships to restructure the Arab-Israeli interactions in order to secure Israeli hegemony over the aggregate of Arab interactions, and boycott Iran economically and militarily through the 'dual containment' strategy. This is the declared strategy of the United States towards Iran and Iraq.

Even though Iran is excluded at the present time from the Middle Eastern project, its establishment will not affect the Arabs alone, but will, necessarily, influence Iran itself – at least with respect to Arab-Iranian economic interactions and Iranian-Israeli nuclear balance. Likewise, the persistence of contradictions in the Arab and Iranian policies *vis-a-vis* Gulf security mainly benefits the leadership of the 'new world order', and creates the appropriate environment for consecrating its presence. Hence, both Arabs and Iranians are in dire need of a new conceptual framework in the context of international transformations. They also need to 'institutionalize' these relations in the framework of agreed rules. The take off point is to give up both the traditional Western concept that holds Iran as just 'a country of geographical proximity' and the traditional Iranian concept maintaining that Iran is the power that should dominate the Gulf. Instead, a new concept should be adopted, based on mutual recognition of interests and avoiding the exclusion of any party from the formula of regional interactions, as long as it behaves within agreed upon rules of conduct.[52]

There are indicators suggesting Arab and Iranian awareness of the importance of modifying the intellectual paradigm governing their relations. The most prominent of these indicators might be the current positive development in Egyptian-Iranian relations.[53] It is possible to activate Arab-Iranian interaction either in the framework of standing institutions – such as the Islamic Conference Organization – or the creation of a council for Arab-Iranian cooperation open for the participation of those Arab states wishing to crystallize and develop this cooperation, regardless of whether they are Gulf states or not.

Notes

* Director of the Centre for Asian Studies, Faculty of Economic and Political Sciences, University of Cairo, Cairo, Egypt.

1.   Ole Holsti, 'The Three-headed Eagle: The United States and System Change', *International Studies Quarterly*, vol. 23, no. 3 (September 1979), pp. 339–59.

2.   *Al-Taqrir al-Istratijy al-'Araby li Sanat 1993* ('The Arab Strategic Report for 1993'), (Cairo: Centre for Political and Strategic Studies, Al-Ahram, 1994), p. 231.

3.   *Ibid.*, pp. 230–1.

4.   Review of King Hassan the Second's speeches at the inauguration of the Casablanca summit in October 1994 (in *Al-Ahram* daily, 31 October 1994), and in the closing session of the conference (*Al-Ahram* daily, 1-2 November 1994).

5.   Review of King Hussein's declarations and speech in the conference on the future of the Mediterranean following the peace process (in *Al-Ahram* daily, 31 October 1994), and in the closing session of the conference (*Al-Ahram* daily, 20 October 1994).

6.   Mahmoud Wahba, *Isra'il wal 'Arab wal Suq al-Sharq Awsatiyyah* ('Israel, the Arabs and the Middle Eastern Market'), (Cairo: Al-Maktabah Al-Acadimiyyah, 1994), pp. 77–80. Similar orientations were expressed by the Egyptian businessmen Sherif Dolar, Mohammed Junidy, Ahmad Bahjat and others. They pointed out that we should take part in the new construct of the Middle East, that we should not fear Israeli competition, because Israeli advancement is exaggerated. See *Al-Ahram* daily, 12 February 1995 and 8 January 1995.

7.   Fahd Al-Fank, *'Al-Ab'ad al-Iqtisadiyyah lil Hal al-Silmy'* ('The Economic Dimensions of the Peaceful Settlement'), paper presented to the project on the regional results of the peace settlement in the Middle East, *Muntada al-Fikr al-'Araby*, Amman, 1992.

8.   Ali Shafiq Mahana, *'Al-Sharq Awsatiyyah Laysat Wahman'* ('Middle Easternism is not an Illusion'), *Al-Ahram* daily, 1 November 1994.

9.   Abdul Mon'eim Sa'id, *'Badlan min al-Khawf'* ('Instead of Fear'), *Awraq al-Sharq al-Awsat* (*Middle East Papers*), Cairo, 12 July 1994, pp. 59–82.

10.   Speech of 'Amr Mousa, Egypt's Foreign Affairs Minister, before the Casablanca summit, *Al-Ahram* daily, 2 November 1994. Also, discourse of Ahmad 'Esmat 'Abdul Meguid, Secretary General of the Arab League, to Ihsan Bakr, *'Idah min al-Amin al-'Am* ('Clarification from the Secretary General'), *Al-Ahram* daily, 13 November 1994.

11.   Discourse of Egypt's Foreign Affairs Minister to *Al-Ahram* daily, 28 October 1994.

12.   Discourse of the Secretary General of the Arab League to *Al-Ahram* daily, 23 January 1995. Also, Ibrahim Nafi', *'Khawatir 'an al-Suq al-Sharq Awsatiyyah'* ('The New Middle Eastern Market'), *Al-Ahram* daily, 31 October 1994.

13.   Saad El-Din Ibrahim, *'Al-Qimma al-Iqtisadiyyah wa Fan Idarat al-Hawajis'* ('The Economic Summit and the Art of Managing Apprehensions'), *Al-Ahram* daily, 31 October 1994.

14.   Sa'id Al-Naggar's commentary in *'Al-Tahaddiyyat al-Sharq Awsatiyyah al-Jadidah wal Watan al-'Araby'* ('The New Middle Eastern Challenges and the Arab World'), (Beirut: Centre for Arab Unity Studies, 1994), pp. 197–200.

15.   Ghassan Salamé, *'Afkar Awwaliyyah 'an al-Suq al-Awsatiyyah'* ('Preliminary Ideas about the Middle Eastern Market'), in ibid., pp. 32–57.

16.   Abdul Raouf Al-Ridy, *'Qimmat al-Iskandariyyah wal Sharq al-Awsat al-Jadid'* ('The Alexandria Summit and the New Middle East'), *Al-Ahram* daily, 1 January 1995.

17.   Lutfy al-Khuly, *'Arab? Na'am, wa Sharq Awsatiyun Aydan* ('Arabs? Yes, but also Middle Easterners'), (Cairo: Markaz al-Ahram lil Tarjama wal Nashr, 1994), pp. 69–85.

18.   In his previously mentioned study, Ghassan Salamé summarized systematically most sayings of the Arab rejectionist trend, Ghassan Salamé, *'Afkar Awwaliyyah 'an al-Suq al-Awsatiyyah'*, op. cit., pp. 40–7.

19.   In deducing the Libyan policy, we are relying on President Qaddafi's speech on the occasion of the 1st of September *Al-Thawra* ('The Revolution'), 2 September 1994, in addition to the discourse by Ibrahim Al-Ghuwayl, a leader of the Islamic Call Association in Libya, in *Al-'Araby* (Cairo), 2 February 1995, and the editorial of *Mustaqbal al-'Alam al-Islamy* (*Future of the Islamic World*), no. 14 (Fall 1995), pp. 2–6, a magazine very closely associated with the Libyan government.

20.   Review his declarations in *Kihan al-'Araby* (Tehran), (in Persian), 18–21 December 1994.

21.   Mohammad Zakariyya Isma'il, *'Al-Hawiyyah al-'Arabiyyah fi Muwajahat al-Salam al-Israili'* ('The Arab Identity Versus Israeli Peace'), *Al-Mustaqbal Al-'Araby*, no. 190 (December 1994), pp. 26–44.

22.   *Al-Ahram* daily, 1 November 1994.

23.   *'Ru'ya Qawmiyyah li Hal al-Ummah: Waraqat 'Amal'* ('A Nationalist Reading of the Nation's Conditions: A Working Paper'), *Al-Mustaqbal Al-'Araby*, no. 189 (October 1994), pp. 19–30. *'Ru'ya Islamiyyah li Hal al-Ummah: Waraqat 'Amal'* ('An Islamist Reading of the Nation's Conditions: A Working Paper'), ibid., pp. 31–40.

24.   Mohammed Hassanein Heikal, *'Al-'Arab 'ala A'tab al-Qarn al-Wahid wal 'Ishrun'* ('The Arabs on the Eve of the 21st Century'), *Al-Mustaqbal Al-'Araby*, no. 190 (December 1994), pp. 4–20, and his discourse in *Al-Ahram* daily, 29 October

1994.

25.   Ahmad Sudki El-Dajani in his commentary published in *Al-Tahaddiyyat al-Sharq Awsatiyyah al-Jadidah wal Watan al-'Araby,* op. cit., pp. 69–70.

26.   Siyar Al-Jumayil, *'Al-Majal al-Hayawi lil Sharq al-Awsat Isa' al-Nizam al-Dawly al-Qadim'* ('The Vital Arena of the Middle Eastern System in the Coming International Order'), *Al-Mustaqbal Al-'Araby,* no. 184 (June 1994), pp. 22–3.

27.   Samir Al-Tiqi, *'An Akhtar al-Ittifaq wa Taghyib al-Mashru' al-Qawmy'* ('Concerning the Dangers of the Agreement and the Concealment of the National Project'), *Al-Tariq* (Beirut), lst issue, January 1994, pp. 48–52.

28.   Mahmoud Abdel Fadil, *'Mashari' al-Tartibat al-Sharq Awsatiyyah: Al-Tasawwurat, al-Mahazir, Ashkal al-Muwajaha'* ('Projects for the Middle Eastern Arrangements, Visualizations, Warnings and Forms of Confrontation'), in *Tahaddiyyat al-Sharq Awsatiyyah al-Jadidah wal Watan al-'Araby,* op. cit., pp. 127–65.

29.   Ahmad Yussuf Ahmad, *'Al-'Arab wal Tahaddiyyat al-Nizam al-Sharq Awsaty, Munaqasha li ba'd al-Ab'ad al-Siyasiyyah'* ('The Arabs and the Middle Eastern Market, a Discussion of Some Political Dimensions'), ibid.

30.   Saad El-Din Wahba, *'Raja'a al-'Arab bi Khuffai Rabin'* ('The Arabs Have Returned with Empty Hands'), *Al-Ahram* daily, 12 November 1994; *'Mu'tamar Iqtisady am Kayan Israily?'* ('Economic Conference or Israeli Entity?'), *Al-Ahram* daily, 15 October 1994.

31.   Among the examples expressing the general Islamist view of the Middle Eastern system, it is possible to cite the following: Magdy Hussein, *'Na'am, al-Salam 'ala Hafat al-Hawiyah'* ('Yes, Peace is on the Edge of the Cliff'), *Al-Sha'ab* daily (Cairo), 7 March 1995; Discourse of Laith Shbeilat, Chairman of the Jordanian Engineers Syndicate and ex-Islamist MP, in *Al-'Araby* (Cairo), 20 February 1995; Nevine Mustapha, *'Al-Mashru' al-Sharq Awsaty wal Mustaqbal al-'Araby'* ('The Middle Eastern Project and the Arab Future'), *Al-Mustaqbal Al-'Araby,* no. 193 (March 1995), pp. 4–18.

32.   Khalid Mohy al Din in his declarations to *Al-'Araby* (Cairo), 31 October 1994.

33.   Hussein Abdel Raziq, *'Al-Mu'aradhah wa Mu'tamar al-Dar al-Bayda'* ('The Opposition and the Casablanca Conference'), *Al-Yassar* (Cairo), December 1994, p. 44.

34.   Fawzy Mansur, *'Al-Sharq Awsatiyyah Mashru' wal Laysa Suqan'* ('The Middle Easternism is a Project, Not a Market'), *Al-Ahaly* (Cairo), 26 October 1994.

35.   Mohammad Sid Ahmad, *'Hal lil Atraf al-'Arabiyyah Awraq Tafawudh?'* ('Do the Arab Parties Possess Negotiating Cards?'), *Al-Ahram* daily, 20 October 1994; *'Al-Qawmiyyah wal Sharq Awsatiyyah'* ('Nationalism and Middle Easternism'), *Al-Ahram* daily, 15 February 1993; *'Li Munahadat al-Khalal fi al-Suq al-Sharq Awsatiyyah'* ('In Order to Fight the Flaws in the Middle Eastern Market'), *Al-Ahram* daily, 17 November 1994; *'Hawl Khalal fi Muwajahat al-Khalal'* ('Concerning the Flaw in Confronting the Flaw'), *Al-Ahram* daily, 24 November 1994.

36.   Text of the statement in *Al-Ahaly* (Cairo), 15 February 1995.

37.   Mohammad Al-Said Abdul Mou'men, *'Al-'Ilaqat al-Iraniyyah al-Misriyyah'* ('Iranian–Egyptian Relations'), research paper submitted to the Conference on the Regional Role of Egypt in the Middle East, (Cairo: Markaz al-Buhuth wal Dirasat al-Siyasiyyah, Cairo University, 1994), pp. 29–30. Also, Pakinam Al-

Sharqawy, *'Al-Ru'ya al-Iraniyyah lil Musalaha al-'Arabiyyah'* ('The Iranian View of the Arab Reconciliation'), research paper submitted to the 2nd Annual Conference for Young Scholars, (Cairo: Markaz al-Buhuth wal Dirasat al-Siyasiyyah, Cairo University, 1994), pp. 29–30.

38.   Abbas Maleky, 'Myth and Reality of the New World Order,' Challenges to Iranian Foreign Policy, *Iranian Journal of International Affairs*, vol. 5, no. 2 (Summer 1993), pp. 311–17.

39.   Mohammad al Sa'id Abdul Mo'mein, ibid., pp. 34–5. It is to be noted that Iran officially updated this policy following the Israeli–Palestinian agreement in 1993. Previously, it used to affirm its opposition to any acknowledgement of Israel because it looked on it as an outlaw country that should be isolated. A discourse for the Iranian President was published in *The Iranian Journal of International Affairs*, vol. 5, no. 2 (Summer 1993), p. 79. Similar declarations for the president and the foreign minister may be found in *Majalleh-e Siyasat -e Khariji*, (Tehran), nos. 1 and 2, 1994, pp. 208–10 (in Persian).

40.   The complete text of the discussions of the conference is published in Persian in *'Friand Sulh Myan Saf-Israil'*, *Fasilnama Khawarmiana* (Tehran), vol. 1, no. 1 (Summer 1994), pp. 5–25.

41.   Mohammad al Sa'id Abdul Mo'mein, op. cit., pp. 3–32.

42.   *Kihan* daily, 8 January 1995.

43.   *Itila'at* (in Persian), 19 January 1995.

44.   Mohammad El-Sayed Selim, *'Al-Ru'ya al-Sa'udiyyah li Amn al-Khalij'* ('The Saudi Conceptualization of Gulf Security'), in Abdel Mon'eim Al-Mashat, ed., *Amn al-Khalij al-'Araby: Dirasah fil Idrak wal Siyasat (Arab Gulf Security: A Study in Perception and Policies)*, (Cairo: Markaz al-Buhuth wal Dirasat al-Istratijiyyah, Cairo University, 1994), pp. 34–73. Also, Hassan Abu Talib, *'Tasawwurat Duwal Majlis al-Ta'awun al-Khaliji li Qadaya al-Amn fil Khalij ba'd al-Harb'* ('The Gulf Cooperation Council States Visualizations about the Security Cases in the Gulf in the Post War Era'), in Mustapha 'Ilwy, ed., *Misr wa Amn al-Khalij ba'd al-Harb (Egypt and Gulf Security in the Post War Era')*, ibid., pp. 119–52.

45.   Sam'an Butros Farajallah, *'Al-Ru'ya al-Kuwaitiyyah li Amn al-Khalij'* ('The Kuwaiti Conceptualization of Gulf Security'), in Abdul Mon'eim Al-Mashat, ed., op. cit., pp. 73–147.

46.   Ahmad Yussuf Ahmad, *'Al-Ru'ya al-Iraqiyyah li Amn al-Khalij'* ('The Iraqi Conceptualization of Gulf Security'), in Abdel Mon'eim Al-Mashat, ed., ibid., pp. 265–88. Also, Joseph Kechichian, *Political Dynamics and Security in the Arabian Peninsula through the 1990s*, (Santa Monica, Calif.: Rand Corporation, 1993), pp. 7–38.

47.   We are referring to a study by 'Adayy Saddam Hussein, in the first issue of the magazine *Shu'un Siyasiyyah (Political Affairs)*, January 1994; from: Ahmadd Yussuf Ahmad, ibid., p.281.

48.   Mohammad Al Sa'id Idris, *'Ru'yat Oman wal Imarat wa Qatar wal Bahrain li Amn al-Khalij'* ('The Conceptualizations of Oman, the Emirates, Qatar and Bahrain of Gulf Security'), in Abdel Mon'eim Al-Mashat, ed., ibid., pp. 148–264.

49.   Wahid Abdel Majid, *'Ru'yat Misr wa Suriyyah li Amn al-Khalij'* ('The Egyptian and Syrian Conceptualizations of Gulf Security'), in Abdel Mon'eim Al-Mashat, ed., ibid., pp. 148–264. See also: Nazly Mu'awad Ahmad, *'Al-Tasawwur al-Masry li Amn al-Khalij ba'd al-Harb'* ('The Egyptian Conceptualization of Gulf

Security in the Post War Era'), in Mustapha 'Ilwy, ed., op. cit., pp. 251–84; Mustapha 'Ilwy, ed., *Harb al-Khalij wa Amn al-Khalij ba'd al-Harb* (*The Gulf War and Egyptian Politics in the Post War Era*), Cairo: Markaz al-Buhuth wal Dirasat al-Siyassiyah, Cairo University, 1992; Mary Morris, *New Political Realities and the Gulf: Egypt, Syria and Iran*, Santa Monica, Calif.: Rand Corporation, 1993; Hooshang Amirahmadi, *'Siyasat Iran al-Iqlimiyyah'* ('The Regional Policy of Iran'), *Shu'un al-Awasat*, Beirut, March 1994.

50. Niveen Masaad, *'Al-Ru'ya al-Iraniyyah li Amn al-Khalij'* ('The Iranian Conceptualization of Gulf Security'), in Abdel Mon'eim Al-Mashat, ed., op. cit., pp. 289–336. See also: 'Ola Abu Zayd, *'Al-Tasawwur al-Irany li Amn al-Khalij ba'd al-Harb'* ('The Iranian Conceptualization of Gulf Security in the Post War Era'), in Mustapha 'Ilwy, ed., op. cit., pp. 153–92; Hooshang Amirahmadi, 'Iran and the Persian Gulf: Strategic Issues and Outlook', *Iranian Journal of International Affairs*, vol. 5, no. 2 (Summer 1993), pp. 366–407.; James A. Bill, 'Regional Security and Domestic Stability in the Persian Gulf', *Iranian Journal of International Affairs*, vol. 5, nos. 3 and 4 (Fall-Winter 1993-94), pp. 561-574; N. Schagoldion, *Iran and the Post-war Security in the Persian Gulf*, Santa Monica, Calif: Rand Corpporation, 1994.

51. Mohammad El-Sayed Selim, 'Reconceptualizing Gulf Security in the Post Cold War Era, Towards a New Model', paper presented at the Conference of the Centre for Persian Gulf and Middle Eastern Studies, the Institute for Political and International Studies, Tehran, 1994.

52. Mohammad El-Sayed Selim, *'Itar Muqtarah li Manzuma Iqlimiyyah'* ('A Suggested Framework for a Regional Order'), *Shu'un al-Awsat* (Beirut), 53. We draw attention here to the visit of Mr Abbas Maliky, Iran's Deputy Foreign Minister, to Egypt in 1994, and the settlement of some lingering cases in Egyptian-Iranian relations, such as the issue of Egyptian debts, the participation of some Egyptian companies in programmes of industrialization in Iran, the declaration of the Arab Republic of Egypt's Foreign Affairs Minister that Egypt condemns the Israeli threat to the Iranian nuclear plants, the participation of some Egyptian researchers in the conferences of the International and Political Studies Institute (a subsidiary of the Iranian Foreign Ministry) and the Egyptian-Iranian Coordination in the 7th Islamic Summit Conference held in Morocco in 1994. We have focused on Egyptian-Iranian relations because they used to represent the nadir in Arab-Iranian ties. We also draw attention to the Iranian President's declarations on 19 December 1994, concerning the necessity for adopting an Iranian-Arab initiative towards Iraq.

25

Arabs and Iranians and the Concept of a 'Middle East Order'

MOHAMMAD ALI MUHTADI

Introduction

What I will be presenting here is not a systematic study in the academic sense, but rather a collection of thoughts and impressions, accompanied by apprehensions and fears that have accumulated as I have followed developments in the Middle East from the Iranian capital.

Although the term 'Middle East' has been known for some time, this expression jumped to the forefront in the Western press and in academic and political circles after these groups began discussion of the peace settlement in the region between Israel and the Arabs, starting with the Madrid conference towards the end of 1991.

Let us take, for example, the famous study by the American Jewish researcher, Bernard Lewis, entitled 'Rethinking the New Middle East'.[1] Lewis found that adopting the term 'Middle East' and widening its definition to include the entire Islamic East, including the Islamic republics in Central Asia and the Caucasus, constituted a strategic focus for the organization of Israel's defences and its relations with its immediate surroundings and the world. Using this concept, and insisting on it, Lewis resolves the problem of the creation of Israel as a foreign body in a region that is described as Islamic, by designating a wider geographic, political and cultural definition for the region to replace the civilizational name it used to be known by, so that if the word 'Israel' is brought up on the map of the region, the word 'Middle East' correspondingly drops from circulation, as one Egyptian scholar in a special study on this subject has affirmed.[2]

While the attempt to merge Israel into this region within special projects that suppress the Arab–Islamic identity, tighten the grip on the Muslims' resources and wealth and plunder them, is nothing new; the international and regional developments that have occurred, foremost among them the collapse of the Soviet Union and a free hand for the US, in addition to the

Iraqi invasion of Kuwait – and what followed this operation by way of destructive results, regressions and collapses in all fields – have presented a golden opportunity for the enemies of the *ummah* to begin application of a plan that was designed with extreme precision, and which carries the title of 'the New Middle East'.

The Features of the New Order

Actually, the form of this order is not altogether clear, and there are differences between what Israel wants and what it can obtain. But to extract the features of the new order, we should look carefully at the so-called multilateral negotiations that began in Moscow in January 1992, that is, two months after the bilateral negotiations in Madrid.[3] The purpose of these negotiations was to build confidence and create relations of cooperation and peace between Israel and the Arab world on the grounds that progress in the bilateral negotiations is linked to the results of the multilateral negotiations.

It is clear that the bilateral negotiations, founded on the principle of 'land for peace', could not possibly yield results. Their objective was, rather, to create an atmosphere conducive to the initiation of multilateral negotiations as a mechanism for designing the future of the region, and to strip the Arabs of everything, without any Israeli concession in the matter of withdrawal from the Occupied Territories.

Shimon Peres said, in his meeting with Egyptian intellectuals at the end of 1992: 'Against the bilateral negotiations there are also Israeli–Arab multilateral negotiations of five independent working groups discussing such issues as resolving the regional water problem, developing the regional economy ... Any discussions of the challenges relating to the future and not dealing with the past.' He added, speaking to one of the Egyptian intellectuals: 'You are educated. You should look to the future, as one of the new generation; knowledge in it is more important than land'.[4]

This means, quite simply, that you should forget there is an occupied land and a dispersed people; it is backward to demand land and the return of refugees; indeed, you must prepare to relinquish your independence, sovereignty, water, oil and wealth, disarm, and walk into an unknown future without looking back. For 'peace in the Middle East', according to Shimon Peres, 'is not a surgical operation; it is not an amputation or an organ transplant from one body to another; it is giant civil engineering projects to build a new Middle East, free of the conflicts of the past, ready to take its place in the new age, the age that does not tolerate the backward or forgive the ignorant!'[5]

In any case, after the bilateral negotiations reached an impasse, there was universal surprise at the announcement of the Oslo agreement, resulting from secret talks that continued for nine months between representatives of Israel and the Palestine Liberation Organization; this despite the Arab agreement at the foreign ministers meeting in Beirut that no one should depart from the circle of solidarity and joint effort in the bilateral negotiations. It was later proven that the Gaza–Jericho agreement did not constitute for the Israelis any more than a Trojan horse, to break the barriers to their entry of the Arab world, especially the Persian Gulf area. For they did not give the Palestinians anything worth mentioning, except administration of the internal affairs of the Gaza Strip, this area that is overpopulated, empty of any resources or wealth, and an administrative nightmare for Israel.

What is surprising to anyone following the conduct of the Palestinian negotiator – or who reads *The Road to Oslo* – is that he views the Palestinian and American negotiators with admiration; he is overwhelmed just by seeing himself greeting 'Mr Peres' or 'Mr Ross', a joy that climaxed when 'Mr Clinton' passed him a chair to sit on and while he delivered his signature.[6] Edward Said says: 'Their only wish was to embrace the US Secretary of State. They do not want work, strain or even equality; they only want that he accepts them, the white man.'[7]

Among the negotiators one man saw that the Arab situation was finished. Even in its hey day, he concluded, it gave the Palestinians nothing. He therefore began work to develop the Palestinian asabiyah in order to entrench the Palestinian trend towards Palestinian–Israeli partnership, wherein the Palestinians play a vanguard role, being spread out and of Arab background, backed by Israeli experience and technology and Jewish extensions into the capitals of money and political and economic decision-making. Or, to put it briefly, a partnership in which the Palestinians become a bridge and intermediary for the phase of normalization and of Israeli economic and cultural hegemony over the entire Arab–Islamic region.[8]

There is an abundance of studies on the five working groups branching out of the multilateral negotiations which confirm the results of the disaster that flowed from their own aims vis -à-vis the Arab and Islamic world, especially in particular so far as the economy and water are concerned.

The economies of the Arab countries are not equipped for this new Middle Eastern order for a number of reasons: The absence of techniques and modernization in methods of management, the hegemony of the oil economy in a large number of these countries and the absence of internal integration between them, all of which has lead to Israeli hegemony over them. This new Middle Eastern order does not, consequently permit balanced development among the different parties involved, nor does it achieve development for the less advanced parties, or help some countries out of the trap of dependence on Western states and financial institutions.

As for the issue of water, it is clear that Israel wants to dominate Arab water resources. The continued occupation of south Lebanon is primarily driven by the need to control the water. The Israeli refusal to withdraw from Golan is due to the fact that Israel wants to maintain dominance over the waters of the Yarmouk, Banias, Humma area and Hasbani and Wazzani Rivers, in addition to maintaining dominance over ground water resources in the Occupied Territories where the Palestinian Authority does not have the power to control water resources. In this context, the words of Shimon Peres in his meeting with Egyptian intellectuals – 'We need only more water, not more land'9 – are of special significance.

The Iranian Position

As for Islamic-Iran's place in the Middle East plan, it is from the start against this plan in its entirety, above all for religious reasons. It is inconceivable that Iran could occupy a place in Shimon Peres's design, especially in view of the so-called international decision that has placed Iran and Iraq within a policy of 'dual containment', despite Iran's geo-political importance as a bridge to the independent republics and its role in the Economic Cooperation Organization (ECO).

In fact, Iran's concern with the settlement process – or new Middle East – and its position on it, rests on two basic considerations:

(1) The importance of the cause of Palestine and the Holy Land, and the impermissibility of neglecting this central issue that concerns all Arabs and Muslims.
(2) The strategic importance of the Persian Gulf area and Sea of Oman, as a vital artery for Iran. The extension of the Israeli plan to this area is regarded as against higher Iranian interests. Hence Iran's support for the intifadah in the Occupied Territories, and for the forces opposed to the Zionist plan. This is also the reason for Iran's insistence that Gulf security is the responsibility of the states overlooking it; any foreign military presence in this area, under pretext of security, is provocative and destabilizing and does not serve the interests of the peoples of the area.

There is another consideration circulating in religious intellectual circles. Namely, that irrespective of the above two considerations, Israel's hegemony over the Arab region and weakening of the Arabs politically, economically and culturally, is tantamount to weakening the Muslims and the heartland of the Islamic world. This should, therefore, be confronted in every way. This view, even if it has not reached the level of a decision – perhaps because of the Iranians' disappointment with the general Arab position towards the Islamic revolution in Iran, and with continuous Arab retreat before the Zionist plan – nevertheless prevails in the psyche of the majority of religious Iranians. The researcher can find many individual terms and expressions that reflect this perception in the statements of government officials, and in the orations of Friday prayers.

The important aspect of this perception is that it cannot but welcome any kind of union with the Arab counties, or any step to such a union, not on the basis of 'asabiyah' or ignorant dogma, which constitutes a closed nationalism and tribalism – a condition censured by Islamic writ. Rather, on the basis of integration, cooperation the defence of the Islamic *ummah* against all threats and the furthering of its glory and sovereignty.

Many who hold this point of view are today in responsible positions in Iran. They are the ones who, during the 1960s, listened to the speeches of Gamal Abdel Nasser on the 'Voice of the Arabs' with enthusiasm and relish, as though – despite the fact that they were not Arabs – he was speaking to them. What is important is that this perception exists and, in my view, warrants study and encouragement so that it can become a focal point from which to launch a renaissance in Iranian–Arab relations.

Against this, there is the secular nationalist current that does not recognize religious motives as a basis for the new Middle East plan. It does not see this plan as a threat to the historical and cultural entity of the Iranian people. According to this outlook, should Iran enter the new project it would occupy a prominent place in view of its potential in terms of material, technical and human resources. Some members of this school of thought look to the plan as an alliance between Semite elements, after they had differed for tens, even hundreds, of years past, and therefore ignore the need to beware of the coming danger from this alliance to Iranian interests, especially as both sides, Arab and Israeli, accuse Iran of fundamentalism and supporting terrorism, perhaps as an excuse to contain and strike at Iranian interests in the region.[10] This current exists among non-religious intellectuals, especially the few remaining supporters of the Shah's regime, most of whom live outside Iran, but are not represented in the state and have no prominent figureheads.

This very fact clarifies the importance of Islam as a principal factor for bringing the Iranian nearer the Arab, not out of historical memory or sharing in the making of Islamic civilization, but because of the religious commitment of the Muslim. If we strip away this commitment, we find no reason for this affinity, save perhaps in joint interests in the commercial sense of the word, far from sacred moral sentiments and feelings. Who wants to affirm this point need only ask our colleague Hani al-Hasan or re-read *Iran From Within* by Fahmy Howeidy.

The Place of Iran in the Israeli Perspective

Those who keeps up with the writings of Israeli leaders and officials and their statements, find that there is a massive amount of propaganda about the coming fundamentalist danger from Tehran – the alleged capital of Islamist fundamentalism. This is designed to 'market' the Middle East plan and persuade Arab regimes of the need to enter it in order to safeguard their own continuation, existence and gains. Israel never lets an opportunity pass without warning of the fundamentalist danger, tying every part of its plan to the need to repel this destructive danger. Let us look at the case of Shimon Peres, the Israeli foreign minister. In his book *The New Middle East.*, Peres confirms that 'the ultimate aim of the plan is to create a regional family of nations with a common market and selected central agencies, and the need for this regional framework derives from four fundamental factors: political stability, which necessarily requires opposing the danger of fundamentalism; economy, or the erection of a regional cooperation organization that moves above the nationalist platform ... and which is the only response to fundamentalism; national security, which is a regional alliance assisting in preventing one party from pushing the doomsday button, and finally the spread of democracy, which works to eliminate the factors underlying fundamentalist incitement.[11]

In the past, the Israelis would say: 'The Arabs do not read'. It seems that they continue to talk about the Arabs in the same way, ignoring their many advances in research, science, intellectual output, the media, and university education.

It is clear that Islamic Iran – in the view of the Israelis and their Western allies – constitutes a means for pressuring and frightening the Arabs, just as the 'Communist threat' was used in the Cold War era. By this they seek to push the Arabs into the new Middle East order, forcing them to sign bilateral security agreements and selling them enormous quantities of weaponry costing billions of dollars.

Thus, any bid to build confidence and understanding between Iranians and Arabs is regarded as a harsh blow to the Middle East plan of the Israelis and their allies, and to the possibilities of implementing it in our Arab and Islamic region.

Notes

The author is a member of the Centre for Arab–Iranian Studies, Tehran, Iran.

1.   Bernard Lewis, 'Rethinking the New Middle East', *Foreign Affairs*, vol. 71, no. 4 (Fall 1992).

2.   Ala' Abdel Wahhab, The New Middle East: Scenario for Israeli Hegemony, Cairo: Ibn Sina, 1995.

3.   Joel Peters, 'Building Bridges: The Arab–Israeli Multilateral Talks', London: Royal Institute of International Affairs, Chatham House, 1994.

4.   Minutes of Shimon Peres meeting with Egyptian intellectuals in the National Institute for Middle East Studies, published in *Davar* daily, 20 November 1992, translated into Arabic at the Centre for Arab–Iranian Studies, Tehran.

5.   'A New Era that Does Not Tolerate Backwardness and Does Not Forgive the Ignorant' – a title of an article in Arabic by Shimon Peres, delivered to Al-Ahram Centre for Translation and Publishing, Cairo, and published in Michel Jobert et al., *What's After the Gulf Storm: A Global View of the Future of the Middle East*, preface by Ibrahim Nafe', (Cairo: Al-Ahram Centre for Translation and Publishing, 1992), pp. 97–111.

6.   See Mahmoud Abbas ('Abu Mazen'), *The Road to Oslo: The Place of the Agreement Tells the Actual Secrets of the Negotiations*, Amman: [n.pb.], 1994.

7.   Edward W. Said, 'Symbols Versus Substance Year after Declaration of Principles', interview with Mouin Rabbani, *Journal of Palestine Studies*, vol. 24, no. 2 (Winter 1995), pp. 60–72.

8.   See Bashir Nafe', 'Preliminary Remarks on the Gaza–Jericho Agreement', *Political Readings*, vol. 4, no. 1 (Winter 1994).

9.   *Ibid.*

10.   See David Pound, 'Pan-Semitism', a presentation to the Seminar on Israeli Policies, published in its proceedings in *Middle East Quarterly* (in Persian), no. 3 (Fall 1994).

11.   Shimon Peres and Arye Naor, *The New Middle East*, Longmead, UK: Element Books; New York: Henry Holt and Co., 1993.

Thirteen

The Place of Arab–Iranian Ties in the Islamic World Frame

26

The Place of Arab–Iranian Relations in the Islamic World Frame

MOHAMMAD ALI AZARSHAB*

The subject of Arab-Iranian relations in the Islamic world, is, for me, a highly emotive one. I am deeply concerned as to whether the Islamic *ummah* can ever reoccupy a central place in human history and must state from the outset that this personal concern lies at the heart of my academic researches into Arab-Iranian relations. I therefore apologize in advance in the hope that this emotional thread in my work is not the result of 'the imagination of a visitor', as an Arab poet once said.[1] Rather, I hope that they are the result of a true determination to bridge the differences between the various peoples of the Islamic *ummah*.

The Islamic Ummah: United or Divided?

Before tackling the issue of contemporary Arab–Iranian relations, we must shed some light on the geography and civilizations of the region, so as to pinpoint similarities and dissimilarities. This should help to define the respective positions of Arabs and Iranians in the Muslim world.

Needless to say, there is a common identity that binds the members of the Islamic *ummah*. However, the strength of this common bond varies according to the status of Muslims in the international arena. This shared identity is embodied in a belief in the invisible world. The great Islamic thinker Mohammed Baqr El-Sadr said: the belief in the invisible world was illustrated on the intellectual level, targeting the intellectual side of human knowledge without the tangible one'. He, furthermore, believed that the invisible world in the Muslim mind is a response to the temptation of the matter to which every person is subject. This temptation is so strong that it can excite the hearts of human beings. So, when Muslims resist temptation, they adopt a negative position taking the form of asceticism, utter satisfaction, contentment or laziness'.2 Any attempt to study this

517

issue is useless, he says, unless we take this dimension into account. And, as it were, the earth dons the garment of the skies.

Theoretically, all Muslims believe that Muhammad is a prophet, that the Qur'an is holy and that the laws laid down by Prophet, and the Islamic sites, are holy as well. Thus, the Islamic *ummah*, over the years, has striven to adopt a united position in the face of any aggression directed against these sanctities.[3] It also holds all the laws laid out in the Qur'an and the Shari'ah as sacred; these laws link the human being to God, and link human beings to one another.

Moreover, literature was written based on the Qur'an, Hadith and the Arabic language, grammar and sciences. These literary works have left a mark on Islamic poetry and arts. Translation introduced Islamic literature, past and present, to all Muslims. We can even say that the prevalence of the Arabic language in the Arab world permitted Arabic literature to go beyond geographical boundaries.[4] Finally, the humanitarian character of the literary works allowed them to affect even European literature.[5]

Islamic culture is also characterized by a common intellectual legacy, both in philosophy and, in particular, history. Indeed, the ideas of certain prominent figures have travelled beyond geographical borders, both in and outside the Islamic world. Chief among these figures are Ibn Rushd, Al-Farabi, Ibn Khaldun and Al-Ghazzali.[6]

The same shared Islamic spirit left its mark on architecture and the other Islamic arts. Richard Athenghawzen said: Despite the differences 'in the dialects', so to speak, all works of art in Islam use the same language'. He added that the Islamic cachet is present in arts and industries, for instance, in Sicily and Andalusia, even after the return to Christian rule. Any change of government will lead to a change in the art-making. But, still, the Islamic influence remains. So, it is obvious that Islam had a big impact, even a vital impact, which affected all forms of art which flourished under Islam'.[7]

The common feature in the Islamic world is the Islamic revival'. What is meant by this, is that, in a sense, the Islamic spirit is returning to the body. There was an attempt to paralyze this collective body. However, it is now trying to regain its identity, its pride and its honour. This revival is evident from Tangiers to Jakarta, where the language used is one and where aspirations are one, even if the means advocated to achieve them are different. These similarities mean that, despite political, national and religious divisions, the people in the Islamic world stand united when faced with a decisive issue. The challenges they face are also very similar.

The divisions in the Islamic world are, first of all, political. I do not mean by political divisions, the existence of a multitude of parties, governments or groupings. What I mean by this is that there exists a conflict of interests between certain groups of modern Muslims. This conflict stems either from a personal reason, or can be ascribed to a foreign source' that has imposed its will on the political arena. It could even be the result of a combination of these two factors. The organization of Arab unity was unable to put an end to this conflict, because it was the result of a public outcry, an outcry the authorities wanted to contain following the burning of the Aksa Mosque. For years now, the Islamic people have avidly followed summit, ministerial and academic meetings on various issues; however, the political situation has continued to deteriorate. It will continue to deteriorate until precedence is given to Islamic interests over personal ones, and over the interests of the big powers – only then will these factional conflicts disappear; only then will the people commune with their governments so as to take the right decisions, in line with the true condition of Islam in the world. We hope to witness this very soon, thanks to the Islamic revival.

In this meeting, we can only recommend that decision-makers, prime ministers, party leaders and group leaders rise up to the occasion and fulfill the expectations of the *ummah*, while preserving our pride and honour. We wish them all the success in the world.

Other manifestations of divisions can be overcome with the help of the people attending this Arab-Iranian meeting, today. The divisions I am referring to are both national and religious in character.

I will devote a section to each category. We can, in this meeting, help to protect the *ummah* itself from exacerbating these divisions. To this end, we have to rectify the image of the Islamic world.

By doing so, Islamic communities will be able to carve their proper niche in the new world order (a subject which will be discussed in the course of this paper). However, I shall begin by discussing relations between Arabs and Iranians, so as to highlight the capacity of the Iranians and Arabs to fulfill the expectations of the Muslims when they pool their resources together.

The Characteristics of the Relationship between Iran and the Arab World

By relations, I do not means political, commercial or touristic relations. These are only the tip of the iceberg. For relations to endure, they should have a human dimension. Any rapprochement between two Islamic states will enjoy a human dimension if it can occur through the educated elite, provided that the elite expresses the conscience of the people in the Islamic world. However, the relationship between the Arabs and Iran is unique. Arabs and Iranians constitute the cement that holds the edifice of Islamic civilization together. Hence, the dialogue between them stands on solid ground, a rare occurrence, not only in the Islamic world but also in the international community.

Allow me to dwell on the party that contributed most to the founding of Islamic civilization. Who contributed more: was it the Arabs or the Iranians? This discussion usually takes place in the studies conducted by Arab and Iranian researchers. Some Iranian nationalists have said that the so-called 'Arab conquests' destroyed a great international civilization erected by the Iranians since the establishment of their empire. They add that the same Iranians have rebuilt another Iranian civilization after the advent of Islam, which was called the Islamic civilization'.[8] Iranian nationalists ascribed the cultural, scientific and Islamic activities in Iran to a nationalistic, rather than a purely religious, identity. It is regrettable that a number of Arab researchers have endorsed this line, and added that the Shu'ubiyyah – a hard-line anti-Arab movement – was the driving force behind the participation of Iranians in the building of the Islamic edifice of science and culture.[9] A number of Iranian and Arab researchers have underestimated the role of various other factors in the building of the Islamic civilization.[10]

When I listen to similar discussions, I submit an opinion, which is that of Islam, the Qur'an and history. I say the following: the credit for building Islamic civilization goes to Islam itself and not to any other community. Indeed, Islam paved the way for an interaction between Iranians and Arabs. This interaction or 'acquaintance' (as in the Qur'an) led to the prosperity of Islamic civilization, and to cultural and intellectual maturity. God has decreed that continuation of life on earth is only secured through the interaction between men and women; likewise, He has decreed that the continuation of civilizations is dependent on the interaction between the various communities and peoples.

The Holy Qur'an linked the interaction between people with the interaction between men and women. Thus, human survival is dependent on that interaction: 'O mankind! We created you from a single [pair] of a male and a female, and made you into nations and tribes, that you may know each other [not that you may despise each other].'[11]

The mere fact that international civilizations, along with the Islamic one, have thrived throughout history is testimony to the fact that the edifice of civilization will only be built through the efforts of many peoples.

Here is the gist of my thought: any rapprochement between the Iranians and the Arabs will restore to them the role they used to play in the march towards civilization. We have seen the fruits yielded by such a rapprochement in the past – in Basra, Kufa, Baghdad, Khwarazm, Nishapur, Isfahan, Hamadan and other cities. So, thanks to modern communication, we can extend these fruits to all Islamic countries, but only if the rapprochement between Iran and the Arabs occurs in a constructive framework.

Despite the divisions that plague relations between Arabs and Iranians, and despite religious and nationalist tensions that are artificially induced between the two peoples, their relations remain unique. Iran is among the first to express concern and support on any issue involving the Arabs. Even under the Shah who, for very well-known reasons, tried to drive a wedge between Arabs and Iranians, the Iranian people were very close to the Arabs and shared their concerns.

When the burgeoning Islamic revival began to take shape in the Arab world, the Iranian people were quick to respond, a response best illustrated by Nawab Safawi and Ayatollah Kashani. When the Iranian people called for the nationalization of oil, the Arabs greeted this suggestion with enthusiasm.[12] Needless to say, the position of the Iranian people is to support the Palestinian cause. On the other hand, many Arabs have expressed their support for the Islamic revolution in Iran.

It might seem strange that Nasser, who spearheaded the move to pan-Arabism, was very popular in Iran. Islamist prisoners used to listen very attentively to his positions. Indeed, a great Islamic leader has said to me: 'I wept when I heard of the death of Nasser, and I was in solitary confinement. I was very worried. My only comfort came from the radio; I was listening to recitations from the Qur'an on the station 'Voice of the Arabs'. When I asked him about his respect for Nasser – especially as he is a big admirer of Sayyed Qotb – he answered: 'What matters to me is the pride of the Arabs, because the pride of the Arabs is tightly linked to the pride of the Muslims. Nasser was the symbol of that pride. His death heralded the disappearance of that pride.'[13]

Finally, each side can build on its experience in order to facilitate a rapprochement between the various members of the Islamic fraternity. This can be achieved through unofficial dialogue – the sharing of language, culture and history, with the help of educational institutions and centres of scientific research – in addition to the official channels that are governed by political, economic and security considerations.

These unique characteristics give the Iranians and Arabs great leverage in the Islamic world. At the same time, Muslims are going to be subject, more than ever, to cultural invasion and attempts to distort their image in the eyes of the general public. I will demonstrate this point in the part entitled 'The rectification of the image'.

I would now like to return to the manifestations of divisions in the Islamic world. I will begin with nationalism.

The Phenomenon of Nationalism

Nationalism is a positive idea when it seeks to defend the pride of a community. However, it becomes a negative force if it collides with any other community. In the Islamic world this whole issue has an additional dimension, since certain forms of modern nationalism have aimed at the revival of the cultural heritage of the *jahiliyyah* era that preceded Islam. This revival clashes with Islam, especially as far as non-Arab communities are concerned. The result would be the emergence of a splinter of nations and the elimination of any similarities binding them. This sad situation reinforces the divisions imposed on the Islamic world, and paves the way for those who have designs on the region to sew conflict in the Islamic world. The revival of nationalism in the Islamic world is bound to cause divisions, along with a loss of interest in the big Islamic issues, in the cultural heritage written in Arabic, even in Arabic script. This would be a loss for Muslims in general, and Arabs in particular.

In Iran, there was a time when the Shah was very wary of the spread of Arab nationalism. He therefore harnessed academic energies to whip up nationalist sentiment.

Much ink flowed on extolling the virtues of Korush and Darius, and accusing the Arab conqueror of committing the worst acts.[14] While the plan to eliminate Arabic in Iran failed, however, it succeeded in Turkey and in parts of Africa.

The Islamic revolution uprooted nationalism the moment it came to power, eliminating any reference to it from the official emblem, the flag, official buildings and textbooks. What is both laughable and saddening is that the Islamic revolution came under fire for not decimating the Persian magus. This is indicative of the importance of nationalism, and its effect on events in the region.

The rapprochement between Arabs and Iranians has been, over the centuries, a model of forsaking nationalism in favour of promoting an atmosphere of understanding among the various communities. Arabs who had emigrated to Iran over the past centuries learned to speak Persian. Their children grew up speaking Persian as well.[15] Iranian scholars used Arabic to write their scientific findings.[16] Iranians even used Arabic in Islamic tax-collection departments.[17] In fact, the two languages cohabited and the mixture that resulted became the language of the Muslims in East and Central Asia. So, all scholars and writers, even the common man on the street, became familiar with both languages, Arabic and Persian.

One of the great images of the rapprochement between Arabs and other Muslims is when certain Arabs protected the Iranians from the discrimination and injustice prevalent under a number of Islamic rulers.[18]

The Iranians themselves have destroyed a few Iranian nationalist movements over the years.[19] Even today, any attempt to cast aspersions on the Arabs and the Arab conquest of Iran is firmly rejected by most Iranians.[20]

Needless to say, whipping up nationalist and anti-Islamic sentiments in the Islamic world is by no means restricted to Iran. These attempts were also registered in Indonesia and Turkey. Moreover, there was even an attempt to turn Arab nationalist advocates against Islam.

Islamic countries that have recently been freed from Soviet occupation are experiencing an identity crisis, torn between their national and their Islamic identity. The position of the Arab world, in this respect, has been regrettable. Most Islamic countries gave precedence to nationalist factors over Islamic ones. Tremendous efforts were made to keep the six independent states from acquiring the Arabic alphabet. They adopted the Latin alphabet instead of Arabic, alleging that the Latin alphabet is necessary in order to assimilate the concept of modern technology.[21]

A number of these same countries adopted a more positive position. However, the outcome remained dissapointing. The idea, according to certain reports, was to promote spontaneous cooperation between Iran and the Arabs, in order to make the Arabic alphabet available in these new republics. This spontaneous coordination has significance. The idea, however, was doomed to failure. The project consisted of sending typewriters with Arabic letters to the Islamic republics, with the help of the Islamic Development Bank. However, this project did not take shape because the Turkey convinced the Arabs that the spread of the Arabic alphabet would serve Iranian interests in central Asia.[22]

This is only an example of the national divisions plaguing the Islamic world, and of the opportunities that have been wasted as a result. However, a rapprochement between Iranians and Arabs represents the best opportunity available for moving beyond nationalist sensitivities, and establishing a framework of cooperation between the various Islamic communities.

Religious Divisions

The Islamic world is divided into Shi'a and Sunni. These divisions began in the 1st century AH. They were reinforced and strengthened as the years went by. These divisions can be ascribed to a disagreement over the interpretation of certain historical events, and over some religious principles. However, that is not the end of the story; in fact, this schism entails complex scholastic disagreements, much discussed by scholars. They might agree or they might differ. This comes as no surprise, for it is common in such discussions. But the matter has yet another dimension. One the one hand, we find the Shiite community, on the other, the Sunni. The allegiance of the people to either community is not based on creed or school of thought; it is far more emotive in character than that. Thus, scientific discussion would not solve the issue; there is a need for discussion at a more basic and populist level. I personally think that the Iranians and Arabs are more than able to tackle this issue.

It is worth mentioning that some studies conducted by certain extremists claim that the conversion to Shi'ism started in Iran. The Arabs who made these allegations sought to slander Shi'ism. Whereas Iranians have tended to commend their national spirit, which was able to resist pressure and maintain its strength in a religious framework – modelled on the Sassanian culture – and taking the form of conversion to Shi'ism.[23] Moreover, a number of commentators have said that the Iranian allegiance to 'Ali was due to the fact that he had Iranian blood in his veins; in fact his mother was an Iranian princess by the name of Shahrabanu, the daughter of the last Sassanian King, Yazdigird.[24]

I am not trying to refute every single allegation made on this issue. Rather, I am merely trying to highlight the point that these religious divisions were not caused by nationalism. History confirms that Iranians converted to Islam gradually, of their own volition. They were in no way coerced, as has been alleged.[25]

The last Iranian King, Yazdigird, had to flee his throne. He roamed Iranian cities, seeking shelter. However, he was not taken in by anyone. This is a testimony to the fact that the Iranian people loathed their unjust ruler.[26] If the Iranians were forced to hide their identity over the first two decades of Arab rule, as some allege, why did they continue to serve Islam and reinforce their Islamic identity after the decline of the caliphate?![27]

It is also worth mentioning that the notion that Shahrbanu was married to Hussein bin 'Ali is far from certain and is not backed by historical facts. Had the deference the Iranians had towards 'Ali been due to the fact that one of his descendants is of Sassanian origin, then it would have been more logical for them to swear their allegiance to the Caliph al-Walid bin Abdel Malek and his son Yazid bin al-Walid, for the caliph was married to an Iranian princess, who gave birth to Yazid. Or, they would have sworn allegiance to Obeid Allah bin Ziad, because his mother, Merjana, was Iranian. Or they would have sworn allegiance to the Abbasid caliphs, because most of their mothers were Iranian.[28]

Most importantly, most Iranians used to be Sunni; some of them were even anti-Shi'a. They refused to stop swearing at 'Ali even after the Caliph Amr bin Abdel Aziz prohibited it. Most Iranian scholars were also Sunni.[29] The strange thing is that the people of Egypt used to abide by the edict (*fatwa*) of an Iranian scholar by the name of Leith bin Said. However, most Iranians used to abide by the instructions of an Arab scholar by the name of Shafi'i. A number of Iranian scholars, like Juwaini and Ghazzali were opposed to the doctrine espoused by Abi Hunei fah from Iran, whereas they were in favour of Shafi'i's doctrine.[30]

It is curious to note that Abu Huneifah decreed that Iranians were inferior to Arabs; therefore an Arab should not marry an Iranian. However, Malek bin Anas rejected this edict and thought Arabs and Iranians equal.[31]

The list goes on and on. The bottom line is that the conversion to Shi'ism was rarely due to nationalist causes. This situation, however, changed as a result of the conflict between the Ottoman and Safavid Empires. During the Safavid era, Iran became the representative of the Shi'a; the Ottoman Empire, on the other hand, became the representative of the Sunni. There is evidence that these divisions were fostered by countries with designs on the Islamic world. Regrettably, nationalist groups in Iran and the Arab world, along with Orientalists, went out of their way to find the historical terms that would exacerbate religious sensitivities. These trends – taken alongside the general anti-Islamic sentiment that was being fostered at the time – were extremely divisive, and militated against attempts to replace the conflict between these two civilizations with a dialogue between Islam and the West. All of these tendencies have served to legitimize and strengthen the views of Western thinkers such as Samuel Huntington.[32]

Whether we ascribe the religious turmoil raging in the Islamic world to internal or external factors, the fact remains that massacres have occured in Pakistan and Afghanistan. Moreover, the Islamic world is the scene of bloody conflicts in North Africa and Central Asia, in which Islamic language and symbols play a significant part. These conflicts have had dire consequences for those Muslims who have strayed in the past, and for the adherents of other religions. There are, indeed, many people who wanted to convert to Islam, but have been dissuaded by these scenes of violence and civil war.

It is possible that the future dialogue between the Iranians and the Arabs will revolve around religion. Irrespective of the outcome, a dialogue that focuses on religion per se will produce a more constructive and rational dialogue.

The Arabs and Iranians have succeeded in this respect, in the past, through the Establishment for Rapprochement between Islamic Sects in Cairo.[33] Today, attempts are being made to build on this experiment in Iran through the 'international academy'. We hope, finally, that the dialogue between the Arabs and Iranians, particularly between university graduates and intellectuals, will be another step in the way of overcoming religious divisions in the Islamic world.[34]

The Rectification of the Image

The Islamic world is at present the subject of a massive propaganda attack aimed at distorting its image, especially in Central Asia, so as to dissuade Central Asian countries from embracing the Islamic fraternity. The propaganda revolves around three axes: backwardness, terrorism, and threats to civilization. Furthermore, it continues despite the contradiction existing between the first point and third and the deception that surrounds the second point.

There is nothing new about this campaign of distortion. Indeed, the image of the Arabs and Muslims that is etched in the minds of Europeans is one of Saracens and tent-dwellers,[35] uncivilized people who make their living by plunder. On the eve of European triumphs, the Europeans used to give free rein to their imagination, portraying the Arabs as 'ignorant' or the 'ignorance of the triumphant rider', as Southern said.[36] Muslims were blamed for every atrocity. However, when the tables were turned and the Arabs were the winners, the Europeans were quick to propose negotiations. For example, when Constantinople was overrun by the Muslims, Juan de Segovia (1400–1458) proposed a series of conferences to which Islamic scholars would be invited. He was convinced that this was a constructive idea, even if the various parties kept to their religious beliefs.[37] If Muslims do not show respect for themselves and protect their pride, how can they expect others to respect them?

In my opinion, the Islamic world will remain vulnerable to attacks so long as it remains weak. Furthermore, I think that the Islamic revival must be harnessed to improve the image of Islam in the eyes of the world, and in the former Soviet Islamic republics in particular. In addition to this, it is necessary that we allow Islam to carve its proper niche in the new world order.

When we say we have to improve our image, I do not mean by that we have to tailor it to please the West. That would be illogical, and a testimony to our defeat and dependency on the West. What I mean is that it is necessary to clear the true and real image of any impurities that may have resulted from improper internal conduct or misguided external acts. I will expand on this issue, focusing on three imperatives: Rectifying the Islamic message; unveiling the human face of Islam; calling for a dialogue between civilizations.

The Islamic Message

The Islamic message was consistent with social developments during past centuries. Islam has always been portrayed in a language understandable to all; it was able to assimilate all new discoveries and knowledge. Reason was used to solve many intractable problems. However, Islam always recognized that there are limits constraining the mind and reason. This commendable position was later undermined. As a result, ijtihad was rejected, and there emerged schools that rejected the role of logic or reason. There was a refusal – based largely on fear – to open up to others. Islam was confined to an image devoid of content and spiritual aspects. The schools were unable to portray the true image of Islam; they depicted a distorted image that did not respond to the aspirations of the Muslims, who wanted to play a role in the march towards human civilization. This stagnation in the Islamic message is still seen, even in newly converted communities.

Information trickling from Central Asia has it that the missionaries are calling on people to stop shaving, to wear short outfits and to stop visiting the cemeteries. Despite their good intentions, those missionaries are doing more harm than good by clashing with reality and leaving a bad impression on people.

On the other hand, there have been reactions against this stagnation. We have heard people calling for modernization. However, this reaction was blown out of proportion, as is usually the case with such trends.

It is impossible to rectify this image, and to protect against stagnation, unless Islamic studies re-adopt ijtihad and abide by its Islamic rules and constraints. Ijtihad is the norm within Shiite circles. Iran can build on its experience in this aspect of Islamic jurisprudence and can, therefore, direct the Islamic message in the right direction, away from the negative aspects of the current situation. Moreover, the Arab world should open up to international trends, in order to make the content of Islamic rhetoric more modern, and more in line with the needs of contemporary life.

All new attempts made to combine the old values with modernization should be met with enthusiasm and respect.

The Human Face of Islam

In the West, people tend to equate Islam with terrorism. Indeed, much ink has flowed concerning the forced conversion of people to Islam. These allegations have been given credence by many fabrications concerning the Islamic world.[38] The best examples are the tales told by certain Orientalists, and by nationalist movements in non-Arab Islamic countries, that are hostile to Islamic conquests. These stories usually overlook the atrocities experienced by Muslims during the Crusades, during the European colonization of Islamic territories and, currently, in Bosnia-Herzegovina at the hands of the Serbs. Instead, these stories highlight the operations conducted by the Lebanese and Islamic resistance movements and the actions of some Islamists in Europe.

I would like to draw your attention to a very important idea. Following the victory of the Islamic revolution, and during the war between Iraq and Iran, the media in the West went out of their way to link the Islamic revolution to terrorist actions. As this revolution, in the view of supporters and detractors, is one of the main achievements of the Islamic revival, it seems that the Islamic revival is being equated with terrorism. Indeed, this is a conviction that is acquiring more and more circulation: Terrorism and Islamic revival go hand in hand. The impact of such a conviction is as follows: a growing fear of the Islamic revival and its leaders, who are deemed to be very dangerous.

A number of small groups have carried out terrorist acts to achieve their goals, thinking that they are following in the footsteps of the Islamic revolution in Iran. These groups are surprised to hear that the Islamic revolution did not take up arms to achieve its goals. Khomeini sidelined those who took up arms and promoted peaceful actions. He instructed his followers to replace fire with flowers. His slogan was always that blood will triumph over the sword. This latter statement may surprise some, for the media has been repeating for years that the revolution triumphed through massacres and coercion.

Undoubtedly, the goal behind equating terrorism with Islam is to suppress the Islamic identity and dignity. The people making these allegations are fully aware of what they are doing. It is obvious that they want to incite the Europeans against the Muslims. As Roufeil said in his book *The Revival of Democracy*: 'We cannot allege that a religion is clement when we see that diversity leads to elimination according to its teachings ... Islam is the main source of terrorism.' He then adds: 'Do we have to protect our theatres, offices and museums from fanaticism? They want to control our culture retroactively.'[39]

There is an attempt, as well, to stir in the minds of the Europeans memories of terrorist acts carried out by local groups, and exploit these memories in order to turn them against Islam. Claire Hollingworth, a journalist who is an authority on military issues, wrote an article entitled 'Another Despotic Religion tries to Infiltrate into the West'. In it she wrote: 'Islamic fundamentalism is becoming very quickly the main threat to world peace and security and the main cause of internal turmoil. Islamic fundamentalism is a threat similar to Fascism and Nazism in the thirties and Communism in the fifties.'[40]

A constructive dialogue between Arabs and Iranians could unveil the human aspects of Islam as regards *jihad* (struggle) conquest and the use of force. Iranians and Arabs are more equipped to achieve this goal, because they have a common cultural heritage and a common history stretching as far back as Iranian-Arab cooperation on the eve of the conquest of Iran.

Dialogue between the Civilizations

There is a radical difference between Western and Eastern civilization; the former being very materialistic, the latter, the birthplace of many prophets.[41] This difference degenerated into wars over the years, starting with the Crusades. Today, with the Islamic desire to regain its true identity in the new world order, this tension is taking another form; warnings are being issued against the spread of Islamic culture in the West. In his famous paper 'The Clash of Civilizations?', Samuel Huntington stated that the main source of future conflict will be culture and that World War III, if it happens, will rage between Western civilization and the Islamic one'.[42] The fears gripping the Western world are expressed in the crudest forms – as was the case with the female Muslim students wearing veils to school in France. Some in the West go so far as to say: if we give ground now, Muslims will force us to wear the veil in the near future. A Swedish politician expressed her concern about the spread of Islam in Scandinavian countries by saying: How long will it take before our children in Sweden kneel turning their heads to Mecca for prayer?'[43]

Some Western analysts have exposed what they believe to be the reasons behind this fear of Islam. They think that the danger lies in the vacuum caused by the lack of faith and values in the West.[44]

The West refuses to acknowledge the presence of the other party; it is bent on drafting plans to uproot and eliminate it. Richard Nixon, the former US President, proposed support for the advocates of modernization in the Arab world as a means to fight off the Islamic threat.[45] By advocates of 'modernization' he meant those who want to distance themselves from the Islamic identity and become integrated in Western culture. Huntington thinks that democracy will favour anti-Western forces. This means that the will of the people will favour the establishment of the Islamic identity. He goes on to call for the adoption of alternatives that will drain the potentialities of the Islamic world.[46]

Had these calls been sparse, it would not have mattered. But it is certain that these views are affecting the decisions taken about the Islamic world. Hence, there is a need to replace 'The Clash of Civilizations' with the dialogue between civilizations'. This dialogue should be based on Islamic principles, which favour the use of peaceful means of 'persuasion and wisdom and good advice'. Islam says: 'come and take part in an equal dialogue', and you and I are either right or wrong together'.

After the success of the revolution, Iran started a serious dialogue with the Christians of the West. Furthermore, there are links binding the Arabs to the West – particularly in the realm of intellectual heritage. We hope that the dialogue between Arabs and Iranians will lead to a plan to open a dialogue with Western intellectuals, so as to improve the status of the Islamic world in the new world order, and to spare Muslims the disasters caused by any future clash of civilizations.

Conclusion

Despite its divisions, the Islamic world is one civilization with clear-cut characteristics and features, and a unified position when faced with internal or external pressure. Given this unity, it seems that the whole world has adopted a united stance as regards Islam, and it seems that the whole Islamic world is being placed under pressure in the new world order.

The Islamic world will be able to carve its place in the world when it strengthens its identity and overcomes all the impediments preventing it from asserting itself and presenting a united front. Given their history, and the important role they play in the Islamic revival, both Iranians and Arabs occupy centre place in the Islamic world. They also stand together on the frontline of the Western onslaught.

The dialogue between Arabs and Iranians can help them achieve the goals that all Muslims desire: to enable Muslims to live in dignity, reclaim their former role, and participate in the progress of human civilization.

Notes

* Centre for Arab-Iranian Studies, Tehran, Iran.

1. The poet is Soueid Ben Abi Kahel Alichekri. He says in his poem: 'Longing provoked the imagination of a visitor from a lover, shy and timid.' See: Al-Mafdaliat, pp. 191–2.

2. Mohammed Baqr El-Sadr, Our Economy, ([n.pb.]: Association of the Martyr Al-Sadr for Scientific and Cultural Studies, [n.d.]), p. 21.

3. The events that took place prior to the attack on the Aksa Mosque, and the attack on the Prophet (in the Sulman Rushdie case).

4. The poems written by Al-Mutanabbi are widespread in Iran, and critical of his own life. El-Saheb ben Abbad wrote a book entitled The Disclosure of Mutanabbi's Deficiencies.

5. See Franz Rosenthal, in: The Heritage of Islam, annotated by Shakhth and Bozorth, translated by Hussein Moueness and Ihsan Sadki El-Amad, reviewed by Fouad Zakaria in The World of Knowledge, 2 vols., 2nd ed., (Kuwait: National Council of Culture, Arts and Letters, 1988), vol. 2, chpt. 7 (Literature).

6. See George Kanawati, in ibid., vol. 2, chpt. 8 (Philosophy, Scholastic Science and Asceticism).

7. See The Heritage of Islam, annotated by Shakhth and Bozorth, translated by Mohammad Zuhair El-Samhoury, Hussein Moueness and Ihsan Sadki al-Ahmad, commentary and research by Chaker Mustafa, reviewed by Fuad Zakaria in The World of Knowledge, op. cit., vol. 1, ch. 6 (Architecture and Art), pp. 406–8.

8. Fereidun Adamiyat, A Great Prince and Iran, vol. 1, pp. 74-75, and Murtadha Mutahhari, Mutual Services between Islam and Iran, 12th ed., (Tehran: Sadra Publications, 1362 AH), p. 384.

9. See Hussein Atwan, Atheism and Shu'ubiyyah in the Abbasid Era.

10. See Mutahhari, op. cit., p. 384 ff. Also: Omar Faroukh, The History of Arab Thought until Ibn Khaldun, Beirut: Dar El-'Ilm lil Malayeen, 1972; Ali Husni Kharbotalli, The Islamic Arab State, Cairo: Revival of Arab Books Publishing House, 1960; Samira Mukhtar Lissi, Atheism and Shououbia and the Triumph of Islam, Cairo: Angelo Library, 1968; Mohammad Nabih Hijab, The Manifestations of Shououbia in Arab Literature until the End of the 13th Century (A.H), Cairo: The Renaissance of Egypt Library, 1961.

11. The Holy Qur'an, Surat al-Hujurat, ayah 13.

12. See, for instance, the poem 'The Vanguard', written by Ahmad Zaki Abu Shadi, in the eulogy of Dr Hussein Fatemi, one of the ministers in the government

headed by Dr Musaddiq, who was assassinated in 1954: Mohammad Abdel Menhem Khafagi, *The Vanguard of Modern Poetry*, (Cairo: [n.pb.], 1955), vol. 2, p. 361.

13. I ask the reader's forgiveness in not revealing his name, knowing that he would not agree to my doing so. However, I hope that his memoirs will be published in Arabic (his native tongue) very soon, including this information.

14. The Shah organized a number of festivities, to celebrate the 25th anniversary of the advent of the Shahanshahi, by the tomb of Kurush. He, furthermore, replaced the Islamic calendar with the Shahnashahi calender. Iranian academic circles went on to study the history of Iran before the advent of Islam.

15. Abiordi was an Arab poet, born in Abiord in Khurasan. Though an Arab poet, his mother tongue was Persian. He said: 'I spent twenty years in Baghdad so as to adapt myself and acquire an Arabic accent, because I have a foreign accent when speaking in Arabic.' See Shawki Deif, *The History of Arabic Literature*, (Cairo: Maaref Publishing House, [n.d.]), section 5, p. 600.

16. Until today, they do not match, for example, Tabataba'i and his interpretation of *The Balance* into Arabic, or Khomeini's interpretation of *To Free the Means* into Arabic..

17. Saleh Abdel Rahman translated it into Arabic from Persian. He is Iranian. See Abu El-Farag Mohammad Ben Ishaq Ben Al-Nadim, *An Index Containing the Names of Old and Contemporary Scientists as Well as the Titles of the Books They Wrote*, seventh article (the article of the philosophers), pp. 252–3.

18. See Tabari (9/1352) about a complaint lodged by Abi El-Saida to Amr Ben Abdel Aziz. El-Saida went to see Ben Abdel Aziz from Khurasan. He complained that 20,000 non-Muslim fighters had been raiding hamlets alongside the Arabs and that some of them had converted to Islam and were paying taxes. He also complained about the fact that the Amir was stand-offish and very nervous.

19. Mutahhari, 'Mutual Services between Islam and Iran', op. cit., p. 115.

20. Ibid. Shahid Murtaza Mutahhari strongly defends the Arab–Islamic conquest and Islamic civilization against Iranian nationalists like Purdavud and Fereidun Adamiyat.

21. Central Asia: 'The Battle of the Alphabets and the Turkish Scalpel', *Turkish Affairs*, no. 8 (1993), p. 66.

22. *Ibid.*, p. 68.

23. Mutahhari, op. cit., p. 140 ff.

24. Parviz Sani'i, *The Law*, (Tehran: University of Tehran Publications, [n.d.]), p. 157, and Edward Brown, *History of Iranian Literature*, Persian translation, p. 195.

25. Mathari, op. cit., chapter entitled The Gradual, Calm Spread', p. 103 ff.

26. The Persian translation of the book written by Arthur Christensen, *Iran under the Reign of the Sassanians* , p. 528.

27. Mutahhari, op. cit., p. 145 ff.

28. See Jalal El-Din Abdel Rahman bin Abi Bakr Siouti, *The History of the Caliphs*.

29. Mutahhari, op. cit., p. 145 ff.

30. *Ibid.*, p. 34.

31. *Ibid.*, p. 134.

32. Samuel Huntington, 'The Clash of Civilizations?', *Mountalak magazine*,

no. 106 (Winter 1994); an extract from *Middle Eastern Affairs*, no. 34 (October 1994).

33.   Abdel Magid Salim, 'A Manifesto for Muslims', Letter from *Islam Magazine*, no. 1. Abdel Magid Salim is the Chairman of the Fatwah Committee at Al-Azhar and the responsible official of the Rapprochement Group: Mahmoud Shaltout (imam at Al-Azhar, 1958-1964), Mahmoud Abu Zahra, Mohammad Mohammad Al-Madani, and Abdel Aziz Issa.

34.   The locale of this academy is Tehran. It publishes a quarterly journal under the title *The Message of Rapprochement*. Its higher council consists of scholars and thinkers. It adopts comparative studies according to the seven schools of thought: Shafi'i, Hanbali, Maliki, Hanafi, Imami, Zeidi and Abadi.

35.   Les Sarrazins, from Saracenus in Latin (Sarakenos in Greek), meaning tent-dwellers'.

36. Maxime Rodinson, 'Western Image and Western Islamic Studies', in: *The Heritage of Islam*, op. cit., vol. 1, chpt. 1, p. 27 ff.

37.   *Ibid.*, p. 54.

38.   Murtaza Al-Askari discussed these stories, showed their falseness and considered them as contrived by Seif bin Omar. See Abdullah bin Saba's book, vol. 2.

39.   Joseph Smaha, 'The End of History and the Various Reactions', *Ijtihad*, vol. 4, nos. 15-16 (Spring-Summer 1992), p. 303, from *Middle East Affairs*, no. 34 (October 1994).

40.   Fred Halliday, 'Ideologies or Anti-Islamic Ideologies', *Al-Hayat* daily, 11 May 1994, from *Middle East Affairs*, no. 34 (October 1994).

41.   See *Our Economy*, introduction.

42.   The Clash of Civilizations?', first published in 1993 in *Foreign Affairs*; from *Middle East Affairs*, no. 34 (October 1994).

43.   Halliday, Ideologies or Anti-Islamic Ideologies', op. cit.

44.   *Ibid.*

45.   In his book entitled *Seize the Moment*; from *Middle East Affairs*, no. 34 (October 1994), p. 38.

46.   'The Clash of Civilizations?', p. 195.

27

The Place of Arab–Iranian Relations in the Islamic World

MICHEL NAWFAL*

Introduction

This study of the position of Arab–Iranian relations in the geo-politics of the Islamic world rests on an analysis of both the facts, and the conventions, of inter-state relations in the heartland of the Islamic world; that is, the whole space in which the three Arab, Iranian and Turkish circles intersect and adjoin. This vital space is what the Egyptian geographer, Gamal Hamdan, calls 'the regional power triangle'.[1]

The study has also chosen to consider the nature of the correlation between the regional and the international spheres as a prelude to an examination of the impact of the world transformations on the regional relations, and specifically Arab–Iranian relations. The main purpose of this examination is to attempt to establish new criteria for the analysis of international relations in the region, in the light of the changed priorities and perspectives of the post-Soviet age.

The major transformations in the world arena, since Mikhail Gorbachev came to power in the former Soviet Union in 1985, have come to be considered as a full-blown revolution in the framework of international relations. These changes have affected both global balances of power the international division of roles and distribution of resources.[2] The most significant of these changes is, of course, the end of the bipolar framework of international relations. As a consequence of this change, the geo-political concepts in the whole world have undergone a process of radical transformation.[3] This process has altered the 'traditional' balance of power in the Middle East region, an area of the world that was particularly deeply enmeshed in the politics of the bipolar system.

In addition, the disintegration of the Soviet Union towards the end of 1990 made the Islamic geo-political space – that was closed from the north by the Soviet borders – open to the regions of Central Asia and the Caucasus. As a result of this, the Iranian and Turkish spheres became closer to the heartland of the political geography of the Arab world.[4] Some analysts have claimed that this transformation in Islamic geo-politics has led to the transfer of the centre of Islamic geo-politics,[5] and that the Arab order is now threatened with retreat to a marginal position.[6] One of the main indications of this trend could well be the acceptance by the Arabs and the Israelis of the principle of the comprehensive settlement that was established in Madrid in the fall of 1991, and the attempt to legitimize the new role of Israel as a normal state and a partner in the new regional order of the Middle East.[7] Relying on this analysis, the Arab-Israeli peace is likely – if it becomes comprehensive – to diminish the role ofthe Arab Mashriq in the regional and international equation.

Even before the Arab-Israeli settlement entered its current course, many commentators felt that the international transformations mentioned above had made both the Arabs and the Iranians face the challenges of a new regional order that could marginalize both their roles. If a Middle Eastern market – including a fully integrated Israel – becomes a fact, then the Arab states risk a sharp decline in their geo-political importance. At the same time, Iran faces continued isolation, due to its perceived role as the major global representative of political Islamism and 'Islamic terrorism'.

A counter argument is supported by certain Egyptian researches, which suggest that the Arab regional order has acquired enough historical flexibility to maintain an active and significant role in global politics. Nevertheless, these same sources also conclude that such an outcome is dependent on the level of coordination or solidarity between the Arab positions, based on their sound evaluation of the actual opportunities and restraints in the international order.[8] However, if the current stage of development of relations between the two orders is characterized by acuteness of the Arab divisions, we should also realize that the international order itself is still in a transitional stage, with every indication that the world is moving towards a multi-polar order.[9]

Thus, we can clearly see that, in order to analyze contemporary Arab–Iranian relations, it is necessary to begin by examining the results of these global transformations, and their impact on Arab and Iranian policies. This is particularly important, since the Palestinian cause – and what it represents in the Arab-Israeli struggle – has been, for a long time, the most constant and binding factor in the political relations (and rhetoric) of the region.

In light of what has been stated above, this study can be divided into three main axes:

1. Defining the conceptual and value frameworks of the analysis.
2. Analysing the international phenomena that affect Arab–Iranian relations.

3. Observing the various patterns of interaction between Iran and the Arab system.

The Conceptual and Value Framework

In formulating its view of the Islamic neighbouring countries, and especially Iran and Turkey, nationalist Arab thought has relied on certain structured conceptions. The most dominant of these conceptions holds that the region that extends from Mauritania to the Gulf is controlled by an Arab system that is characterized by cultural, linguistic and ethnic homogeneity, as well as intensive and positive interactions between its members. This system is held to be an 'Arab regional order', with all the characteristics of a regional order.[10] Consequently, the states that do not belong to this Arab order came to be considered as 'geographically neighbouring countries'. Thus, Iran and Turkey were considered as such, as were Israel and Ethiopia.

This nationalist conception of the regional order made these neighbouring countries appear as a threat to the identity and national security of the Arab regional order.[11] This perception was, in part, justified by the foreign policies of Turkey and imperial Iran, whose actions were in general hostile to the Arab liberation movement – especially their coordination with the Western strategies, their collaboration with Israel and their rejection of non-alignment policy.

This view was also justified by the mechanisms of the bipolar order, which reproduced the global US–Soviet conflict in the form of a regional tension between Iran and the majority of the Arab states. Yet some observers have criticised this conceptual framework for failing to distinguish between the inclinations of the ruling establishments in Turkey and Iran, and the religious, cultural and geo-political links between the Arab, Turkish and Iranian peoples. Consequently, this common basis has not led to investment in building regional cooperation organizations. This failure, in turn, increased foreign infiltration into the region, and the spread of the phenomenon of regional polarization.[12] Other observers adopt a different analysis, linking the reasons for this inability to the strategic and Islamic positions of the Arab countries, and to their subjective ability to become superpowers. That is why those observers have stressed the necessity of understanding 'the specific way by which Western colonialism has dealt with the regional power triangle', and especially the strategic decision of the superpowers to divide the region.[13]

When the Islamic transformation took place in Iran in 1979, the Arab nationalist crisis was at its peak in the aftermath of the split that was caused by Egyptian recognition of Israel in 1978. This had led to a severe questioning of the effectiveness of the common defence treaty and economic cooperation between the Arab countries. The Islamic elite in Iran believed that the time was ripe for a reshaping of Arab policies. For it saw that the new Iranian policy, which opposed Israel and US hegemony, could have an impact on the Arab region, especially through the adoption of the Palestinian cause and the Arab resistance against the Israeli occupation as the fundamental cause of the Islamic struggle on both the political and the religious levels. Thus, the Islamic republic in Iran made it clear that it saw the Israeli presence in the region as a threat to the entire Islamic *ummah*, rather than as a specifically Arab concern.[14]

Until recently, the Iranian approach to the Arab region was dominated by the view of the 'Jihad in Palestine', despite the fact that the importance of national interests was visible in many of the Islamic government's decisions in the period that followed the war with Iraq.[15]

The intellectual climate in post-revolutionary Iran, however, led to an overestimation of the role of the Islamic awakening, and a lack of readiness to view the relationship between Islam and Arabism through an objective approach that takes into consideration the experiences of Arab history and society.[16] This conceptual outlook also failed to give proper weight to the changes that had occurred in the dominant values in the Arab order, which represented the political and cultural climate in which the various Arab policies were developed in the 1950s and the 1960s, the most significant of which being the change towards Israel and the willingness to recognize the Zionist entity. Such a transformation might have started when most of the Arab countries accepted UN Security Council resolution 242, providing for the recognition of secure and recognized borders of all the countries in the Middle East, including Israel.[17]

The Arab order has entered, of late, into a new stage in the long struggle against Israel, in which its options and capacities appear radically diminished.[18] This stage, in contrast to the previous stages – that drained Arab resources but boosted their morale – seems to be a last confrontation that is geared towards the imposition on the Arab order of an unbalanced settlement. Such a settlement threatens the perceived cultural legitimacy of the regional Arab order. The first condition is that the US-sponsored negotiations should take place on a bilateral level between Israel on the one hand, and each of the Arab states and entities concerned, including the Palestine Liberation Organization, on the other. Furthermore, each bilateral track should end in an agreement that provides for securing a new peaceful relationship, or so-called 'normalization'.

The second condition involves securing the necessary guarantees to ensure that Israel is no longer a marginal power outside the Arab order. For Israel will no longer deal with an 'order' in the region unless it is a full member of that order. Thus, a new order will emerge, the 'new Middle

East' order that is based on the following hypothesis: 'Peace between Israel and its Arab neighbours will create an adequate environment for a radical re-organization of Middle Eastern institutions, and reconciliation and the Arab acceptance of Israel as a nation that enjoys equal rights and duties, will trigger a new kind of cooperation...'[19] But if this cannot be achieved in the near future, then Israel will guarantee, through bilateral agreements, the building of a series of bilateral and trilateral 'orders' that would include Israel as one of their members. Moreover, the interaction of these sub-orders would, in effect, take priority over the interaction of their Arab members with other Arab states which do not interact with Israel.[20]

The third condition enables the bilateral negotiations, and the settlements they lead to, to be conducted under the *fait accompli* of Israeli supremacy, so that the resulting settlements and commitments are pre-designed to reflect the existing regional imbalance.

The fourth condition is to bring about a major change in Arab political thought and collective consciousness by means of opening Arab states and their populations to the Western concept of the Middle East, thus negating the Islamic and Arab identity of the region. It also calls for the reformation of the Arab concept of Zionism – whether as an ideology or a political movement – and of Israel, in order to justify the legitimacy of its existence in the region.

In light of the bilateral Israeli-Palestinian agreements, and the Israeli-Jordanian treaty, it could be said that Arab fragmentation has reached an unprecedented level, especially since, in the aftermath of the second Gulf war, the region has come under the hegemonic influence of the US. Many major Arab states have been forced to isolate themselves, thus confirming the inability of the Arab order to formulate a unified nationalist strategy,[21] Many states are also faced with internal turmoil, that may pave the way for a state of chaos in the region, similar to that which has characterized the Balkans in recent years.

An exceptional situation has thus arisen in the contemporary history of the Middle East, at the centre of which lies the abandonment, on the part of the Jewish state (a state that represents, from a geo-political viewpoint, a Western 'hermitage' in the middle of the Arab regions) of the garrison state/sanctuary concept, in order to adopt a concept of integration into the region on the basis of exchanging occupied lands for peace and recognition (the Israeli-Palestinian Declaration of Principles regarding the interim measures for self-rule, signed in Washington on 13 September 1993).[22] In view of this geo-political transformation, Iran is shielding itself behind the rejection in principle of any settlement of the Arab-Israeli conflict through negotiations. But it seems to lack a realistic overall strategic vision of the region, especially in the field of regional cooperation that the Israeli suggestions concentrate on.[23] The most dangerous of these suggestions is the call for a conference on security and cooperation in the Middle East similar to the one established in Europe.[24]

Some might say that the Islamic religious view regarding Palestine and Jerusalem dictates that the Islamic government in Iran should distance itself from all policies, measures or plans that aim to review the alleged *Shari'ah* judgement concerning the land of Palestine, which sees Israel as an aggressor and usurper.[25]

But the Clinton Administration's approach towards the Middle East makes one believe that the attempt to reach a disengagement in the Middle East (by finding a settlement for the Arab-Israeli conflict) that coincides with the rush of some members of the Arab order to establish good relations with Israel, aims at separating Iran from regional Arab policies. Such an attempt, if successful, would clearly weaken the link that equates common Islamic identity with the Palestinian cause, as the 'first or central cause' of Arabs and Muslims alike.[26]

Furthermore, some Western diplomats believe that the same policy considerations that impelled the US to dictate a certain timing for 'a comprehensive settlement' in the Middle East, after having contained Iraq in the second Gulf war (in order to attend to the 'Islamic threat' that is manifest in Iran and the Islamic upheaval), are directly mirrored by the considerations that urge the Islamic Republic to maintain its correlation with the Palestinian/Israeli issue, through its emphasis on the concept of Islamic solidarity and its support of the Islamic Arab and Palestinian movements opposed to both the settlement and normalization with the Jewish state.[27]

The International Environment and Rebuilding Relations

The divergence in Arab–Iranian relations was nourished by the colonial partitions of the region that took place after the First World War. These partitions created a distance between the parties of the 'regional power triangle'. However, the changes the world order has undergone since the beginning of the nineties militate in the direction of ending such a state of affairs. The most prominent of these changes are the collapse of the Socialist bloc, the disintegration of the Soviet state and, consequently, the end of the Cold War and the bipolar system. The world order has entered a transitional phase that is characterized by competition between the US, Japan and Europe within the framework of the seven industrialized states. Whilst, on a global level, this group of states seeks to impose its political and economic hegemony over the states of the South.[28]

The second half of the eighties witnessed a convergence of a number of gradual changes, which resulted in certain radical transformations to the international order. The most important of these transformations was the collapse of the Soviet Union as a global power.[29]

This was also linked with the swift and concerted action of the US to dismantle the military and political mechanisms of the Cold War, which led to a series of nuclear and conventional non-proliferation agreements, as well as a political and ideological rapprochement that was manifest in the US–Soviet summits, and other larger European ones within the framework of the Conference for Security and Cooperation in Europe.[30] These initiatives were accompanied by the emergence of an ideological vacuum, following the perceived collapse of the Marxist alternative to liberal capitalism. This vacuum has precipitated a state of chaos, which expressed itself most clearly in the rebellion of Soviet nations and their internal ethnic struggles. Thus, the Soviet Union disintegrated (after the coup of August 1991 was thwarted) and was replaced by a commonwealth of independent states.[31]

The collapse of the Soviet Union represented a strategic gain for Iran, which had suffered, since the late nineteenth century, from the problem of a strong neighbour to the north. When the Islamic revolution was victorious in 1979, the Soviet Union held fast to the terms of the treaty it had signed with Iran in 1931, especially articles 5 and 6 giving the Soviet Union the right to interfere militarily in certain circumstances.[32]

Thus, it seems that these developments have freed Iran from its security concerns and enabled it to revitalize its role in the Gulf and the Arab East. Moreover, the demise of Communism amounted to an ideological triumph for Iran, since the Islamic revolution emphasized from the very beginning its rejection of the communist and capitalist models, and advocated Islam as a means of liberating the 'oppressed' from the hegemony of the oppressors in both capitalist and socialist camps.

But the disappearance of the Soviet Union also created new challenges for Iran. The first of these challenges was Tehran's loss of the ability to make use of the ideological differences between the two superpowers. During the bipolar system, Iran was in a position to exploit the US concern over Soviet expansion in the Middle East, especially the Gulf, on the one hand, and to blackmail the Soviet Union, which was opposed to Western policies, on the other.

The situation became different when the Russian President Boris Yeltsin signed, in February 1992, a cooperation agreement with the US that underscored their alliance and their mutual stand on such issues as weapons of mass destruction and the question of human rights, which were the very same issues that dominated Iranian-US relations.[33] Iran's margin for political manoeuvre was narrowed, and it no longer had the necessary freedom to support perceived Islamic causes, whether in the neighbouring Islamic states or in other world regions harbouring Islamic

minorities. Thus, when pressure mounted inside Iran, demanding intervention on the side of the 'brethren' in Azerbaijan, Moscow issued an
ultimatum to Tehran, regardless of the fact that the military Armenian
advance was approaching the Iranian borders. The intricate geo-political
crisis in the Balkans, and the need to respect the Russian role in the traditional geo-political space of the Orthodox, muted the Iranian response to
the position of the Bosnian Muslims.

The success of the Western strategy in containing Russian power, albeit
temporarily, posed a second challenge to Iran, represented by a shift in the
rhetoric of international politics, from the language of ideology to that of
culture and 'civilizations'. As a result of this shift, Islam came to replace
communism as the main perceived enemy of the West. This represented an
attempt to consolidate the alliance of the Western industrialized states,
and contain their nationalist struggles or, at the very least, to limit their
repercussions.[34] Talking about the 'Islamic peril' and the necessity of facing
it has become, of late, rather fashionable in establishment circles in Washington.[35] Thus, the Islamic regimes, such as Iran and the Sudan, which call
for 'cultural authenticity' on the basis of holding fast to the principles of
sovereignty and independence, are liable to become a target of a Western
campaign that seeks to limit the role of Iranian foreign policy in the Arab
region.

The third challenge is the emergence of the Islamic republics in Central
Asia and the Caucasus. In addition to the fact that this region of Central
Asia represents the 'backyard' of Iran. In terms of common civilizational
heritage, demography and resources, Iran is closely tied to Tajikistan and
Azerbaijan.[36] Some analysts have even predicted that the six Islamic republics will become members of a regional system extending southward to
include the Gulf states, whose centre will be Iran. Iran has already established a network of economic relations with these republics, especially
Turkmenistan (food and textile industries, and the transport of gas to the
Gulf). It has also proceeded to preserve the Persian language in Tajikistan
and Afghanistan. In addition, Iran has sought to revive the Islamic-Persian
civilizational components in certain countries, such as Uzbekistan and
Turkmenistan.[37]

In the new climate of awareness of the historical bonds between Iran
and the region that is now called 'Central Asia',[38] Tehran adopted a view
derived from the general Islamic position, calling for a return of the newly
independent Islamic states to the 'domain of Islam' (Dar al-Islam).

In this respect, Iranian diplomacy sought to ensure that these countries
become members of international Islamic organizations, especially the
Islamic Conference Organization. When the Islamic summit was held in
Dakar, at the beginning of December 1991, Iran called for the inclusion of
the six republics into the Islamic Conference Organization.

Moreover, the acceptance of Azerbaijan, Uzbekistan, Turkmenistan, Tajikistan and Kirghiz as members in ECO[39] during the Organization's summit in Tehran (16–17 February 1992), was a move that led to contradictory contemplations about the possibility of transforming an extended ECO into an Islamic common market of 250 million souls.

The Iranian approach towards the Central Asian republics clashed, from the start, with Turkish overtures in the area (which benefited from the fact that most of the peoples of the region are Turkish-speaking). Observers soon noted that the initial wave of Islamic solidarity, aroused by the independence of the six republics, was quickly replaced by signals from the dominant elites in these states – who had lived for 70 years under the Soviet regime – that they were happier, both politically and intellectually, to move toward the Turkish model of the relationship between state and religion. Talk of Turkish-Iranian rivalry began to circulate at the international level when the Iranian President Hujjat al-Islam Hashemi Rafsanjani announced, during the ECO summit, the establishment of an independent organization comprising the states of the Caspian Sea (Iran, Russia, Azerbaijan, Turkmenistan and Kazakhstan). This organization overlapped with the ECO and the Organization of the Black Sea countries, established by a Turkish initiative in January 1992. As time passed, it became evident that the Asian republics preferred to follow a policy of balance between the Turkish and Iranian poles of the 'power triangle', and that they were fully prepared to exploit the rivalry between Tehran and Ankara in order to further their own interests.

Lastly, it should be mentioned that the Islamic republics, being newly independent – and because of the intertwining of their social structures with their counterparts in Iran – have become a severe threat to security in Northern Iraq. Moreover, they re-impose the Soviet challenge in a different context. Iran now finds itself alone, in the absence of the Soviet presence, in the struggle to reinforce security and maintain order in the area surrounding its northern frontiers.

But where does the Arab order stand in these international changes? There is no doubt that the collapse of the bipolar order has destroyed an important source of the global status of the Arab order. Although there were many difficulties facing the economic and political development of the Arab homeland after independence, the big Arab countries were able to enter the first industrial revolution and some branches of the second industrial revolution. Moreover, the oil-exporting Arab countries were able to free themselves from that pattern of relationship with the seven giant oil companies that was based on concessions. They even took control of the fundamental decisions related to production and pricing. These successes were largely due to the mechanism of the bipolar order, which left a wide margin for manoeuvre, whether directly or indirectly. On the political level, most of the Arab countries gained their independence within the framework of this mechanism, which also enabled many of them to enter the field of modern military technology, whether by importing weapons or producing them locally.[40]

At the same time, the collapse of the bipolar order led to the loss of a strategic ally for most Arab states (the Soviet Union and the Socialist bloc). Yet, the collapse of the bipolar system was not entirely bad. The disengagement between the international struggles and the regional ones has automatically disengaged the artificial link between the international struggle and the major Arab causes, especially the Palestinian cause. In the bipolar system – and in accordance with the logic of the struggle of the two superpowers – all the Western support, and the US support in particular, went to Israel – in a way that exceeds what US–Israeli relations, or US–Arab relations now require. Therefore, as much as the bipolar system gave the Arabs the chance to achieve their independence and develop their military abilities, it might have harmed their political interests by making them a victim of Israel's artificially enhanced status as a Cold War weapon for the US.

New opportunities might emerge in the post-Cold War period as competition between the major Western blocs intensifies, bearing in mind that for the time being, such competition is still confined to the economic field. But whereas these opportunities are still limited due to US hegemony, and the European and Japanese dependence on the US, an ample chance exists today for these opportunities to expand with the growth of the European and Japanese powers. These opportunities are clearly manifest, particularly in the economic field, due to the fact that the formation of competing trade blocs in the industrial world, and the narrowing of the chances of expansion of each bloc in the market of the others, increase the importance of the Arab market in general.[41]

It should be noted, however, that the Arab region is still considered too close to regions where regional, international and ethnic rivalries are liable to explode (like Central Asia and the Caucasus). Central Asia remains particularly dangerous, in the eyes of the Western powers, as an arena in which Russia may attempt to revitalize its status as a global power, in the context of Orthodox geo-politics.[42] This, in turn, could pose an indirect security threat to the Arab East and the Gulf area, although these are, of course, very long-term considerations.

It is most likely that the growing dependence of the advanced industrialized economies on Arab oil in the coming period, and the absence of any economic and practical energy alternatives, will increase the strategic importance of the Gulf area and the Arab region as a whole, since they hold the biggest world oil reserves, whose supplies and transport routes have to be secured.

Patterns of Interaction and Adaptation

There are many diverging patterns of Iranian-Arab interaction, since Arab–Iranian relations are not, as is well-known, a result of a unified Arab strategy, but rather are motivated by the specific circumstances of each Arab country and its geo-political vision of the potential threats to its security. The relationship was also subject to competition between the big Arab states on the one hand, and to the polarization trends of both the Arabs and the Iranians on the other. For instance, the policy of the states of the Gulf Cooperation Council during the first Gulf war (1980-1988) ranged between full financial and military support for Iraq (Kuwait) to maintaining diplomatic relations with Iran and playing the role of mediator between the two warring countries (Oman). The policy towards Iran varied even in the same federal entity, as Dubai and Ras al-Khaimeh supported Iran while Abu Dhabi sided with Iraq.

This phenomenon continued to prevail after the second Gulf war. While Iranian relations with Sudan were qualitatively developed, although they did not reach the level of cooperation and coordination that exists between Syria and Iran, attempts to normalize Egyptian-Iranian relations failed. And while Iranian relations with Syria witnessed a new level of cooperation and coordination – and reflected an ability to respond, and then to adapt, to the challenges of the regional realities in the aftermath of the Madrid peace conference – Iranian relations with Algeria witnessed a radical change, to the extent of a complete breakdown, following the Algerian military crackdown after the victory of the Islamic movement in the general elections in January 1992.

The Security System in the Gulf

In assessing the positive development of Arab–Iranian relations, after Iran accepted the cease-fire resolution in August 1988, it is noted that the Gulf, being the vital space of Iranian geo-politics, represents the first test case of this development. In principle, Iran did not exclude Iraq, its old enemy, from its efforts to develop cooperation with its neighbours. For Iran considers that the regional security of the Gulf area is an issue that concerns all the Gulf countries, to the exclusion of all foreign intervention.

This Iranian attitude was quite visible on the eve of the Iraqi invasion of Kuwait. In the beginning of June 1990, the ministerial meeting of the Gulf Cooperation Council supported holding a meeting at the summit level between Iran and Iraq. A month later, the Iranian Foreign Minister, Ali Akbar Velayati, visited Kuwait in what seemed a decisive turning point in the attempt to improve relations between Iran and its old adversaries. And when

Iraq blamed the Gulf countries for flooding the world market with cheap oil, Iran supported the Iraqi stand. Moreover, Iran maintained its position regarding security until the eve of the Iraqi invasion of Kuwait. It strongly emphasized its rejection of the presence of any foreign troops, at a time when the Iraqis deployed 30,000 soldiers at the Kuwaiti borders, and the Emirates had been conducting joint manoeuvers with the US marines since 24 July 1990.43

The Kuwait crisis and the second Gulf war consolidated Iranian efforts to impose itself as the major partner in the Gulf cooperation and security system. After his invasion of Kuwait in August 1990, Saddam Hussein offered Iran certain strong incentives for a peace settlement, including – a point of special interest to the Iranians – Iraq's expressed readiness to recognize the borders at the Shatt al-Arab as they were before the Iran-Iraq war. Nevertheless, Iran insisted on its firm stand condemning the invasion of Kuwait. On the other hand, Iran remained in contact with Iraq, and restored diplomatic relations on 14 October 1990. But through all that, Iran never missed a chance to condemn the presence of 'foreign troops' in the Gulf.

The former adversaries of Iran acknowledged this development in its position at the summit conference of the Gulf Cooperation Council, held at Doha in December 1990. The Gulf Cooperation Council stressed the efforts to settle the differences with Iran, emphasizing the importance of developing cooperation with the Islamic Republic on the basis of good neighbour policy, non-interference in internal affairs, and respect for sovereignty and independence on the basis of religious and historical bonds between the countries of the same region. The Kuwait summit of 1991 was the most important indicator of the phenomenon we have referred to above. For it reinforced the principle of pluralism in Iranian-Gulf relations, allowing each country of the Gulf Cooperation Council to freely conclude bilateral agreements with any other, since there existed a 'disparity in the relations of each country between the Gulf Council and Iran due to the nature of the interests they share together.'44

Iranian officials believe that the second Gulf war was itself a means for enabling the US to maintain its hegemony over the region. For this reason, Iran adopted a course of neutrality throughout the crisis. And this, in effect, meant that Iran was avoiding any head-on collision with the international alliance against Iraq. One of the benefits of this realistic policy was that it created, immediately after the war, a favourable climate for the restoration of diplomatic relations with Saudi Arabia (March 1991), which had been severed since the events of the Mecca Holy Shrine (Al-Haram Al-Sharif) in 1987. In June 1991, the Saudi Foreign Minister, Prince Saud al-Faisal, visited Tehran, and a network of cooperative relationships began to emerge between Iran and the Arab Gulf countries, especially in the fields of transport and communication. Iran also avoided making the oil issue – one of the most complicated issues of Gulf-Iranian relations – a cause for an acute confrontation within OPEC. In the first half of 1992, Iran decreased its extra share of oil production from 300, 000 barrels per day to 120, 000.[45]

However, the second Gulf crisis, which served Iran's interests, alternatively opposed these very interests in one vital area. The US intensified its military presence in the Gulf region, and it even gave this presence a kind of continuity, through the treaty signed with Kuwait in September 1991, providing for certain US troop facilities at Kuwait ports, the storage of military equipment, and joint manoeuvres to be conducted over a period of 10 years.

But if Iranian frustration in this respect translated into intransigence over the settlement of the issue of Abu Musa Island,[46] yet there is a consensus of opinion that a system of viable security arrangements in the Gulf presupposes the presence of a regional structure that includes Iran as a fundamental and active partner. For the time being, however, US pressures connected with the policy of dual containment of both Iraq and Iran[47] and Saudi reservations are not the only obstacles facing the establishment of a regional security and cooperation system.[48] There is also the problem of the three islands that Arab elites consider to be the major obstacle to restoration of normal relations between Iran and the Arab Gulf countries.[49]

Any observer of the Gulf countries' attitudes would notice a traditional difference between the positions of Saudi Arab on the one hand, and those of the rest of the Gulf countries on the other. While Saudi Arabia sees in Iran a traditional regional rival, and views with caution any Iranian rapprochement with any Council member, the others, especially Qatar, Oman and the UAE, have exhibited, at varying levels, a desire to develop their relations with Iran. And while it was expected that the second Gulf war would melt the ice between Tehran and Riyadh, the course of events did not satisfy these expectations. This failed rapprochement was the result of certain key factors, such as the attitude regarding Iraq and its future, the Saudi dependence on direct US military presence, and the Saudi participation in the multilateral Middle East talks (in contrast with the Iranian position that opposes the Arab-Israeli settlement).[50]

The Arab–Israeli Conflict

The Gulf crisis and the second Gulf war have, among other things, revitalized the Iranian role in Arab causes, and the Palestinian question in particular. The defeat of Iraq, and the consequent severe limiting of its regional role, gave Iran room for manoeuvre which it lacked throughout the years of confrontation with Iraq. It even made its role more acceptable within the framework of the balance of power. Moreover, what occurred made it possible to launch the 'peace process', which Iran emphatically opposed.

Thus, it was only natural that such an Iranian policy would anger the Israelis as well as the US Administration; all the more so because the latter is expending a considerable amount of money, effort and prestige to make a peaceful settlement of the Arab–Israeli conflict possible. Ironically, this Iranian policy, that is supposed to enhance Arab rights, is faced by opposition and rejection from many Arab states, as well as the PLO itself.

According to the US view, Iranian opposition to peace negotiations between the Arabs and Israelis aims at promoting radical political Islam and undermining the stability of pro-American regimes in the region. In this context, some Israeli leaders, in light of increasing activism by Islamic movements in the occupied Arab lands – and the attacks on Jewish and Israeli institutions in South America and Europe two years ago – have gone so far as to equate Islam with Communism, and put the Islamic Republic of Iran on the same footing as the former Soviet Union. Yet this campaign has ignored the fact that some Iranian officials have stressed that Tehran is no longer concerned with stopping the peace process, although it still adopts a principled ideological position against 'Israeli injustice'.[51]

On the other hand, Iranian policy on the Palestinian cause seems, from the Arab viewpoint, to lack coherence and consistency. The only consistent stand in the Iranian approach has been the rejection of Israel as an illegitimate entity.

The absence of political planning is reflected in the current Iranian attitude towards the Israeli-Palestinian declaration of principles known as the 'Oslo Agreement'. While it is believed that Iranian officials generally hope that this agreement will yield certain satisfactory results for the Palestinians, they have, publicly, adopted a rather contradictory rhetoric.[52]

Yasser Arafat was the first foreign leader to visit Iran and meet with Imam Khomeini after the success of the Islamic revolution in 1979. Arafat's visit was preceded by turning the Israeli Embassy into the 'Embassy of Palestine', in what was considered to be the first move of the Islamic Republic in the field of foreign policy towards the Arabs. The Iranian stand concerning the Palestinian question was crystal clear in its hostility towards Israel from the very first day of the Islamic revolution. As soon as the revolutionary forces took control, Imam Khomeini insisted that the liberation of Palestine should be considered one of the main foreign policy goals of the Islamic regime.[53]

To realize the importance of this transformation, it is sufficient to remember that there was no Palestinian mission during the reign of the Shah, whose main concern was to maintain good relations with Israel and its ally, the United States. On the other hand, sympathy for the Palestinian struggle was one of the main factors that led to the outbreak of the revolution that toppled the Shah, whose Israeli regional policy gave an image to his regime as having a Persian nationalism hostile to the Arabs. As a matter of fact, the successive Israeli wars with the Arabs and the Israeli occupation of Arab lands were coupled with the continuous growth of trade relations between Iran and Israel. And when the Arab system declared a ban on oil exports to the supporters of Israel in the West, Iran distanced itself from this historical initiative, and began to increase its production to make up for the shortage. The view that Iran was an enemy of the Arabs was particularly strong among the Palestinians, who considered the Shah a major opponent of their movement.

The substantial change that moved Iran to the Arab side of the equation was supposed to improve and strengthen relations between Iran and the Arab countries. But this scenario did not materialize, since none of the Arab countries – with the exception of Syria, South Yemen, Libya and Algeria – made any move to improve relations with the nascent Islamic Republic. And although Arab–Iranian tensions resulted from many complex factors, the chief reason was the popular and Islamic nature of the new regime, and its alleged attempts to export the revolution. Hence the support of many Arab states for Iraq, during the first Gulf war of 1980-88. During this conflict, the Gulf Arab states gave financial support to Iraq, while some other Arab countries, such as Jordan, Sudan and Morocco, contributed with troops and equipment.

Although the Islamic Republic of Iran continued to be committed ideologically to the Palestinian cause, the close relations between the Islamic Republic and the Palestine Liberation Organization proved to be short-lived. The PLO was, from the start, against the war between Iraq and Iran, arguing that this war benefits the superpowers and Israel and weakens the 'two revolutionary states'. They were even afraid that it would distract attention from their struggle for independence. On the other hand, Iran expected the PLO to take a principled stand, just as Iran had taken towards the Palestinian cause, by declaring the Iraqi side as the aggressor. But the PLO tried to avoid taking such a stand and, as time passed, Arafat had to go along with the Arab Gulf countries, which adopted a generally pro-Iraqi stance. Palestinian-Iranian relations faced further difficulties when the Syrian-Palestinian conflict broke out, due to the fact that Iran and Syria were allied against Iraq.

The Israeli invasion of Lebanon in the summer of 1982, the movement of the Palestinian leadership from Beirut to Tunis, and the mounting external pressure on Arafat and his followers in 'Fateh', led to a gradual transformation of Palestinian policy towards recognizing Israel. These changes were accompanied by a growing stress on the secular nature of the

Palestinian national movement. This gap, which was further deepened by the PLO's recognition of Israel, convinced Iran of the necessity to develop a new Palestinian policy. This new Iranian policy focused on the Islamic movements that are active in Palestine, providing them with aid and sponsorship. These movements included, in particular, Hizbullah (Party of God) in Lebanon, al-Jihad al-Islami and the 'Hamas' movement in the occupied territories. Furthermore, this new policy enabled the Islamic Republic to renew and emphasize its association with the Palestinian cause and the Arab-Israeli struggle. In addition, and in the context of mutual interaction, the emergence of the Islamic forces during the course of the popular *intifadah* had a strong impact on Iranian policy towards the Arab-Israeli struggle.

The Iranian government recently gave some indications suggesting an alteration of its Palestinian policy, moving towards a more realistic stance on the peace negotiations and the Arab-Israeli settlement. President Hashemi Rafsanjani declared, in a press conference on 7 June 1993, that his country does not approve of the settlement, but 'it will not interfere practically and materially to obstruct it'. He then repeated in an interview with the American magazine *Time*, in June 1994, that Tehran does not intend to interfere in practice with the course of peace, and that it will not take any action to impede the Arab-Israeli negotiations.

It seems that there were certain regional considerations that impelled an apparently contradictory Iranian attitude towards the different tracks of the peace negotiations. For, while Iran took an evidently adamant position towards the Jordanian-Israeli track, and consequently the Israeli-Palestinian track that yielded the limited self-rule agreement, there was considerable flexibility concerning the Syrian-Lebanese-Israeli track. This was due to the requirements of the Syrian-Iranian alliance and the necessity of adapting to the development of Syrian policy, especially in view of the fact that the performance of Islamic resistance in south Lebanon was linked with the extent of the progress in the peace process.[54]

This interaction between Iran and Syria represents a clear case of realpolitik in action. Damascus is, after all, the pivotal point of Iranian diplomacy in the Arab Mashriq, and the partner that acts as a mediator between Iran and the other Arab countries.[55]

The change in Syrian policy is probably one of the factors that has weakened the ideological stance of Iran towards the peace settlement. Before the outbreak of the second Gulf war, Syria clung to a consistent position that refused to negotiate with Israel before it completed its withdrawal from the occupied Arab lands. But the diminishing prospects of the possibility of reviving the strategic balance with Israel – in the aftermath of the Iraqi defeat and the disintegration of the Soviet Union – required a comprehensive review, and raised the possibility of taking part in the negotiations

without abandoning the concept of a 'balanced settlement' on the basis of
UN resolutions 242 and 338.

Iran (and the Islamic resistance) will remain the main Syrian pressure
card on Israel throughout this difficult stage, in which the fate of the regional settlement depends on achieving tangible progress in the
Syrian-Lebanese-Israeli track. Meanwhile, Syrian-Iranian cooperation is
acquiring a dimension that calls on the other Arabs to try in earnest to put
an end to the estrangement of Iran.

Conclusion

The Gulf crisis and war that followed the Iraqi invasion of Kuwait in 1990
have shattered the mechanisms of the Arab regional order, just as the international coalition succeeded in destroying the Iraqi force. These
developments have had a great impact on the Middle Eastern equation.
They have changed the regional balance of power in light of the Western
military deployment in the Gulf, and paved the way for the peaceful settlement of the Arab-Israeli struggle, raising once more the issue of re-drawing
the borders of the Middle East region.

It could also be said that the international and regional transformations
mentioned above have brought about the possibility of the 'marginalization'
of Arab and Iranian roles in the 'regional power triangle'. This potential
marginalization is a result of the collapse of the bipolar system, and the
tendency of the active forces in the West to concentrate on the new partners in the League of Independent States and Eastern Europe.

It was natural that the regional repercussions of these changes would
differ in their effects. It was also to be expected that reactions to these
changes would be extremely varied. In fact, the effects of these changes on
the units of the Arab order were much more negative than their effect on
Iran and Turkey. As we have already seen, Iran and Turkey have actually
made some gains, especially in the Gulf and Central Asia.

The conclusion that follows from these negative results is that the parties of the 'regional power triangle', especially the major Arab countries and
Iran, have found themselves facing similar challenges that necessitate the
development of a new conceptual framework that surpasses the classical
one, which was dominant before the collapse of the bipolar system. There
are favourable elements that encourage the adoption of a new framework
for Arab–Iranian relations. Of these factors, the one that could prove to be
most important is the general awareness amongst Arab and Iranian elites
of the importance of developing a new framework for the relations between Islamic states.[56]

As for the Arab side, there are growing indications of the presence of an ideological/political trend that calls for an acceleration in the re-building of Arab–Iranian and Arab-Turkish relations on a new basis, that takes into consideration the recent regional and international transformations.

This trend benefits from the accumulated experience in the field of Syrian-Iranian cooperation, and from some aspects of Gulf-Iranian dealings.[57] But the genuinely new development is that the ruling Egyptian elites have begun to express a growing desire to reach a framework for dialogue with Iran, in order to cope with the new issues in the Gulf and Middle East.[58]

As for the Iranian side, it is noted that the regional framework of Iranian foreign policy has been changing since the end of the Iraq-Iran war in the summer of 1988. And because the task of reconstruction has become a priority, the acceptance of UN Security Council resolution 598 (dated 7 August 1988) calling for a cease-fire with Iraq, represented a decisive step through which Iran could free itself from the total isolation it found itself in due to the war. Political as well as economic openness became necessary. However, it should be emphasized that what motivated this openness was not only the will to reconstruct the country, but also (more importantly) Iran's geographic position and its bearing, at the economic and political levels, of the characteristics of a rentier country that lives largely on oil revenues. Hence the primacy of foreign policy in Iran, which represents a distinctive, and continuing feature of its modern history.[59]

Moreover, the reformulation of the goals of Iranian foreign policy at the end of the Cold War has coincided with the emergence of various circumstances that have enhanced Iran's regional role. The demise of the Soviet Union and the emergence of the new Islamic republics, within the framework of the League of Independent States, have opened a new field for Iranian foreign policy in which not only the geographical neighbourhood but also historical and cultural relations, play a strong and influential role. In this respect, Iran should pursue a course that eventually leads to the formation of a sub-regional group consisting of the southern states of the former Soviet Union, in addition to Iran and Turkey. It is a group in which Iran should occupy a fundamental position, similar to its role in the Gulf region.[60]

As Iran is suffering from the problem of its foreign image, and since it has now realized the scope of its isolation and marginalization, it may reach the conclusion that one of the means to enable it to change its image in the world at large is realistic openness to the Arab homeland, and a concerted effort to build normal bilateral ties with the strong Arab countries, especially Egypt and Saudi Arabia. Some Iranian academics believe that the dual ideological/nationalist approach to Iranian interests would be better served by enhancing cooperation with the Arabs, for such cooperation would also help in changing the Iranian image in the world.[61]

This does not mean, of course, that the road has been paved for the emergence of a favourable climate for building a conceptual framework enabling a radical transformation in the course of Arab–Iranian relations. Rather, it should be realized that the actual state of affairs presents a thick regional wall of ideological and psychological prejudice, largely due to an extremely nationalist culture on both sides. Such a state of affairs provokes mutual suspicion about the intentions of each side, and contributes to a climate of misunderstanding and negative images. For proof of this, we can go back to the minutes of the dialogue held in Cairo between Mohammed Hassanein Heikal and some Egyptian journalists on the occasion of the seminar on Arab–Iranian relations.[62] The mere fact that the seminar was held is considered, along with the implications of its timing and the issues discussed, an indication of the change in the conditions of Egyptian-Iranian dialogue, as well as the concern felt by Egyptian political elites towards the continued suspension of relations with Iran while normalization progresses with Israel.

In this respect, it was not a mere coincidence for some Iranian academics to come to Beirut in these difficult times and publicly call for direct dialogue between Iranian and Arab societies. Also significant was the taking of this opportunity to suggest that the problem of Arab and Iranian academic and intellectual circles is that their main sources of information and conceptions about one another are Western.[63]

The circles who are concerned with the future of Arab–Iranian relations have realized that official quarters in Tehran – in the aftermath of the Iran-Iraq war and the confusion that resulted from attempts to find a peaceful settlement to the Arab-Israeli conflict – are asking themselves with doubt and bitterness just how meaningful or feasible is it to continue insisting on Arab–Iranian rapprochement and cooperation. Such questions, raised by certain cross-sections of civil society, put the Islamic government on the defencive, when advocating the strongest of ties with the Arabs and a credible solidarity with them, against those who argue for 'Iranian interests' first and find ample justification for disappointment and frustration in the present experience of Arab–Iranian cooperation. The latter cross-section, according to some sources, have neither the weight nor the influence to decisively influence Iranian policy. Observers of this phenomenon in Tehran agree that it reveals how much the state is ahead of society when it comes to Iranian policies on Arab affairs.

It is worth concluding with one last remark derived from field observations throughout the period 1979–1989 and after: most Western media reports deal with Iranian rearmament, in a country whose annual income is about $16 billion, with more than two-thirds of it spent on developing the agricultural and industrial sectors. Such reports are therefore exaggerated for the express purpose of reinforcing, in Arab opinion, an image of Iran as hegemonial and expansionist in intent. Those who are in the least familiar with the views of the Iranian political elite realize that the emphasis on the concept of regional sovereignty in the Gulf and the curbing of Israeli strategy in the Arab Mashriq and Gulf, is a product of the dual approach that governs Iranian foreign policy. This approach links Iranian national security with neighbouring Islamic states, and it is based on purely defensive considerations.

According to some neutral Western studies, Iran was able, by the end of the second Gulf war, to take advantage of a diminished Iraqi threat and rebuild its infrastructure, which was almost devastated during the first Gulf war (1980-1988). Iran finds itself now – even without being interested in the arms race – forced to rebuild and modernize its military forces, and develop its military industries. Iran cannot rely (as Kuwait and Saudi Arabia did) on protection from Western states in the event of of a renewed Iraqi attack. Nevertheless, it is rather difficult for the Arab Gulf countries to view this Iranian armament with comfort, even if it is not necessarily directed against them.[64]

In any case, the political behaviour of the leaders of states and societies is not only determined by the objective facts of the geo-political environment, but also by the perception of the ruling elites of the chances, limitations and obstacles of geo-politics and historical geography in a given time and place. The negative implications of this strategic culture are evident in the conception of the Egyptian media, which contends that there exists an Iranian-Sudanese axis that threatens Egyptian national security throughout the depths of the Nile Valley; or a Saudi Arabian conception of getting around the 'Iranian barrier', to reach the Islamic republics in Central Asia; or a revolutionary Iranian conception of the possibility of transforming the defensive posture against Iraqi aggression in 1980 into an offensive attitude that could topple the regime in Baghdad or turn the 'holy shrines' in Iraq into a base for the liberation of Palestine, etc.

An exceptional effort should be made to ensure that political thinking is compatible with realistic equations, followed by planning and hard work, when re-building Arab–Iranian relations in the context of the 'regional power triangle' and renewing its historical unifying culture. And the dialogue within the context of which this paper is here presented may, God willing, provide a mechanism for furthering acquaintance and contact between Arab and Iranian elites who are equipped to dismantle the mutually harmful prejudices that persist to this day.

Notes

* Editor-in-Chief, *Shu'un Al-Awsat* magazine, Centre for Strategic Studies, Research and Documentation, Beirut, Lebanon.

1.   Gamal Hamdan, *The Strategy of Colonialism and Liberation*, (Cairo: Dar al-Shuruq, 1983), p. 416.

2.   Muhammad El-Sayed Said, ed., *The Arab Homeland and the International Changes*, (Cairo: Institute for Research and Arab Studies, 1991), pp. 10–31.

3.   For a review of the conclusions of the French strategic analyst, Pierre Lellouche, regarding the transformation process from the Yalta order to the new world instability, see: Pierre Lellouche, *Le Nouveau Monde*, (Paris: Grasset, 1992), pp. 482–532. See also: Philippe Moreau Defarges, *Introduction a la geopolitique*, (Paris: Seuil, 1992), pp. 144–51.

4.   The concept of the heartland in geo-politics indicates the pivotal region in a coherent regional space, where the factors of force are intensified. These forces include the points of support whose domination enables the control of the whole region. The heartland we are talking about here is the intermediate Arab region that links, and at the same time separates, between the East and the West. It comprises Greater Syria, the Nile Valley, the Arabian Peninsula and the Gulf, and draws its geo-political value from the ongoing struggle on the function of the 'Israeli bastion' and the control of the energy resources relevant to the international strategies.

5.   'The Changes in Islamic Geo-politics and the Transfer of the Central Leadership', a paper presented to the seminar, 'Towards an Equitable Dialogue between the Arab Countries, Iran and Turkey', *Shu'un al-Awsat*, no. 33, September 1994.

6.   By the 'Arab order' we mean the system of international interactions in the Arab countries, whose unites are composed of the members of the Arab League, which represents the order's general organizational framework. This order that adopts Arabism as its regional identity is composed of some countries that play a major role in the process of interaction (the central countries) and some minor countries called the 'peripheral countries'.

7.   The logic of the settlement requires two transformations of an enormous impact. The Arabs should firstly accept Israel as a legitimate component of a regional order whose identity is a Middle Eastern identity instead of an Arab one. Secondly, Israel should agree to change into a normal state in the region, which means that it should abandon its garrison state concept, the basis of the legitimacy and coherence of its entity for more than half a century.

8.   Ahmad Yousef Ahmad, in Muhammad El-Sayed Said, ed., *The Arab Homeland and the World Changes*, op. cit., pp. 33–40.

9.   Maxime Lefevre et Dan Rotenberg, *La Genese du nouvel ordre mondial*, (Paris: Ellipses, 1992), pp. 115–45.

10.   The concept of a 'regional' order is a relatively recent one in the field of international relations. It usually denotes the system of interaction between a set of neighbouring countries that are linked by economic, social and cultural ties. There has been a general consensus since the sixties that the term 'the Arab regional order' denotes not only a geographical area, but also a national affiliation and a cultural and civilizational identity: Jamil Malat and Alieddine Hilal, *The Arab Regional Order: A Study of the Arabs Political Relations*, (Beirut: Centre for Arab Unity Studies, 1983), pp. 17–21.

See also Muhammad El-Sayed Said, *The Future of the Arab Order after the Gulf Crisis*, 'Alam al-Maarifah (Kuwait: The National Council for Culture, Arts and Letters, 1992), pp. 14 and 21.

11.   Abdul Mon'eim Said, *The Arabs and the Neighbouring Countries, the Project of Foreseeing the Future of the Arab Homeland*, (Beirut: Centre for Arab Unity Studies, 1987), pp. 42–5.

12.   Mohammad El-Sayed Selim, 'Interaction in the 'Power Triangle', An Intellectual Institutional Framework', a paper presented to the seminar, 'Towards an Equitable Dialogue between the Arab Countries, Iran and Turkey', *Shu'un Al-Awsat*, no. 33, September 1994.

13.   Mounir Shafik, *On Arab Unity and Fragmentation*, (Beirut: Dar Al-Tali'ah, 1979), p. 158.

14.   Fehmi Houwaidi, *Iran from the Inside*, (Cairo: Al-Ahram Centre for Translation and Publication, 1987), p. 365.

15.   Mahmood Sariolghalam, 'The Future of Arab–Iranian Relations', *Al-Mustaqbal Al-'Arabi*, vol. 16, no. 177 (October/November 1993).

16.   Ibid.

17.   Jamil Matar and Alieddine Hilal, *The Arab Regional Order: A Study of Arab Political Relations*, op. cit., p. 195.

18.   Abdul Mon'eim Al-Mashat, 'The Arab National Security: There is Still a Chance', *Shu'un Al-Awsat*, no. 36 (December 1994).

19.   Shimon Peres, *The New Middle East*, (Shaftesbury, England: Element, 1993), p. 61.

20.   This disintegrating and fragmented picture was reflected by the Economic Conference for Development in the Middle East and North Africa, held in Casablanca in October 1994. The conference was overwhelmed with Israeli projects that were supported by the relevant maps and pictures, especially one entitled 'Development Alternatives for Regional Cooperation'. In these projects the Israelis spoke of dividing the Middle East into five regions: The Arabian Peninsula and the Gulf, to be composed of the states of the Gulf Cooperation Council in addition to Iran, Iraq and Yemen; the Eastern Mediterranean region that consists of Egypt, Syria, Lebanon, Jordan and Israel; the North African region that includes Algeria, Tunisia, Morocco, Libya and the Sudan; the Arab Homeland (which includes all the Arab countries but not Iran and Israel), and the Middle East and North Africa Region, consisting of all the above countries.

21.   Haytham Kilani, 'The Dilemma of Arab Security', *Shu'un Al-Awsat*, no. 31 (October 1994).

22.   For an elaboration on these scenarios, see also: *Defarges, Introduction à la géopolitique*, op. cit., pp. 145–7.

23.   In spite of the 150 Israeli projects submitted to the Casablanca conference to achieve regional cooperation in the 'New Middle East', the Israeli strategy is still based on the notion of dividing the Arab homeland into a number of strategic circles. The traditional division encompasses three strategic circles: The Gulf and the Arabian Peninsula; Syria and Iraq; and the Nile Valley that includes Egypt and Sudan. This Israeli strategy aims at preventing the establishment of an alliance between any two circles.

24.   According to the Israeli suggestion that was endorsed by the US, the main function of the conference was to ensure coordination and exchange of information, as well as recognizing the existing borders.

25.   For the Imam's rules and statements regarding Israel and the occupation of Palestine, see: Ibrahim Al-Dasouki, *The Winter of the Iranian Revolution, the Ideo-*

logical Roots, (Beirut: Maktabat Dar al-Kutub, [n.d.]), pp. 160-3. See also: *The Islamic Edicts Regarding the Issue of Palestine and the Peace Settlement with the Zionist Entity, Beirut*: Kutub al-Taqrir lil Tiba'ah wal Nashr, Al-Jihad Al-Islami Publications, [n.d.].

26. Martin Indyk, 'Clinton's Policy towards the Middle East', *Palestine Studies*, no. 15 (Summer 1993).

27. For a recent Islamic synthesis of this concept, see: Munir Shafik, *The New International Order and the Confrontation Option*, (Beirut: Al-Nashir, 1992), p. 84.

28. Lefevre et Rotenberg, *La Genese du nouvel ordre mondial*, op. cit., pp. 97-8.

29. The Ahram Centre for Political and Strategic Studies, *The Arab Strategic Report 1990*, (Cairo: The Ahram Centre, 1991), pp. 47-8.

30. *Ibid.*, pp. 49–50.

31. Hassan Nafiat, 'Nationalistic Uprising in the Soviet Union', *Al-Siyasat Al-Dawliyyah*, vol. 17, no. 66 (October 1981).

32. Shereen T. Hunter, 'Soviet-Iranian Relations in the Post-revolutionary Period', in R. K. Ramazani, ed., *Iran's Revolution*, (Bloomington: Indiana University Press, 1990), p. 86.

33. 'The Clinton Administration and the Future of US–Iran Relations', *Middle East Insight, Special Iran Conference Issue*, Washington D. C., 14 January 1993.

34. We can consider the debate launched by Foreign Affairs in its Winter/Summer 1993 issues about Huntington's concept of 'clash of civilizations' as the culmination of the theoretical and academic effort that provides a basis for this strategic trend in American politics. The US Congress had previously held hearing sessions for experts and specialists in contemporary Islamic studies. Moreover, *Foreign Policy* published in its Fall issue, no. 89, 1991, an interesting article entitled 'Defending the Western Culture'.

35. It is no longer a secret that one of the security pillars that the current peace process is based on is combating the so-called 'fundamentalist terrorism', and the costs and capabilities that are required have occupied an important part of the peace settlement and security arrangements between Israel and both the Palestinians and the Jordanians.

36. Graham Fuller, 'Emergence of Central Asia', *Foreign Policy*, no. 78 (Spring 1990).

37. Ibrahim Arafat, *The Iranian-Turkish Contest over Central Asia*, Cairo: Centre for Political Research and Studies, Cairo University, 1933.

38. 'Central Asia' is the new name of the region the Muslim geographers knew as Khurasan and the 'countries beyond the river'. Khurasan is divided today between Iran, Afghanistan and Turkmenistan, while the 'countries beyond the river' means the region of Iran to the north-east of the Amu Darya River. Iran has played a major political and cultural role in the region for more than two thousand years. The Persian heritage is still a deeply rooted aspect of cultural life in Uzbekistan, Tajikistan, Kirghiz and Kazakhstan, despite the fact that the Turkish languages have replaced the Persian language. The Iranian Foreign Minister, Ali Akbar Velayati, stressed in the inauguration of the seminar, 'Transformation of the Soviet Union and Its Impact on the Third World', held in Tehran in March 1992, the vital role of the Islamic Republic of Iran in the region, because of 'the geographical, historical and cultural relationship'.

39. The Economic Cooperation Organization (ECO) was founded in 1965, with

Iran, Turkey and Pakistan as its members. The three countries have tried, since 1975, to revitalize the Organization, but its activities have been practically frozen since the outbreak of the Islamic revolution in 1979.

40.   Muhammad El-Sayed Said, *The Future of the Arab Order after the Gulf Crisis*, op. cit., pp.235-237.

41.   Muhammad El-Sayed Said, 'The International Trade Blocs and Their Effect on the Arab Homeland', in: Muhammad El-Sayed Said, ed., *The Arab Homeland and the International Changes*, op. cit.

42.   Francois Thual, *Geopolitique de l'orthodoxie*, (Paris: Institut de relations internationales et strategiques: Dunod, 1993), pp. 31-84.

43.   Shahram Chubin, 'Post-war Gulf Security', *Survival*, vol. 33 (1991).

44.   For the resolutions of the Gulf summits from 1990 to 1992, see: Bibliography of Arab Unity in *Al-Mustaqbal Al-'Arabi*.

45.   *Al-Wasat* daily (London), 7 May 1993.

46.   In response to apparent Iranian intransigence since 1991, the Gulf Cooperation Council declared its solidarity with the UAE, against Iran. This stand coincided with two condemnations issued by two different bodies dealing with organizing Arab–Iranian relations: The Arab League and the states of the Damascus declaration. Although the mediation, conducted by Oman and Syria, resulted in holding official Iranian-UAE talks in September 1992, no progress was achieved.

47.   See Indyk, 'Clinton's Policy towards the Middle East', op. cit.

48.   Johannes Reissner, 'L'Iran el les changements au Moyen-Orient', in: Elizabeth Picard, *Direction, La Nouvelle dynamique au Moyen-Orient*, Paris: L'Harmattan, 1993.

49.   Bakinam El-Sharkawi, 'The Iranian Vision of the Arab Reconciliation', a paper presented to the Second Annual Conference of Young Researchers, Cairo: Centre for Arab Research and Studies, 14-15 November 1994.

50.   Abduljalil Marhoun, 'The Gulf Cooperation Council and the Project of Regional Order', *Shu'un Al-Awsat*, no. 11 (August 1992). See also Abdulalim Muhammad, 'The Invasion of Kuwait and the Gulf War', *Shu'un Al-Awsat*, no. 11 (August 1992).

51.   Hoochang Amirahmadi, 'Iran and the Islamic Threat: The New Israeli Approach', *Shu'un Al-Awsat*, no. 34 (October 1994).

52.   Hoochang Amirahmadi, 'The Islamic Republic and the Question of Palestine', *Middle East Insight* , Washington, May-August 1994.

53.   For the Imam's statements and appeals regarding Palestine and Zionism, see: *The Imam Confronting Zionism*, 2nd ed., Tehran: Ministry of Islamic Guidance, 1404 AH.

54.   Niveen Masaad, 'The Impact of the New World Changes on the Iranian-Arab Relations 1989-1993', in: *Arab–Iranian Relations*, by a group of researchers, Cairo: Centre for Arab Research and Studies, 1993.

55.   Bakinam El-Sharkawi, 'The Impact of the Iranian Islamic Revolution on Arab Relations', op. cit.

56.   For a systematic synthesis of this trend, see Mohammad El-Sayed Selim, *Relations among the Islamic Countries*, Riyadh: King Saud University, 1991.

57.   Cairo and Beirut have witnessed in the last two years a series of seminars and research workshops that deal with Arab–Iranian and Arab–Turkish relations, and the limits and opportunities that control the tripartite dialogue between Ar-

abs, Iranians and Turks.

58.   Mohammad El-Sayed Selim, 'Interactions in the 'Power Triangle', an Intellectual Institutional Framework', op. cit.

59.   See Michel Nawfal, 'Iran Faces the International Changes', *Al-Nahar* daily, 26-29 June 1990.

60.   Seminar on Russia, Central Asia and the Arabs, organized by the Centre for Research and Political Studies, Faculty of Economic and Political Sciences, Cairo University, Cairo, 26-28 April 1993.

61.   Mahmood Sariolghalam, 'The Basis of the Iranian Post-revolution Foreign Policy', *Shu'un Al-Awsat*, no. 21 (July-August 1993).

62.   For the minutes of the dialogue, see *Al-Safir* daily, 24 June 1995.

63.   We are referring here to the initiative of Dr Mahmood Sariolghalam, a consultant to the National Academic Council in Iran, and the visit he made to Beirut in July 1993. He was invited jointly by the Centre for Strategic Studies and Documentation and the Centre for Arab Unity Studies. During his visit he gave two lectures on Iranian foreign policy and the future of Arab–Iranian relations. We are also referring here to the joint Arab–Iranian efforts and contacts that made this present seminar possible.

64.   Volker Perthes, 'The Dynamics of Armament in the Near and Middle East', *Shu'un Al-Awsat*, no. 21 (July–August 1993).

Index